The Journals of William E. McLellin
1831–1836

Countryside near Kirtland, Ohio, about 1872. W. A. Faze. Courtesy of John Waldsmith.

The Journals of William E. McLellin
1831–1836

Edited by
Jan Shipps and
John W. Welch

BYU Studies
Brigham Young University
Provo, Utah

and

University of Illinois Press
Urbana and Chicago

Library of Congress Cataloging-in-Publication Data

McLellin, William E. (William Earl)
    The journals of William E. McLellin, 1831-1836 / edited by Jan
    Shipps and John W. Welch.
        p.   cm.
    Includes bibliographical references and indexes.
    ISBN 0-8425-2316-2 (alk. paper) : $29.95
    1. McLellin, William E. (William Earl)—Diaries. 2. Mormon Church—
Clergy—Diaries. 3. Mormon Church—History—19th century. I. Shipps,
Jan, 1929-   . II. Welch, John W. (John Woodland), 1946-   . III. Title.
BX8695.M28A3   1994
289.3'092—dc20   94-37387
[B]   CIP

Printed in the United States of America
10 9 8 7 6 5 4 3 2 1

To our faculty and administrative colleagues at Indiana University-Purdue University, Indianapolis, and at Brigham Young University

Contents

Foreword by Laurel Thatcher Ulrich x

Editors' Preface xiii

Part I: Introduction

JAN SHIPPS
"Another Side of Early Mormonism" 3

JOHN W. WELCH
"The Acts of the Apostle William E. McLellin" 13

Part II: The Manuscripts of
William E. McLellin (1831–36)

Journal I, July 18, 1831-November 20, 1831 29

Journal II, November 16, 1831-February 25, 1832 61

Letter to Relatives, August 4, 1832 79

Journal III, January 28, 1833-May 24, 1833 89

Journal IV, July 9, 1834-April 17, 1835 131

Journal V, May 4, 1835-September 3, 1835 171

Journal VI, April 9, 1836-June 7, 1836 213

Letter to Apostles, January 24, 1837 229

Doctrine and Covenants Sections 22 (RLDS 20),
45, 65, and 66 233

Part III: Supplemental Resources

RICHARD E. TURLEY, JR.
"The Provenance of William E. McLellin's Journals"   257

WILLIAM G. HARTLEY
"The McLellin Diaries and Early Mormon History:
Contributions and Questions"   263

LARRY C. PORTER
"The Odyssey of William Earl McLellin:
Man of Diversity, 1806–83"   291

M. TERESA BAER
"Charting the Missionary Work of William E. McLellin:
A content Analysis"   379

Appendix I: Articles in Early LDS Periodicals on
Subjects of Preaching in McLellin's Journals   406

Appendix II: Other Early Mormon Missionary
Journals and Accounts   408

Appendix III: Baptism Register   413

Biographical Register   415

Gazetteer   475

Scripture Index   487

Subject Index   493

Maps and Illustrations

Maps

McLellin's travels, 1831	28
McLellin's travels, 1831-32	60-
McLellin's travels, 1833	88
McLellin's travels, 1834–35	130
McLellin's travels, 1835	170
McLellin's travels, 1836	212

Illustrations

Kirtland, Ohio countryside, c. 1872	frontispiece
Page 1, Journal I	xii
Page 7, Journal V	xix
Page 6, Journal I	2
Page 23, Journal III	87
Painesville, Ohio, c. 1846	150
Main Street, Painesville, c. 1850	151
Grand River Shipyard, Fairport, Ohio, c. 1858	172
Fairport Harbor, c. 1858	173
The Kirtland Temple, c. 1904	211
Steamboats, Cincinnati, Ohio, c. 1848	220
Cincinnati waterfront, c. 1848	221
Manuscript of Doctrine and Covenants 65	242
Page 21, Journal I (Doctrine and Covenants 66)	247
William E. McLellin, c. 1870	256
Page 9, Journal II	262
William E. McLellin, c. 1875	290
John Johnson farm, prior to 1874	298
Tombstone of William E. McLellin	356
Page 10, Journal IV	486
Page 15, Journal VI	492

Foreword

William McLellin's journals belong to several genres of early American expression. They are part travel journal, part account book, part religious meditation, part memoranda. As the editors of this volume make clear, they give us access to early Mormonism at the grass roots. But they do much more. McLellin's journals radiate the spiritual hunger, the intellectual curiosity, and the frontier pragmatism that defined rural Americans in the early nineteenth century.

McLellin's opening, alternately matter-of-fact and filled with mystery, sets the tone. "At this time I was living in Paris, Illinois. Teaching school," he began, moving quickly to the seemingly casual information that changed his life. Two men had come with a book they claimed was a revelation from God. They were to preach "2 1/2 miles below Paris at N. W. Nunally's." McLellin taught school until noon, then "saddled Tom" and rode off to "see and hear those quear beings." Yet judging from his own description, the message he heard was not so much *quear* as *plain.* It was "the plainness of the truths they declared," he wrote, that induced him "to believe something in their mission."

This same combination of strangeness and familiarity characterized McLellin's accounts of his own missionary journeys. He methodically recorded miles traveled, the number of people gathered in each country meetinghouse or barn, meals eaten, and hours spent studying or preaching, alongside his experiences of the divine. A remarkable entry for March 8, 1833, when he and his companions ascended a "mount" near the Mississippi, conveys the mixture of secular and sacred images that permeate his journals. Into a predictably literary nineteenth-century description of a picturesque village with its curling smoke in a receding landscape of "tall timbers," "extended plains," and "winding" river, McLellin placed a "wandering Lamanite," and he explicitly linked his own spiritual quest to that of "Holy men of old" who "sought Mountains and solitary places."

What we have then is a remarkably detailed and honest account of an ordinary American deliberately seeking and sometimes finding the sacred. For all their questing, the journals never abandon the factual and everyday. McLellin tells us how much he paid for a watch or a cloak and how he treated his sore throat with vinegar, butter, and honey; he comments wryly on the vicissitudes of traveling with donated shoes—one pair too big, the other too little. Through his journals, we learn about the spiritual yearnings and skepticisms of other ordinary folk, including those who called upon him to heal an old lady with "the Phlhisis" or a young boy "who had fitts and who some times raged and foamed like a mad man." There are also pithy descriptions of the troubles of would-be saints. "It was big I and little u̲," he wrote, after trying in vain to mediate one squabble.

McLellin and his companions faced less persecution than indifference (they handled both forms of rejection by washing their feet clean as they moved from one settlement to another). From a social history perspective, what seems most telling is the way these Mormon Apostles depended on an old ethic of neighborly trade. The unquestioning generosity of ferrykeepers, housewives, and country craftsmen suggests that McLellin and his companions had something real to exchange—a vision of life, a "quear" story, a rousing sermon; that people offered dinners, shelter, transportation, clothing, and beds for the night, not just out of Christian benevolence, but from an honest desire to give value for value received. If few of those people took up their packs and followed, they nevertheless listened with interest and respect.

McLellin's journals are filled with real people—a Baptist housewife who was too busy doing her wash to listen to their message; a "little foppish Methodist" preacher who observed that the God of the Book of Mormon "was not a Grammarian"; a country doctor who insisted that the poor gathered in Zion "lived on water porage Salted," and many others. McLellin himself is a real man trying to talk down Satan and to listen to God. Through this fine edition, he continues to speak.

LAUREL THATCHER ULRICH
University of New Hampshire

Page 1, Journal I (actual size). McLellin's journals begin on July 18, 1831, the day he heard David Whitmer testify to "having seen an Holy Angel" who had made known to him the truth of the Book of Mormon. Whitmer's testimony changed the course of McLellin's life. Courtesy LDS Church Archives.

Editors' Preface

The publication of the McLellin journals is the product of an extensive cooperative collaboration between two research teams that came about in the following manner. The journals of William E. McLellin, which had been presumed lost, were located in the vault of the First Presidency of The Church of Jesus Christ of Latter-day Saints in March 1986. Given the connection between McLellin's name and the Mark Hofmann affair, the LDS Church anticipated that any announcement that the journals had been located would generate inquiries from the press about their contents. So that inquiries could be directed to historians not connected with the LDS Church Historical Department, Jan Shipps and Richard Bushman were asked in 1991 to read the manuscripts. Sensing their inherent worth to a wide variety of scholars, Jan asked for permission to prepare a scholarly edition of these documents. Upon receiving permission, she mobilized a research team at Indiana University–Purdue University, Indianapolis (IUPUI), and before the Church made a public announcement that these journals had been found she started to work on the initial tasks in the creation of such an edition.

At this point, John W. Welch and *BYU Studies* entered the picture. Seeing the *Church News* article on October 24, 1992, that announced the location of these documents, he immediately contacted the Church Historical Department to ask if *BYU Studies* might undertake the publication of these papers as a part of its ongoing program of publishing important LDS documents, especially since a new *BYU Studies* monograph series had recently been launched. When he was informed that Jan was already working on them, he called her and proposed a collaborative editing arrangement. Jan readily agreed. This proposal was then approved by the Church Copyrights and Permissions Office, and a team of historians and editors was organized by *BYU Studies.*

We held an initial meeting in Indianapolis to plan the project as a joint enterprise of the two research teams. In this working session, primary responsibilities were allocated between the two groups, and a work schedule was established. After further consultation at the 1993 Mormon History Association meeting at Graceland College in Lamoni, Iowa, we proposed a copublication arrangement with the University of Illinois Press to Elizabeth G. Dulany, assistant director of the press, who has built that press's extensive Mormon list. The press accepted our proposal and Liz became a consultant to the project. Accordingly, these journals are appearing as a work coedited by a Methodist professor of history and religious studies in a public university and by a Mormon professor of law and editor of an LDS scholarly periodical. Additionally, this book is copublished under the joint imprint of Brigham Young University's *BYU Studies* and the University of Illinois Press, that is, of both LDS and non-LDS publishing outlets.

The primary responsibilities first undertaken by the team at IUPUI included preliminary transcription of the enlarged photocopies of all the McLellin papers supplied by the Church Historical Department. These documents included not only the six missionary journals, but also three revelations that became sections in the Doctrine and Covenants plus miscellaneous papers and notes written by McLellin in the 1870s. To prepare the transcriptions of the journals for initial proofreading, the team carefully represented the features of the handwritten text as far as possible in a typed version. Also, the IUPUI team took responsibility for preparing the maps and gazetteer and for researching the libraries in the Midwest for information about the people mentioned in the journals who never became members of the LDS or RLDS churches. A computer program was designed at IUPUI to conduct statistical analyses of many types of data found in the journals.

The primary responsibilities of *BYU Studies* included the formatting, typesetting, and technical editing of the transcribed texts as well as the two letters written by McLellin in the 1830s, preparing the historical notes to these documents, researching the libraries and archives in Utah for facts about all individuals named in the journals, and locating photographs for possible publication in this volume. In addition, *BYU Studies* recruited several BYU historians to prepare a biography and commentaries on the McLellin materials.

After working drafts of these various materials were prepared by both teams, thorough cross-checking, revising, and refining ensued. We met in Salt Lake City to proofread all of the typeset documents against the original manuscripts in the LDS Church Archives. Keeping in close contact by phone, mail, and fax, we also arranged time for consultations at professional meetings, including the meeting of the Society of Biblical Literature and American Academy of Religion in Washington, D.C., in November 1993, and the Mormon History Association meeting in Park City, Utah, in May 1994. We welcomed the opportunity to present a full session at the latter meeting on this project that impelled all the principals to finalize their contributions and allowed them to receive helpful comments. We reviewed together all details in the notes and made revisions and further additions. We then jointly edited and finalized the biographical register, gazetteer, maps, and all other supplementary essays and materials in extended working sessions in Provo in August 1994.

Description of the McLellin Journals. Physically the journals appear as follows: The six McLellin journals are very nearly the same size. The journals are rather small (typically 3 7/8" x 6 3/16") and would easily fit inside of a Bible or a book about the size of the first edition of the Book of Mormon. Since the papers are not tattered, McLellin must have kept them inside of something such as a book in order to protect them.

With the exception of Journal V, which has been given a simple paper cover, all of the journals are written on folded, unbound pieces of paper. McLellin typically took a large sheet of paper, folded it several times, and trimmed the edges to make little booklets, on which he wrote his journal entries. The shorter journals may have been the result of a single piece of paper folded three times. The longer journals appear to have been written on several pieces folded and gathered. He wrote on the front and back of each page.

The handwriting in Journal I is particularly small. Nevertheless, the letters are quite clear, and the writing is very deliberate. Apparently paper was hard to come by, for these pages appear to be precious and are filled to the maximum. Journal I is twenty-four pages long.

Journal II is eighteen pages long, all of uniform size. The script is more cursive and somewhat larger and, thus, is easier to read than the writing in Journal I.

Journal III is composed of three gathers. The first is sixteen pages long, sized 3 7/8" x 5", and numbered 1–9 and 11–17 (whoever later added the numbers skipped page number 10). The paper used for the second gather is slightly larger (3 7/8" x 5 1/4"), comprising another sixteen pages (numbered 18–33). The third and last gather is a bit larger (4" x 6") and is twenty pages long (numbered 34–53). The numbers written at the top of the pages in Journal III are in a blacker ink than the script.

Journal IV begins on July 9, 1834. The first page ends midsentence, and the back of this page is uncharacteristically blank. The ink on this page has bled through more than on most pages, and perhaps McLellin decided that the quality of this paper was too poor, did not write on the back of that page, threw away the rest of the sheet like it, and on July 22 started over with page number 1 on different paper. Beginning again at that point, that group of sheets is twenty-four pages long, running to the end of that journal.

Journal V has a dark brown, lightweight paper cover on its front and back. The main contents consist of thirty-two pages, but four of the last six are blank, and the final two were written later. In addition, a final loose page was inserted containing a chronology, written on vertically lined paper. Half of these pages are quite faded.

Journal VI is thirty-six pages long. Unlike almost all of the other pages, the paper used for Journal VI was lined horizontally by the manufacturer. These pages are slightly smaller than most of the others (3 7/8" x 5 15/16").

The five sheets of paper on which McLellin transcribed sections 22, 45, and 65 of the Doctrine and Covenants are 3 5/8" x 6 1/4" and are similar to the paper used in the early journals. Like the pages of the journals, these five sheets have writing on both their front and back sides, totalling ten pages of text.

Editorial Procedures. Along the way, we made many editorial decisions, especially as we worked with the original manuscripts. As can be seen in the reproduced pages included in this volume, McLellin's handwriting is usually not difficult to read. Yet because he was using small pages and quill pens, words are occasionally written between lines and contractions and abbreviations are often employed. Spelling is usually adequate but somewhat erratic and inconsistent. In some instances, the ink has bled through or is faint or blotted, or words have been crossed out or overwritten. Marks and odd strokes appear beneath and above many letters, particularly the *s*'s.

In order to make the journals accessible to our readers, we made the following editorial decisions:

- to use a consistent spelling for William McLellin's name, even though he spelled it in various ways throughout his life;

- to leave all other spelling and capitalization as written by McLellin, including the spelling of proper names, the correct spellings of which can be found in the biographical register or gazetteer;

- to bring down all raised letters or interlinear words that McLellin wrote above the line;

- to render apostrophes as such, rather than as the commas McLellin used;

- to omit all odd strokes that appear beneath or above many letters;

- to insert punctuation and restore worn letters in order to facilitate readability;

- to standardize the various lengths of dashes as either long or short;

- to leave blank spaces where McLellin did, presumably intending to fill in the missing names or data later;

- to retain McLellin's emphasis on certain words or letters by the use of bold type;

- to identify names of people or places rendered by McLellin as initials, by identifying them the first time they appear on a page by enclosing the information in square brackets;

- to show crossed-out words with a simple overstrike;

- to place in brackets and to cross out underlying words that McLellin wrote over with other words, and to follow them in plain text with the revisions: for example, [~~Friday~~] Thursday;

- to indicate page breaks by showing manuscript page numbers in square brackets;

- to begin each day as a separate paragraph.

Although these journals contain very little in the way of drawings or symbols, on one occasion in the fifth journal McLellin wrote half a line of characters which may be shorthand, cryptograms, or even attempts at writing reformed Egyptian or some other language. Despite several efforts, we have not found anyone who can decipher these. We include here a facsimile of that page and welcome suggestions about the meaning of these characters.

We have deposited in the libraries of IUPUI, Brigham Young University, and the LDS Church Archives the photocopies from which we have worked and our original transcriptions of the journals that represent as far as possible all features of the holographs. Anyone interested in examining these working materials may contact those repositories.

Running heads on the top of each journal page in this edition reflect all dates described on those pages, even if the entry for that date begins or ends on another page. In a few cases, a single entry may span several days in retrospect. In these cases, the headers reflect the date on which the entry was written, not the dates covered.

Just as we have created with these changes a relatively straightforward text for reading, we have added notes whose purpose is to make the meaning of the text as clear as possible without overburdening the journals with material we have placed elsewhere in the volume, for example in the biographical register, gazetteer, or in the biography of McLellin. In the notes, we have drawn from contemporaneous sources correlative information about the events that McLellin describes, but we have quoted those sources extensively only if they are not readily available in print. We believe that readers will often find it helpful to consult the *Encyclopedia of Mormonism* for general information about many Mormon terms, practices, doctrines, institutions, and beliefs mentioned by McLellin. No effort has been made to reproduce in the notes modern information found in the *Encyclopedia* or other similar standard sources.

In the years after McLellin left the Church, he often wrote on the subject of Mormonism. Many of his writings in the 1840s were published in the *Ensign of Liberty,* and several of his letters from the 1860s and 1870s appeared in the *Saints' Herald* and other magazines. His unfinished essays from the 1870s are held in the LDS Church Archives. We decided not to include these materials mainly because of their length, because of their late dates, and because some to Elder Nickerson's here we found Elder B. Young & Jo. Smith who had been labouring this Church and region round about — They had a meeting this evening and Elder Young preached about an hour to them on the principles of our faith.

Tuesday we began again to wend our way easterly we travelled about 19 miles and staid with a Mr. Drue, a lame man who treated us with the best that he had & c & on...

Wednesday 20. we proceeded on and took breakfast in little valley with a Mr. Gray who was a cousin to Elder J. Elliott, thence to Ellecottville thence to a Mr. Wissel's who received us to lodge with him during the night after we had been turned away from three or four houses and that too while it was raining quite hard — but they were quite poor — About 24 mls.

Thursday 21. We passed on about a mile in the rain and called at a widow Love lip's and took breakfast and there seemed to be an anxiety to hear us preach insomuch that the neighbours soon gathered in and Elder Hyde preached to them 1½ hours from Mark 13- 21-22 They seemed much affected and quite believing. After which we passed on about 10 miles and staid with a bro. till morning.

Friday 22. We passed on to Elder Cowdery's and there we met with our brethren the twelve and found them all well and proceeded to business and opened our Conference Elder J. W. Patten presiding and W. E. McLellen Clerk — some minutes instruction was given respecting Tongues &c.

Saturday commenced public preaching at 10 o'clock in a large barn Elder Kimball arose and read the 14 chap. of John and spoke to the people about half an hour very feelingly indeed of them are derivative or not even original with McLellin. All of these materials, however, are quoted or described in the notes to this volume or to Larry Porter's biographical treatise.

Acknowledgments. In carrying out these many editorial decisions and accomplishing the many tasks necessary to prepare this volume for publication, we have incurred many debts. We are especially grateful to BYU professors Larry E. Dahl, William G. Hartley, and Larry C. Porter for the pages they prepared for this volume on D&C 66, on the historical significance of the journals, and on McLellin's biography, respectively. From IUPUI, we owe special thanks to Teresa Baer (statistical analysis, biographical register, gazetteer, archival transcript); Evelyn Oliver, secretary to the Religious Studies Department (initial transcription of the McLellin papers); Kevin Mickey and the staff of the Laboratory for Applied Spatial Information Research (maps); William Stuckey, director, and staff members Melody Johnson and Stuart Schleuse of the Computer Aided Research Laboratory in the IUPUI School of Liberal Arts; and Allen Baer (numerous research tasks). From *BYU Studies,* we recognize the productive contributions of Executive Editor Doris Dant and other members of the editorial board; publishing specialists Marny K. Parkin and Karl F. Batdorff; several editorial and research assistants, notably Angela Ashurst-McGee (editing), Steven C. Harper (commentary on D&C 22 and 45), Kristina Labadie and Douglas Larson (biographical register), Trevor Packer (historical notes, commentary on D&C 65), Jonathan Lofgren, John E. Miner, and Chad Poulson (research); and volunteers, including Kristen Betz (proofreading). Ronald Romig, Church Archivist for the Reorganized Church of Jesus Christ of Latter Day Saints in Independence, Missouri, kindly supplied several helpful documents. Howard A. Christy of BYU Scholarly Publications assisted in final editing, especially on the gazetteer and maps. We express appreciation to Richard Neitzel Holzapfel for his unique assistance with photographs and to the staff at the LDS Church Archives and Historical Department in Salt Lake City, notably Bill Slaughter, Steven Sorensen, and Richard Turley (who prepared the statement of provenance). Special appreciation is due to Liz Dulany. Finally, we have recognized the generous support of our respective universities by our dedication of this volume to them and to our academic and administrative colleagues.

Perhaps above all, we are grateful to each other for the opportunity to work together on these engaging materials in the spirit of friendship and mutual concern for getting matters straight. We hope that this project typifies the kind of "love, peace, harmony and humility" that William E. McLellin found among those people who had gathered from different backgrounds to Independence, Missouri, which qualities so deeply impressed him on Friday, August 19, 1831.

Jan Shipps
John W. Welch

Provo, Utah
August 19, 1994

Part I: Introduction

I met with D. Whitmer & Martin Harris who accompanied me about 10 miles further westward where I found. The Bishop E. Partridge and his council Isaac Morley and John Corrill with several other Elders and a number of private members both male and female. I spent the evening with them and had very agreeable conversation.

Friday 19th I rose early, talked much with those people: Saw Love, Peace, Harmony and Humility abounding among them. A rare circumstance occurred while attending family prayer which convinced me that the Elders had the power of discerning spirits. It affected me so that my weakness was manifest. I took Hiram the brother of Joseph and we went into the woods and set down and talked together about 4 hours. I inquired into the particulars of the coming forth of the record, of the rise of the church and of its progress and upon the testimonies given to him &c. This evening I went to one of their prayer meetings. Here I saw the manner of their worship; heard them converse freely upon the things of religion. After meeting I returned to Mr. Lewis' and staid all night.

Saturday the 20th I rose early and betook myself to earnest prayer to God to direct me into truth, and from all the light that I could gain by examinations, searches and researches I was bound as an honest man to acknowledge the truth and validity of the book of Mormon and also that I had found the people of the Lord — the Living Church of Christ. Consequently as soon as we took breakfast I told Elder H. Smith that I wanted him to baptize me because I wanted to live among a people who were based upon pure principles and actuated by the spirit of the Living God. I went with the Elders present to the water and was immersed according

Page 6, Journal I (actual size). McLellin describes his conversion, which involved prayer, examination, and feeling the spirit of love, peace, harmony, and humility among the Saints. Courtesy LDS Church Archives.

Another Side of Early Mormonism

Jan Shipps

A certain discrepancy between expectations and what transpires is normal, even predictable. Acute incongruity between anticipation and what actually happens is rarer, less routine. Real irony, however, is unusual, something sufficiently out of the ordinary to be regarded as exceptional. Considered from one standpoint, the journals of William E. McLellin that had been reposing in a safe of the LDS Church Historian or of the First Presidency since 1908 meet the irony test; their content seems genuinely ironic in view of the circumstances surrounding their discovery.

The papers of McLellin, an Illinois schoolteacher who converted to Mormonism in 1831, became an apostle in 1835, but afterwards left the Church and was branded apostate, had long been presumed lost until the nefarious document dealer Mark Hofmann reported in the mid-1980s that he had found them. This was the same document dealer whose production—I use the term advisedly—of both a forged agreement alleging the involvement of the Joseph Smiths, Senior and Junior, in a gold-digging enterprise and the so-called "salamander letter," which implied a direct connection between the Book of Mormon and white magic, had concentrated substantial attention on Mormonism's enigmatic beginnings both inside and outside the movement. Many therefore expected—and some feared—that any contemporaneous documents in a collection of McLellin's papers would be filled with information that would add to a perception of early Mormonism as a hotbed of occultism and hermetic hocus-pocus. Instead, what these narratives from the 1830s depict is a struggling missionary band preaching not only a millennialist message that, to be sure, reflected the importance of the coming forth of the Book of Mormon as a signal that the end was near, but also a message whose true anchor was nonetheless the Christian scriptures.

As the earliest extended account of the Mormon experience, McLellin's missionary journals are significant documents. They are not significant because they either extend knowledge about or challenge early Mormonism's radical and esoteric aspect; they do not speak to this side of the story at all. They are important historical documents because they point to an often overlooked (or summarily dismissed) part of the story of early Mormonism, i.e., the movement's rootedness in Christianity and the extent to which its representatives preached the Mormon gospel within that familiar framework. What McLellin wrote is historiographically significant on two additional accounts: these missionary journals direct the spotlight toward a neglected, but crucially important, dimension of early Mormonism, and they reveal a great deal about religion in that period between the American Revolution and the Civil War usually referred to as the early republic. At the same time, the journals comprise an extraordinary spiritual autobiography that discloses much about the experiential dimension of a religious movement that is usually described in terms either of particular personalities—Joseph Smith, Brigham Young, Parley P. Pratt, Heber C. Kimball, and so on—or of the distinctive, even radical, nature of its theology, doctrine, and institutional makeup.

The focal point of nearly every existing account of early Mormon history (including my own) has been, as the title of Richard Bushman's 1984 study put it, *Joseph Smith and the Beginnings of Mormonism*.[1] Because this is the case, authors have naturally directed attention to the coming forth of the Book of Mormon and Smith's prophetic career. In following the Prophet from western New York to Kirtland, Ohio, historians have been inordinately concerned with the Saints at the heart of the movement. Hence much notice is also directed to the story of the Mormons sent by the Prophet to establish a Mormon settlement in Independence, Missouri. As a result, regardless of whether the Prophet is depicted as a man who spoke with and for God or as one who was a crafty and devious practitioner of the magic arts, existing histories of Joseph Smith and his followers during Mormonism's early years paint a picture that, more often than not, portrays an unconventional and iconoclastic movement with two centers where all adherents to Mormonism were concentrated.[2]

Such history is a seriously foreshortened picture, especially of Mormonism during its first decade.[3] But the distortion is understandable because the sources that portray the introduction and, at times, subsequent flowering of this new form of Christianity in the hamlets, villages, and small towns of the early republic have been too skimpy and too scattered to allow a satisfactory full-scale account of the story of this dimension of the movement to be written. Since they furnish a full and reasonably systematic description of Mormonism as it emerged connected to, yet apart from, Kirtland and Independence, McLellin's unusually full and literate journals provide a basis for filling this lacuna.

At the same time, these documents provide convincing evidence that an actual religious marketplace existed in the United States in the middle years of the first half of what has been designated as the Christian century. These six journals of McLellin's missionary tours—one in each year between 1831 and 1836—describe how preachers of every stripe were proclaiming the gospel in the schoolhouses, courthouses, meetinghouses, and even barns that formed the public square in the towns, villages, and hamlets of the 1830s hinterland. They characterize, as well, the "product" offered by the Saints in the new nation's spiritual emporium.

Rehearsing the topics and circumstances of his own discourses and those of other LDS missionaries with surprising fullness, McLellin often recorded the subject matter of sermons and sometimes indicated how listeners responded. He also frequently designated the precise biblical texts on which he and his compatriots preached. Such information makes possible a comparison of the Saints' message with those preached in the same arena, and often from the same pulpit, by the representatives of other Christian faiths. The accounts in these journals also impart a sense of how central to the message being preached by the followers of the Prophet was their understanding that theirs was "the Church of Christ."

They reveal, as well, that preachers from many other groups were equally convinced that theirs was Christ's church. To complicate matters in these years, the Disciples of Christ (Campbellites), whose church was also organized in 1830, were likewise named the Church of Christ. This meant that the Saints sometimes had difficulty in differentiating themselves from other Christians who were in the field at the same time. In particular, they often faced the demanding task of distinguishing themselves from the followers of Thomas and Alexander Campbell, Barton Stone, and others, who had somehow managed to take possession of the name Christian. About midway through the text of these journals, McLellin describes an episode that dramatizes the competitive temperament of the United States religious arena during this period. On April 15, 1833, McLellin and Parley Pratt were at the water's edge with several converts who were ready "to be baptized in the faith of the Church of Christ" when they were interrupted by a representative of a competing denomination who hailed one Sophia White and calling her "Sister . . . urged her to not throw herself away or out of the church of Christ, as he called it."[4] In view of this confusion, it is not surprising that, by 1834, Smith's followers had started calling themselves Mormons and calling their church the "Church of Latter Day Saints."[5]

If the Mormons had to share the name of their institution with other groups, however, their possession of a modern work of scripture made their message unique. These McLellin journals convey the extraordinary importance of the usual pattern of LDS preaching of the existence of the Book of Mormon as support for the gospel set forth in the New Testament; they likewise make clear how Smith's followers used the book in their preaching in those early days. Although the Book of Mormon is almost always mentioned, at only three points does this extended account of six years of Mormon preaching in the early 1830s indicate that this scripture was used as a source for sermon texts. For all that, the Book of Mormon was critically important. McLellin himself seems always to have emphasized it and, at one point, complained when a missionary companion did not even mention it. But how was the Book of Mormon used by the early Mormon evangelists? LDS preachers seem to have pointed primarily to the *fact* of the book, to its very existence, as verification for the validity of the Bible. Of greater significance, they pointed to its coming forth as the opening event in the dispensation that was serving as the "winding-up scene" before the curtain rose on the *eschaton*. The Book of Mormon was therefore presented as the ultimate sign of the times, indicating the Saints' conviction that people in the United States in the 1830s were living at the end of time.

Although their author was often in Kirtland, Ohio, these documents are totally silent about the building of a temple in that place;
he attended, but does not mention the dedication of the temple, an
event which is sometimes described as the Mormon Pentecost.
There is no allusion in the journals to the calling of a church patriarch
nor to Zion's Camp, the military expedition the Prophet led to
Missouri in an attempt to preserve the Independence "stake of Zion."
And the Kingdom of God is mentioned only in the context of a
sermon on Mark 1:15, not in connection with the organization of the
Kingdom of God that accompanied the dedication of the Kirtland
Temple.[6] Considering the neglect of these Hebraic elements that
were being introduced into Mormonism and McLellin's relative
silence about continuing revelation and the prophetic aspect of Mormonism generally, as well as the stress placed on the Book of Mormon
as the herald of the kingdom, these documents suggest that the primary
message of early Mormon preaching was millennialist Christianity.[7]
Those whose ears were attuned heard that the end was near, a
not unfamiliar message. Unlike the messages of other millennialist
preachers, however, this one was distinguished by the claim that the
coming forth of the Book of Mormon signaled the imminence of
the Second Coming. These Mormon good tidings also emphasized
that the Church of Christ had been restored and that through this
institution humanity could, as promised in the text of the first chapter
of the second letter of Peter on which these preachers often spoke,
"escape from the corruption that is in the world . . . and become
partakers of the divine nature."[8] Incidences of unaccountable healings
and speaking in tongues were interpreted by LDS preachers and their
listeners alike as testimony to the authenticity of this version of the
Christian message.[9] But most importantly, these journals show that
the existence of the Book of Mormon is what initially set LDS
preaching apart from the exhortations of the "sectarians," as Protestants and Catholics were classified by the Saints.
Yet McLellin's writing, especially in Journals IV and V, also
makes it clear that the patterns of Mormon life in the countryside
were not particularly distinctive, however much the content of the
Saints' message might differ from other Christian preaching. By 1834
and 1835, the religious lives of the Mormon converts who did not
gather to Zion were being lived within the context of small

congregations presided over by what amounted to lay leaders. This arrangement meant that McLellin and other church dignitaries who filled missions were functioning somewhat in the manner of circuit riders, filling the roles of both traveling evangelist and priest.

A dramatic contrast materializes if McLellin's report of what was going on in the countryside is compared with what was happening in the gathering centers where the focus was on the Prophet and on institutional elaboration. Initially pouring into Kirtland where their leader was in residence, Joseph Smith's followers created the first of a series of gathered communities which obliterated the boundaries between civil society and the sacred that were being so clearly drawn elsewhere in the United States as state and church became separate at the local as well as the federal level. In Kirtland (and later in Independence) citizens of rather ordinary midwestern towns daily came into face-to-face contact with one who could speak for God.[10] If revelations from on high were not announced every day, Kirtland settlers had the medium for receipt of such communications in their presence. This fact separated them from the citizens of nearby Mentor and Painesville. It likewise separated Smith's followers in Kirtland from the Saints in a settlement such as Amherst, Ohio, not fifty miles away. There the Mormons organized a local church to which the Saints came for meetings but from which they returned to their homes in the vicinity roundabout, apparently managing their church membership much as it was managed by Baptists, Methodists, and other Protestants in the area.

The new converts to the Mormon movement shared acceptance of Joseph Smith's prophetic claims as well as the claim that the church he organized and led was Christ's only true church. They also all embraced the Book of Mormon as an additional work of scripture whose coming forth signaled the opening of the final dispensation of time. The journals nonetheless make it clear that while many converts gave up everything to settle with other Saints in Zionic enclaves, many who believed did not do so, but continued to live apart from their gospel siblings. This contrast can best be articulated in terms of *difference* and *otherness*, concepts whose use in making distinctions within Mormonism can clarify and illuminate the relationship between this movement and the incipient Protestant mainstream in America, not only in the 1830s, when William McLellin was recording his missionary experiences, but at every point in time since then.

While *difference* and *otherness* are mainly perceptual from within and without, both are manifested actually as well as symbolically. *Difference*, however, is most often evidenced in doctrine and ritual—religious dimensions in Ninian Smart's terminology. Thus in this case the disparity is likely more rhetorical and symbolic than actual. *Otherness* is likewise exhibited in doctrine and ritual, but genuine *otherness* is more often imputed to persons and groups whose beliefs take literal shape visible enough to be recognized by persons without as well as within a community, religious or otherwise.[11]

Although Mormonism's original and distinctive beliefs were not unimportant in engendering Protestant antagonism both in the gathering centers and in the countryside, it is this last, the behavioral aspect of the gathered Mormon community, that generated the overt and sometimes violent opposition that resulted in the Saints' hegira from New York to Ohio and Missouri, from Missouri to Illinois, and from Nauvoo to the Mountain West. McLellin's account of the emergence of Mormonism in the rural and semirural areas of the Midwest and Northeast during these years in which religious patterns were being set in the early republic describes verbal hostility to the Mormon messengers rather than the type of open persecution against those who heard and believed that would come to characterize the relationship between the Saints in the gathering centers and their neighbors.

Read with foreknowledge of the divisions in the Mormon movement that occurred after the death of the Prophet, these journals are prescient because they disclose striking variation *within* the Mormon movement. While personalities were critically important, the disagreements that would lead to fission in the years after the Prophet's death reflected a division between the Saints like McLellin who were content with *difference* and those like Brigham Young who would hold to the profound *otherness* emerging in Kirtland during the period when the new theology and practice that were part and parcel of the "restoration of all things" took shape.

Foreknowledge of what would occur in Mormonism more than a century later also makes McLellin's picture of Mormonism in the countryside in the 1830s seem surprisingly contemporary. Although those of Joseph Smith's followers who would come together under the leadership of the Prophet's son would adopt (and/or return to) the pattern exemplifying *difference* that these journals make so manifest, the Saints who went west created and lived within gathered communities as peculiar people. Their history across the first 150 years of Mormonism has become so familiar to the Saints—and to students of Mormonism—that the modern pattern in which Saints worship together in block meetings on Sunday and afterward go their separate ways until the next time of meeting has appeared to be a dramatic departure from normative Mormonism. McLellin's account of the Saints who lived in the mission fields in the early years suggests instead that modern Mormon patterns of worship and living in the world are close to the pattern that existed in the countryside in Mormonism's early years. Thus these revealing journals are further evidence of the richness and complexity of this extraordinary religious movement. They will be of great interest to all types of Latterday Saints. And they are a significant resource for all who wish to understand the history of Mormonism and the history of American religion in the years between 1831 and 1836.

NOTES

[1] Emphasis mine. This work was published by the University of Illinois Press in 1984. For other recent works, see also Shipps, *Mormonism: The Story of a New Religious Tradition* (Urbana: University of Illinois Press, 1985); Marvin S. Hill, *Quest for Refuge: The Mormon Flight from American Pluralism* (Salt Lake City: Signature Books, 1989); Kenneth H. Winn, *Exiles in a Land of Liberty: Mormons in America, 1830-1846* (Chapel Hill: University of North Carolina Press, 1989); John L. Brooke, *The Refiner's Fire: The Making of the Mormon Cosmology, 1644-1844* (New York: Cambridge University Press, 1994). Treatment of Mormon beginnings in the most important recent surveys of Latter-day Saint history also center on Joseph Smith and developments in the areas where his followers gathered, i.e., James B. Allen and Glen M. Leonard, *The Story of the Latter-day Saints,* 2d ed. (Salt Lake City: Deseret Book, 1992); and Leonard J. Arrington and Davis Bitton, *The Mormon Experience: A History of the Latter-day Saints* (New York: Alfred A. Knopf, 1979).

² This is as true for much of what might be called the official historiography of the movement, i.e., works issued by the various church presses, as for non-canonized and even antagonistic accounts of the first years of Mormonism.

³ If the measurement is from the publication of the Book of Mormon and the organization of the Church, the first decade extends from 1830 through 1839, but if the starting point is the Prophet's translation of the Book of Mormon and the initial preaching of the gospel which effectively inaugurate this movement, the first decade opens in 1829 and closes in 1838, the year Joseph Smith fled from Ohio to Missouri.

⁴ Note the uppercase *C* in the reference to the Saints' church and the lowercase *c* in the reference to the competing denomination. Throughout these journals the author continues to refer to his church as the "Church of Christ," but on August 1, 1834, he writes of preaching about the "church of the Latter day Saints" for the first time. In making such references afterward, he indicated that this was not the Church's official name by writing these three words without capitalizing either the *L* or the *S* and by placing single quotes around them.

⁵ In these documents, this designation appears first in Journal IV and again in Journal V. An 1838 revelation confirmed that the Church of Jesus Christ of Latter-day Saints should be the official name of the Church, a matter that was so troubling to McLellin that it figured in his leaving the Church.

⁶ Zion's Camp is the name the Prophet gave to the 1834 military expedition he mounted from Kirtland to go to the assistance to the beleaguered Saints being driven out of Independence. The reference to the Kingdom of God is found in the journal entry for August 3, 1835.

⁷ These journals likewise reveal an intense biblicism and concern with spiritual gifts, especially healing and speaking in tongues.

⁸ In the most recent work on the radical and hermetic features of early Mormonism, John L. Brooke suggests that the use of this particular text would have been a reference to the radical theological concept of eternal progression toward godhood which was introduced into Mormonism in the 1840s. Tracing the history of this notion in radical theologies from the sixteenth century forward, as well as in popular forms of Masonry, Brooke argues that the concept of partaking of the divine nature as gods was present in Mormonism from the very beginning. See *The Refiner's Fire*, chapter 8. Although the McLellin journals record the use of this text on several occasions, such a reference to eternal progression or to Smith's followers' becoming gods is nowhere indicated.

⁹ Not surprisingly, accounts of the sermons that were preached suggest that Mormon preachers asserted that the manifestation of spiritual gifts was evidence that the followers of Joseph Smith had the "true" Church of Christ. More interesting to those who read documents closely is the extent to which these are the journals of a literate writer. The entries

that reflect manifestation of spiritual gifts either to McLellin personally or in the context of a preaching "appointment," however, are sometimes filled with sentence fragments, misspelled words, and misplaced or missing punctuation.

[10] This lent to Kirtland an extraordinary character that found expression in the construction of a temple rather than the usual Protestant steepled meetinghouse. Thus the Kirtland "built environment" differed from that of nearby settlements. The same cannot be said for the Mormon settlements in Missouri, but only because the Saints were driven from the area before their imprint on the built environment was manifested.

[11] See the discussion of the dimensions of religion as they are manifested in early Mormonism in Shipps, *Mormonism*, chapter 3.

The Acts of the Apostle William E. McLellin

John W. Welch

The discovery of the William E. McLellin journals is as significant to Latter-day Saint history as the discovery of an original diary of an early Christian apostle or bishop would be to New Testament studies. Just as Luke, Barnabas, and Silas journeyed and preached with Paul during the earliest years of Christianity, so McLellin traveled and proclaimed the gospel with many significant early Mormon figures from 1831 to 1836. His companions included such prominent men as Hyrum Smith in Journal I, Samuel Smith in Journal II, Parley P. Pratt in Journal III, and his brethren in the Quorum of the Twelve Apostles in Journal V. Although the McLellin documents can be approached and studied in many ways, viewing them as primary sources for the study of the emergence and rapid propagation of a young Christian movement can help readers gain a sense of the spirit that impelled the rise of early Mormonism.

Because they are so clear and engaging, the McLellin journals require little introduction in many respects. They tell modern readers many details about the miracles, conversions, doctrines, beliefs, difficulties, and successes of these Latter-day Saint adherents. During the early 1830s, McLellin wrote informatively and sincerely about Mormon worship, as well as about his personal religious practices, his apostolic joys and sorrows, his challenges and results. Moreover, he faithfully recorded the specific topics that filled the lengthy sermons delivered mostly by himself, but also by the others who were with him. Luke's Acts of the Apostles likewise tells of the spiritual experiences, successes, hardships, and messages of the early disciples of Jesus Christ. In early Mormon documents like McLellin's journals, one finds all of the makings of a modern Acts—a point that was not lost on the early Saints themselves. For example, Reynolds Cahoon, one of McLellin's first Mormon acquaintances, ended his 1832 journal with the attestation: "Wherefore these are the Acts of Reynolds up to August 19th, 1832."[1]

While it is unknown when the accounts in the book of Acts were first committed to writing,[2] the McLellin papers commence in July 1831, only fifteen months after Joseph Smith organized the newly restored Church of Jesus Christ of Latter-day Saints on April 6, 1830. Thus, the contemporaneous daily entries in these journals have the advantage of not being a compiled or edited history; they were not influenced from the outset by the fact that the writer knew the end of the story from its beginning.

Accordingly, for Latter-day Saints and all readers interested in the beginnings of new religions, the events reported by McLellin offer a rare and significant glimpse into the details of the day-to-day, real-life experiences of the earliest Mormon missionaries and apostles as they proclaimed their message of restored Christianity to all who would listen. These journals are well-written, readable, vivid, and interesting. McLellin supplies enough information about many episodes to enable the reader to picture the setting and, even from a distance, to share something of these experiences with the original participants.

By briefly relating some of the main elements that characterize the acts of William E. McLellin to the New Testament book of Acts, I hope that these introductory comments will draw attention to a few of the strong religious themes in these journals.[3] First, some of the similarities between the New Testament book of Acts and the McLellin journals are explored. Then the topics of the sermons mentioned in the journals, which offer significant insights into the nature and content of early Mormon preaching, are discussed. I am especially impressed, after working with these journals, by their religious content. These documents confirm that the early Mormon experience was not eccentric or aberrational, but was deeply rooted in the Christian Bible, in the gospel of Jesus Christ, and in the spirit of revelation and prophecy. As my colleague Jan Shipps has pointed out above, the McLellin journals allow us to see an important but rarely seen side of early Mormonism growing in the outlying countryside. Many of the following principles, practices, and doctrines tied that side of early Mormonism to its central stakes in Ohio and Missouri, just as they have continued to supply coherence to Mormonism down to the present day.

The Acts of William E. McLellin

Although these journals cannot aspire to the status of scripture, many readers conversant with the book of Acts will be struck by the similarities between McLellin's nineteenth-century records and the earliest Christian history in the New Testament. For example, the book of Acts, although not primarily intended as an exposition of the teachings of the early Christians, contains—especially in the middle chapters—important keys to understanding the doctrines and basic practices of first-century gentile Christianity established by Paul among the Greeks, away from the early centers of Jerusalem and Antioch. McLellin likewise mainly chronicles the growth and progress of one part of early Mormonism, located away from the LDS centers in Kirtland and Independence.

Of primary importance to the ancient Apostles were the fundamental practices and ordinances of faith, repentance, baptism, and bestowing the gift of the Holy Ghost by the laying on of hands.[4] McLellin preaches the same basic principles and ordinances of the gospel, baptizes, and bestows the gift of the Holy Ghost by the laying on of hands.

At the same time, little reference is made in the book of Acts to the stories of Jesus, his miracles, his resurrection; the writer assumes that the reader knows these foundational elements. McLellin does likewise: He offers few details about the founding events and visions of the Restoration, evidently taking those essentials for granted as he makes his personal day-by-day entries.

In addition, both works share an essential enthusiasm for the new gospel dispensation that each proclaims. The book of Acts begins at the time of the ascension of Jesus and of the angel's promise that Christ would come again (Acts 1:11).[5] The same impending millennial expectation permeates the early McLellin journals.

As they shared the gospel, the early Christians made substantial use of the scriptures accepted by their hosts, primarily as they quoted from the prevailing Septuagint translation of the Hebrew

Bible to prove their points and to buttress their claims of doctrinal correctness.[6] Such references were intended to persuade listeners that they should accept the new revelation in Christ by pointing them to evidence in their own authoritative scriptures. McLellin similarly relies heavily on the Bible to justify his religious teachings and to convert and convince his audiences that they should believe in the new revelations proclaimed by Joseph Smith.[7]

Acts emphasizes spiritual outpourings, notably on the day of Pentecost in Jerusalem, when all who were present were "filled with the Holy Ghost, and began to speak with other tongues, as the Spirit gave them utterance" (Acts 2:4). In Acts 10:44-46, Peter speaks to the Gentiles and the Holy Ghost falls "on all them which heard the word . . . for they heard them speak with tongues, and magnify God." In a like fashion, McLellin on several occasions reports magnificent manifestations of the power of God and speaking in tongues.[8]

This list of similarities can be extended greatly. Both works involve revelations, prophesying, seeing visions, and dreaming dreams.[9] Just as McLellin speaks often about the signs of the times, Acts likewise points out the signs in the earth.[10] Both texts feature extraordinary healings. For example, Peter and John heal a lame beggar in the temple (Acts 3:1-11), and later the "multitude" brought "sick folks, and them which were vexed with unclean spirits; and they were healed every one" (Acts 5:16).[11] Acts is also characterized by dreams and new revelations about the law, about what to do and where to go. At almost every turn, McLellin's daily entries partake of the same miraculous characteristics: he reports some twenty-three cases of healing the sick, several other physical manifestations of the power of God, one instance of discerning of spirits, two acts of casting out devils, seven occurrences of speaking in tongues, and four times when divine help was received along the way. Journals I through IV are relatively consistent in reporting manifestations of the spirit or miraculous occurrences (by my count, fifteen, seven, eleven, and fourteen times, respectively in these four journals). Fewer instances are reported in Journals V and VI (six and three events each).

From the book of Acts, readers sense the strong bonds of fellowship, worship, and prayer that forged a unity among the early Christians (Acts 2:42). An early Christian objective was to be "of one heart and of one soul" (Acts 4:32). So also, from the time of his conversion on August 20, 1831, and throughout his ministry, McLellin similarly placed a high premium on cultivating the virtues of peace, harmony, and humility.

At first the early Christians gathered at Jerusalem, but soon the leaders of the young Christian religion had to deal with congregations gathered in many locations. Growth was a crucial concern for survival and viability.[12] McLellin reflects the same conditions among the members of the early Mormon movement, who were concerned about united gathering as well as dispersed growth.

In several instances, the author of Acts revels in occasions when the young Christian church was opposed or oppressed by the established religion but emerged victorious.[13] McLellin savors similar successes.

The New Testament history depicts early Christianity as being accepted at first by Jewish leaders, such as Gamaliel, who argued that Christianity should not be seen as a threat (Acts 5); but persecution of the Christians intensified as they began to succeed (Acts 14:1-7). In much the same way, the initial reception of Mormons by some Christian congregations was quite hospitable: McLellin and his companions were often allowed to preach in the buildings of other churches, being preferred over other speakers by vote of those congregations. Before long, however, reactions to the burgeoning Mormonism became increasingly antagonistic.

All of the McLellin journals and much of Acts (chaps. 16-20) report missionary journeys. The early Christian leaders typically stayed at the homes of hosts, as Peter did at the home of Cornelius in Caesarea. McLellin followed the same practice.

The Acts of the Apostles, as its name indicates, tells principally about the work and conduct of the Twelve Apostles, their duties, discussions, councils, and actions. The McLellin journals, especially in 1835, also disclose new and interesting details about the newly organized Quorum of the Twelve and its first mission to New York, Canada, and New England.[14] Of course in the book of Acts, not all of the Twelve are equally represented; Peter, John, and Paul receive most of the attention. Likewise, McLellin's picture is understandably selective and incomplete.

Dissension soon developed within early Christianity as doctrines—such as the use of circumcision or the proper relationship of
Christians to the law of Moses (ch. 15)—needed to be further
defined. Pharisees who believed in Christ continued to promote their
own ideas about the observance of the law (Acts 15:5). Fledgling
branches of the Church in Greece and Asia Minor needed direction
and strengthening. In much the same way, McLellin finds himself
dealing with problems in the young branches of the restored Church,
notably in Florence, Ohio.

Acts gladly reports Paul's hardships. Early Christians were
proud to be "counted worthy to suffer shame" for the name of the
Lord (Acts 5:41), and sharp contrasts were drawn between the righteousness of the believers and the wickedness of the surrounding
world.[15] McLellin likewise reports his difficult journeys across dry
and desolate prairies, his dignified penury, and his disdain for the
luxuries of the world's ways.

Without overstating the significance of these similarities, and
while allowing for normal historical differences, these basic factors
in the history of early Christianity are substantially congruent with
the most visible characteristics of the McLellin journals. Whatever
implications or conclusions one may choose to draw from these
points, the parallels between the experiences reported in Acts and
in the McLellin journals are extensive, pervasive, and illuminating.

The Content of Early Mormon Preaching

Of all that is found in these journals, among the most valuable
elements are McLellin's descriptions of the sermons that he and his
companions preached in the earliest years of Mormonism. Fortunately, during the six years spanned by these journals, McLellin was
diligent and consistent in recording in his journals the topics covered
in almost every sermon that he mentioned. The composite listing of
these topics, sermon after sermon, provides a rare profile of the
content of early Mormon preaching. Prior to the discovery of these
documents, little was known about typical Mormon sermons in the
initial period of LDS Church history. Never before have historians
been able to learn so much about what was preached in the town
assemblies or LDS meetings in the early 1830s. These basic messages

are those that have consistently articulated and propelled the essence of Mormon enthusiasm, dreams, doctrines, and concerns.

McLellin was remarkably constant during his early missionary years with respect to his main themes and primary religious interests. By far the most frequent topic in his sermons was the Book of Mormon, evidences in its behalf, prophecies about its coming forth, testimonies of its divinity, and validations of its worth in opening the glories of the latter days (his theme in over thirty-three sermons). The next most commonly treated subjects in his discourses were the articles and covenants of the Church (some eighteen occurrences), faith (at least seven times), the gathering of the Jews and of the Saints in two respective locations (fifteen times), the gospel (fifteen or more times), the impending judgments of God (five times), the Kingdom of Christ (six times), priesthood authority or priesthoods (nine times), the rise and establishment of the Church (nine times), and the second coming of Christ (nine times). Also treated on several occasions were charity, Christian perfection, the Church of God in all ages in the Bible, communion, the divine authenticity of Mormonism, forgiveness, gifts of the spirit, glories of heaven, the Holy Ghost, laying on of hands, the Millennium, obedience, ordinances, parables, the plan of redemption, prayer, prophecy, repentance, signs of the times, the workings of the Spirit, knowing the truth, and confusion in the world. Among McLellin's favorite scriptures were 2 Peter 1 (on divine nature), 1 Corinthians 12 (on the gifts of the spirit), and Psalms 37:37 (on the perfect man, whose end is peace). These topics and scriptures are similar to those also appearing in the sermons of McLellin's traveling companions.[16] Although his views about many of these subjects changed over time, McLellin retained throughout his lifetime an interest in many of these topics, especially the Book of Mormon.

Readers may wish to follow McLellin's preaching from year to year.[17] Subtle shifts in the topics that he chose to emphasize may disclose instructive insights into developments in McLellin's own thinking, as well as the prevailing concerns of the Church as a whole.

In 1831, McLellin's two dominant preaching topics were the Book of Mormon and the judgments of God to occur at the impending second coming of Christ. Other complementary subjects included the gathering of the Saints to Zion and the Jews to Jerusalem, the restoration of the ancient gospel in its glorious plainness, spiritual gifts in the Church, and the duties required of people by the Lord. Thus, in his initial year the new convert was single-minded in his proclamation of the Book of Mormon as ushering in the coming of Christ and the establishment of Zion—key elements in McLellin's own conversion. In trumpeting this eschatological news in Journal I, McLellin mentions no specific biblical references in connection with his preaching, although he reports that he cited biblical scriptures in support of the Book of Mormon. Other LDS speakers, who likewise emphasized the Book of Mormon, gathering, and prophecies of danger, made brief use of Galatians 1 in proclaiming the truth of only one gospel of Jesus Christ.

In 1832, McLellin continued to proclaim these themes, but his preaching as reported in Journal II became more specific and Church-oriented. Rather than simply mentioning the evidences and testimonies concerning the coming forth of the Book of Mormon, McLellin now stressed the utility and importance of the book as well, and he spoke often about ecclesiastical themes that would build the Church and lead its members to peace and glory in Christ: covenants, obedience, ordinances (particularly the laying on of hands), prophecies, the fulness of the gospel, the plan of salvation, and the glories of heaven, as well as Christian perfection and gatherings in Zion and Jerusalem. He contrasted the Church with the world in all biblical ages, and he compared the restored Church to the first establishment of the Church in New Testament times. Several of these church themes probably reflect McLellin's recent experiences with church leaders, as he lived close to Joseph Smith in Ohio at the end of 1831 and the beginning of 1832. Some of McLellin's topics even correlate with revelations that were being received around this time by Joseph Smith. For example, Doctrine and Covenants 76 was received in February 1832, at the end of Journal II, and revealed information about salvation and the glories of heaven, topics taught at that time by McLellin. He also expounded the signs of the Church of Christ mentioned in Doctrine and Covenants 46 (compare 1 Corinthians 12).

McLellin did not complete his mission to the South described in Journal II, and in December 1832, he was disciplined by Joseph Smith, evidently for neglecting this calling. In January 1833, a repentant McLellin embarked with Parley P. Pratt on a fervent mission in the South (around Missouri). During this mission, McLellin preached the primitive faith once delivered to the early saints, repentance, and the plainness of the gospel contained in the Bible and the Book of Mormon. He invited all to come unto Christ, to receive the truth, and to experience the witness of the Spirit. In Journal III, he continued to praise the Book of Mormon, to warn people of the signs of the times, and to extol the beauties of the regulations within the Church. He also added new themes to his repertoire: prayer; trusting in God and not in man (a message that long remained important to McLellin personally); eschewing the mistakes of the flesh; understanding the nature of parables, communion, and the priesthood; and establishing what McLellin called "the Kingdom of Christ."

During this time, by way of contrast, Pratt's themes were much broader than McLellin's messages of fundamental simplicity and austere spirituality. Pratt spoke expansively of such things as the creation from the beginning to the end; who Jesus was, is, and will be; the nature of revelation from the creation to the present; Enoch's prophecy; and the restitution of all things spoken of by all the holy prophets. Apparently Pratt and the authors of articles from this time in the Church's periodicals also used more explicit recitation and exposition of scripture. Pratt read or gave definite sermons on such passages as Alma 9-16, Isaiah 49, Ezekiel 6-9, 3 Nephi 11-18, and Psalm 102, whereas McLellin seems to have dwelt more on plain and basic elements of the Spirit and of building the kingdom.

Journal IV covers ten months following the arrival of Joseph Smith and Zion's Camp in Missouri. During these months, McLellin preached on virtually all of the subjects found in his first three journals, as well as several new topics. He preached several times on 2 Peter 1 and the attributes of godliness. He delivered messages on specific virtues of charity, humility, endurance, forgiveness, unity, joy, and the laws of Zion. He spoke more openly than before about the beneficial effects of these virtues on society, on the one hand, and about the confusion and falsehood of the world, on the other hand. In connection with the nature of the kingdom of Christ, McLellin spoke pointedly in Journal IV about the authority given by God to the Church of the Latter-day Saints, specifically about the two priesthoods. In reasoning about the Book of Mormon, McLellin argued more directly than before about the comparisons and unities between it and the Bible. He also spoke once on the covenants of Abraham and Joseph.

During this time, McLellin recorded relatively few comments about the preaching of the others who accompanied him. Growing somewhat impatient with John Boynton, McLellin commented on November 14, 1834, that Boynton had delivered "a fine discourse but he never mentioned the Book of Mormon once." This is an important disclosure that, at least in McLellin's mind, no Mormon sermon was complete without at least one reference to the Book of Mormon.

In Journal V, while he was traveling with the newly organized Quorum of the Twelve Apostles during the summer of 1835, McLellin's preaching seems to have settled on a few main messages that he repeated on several occasions. Against the steady backdrop of sermons about the gospel, the Book of Mormon, the priesthoods, authority to act in the name of Jesus Christ, the Kingdom of God, and the second coming of Christ, the new apostolic witness gave precedence to the twin themes of perfection and truth. He expounded on Abraham and perfection, perfection in the Psalms, and Christian perfection. He discoursed on evidences of truth, the effects of truth, the Holy Ghost as the source of truth, the Book of Mormon and the truth, and the plainness of truth, occasionally as contrasted with the religions of the day.

Others sharing the pulpit with McLellin in 1835 spoke on similar topics: faith, truth, the religions of the day, the Book of Mormon (notably the Savior's teachings in 3 Nephi), the two priesthoods, the gift of tongues, superfluous dress, immortality, "the Vision" (D&C 76), the gathering of the Jews, and the Kingdom of Christ, although no explicit mention is made of gathering to Zion.

McLellin's brief final mission began in April 1836, only a few days after the dedication of the Kirtland Temple. Later McLellin would voice complaints about the conduct of some of the brethren in celebrating the completion of this edifice, and he would express disappointment in the temple endowment that he received at that time; but his 1836 journal contains no hint of any such disapproval. By the same token, Journal VI never mentions the temple at all, at least directly. Some of his preaching, however, may reflect themes connected with the dedicatory experiences in Kirtland. Two of McLellin's first sermons in 1836 were on the dispensations that established the religions of Moses, Jesus (or Peter), and Joseph. This topic may echo the restoration of keys to Joseph Smith by Moses on April 3, 1836, and by Peter in 1829. He also spoke on the glory of the new work. At the same time, McLellin carried on with a few of his old standbys: evidences of the Book of Mormon, perfection, revelation, the covenants and articles, and the rise and establishment of the Church.

One may also begin to detect in McLellin's final journal evidence of a subtle distancing between McLellin and his brethren in the Church.[18] Although we know virtually nothing from early Christian times about the religious life of doubting Thomas or several other of Jesus' disciples who may or may not have remained faithful to the main body of Christians, McLellin's subsequent history is well-known.[19] The brewing estrangement between McLellin and his brethren is perhaps most strongly indicated by the fact that in Journal VI, for the first time, McLellin travels alone, manifests fewer gifts of the Spirit, and never mentions the topic of any sermon by anyone except himself.

Despite this interesting body of information about the content of early Mormon preaching, McLellin's entries are unfortunately always very brief. Typically he gives in very short compass only one, two, or three main topics of each of his sermons. Thus, readers are left to wonder exactly what he said about these important themes. For example, when he spoke about the witnesses for the Book of Mormon, how much detail did he give about the appearances of Moroni to the Book of Mormon Witnesses (most of whom he came to know personally)? When he spoke about "the rise and progress of the Church," how many of the visions of Joseph Smith were recounted? When he spoke about the two priesthoods or about Peter and the divine authority given by God to the Church, did he comment on the restoration of the Aaronic and Melchizedek Priesthoods at the hands of heavenly messengers? His failure to record any of these details cannot be taken as evidence that he did not mention such points, since his entries never elaborate on the topics of his sermons.

Luckily, however, one may turn to other contemporaneous sources for information about the typical points of doctrine that were being taught in early Mormon sermons. These other sources supply much substantive information that probably parallels the content of these sermons mentioned only briefly by McLellin in his journals. In particular, many of the topics on which McLellin and his companions delivered sermons were also the subjects of articles and editorials published in the two Church periodicals at that time. Indeed, the list of topics that were expounded over the pulpit by McLellin corresponds closely with the subjects treated on the printed pages of the two Church periodicals of the day, *The Evening and the Morning Star* and *The Messenger and Advocate.*[20]

Although the McLellin journals are among the earliest and the most extensively detailed LDS missionary diaries, his journals are not the only Mormon records of this general kind from this historical period. At least fifty other missionary journals from the 1830s are housed in the LDS Church Archives in Salt Lake City. Like McLellin's writings, many of these early journals include descriptions of the writer's conversion to Mormonism, interactions with other members of the Church, and extracts from revelations later published in the Doctrine and Covenants. Anyone interested in comprehensively studying this genre of religious and historical documents should consult these sources.[21]

The McLellin journals are clear, engaging, and authentic (in both senses of that word). They will be essential primary sources for anyone researching the history of The Church of Jesus Christ of Latter-day Saints in the early 1830s.

NOTES

[1] Reynolds Cahoon Diary, No. 2, typescript p. 4, LDS Church Archives. For a somewhat comparable literary approach to writings of eight apostles in 1839–40, see Eugene England, "A Modern Acts of the Apostles, 1840: Mormon Literature in the Making," *BYU Studies* 27, no. 2 (1987): 79–95.

[2] Regarding the problems of ascertaining the time of composition of the book of Acts, see any good commentary on Acts. Johannes Munck, *The Acts of the Apostles* (Garden City, N. Y.: Doubleday, 1967), xlvi–liv, for example, argues for a relatively early date, "at the beginning of the sixties," liv.

³ To locate many specific page references for these themes in the McLellin journals, see the respective entries in the subject index at the end of this volume.

⁴ In addition to the teachings of Peter on the day of Pentecost (Acts 2:38), several accounts in the book of Acts, such as Philip's baptism of the eunuch in Acts 8, follow this pattern. "Then laid they their hands on them, and they received the Holy Ghost" (Acts 8:17).

⁵Especially the early chapters of Acts reflect the attitudes of a community preparing for the imminent return of the Lord and living in anticipation of the promised coming of his kingdom (Acts 2:39).

⁶ Thus, for example, Acts 2:16 quotes Joel's words, "Pour out my spirit upon all flesh," and Acts 2:25 quotes David's claim of "seeing the Lord," in both cases interpreting the older biblical passages Christologically.

⁷ Biblical scriptures mentioned explicitly by McLellin include: Gen. 17:1; Ps. 37:37; Isa. 8:20; 11; Matt. 24:3; Mark 1:14-15; 13:21-22; Luke 6:20-26; John 3; 5:30, 39; 14:26; Acts 20; Rom. 8:14; 1 Cor. 2:13; 12; Gal. 1:8; 1 Thes. 1:5; Philip. 3:15; 2 Tim. 4:2; Heb. 12:14; 2 Pet. 1:1-7. See also Teresa Baer's statistical data in this volume for further information regarding the use of these scriptures in McLellin's preaching.

⁸ Discussed further by William G. Hartley below in this volume.

⁹ See Acts 2:17. Consult the index to this volume for occurrences of these topics in the journals.

¹⁰ Compare McLellin's interests with Acts 2:19.

¹¹ In addition, Peter heals Aeneas of palsy and raises Tabitha from the dead (Acts 9:34, 36-43). Other miracles are reported: handkerchiefs are sent to heal, evil spirits are cast out (Acts 5:12; 19:11-12), and Paul heals a woman with an unclean spirit (Acts 16:16-18).

¹² "And the Lord added to the church daily" (Acts 2:47), and thus they preached to all and emphasized that God is no respecter of persons (Acts 10:34).

¹³ In Acts 4, the Sadducees unsuccessfully attempted to silence the Apostles; and in Acts 12, Peter and others were imprisoned but were soon delivered. Stephen's argument before the Jewish leaders in Jerusalem in chapters 6-7 is presented as a rhetorical triumph, even though it resulted in the first Christian martyr's death.

¹⁴ Material relevant to the Twelve is covered further by William G. Hartley and Larry C. Porter, part III below.

¹⁵ Acts 3:14-15 speaks of the wicked people of the world who "denied the Holy One and the Just and desired a murderer to be granted unto you; and killed the Prince of life."

¹⁶ McLellin's companions spoke about belief in the Bible; the Book of Mormon, its coming forth and evidences and testimonies of it; the nature of revelation from the Creation to the present; prophecies; the Kingdom of Christ; the covenants of God; priesthoods; the restitution

of all things spoken by all the holy prophets; Enoch's prophecy; the testimony that Jesus is, was, and will come; faith; gifts; the abuse of tongues; instruction regarding tongues; giving heed; the gospel; superfluous dress; the Methodist discipline exposed; creeds; false religions of the day; warnings of danger; Jews and Gentiles; gathering of Jews and scattered Indians; life and immortality. The scriptures they cited included Ps. 102; Isa. 11; 49; Jer. 31:31; Ezek. 6-9; John 10; 14:2; Rom. 8; 1 Cor. 2; 12; Eph. 1; Gal. 1:6-10; Heb. 11; and 2 Tim. 4. The early Mormon preachers also read from 3 Nephi about Christ's ministry, Alma 9-16 about Alma and Amulek's suffering in Ammonihah, and the Vision in what is now known as D&C 76.

[17] For many other approaches to the preaching data found in the journals, see the studies by Teresa Baer in part III below.

[18] Already in Journal VI, he becomes more defensive when dealing with his audiences, eager to argue that the Book of Mormon is not a delusion and more concerned about removing objections to his message. He also takes up the new practice of speaking about his religion in possessive and exclusive terms, offering "evidences of *my* religion," proclaiming the "truths of *my* religion," and asserting "the divine authenticity of *my* holy religion."

[19] See Larry C. Porter's chapter in part III below.

[20] See appendix I and notes to the journals.

[21] An extensive list of these early missionary journals or accounts appears as appendix II.

Part II: The Manuscripts of William E. McLellin (1831–36)

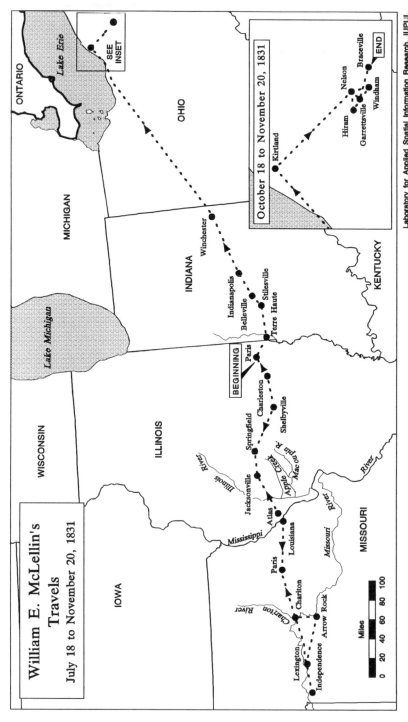

William E. McLellin's
Travels
July 18 to November 20, 1831

WISCONSIN

IOWA

ILLINOIS

MICHIGAN

ONTARIO

Lake Erie

SEE
INSET

OHIO

INDIANA

Winchester

Indianapolis
Belleville
Stilesville
Terre Haute

Lake Michigan

BEGINNING
Paris

Charleston
Shelbyville

Springfield

Jacksonville

Illinois River

Apple Creek

Macoupin R.

Atlas

Mississippi

Louisiana

Paris

Missouri River

MISSOURI

KENTUCKY

Chariton

Chariton River

Lexington

Independence
Arrow Rock

October 18 to November 20, 1831

Kirtland

Hiram
Garrettsville
Nelson
Braceville
Windham

END

Miles

0 20 40 60 80 100

Laboratory for Applied Spatial Information Research, IUPUI

William E. McLellin Journal I
July 18, 1831–November 20, 1831

1. Wm E McLelin's Journal.
Commenced the 18th of July 1831.

At this time I was living in Paris, Illinois. Teaching school——
This morining I heard very early that two men (who said they
were traveling to Zion which they said was in upper Missouri.[1]
They had also a book with them which they sd was a Revelation
from God. calling it the book of Mormon) were to preach 2¹/₂
miles below Paris at N. W. Nunally's. I taught school until 12 o'clock.
I saddled Tom and rode there with speed, Anxious to see and hear
those quear beings. Their names were Harvy Whitlock & David
Whitmer— The people were assembled in a beautiful sugartree
grove. Mr Whitlock arose and gave some particulars respecting the
book and some reasons why he believed it to be a divine revelation. Spoke some of the Signs of the times[2] then he expounded
the Gospel the plainest I thot that I ever heard in my life, which
astonished me. D[avid] Whitmer[3] then arose and bore testimony to
having seen an Holy Angel who had made known the truth of this
record to him. all these strange things I pondered in my heart.

I invited them to go and preach in Paris, which they did next day.
Though it had but little effect. I then went with them about 5 ms
to T. Hicklin's and staid with them all night. I made many enquiries
and had much conversation with them thence I went with them
to their appointment [*page 2*] it being (Sundy). A large congregation attended. And from the solemnity which attended those men
in giving their testimony and the plainness of the truths which
they declared I was induced to believe something in their mission.
People seemed to be anxious for them to stay longer & they told

me that Joseph Smith, the man who translated the book and a number of others had gone to Jackson Co. Mo.[4] and if I would go there I could see them. They said also that Smith was a **Prophet**. Finally I told them if they would stay one week longer that I would go with them. They agreed to stay. Then H[arvey] W[hitlock] arose and spoke about three hours. I never heard such preaching in all my life. The glory of God seemed to encircle the man and the wisdom of God to be displayed in his discourse. Some of the people seemed to be much affected. The meeting was closed by a few observations of D[avid] W[hitmer] a solemn testimony also of the thruths which they had just heard. They made some other appointments and filled them that week. I returned home and taught school and settled some business during the week.

On Friday I closed my school and on Saturday the 30th after being much hurried during the day, I left Paris E[d]g[ar] Co. Ill. about 6 o'clock P. M. & started for Jackson Co. Mo. I rode 14 ms. to a Mr Wilhites. I reached there about 10, at night. I had my supper, bed and horse fed.

I rose early paid 37 cts. and pursued my course 23 ms. to Wm Whites Coles Co. by 11 in the morning. Here I met again with my friends the strange preachers. They had an appointment here for the day, a number of people collected and H. W. preached about 2 hours. This evening I had the sick head ache [*page 3*] very badly.

Monday the 1st day of August I rose early felt well, took breakfast and went to Col. Fleener's to an Election. I settled some business, returned and took dinner with Uncle Nathan Wood who was much taken with those young men. I then took them with me about 5 ms to my good old friend Jesse Fuller's, we staid all night with them. had a pleasant visit— I also took them with me to the grave of my departed and dear companion Cinthia Ann and there they see seemed to mourn with me for the loss of my dearest friend and her blessed little infant.

August 2nd We took breakfast and pursued our course to about 3 ms to Esqr G. M. Hansons (a Methodist[5] Preacher) and took dinner, thence 9 ms. and called on John Price, the neighbours collected and H[arvey] W[hitlock] spoke to them about an hour.

A. 3rd we arose early and took breakfast, thence 10 ms to Esqr Wm T. Bennetts in Shlby Co. and took dinner. Here I bought from them the last book of Mormon which they had. Here we parted. They intended to go throu Vandalia, St Louis &c. and I intended to go through Springfield &c. My object was to get to Independence before them[6] and see if the testimony of the other witnesses[7] would agree with theirs. Thence I rode on 3 ms. to Shlbyville. Thence 5 ms. to the widow South's and staid all night. I read some in the book of Mormon to them and told them what I knew about it. The[y] seemed to be some what interested about it.

Aug. 4th I rode on 26 ms to a Mr Dolson's and took breakfast and fed Tom & paid 25 cts. Thence 30 ms to Uncle Wm Moore's and staid all night. In Sangamo[n] Co.[8]

August 5 I went to Springfield and gave 2 dollars for a pocket Bible and 75 cts for the repairing of my watch. I returned and talked considerable with my Uncle and my brother Israel concerning the book, the people and what they believed. My uncle gave [*page 4*] me some very good advice and seemed to be anxious to know the truth of what I had told him.

Augst 6th I rose early, took breakfast, though I felt some unwell yet I pursued my course. My brother rode with me about 10 or 12 ms. Thence I rode on Westerly about 30 ms. to Mr Reeves in Morgan Co. I was so unwell it seemed to me I could not get any further. I took but little supper and went to bed. I was very sick had high fevers and I also had some very singular dreams about my journey (which afterward proved true). I lay here until the 11th. I called on two Doctors, took considerable medicine. The fever abated some and I was so anxious to go forward that I [paid] Mrs Reeves $2 for their trouble and paid the physicians $2.50.

And August 11th I rode on 4 ms to Jacksonville Morgan Co. thence 12 ms. I stopped to take a little refreshment and feed my horse.

I paid 25 cts. thence 10 ms to the Illinois River. I crossed paid 12 cts and staid all night on the west bank.

A. 12. I rose early and took breakfast and paid 25 cts and rode on 23 ms and fed Tom (I did not feel to eat myself) and paid 12 cts. and rode on 3 ms to Atlas, Pike Co. Thence 6 ms to the Mississippi River. I crossed in a horse boat, pd 50 cts and landed in Misouri Pike Co. in Louisiana a little town on the bank. Thence 12 ms through a dreary region all alone and it dark, to Esqr McCune's & staid all night and until after breakfast, pd 50 cts and rode on (though yet weak) 31 ms to Mr. Rogerses, staid all night.

Augst 14 I rose early paid 50 cts and rode on 3 ms to a Mr Ivey's and fed my horse and took breakfast. Here two Elders had staid about a week (viz) Hiram Smith and John Moredock though they were gone.[9] They had no book with them and when Mrs Ivy found out that I had a book she said she must see it and when she saw it she said I must sell it [*page 5*] to her which I did and then pursued my course toward the western horizon 32 ms to Mr Milligin's and took dinner in Monroe Co. paid 12 cts. Thence 13 ms to S. Brockmans in Randolph Co. Staid all night.

Agst 15. pd 31 cts. and rode on 13 ms. to G. S. Foster's and took breakfast and fed Tom. Here I heard of two more Elders Simeon Carter & Solomon Hancock.[10] They had preached here some and baptized one or two— I pd 37 cts. (This was in Howard Co) and rode on 12 ms. to old Charatin, Thence one ml. to Mount Pleasant ferry. Here I heard that Joseph, Sydney, Oliver and about a dozen of others,[11] had left there the day before and gone to the East. Now I was very much disappointed. Yet Mr Thornton told me that H[arvey] W[hitlock] D[avid] W[hitmer] H[iram] S[mith] and others[12] had gone on to the west. consequently I crossed paid 25 cts. and pursued my course 16 ms to a widow McCafferty's Saline Co and staid all night.

Augst 16. I rose early pd 50 cts and rode on through the prairies 19 ms to Mr Demoss' and I stopped fed my horse, took breakfast. I felt some fatigued. Therefore I rested about 4 hours. pd 37 cts. Thence 17 ms to Mr Fulkersons and staid for the night.

Agst 17 I rose early paid 25 C. and rode on 9 ms to Lexington Lafayette Co. had my breakfast and horse fed pd 50 C. Thence 30 ms. to Mr. Patton's staid for the night.

A. 18th I rose and paid 37 C. and rode on 10 miles to **Independence**[13]—— Jackson Co. I stopped and took breakfast and fed my horse and rested about 5 hours, in which time I conversed with a number in the villagers about those people that they called Mormonites. They though[t] they were generally a very honest people but very much deluded by Smith and others.[14] Notwithstanding all I felt anxious to see them and examine for myself.[15] I bought Brown's Concordance for 75 cts. I then started but before I got out of the village [*page 6*] I met with David Whitmer & Martin Harris[16] who accompanied me about 10 miles further westward where I found: The Bishop E. Partridge[17] and his council Isaac Morley and John Corrill[18] with several other Elders and a number of private members both male and female. I spent the evening with them and had very agreeable conversation.

Friday 19th I rose early, talked much with those people: Saw Love, Peace, Harmony and Humility abounding among them. A rare circumstance occured while attending family prayr which convinced me that the Elders had the power of deserning spirits.[19] It affected me so that my weakness was manifest. I took Hiram the brother of Joseph and we went into the woods and set down and talked together about 4 hours. I inquired into the particulars of the coming forth of the record, of the rise of the church and of its progress and upon the testimonies given to him &c.[20] This evening I went to one of their prayr meetings. Here I saw the manner of their worship, heard them converse freely upon the things of religion. After meeting I returned to Mr J. Lewis'[21] and staid all night.

Saturday the 20th I rose early and betook myself to earnest prayr to God to direct me into truth; and from all the light that I could gain by examinations searches and researches I was bound as an honest man to acknowledge the truth and Validity of the book of **Mormon** and also that I had found the people of the Lord—The Living Church of ~~Jesus~~ Christ. consequently as soon as we took breakfast I told Elder H. Smith that I wanted him to baptize me because I wanted to live among a people who were based upon pure principles and actuated by the Spirit of the Living God. I went with the Elders present to the water and was immersed according [*page 7*] to the commandments of Jesus Christ by H[iram] S[mith][22] and was confirmed by the watter's edge by the laying on of the hands. We returned to brother Lewis's. I felt very happy, calm and pleasant during the day until evening, then the Enemy of all righteousness made a mighty struggle to persuade me that I was deceived until it seemed to me sometimes that horror would overwhelm me. I did not doubt the truth of the things which I had embraced, but my fears were respecting my own salvation. The time for evening prayr came, and I was glad, I told my brethren that I felt bad and they prayed for me. Bro. N. Knight[23] after arising from prayr came and by the spirit of God was enabled to tell me the very secrets of my heart and in a degree to chase darkness from my mind, I went to bed, rested well—

Sunday 21st The Brethren met at brother Lewis's and had a sacrament meeting.[24] bro. J. Corrill Lectured from the 1st Chapter of Gallatians.[25] His remarks were very plain and conclusive. A number of brethren and sisters spoke of the marvelous works of God & of their willingness and determinations to serve him & keep all his commandments. I spoke and gave a few among the many reasons which induced me to join with them in religious faith. The meeting was dismissed and we assembled again at a schoolhouse,[26] near, that evening and held a prayrmeeting, Where I was much disappointed, instead of shouting, screaming, jumping or shaking of hands in confusion.[27] Peace, order, harmony and the spirit of God seemed to cheer every heart, warm every bosom and animate every Tongue. I really felt happy that I had seen the day that I could meet with such a people and worship God in the beauty of Holiness, For I saw more beauty in Christianity now than I ever had seen before.

[*page 8*] Monday and Tuesday I spent in reading and in social conversation with my brethren. Brother S[imeon] Carter and others told me that it was my duty to become an Elder in the church and go and preach the Gospel. Tuesday night I staid at the schoolhouse with a number of my brethren and sisters who were living there.

Wednesday 24th I rose quite early and walked out and seated myself in a cluster of bushes which grew near the house. There while the stars were yet twinkling I set pleasantly musing until my meditations were interupted by a faint yet plaintive and Solemn voice which was articulated in the grove not many paces from me. And while silently listening, my ear was caught on a different direction by another Similar Sound. But here I have to pause because I cannot give the reflections which I had nor describe the **solomnity** which rolled over my mind, when I knew it was those whom the world called so much deluded enjoying Sweet communion with their God. Certainly said I, here is a reality if the experiance of the world has ever given **One———**! The Elders and brethren met to-day to hold a conference and offer a sacrament to the Most High to fill the commandment which they received at Charatin. And for the first time I went to the grove and made it a subject of solemn Prayr respecting my ordination to the ministry. When I arose from prayr this question suggested itself to my mind "What is your motive?" And this answer seemed to be whispered into my heart. (viz) The glory of God, The Salvation of my own soul, and The welfare of the human family. I returned to the house perfectly resigned to the will of God and seated myself in conference with my brethren,[28] which was opened by prayr, and after doing [*page 9*] some church business and partaking of the Lords Supper, they called on me to know if I had any thing to offer. I arose and told them that I was resigned to the will of God in the matter and that I believed that God would make my duty known to them if they would inquire. I then sat down— Brother H[iram] S[mith] immediately arose & said he had recd a witness of the Spirit that I should be ordained an Elder. This agreed with the minds of all present and Elder H. Smith and Bishop E. Partridge ordained me to be an Elder in the Church of Christ.[29] I felt very solemn while taking this charge upon me. Yet I was willing to proclaim, in my weakness, the glorious Gospel of the great Redeemer which I had received and I trust in an honest heart——

August 25th We arose and made preparations for to start to the east again.[30] I pd 50 cts for 2 1/2 lbs Coffee which I had sent to Indp. for, also $1.25 to E. P[artridge] for a book of Mormon. Then M[artin] H[arris], D[avid] W[hitmer], H[arvey] W[hitlock], H[iram] S[mith], S[imeon] C[arter], and myself bid farewell to our precious brethren and sisters in the Lord, (it was truly an affecting time) and we walked on to Independence. Here I paid 75 cts at the tavern for the keeping of Tom 3 days. Thence 10 ms to Mr Pattons and staid all night. They were very hard, the truth had but little effect on their minds.

Friday 26. We traveled on all day and staid all night with a Mr. Jennings

Saturday 27 Here we heard that brother Harvey's wife was coming on. And this morning he bid us farewell and returned to Zion. And we pursued our journey 11 ms. to Mr Easters' and took dinner. Here we proposed to preach the next day. They were willing and sent out and informed their neighbours—

Sunday 28. The people collected for to hear [*page 10*] preaching, brother Hiram opened the meeting & addressed them about and hour "on the Gospel." I then arose for the first time to attempt to preach. Now I can give but a faint description of this scene Though one thing I know. I had some desire to address the people and with prayr in my heart, I arose: and it seemed to me that the whole volumn of Truth was opened before me. My heart was animated and burning; and my tongue seemed to be untied. I spoke about an hour and a half. Many hearts were affected and many eyes filled with tears. I ceased to proclaim and seated myself. Filled with astonishment to behold the wonderful works of the Mighty God while wrapped in his Eternal Spirit.[31]— Here we sold 5 books of Mo. and answered many queries, Mr Demoss invited us and we traveled on 6 ms. and staid with him all night and until after breakfast. Without charge. brother Carter had left us and gone on.

Then Monday 29th Martin, David, Hiram and myself pursued our journey about 20 ms near the Arrow Rock[32] we met a company of our brethren and Sisters, who were journeying to the land of Zion. We staid with them and had a meeting. I spoke by way of exortation about an hour. The other brethren also delivered short exortations. The brethren seemed to enjoy the meeting well.

Tuesday 30. We traveled through rain & mud up to Mount Pleasant and crossed the Missouri river and staid all night with Mr. Thrash.

Wednesday 31. This morning early brothers Martin and David left us and took their journey to go through St Louis, Vandalia, Terre-Haute Indianopolis thence to Kirtland &c. We sent an appointment up to Charatin for Thursday— brother Hiram was quite unwell to day with a diarhoea.

[*page 11*] September 1st We attended our appointment. the people collected in the court-house. I arose and addressed them about Two hours. bro. H[iram] Then bore testimony to the truths which had been delivered and gave in his testimony respecting the truth of the book. I then arose and read the testimony of the three witnesses[33] and reasoned upon the power and force of it until many of the hard hearted were astonished and some dropped the crystal tear. The people were dismissed. But a little arogant Methodist Priest who was present though without my knowledge, observed that we taught a supernatural Religion, Therefore we must give supernatural evidence in favour of it—— Being inflated with self conceit and with the Spirit of the Devil, he ordered a Physian who was present to administer to me a glass of poison to test the power of my faith and the truth of my mission.[34] But the Doctor very calmly and solemnly said to him "Don't you **Tempt God**." The little Priest seemed to be confused and left the room in haste. The people dispersed. And we returned to Mr Thrash's again. Some of the neighbours came in and solicited another meeting. Bro. H[iram] was still unwell. After much solicitation I consented. The villagers &c soon gathered in. The house was filled. Here I was brought to a strait, to know what to say. But I arose with confidence in God. And my mind seemed to be filled with truth and my tongue again let loose. I addressed them about one hour and a half. Their minds seemed to be inquiring, but none were willing to obey, Therefore we made no more appointm[ents.]

Friday 2nd We pursued our course and traveled on that day and the next,

Saturday eve we called at Esqr Davis' on the head waters of Salt river. he wished us to hold a meeting and we agreed to [*page 12*] next day. He went and sent out and informed the people.

Sunday 4th Bro. H[iram] had obtained relief of his Diorhoea. The people collected, and he arose and addressed them a few minutes— I then got up and warned them of the judgements of God which would fall on them unless they would repent. But there seemed to be an impenetrable gloom hanging over their minds. They seemed to be willingly and willfully wicked. Therefore we dismissed them and got our horse and traveled on about 8 ms and staid all nigh[t].

Monday 5. In the afternoon we reached Mr Ivey's. Their friends gathered in, in the eve and we had much social conversation with them. They seemed to be somewhat believing. I arose to address them and was filled with the spirit to that degree that I spoke with much warmth. After I ceaced, one of the females present did shout with a most tremendious acclamation. but none seemed willing to go forward in obediance —

Tuesday 6th We bid our friends Fare-well and pursued our course Eastward; and staid all night with a man who believed that all the various races of beings in the world sprung from different **Adams**.

Wednesday 7 we traveled on across the Mississippi river at Louisiana. Thence to Atlas and staid all night.

Thursday 8th We crossed the Ill. river at Philips' F[erry].

Friday 9. This morning we took breakfast with a Christian preacher (as he called himself). He charged us with being false prophets.

Reason or Testimony had no influence on his mind; he charged us fifty cts. for breakfast and his heart seemed so hard and wicked that he would have struck us dumb if he had had it in his power, but we left him raging and when we came to a brook Bro. H. washed his feet for a testimony against him.[35] [*page 13*] This evening we reached Jacksonville Morgan Co. Ill. The court was sitting and there were a great many country people in the village. And as soon as they found out who we were, they gathered around us; we seperated and talked with them about two hours. I cut some of them so close with the truth that a ruffian fellow rolled up his sleeves and swore that he could give it to me but a gentleman prevented him and took him away. We gave an appointment that we would preach next day in the Court house. A Mr Dewitt invited us in and we staid with him all night—

Saturday 10. we attended our appointment. A numerous concourse of people attended,—I think about 500— If ever I felt small, and felt my dependence on God, now was the time. To have to ascend the judges bench and face Judges, Lawyers Doctors Priests and people. But I arose with confidence in Elijah's God and gave them a brief history of the book of Mormon, of its coming forth &c, Then reasoned upon and expounded prophecy after prophecy and scripture after scripture, which had reference to the book and to these days and after speaking with great liberty [and] about 3 hours I concluded with a warning to them to flee from the wrath to come and gather themselves to **Zion** and prepare to meet the Lord at his second coming which was nigh at hand. Bro. H[iram] Then arose and bore testimony to the truths which they had heard and gave them his evidence of the truth of the book and then dis[mis]sed [them] the people. Perfect silence and good attention seemed to pervade the house during the service.[36] A general enquiry was heard in the multitude respecting the things which they had heard. I was offered by one Gentleman as much as two dollars for a book but I had none for sale— [*page 14*] We had many solicitations to make other appointments. brother H. made one for the next day about 7 ms. N. E. We spent the evening with Mr Dewitt.

Sunday 11 We attended our appointment. Bro. H. arose address[ed] the people for about 2 hours. it seemed to have but little effect. I then exorted them for about half an hour with great Zeal and firmness, it still had but little effect. We made another appointment for next day about 8 ms S. E.

We attended our appt. Nothing material occurred.

Tuesday 13 we traveled on to Uncle Wm Moore's about 6 ms south of Springfield. But to my sorrow my uncle had left that morning for Tennessee. Though my bro. Israel was there. He intended to start in about a week for Ten. also. I gave to him a book of Mormon to carry to my bro. Samuel.

Wed. 14. I left my brother in tears and we traveled about sixteen ms. and I became so unwell that I could not get farther. we put up, and I had a considerable shake of the Ague,[37] a high fever ensued which lasted the most of the night—

Thurs=15. We started on, though I was quite sick, about noon I felt so much worse that I lit from my horse in the prairie and lay down on my great coat and blanket and gave up to shake again. But immediately I began to think that God had not called me to proclaim the 'Gospel' and then would suffer me to be sick because I had to pass through an unhealthy country in the sickly season. I opened my mind to bro. H[iram] We immediately bowed before the Lord and with all the faith which we had, we opened our hearts to him. bro. H. arose and laid his hands upon me. But marvelous for me to relate that I was instantly healed [*page 15*] And arose and pursued my journey in health with vigour. And about 3 oclock we reached Mr. Dolson's. He sent out and informed his neighbours. They came in and we held a meeting. I spoke about an hour and a half. I felt well.

We pursued our course until Saturday about noon we reached Shlbyvill. When the people found out who we were they solicited us to preach — We consented. They immediately gathered into the court house. I arose and addressed them about 3 hours. There was a Methodist Preist present who took notes of my discourse. We closed our meeting. He then arose with all the rage & fury which it seemed the evil one could invent. I sometimes thought that he would break the stand. When he closed, I arose and showed the people his mistakes, and they seemed to be ashamed for him. bro. H. also made some observations precisely to the point. He said no more—— We made another appt. for next day about 7 ms N.E.

Sunday 18. We attended our appt. Bro. H. preached about 2 hours. we took dinner and Thence to Coghhorn's grove and held a meeting in the evening. I arose and attempted to preach, but could not, I had no animation in it, no memory, and in truth I had lost the spirit of God. Hence I was confounded, I set down and told bro. H. to preach for I could not. He, although, he had laboured so hard during the day, yet he preached.

Monday morning I went into the woods and bowed before the Lord and cried and prayed & prayed until I found out what was the matter. One thing, It was to show me, my own weakness and that it was not me who had preached so many gre[a]t sermons— [*page 16*] But that the Lord had given me Light & Liberty. And I found too by close examination that my whipping out the Methodist P. so completely the day before had tended to lift me up. This was the whole secret.

Monday 19. We proceded on & called on my good old friend Mrs. Fuller and found that her and her family were afflicted some with the Ague. The Esqr was gone to Virginia. Thence to Wm Whites and we gave an appt to preach there on Wednesday.

Tuesday I went to Charleston on business.

Wednesday we attended our apt and some appeared quite believing. Here I bought a horse for bro. H[iram] for $35,00.

Thursday 22. While here we visited my dear Cinthia Ann's grave— which called to my mind the many pleasures we had seen together and also the uncertainty of all earthly Objects—— Thence to Paris, the place from whence I started and found my old friends

Milton and Hetty somewhat disconsolate. They had lost their little
Mary Ann. But they inquired much concerning my faith in the
things which I had been to examine. We gave them all the light
that we could. Their minds were quite tender——

Friday 23. We gave an appt to preach in my old schoolhouse at
candle light, and I spent the day in settling business and in talking
with my friends, trying to convince them that the day of Christ
was near at hand. Evening came on and we attended our appt. The
house was full. I arose and addressed them about two hours—
Some mocked, while others were astonished and others were
desirous to know the truth. We made an other appt at T. Hicklin's
for Sunday—

[*page 17*] Sunday 25th We attended our appointment. the people
attended and I arose and addressed them about 2½ hours and
unfolded to them many things concerning the works of the Lord
in these Last days. Br Hiram spoke to them a few minutes— They
were dismissed. But some were angry, some were inquiring, but
the more part were careless about it——

Monday 26th I left Br Hiram at friend Hicklin's and returned to
Paris and spent Tuesday & wednesday in settling my business which
I left undone when I started to examine for the **truth** and in
collecting the money which was due to me, and in talking and
reasoning with my acquaintance, trying to convince them that the
book of Mormon was a true revelation from God; but they seemed
to be affraid that it was a speculation, and not true—

Thursday 29th We left friend Hicklin's— who with his wife seemed
very tender and quite believing— Thence Eastward and staid all
night a few miles north of Terre-Haute.

thence we staid all night with a Methodist man who was very hard
and unbelieving a little east of   in Indiana.

Thence Saturday to Stilesville, a small village on the national road[38]
and called on   Wood a preacher of the Christian order. he

was just preparing to go to a two days meeting and he was very anxious that we should go with him to the meeting, that is, after we had told him who we were and what we believed. And we concluded to go. Thence 3 miles south to the place. One of their minister's was speaking, who seemed to be confused when he looked upon us, [*page 18*] And he soon closed, then the preachers present held a council whether we should preach among them, and they agreed we should, and invited us into the stand. And I arose and addressed them on the subject of the coming forth of the book of Mormon about 1½ hours and also on the subject of the ancient faith, concerning the spiritual gifts in the church,[39] &c, &c.— After I was done old father   Wood asked us if we believed in the gift of Healing by the laying on of the hands of the Elders, and we answered that we did most firmly, he then invited us home with him; saying that his daughter's child was very sick. We went without hesitation about 2 miles further South. The child was very sick and had been for some time. Its mother was sitting nursing of it, and after we had spoken upon the nature of faith; The family seemed to be quite believing, and we all bowed before the great Jehovah and implored his mercy upon the child, we then arose and brother Hiram & I laid our hands upon it, and in a few minutes the little child got down from its mother's lap and went to play upon the floor. This caused them to rejoice and the old gentleman got down & prayed mightily, then arose & said that he believed that the Lord was there. We then more fully explained the nature of the rise of the ~~rise~~ church of Christ and the things believed in it. They were very friendly, but did not lay hold.

Sunday 2nd October——— We attended their meeting and they invited us to preach, Br Hiram said it was my duty to preach again, A numerous concourse of people being collected. [*page 19*] I arose (but O! I felt very small) yet knowing that the Lord was all Wisdom I felt to put my trust in him consequently I opened my mouth and by the power of the spirit of the Lord, I unfolded to them the plainness of the Glorious gospel and also the requirements of the Lord of them or their duty and also the opening glories of the latter days by the coming forth of the book of Mormon and the gathering of the saints to mount Zion and the

Jews to Jerusalem.[40] I spoke about 2 1/2 hours. Br. Hiram bore testimony to the things delivered and also to the book of M. and warned them of their danger— But notwithstanding all, they went on in their old way to administer the sacrament. But we made an appointment to preach at Bellville next day then left them.——

Monday 3rd We came to Bellville. The day was very rainy, yet a number collected. Br Hiram spoke to them about one hour & a half and unfolded many prophecies to them plainly, to their great astonishment. I also spoke by way of warning and exortation to them about half an hour——

Tuesday 4. We pursued our course Easterly. though because of the much rain which had fallen and the bridges on the road being not yet made We had to swim two of the creeks, and we were preserved. This evening we came to Indianopolis and I called on my Uncle Doctor S. Mitchel and spent the evening with him and Uncle J. [*or* I.] Mitchel.

Thence we traveled a North East coarse for two days and a half until we reached the neighbourhood of Winchester in which we found that [*page 20*] Brothers Zebidee [Coltrin] & Levi [Hancock] had preached and baptized a number of Deciples.[41] Here we staid and preached and exorted and strengthened our brethren, and ordained brother Jarvis Lee to be a Priest in the church. We were with them several days and before we left them we called the Elders and other officers together & gave the instructions to them as which the spirit gave utterance to us &c, &c. —

Wednesday 12. We again took our journey Easterly for the church in Ohio where brother Hiram had left his family. We did not preach any more until on the 18th in the morning we reached of Father Smith's in Kirtland[42] and found them all well and strong in the faith and good works; rejoicing in the hope of the second coming of the Lord with all his saints.

Here I staid in the church, reading, learning and teaching &c. until I attended a conference about 20 miles from Kirtland[43] on Tuesday 25. Here I first saw brother Joseph [Smith] the Seer, also brothers Oliver [Cowdery], John [Whitmer] & Sidney [Rigdon] and a great many other Elders &c. This conference was attended by me with much spiritual edification & comfort to my heart.[44] And Tuesday night in conference, a number of Elders were ordained to the High-Priesthood[45] of the Holy order of God among whom though I felt unworthy I was ordained and took upon me the high responsibility of that office[46]— A number of others present were ordained to the lesser Priest-Hood[47]——

Wednesday 26. a large number of people collected to hear preaching and brothers Sidney & Oliver preached and brothers Hiram & Orson followed by a few remarks and exortation, &c, &c,[48] [*page 21*] From thence I returned to Kirtland, but I had caused old Father Smith to ride Tom and as I was walking on I stepped off of a large log and strained my ankle very badly— thence I rode; and just as I was abo[u]t to start to bed I asked brother Joseph what he thought about my ancle's being healed. He immediately turned to me and asked me if I believed in my heart that God through his instrumentality would heal it. I answered that I believed he would. He laid his hands on it and it was healed although It was swelled much and had pained me severely ——

Thence I went home with him[49] on Saturday 29th. Early in the morning we reached there having staid Friday night in the Nelson church[50]— This day the Lord condecended to hear my prayr and give me a revelation of his **will**, through his prophet or seer (Joseph)— And these are the words which I wrote from his mouth,[51] saying, Behold thus saith the Lord unto you my servant Wm blessed are you, in as much as you have turned away from your iniquities and have received my truths, saith the Lord, your Redeemer, The Saviour of the world; even of as many as believe on my name. Verily I say unto you, blessed are you for receiving mine everlasting Covenant, even the fulness of my Gospel sint forth unto the children of men, that they might have life, and be made partakers of the glories which are to be revealed in the last days as it was written by the Prophets & Apostles in days of old. Verily I say unto you my servant William that you are clean but not all. Repent therefore of those things which are not pleasing in my sight Saith

the Lord; for the Lord will show them unto you. And now, verily
I the Lord will show unto you what I will concerning you: or what
is my will concerning you. Behold verily I say unto you that it is
my will that you should proclaim my Gospel from land to land,
and from city to city: Yea in those regions round about where it
hath not been proclaimed — Tarry not many days in this place. Go
not up unto the land of Zion, as yet. But in as much as you can
send; Send. — otherwise think not of thy property —— [*page 22*]
Go unto Eastern lands. Bear testimony in every place, unto every
people and in their sinagogues: reasoning with the people. Let my
servant Samuel go with you; and forsake him not, and give him
thine instructions: and he that is faithful shall be made strong in
every place. And I the Lord will go with you. Lay your hands upon
the sick and they shall recover. Return not until I the Lord shall
send you. Be patient in afflictions. Ask and ye shall receive. —
Knock and it shall be opened unto you. Seek not to be cumbered.
Forsake all unrighteousness. Commit not Adultery. (A temptation
with which thou has been troubled.)— Keep these sayings true
and faithful and thou shalt magnify thine office, and push many
people to Zion, with songs of everlasting Joy upon their heads.
Continue in these things even unto the end; and you shall have a
crown of Eternal life on the right hand of my Father, who is full
of grace and truth. Verily, thus saith the Lord your God, your
Redeemer even Jesus Christ—— Amen—— A revelation given to
William E. McLelin a true descendant from Joseph who was sold
into Egypt down through the loins of Ephraim his Son —
Given in Hiram, Portage Co. Ohio. 29th Oct 1831——
This revelation give great joy to my heart because some important
questions were answered which had dwelt upon my mind with
anxiety yet with uncertainty[52]——

Sunday 30th This day the brethren & sisters collected at Bro.
J[ohn] Johnson's. And the brethren called on me to preach. But it
seemed to me as if I could not. Here was the church who had
been instructed by the first Elders in the church. Here was Brothers John, Sidney, Oliver and Joseph and it did not seem to me as
if I could instruct them or even entertain the Congregation; but
with confidence alone in Enoch's God I arose and addressed them

about one hour and a half. And it was not I but the spirit and power of God which was in me and it did seem to me before I finished as though it was not I or that I had got into another region where all was light & glory.

I had expected to remain here and read and write [*page 23*] for some weeks and probably months,[53] but having received ~~the will of the~~ will of the Lord[54] I determined to obey it, consequently I only remained here about three weeks[55] during which time I preached in the church at Nelson on one Sabbath, at Windham on the next &c. I read and copyed revelations, &c. and in preparing for my tour to the East, and Bro Samuel having heard the revelation and all things being prepared we left Br. Joseph's on 16th of Nov.[56] Thence 5 mls. to Nelson and ~~evening meeting be~~ attended an evening meeting among the brethren. Br. Samuel opened the meeting and I then spoke about one hour, The brethren were much animated and made known their good determinations and resolutions to serve the Lord[57] ——————

Thursday 17th—— We went 3 miles to Garrettsvill and held a meeting in the even and had a large congregation. I opened meeting and spoke about one hour and some wicked wretch or Wretches interrupted the people by burning some odious smelling stuff, so that it raised confusion in all the house and broke up the meeting[58]——

Friday 18 We spent in talking with some who wished to learn[59] and in the even we attended a Campbellite meeting. The Priest spoke from John [~~for~~] 4th[60]— and then gave liberty to others. I then spoke and told them my mission, but they spoke out and said that they did not want to hear any more — They called a vote and I was requested to say no more. And I ceased after I had born testimony to the book of Mormon and to the Judgements of God which would fall upon them unless they would repent. By request they granted bro. Sml ten minutes to speak, in which time he bore testimony also. But the[y] rejected all with disdain and desired us to depart out of their coasts. Which we did and wiped the dust of our feet against them.

Saturday 19. We callcd on bro Miller and took dinner and passed on 6 miles to Nataniel Lane's. they received us kindly and sent out and circulated an appointment for next day.——

[*page 24*] Sunday the 20th a considerable congregation assembled at a schoolhouse in Braceville. they were attentive and appearantly serious.[60] I opened the meeting by prayr and expounded the gospel in plainness to them. Several persons invited us home with them but we returned to Mr Lane's and staid all night they still remained very friendly. Mr Lane himself was a professed Universalist, and we could not move him from his principles.

The continuation of the account of the mission of the Doctor and Sam. H. Smith will be found under the head of <u>"A Diary of Our Tour to the East."</u>

NOTES

[1] The Book of Mormon teaches that in the last days, a holy city will be built in the Americas (3 Ne. 21:23). A revelation to Joseph Smith in September 1830 indicated that this Zion, or New Jerusalem, would be situated on the western Missouri frontier, on the borders by the "Lamanites," i.e., Native Americans. See Doctrine and Covenants 28:9 (one of the standard works, or scriptures, of The Church of Jesus Christ of Latter-day Saints; the 1981 edition is hereafter cited as D&C). A revelation to Joseph Smith on March 7, 1831, prophesied that the second coming of Christ would follow the building of this city and the gathering of the righteous within its borders (D&C 45:43-44, 66-71). Three months later, another revelation (D&C 52) directed fifteen pairs of elders to travel to Missouri, where a conference would be held and where the Lord would reveal the exact location of Zion. These elders were charged to "go two by two, and . . . preach by the way in every congregation, baptizing by water, and the laying on of the hands by the water's side" (D&C 52:10). The two men to whom McLellin refers were a part of this contingent of missionaries.

[2] Across the centuries, Christians have interpreted certain events and situations—wars, rumors of wars, abundant iniquity, desolation, sickness,

earthquakes, the sun darkening, the stars falling, and the moon turning to blood—as "signs of the times" that would precede the second coming of Christ. The followers of Joseph Smith regarded the coming forth of the Book of Mormon as a decisive event in the eschatological calendar leading to Christ's return. For that reason, Mormon elders often connected the appearance of their new scripture with the end times. See the August 4, 1832, letter that McLellin wrote to his relatives (page 80 below) about Mormon elders coming "into the neighbourhood proclaiming that these were the last days, and that God had sent forth the book of Mormon to show the times of the fulfillment of the ancient prophecies When the Saviour shall come to destroy iniquity off the face of the earth, and *reign* with his saints in Millennial *Rest.*" Perhaps Harvey Whitlock also referred to the March 7, 1831, revelation that described the signs of the times and predicted the imminence of the second advent (D&C 45:26-47).

[3] David Whitmer, one of the Three Witnesses to the Book of Mormon, said he had been shown the Book of Mormon plates by an angel in 1829. Half a century later, McLellin recalled the impression Whitmer's testimony had upon him: "I saw [David Whitmer] June 1879, and heard him bear his testimony to the truth of the book as sincerely and solemnly as when he bore it to me in Paris, Ill. in July 1831. I believed him then and still believe him." William E. McLellin to James T. Cobb, August 14, 1880, RLDS Archives. Reprinted in Lyndon W. Cook, ed., *David Whitmer Interviews: A Restoration Witness* (Orem, Utah: Grandin Book, 1991), 240.

[4] The complete list of the men assigned to travel to Missouri at this time is found in Doctrine and Covenants sections 52 and 55. Of the thirty-one men who were named, apparently Wheeler Baldwin, William Carter, Edson Fuller, Jacob Scott, and Ezra Thayre did not go at this time. Lyndon W. Cook, *The Revelations of the Prophet Joseph Smith* (Salt Lake City: Deseret Book, 1985), 48, 72-83. Joseph Smith and his party left Kirtland, Ohio, on June 19, 1831.

[5] At this time, the Methodist Episcopal Church was the most populous religious organization in Illinois. S. Augustus Mitchell, *Illinois in 1837* (Philadelphia: Grigg and Elliot, 1837), 62. For more information on religion in Illinois in the early 1830s, see Edwin Scott Gaustad and Philip L. Barlow, *New Historical Atlas of Religion in America* (New York: Oxford University Press, forthcoming).

[6] McLellin did not succeed in reaching Independence before Whitmer and Whitlock. A short distance east of Independence, Whitlock and Whitmer met Joseph Smith on his return trip to Kirtland; McLellin missed that encounter by one day. See McLellin's journal entry for August 15, 1831.

[7] Oliver Cowdery and Martin Harris also reported having been shown the Book of Mormon plates by an angel. Both were in Missouri at this time; Cowdery had been there since an 1830 mission to the Lamanites in western Missouri and the Indian Territory beyond, and Harris had traveled there with

Joseph Smith's party in July 1831. Perhaps McLellin is referring directly to these two Book of Mormon witnesses, or perhaps he simply wanted to talk with other prominent church members who would have been in Missouri at this time (Joseph Smith, Sidney Rigdon, Hyrum Smith, Newel Knight, etc.).

[8] For a somewhat contemporary account of a journey from Paris to Sangamon County, see Mary Washburn Parkinson, "Travels in Western America in 1837," *Journal of American History* 3, no. 4 (1909): 511-16.

[9] Hyrum Smith and John Murdock were two of the elders traveling to the conference in Missouri. According to John Murdock's journal, John became very sick and remained with the Ivies at Salt River from August 4-11. Murdock then gave his watch to William Ivie in payment for Ivie transporting him to Chariton some seventy miles away. Andrew Jenson, Journal History of the Church (a set of scrapbooks containing both typewritten transactions and printed documents maintained in the LDS Church Archives), June 14, 1831, 3 (hereafter cited as JH).

[10] Solomon Hancock and Simeon Carter were another missionary pair directed to preach while traveling to the Missouri conference. They "raised up a branch in Indiana as they traveled through (either in Tippecanoe or Warren county)." JH, June 19, 1831, 2.

[11] Joseph Smith left Independence on August 9, 1831, in company with Sidney Rigdon, Oliver Cowdery, Samuel H. Smith, Reynolds Cahoon, Sidney Gilbert, William W. Phelps, Ezra Booth, Frederick G. Williams, Peter Whitmer, Jr., and Joseph Coe. See D&C 52:3; Joseph Smith, Jr., *History of The Church of Jesus Christ of Latter-day Saints*, ed. B. H. Roberts, 2d ed. rev., 7 vols. (Salt Lake City: Deseret Book, 1971), 1:202 (hereafter cited as *HC*). While he was in Independence, the Prophet dedicated the land of Zion and the land for the temple. *HC* 1:189-202. Most of the elders were then commanded to return to Kirtland, "two by two, and preach the word, not in haste, among the congregations of the wicked, until they return to the churches from whence they came" (D&C 58:58-59; 60:1-17). For details of their return journeys, see *HC* 1:202-6; and JH, August 13, 1831, and September 1, 1831.

[12] John Murdock is the only other person known to have been with Whitlock, David Whitmer, and Hyrum Smith. JH, June 14, 1831, and August 13, 1831. When Joseph Smith met this group at Chariton, he announced a revelation (D&C 62) which commanded these elders to continue traveling west to Zion and to hold a meeting there before returning to Ohio. *HC* 1:205-6. This meeting was held August 24, 1831. See McLellin's journal entry for that date.

[13] Historian B. H. Roberts observed that

> Independence in 1831 . . . was a frontier town with all the disadvantages implied by that term. It had a mixed population of white men from many sections of the Union, chiefly, however, from the south, some

of whom had moved into the western wilderness to escape the consequences of unlawful deeds committed elsewhere; vagabond Indians and renegades who had mingled with them; besides a number of negro slaves. Society was as varied as the character of the population, but on the whole may be described as being without stability, regard for law, or religion. (B. H. Roberts, *Missouri Persecutions* [Salt Lake City: Bookcraft, 1965], 50, see generally 48-49; and *HC* 1:197-98)

Early Mormon Ezra Booth described Independence in 1831 as a new town with

a court house built of brick, two or three merchant stores and 15 or 20 dwelling houses built mostly of logs hewn on both sides; and situated on a handsome rise of ground, about three miles south of Missouri river, and about 12 miles east of the dividing line between the United States and the Indian Reserve, and is the county seat of Jackson county. West of the line lies the territory selected by the government of the United States for the future residence of the Indians, to which place a number of tribes have already emigrated. (JH, August 3, 1831, 2)

[14] The most complete description of relations between Mormons and non-Mormons in Jackson County during this time is Warren A. Jennings, "Zion Is Fled: The Expulsion of the Mormons from Jackson County, Missouri" (Ph.D. diss., University of Florida, 1962).

[15] During this time, McLellin visited the temple lot, which McLellin later stated was "covered with young poplars, thickly standing." According to McLellin, Joseph had

cut his way in through this thick growth of trees, brush and saplings, and marked the spot by blazing a tree near by, cutting away the under brush for a few feet around and setting up a small stone that had been picked up in the ravine below. This was all the corner stone that was ever laid upon it, and it only to mark the place of the corner. (William H. Kelley letter, January 16, 1882, *Saints' Herald* 29 [1882]: 67)

[16] Harris, who had traveled to Independence with Joseph Smith's group, was commanded in a revelation given through Joseph Smith on August 1, 1831, to donate his money to the Church; in return, according to the law of consecration, he would receive an inheritance in Zion (D&C 58:35-38). See Karl Ricks Anderson, "[Law of] Consecration in Ohio and Missouri," in *Encyclopedia of Mormonism,* ed. Daniel H. Ludlow, 5 vols. (New York: Macmillan, 1992), 1:314-15 (hereafter cited as *EM*).

[17] On February 4, 1831, Edward Partridge was called to be the first bishop of the Church and he was ordained by Sidney Rigdon that day (D&C 41:9). Certificate in Joseph Smith collection, LDS Archives. As bishop, Partridge's responsibilities primarily involved overseeing the practical implementation of the law of consecration. In a revelation given in Zion on

August 1, 1831, Partridge was commanded to remain in Missouri and "divide the lands of the heritage of God unto his children" (D&C 58:17, 24). See also William G. Hartley, "Bishop, History of the Office," in *EM* 1:119-22. Later in his life, McLellin felt that these responsibilities of the bishop were corrupt innovations. He wrote, "[Joseph Smith's] appointing and ordaining Edward Partridge a Bishop to take care of church property has no warrant in the word of God, nor in church history either." William E. McLellin to President Joseph Smith [III], July 1872, RLDS Archives.

[18] At a conference in Kirtland on June 3, 1831, Morley and Corrill "were ordained assistants to the Bishop under the hand of Lyman Wight." Donald Q. Cannon and Lyndon W. Cook, eds., *Far West Record* (Salt Lake City: Deseret Book, 1983), 7. Sent to Missouri along with the other elders assigned to journey to Zion, they were instructed to remain in Zion, the "land of [their] residence" (D&C 52:7, 23; 58:24).

[19] This is one of the gifts of the spirit, mentioned in 1 Corinthians 12:10. According to Joseph Smith, this gift enabled people to

> detect [evil spirits'] mischievous and mysterious operations when trying to palm themselves upon the Church in a religious garb, and militate against the interest of the Church and spread of truth . . . A man must have the discerning of spirits before he can drag into daylight this hellish influence and unfold it unto the world in all its soul-destroying, diabolical, and horrid colors; for nothing is a greater injury to the children of men than to be under the influence of a false spirit when they think they have the Spirit of God. (Joseph Fielding Smith, comp., *Teachings of the Prophet Joseph Smith* [Salt Lake City: Deseret Book, 1979], 205-6)

[20] Hyrum Smith, one of the Eight Witnesses to the Book of Mormon, is listed among the group who saw and handled the golden plates from which the Book of Mormon was translated.

[21] Lewis's home was in Kaw township, west of Independence; it was the site of "the first conference in the land of Zion," held August 4, 1831. *HC* 1:199.

[22] Some sources have erroneously stated that Samuel Smith baptized McLellin; for example, Lawrence R. Flake, *Mighty Men of Zion* (Salt Lake City: Deseret Book, 1974), 197. Others have mistakenly indicated that he was baptized "on the way" to Jackson county. Andrew Jenson, *Latter-day Saint Biographical Encyclopedia: A Compilation of Biographical Sketches of Prominent Men and Women in the Church of Jesus Christ of Latter-day Saints,* 4 vols. (Salt Lake City: Andrew Jenson History Co., 1901-36), 1:82.

[23] Newel Knight had been commanded to journey to Missouri, along with the other members who had emigrated from Colesville, New York, to Thompson, Ohio (D&C 54). "This group of about sixty members left Ohio on 3 July 1831 and arrived in Independence on 25 July." Cook, *Revelations*

of the Prophet Joseph Smith, 85. William G. Hartley, *"They Are My Friends:"*
A History of the Joseph Knight Family, 1825-1850 (Provo: Grandin Book,
1986), chs. 8-10.

²⁴ An April 1830 revelation on church organization, ordinances, and
administration instructed the members of the newly restored institution to
"meet together often to partake of bread and wine in the remembrance of the
Lord Jesus" (D&C 20:75). As had been true of the primitive Christian church,
such gatherings became the basic worship service of the new Church.

²⁵ This chapter focuses on Paul's conversion story, especially empha-
sizing the divine source of Paul's conversion: "For I neither received it of
man, neither was I taught it, but by the revelation of Jesus Christ" (Gal. 1:12).
There is no way to know whether Corrill's lecture drew connections
between Paul's learning the truth directly from Christ and Joseph Smith's
similar learning from Christ, but Galatians 1:8 was undoubtedly used to
affirm the restoration of the original gospel of Jesus Christ: "But though we,
or an angel from heaven, preach any other gospel unto you than that which
we have preached unto you, let him be accursed." Mormons, along with
other Christian primitivists, sought to practice Christianity quite literally as
it is defined and prescribed in the New Testament.

²⁶ It is likely that this refers to a house built twelve miles west of
Independence in Kaw Township, "as a foundation in Zion." On August 2,
1831, a log, "carried and placed by twelve men, in honor of the twelve tribes
of Israel," was laid for a house which was built to serve as "a house of
worship, [and] was also used as a school and was the first school to be
erected within the present boundaries of Kansas City, Missouri." At this site,
following the placement of the log, "the land of Zion was consecrated and
dedicated by Elder Sidney Rigdon for the gathering of the Saints." *HC* 1:196;
Richard Neitzel Holzapfel and T. Jeffery Cottle, *Old Mormon Kirtland and
Missouri* (Santa Ana, Calif.: Fieldbrook, 1991), 203-4.

²⁷ A tongue-in-cheek comparison with some of the more extreme
worship practices of the Second Great Awakening.

²⁸ See note 12 above. The details of this conference are recorded in
Cannon and Cook, *Far West Record,* 13-14.

²⁹ In later years, McLellin came to disagree with this process of
ordination, believing that priesthood authority was not to be given by the
laying on of hands. William E. McLellin to Elder M. H. Forscutt, October
1870, RLDS Archives.

³⁰ The revelation given at Chariton commanded the elders to return
to Kirtland following the meeting in Missouri, proselyting along the way
(D&C 62:5; also 58:63; 60:14).

³¹ In 1832 McLellin wrote to his family about this "first discourse." See
page 79 below.

³² According to Joseph Smith, Arrow Rock, a landmark in Saline
County, Missouri, was "so called from the Lamanites [Native Americans]

coming from all quarters to get a hard rock from the bluff out of which to make arrow points." *HC* 3:363.

[33] In the first edition (1830) of the Book of Mormon, the "Testimony of Three Witnesses" and "Testimony of Eight Witnesses" were printed on the last two pages of the book.

[34] This challenge is based on a New Testament text: "And these signs shall follow them that believe; In my name shall they cast out devils; they shall speak with new tongues; They shall take up serpents; and if they drink any deadly thing, it shall not hurt them: they shall lay hands on the sick, and they shall recover" (Mark 16:17-18).

[35] The Apostles' practice of shaking the dust from their feet as a testimony against those who would not accept the message they preached (Luke 9:5; also Matt. 10:14; Acts 13:51) was incorporated into early Mormonism. A July 1831 revelation to Joseph Smith and Oliver Cowdery commanded: "And in whatsoever place ye shall enter, and they receive you not in my name, ye shall leave a cursing instead of a blessing, by casting off the dust of your feet against them as a testimony, and cleansing your feet by the wayside" (D&C 24:15). This charge was renewed in a revelation to the elders who were preparing to make the return trip from Independence to Kirtland in August 1831. Neither McLellin nor Hyrum Smith was present when the revelation was given instructing the elders departing for Kirtland to "speedily return, proclaiming my word among the congregations of the wicked, not in haste, neither in wrath nor with strife. And shake off the dust of thy feet against those who receive thee not, not in their presence, lest thou provoke them, but in secret; and wash thy feet, as a testimony against them in the day of judgment" (D&C 60:14-15). But it is likely that these instructions were passed on to them.

[36] McLellin gives a similar description of this meeting in his letter to "Beloved Relatives," page 79 below.

[37] An intermittent fever in which the sick person progresses through stages of coldness, hotness, and sweating, each stage accompanied by paroxysms. Robert Hooper, *Lexicon Medicum; or Medical Dictionary*, 2 vols. (New York: J. and J. Harper, 1829), 1:37, 353.

[38] Begun in 1811, the construction of this road was funded by the federal government. The road was conceived as an aid to westward expansion and greatly decreased travel time. The road started at Cumberland, Maryland, and gradually expanded westward, reaching Vandalia, Illinois, in 1838. It was built with a stone surface, but the western end, on which McLellin traveled, was unsurfaced during this time; the stone road at this time ended at Zanesville, Ohio. U.S. Highway 40 and Interstate 70 now parallel the National Road's route. M. G. Lay, *Ways of the World* (New Brunswick, N.J.: Rutgers University Press, 1992), 115-16.

[39] There is no way to tell whether McLellin referred to Mark 16:17 or 1 Corinthians 12.

[40]The Book of Mormon teaches that Jerusalem will be reestablished as a gathering place for the Jews, while another city, the New Jerusalem (here referred to as "mount Zion") will be built in the Americas as a gathering place for "the remnant of the seed of Joseph" (Eth. 13:6; also 3 Ne. 20:29-33; D&C 45:64-69). This conception of the two cities became an important component of LDS theology and, in the early years, was often mentioned in discussions of the end time.

[41] "Levi Hancock and Zebedee Coltrin traveled together to Missouri, and performed successful missionary labors in Ohio, Indiana, and Illinois." JH, June 19, 1831. The companions were in Winchester during July and August 1831 and there they "raised a large branch of the Church" (about one hundred members), in addition to baptizing about one hundred others, including one of George Washington's bodyguards, in nearby Ward township. Levi W. Hancock, "Life of Levi Hancock," typescript, Special Collections, Harold B. Lee Library, Brigham Young University, Provo, Utah, 37-40.

[42]At this time, the population of Kirtland, Ohio was 1,140, of whom 90 were Mormons. The Kirtland branch consisted of 100 members, including those who lived in the vicinity. Milton V. Backman, Jr., *A Profile of Latter-day Saints of Kirtland, Ohio and Members of Zion's Camp 1830-1839: Vital Statistics and Sources* (Provo, Utah: Brigham Young University, 1982), 83. See generally Milton V. Backman, Jr., "Kirtland, Ohio," in *EM* 2:793-98.

[43]This conference was held in Orange, Cuyahoga County, Ohio, at the home of Sirenes Burnet. *HC* 1:219; Cannon and Cook, *Far West Record,* 19. Orange is seventeen miles south of Kirtland, and by the end of 1830, approximately 65 members constituted the Orange Branch. Holzapfel and Cottle, *Old Mormon Kirtland and Missouri,* 122.

[44] Subjects discussed at this conference included the importance of the work of Joseph Smith on the Bible and the need to provide for the families of traveling elders. Following several speeches, the men bore testimony. McLellin said "that he had the greatest reason to rejoice of any present and that he also would be subject to the will of God even unto death" and he also gave the closing prayer. See conference minutes, Cannon and Cook, *Far West Record,* 19-24, quote on 21.

[45]The first ordinations to the office of high priest had been performed on June 3, 1831. *HC* 1:175-76. Later in his life, McLellin felt that only one person at a time could hold the office of high priest: "Under the Law but one High Priest could legally exist at the same time. So if that was a shadow or type, then the substance and anti-type, the Gospel dispensation, can have but One High Priest—Christ Jesus!" McLellin to Joseph Smith [III], January 10, 1961, RLDS Archives. McLellin seems to have struggled with all additions or changes that Joseph Smith made in Church

organization and structure after the first year. McLellin argued that since the original Articles and Covenants of the Church did not mention high priests, the office was merely Joseph Smith's own invention, added to later transcripts of the Articles and Covenants. "Hence," he said, "I am no believer in High Priests." McLellin to Joseph Smith [III]; also McLellin to M. H. Forscutt, October 1870, RLDS Archives.

[46] At this conference, Sidney Rigdon told the candidates "that if they [after being ordained] should doubt God would withdraw his Spirit from them." McLellin and fourteen others were called and seated. Joseph Smith "was appointed to examine these brethren, presenting themselves for ordination, [and] after prayer said that he had a testimony that each had one tallent and if after being ordained they should hide it God would take it from them; [he] exhorted them to pray continually in meekness." Oliver Cowdery then ordained McLellin and the others to the office of high priest. Cannon and Cook, *Far West Record,* 24–25.

[47] McLellin later believed that there should be no such thing as "Levitical Priests . . . in this age or dispensation" since they should have been done away with, like the law of Moses was, when Christ established his Church in the meridian of time. He felt that the Melchizedek Priesthood was a replacement of the lesser priesthood, and that there was no need for the lesser priesthood since the higher priesthood was available. McLellin to Joseph Smith [III].

[48] The last session of the conference, which met at 8:00 a.m., is described in Cannon and Cook, *Far West Record,* 25–26.

[49] At this time, Joseph Smith, Jr., was living at the John Johnson home in Hiram, Ohio. *HC* 1:215, 219.

[50] John Whitmer and Lyman Wight had established a branch of the Church in Nelson, 5 miles east of Hiram, in February–March, 1831. Meetings were possibly held at the home of Charles Hulet, an early convert. Cannon and Cook, *Far West Record,* 12, note 1.

[51] McLellin later described his experience as scribe in the *Ensign of Liberty,* 98–99:

> The scribe seats himself at a desk or table, with pen, ink and paper. The subject of enquiry being understood, the Prophet and Revelator enquires of God. He spiritually sees, hears and feels, and then speaks as he is moved upon by the Holy Ghost, the 'thus saith the Lord,' sentence after sentence, and waits for his amanuenses to write and then read aloud each sentence. Thus they proceed until the revelator says Amen, at the close of what is then communicated. I have known [prophets] to seat themselves, & without premeditation, . . . thus deliver off in broken sentences, some of the most sublime pieces of composition which I ever perused in any book.

[52]Writing in 1848 in the *Ensign of Liberty*, no. 4 (January): 61, McLellin described his experience in receiving this revelation:

> I had expected and believed that when I saw Bro. Joseph, I should receive [a revelation]; and I went before the Lord in secret, and on my knees asked him to reveal the answer to five questions through his Prophet, and that too without his having any knowledge of my having made such request. I now testify in the fear of God, that every question which I had thus lodged in the ears of the Lord of Sabbaoth, were answered to my full and entire satisfaction. I desired it for a testimony of Joseph's inspiration. And I to this day consider it to me an evidence which I cannot refute.

He also said, "In Oct. 1831 I wrote a revelation as [the Prophet Joseph Smith] delivered it. And I know he used no [seer] stone to see then." McLellin to President Joseph Smith [III]. Later, however, McLellin had questions about this revelation. In his 1870 letter to Forscutt, he said, "The revelations given by or through J. Smith after he ceased to give them by the use of the Interpreter, by which he the book of Mormon was translated, cannot be altogether depended upon, after he ceased to give them in that way."

[53] The events during this interval turned out to be critical with regard to later perceptions of McLellin's life as a follower of Joseph Smith. The newly ordained elder attended a November 1-2, 1831, conference in Hiram, Ohio, at which it was decided to print 10,000 copies of the Prophet Joseph Smith's revelations. The volume, which would not be issued until 1833, would be called the Book of Commandments. Between sessions of this conference, by inspiration, the Prophet received the "Lord's Preface" to this work. This preface was published as the book's first section; it is also the first section of the 1835 book of Doctrine and Covenants, which is an expanded version of the Book of Commandments. Another revelation (D&C 67), likewise received by the Prophet during this conference, addressed the matter of whether his seemingly uneducated language called into question the status of his revelations as God's word. Apparently some of his followers wished to edit the Prophet's revelations. This new revelation instructed elders who were worried about the imperfections of Joseph's language to select the least perfect of the revelations in the Book of Commandments and to "appoint him that is most wise among you" to write a revelation, i.e., "make one like unto it." If the revelation written by the person chosen as the wisest of the elders did not appear to be from God, then the elders would be "under condemnation" if they did "not bear record that they [the Prophet's revelations] are true" (D&C 67:6-8).

Perhaps because he was a schoolteacher, McLellin was the elder who "endeavored to write a commandment like unto one of the least of the Lord's." Instead of being convincing as God's word, McLellin's ineffectual attempt "to imitate the language of Jesus Christ" was understood as evidence that the Prophet's revelations read true. Thus McLellin's effort had the effect of renewing the faith of the elders "in the fulness of the Gospel, and in the truth of the commandments and revelations which the Lord had given to the Church through [Joseph Smith's] instrumentality." Consequently, the elders "signified a willingness to bear testimony of their truth to all the world." The passages quoted here are taken from a section in the *History of the Church* 1:226, dated November, 1831, but written shortly after McLellin had left the Church. This same section makes it clear that McLellin's effort to write a revelation was later interpreted as an act of self-aggrandizement. A recent analysis of this episode suggests, however, that in attempting to write a revelation McLellin was simply complying with the injunction that one among the elders should "make one like unto [the least persuasive of Smith's revelations]." Mark R. Grandstaff, "Having More Learning than Sense: William E. McLellin and the Book of Commandments Revisited," *Dialogue: A Journal of Mormon Thought* 26 (Winter 1993): 23-48. See further, page 253, note 15.

Later, in 1870, McLellin argued that the decision to print the Book of Commandments was "contrary to the Lord's directions," since "it was often said in those [revelations] given before to 'Keep these things from the world.'" McLellin to Forscutt.

[54] In response to the desire of McLellin and three other elders "to know the mind of the Lord concerning themselves" (*HC* 1:227), Joseph Smith inquired of the Lord and received a revelation which instructed the elders to "preach the gospel to every creature" (D&C 68:8).

[55] For McLellin's activities during this interval, the following timetable can be constructed:

November 1-2: He attended the conference in Hiram, Ohio. Conference minutes are reprinted in Cannon and Cook, *Far West Record,* 26-28.

November 6: McLellin preached in the church at Nelson.

November 8: McLellin attended a conference in Hiram at which it was decided to revise and correct errors which had crept into the revelations that were to be published in the Book of Commandments. Conference minutes are reprinted in Cannon and Cook, *Far West Record,* 28-29. Several letters written late in his life convey McLellin's grievances against the LDS Church. These letters indicate that the revisions made in the revelations were frustrating to McLellin, who saw these additions and subtractions as a sign that Joseph Smith was tampering with the word of the Lord. McLellin to President Joseph Smith; McLellin to Forscutt.

November 11: McLellin attended a conference in Hiram. Conference minutes are reprinted in Cannon and Cook, *Far West Record,* 30-31.

November 12-13: McLellin was the moderator at another conference in Hiram, Ohio. He offered the opening prayer. This conference appointed Oliver Cowdery and John Whitmer to carry the revelations to Independence to be published. See conference minutes in Cannon and Cook, *Far West Record*, 31-32.

November 12: McLellin preached at Windham. Reynolds Cahoon recorded in his journal: "I attended two conferences in Hiram [possibly the November 11 and November 12 conferences], after which I journeyed with Brother Wm. E. McLellin to Windom, where we held a meeting on Saturday, Nov. 12th, and on the Sabbath (Nov. 13th) returned to Hinnan [later spelled Hinman]." JH, November 1831, 1.

[56] McLellin's entries for November 16 through November 20 are repeated with slight changes in Journal II.

[57] Samuel Smith similarly described this congregation as "very large and attentive." JH, November 16, 1831, 1.

[58] Samuel Smith recorded the following: "In the evening of the 17th we held another meeting at Garretsville, Portage Co, Ohio. Here the people seemed to be very hard hearted as they interrupted us a number of times, but we left our testimony with them, and stopped over night at the house of Bro. Cowens." JH, November 16, 1831, 1.

[59] These were a Mr. and Mrs. Richards and Mrs. Cowin. See McLellin's entry for November 18, 1831 in Journal II. Samuel Smith said of this day, "We spent [the day] . . . conversing with those who came to enquire." JH, November 16, 1831, 1.

[60] John 4 contains the account of Jesus' words to the woman at the well in Samaria: "Whosoever drinketh of the water that I shall give him shall never thirst" (4:14); "ye worship ye know not what: we know what we worship" (4:22); "God is a Spirit: and they that worship him must worship him in spirit and truth" (4:24). These and several other passages in John 4 could have been interpreted and used by the Campbellite minister to oppose such Mormon doctrines as the need for new revelation or the physical appearance of God.

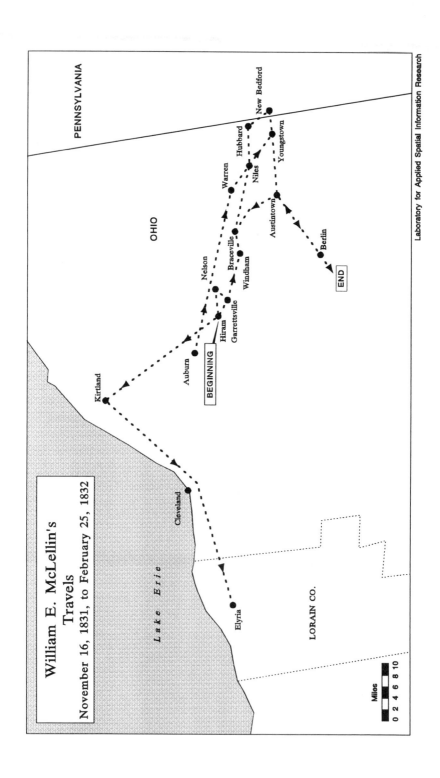

William E. McLellin's
Travels
November 16, 1831, to February 25, 1832

PENNSYLVANIA

OHIO

New Bedford

Hubbard

Warren

Youngstown

Niles

Nelson

Braceville

Austintown

Windham

Auburn

Hiram

Berlin

Garrettsville

Kirtland

BEGINNING

END

Cleveland

Lake Erie

Elyria

LORAIN CO.

Miles
0 2 4 6 8 10

Laboratory for Applied Spatial Information Research

William E. McLellin Journal II
November 16, 1831–February 25, 1832

A diary of our tour to the East[1]

We left Brother Joseph Smiths[2] in Hiram Portage County Ohio on the 16th Novr. thence to Nelson 5 ms and in evening meeting among our brethren B[rother] S[amuel Smith] opened the meeting by a few observation[s] and Prayr. Then I spoke about one hour the brethren were much animated and made known their good determinations and zeal for the cause of thruth.

Thence the [18th] 17th we went 3 ms. to Garrettsvill and held a meeting in the evening. We had a very attentive congregation. I opened meeting and spoke about and hour and some wicked wretch or wret[c]hes interupted the congregation by burning some odious smelling thing in the so that raised confusion in all the house and broke up our meeting.[3]

Friday [17th] 18th we spent in talking with Mr & Mrs Richards and Mrs Cowin. in the evening we went to a Campbellite meeting the Priest spoke from John 4th[4] and then gave liberty to others. I then arose and told them my mission they then spoke and said they did not want to hear any more. I was to silence and I did so after bearing testimony to the truth of the book of Mormon and to the judgement of God which would come upon them if they did not repent. [*page 2*] They granted B. Saml ten minutes to speak. He bore testimony also. [by] but they rejected all with disdain and desired us to depart out of their coasts. We did so and wiped the dust of our feet against them.

[F] Saturday 19th We called on Brother Miller and took dinner and passed on 6 ms to Mr Lane's. they received us kindly and sent out and notified the people.

Sunday 20 a congregation attended at schoolhouse in Braceville. They were attintive and apparently serious. I opened the meeting and expounded the Gospel to them. Several persons invited us home with them. We returned to Mr Lane's and staid all night they were still very friendly. Mr Lane was a universalist. we could not move his principles.

Munday 21th we visited Mr Barnum and spent the day in conversation with him and family. We attended another meeting that evening at the same schoolhouse. the house was full though the evening was unpleasant in consequence of snow. The people were attentive & requested another Meeting. We appointed another on Thursday next and spent the time with the neigh[*page 3*]bours in conversation, in reading writting and studying the scriptures.[5]

Thursday ~~evening~~ afternoon we attended our appointment. ~~Samuel opened the meeting and spoke about an hour~~ I spoke on the covenants and promises, the glories of the Millenniel day[6] and exorted the people to obey. Samuel bore testimony to the truths which they had heard. We then gave an invitation for any to do their duty. Irene Barnum arose and expressed her determination to serve the Lord and wished to be eniceated [initiated] into his Kingdom by the ordinances of the Gospel. Reuben Fields also joined. There was a general affection throughout the room— We appointed a meeting in Warren on Friday afternoon— also at the same house for on Sunday nex[t] for the purpose of Baptizing those who joined. we went to Mr Barnum's that night. the old man was changed from agreeable to appear a little cross.

We left there after breakfast and went to Warren. We held our meeting by candle light in the court house. We had a large congregation though a majority of them were Deists but they treated us civily.[7] I arose and opened [*page 4*] the meeting by prayr and addressed the assembly on the propriety of new Revelations and explained the utility of book of Mormon and opened the plan of Salvation by the Gospel and exorted them to obedience.

Saturday we returned to Mr Lane's. that evening Mr Barnum sent our clothes to Mr Lane's and sent word that we could have no further admittance in his house. I endured it patiently.

Sunday we attended our appointment and I opened the meeting by prayr and exortation. I then opened a door for the reception of members. brother Rueben Field's wife came forward. we then repaired to the water about 2 ms distant. I baptized them[8] though it was a cold day and considerable snow on the ground. we then appointed a confirmation meeting at Br Fields that evening. we attended Br. Harrison[9] opened the meeting by prayr and exortation. I then spoke by way of exortation and prayed for my Br and Sister and laid my hand upon them. Br Rueben received a great witness & exorted his neighbours to obidience. We appointed another meeting on next Tuesday eve at Br Fields——

We attended Brother Saml opened the meeting by exortation. I then prayed and spoke on the establishment of [*page 5*] the church of christ in these last days. I then exorted them to embrace the truth and flee from the wrath to come. Bro. Reuben bore testimony to the truths which the people had heard. We closed our meeting without making another appointment——

Wednesday the 30 Nov. We started from friend Lane's on our course to the east. The day was very cold and we stopped frequently to warm and we declared our mission to all we saw. we called to see Mr Avery 1/2 ml from the center of Braceville. we talked a while and started but he followed us out and invited us to spend the eve and night with him— Nothing remarkable.

Thursday 1st day of Dec we took breakfast and pursued our tour to the east. Thence to Warren. Thence East. we tried [for] at three or four houses to get the people to keep us all night and call the neighbours together, but they would not. We traveled till night before we could [find] any man to keep us. at length we came to a Deists by the name of W. Suse. he kept us. we talked with him but he would not believe unless We would do a sign among the wicked to convince his carnal mind.

We took brakfast. Thence F[riday] 2nd one mile to D Eatin's Esq. He is a professed and hardoned Deist though a very friendly [*page 6*] man. It was very cold and snowing. He invited us to stay. he called his neighbours together that evening a number collected.

Br S[amuel] opened the meeting by prayr and gave a History of the book and made some observations from prophecies. I then spoke about an hour on the manifest difference between the church of God and the world in all ages that the Bible gives account of. I then closed by offering to address the people again. a Mr. Edwards opened his heart and door and invited us to preach there. We appointed a meeting for Sunday.

Saturday 3 we spent with Mr Eatin in reading and studying.

Sunday 4 we attended our appointment about 4 miles from Warren.[10] The house was full. it was extremely cold. I arose and addressed the people one hour and a half on the importance of the book of Mormon and their becoming true Christians. We closed the meeting without making another appointment——

Monday 5th By pressing request we made another appointment for Tuesday eve ne near the same place at Jms St John's.— I went about two miles from Mr Edward's to a Grammar School and spent the day pleasantly until 2 Oclock. A Campbellite Preached about an hour and a half on the 10th Rom. he made some very wild shoots.[11] It was too late when he finished for me to make any remarks. I only gave out my appointment for Tuesday evening. [*page* 7] Thence I went to Dan. Eatin's and we staid all night.

Tuesday 6th I went to Mr Read's and conversed with his wife about an hour who is a Roman Catholic though quite reasonable and senseable. Thence in search of the Apochryphal Testament and to examine an Iron furnace and forge and a large mill &c. We attended our appointment.[12] Br S. opened the meeting by prayr and I spoke about 2 hours first some general observations then on the prophecies and then the Gospel and then Br. S. exorted and invited the people to embrace the truth. None expressed a desire. I then exorted a while and closed without making another appointment. But by pressing requests we made an appointment for next evening at the schoolhouse where I heard the Campbellite and also on next Sunday at Heatin's Mill.[13] The people were much excited and appeared anxious to hear and learn the truth.[14]

Wednesday 7th in the evening we attended our appointment.[15] I opened the meeting and we both exorted considerable and closed without opposition.

Thursday Friday, and Saturday we spent in preaching from house to house.

Sunday 11th We attended our appointment.[16] A large assembly collected. I opened the meeting and spoke about 2 1/2 hours on the Covenants, the evidences of the book of Mormon, and of Zion and Jerusalem the two places of the gathering in the last days and of [*page 8*] The nature of the two gatherings on Zion and Canaan and of the glories of the Millenniel reign and closed by speaking the glories of the gospel and exortation. Brother Saml arose and bore testimony to the truth of what had been said and of the book of Mormon. We made an other appointment at Mr St. John's for Tuesday evening following. The people were attentive and very serious in part but none joined with us tho many said they believed we preached the truth——

Tuesday eve we attended our appointment. the house was full of people. I opened the meeting by prayr. Saml then spoke a while on the 12 Chap of 1 Cor.[17] I then arose and made some general observations——I had preached so much to the people before and several there believed that we had declared the truth to them and I exorted them to obedience and unfolded the glories of heavedn and of Zion until the Lord poured out his spirit in [h] my hear[d]t till I ceaced to exorted and I just shouted and praised the Lord and offered my hand to all to go with me to Zion. there were many who shed tears freely and many more who were very serious. Mother C. Reed gave [me] us her hand and S[ister or Sarah] St. John and declared themselves candidates for the new Kingdom by Baptism. we closed our meeting and appointed [an] to meet at or near Heatins Mill at two hours by the sun next eve for the purpose of baptizing the two ~~Reed~~ Sisters who had joined. [*page 9*] We dismissed. There were two Campbellite Preachers there who had come to contend with us. one of them arose and requested the privilege to speak of the man of the house, he went on though the people were not much attentive. I set and watched him till he was done. I then arose and removed the difficulties he mentioned and I believe I gave general Satisfaction—[Wednesday] We attended our appointment. It was snowing considerable. And though we had to break the ice. I went down in the watter and baptized the two Sisters who had joined. There was a considerable congregation present. We appointed a prayr meeting that night at friend Reed's for the purpose of confirming those baptized. The house was full. Br Saml opened the meeting and spoke about half and hour. I then rose and spoke about an hour on the first establishment of Christianity then on the rise and progress of the church of Christ in these last days and the importance of the ordinances of the gospel but particularly that of the Laying on of the hands for the reception of the Holy Ghost. I then prayed and laid my hands on them and they said they rejoiced that they ever heard the plan of salvation—I then exorted the people to embrace the truth and Elizabeth Everhart come forward and we repaired to the water and I baptized her and as we came out of the water Saml Burwell came to me and [*page 10*] I took him down and immersed him and then we returned to Mr Reed's and prayed with them and I laid my hands upon them.[18] We then appointed another meeting at Mr Edwards' for next Tuesday eve and we also ~~we~~ sent an appointment about five or six miles East by pressing request to preach next Saturday and Sunday——

Thursday 15. in the morning I was taken with a diarhoea and was quite unwell with a violent cold——

I ought to have mentioned that on last S[un]aturday eve [B] Sister Sarah St John's child was scalded badly and Br Saml was there and laid his hands upon it and healed it in so much that it did not even so much as blister—

Sunday eve Mrs Smith was taken very sick [~~very~~] where I was and I prayed for her and laid my hands upon her and she was restored to health ~~in a few~~ We also prayed for and laid our hands upon a Mr Campbell's child who had a most remarkable sore face and next morning it was almost well—

[ɬ] We went Saturday morning to our appointment but it was put off for or till evening. we attended at eve in a schoolhouse in Youngstown. the house was full. I opened the meeting and spoke about an hour. Br Saml bore testimony. we dismissed without making another app.

but next day we appointed to preach in Austentown[19] at Peter Lantermans. in the eve we attended Though I was very unwell and laboured under a great pressure in my breast I arose and spoke about an hour and had considerable [*page 11*] liberty both of body and mind but I suffered unaccountably during the night. Cold had settled on my lungs and I was much agitated with trembling &c.

Tuesday 20th After Bro Saml had prayed for me and laid his hands upon me I was enabled to ride in our slay back to Weathersfield—— and that eve we attended our ap. at Friend Edward[s] Though weak after brother Saml opened by prayr I was enabled to speak about an hour——

Wednesday 21th my cold increased and my breast and lungs became so exceeding sore I was cast down upon my bed and mostly confined[20]

until Tues 27th Brothers Joseph [Smith], Hiram [Smith], Reynolds [Cahoon] & Lyman [Johnson] visited me[21]

and Wedns 28th in the morning Brother Joseph came to my bed side and laid his hands upon me and prayed for me and I was healed so that I got up and eat breakfast and attended an ap. made for them. the brethren spoke. I then arose and was enabled to speak about half an hour and I gave opportunity to any and all to join us. bro S. Burwell's wife (Celia) came forward and joined. We ap[pointed] another meeting to be that eve at friend Reed's. we met and I baptized sister Celia. Br Hiram and myself preached to a large company. I then dismissed and after the wicked went away. I arose & spoke about half an hour. Bro. Jos[eph] then prayed & laid his hands upon sister Celia and she expressed great joy in the reception of the Holy spirit.

Thurs. 29th we came to Hiram Town to bro. Johnson's and had a prayr meeting that eve.

Friday 30th The Elders present held a council [*page 12*] at father Whitmer's which was attended with much mutual benefit and edification.

Sat 31 I went to Kirtland.

[~~Sunday~~] January 1832. Sun. 1st I attended a meeting with the brethren where I recd much edification & comfort to my heart. Elder T. Marsh[22] lead the meeting. I also became acquainted with some good brethren that I had not seen —— I atten. another mee. that eve at the sam[e] place. I was appointed to lead. we had a good meeting. I att. their general crurch [church] mee & conference.

Mon. 2th I was appointed to lead again. The conference was conducted with general harmony. We had much labour with some disobedient members. one was restored and some cut off.[23] the council closed after night by prayr of Br Coe——

Tuesday and Wednesday I spent in visiting the brethren and in talking with some unbelievers and in reading and s[t]udying the scriptures.

Thursday 5. I attended a council of Elders at B. Cahoon's for the purpose of mutual edification. Br Hiram Smith Led the council. It lasted till after night and was dismissed by prayr of Br Williams. I went home with Br Coe and spent the time reading the prop[h]ecies and conversing with him and family until

Saturday 7th I attended a church mee. at Br Billings. Br Coe lead the mee—— I[t] was conducted with general peace, harmony and satisfaction & closed by prayr of Br T[homas] Marsh.

<u>Sun</u> 8th [*page 13*] Sunday 8th Jan. I attended with the church. Br Coe delivered a discourse upon the prophecies, very edifying to me. I then spoke about an hour upon the distinguishing qualities of the church of God. We had a very good mee. We had another meeting the same eve. I spoke about half an hour on Christian perfection.

Br N[ewel] Whitney the Bishop[24] called a council Monday eve to enquire into the case of Br Ezra Thair.[25] We had a ve[r]y mutual council attended with much benefit——

[~~Tues~~] Wednesday 11th I mostly spent in talking with a Ms [Mr.] Bennett a Campbellite Priest. I took him on my slay

and Thursday and Friday I brought him to Hiram to see Jos[eph] & Sidney, Friday eve he talked considerable with Br Joseph.[26]

Saturday I spent in reading & talking with the brethren.

S[unday] 15th I went to Auburn with B. Sidney. He opened the mee- & spoke about 2 hours. I spoke about 15 minutes. the people did not hearken to the councils of Heaven at all.

Monday 16th Br Sidney & wife & I went to Warren. Br Sidney & I went on to Weathersfield and staid all night at friend Reed's ——

Tuesday 17th I spent in visiting the members, there and that eve we held a meeting at John Edward's. Br Sidney preached and we appointed a mee — for next day at Mr Reed's. Brother Sidney again and we left there about one oclock [*page 14*] and came to Warren thence to Hiram——

Thursday 19th I spent in Reading and Writing Letters.

Friday 20 I came to Kirtland.

Saturday I spent writing.

Sunday 22 I attended with the Kirtland brethren and preached about 2 hours to them and administered the Lord's supper & Sunday eve I attended a prayr meeting at the flats[27]—

Monday 23 I had an appointment at Br. Billings early in the morning. I attended and baptized 9 children.[28] I then started for conference in Lorane Co W. reserve.[29]

I attended on Wednesday 25. There I recd a commition to go to the South. Brother Luke Johnson was appointed to go with me.[30]

Thursday & Friday I ret[t]urned to Kirtland. I was sorely tempted of Devil But Friday night I made a hard struggle a[nd] shook him off my back.

Saturday I wrote commandments & revelations at Father Smiths.

Sunday I attended with the Kirtland Brethren. Brother Orson Hyde Preached about an hour. I spoke about half an hour.

Monday I Baptized Shadrick Roundy[31] from New York.

Tuesday I went to Hiram to Br Joseph's.[32]

Wednesday eve we held a meeting at father Johnson's for a farewell to the brethren.

[F] Thursday the 2 of February Br Luke Johnson & I started on our mission to the South. We staid with Br Thos Cowan, The neighbours come in and we laboured with them and prayed [f] with them & exorted them to believe and obey the fulness of the Gospel.

[*page 15*] Friday 3 We left Garretsvile. thence to Brother Miller's. thence to Br R. Fields. he was doubting some but we exorted them to faithfulness and they seemed much encouraged and they said they would visit Br. Joseph. Thence we went to Mr. G. Millers a Campbelite, univer[s]alist and staid all night.

Saturday we went to Weathersfield

and Sun & Mon- I wrote letters.

Tuesday 7 I visited Danl Eatin a profound Deist――――

Wednesday eve we had an appointment at James St. John's. we attended and I spoke about an hour with Zeal & warmth and mighty exortation. some were much affected. the brethren were much comforted but none joined.

Thursday It eve we had an appointment in Howland but it rained so hard and raised the watters so I did not go.

Friday I continued writing reading and studdying.

[Sunday] Saturday Brother Luke crossed the creek and the bridge was shortly taken away and [he] got on Tom and went 8 or 10 miles to Fowler to a Mr Terrill's and made an appointment for us next Tuesday eve & returned to me.

on Sun I had an appointment at J. Edwards' and I spoke to a few on the covenants, prophecies and the new Covenant on the fulness of the Gospel. I dismissmissed [*sic*] by prayr of Br Luke. the friends seemed considerabley affected.

Monday Br Luke was at father Everharts. Sister Elizabeth was sick and he prayed for her and laid his hands upon her and she was immediately healed.

Monday eve old Mother Edwards told us she had had a vision and she knew the book of [*page 16*] Mormon was a divine revelation. she had a foot and leg which had been struck with the num[b] palsy. she believed we were the servants of God & requested us to pray for her. we did so and she was immediately healed. Monday eve I preached again for them at J[ames] St. John's. I spoke about an hour and a half and we bid them finally Adieu.

Tuesday eve we attended our appointment. a large company collected. I spoke about two hours. there was entire silence and attention. they appeared as if they were pinned to their benches. Brother Orson [Pratt] and Lyman [Johnson][33] had preached there about a week before.

Wednesday 15 There were three afflicted persons [who] p[r]ofessed faith in christ to be healed. We prayed and laid our hands on them— Thence about 15 ms to a Mr Burnett's near the Pennsylvania line in Hubbard Town

and Thursday eve we had an appointment at a schoolhouse. an assembly of Campbellites, Methodists Presbyterians and deists attended. I spoke 1 hour & 3/4 but was called a liaar while speaking and interutpted two or three times more by the wicked wretches. we dismissed and I shook the dust off my feet as a testimony against the rebelious and we returned to Mr Edmund Burnetts Jr and staid all night and were treated particularly friendly and they were much believing in the book and work.

Thence [*page 17*] Thence Friday we went about 5 ms to Silas Burnet[s] an old regular Baptist's.

Saturday it rain[e]d almost all day. we had an appointment in the eve. only a few attended. I spoke about an hour. they were very inattentive and careless.

Sunday 19th we went to a baptist meeting about 4 miles. the Priest did not come. I asked for the privilege of speaking but was forbid Though we bore testimony to the truth of the works of God in these last days ———————

Monday 20 thence to New Bedford in Pennsylvania eve to have the people to hear us but they would not and desired us to depart out of their coasts which we did speedily. Thence to Erastus Cowdery's [an] in youngstown and staid all night. He was quite unwell and quite unbelieving. we talked much with him and family but to little effect.

Tuesday 21 thence west to Berlin. we tried six or seven places before we could find entertainment.

Thence Wednesday we continued west and staiad all night in Springfield with some Methodist people who treated us kindly but did not believe in our religion.

Thence Thursday we went to brother George Boosinger's. it snowed and was extremely cold. we staid all day. he went to Middleberry village and made an appointment for us to fill on Friday. we staid all n night and I talked much with his unbelieving family—

Friday 25 We attended our appointment in Middlebury. a respectable audience collected. I arose and addressd them two hours and 30 minutes and I [*page 18*] reasoned with them and expounded prophecy after prop[h]ecy and scripture after scripture after scripture until my natural strength was much exausted. I ceased and left it with them and retired to Esq Charles Sumner's country residence to spend the eve. I conversed with the family some and retired to rest but a query rise in my mind whether man or the fountain of all wisdom had called me to preach. many were my reflections. I finally while the soft whisper's of night were inviting me to rest I determined to cease proclaiming until I was satisfied in my own mind——[34]

NOTES

[1] Journal entries for November 16 through November 20, 1831, appear to have been copied from Journal I. In some cases, however, additional information is given. The events of this mission are also recorded by McLellin's companion, Samuel Harrison Smith. Andrew Jenson, Journal History of the Church, housed in LDS Church Archives, November 16, 1831, 1–2 (hereafter cited as JH).

[2] The Prophet and his family were living in the home of John Johnson. Joseph Smith, Jr., *History of The Church of Jesus Christ of Latter-day Saints,* ed. B. H. Roberts, 2d ed. rev., 7 vols. (Salt Lake City: Deseret Book, 1971), 1:215, 219 (hereafter cited as *HC*).

[3] McLellin and Smith slept this night at the home of a Brother Cowens. JH, November 16, 1831, 1.

[4] See note 60, Journal I.

⁵ During the interim between November 21st and 24th, McLellin and Smith "spent much of [their] time at the house of one Mr. Barnum in Braceville . . . and labored much with him and his family." JH, November 16, 1831, 1.

⁶ These "glories" would include the privilege of living in a world of great peace and righteousness. According to the Book of Mormon and revelations given to the Saints through Joseph Smith in 1830 and 1831, during the thousand-year period of the Millennium, Christ will rule personally upon the earth and Satan will be bound (1 Ne. 22:26; and D&C 29:11; 45:58).

⁷ According to Smith's account, "We found the people in that place very wicked, so we returned the next day to Braceville." JH, November 16, 1831, 1.

⁸ Samuel Smith's account makes it clear that both Reuben Fields and his wife were baptized on this date. In addition, he writes, "Irene, the daughter of Mr. Barnum, would have been baptized also, but her father would not permit her, as he had become hardened against the truth." JH, November 16, 1831, 1.

⁹ This is probably a reference to Samuel Smith, whose middle name was Harrison. In other journal entries, McLellin similarly mentions Smith opening meetings with prayer or exhortation.

¹⁰ This meeting was held in the home of John Edwards in the vicinity of Weathersfield, Ohio. JH, November 16, 1831, 1.

¹¹ Since the followers of Thomas and Alexander Campbell held that salvation was available to all on the basis of a confession of faith and not nonrational experience, the Campbellite minister may have elaborated upon some of the following verses from Romans 10: "For Christ is the end of the law for righteousness to every one that believeth" (10:4); "with the mouth confession is made unto salvation" (10:10); "whosoever shall call upon the name of the Lord shall be saved" (10:13). See Benjamin Lyon Smith, comp., *The Millennial Harbinger Abridged,* 2 vols. (Rosemead, Calif.: Old Paths, 1902), 2:40–47.

¹² This appointment was held, as planned, at the home of James St. John in the Weathersfield area. JH, November 16, 1831, 1.

¹³ A grist mill owned by James Heaton. JH, November 16, 1831, 2.

¹⁴ Samuel Smith wrote, "The prejucices of many began to break down and the spirit of the Lord commenced to work upon the hearts of the people, and we began to hope that they would receive the truth and that the Lord would build up a church in this place." JH, November 16, 1831, 1–2.

¹⁵ This appointment was "held in the nieghborhood of a Mr. Cherry." JH, November 16, 1831, 2.

¹⁶ This appointment was held as scheduled at the Heaton grist mill. JH, November 16, 1831, 2.

[17] 1 Corinthians 12:1-11 speaks of the "spiritual gifts," a subject of paramount interest to McLellin and his companions, to whom Paul's words gave assurance that "no man speaking by the Spirit of God calleth Jesus accursed: and that no man can say that Jesus is the Lord, but by the Holy Ghost." Paul acknowledged many gifts of the "same God which worketh all in all," manifestation of which included "the word of wisdom," "the word of knowledge," faith, healing, the working of miracles, prophecy, discerning of spirits, tongues, and the interpretation of tongues. Promises to the Saints of virtually the same gifts of the Spirit were given in a revelation Joseph Smith received on March 8, 1831 (D&C 46).

[18] Samuel Smith confirms that these four people were baptized on December 14, 1831. Smith refers to Sarah St. John as Mrs. St. John; most likely, she is the wife of the previously mentioned James St. John. JH, November 16, 1831, 2.

[19] Samuel Smith indicates that they held a meeting in the town of Orson on either December 17 or 18. Perhaps Orson is a misnomer for Austen. JH, November 16, 1831, 2.

[20] Samuel Smith left McLellin and returned to Hiram, Ohio, on December 24, 1831. JH, November 16, 1831, 2. Of the end of this mission, Smith wrote, "[We] went a short distance but becaus of disobediences our way was hedged up before us Brother William was taken sick & I returned." Samuel Smith, "Events in the Life of Samuel Harrison Smith including His Missionary Journal for the Year 1832," microfilm, Special Collections, Harold B. Lee Library, Brigham Young University, Provo, Utah (hereafter cited as BYU Special Collections).

[21] At this time, Joseph Smith was on a mission around Hiram, Ohio. JH, December 3, 1831. Joseph most likely heard of McLellin's ill health from his brother Samuel, who, after leaving McLellin, attended a meeting with a group of elders in Ravenna. Joseph Smith was probably at this meeting. JH, November 16, 1832, 2. Hyrum Smith and Reynolds Cahoon were also on a missionary journey together at this time. JH, December 13, 1831. Hyrum briefly mentioned this visit to Weathersfield: "[We] labored and Bore testamony unto them of the works of god in these last Days." Hyrum Smith, "Diary and Account Book, 1831 and 1832," BYU Special Collections.

[22] More than thirty years later, Thomas Marsh wrote: "Sometime in January, 1832, Bishop Partridge having furnished me with an Indian pony, I returned [from Missouri] to Kirtland, accompanied by Cyrus Daniels." *Millennial Star* 26 (June 11, 1864): 376.

[23] According to Reynolds Cahoon, "At the public meeting held at Kirtland, Ohio, Elders Orson Pratt and Reynolds Cahoon were appointed to visit the doubting members in the different branches in certain parts of Ohio. . . . Several members, who had transgressed the laws of God, were excommunicated from the Church." JH, January 1, 1832. Cahoon

was probably referring to the three meetings that took place January 1–2, 1832. McLellin mentions the excommunications occurring on January 2, 1832.

²⁴ After the first bishop of the Church, Edward Partridge, was sent to Missouri in June 1831, Newel K. Whitney was called in September 1831 to act as the bishop's agent in Kirtland. When the need for another bishop arose, Whitney was ordained on December 4, 1831. Lyndon Cook, *The Revelations of the Prophet Joseph Smith* (Salt Lake City: Deseret Book, 1985), 102; see also D&C 72.

²⁵ Although the nature of this enquiry is not clear, it stands to reason that it pertained to a land dispute in which Ezra Thayer, Frederick G. Williams, and Joseph Smith were involved. That matter had been considered at an October 10, 1831, church conference which, after deliberation, reproved both Joseph Smith and Thayer and concluded that the family of the latter could remain where they were until spring 1832. Donald Q. Cannon and Lyndon W. Cook, eds., *Far West Record* (Salt Lake City: Deseret Book, 1983), 15–16; see also D&C 56:8–9.

²⁶ A January 10 revelation instructed the elders of the Church, which would have included McLellin, to "continue preaching the gospel, and in exhortation to the churches in the regions round about." Joseph Smith and Sidney Rigdon were instructed to return to the work of translating the scriptures, while still preaching "inasmuch as it is practicable" (D&C 73:1–2, 4).

²⁷ The Kirtland Flats area was "the center of the industrial and merchandising life of the township, . . . adjacent to the East Branch of Chagrin River." Milton V. Backman, Jr., *The Heavens Resound: A History of the Latter-day Saints in Ohio, 1830-1838* (Salt Lake City: Deseret Book, 1983), 37. Most meetings "at the flats" were held in Newel K. Whitney's store or home.

²⁸ At this time, Titus Billings was a deacon, so he did not have the priesthood authority to baptize. JH, December 31, 1831, 5. He had five children old enough (eight years or older) to be baptized. Perhaps McLellin baptized these five: Samuel Dwight, Thomas, Ebenezer, Emily, and Martha. The identity of the other four children he baptized on this day is unknown. Susan Easton Black, *Membership of The Church of Jesus Christ of Latter-day Saints, 1830-1848,* 50 vols. (Provo, Utah: Religious Studies Center, Brigham Young University, 1989), 5:304.

²⁹ This conference, which had been scheduled during the October 26, 1831, conference in Orange, was held in Amherst in Lorain County. Cannon and Cook, *Far West Record,* 26. Amherst is approximately fifty-five miles west of Kirtland and only eight miles from Oberlin, where Congregationalists established Oberlin College in 1832. Parley P. Pratt was one of Amherst's early settlers; following his conversion to Mormonism, he preached to the inhabitants of Amherst in 1831. Simeon Carter was baptized, and within a short time, a branch of the Church was organized

in Amherst. Richard Neitzel Holzapfel and T. Jeffrey Cottle, *Old Mormon Kirtland and Missouri* (Santa Ana, Calif.: Fieldbrook Productions, 1991), 128-31.

[30] At this conference, Joseph Smith was sustained as President of the High Priesthood, and was ordained by Sidney Rigdon. JH, January 25, 1832, 2. Joseph Smith recorded: "At this conference much harmony prevailed, and considerable business was done to advance the kingdom, and promulgate the Gospel to the inhabitants of the surrounding country. The Elders seemed anxious for me to inquire of the Lord that they might know His will, or learn what would be most pleasing to Him for them to do, in order to bring men to a sense of their condition; for, as it was written, all men have gone out of the way, so that none doeth good, no, not one. I inquired and received [Doctrine and Covenants 75]." *HC* 1:242-43; see also Dean C. Jessee, ed., *The Papers of Joseph Smith*, 2 vols. to date (Salt Lake City: Deseret Book, 1989-), 1:371.

The revelations in Doctrine and Covenants 75 were "given and written" before the entire assembly. JH, January 25, 1832, 2. Of the elders mentioned, McLellin received the most lengthy and specific counsel: "Therefore, verily I say unto my servant William E. McLellin, I revoke the commission which I gave unto him to go unto the eastern countries; And I give unto him a new commission and a new commandment, in the which I, the Lord, chasten him for the murmurings of his heart; And he sinned; nevertheless, I forgive him and say unto him again, Go ye into the south countries. And let my servant Luke Johnson go with him, and proclaim the things which I have commanded them—Calling on the name of the Lord for the Comforter, which shall teach them all things that are expedient for them—Praying always that they faint not; and inasmuch as they do this, I will be with them even unto the end. Behold, this is the will of the Lord your God concerning you" (D&C 75:6-12). Doctrine and Covenants 75 also reminded all of the elders of the blessings of missionary work (vv. 1-5), and contained a charge to leave blessings upon the homes of those who accept their message, while dusting their feet at the homes of those who reject the message (vv. 19-20).

McLellin's description of the conference relates, "There were between 70 and 80 official characters there from different states. The Elders received a commandment there to travel two by two. East, West North and South and proclaim the things which they had learned and which should be given them by the spirit." William E. McLellin to "Beloved Relatives," August 4, 1832, RLDS Archives, see page 82, below. McLellin later stated that at this conference "for the first time in the church Joseph was appointed and ordained under the hands of S. Rigdon to the first presidency of the whole church, as they professed to be directed of the Lord; which was acknowledged by the whole conference." William E. McLellin, ed., *Ensign of Liberty of the Church of Christ*, nos. 1-7 (Kirtland, Ohio: W. E. McLellin, 1847-49), 61.

[31] This is the only known first-hand reference to Shadrach Roundy's baptism. Other, presumably less-accurate, sources say his baptism was on January 23, 1831, an entire year earlier.

[32] At this time, Joseph was still at the John Johnson home, working diligently on the Bible translation. *HC* 1:245. Also on this day, McLellin purchased eight copies of the Book of Mormon from Hyrum Smith for ten dollars. Smith, "Diary and Account Book."

[33] Orson Pratt and Lyman Johnson had been assigned at the Amherst conference to serve a mission to the East together (D&C 75:14).

[34] Of the end of this mission, Luke Johnson wrote: "We preached several times, and arriving at Middlebury, Portage (now Summit) County, Ohio. Brother McLellin got a situation behind a counter to sell tapes, etc., and I, preferring not to preceed alone, returned to the town of Hiram, and the Prophet appointed Seymour Brunson in his stead." JH, January 31, 1832, 2.

McLellin himself described the end of this mission in greater detail in his August 4, 1832, letter. He mentions bad weather, ill health, insufficient faith to be perfectly healed, and working as a store clerk until the end of April. During this time he did not preach in public, but "examined the evidences of Inspiration or of the scriptures. I reasoned much with Deists, Scepticks, Infidels, &c. &c. For I tell you that a majority in many eastern villages belong to those classes. My longs [lungs] still continued weak and I finally determined to cease traveling to preach for a while." See page 82, below.

Nevertheless, Joseph Smith did not consider the mission successfully completed. His letter to Emma Smith on June 6, 1832, suggests that McLellin ended his mission to marry Emeline Miller. Dean C. Jessee, ed., *The Personal Writings of Joseph Smith* (Salt Lake City: Deseret Book, 1984), 239. See note 2, McLellin's 1832 letter below.

Letter of William E. McLellin
to Beloved Relatives

Jackson County. Missouri. Independence.

4th August 1832

Beloved Relatives.

Long! Long has it been since I've heard from you.—And no doubt, you have thought the time long since you have heard from me. Probably, you have thought that I was no more.!. Distracted, Cast away or that I had forgotten you forever.—But I can assure you that I yet Remember you with the warmest feelings of heart. I wrote a letter to you the last of last November but I think it uncertain whether you recd it; at least, I will now give you a short account of my peregrinations and the scenes that I have experienced for one year past.

Some time in July 1831. Two men came to Paris & held an evening meeting, only a few attended, but among the others, I was there. They delivered some ideas which appeared very strange to me at that time. "They said that in September 1827 an Angel appeared to Joseph Smith (in Ontario Co. New-York) and showed to him the confusion on the earth respecting true religion. It also told him to go a few miles distant to a certain hill and there he should find some plates with engravings, which (if he was faithful) he should be enabled to translate. He went as directed and found plates (which had the appearance of fine Gold) about 8 inches long 5 or 6 wide and alltogether about 6 inches thick; each one about as thick as thin paste Board fastened together and opened in the form of a book containing engravings of reformed Egyptian Hieroglyphical characters. which he was inspired to translate and the record was published in 1830 and is called the book of Mormon. It is a record which was kept on this continent by the ancient inhabitants." Those men had this book with them and they told us about it, and also of the rise of the church (which is now called Mormonites from their faith in this book &C.) They left Paris very early next morning and pursued their journey Westward. But in a few days two others came into the neighbourhood proclaiming that these were the last days, and that God had sent forth the book of Mormon to show the times of the fulfillment of the ancient prophecies When the Saviour shall come to destroy iniquity off the face of the earth, and **reign** with his saints in Millennial **Rest.** One of these was a witness to the book and had seen an angel which declared its truth (his name was David Whitmer). They were in the neighbourhood about a week. I talked much with them by way of enquiry and argument, They believed Joseph Smith to be an inspired prophet. They told me that he and between 20 & thirty other Preachers were on their way to Independence. My curiosity was roused up and my anxiety also to know the truth.—And though I had between 30 & 40 students and the people generally satisfied with me as Teacher—yet I closed my school on the 29th July and on the 30th I mounted Tom and left for Indepen- August the 4th I visited Uncle Wm Moore's and spent the 5th with him and family & brother Israel. I gave Uncle Wm. $10 to carry to you. The 6th I pursued my journey until evening I was taken severely with the fever. I applied to two Physicians. I stopped near a week, then pursued my course though through great weakness. I crossed the Illinois river about 100 miles above [*page 2*] St Louis, thence accross the Mississippi at Louisiana about the same above. Thence across the Misouri at the mouth of Chariton. Thence [to Indep.] August the 18th I took breakfast in Independence (after having rode about 450 miles from Paris) But to my sorrow I learned that Jos S. and 12 or 15 others had done their business and started to the east again a few days before. But there had a church come on of about 60 from York State and there were about a dozen Elders who had not gone back. I examined the book, the people, the preachers and the old scriptures, and from the evidences which I had before me I was bound to believe the book of Mormon to be a divine Revelation; and the people to be christians Consequently I joined them. And on the 24th I was Ordained and Elder in the church of christ and on the 25th I started to the east with brother Hiram

Smith a brother to Joseph: and on the 28 I preached my first discourse to the world. I spoke one hour and 1/2 which astonished the multitude! some sd I had been a preacher, some sd A Lawyer &C, &C, But the secret was God assisted me by his Spirit and it reached their hearts Thence we traveled on proclaiming by the way until we got to Jacksonville Ill. (in court tirm) on Friday and gave an appointment to preach next day in the court house. We attended. the house though large was full of Judges, Lawyers, Doctors, Priests and People I think about 500. I spoke 3 hours and when done I cannot describe the joy of some, the consternation of others, and the anger of others—Thence to Uncle Wm Moore's But O! that morning he had started to Tennessee. Br Israel was there I talked considerable with him. I gave him a book of Mormon to carry to you.[1] He intended leaving for Arkansas in about a week and thence to Tennessee—— Thence we went to Paris. I settled the most of my business, and left the other with Lawyer Shelledy. I purchased a horse for Br. Hiram. We preached the truth to the people round about and thence we traveled immediately on to the Northeastern part of Ohio, and on the 18th of Oct we reached old Father Smith's Geauga Co. O.—After the book was translated and the church established, Persecution raged so against them that the most of the believers either come to Ohio or to (Zion). The american people boast of republicanism and often speak very contemptuously of the dark ages of perscution against the Saviour and his Apostles. But let a man now reasonably expose the errors and false notions of God and touch a man's traditions— and the same Devil or persecuting spirit is stirred up as was anciently; and all that is wanting is Power—But O! awful to relate, that the want of Authority does not stop them, amidst all the blaze of light they rise in mobs, black themselves, waylay houses and even break in and drag the the servants of God from their beds, and families into the streets, and abuse and torture them, for no other reason only their religion differs from the popular—(as was the case last April with Jos. Smith and Sidney Rigdon in Portage Co. O.) On the 25th Oct I attended a conference, where I first saw and became acquainted with Joseph. About 40 Elders attended. General peace and harmony pervaded the conference and much instruction to to me. From thence I went home with Jos and lived with him about three weeks; and from my acquaintance then and until now I can truely say I believe him to be a man of God. A Prophet, a Seer and Revelater to the church of christ—[*page 3*] My labours were mostly confined, During last winter, to the Western Reserve O. in the churches and [rou] round-about in the congregations of the wicked. Though I took one tour into Pennsylvania proclaim- the truth and baptizing the believers. I attended another conference in Lorane Co. west of Cleveland on the 25th of January. There were between 70 and 80 official characters there from different States. The Elders received a commandment there to travel two by two. East, West North and South and proclaim the things which they had learned and which should be given them by the spirit. I started to the south preaching by the way until I came to Middlebury a village in Ohio. I preached in it on the 25 of February and by traveling and labouring During such inclement weather, my health became impaired and I could not at that time exercise faith enough to be perfectly healed (neither could Timothy of old I T. 5,23) Consequently I stopped there and kept store for Col. Sumner until the last of April. During which time I preached none in public, but I examined the evidences of Inspiration or of the scriptures. I reasoned much with Deists, Scepticks, Infidels, &c. &c. For I tell you that a majority in many eastern villages belong to those classes. My longs [lungs] still continued weak and I finally determined to cease traveling to preach for a while. And in order to be useful I also determined to seek a companion and come to Zion & settle at least for a while. I returned to Hiram Township. Portage Co. O. to my brethren, and on the 26th of April I was married to a young Lady by the name of Emiline Miller[2] You have often heard of short courtships but I was married the 4th day after I first even hinted to subject to my partner. Emiline's hight is 5 feet 1 inch. She generally weighs between one hundred and ten and twenty. She was born in the State of Vermont Though she left there when quite small and came to Ohio. She was twenty two years old the 4th of last September. Her education is common English. She has taught school some, though her principle business has been tailoring. The 30th of July 1829 I married Cinthia Ann, but I was deprived of her most lovely endeavours to render me happy and agreeable, in consequence of which I spent many lonesome & sorrowful hours. But Emiline renders me happy, and I hope notwithstanding all to spend the remainder of my days tranquilly as it respects matrimonial subjects.—

On the 2nd of May we, in company with near 100 of our brethren (viz) men, women & children, left Portage Co. for this place.[3] We took watter (on Stemboat) 20 ms below Pittsburg which conveyed us (and ours) to St Louis in 8 days & nights. We brought our waggons and some horses with us, and we bought some oxen at St Louis and from thence we traveled up by land; 14 waggons in company. This was fulfilling the propecies Isa 2,3—"And many people shall go and say Come let us go up to the Mountain of the Lord." &c..&c On the 16th of June we arrived in Independence (the centre of Zion or of the gathering of the righteous on this continent) to prepare for the second coming of Christ)—Independence is situated on a high rise 3 miles south of Missouri river, 12 miles from the west line of the state, near 300 ms above St Louis. The local situation of the country round about it, for health, richness of soil, good spring watter, and other conveniences—is as good, it seems to me, as heart could wish—I have purchased to Lots on Main street with a small cabin on them for $100.[4] a fifty dollar horse and $50 in cash. This is my home, from which I never expect to move, Though I may travel hundreds and Thousands of miles—I otained a school here and commenced teaching the 8th of July, for three months. I have generally about 30 stu[dents] Crops here are very flourishing at this time, more so than any place from which I have heard. Though produce is scarce in consequence of the flood of emigration. Flour is $2.50 per hund[red] Corn meal 75 cts. per bushel. Bacon 8 cts per lb. &c. Coffee 20 and Sugar 10—[*page 4*] I will now give you some of our religious views. We believe, that the Bible, the New Testament and the book of Mormon, are of divine origin and Authority. We believe, that faith in God, Repentence and Baptism (by immersion) in the name of the Lord Jesus, for the remission of sins and Laying on of the hands of the Elders for the reception of the holy Spirit, is the plan by which sinners may become reconciled to God or become christians We believe, that God is unchangeable: consequently his servants may call upon him and he will answer as in days of old. And when they ask in faith and receive his holy Spirit they may Prophesy, See Visions, Discern Spirits, Do Miracles, Cast out Devils, Heal the sick, &c. and even (as Paul 2 Cor 12. 1-2 or John Rev 4.1) by faith to be enwrapped in the spirit and caught up to behold the wonders and glories of God's Throne and the order of the eternal world. We belive that Joseph Smith is a true Prophet or Seer of the Lord and that he has power and does recieve revelations from God, and that these revelations when received are of divine Authority in the church of Christ. For further information I refer you to the Star,[5] which I have sent you with this letter. My Dear Brother and all my relations, I entreat you as a Brother to Lay asside prejudice and examine for truth. For truth alone is all that will benefit us here or hereafter—The reason why I have not written to you oftener is because I was determined to visit you. But when disappointed I then thought I would not till I got here and settled myself.

Independence. Mo
Aug 4th

                    Mr. Samuel McLelin
                        Carthage——
                        Smith County
                        Tennessee——

I had 3 or 4 days touch of the fever while at St Louis but I recovered and since I have had as good health [and] as I generally have for 4 or 5 years, my longs are affected which causes me great weakness especially in warm weather. Emiline never has had any sickness and has been particularly healthful since we were married. Nothing hinders me from coming to see you only poverty
        Wm E. McLelin
        Br Saml you could come from Nashville Ten in a few days in steamboat.

O that I could see you and change words with you. Come my Br. and visit me! I almost if know you were to see this country you would not live there long—If any of your neighbours wish to take the Star, send their names and cash in your letter. Write to me immediately for you know I want to hear from you. I recd your letter which informed me of Father's sale of land &c. I really want to hear from father, Israel and Nancy of Wm and your little children O do not delay in writing to me, and all about the neighbours, write fine. I hope you have persued the book of Mormon. write your objections to it and the doctrine I advocate if you have any (But be reasonable) write also about Father Wood's people, for I have not heard from them lately. Fain would I mingle my thoughts with yours and learn from your pillows the exercises of that which is never in active. Gladly would I be conveyed to your friendly bosoms by some kind spirit and write upon you breasts these words—Time is short!——

Emiline is very anxious to see my relations and joins with me to invite you to come to this country.

I must cease for want of paper—Wm E. & Emiline McLelin—

NOTES

Typescript by RLDS History Commission, November 1985. Printed by permission of the Library-Archives, Reorganized Church of Jesus Christ of Latter Day Saints, Independence, Missouri.

[1] Samuel McLellin. See McLellin's journal entry for September 13, 1831, above.

[2] When Joseph Smith later heard of McLellin's marriage, he expressed disapproval at McLellin's leaving his mission in order to marry. In a letter to Emma, June 6, 1832, he wrote, "I am not pleased to hear that William Mclelin has come back and disobayed the voice of him who is altogether Lovely for a woman. I am astonished at Sister Emaline yet I cannot belive she is not a worthy sister. I hope She will find him true and kind to her but have no reason to expect it. His Conduct merits the disapprobation of every true follower of Christ. but this is a painful subject. I hope you will excuse my warmth of feeling in mentioning this subject and also my inability in convaying my ideas in writing." Dean C. Jessee, ed., *The Personal Writings of Joseph Smith* (Salt Lake City: Deseret Book, 1984), 239.

[3] During the spring of 1832, a flood of Mormons immigrated to Missouri, as soon as the weather and road conditions permitted. Warren A. Jennings, "Zion Is Fled: The Expulsion of the Mormons from Jackson County, Missouri" (Ph.D. diss., University of Florida, 1962), 63.

[4] The two lots consisted of a "small irregular strip of about seven acres." Pearl Wilcox, "Early Independence in Retrospect: Part VII," *Saints' Herald* (February 16, 1959): 14.

[5] In the fall of 1831, the Church decided to publish a monthly newspaper at Independence, *The Evening and Morning Star.* Joseph Smith, Jr., *History of The Church of Jesus Christ of Latter-day Saints,* ed. B. H. Roberts, 2d ed. rev., 7 vols. (Salt Lake City: Deseret Book, 1971), 1:217 (hereafter cited as *HC*). A prospectus was penned by W. W. Phelps in February 1832, and a summary of this prospectus indicates the *Star's* goals:

> *The Evening and Morning Star*—in addition to being a herald of Israel's return to the favor of God, and a messenger of the everlasting Gospel—will also contain whatever of truth or information that will benefit the Saints of God temporally as well as spiritually, "without interfering with politics, broils, or the gainsaying of the world." It is also announced that from the *Star* press it may be expected, as soon as wisdom directs, that there will be issued "many sacred records which have slept for ages." The Star [*sic*—no italics in the original] was to be a royal quarto sheet, issued monthly, at one dollar a year. (*HC* 1:259n)

The first number was printed in June 1832. The paper contained some national news items, but mostly consisted of theological essays, original poems, and descriptions of catastrophes. Jennings, "Zion Is Fled," 60. Excerpts from the first three numbers of the *Star* are included in *HC* 1:273-84.

we reached the borders of the great
Mississippi and while we were journeying
on to do our Father's business, walking together
silently meditating on the works of God
and the holiness of heart required of those
who travel to proclaim the fulness of his gos
:pel in this wicked generation. while thus
meditating, we looked to the right and
Lo! a tall peak of a Mount stood above
us some hundreds of feet. "There, said
Br Parley, is the place for contemplation."
We immediately ascended its tall summit and
seated ourselves on its peak. And of all pla:
:ces for scenery that I had ever seen, This see:
med to be the most complete. In the surroun:
:ding Landscape (which we could view for miles)
the tall timbers had been fell by the healthful
and vigorous farmer, and mansions reared from
whose of stone, Brick or wood from whose
tall chimnies into the pleasant atmosphere of the regions of the the blue smoke was curling
While viewing those vast extended plains
we could turn our eye a little to the left and
look down upon the little Village of Clarkes-
:ville situate immediate on the bank of
the Long famed Mississippi whose winding
Course we could behold for many miles up and
down, and contemplate its many resources in the
far, regions of the North, and in imagination
behold the wandering Lamanite drinking of

Page 23, Journal III (actual size). Waxing eloquent, McLellin describes the beautiful countryside that he and Parley P. Pratt viewed from a high "place for contemplation." The "tall peak of a Mount" is what is now called The Pinnacle, which looms 400 feet above Clarksville to the northwest. Courtesy LDS Church Archives.

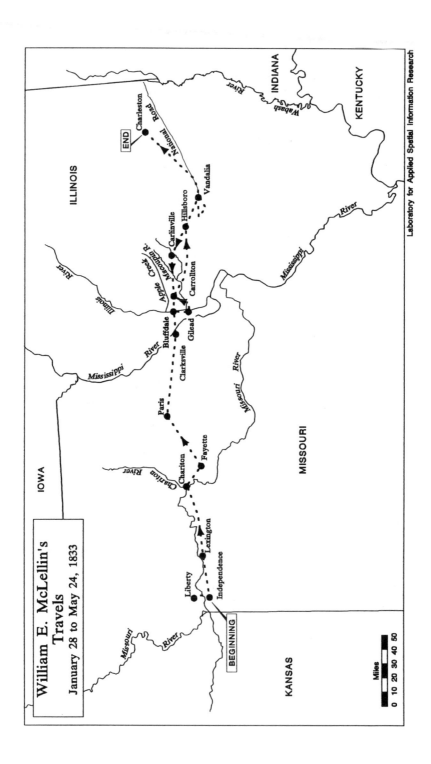

William E. McLellin's
Travels
January 28 to May 24, 1833

IOWA

ILLINOIS

INDIANA

KENTUCKY

MISSOURI

KANSAS

Charleston

END

Vandalia

Carlinville

Hillsboro

Carrollton

Bluffdale

Gilead

Clarksville

Paris

Fayette

Charlton

Lexington

Independence

Liberty

BEGINNING

National Road

Apple Creek

Missouri R.

Illinois River

Mississippi River

Mississippi River

Missouri River

Missouri River

Wabash River

Charlton River

Laboratory for Applied Spatial Information Research

Miles

0 10 20 30 40 50

William E. McLellin Journal III
January 28, 1833–May 24, 1833

A Journal——
of Wm E. McLelin & Parley Pratt[1]

28th [February] January 1833 We took our leave of the favourite village of Independence and its inhabitants about 10 O'clock—— Thence 3 miles to Mr Ivevtts ferry[2] on the Missouri River—— We determined to keep all the commandments of God: Consequently we had taken no money neither two coats for our journey[3]—— But only the glorious gospel Jesus to recommend us—Br P. went to the ferryman and told him our errand. He seemed to hesitate wishing money. I seated myself [listening] listened to Br. P. reasoning with him. I asked the Lord how it was and prayed earnestly that he would open his heart to take us across— While I was secretly lifting my heart to God, he turned to his servant without asking further [*page 2*] questions and told [his] him servant to take us over, We crossed with joy and thanks to God and thence 8 ms to Col. Thornton's. He was gone to the Legislature. we told his lady our errand and asked for entertainment. She received us Though we had not much liberty of Spirit. We took our supper [January 29] and breakfast and thence 6 ms to Liberty—— We introduced ourselves as preechers, An appointment was given out, We took dinner with a Mr Tillery— [And w] We then retired to an adjoining grove and spent a very pleasant afternoon—— We returned. the court house being [illumined] illuminated we entered a very spacious apartment a respectable and attentive" audiance collected. Br. Parley arose and addressed them on various subjects about one hour and a half. I then spoke about 1 hour. Br. P. dismissed them, and we were met before we left the house by Br. T. Billings who informed us that it was our duty to return to

Independence before we persued our journey, We returned again
to Mr Tillery's and staid all night——

[*page 3*] [F] Jan 30th We rose early and took breakfast. It was
raining but we started for Independence and walked through rain
mud and water until we reached Zions seat[4]——

[~~Friday~~] Thursday We spent in council with our Brethren and Friday in attending to other business & in preparing to take our
journey again. Some important things transpired During our stay
at home which I will not here note——

Saturday the 2nd day of February 1833 We bid farewell again about
10 O'Clock and took our journey eastward, and as we did before;
without purse or scrip[5]—— Thence to the little blue.[6] But here
I will note, Just before we reached the creek we met a man from
Ohio who had just waded the C. we then pondered how we
should get over and I asked Br. P. what he thought about it— Said
he "Take no thought."[7] [*page 4*] When we got to the Creek; there
we found a horse saddled, as if waiting to take us across, and the
gentleman was willing to take us over which he did and we went
on our way rejoicing—— Late in the afternoon we called on
Col. Hambright a little North of the Noted Mount Ephraim. We
entered his cabin and told him that we were traveling to preach
the Gospel of Jesus Christ and we asked him if he would entertain
us over night, he hesitated but said "I suppose I can" At first he
seemed very indiferent, as if he did not want to hear any thing
about the things which we had to declare but we introduced the
subject to him in a very curious manner so that it stirred up his
curiosity and set him to inquiring— He entertained us comfort-
ably. We took supper and breakfast with him—— [February 3]
Thence we traveled across Mount E. and Prairie Creek.[8] It being
Sunday we indeavoured to get a meeting but could not, consequently we traveled on about 13 ms. and called in to get dinner
with a widow Renick and staid [*page 5*] all night. But she and her
two Bachelor Sons would not even suffer us to tell them any thing
about our mission or the things which we know are just about to
take place—

Monday morning we rose early and pursued our journey 3 ms to the big Sny.[9] We set down on its bank and pondered how we should get over knowing it would be difficult to wade. But while we were drawing our shoes with prayrs in our heart to God to preserve our healths, Behold a man rode up who proposed to take us over which he did— & now we rejoiced again in the God of Israel to know his promises fulfilled to us— But this morning we traveled until 10 O'Clock and called at four houses to get some breakfast but we were cursed and driven out because we had no money. Neither would they hear our words until we reached a Mr Mitchel's who was gone to the legislature but his lady was quite friendly and had a good meal prepared in a few minutes; which we eat with Joy, then we pursued our coarse until we had traveled 14 ms and called on Mr. Fletcher, The sheriff of Lafayette Co. He entertained us freely and well and we had much liberty in talking. But yet I expect but little fruit——

Thence we traveled where blindness, Ignorance and unbelief seemed to reign; Late we [*page 6*] This day we passed over 16 ms and called on old Mr Esters'— the house where I preached my first sermon after I received the fulness of the glorious Gospel of Jesus Christ—They entertained us but seemed to do it grudgeingly. It seemed to me as if Satan had sealed up their hearts and minds and they had closed their eyes, &c, Lest they should see with their eyes, hear with their ears and understand with their hearts and be converted that the Lord should heal them.[10]

This day we passed over 26 ms and reached the Widow McCafferty's where we were received and well entertained. But no appearance of Repentence among them——

Thurs. 6[11] we traveled 18 ms and crossed the Missouri river at Mount Pleasant and called on Mr. Thrash & Thornton— But O! here our hearts were pained. Here where I once yea, twice had been received with seeming joy and gladness, Where they then seemed to be enquiring, yea joy seemed to sparkle in their eyes while they listened to the servants of the Lord telling of the great things which are about to take place in this generation—— But to

my surprise; Carelesness now and indifference seemed to possess
their minds— We had come praying and expecting that a field of
labour would be opened here, yet so we found it [*page 7*] Here
was a time that we needed the strength of the Lord and after
supper we retired to a lonesome and high hill and while the dark
shad[ows] of night encircled us around, we bowed before him
whose eye sees and peirces all things and we poured out our souls
to him in mighty prayr & again asked that we might have an
opening so as to commence our labours for we had passed through
a region of hard benighted country——— We returned to the house,
the more friendship appeared in them— We proposed to hold a
meeting and said they were willing——— and after praying with
them we retired to rest——— and I really did rest, because I was
weary and sore traveling———

Friday 7th This morning we sent an appointment to Charatin or
word that we would preach at Mr Thrash's at candle light and sent
also to the regions round abouts This day we spent in [praying]
reading, Conversation, meditation and prayr to God——— We took
our Bibles and ascended a very high hill and for scenery and
meditation it is one of the most beautiful places that I ever saw.
The ridges were high and narrow and running in various ways up
and down while the Long and majestic Missouri rolled swiftly by.
The air was calm and pleasant, even as in the morn of May morn
of May [*page 8*] Here upon this high place while all nature seemed
to smile around us and naught to interrupt except the croak of the
passing Raven or the squall of the fleeting wild goose——— Here
we struggled hard in mighty prayr to God that he would open the
the Heavens upon us and minister to us by an holy Angel and we
seemed to draw nigh to the Lord, but yet the veil was not rent.
Notwithstanding we spent a very pleasant day in the service of
the Lord. Evening came on. the people collected. Br Parley addressed them about one hour and a half and I spoke about one
hour. We presented to them the nature of our mission and exorted
them with earnestness to repent and receive the truth and prepare for the coming of the Lord Jesus. We dismissed them, each
went his way, we were not invited to preach again; consequently.

Sat 8th We took our journey—— But I ought to have noted that Friday we saw a Methodist man who lived near Fayette. he invited us to come and see him. This morning we started and after travel over 6 ms we cal[l]ed on a noted Priest [*page 9*] about 2 O'Clock by the name of Haden. he belonged to the order called Christians. We found him sitting in his parlour gravely reading his New Testament—We told him who we were and what was our business— He received us freely and after a few minutes conversation he proposed, if we would preach that he would send for his neighbours to come and hear us, We of course consented and with joy too— We spent the eve in conversation with him, He seemed to be some what tender & inquiring—— He often told us that he was as honest a man as we ever saw, he also said that he earnestly wished to know the truth— Notwithstanding the shortness of the notice yet the house was filled— I arose and spoke about two hours to them with great liberty. Br Parley spoke a few minutes— then Elder Joel Haden[12] got up and made a few observations, they [was] were quite liberal, yet went rather to oppose, the things which we had delivered, He said if the Lord had spoken to men in these days by his own voice and by Angels, Why does not that impartial God speak to me, yet he did not believe that it was a day of miricles—We told them our errand and exorted them to repent— we told them we were willing to preach to them more if they wanted to hear and would open their hearts and houses—— We had a number of invitations and we made an appointment for next [*page 11; number 10 skipped*] Tuesday eve at a Mr. Criglers near this place——

Sunday we went about 6 ms. to a monthly meeting. Old father S. Bradley was preaching when we reached the place but he closed in a few minutes and he and the people insisted that we should preach. Br. Parley arose and addressed them for about 2 hours— some of them began to get very uneasy before he closed. I then arose and give out an appointment to be at Elder Bradley's at candle light—— The house was filled, I spoke about one hour and 3/4. I had almost perfect attention of the whole congregation. Br. Parley dismissed the meeting.

Monday the 11th we returned to Elder Haden's.

Tuesday 12th This day we spent in reading and in conversation, at eve we attended our appointment; the house was filled. Br Parley arose and spoke 1 hour & 1/2. I then spoke 3/4 of an hour— I then gave privilege to any that wished to speak. J. H. Haden then arose and give some of his reasons why he did not embrace the book of Mormon.[13] His observations tended to prejudice the minds of the people against the book. But he flattered us by saying he believed that we were honest and honestly believed in [*page 12*] that book and he acknowledged that the book upheld principles of righteousness entire, and that it spoke against evil entire, but he said this was no evidence to him &c &c. Br Parley then arose and spoke about 30 minutes with plainness and with power" and dismissed the people——

Wednesday 13 We passed on 6 ms. to Fayette— and at eve we attended a meeting of J. H. Haden's. He invited us to neither set with him nor to preach, but we gave out an appointment for next eve in the Court house— James H. Berch introduced himself to us and invited us home with him—— and we accepted—— He lives in a spacious building on a beautiful site near the C[ourt] H[ouse].

Thursday 14th we spent in prayr and raading [reading]——At eve we attended at candle [light] to our appointment in the court house—, a large assembly attended, I addressed them about 13/4 hours concerning our **faith** and various other subjects— Br. Parley spoke 15 or 20 m̄ minutes and I dismissed them— Mr Jam[es] H Birch invited us home with him [*page 13*] again and we went—— He and his little friendly Lady seemed to entertain us freely and Cheerfully——

Friday 15 This morning Mrs Birch Bought from us a book of Mormon and Mr Birch subscribed for the Star[14]— We took breakfast, then bid our friends farewell, praying that they might read the book believe the truth and obey it and flee to Zion and save their souls. Thience 16 ms. to a Mr Lessley's and staid all night, They entertained us freely and we [told] talked with them freely——

Thence 6 ms to Majr Jones' and took breakfast. Thence 2 ms to Anthony Head's. in this place, Br G. Hincle had laboured and had baptized a man and his wife by the name of Goff—— It being Saturday we proposed to stay and hold a meeting next day—— The word was given out——

Sunday 17th a small congregation collected and I preached to them 2 hours with great plainness and they give tolerable attention. Br P. spoke a few minutes. [*page 14*] I dismissed the congregation with but ~~with but~~ little hopes of ever reaping much fruit— Altho, some seemed to be believing among whom was friend Head's family——

Monday 18th we took breakfast, Thence 27 ms Eastward to Mr L. Pool's and staid all night,—— This evening I found lying in the road a *pocket* book containing some valuable papers and also $5 in U.S. paper——, about dusk we called on Br Arterberry but none of the family were at home. we were Weary—And our finding the pocket book, not finding our brethren at home— and having to call on the wicked in their stead, all seemed strang[e] to me [b]ut so it was—And no doubt for a wise [pur]pose in God——At least I intend to watch these signs and see what the event will be——

Tuesday 19th we understood that we had a Sister about 1 mile onward consequently we concluded to go and take breakfast with her, we found her at home, Seemingly strong in the faith and she soon prepared us a good breakfast [*page 15*] Here we spent a few hours and Br Parly finished a letter to send to his wife— Thence 4 ms. to Paris[15] and mailed the letter and inquired for the man whose name was on the papers and being told that his brother in Law lived in the village— thence we repaired. just before we reached the house we saw a man ride up. We walked in and seated ourselves— The gentleman soon began to tell his friends about the looss [loss] of his pocket book and what it contained— I then pulled it out and gave it to him which caused them to rejoice much. Dinner was prepared and we eat heartily of their bounties telling them who we were and what was our business but they gave no heed unto us and we left them. Thence 13 ms to br. George M Hinkel's. we spent the night with his wife but he was not at home——

Wednesday 20th we spent in conversation and in visiting the brethren[16]— at eve we attended a meet[ing] at Br Isaac Allred's. Br. Parley opened the meet[ing] and spoke about 1½ hours & I spoke about one [hour] with Zeal and warmth, the brethren seemed [en]couraged and rejoiced and I ceaced pr[e]aching praying and blessing the name of the Lord for his goodness. Br. A. Dods who had been in this place for some weeks so blinded that he could not see his way because of the sore eyes, came forward and requested the prayrs of the elders for the restoration of his eyes— which was attended to with a great degree of feeling among the brethren & sisters. [*page 16*] After meeting was dismissed I felt somewhat unwell. Pains Acheing and cold chills attackled my system—— We retired to rest and I felt so bad that I asked Br Parley to lay his hands upon me which he did and I dropped to sleep, but in the night when I awaked I was shaking most tremendiously hard with the ague and I shook I suppose as much as 2 hours— then a very violent fever—— ensued, my stomach became very sour, my bowels also we[re] much affected, which caused severe vomiting & purging——

Thursday I was confined to my bed and I think I never was much sicker in my life, in the evening I called for the Elders——

Friday I was some better, &S.

Saturday I am still some better—— Br Parley on Friday night attended another meeting among the brethren [w]here he had great Liberty and unfolded to [them] the dealings of the Lord from the creation down until John said "It is done."

Sunday 24 The brethren and sisters collected at Br. I. Allred's and I took the lead of the meeting. I spoke on the Covenants & Articles on the officer's duty and the beauty of such regulations &c. I spoke about 1 hour and 20 mts. Br Parley spoke a few minutes—— then the meeting was [*page 17*] conducted by various ones speaking.

I gave a lecture on the operation of the Spirit—— Br Parley gave a testimony of the Lord Jesus that he is, that he lives and will come &c. In which he says, he does not recollect to have ever had more of the Spirit and Power of God upon him—— In truth we had a great meeting. It was dismissed about sun set.

Monday 25 The Elders, Priests, Teachers &c met with us (by the request of Br. GHinkle) at Br Hinkle's to hear our instructions— We found by examination that the Elders we[re] young and inexperienced, yet sound in [faith] and good works. There were three. two had fa[ith.] one had not. We unitedly advised them that the time of their mission in the world had not come and that they remain a season at home and search the scriptures and lay up rich treasures in their minds till the time come—— They seemed willing to take our advice. We also unitedly advised Br Dodds to remain here until his eyes were made whole and he concluded so to do— We also advised Brother George & Daniel to visit their churches in Illinois & Indiana and agreed so to do shortly—— Dismissed thence to Br James Allred's and [staid] all night. But have received no news from Zion.——

[*page 18*] Tuesday the 26th We pursued our journey 9 ms. I had recovered my health so that I was again enabled, though weak, to travel and we passed on calling at the private houses and reasoning with the people until we called on a Mr Thos. Wills' and asked for some dinner and while it was preparing the lady said that she thought the people in the settlement would be glad to hear us preach. After dinner Br Par[ley] started to a house-raising to find out and if so to circulate an appointment. An appointment was given out for tommorrow evening and five or six men came in to hear us converse.

Wednesday 27. This morning I left Br. Parley to fill the appointment and traveled on in search of a place to hold another meeting. I crossed a twelve mile prairie and then 6 ms through a very thinly settled place until I reached a Mr Bonham's, The same old gentleman with whom I staid once before who believed in a variety of Adams in the first creation. I was received kindly by His old Lady, the man being not in—— I passed the eve in conversation but the old gentleman still retained his views about the creation. He said that "the book of Mormon was a good moral and rule of life." &c. All I could say had but little effect——.

Thursday 28. This morning it was swowing [snowing] consider-able and I endeavoured to get them to circulate an appointment but they would not. [*page 19*] Consequently I look up my nap sack and pursued my course onward about two miles where was a store & horse-mill and it being cold I turned in thither and reasoned with and expounded the scriptures unto those who were willing to hear. Dinner time came on and Capt Bondurant in-vited me to his house to take dinner with him— where I was conversing and reasoning in the afternoon when Br Parley came on and overtook me and told me that he preached where I left him to the people on Lick creek, he had great liberty and the people gave good attention and desired him to stay longer or at least if he ever came that way he must surely call &c. To day I tried to get a congregation or a place to preach. One man said that I might preach at his house but his wife who was a Baptist said she wanted to go to meeting on Saturday & Sunday and she must wash next day consequently she could not attend to it— Another said he must get up some wood for he must go to the Baptist meeting also and so he could not attend to hear me &c, &c,—— Thus excuses were made.

Friday, March 1st 1833, This morning I commenced to read the Bible through in course regularly. After breakfast we traveled about five miles to George Seely's. Brs. Calvin [Beebe] & Peter [Whitmer] had held a meeting here and Mr Seely was anxious that we should stop and hold another one—— The day was most extremely cold and if we left here we would have to pass through a ten mile prairie. I had not entirely recovered of the sickness which I had at Br Allred's and I concluded to stay and hold a meeting. Word [*page 20*] was circulated but it continued to grow colder—— Br. Parley left me to fill the appointment and went on in order to get another appointment. only one man attended and I talked to him until he acknowledged that he thought my religion was true, but the truth got but little hold of his heart.

Saturday 2nd Mr Seely seemed to be quite believing and subscribed for the Star— Although it was still cold and snow on the ground I set my face toward the South and traveled on across a desolate field 10 miles to Br. Daniel's where I found Br Parley and also a good Brother and his family seemingly strong in the faith. An appointment was circulated for the morrow— This evening I was quite unwell. I had taken a fresh cold and had a very severe cough— About dusk two Sisters from Br. McCord's came in who seemed glad to see us and also rejoiced to hear and learn the things of the kingdom— The eve, was spent in social conversation singing and prayr; and after I had taken a dose of vinegar Butter and honey mixed we retired to rest——

Sunday 3rd This morning my cough & cold was much better— A small congregation collected at Br. Daniel's. Br Parley addressed them one hour and a half. I then spoke about 1 1/4 hours, the Brethren & Sisters seemed cheered and strengthened and the people seemed some affected, We made an appointment for evening in order to break bread[17] with the little few who believed (even 6). A few of the neighbours came in. I opened the meeting by singing and prayr and then spoke about half an hour, The brethren expressed their good determinations and desires to serve the Lord and Br Parley administered the bread and wine and we had a refreshing time— [*page 21*] No more joined but some were so much affected that I have strong hope that they will yet come in——

Monday 4th This morning from singing preaching & Coughing so much, my stomach and lungs are very sore— and we conclude to stay until tomorrow— and rest and read and have some washing done—— Yesterday after noon old Mother McCord and her son Robert came to Br. Daniel's and were at our evening meeting, they seemed quite tender and some what believing— Robert staid all night at Br Daniel's and we talked and reasoned with him considerable——

Tuesday 5. This morning it was snowing quite hard but we determined to go on our way. We took breakfast, bid our Sisters farewell and Br D[aniel] accompanied us a peace [piece] to show us the way and also our friend Robert started with us. When Br. Daniel was about to bid us farewell, he exorted his Nephew Robert to not let this oppertunity of obeying the gospel to pass by. He said he believed and wanted to be baptized & he wanted his neighbours to see it, Consequently we appointed a meeting at his father's for next day and word went out——

Wednesday 6th The people collected, though only few, and I know I never heard Br Parley Preach plainer in my life for about 2 hours. I then spoke about one hour and then invited if any believed, to make it manifest. Robert McCord came forward and we immediately went to the water and I immersed him—— having a very feeling time. Then dismissed the people and returned to the house. Br Daniel & Sister Hannah staid until next morning. After we returned to the house [*page 22*] old mother McCord told me that she firmly believed it was her duty to be baptized. and her objection to going there was; she was affraid to go in the water while it was so cold. But I told her, I feared for her lest by putting it off she would grieve the Holy Spirit, and be left to her self to reject the truth—— Evening came on & we attended to the ordinance of laying of hands for the reception of the Holy Ghost on Bro. Robert, which he received but not so powerfully as I have seen some, we also prayed and sung with the little band of brethren. And I really enjoyed the comforts of the Holy Spirit.

Thursday 7th After early breakfast we again took our leave of the deciples in this place and bro. Robert accompanied us about 2 miles and after we had (in a lonely grove) kneeled before the Lord and prayed with and for him; we parted— For some days something seemed to whisper [to] us that our mission was short until we had reached far away in the East and South, Consequently this day we traveled on Easterly 18 miles to a Mr Mackey's and tarryed all night— This day we reasoned a little with old Satan and had many temptations But thank the Lord we prayed to [the Lord] him and his grace was sufficient and we had strength to bid Satan to get behind us and so it was & we had sweet sleep.

Friday 8th We pursued our course until [*page 23*] we reached the borders of the great Mississippi and while we were journeying on to do our Father's business, walking together silently meditating on the works of God and the holiness of heart required of those who travel to proclaim the fulness of his gospel in this wicked generation while thus meditating, we looked to the right and Lo! a tall peak of a Mount stood above us some hundreds of feet. "There, said Br Parley, is the place for contemplation." We immediately ascended its tall summit and seated ourselves on its peak. And of all places for scenery that I had ever seen, This seemed to be the most complete. In the surrounding Landscape (which we could view for miles) the tall timbers had been fell by the healthful and vigorous farmer and mansions reared ~~from whose~~ of Stone, Brick or Wood from whose tall chimnies the blue smoke was curling into the pleasant atmosphere of the regions of the west. While viewing those vast extended plains we could turn our eye a little to the left and look down upon the little village of Clarksvill[18] situate[d] immediate on the bank of the Long famed Mississippi whose winding course we could behold for many miles up and down, and contemplate its many resources in the far regions of the North; and in imagination behold the wandering Lamanite[19] drinking of [*page 24*] its cool[e]ing fountains to quench his thirst ~~after~~ while returning from his long chase in order to secure food for his hungry family——Here in this delightful place for meditation we recollected that it was recorded of Holy men of old that they sought Mountains and solitary places and there in exceeding high places they purified themselves and fasted and prayed and communed with their God. Consequently we having been strugling for several weeks to keep our selves in perfect obedience to the will and commandments of our Lord and also in mighty prayr that we might commune with the guardian Angel who protected us, and Here we united to make another struggle before the Lord.[20] And the day being clear and pleasant and the air calm and the rays of the sun warm we united in prayr, meditation and reading the prophecies and promises of the Lord to the faithful, in which we continued about five hours. And we wrestled with our mights but yed [yet] the veil was not rent. We returned from the mountain and entered into Clarkesvile (we only traveled 5 miles to day) and called on Mr Runkle a tavern keeper in the place a very wicked man yet curiosity, he said induced him to keep us, he gave out an appointment for candle light, at which time the villagers gathered into a schoolhouse and Br. Parly spoke some over tow [two] hours and I about 20 minutes— But the people seemed to be given to infidelity, Dancing, card playing &c, &c. The truth seemed to take no effect. Curiosity led some to inquire a little about it, but alas! this was all[21]——

[*page 25*] Saturday 9th we applied to the ferryman who hesitated not to take us across the great Mississippi although we were Preachers & without money— Thence 7 miles across the bottom and called on Esqr Jones and proposed a meeting, and although he was no professor in religion yet he went and sent out and his neighbours came in at candle light and I preached to them 13/4 hours in great plainness and simplicity then proposed another meeting and being solicited we appointed one for next day at the same place, (This night we had to sleep on a very little narrow contracted place and did not rest but a little—) But thank the Lord our healths were preserved.

Sunday 10th The people collected, though only a few, and Bro. Parley [spoke] to them in plainness about 13/4 hours—— though all our preaching had but little effect, seemingly, because of the ignorence and great carelessness and indifference of the people. The people being dismissed, we eat a little bread —milk, butter and honey and then started on about 3 O'clock to go over about 12 miles to the next settlement on the Illinois river. After we had passed on about 2 miles we were overtaken by two young men who lived about 4 miles below the place where we preached they had heard us preach. They said that they wanted to examine our book and also to hear us preach again. We turned with them and came to Mr Mun's who received us very [*page 26*] friendly. The old Lady was quite a spiritual minded woman and seemed to firmly believe the things which we told them, Mr Mun had also once been a Methodist preacher, but had become indifferent and cold in the things of God. Yet he listened with seeming joy to our relation.

Monday 11th This morning they were anxious for their neighbours to hear. An appointment was circulated for One Oclock at a Mr Meads near—— [ten] Eight persons collected besides the man and his wife making Ten, I sung considerable, then opened by prayr and addressed them just one hour and a half. The people seemed much interested & more particularly a Mr Benj— Heaton and his Lady, he borrowed a book and between that and next morning he read 138 pages[22] and when he returned the book he said that he believed it and his wife firmly believed it— We returned to Mr Mun's—This evening their Methodist circuit rider came in (Trotter). He would not engage in any friendly converse with us but treated us and all we said, sneeringly with contempt, he even would not stay where we did but went to Mr Meeds— A Baptist preacher also came in to see us who seemed to be very inquiring and asked many questions— he went away he said well satisfied that he had come to see and hear for himself—— The little foppish Methodist P objected to the book of Mormon entirely because of its provintialisms or Yankeeisms as he called them and because the Lord of it was not a Grammarian or the language was not strictly grammatical. [*page 27*] We gave him some solemn warnings & Parley read to him the 564 & 5 pages of the book of Mormon[23] but he gave no heed [and] but treated it very lightly—— This afternoon Mjr. Roberts, Sheriff of Calhoun called and we sent an appointment by him to Gilead the cty seat for Wednesday 2 oclock—

Tuesday 12th This morning our good friends gathered in to bid us farewell (Mr B. Heaton & B. Mun subscribed for the Star) and with tears in their eyes and love twining around their hearts they bid us God's speed while their eyes watched us until out of sight. And Notwithstanding all their seeming faith yet they wanted more time before they obeyed— But we hope we will gather fruits many days hence. Thence 15 miles to a Mr Winship's and called and proposed a meeting. thcy seemed to be glad of an opertunity to hear and though it was late in the afternoon an appointment was, immediately circulated— The people come and brother Parley preached 1 hour & 35 minutes to them and we sung a number of songs and dismissed them in view of their attending tomorrow at the court-house—— There were 18 Persons there.

Wednesday 13th— Thence 3 miles to Gilead we had but but [*sic*] a small congregation considering it to be in town or county seat, but it was the smallest county seat that ever I was in—— The people collected into the courthouse— And our little Trotter was there— I arose and addressed them 1 hour and 40 mts, Being interrupted 3 times by men's speaking and the little impudent Trotter was one. But it mattered not to me and I think they they [*sic*] were ashamed of it before I was done. [*page 28*] Bro. Parley made a few remarks and dismissed by prayr—— I had an invitation to go home with a Methodist man— We were also invited by a Mr Huff— Thence 1 mile and staid all night with him, he was quite believing, but loved this present world more than the things of God—

Thence 3 miles to Smith's ferry on the Illinois river—— Thence 5 miles to a Mr. Watson's up the bottom and proposed a meeting. Word was sent out—— And a small number came in. Br Parley spoke to them 1 hour and 1/4 and I about 20 minutes. Mr. Watson was anxious for us to stay longer but we felt to go on——

Friday 15·= Thence up the bottom or bluff 10 miles to a Mr. Gates' a schoolhouse being in the settlement. We proposed a meeting and it was circulated by the students &c. The people collected at candle light and I address[e]d them on the faith once delivered to the Saints &c for 1 hour & 20 mts. The people seemed very attentive. bro. Parley added a few remarks and they were dismissed.

Saturday 16th This morn. A request was sent to us for another appointment at Mr. Daton's for this even which was given out— To day I walked 9 miles back and forth in order to see and instruct people. I visited a Mr. John Russel who was a Baptist preacher and quite a literary man, but very unbelieving in the book of Mormon.

Yet he desired to hear us preach and ~~for that purpose~~ [*page 29*] This morning Bro Parley went down to Mr. Daton's and I went down in the evening. The house was filled and Bro. Parley spoke to them about 1¹/₄ hours and I 40 minutes, The people seemed to be serious, Yet they did not obey although they were exorted to, and that warmly— An appoincment was also given out for Sunday at the Schoolhouse——

Sunday 17th. We attended our appointment, a multitude came together. Br. Parley opened by prayr and I addressed them 2 hours upon the prophecies and the evidences and testimonies of the book of Mormon &c, &c. The people seemed much interested and searched or went to searching their scriptures to see if these things were so——Another appointment was solicited of us about 4 miles east at Col. Scotts which was given out to be Monday even— I returned to Mr Russel's who received me very friendly

with whom I staid on Monday and wrote a letter to my Emiline. Bro. Parley went and filled our appointment at Col. Scotts and a Baptist Priest (E. Dodson)[24] was there and after Parley was done he got up and spoke with energy and a great sound of words but was very unreasonable in his observations. Br. Parley answered his objections so that they parted friendly.[25] The people requested another [~~appointed~~] appointment at the same place.

Tuesday [~~12~~] 19th I left Mr Russel's and started on in order to find Br Parley and I walked on [*page 30*] 6 miles to Col. Scotts. Br Parley had gone on to town and I pursued on and when I reached Carrollton I found that an appointme[n]t was circulated for candle-light. We were invited by the Clerk of the court to take supper with him (who was a Campbellite Priest). We were received and treated very friendly by a number—— We attended our appointment and had a large number for the time. Br P. spoke 1¹/₂ to them but it rained blowed and thundered so that it was very laborious speaking. I also spoke 40 mts, and offered to preach again if the people wanted to hear and they spoke out immediately for us to preach at eleven o'clock which was given out and we returned to Mr Bledsoe's.

Wednesday 20 we attended our appointment. The principle men of the place and a large nu number collected in the court house. Br. Parley spoke 30 minutes I then spoke 1 1/2 hour's upon the evidences of the Bible & book of Mormon on the prophecies refering to the book of Mormon and on the two gatherings at Zion & Jerusalem and a little of the effects to be produced at each. Some of the more honest seemed astonished and wished to search for truth while others braced themselves against the light and the Priests opposed it and laughed in our faces. We spent this even with a Mr Baker [and] a Lawyer and Campbelite Priest, who was very unbelieving, We also this even went to their meeting and heard Baker Preach or try to preach but it seemed to me dry stuff indeed and it was dry because it had no oil in it, but it was humanism.

[*page 31*] Thursday 21. This morning we were called upon to visit a boy who had fitts and who some times raged and foamed like a mad man and who sometimes tried to kill his nearest friends— —When we went we found him in an outter house chained with a large chain and fastened so that he could not get out of the house—— His intellect was much impaired, Yet he talked with us with some reason and desired us to pray for him, His father and mother who seemed to have some faith being present we all united in prayr Br Parley being mouth & he and I laid our hands upon him &C, &C. Thence to— Tuesday I made and left an appointment at Bluffdale for Thursday even and at Col. Scotts for Friday 12 o'clock—— Thence we left Carrollton to fill these appointments and took dinner with Mr Scotts who was a professed Deist—— &c. Thence to Mr Nail's and took tea, thence to the schoolhouse and it was crowded yea filled with people to hear. Mr Dodson was there also. Br Parley opened the meeting and spoke with clearness and with power for one hour and 20 minutes and I spoke about the same lenght of time with warmth and great liberty. There seemed to be a general affection and solemnity throughout the congregation. None come forward to obey. friend Dodson took notes and when we had dismissed, he made a few observations and said that he thought [that] he could point out

17 mistakes that we had made but he put off the time untill this [*page 32*] next church meeting. I then arose and exorted the people to put their trust in God and not in man for I was sorry if we had committed 17 abominations or made 17 mistakes for that was just the number of the works of the flesh which Paul summed up [in] Gal[atians.][26] A methodist man then arose, [and] who had been much opposed to us and said, "that we had preached the truth, and the signs of the times were sufficient to arouse all and prove what we had said." [The] Our friend Russel then arose and observed that they must not doubt but that we were sincere and that we had traveled and p[r]eached until our shoes were worn out; consequently he thought that they ought to contribute. A Mr Griswould carried around a hat and received and gave to us $3.75. The meeting being dismissed, the people crowded unto us inviting us home with them and also wishing us not to leave them yet— &C. We assured [that] them that we should not leave them so long as they wished to search for truth with honest hearts and that for their soul's salvation—— We went home with Our friend Russel again.[27]

Friday 22. This morn, friend Dodson came in sat down and reasoned with us awhile. Br Parley read Alma's and Amulek's teaching and sufferings to him in Moronihah[28] to him and then the spirit fell on Br us so that Br Parley was melted into tears and his words were powerful even to the cutting of those to the heart who were present and I was filled to [*page 33*] so that I walked through the room praising and blessing the name of the Lord and testifying to his word even the book of Mormon until Sister Russel spoke out and "said that she believed it"— We left our once strong opposer in tears & so affected that he did not utter farewell but shaking us warmly by the hand we parted[29]: friend Russel accompanying us out, insisting that we should return, saying that, "his house should be our home" Thence 6 ms to Col. Scotts, the people being collected I arose and addressed them about one hour and Parley about one hour. There was not much visible effect among them for the better. A Mr Horton invited us to make an appointment about 4 mls south but we did not at this time—— Thence 2 miles

to Mr Osburn's who had once been a methodist Preacher, his wife
was a Sister to bro. D. Francis who lives in Zion—— She is a
reformed M[ethodist]

Saturday 23. I ought to have mentioned that F[r]iday morn——
Mr Griswould called who had heard us preach Thurs= even and
wanted us to go and preach in his settlement and we sent an app.
for Saturday even and Sunday &c. consequently this morn— we
proceeded on   miles to his house and found him very unwell
with sick head ache and aching bones &c. So much so that he was
not able to set up or to converse any with us—— Mrss. Griswould
seemed very believing——[*page 34*] Saturday 23. This even we
attended our appointment at a schoolhouse which was filled and
there were some who did or could not get in. Br Parley preached
one hour and 15 minutes and I spoke about 15 minutes. We made
an app. at Mr. Griswould's Barn for tomorrow at eleven O'clock.

Sunday 24. In a beautiful prairie filled with field's, farms, and
houses, a large—— Audience collected in the barn. I arose (although it was a little cool) and addressed them one hour and a
half on the evidences of Revelation and particularly the book of
Mormon &C. Br Parley spoke in addition about half an hour with
great plainness on the gathering of the Jews and of the Scattered
Indians &c. We made another app. about 4 miles Easterly near
Elder Dodson's. Then dismissed. The people were very friendly
and we had a number of invitations to visit them~~people~~ W[e] took
dinner with a Mr. Robley— Thence to our app. The house was
crowded. Br Parley addressed them one hour on the 49 chapter
of Isaiah[30] and I addressed them about 20 minutes on the plainness of the Gospel in both records— The people were anxious to
hear us again or seemed so at least— A Mr Harper, a Baptist man,
invited us home with him. We went and found them a very fine
family.——

Monday 25. This morn we visited friend Dodson's & conversed
with his Lady who seemed to be unprejudiced and anxious to
learn more of us. Thence 9 miles to Carrillton; but darkness
[*page 35*] seemed to shroud the minds of the people in that

place and there was a manifest carelesness about the things which we had declared. R. S. Negus subscribed for the Star. Thence 4 miles to Col Scotts's and staid,

Tuesday 26. Thence 7 miles to our friend Russel's again and spent the day in talking and in writing a letter to brother Phelps. A general app. was circulated for next Saturday and Sunday in order to give the people time to search, And we calculate to spend our time in the regions round about, conversing with those who desire to hear and learn more particularly, until that time——

Saturday 30. We attended our app. at the schoolhouse and it was full of people. Br Parley expounded the 6, 7, 8 and 9th Chapters of Ezekiel's prophecy[31] to them and I ocupied a few minutes. we spoke in all about 2 hours. Elizjah Dodson was present and had been round among his brethren for two or three days warning them against us and the book of Mormon, he seemed to be stirred up with fear that some of them would embrace the things which we preached and indeed he had reason to fear, for some of his first members professed to believe with all thier hearts. He in order to save them from the delusion (as he called it) made an app. to preach there at candle light. And we felt a little glad, because it would give the people an oppertunity to judge between chaff and sound doctrine——truth and error—— We attended expecting to hear him expose or oppose the things which we had preached, but first we betook ourselves to solemn prayr that he might be [*page 36*] confounded, in as much as he attempted to oppose the truth or pervert the Scriptures,— He spoke 1 3/4 hours. And had it not been for a few [p]mere [mere] positive assertions, I should have thought that he was trying to establish the truth of the book of Mormon. I had expected that he would have brought forward his strong reasoning But here we realized the power and efficacy of prayr & also the thruth of this prophecy "Every tongue that shall rise against the[e] in Judgement, thou shalt condemn."[32]

Sunday 31. We attended at the schoolhouse and between two and three hundred people collected— the house and yard was full, and we had preached in [all] the regions round about from the old and New Testaments, from the book of Mormon and from reason; and today it seemed good unto the Spirit which was in us to read considerable in the book of Mormon; consequently Br Parley arose and read a number of pages concerning the personal ministry of Christ of Christ on this continent,[33] and in all he read, expounded and reasoned about 2 hours and I then spoke about one hour, and read and expounded the covenants— & articles Bro. Parley then asked if any wished to obey, but none came forward. we appointed another meeting for candle light at the same place, The people dispersed and collected again at dusk, the house was filled. I addressed them first on prayr and it was said that some kneeled who were never seen so to do before. I then spoke on the propriety of our praying the Lords prayr now, then on the establishment of the kingdom of Christ & I then read the little revelation[34] given on that subject and spoke of i[t]s contents or of the coming of Christ and of the necessary preparation or supper of the Lamb and invited all to come to Christ &C. &C. and be prepared for the great day to come—— [*page 37*] I then proposed that all those who believed the things which we preached to manifest it by rising up to their feet, and I think about 30 men & women immediately & unhesitatingly arose and after they were seated again We told them it was their privilege to obey as soon as they felt ready— but they seemed to wish to examine a little further, before they leaped— And we told them that we would not leave the regions as yet and they universally (except a few) arose to manifest their wish for us to stay—— But Mr Dodson and Harvey who were present seemed to have great sorrow because they saw so many of their members or brethren receiving us and our teachings and they arose to speak in order to oppose us, but the people immediately began to go out and leave them, which still increased their trouble, We made another app. for Monday even about 4 miles at a Methodist schoolhouse & for Tuesday even at Henry Robley's on Apple creek prarie about 10 miles. We then dismissed——

Monday, April 1. we walked 7 miles and at candle light we attended our app. The house and yard was full, and Br Parley opened and unfolded the nature of revelations from the beginning or creation of Adam down through the various ages of which the revelations speak as far as he knew or as it was revealed— I then made a very few observations on the plainness of the Gospel & exorted them to prepare to meet the Lord for his coming was nigh at hand. We then returned to Col. Scotts and staid all night, And from his conversation I judged that he and his wife were both [*page 38*] a little shaken from their Infidel principles—

Tuesday 2. This morning it was raining considerable. And my shoes were worn entirely out. Yet thanks to the good Lord there was a pair of new ones just finished for me: and a young Lady in the neighbourhood who was afflicted with an evil Spirit even to fits & convultions sent for us to go and pray for her and we went. She [had] was not professed religion but her parents were methodists and quite believing. We prayed with them and laid our handsonon [hands on] here. Thence 10 miles to Henry Robley's through the rain and mud. evening came on and the people collected, a large number & I addressed them on the faith once delivered to the saints about 2 hours. Parley made a few observations and dismissed making an other app. for Thursday 3 oclock at a Mr Walker's 4 miles westerly and at Mr Griswold's barn for Sunday 11 oclock. The people here seem anxious to hear & to believe.

Wednesday 3. I left Parley to visit round and converse with the people and I returned 8 miles to friend Russel's to got our clothes which we had left to be washed and this evening I went to the house where we prayed for the afflicted Girl to hear, see and converse with a protestant Methodist Priest. He preached or tried to, and I by request made a few observations and dismission. I tried to converse with him but among all the unreasonable Priests that I had ever seen, he was the most so, he would not hold still long enough for me to tell him what the book of Mormon purported to be, and after I found that I could not enlighten him any, I left him— [*page 39*] Thence a widow Simmon's and staid all night. she was a Methodist, Yet very believing in the things which we preached.

Thursday 4. Thence 6 miles through the rain and mud to Esqur Walker's to our appointment——The house was filled with people, but Parley did not attend with me and I had no book of Mormon with me, I waited some time to see if Parley would come. I then arose putting my trust in the Living God and addressed a congregation of Baptists, Methodists, Christian order and none professers about 2 hours on the faith once delivered to the Saints and on the nature of the Kingdom of Christ &c. & it seemed to take general effect I then gave out our appointment for Sunday and dismissed them. Several of them spoke and desired [an] to hear again. Consequently I made another app. at the same place for Saturday 12 oclock & then went home with a Mr I. C. Campbell a member of the Christian order and staid all night,

Friday 5. This morning Parley came and said that the rain was all that hindered his attending the app. We spent the day in talking and reading and staid with I. Coon.

Saturday 6. This morning we were called upon and went to old father Coon's to pray for a fittyfied Girl, which we did with all solemnity trusting in the promises of God—— Thence to Esqr. Walker's to our app. The house was crowded again and Parley spoke 2 hours & I 20 mts. The people seemed all attention. Parley left me here and went up to the Prairie and at even I attended a meeting held by old Mr Henderson a Christian Preacher but a Mr. Osburn a Baptist Priest tried to preach from the songs of Solomon 1-8[35] but it was poor preach. then old daddy Henderson exorted a long while, sung [*page 40*] and went round & rou[n]d and shuck each others hands in complete confusion, then he called for (what he named) mourners and wanted them to come and bow down and let him pray for them. I said nothing only gave out our app. for next day, and being dismissed I went in company with Priest Henderson to Mr Campbell's and staid all night and talked considerable with them——

Sunday 7. To day it rained very hard until after 12 oclock, we then went to Henderson's app. to Esq Walker, and he invited me to preach and a few being present; I arose and addressed them about

1¹/4 on various points. the old gentleman then only made a few observations exorting them ~~them~~ to search the scriptures and see if these things were so. I then returned to the prairie & took dinner with my friend H. Robley & E. Dodson had an app. at the schoolhouse for candle light and we went up but Mr Dodson did not come. and the people desired that I should speak to them and I spoke about 1 hour then gave out an app. for Friday at a Mr Burasus' and for Sunday next at Mr. Griswold's barn, in as much as the people were disappointed by the rain, we wished to give them another general app. and give ourselves this week to labour in the regions.

Monday 8. This morn. I mit [met] with Parley again and we concluded to return to Bluffdale again and we set off and I went through the rich woods in order to give out an app. for tomorrow 3 oclock at B[luff] D[ale] School H[ouse] and Parley went on down the bottom to circulate it.

Tuesday 9. This day it was very showery, yet notwithstanding, We attended our app. and quite a number collected. Parley read Enoch's pro[p]hecy[36] and commented upon it and 102 Psalms[37] & was very definite, [*page 41*] I then arose being filled with anxiety for the salvat[i]on of the people, for we had preached to them & preached to them until they understood our mission, the Signs of the times, and their duty and privilege and they professed to believe these things with all their hearts; and yet they seemed to want to stand still. Beholding their stupidity, When I arose I only spoke a little while by way of teaching: and I do not recollect to have ever spoken more powerfully by way of Exortation, for the most hardoned present were cut to the heart and tears flowed apace from the tender and believing; But yet, one waited for another and none proposed or offered themselves as candidates for Zion——— And we dismissed them with heavy hearts I assure you. But our peace returned to us again, having this confidence that we had faithfully discharged our duty &C.

Wednesday 10. This day we gathered togeth~~ereth~~ our books, papers and clothes preparatory to finally leave them until they become ready to obey the **truth**, This day I sent an app. to G. Richards' for Saturday 3 oclock, about 14 mls. and also another to Mr Walkers for Thursday even, dark.

Thursday 11. we walked about 6 miles to our app. It was a very windy afternoon and night; Yet there were a number collected and Parley preached 11/2— and I 3/4 hours. but none seemed willing to obey consequently we left no further app. considering our work done here unless they sent for us to come and baptize them into the Church of Christ—

[*page 42*] Friday 12. We attended our app. at Mr Burrase's and I felt very unwell, having a very bad cold and head ache. Parley preached having a large congregation. I only made a very few observations, then dismissed—

Saturday 13. Last even I suffered much from a severe head ache, but the Lord had mercy on me. To day we walked on 7 miles to our app. at Mr Richards'. [T̶] A small company collected and at 3 oclock I arose and addressed them about 21/4 hours. we then, although late, walked on 5 miles to Mr Griswold's and I to Mr H. Robley's.

Sunday 14. Was a pleasant day and some two or three hundred collected in ~~the bar~~ a large barn to hear and at 11 o'clock Parley arose and addressed them about 2 hours, firstly, of God's dealings with the Jews and then the Gentiles and Lastly of the Gentiles and then the Jews— and I spoke 20 mts and we determined to dismiss the people without making any further app. The people seemed all attention Yet no person moved to obey, notwithstanding all their stir and all our solicitations, they seemed to wait one for another. Consequently we dismissed them finally, as we thought— — But two or three from Bluffdale immediately came to us and said if we would return there they would be baptized. I then called to the people and appointed to preach again at B[luff] D[ale] schoolhouse on Monday even 3 oclock—— and at candle light I attended to hear Mr Dodson. But, behold the Rev. Mr Peck

made his appearance[38] and spoke to the small congregation 1 hour
& 3/4. his whole discourse was intended by him to disprove the
book of Mormon,[39] but I thought that it was a feeble effort particularly, when considered from a learned man. [*page 43*] When he
had dismissed I called the attention & gave out our app.[40] and told
them that we expected to baptize some in the faith of the book
of Mormon and probably some of the good Baptist people— This
made their Priests stare I assure you——

Monday 15. We attended our app. The house was full. I arose and
addressed them about 1 hour & 1/4 having five or six Pri[e]sts
before me but they were not Jethro's. they were only man made.[41]
therefore I did not fear them. Mr. Peck set just by me and took
notes and sneered and whispered to one of his fellow Priests but
it all mattered not to me. Parley made a few observations[42] and we
then proposed that all those who believed and wished to be baptized would manifest it and A. Holden, J. White & his wife Sophia
and Susannah Campbell &c all professed fait[h] and a willingness
to be baptized in the faith of the Church of Christ—— We gave
out 3 appts[:] one 7 miles below for [~~Tuesday~~] Wesday 3 O'clock,
two here (Thursday 3 and on Sunday 11[)]. We then immidiately
went 1 mile to the water and baptized Aaron Holden, James ~~White~~
& Sophia White. Mother Campbell put it off until Sunday to wait
for some of her children— After Sister White was ready to go into
the water Mr Peck hailed her as a Sister and urged her to not
throw herself away or out of the church of Christ, as he called it.
But she stemmed the tarrent [torrent] and went forward with her
husband and was baptized——

Tuesday 16th I commenced writing a letter to Emiline, visited old
friend Calvin's family &c[43]—— and at Candle light we attended
[~~to~~] at the s[c]hoolhouse to hear Mr Peck expose Mormonism as
he [*page 44*] called it, but I assure you he made a weak effort,
considering his learning and ~~tal~~natural talents. In fact, his discourse of 2 hours long was well calculated to throw a veil of
darkness over the whole face of revelation. we made no remarks
only only [*sic*] gave out our appts which we had previously made.

Wednesday 17th we walked 8 miles down the bluff to Mr
Clendenon's to fill our app. A cabin full collected [ԯ] and I preached
near three hours to them on various subjects, but particularly on
the spiritual gifts in the Church of Christ &c.

Thursday 18. We returned and attended at 3 to our app. the congregation was more thin than common. Parley preached 2 hours
& 1/2 trying to get the people to believe their own book[44] and
I assure you he did'nt spare.

Friday 19— I finished my letter, enclosed $10 U.S. paper in it to
my wife and to the post office, and the remainder of the day we
spent in reading news and visiting our friends and brethren——

Saturday 20. At 3 O'clock I attended to hear Mr Peck preach again.
He took the prophecy of Zechariah for his text and I have heard
many men try to spiritual and twist the plain word of God but
I never heard an equal to this. He even said that the mount of
Olivet mentioned in the 14th Ch.[45] meant the Jewish economy
before the distruction of Jerusalem by Titus &c[46] He closed by
prayr of J. Harvy. I made no observations because all who were
present had heard us plainly on this same subject and prophecy
previously[47] &C [*page 45*] Br Parley went to day two or three
miles to a methodist meeting where we had made an app. not
knowing that they had one, he heard them speak a while then
returned to Col. John Scotts's & Mrss. Scott sent out her children
and a few of the neighbours came in and he spoke or preached
to them about 2 hours on various Subjects. he staid with Mr Scott
who told him when we came into the country was a professed
Deist, but said he "I am thoroughly convinced now of the truths
which you preach and Just as soon as I can settle my business
I shall remove to Zion, I shall not join now and the reason is this
I have considerable property in my hands and were I to join the
wicked community would exert themselves to injure me. &C, &C."

Sunday 21. We attended our app. at 11,o. at Esqr. Gates' barn.
A multitude collected probably 300 and we occupied about 2 hours
and a 1/2. Mr Peck being present who gave out or had an app. for

3 at the same place. We then went 1 mile to a creek and baptized Susannah Campbell & Elizabeth Reed I then and had a very solemn time. I then returned to the barn to hear Mr Peck's strang[e] arguments and last shoot, but instead of argument, it was loud assertions, abusive language, exaggerations, missrepresentations and rehearsing many false reports. He also brought up E. Campbell's[48] pamphlet written against it and then read a letter written by Samuel Sherwood (Peck even compared the book to Sinbad the Sailor, Tom thum[b] & Jack the Jiant killer &C &C) &C.[49] and while he was giving his last blow and bid them farewell, as he said he should leave them in the morning; a loud Amen was uttered by some one near by in token of his joy that he was going. We called the diciples together at candle light at Br White's for the purpose of confirming and instructing them. We broke bread among them and then Parley— [*page 46*] prayed with and laid his hands upon them and we had a very solemn meeting, but no more joined——

Monday 22. we spent pretty much, in writing letters to our friends, Parley to his wife & I to my Br. Samuel &C

Tuesday 23. We walked [6] 9 miles and preached 3 mts hours with Liberty and demonstration and baptized 2 Sisters (viz) Mandana Campbell & Mary Ann Clark but their husbands were not quite ready——

Wednesday 24. To day I visited some of the brethren and I walked about 12 mls. and staid all night with R. Scott.

Thursday 25. we walked 5 mls. to Carrollton and attended our app. in the court house at 3 O'clock. a small congregation attended and those who did attend seemed very indifferent but notwithstanding all, in order to clear our garments[50] Parley spoke to them by way of reasoning about 1 hour & a 1/2 and I attempted to speak but I only spoke 10 minutes. for Such manifest indifference & carelessness was manifested among them that I could not preach, consequently I dismissed them, with an impression that we should never again call them together, They did not even [ask] any of them ask us to stay and rest ourselves, consequently we bid

Carrollton fare-ill and walked out easterly about 4 miles and staid with a methodist man. He used us well.

Friday 26. We walked on 6 miles to Mr Wilson's where we had sent an app. for to day 3 O'clock—— about 30 collected and I addressed them about 1 hour but the wind [blowed] blew so hard and the people had so little faith, I can assure you it was hard work to preach—— We made another app here for Sunday, then dismissed.

Saturday 27 we spent in reading &C &C

[*page 47*] Sunday 28. The wind still blew quite hard but yet we attended our app. we had only a small congregation considering the multitudes who had heard us on the preceding Sunday's, however Parley preached to them about 1 hour & a 1/2 but the people were so unbelieving and possesed such bitterness against us that it was hard labour to preach. And after we had dismissed, a yound [young] Doctor Higgins arose & called the attention of the people while he read a copy of a letter written by Saml Sherwood, dated 25, Feb. in Independence, which was filled with falseties and exagerations, this created some anxiety among the hardond wretches and they called on us to know whether it was true or false. I examined the letter and gave a detail of what we believed on the various subjects which it touched. But the most funny of all was, the letter stated that, "the poor in Zion lived on water porage Salted." We then dismissed without any further app. in the neighbourhood——

Monday 29. we passed through to Mr H. Robley's 12 miles and found them still quite believing & friendly. I sold them a book of Mormon which they were glad to get.

Tuesday 30. Mr Rob[y]lly had received the Star up to the 10 number and to day we read until the afternoon then walked on 7 miles to Levi Merick's——

Wednesday. May 1. To day we attended an app at a Mr Bellew's at [3] 2 o'clock and quite a number collected and I spoke to them nea[l]rly 3 hours on various subjects but more particularly on the covenants and the Law &c. We then went to the creek and baptized Levi and [Mrs.?]   Merick. They had belonged to the baptists ever since they were children——

[*page 48*] Thursday 2. We walked 12. miles to our app. at Br Whites at 3. O'clock and brother Parley preached about 1¹/₂ hours. We made another app. here for Sunday next and after we had dismissed 3 more persons told us that they believed and intended to be baptized on Sunday &c. To day we received a letter from Br Phelps from Zion but all the news to us was, It seemed as if he just happened to say "your families are as usual" &c &c——

Friday 3 we walked 10 miles down the bluff to an app. at Mr Watson's. Parly preached again about 2 hours on the, "restitution of all things spoken by all the holy prophets since the world began["][51] &c and I spoke probably 20 minutes on the plan of redemption and by way of exortation and then explanation of what we believed then dismissed and Thomas Turney came to us and told us he was convinced and he should esteem it a privilege to obey the gospel and he wished to be baptized consequently we went [two] 3 miles to the Macaupin and while the moon the queen of night, shone bright ore each earb [herb] and tree about 8 O'clock Parley walked forth and buried him beneath the yielding wave and while all nature seemed to smile in praise to its Eternal Maker we prayed the blessings of our Father upon us, then parted and each went his way rejoicing——

Saturday 4. We spent in visiting our brethren &C

Sunday 5. we attended our app. at Esqr Gates' barn at 10. The brethren & sisters & people being assembled I arose and addressed them about 2 hours on the nature of parables, on the Articles & Covenants and Laws and gathering of the church of Christ &C, &C, I then proposed if any present wished to become— [*page 49*] untited [united] with us that they would manifest it and James H. Reed, Joseph Jackson, Katharine Holden and Nancy Simmons immediately arose—— &c. I then dismissed, to meet again at the creek at 1/2 past 3. and we took dinner with Mr J & J. Calvin then attended at the watter's edge and a large company being present I went down into the water and immersed those who were willing to take upon them the name of Christ and live in obedience to his Laws. ~~Then~~ &c we really had a very solemn time so that many were affected even unto tears, We then collected again at Brother White's and Parley broke bread and we administered to the deciples and then I prayed with, laid my hands on and confirmed the believers and we had a solemn and joyful meeting. The believers rejoiced much &C.[52] [I] We [th] had been cal[c]ulating for some days past to leave the p[l]ace in the morning, Parley for Zion and I for Paris. but the people as well as the brethren were [go] very anxious that I should stay longer. consequently upon reflection I gave out an app. for wednesday at br. Turner's and Friday at Mr Bellew's and for Sunday at Col. Scott's.

Monday 6. This morning I had the painful duty to perform of parting with brother Parley, he determined that he must see his family. consequently he left for Zion[53] and I sent one dollar and 50 cents with him as a remembrance to my little Emeline &C—— and I have given my self till Wednesday to rest, read and visit my friends— and good brethren—— whom I love in the truth and in the bonds of the Gospel of my great Redeemer even the Lord Jesus Christ——

[*page 50*] Wednesday 8th To day I attended my app. [by] below the Macaupin at Br T. Turner's at 2 O'clock, a number collected considering the busy time and the thinness of the neighbourhood. I preached about an hour and a half but I did not have a very great flow of the spirit. Some wished to join but put it off until I shall preach here again next Tuesday.

Friday 10. I attended at Mr Bellew's. I had but a small congregation, yet I arose and preached about 2 hours & a 1/4. And I did preach to[o], I think the greatest sermon that I ever preached in Ill.

Saturday 11. I attended at Bluffdale to the Baptist church meeting but the Rev. Mr. Dodson had only 14 hearers and we had I thought poor preach and a cold meeting.

Sunday 12. To day I attended my app. at Col. J. Scott's at 11 O'clock. I had a lorge [large] congregation and I addressed them about an hour and 3/4 on the two covenant lands, the two places of deliverance and the effects produced by the two gatherings with general remarks &c &c Old Mr Dodson A Baptist Priest then arose and preached or spoke an hour and a 1/4 on a funeral occasion—— "It was a right old fashioned baptist sermon." and it seemed to have but little effect any way. Bro. Merick, his wife and bro. Jackson came ten miles to hear me and they told me that they felt paid for their journey——This evening I visited old Sister Simmons and spent [old] a very interesting evening and morning with her, she had been very sorely tempted the week past but now her faith seemed to be increased and her confidence established and her mind at eas[e]—

[*page 51*] Tuesday 14. I attended my appointment below the Macoupin at brother Turner's. I had but a small con congregation and they were complete Illinoyans. I preached about an hour and a half to them with considerable freedom and clearness. Those who wished to join when I was here before. One was hindered by her Father and an other by her husband so that I baptized none, and left them without any further appointment here: making one for B[luff] D[ale] S[chool] H[ouse] for next Sunday. Brother Turner seemed to enjoy himself well and had a good understanding of the truth and rejoiced much in it——

Wednesday 15. Having heard that one of my second cousins lived in this county east of Carrollton to day I determined to see, and I went and found that her, [that] who was formerly Lucinda White had married Jacob Odel, was here and doing tolerably well. I spent an after noon with her very agreeably, which called to mind many of my youthful scenes of life—— and worldly pleasures.

Friday I received two letters by mail, one from my Emiline (Zion) and one from cousin Saml Baird)(Cantervill) & these were a source of muuth joy to me. Here I give myself two or three days to visit and strengthen my brethren and sisters before my departure from

them which I anticipate will be on Monday morning next——
I ought to have mentioned that my good Sister Russel gave to me
the postage of both of my letters——

Saturday 18. To day I spent pretty much in writing a letter to
my wife——

[*page 52*] Sunday 19. To day I preached in the schoolhouse to a
tolerably large congregation, on The Priesthood, on the operation
of the Holy spirit and on the nature of communion &c. And then
broke bread among the diciples— We had quite an interesting
meeting. To day I received a letter from Sister Nancy Simmons
stating that she had lost her faith, retraced her steps and gone
back and joined the Methodists again—— I ref[l]ected that she
had vountarily joined us she had vountarily left us and I'd
vouluntarily let her go. Consequently I gave myself no trouble
about it——

Monday 20—— This morning and yesterday the good people
gave me $5.62. cents &c and Mr Rogers let me have a horse to
ride as far east as Vandalia and It seemed to me as if my preaching
mission was out. consequently I set off for Paris and rode about
40 mls. to Carlinville, staid all night, but had the sick-head-ache
ve[r]y badly——

Tuesday [20] 21. Paid 37. cts and rode on Felt some better. Took
breakfast with Mr Evans and rode on 25 miles to Hillsboro, thence
14 mls to a Mr Hill's and staid all night but I fared quite poorly—

Wednesday 22. To day I rode 12 ms. into Vandalia, called at
mr. Watterman's, delivered the horse according to directions and
thence on the national road 13 mls. to Mrs Hodges and being very
hungry I called for some dinner, but I assure you it was poor eat,
they gave me a little blue milk, cold fried me[at,] and cold corn
hoe cake, and it all appeared as though there was no respect to
cleanliness while preparing it. But I shut my eyes and swallowed
it down.

[*page 53*] Thursday 23. I took breakfast and passed on 16 miles to Jacob Slover's and took dinner and thence 3 ms to my old friend John Gannaway's and staid all night but ah! here I assure I took a cup or two of old aunt Betsy's coffee![54] and I did too——

Friday 24. After taking a good breakfast, I started about 9 through a 25 mile prairie— and I walked on and walked on, The rays of the sun beat very warmly upon me but I walked on without a cooling shade to rest in and worse than all, without even one drop of watter from the thrilling brook to cool my mouth or quench my thirst— I had often thought that I knew what it was to suffer but I think I'll never forget this prairie. at length I lifted my eyes and Lo! a grove of timber just before me, I wandered down Its drain until I found a little water seaped together and although it looked very blue and was quite warm yet I lay down and sucked a considerable draught—— Thence [to] 9 miles to my good old friend Jesse Fuller's. And I do think that I never was more tired sore and thirsty, but I leave this painful subject—

NOTES

[1] Pratt also wrote an account of this mission. His narrative is contained in Parley P. Pratt, Jr., ed., *Autobiography of Parley P. Pratt*, 4th ed. (Salt Lake City: Deseret Book, 1985), 66–73. Pratt's account is primarily a reconstruction of debates he held with the rival preachers Dotson and Peck.

[2] This may have been "Everett's Ferry," which is mentioned in early Jackson County records. Pearl Wilcox, "Early Independence in Retrospect: Part III," *Saints' Herald* (January 19, 1959): 13.

[3] New Testament instructions to those who carry the gospel abroad (Matt. 10:9–10; Luke 10:4) were reiterated in revelations to Joseph Smith (D&C 24:18; 84:77–81), received in July 1830 and September 1832.

[4] Independence was the center of Jackson County, Missouri, which a November 1831 revelation to Joseph Smith had designated as the land of Zion (D&C 69:6).

[5] See Luke 10:4; 22:35; and D&C 24:18; 84:78.

[6] A blue-water stream which drained the central portion of Jackson County. Warren A. Jennings, "Zion Is Fled: The Expulsion of the Mormons

from Jackson County, Missouri" (Ph.D. diss., University of Florida, 1962), 13.

[7] See Matt. 6:31-34; 3 Ne. 13:31-34; D&C 84:84.

[8] Possibly the creek known as "Fire Prairies Stream." Pearl Wilcox, "Early Independence in Retrospect: Part II," *Saints' Herald* (January 12, 1959): 10.

[9] Probably Sni-a-Bar Creek, which drained the eastern region of Jackson County. Jennings, "Zion Is Fled," 13.

[10] This is almost a direct quotation of Isaiah 6:10. Virtually the same passage is found in Matthew 13:15; Mark 4:12; John 12:40; Acts 28:27; and 2 Nephi 16:10.

[11] The journal is one day off. This would have been Thursday, February 7. Similarly, Friday's and Saturday's dates would have been February 8 and 9.

[12] Haden, the aforementioned "Priest," was a Campbellite minister. His remarks echoed the position of Alexander Campbell, who repudiated the very idea of modern revelation. For a helpful analysis of Mormon and Campbellite preaching, see Richard L. Bushman, *Joseph Smith and the Beginnings of Mormonism* (Urbana: University of Illinois Press, 1984), 180-85.

[13] Haden's remarks may have reflected Alexander Campbell's scurrilous review of the Book of Mormon in *Millennial Harbinger* 2 (February 1831): 86-96. Campbell's observations on the Mormon scripture were subsequently published as a pamplet and widely circulated.

[14] *The Evening and the Morning Star,* a monthly publication of the Mormons in Independence. See note 5, McLellin's 1832 letter above.

[15] Paris, Monroe County, Missouri, not Paris, Illinois, where McLellin taught school.

[16] The Salt River Branch of the Church was organized in 1832 after George Hinkle and others baptized the Allred, Ivie, and other families in the area. John Ivie was the president of the branch. "The Diary of Reddick N. Allred," in *Treasures of Pioneer History,* comp. Kate B. Carter, 6 vols. (Salt Lake City: Daughters of Utah Pioneers, 1952-57), 5:299.

[17] The sacrament of the Lord's supper. See note 24, Journal I above.

[18] It was apparently at this time that McLellin and Pratt were advised by some other religious people "not to attempt a meeting or any religious instruction" in Clarksville, Missouri, "for [the inhabitants] were a hardened and irreclaimable set of blasphemers and infidels, given to gambling, drinking and cursing, etc.; and . . . many different orders of the clergy had attempted to reclaim them, or even to get a hearing." The people who issued this warning nevertheless refused to transport the two elders across the Mississippi for free. Pratt, *Autobiography,* 66-67.

[19] A Book of Mormon term denoting a group of ancient settlers in the Americas who were progenitors of some Native Americans. Commonly used by Mormons in place of the word "Indian."

²⁰ The parallel that McLellin drew with "Holy men of old" and his use of the words "struggle" and "wrestled" to describe prayer suggest that this passage has reference to an account in the Book of Mormon in which Enos, a prophet, withdrew to the woods to pray for help (Enos 1:2–3, 10). Pratt indicates that they prayed for the Lord to open the hearts of the citizens of Clarksville. Pratt, *Autobiography,* 66.

²¹ Pratt's account of the day in Clarksville is slightly more optimistic: "We preached, had good attention, and much of a candid spirit of inquiry was manifest, and we were treated with hospitality and friendship, and even ferried over the river free; and this was more than those religious sectaries would do, who had warned us against them." Pratt, *Autobiography,* 67.

²² He had read through what is now the fifth chapter of the Book of Jacob, approximately one-fourth of the Book of Mormon, which had 588 pages in the first edition.

²³ These pages of the 1830 edition of the Book of Mormon contain the writings of the prophet Moroni, as he expresses his fears concerning his "weakness in writing." He writes, "I fear lest the Gentiles shall mock at our words. And when I had said this, the Lord spake unto me, saying: Fools mock, but they shall mourn." For the complete passage, see Ether 12:22–40.

²⁴ Pratt describes in detail several debates with this minister, whom he describes as "Dotson, who opposed us with much zeal, from time to time, both in public and in private, and from house to house." Pratt, *Autobiography,* 68.

²⁵ Pratt depicts one such discussion with Mr. Dotson. Pratt, *Autobiography,* 68.

²⁶ Galatians 5:19–21 lists seventeen vices: "adultery, fornication, uncleanness, lasciviousness, idolatry, witchcraft, hatred, variance, emulations, wrath, strife, seditions, heresies, envyings, murders, drunkenness, revellings."

²⁷ Pratt also described the generosity of the people in this area:

> John Russell . . . invited us to tarry in the neighborhood and continue to preach; he said his house should be our home, and he called a vote of the people whether they wished us to preach more, The vote was unanimous in the affirmative.
>
> We tarried in the neighborhood some two months, and preached daily in all that region to vast multitudes, both in town and country, in the grove, and in school houses, barns and dwellings. (Pratt, *Autobiography,* 67)

²⁸ The Book of Mormon recounts the story of Alma and Amulek, servants of the Lord, who were imprisoned for many days in a city called Ammonihah, which McLellin mistakenly calls Moronihah. After the righteous women and children, along with all their holy writings, had been burned by the apostate people in that city, Alma and Amulek were

delivered by an earthquake sent by the Lord, and the wicked city was soon destroyed by an invading army (Alma 9-16).

[29] Pratt also describes this spiritual experience:

[Mr. Dotson] was opposing the Book of Mormon with all his power.

We asked him to listen while we read a chapter in it. He did so, and was melted into tears, and so affected and confounded that he could not utter a word for some time. He then, on recovering, asked us to his house, and opened the door for us to preach in his neighborhood. We did so, and were kindly entertained by him. (Pratt, *Autobiography,* 69)

[30] Isaiah 49 was understood by Latter-day Saints to announce the preaching of the gospel of Jesus Christ in the last days to all the nations of the earth, the gathering of Israel with the assistance of gentile kings and queens, and the glorious reign of God. Isaiah 49 is quoted in the Book of Mormon (1 Ne. 21:1-26; and 2 Ne. 10:9-10).

[31] Ezekiel 6-9 prophesies about the scattering of Israel, preservation of a remnant, desolation and destruction of the world and of the wicked in Jerusalem, and identification of the righteous with a mark on their foreheads.

[32] See Isa. 54:17; 3 Ne. 22:17.

[33] The Book of Mormon contains an extended report of a ministry of the resurrected Christ among ancient inhabitants of the Americas. He is said to have taught, ordained ministers, established his Church, and performed miracles (3 Ne. 11-28). Latter-day Saints regard this ministry as one of the most important and spiritually significant parts of the Book of Mormon.

[34] This is the earliest known description and discussion of the revelation now known as Doctrine and Covenants 65. Joseph Smith received this revelation soon after McLellin met him (October 1831), and McLellin made a copy of the revelation. For more information, see pages 241-46 in this volume.

[35] Apparently the Baptist preacher drew his sermon from verses throughout the Song of Solomon.

[36] Shortly after Joseph Smith commenced the work of producing a new translation of the Bible, he received a revelation about the "doings of olden times, from the prophecy of Enoch." *HC* 1:133. Enoch's prophecy, which is included in the Pearl of Great Price (Moses 7), is a vision of God's dealings with his people, from Enoch's era to Christ's second coming and the consequent Millennial peace. This prophecy indicates that a restoration of the gospel would occur before Christ's return, and Zion, a "Holy City," would be established.

[37] Pratt possibly focused on verses 12-28 of this psalm, which describe the establishment of Zion. Psalms 102:16-22, for example, could have been cited as authority for the establishment of Zion, for visions and new

revelations, and, because the plural form of the word *kingdom* was used, as a warrant for the Mormon belief in a gathering of God's people in two places (Zion in the New World and Jerusalem in the Old): "When the Lord shall build up Zion, he shall appear in his glory. He will regard the prayer of the destitute, and not despise their prayer. This shall be written for the generation to come: and the people which shall be created shall praise the Lord. For he hath looked down from the height of his sanctuary; from heaven did the Lord behold the earth; to hear the groaning of the prisoner; to loose those that are appointed to death; to declare the name of the Lord in Zion, and his praise in Jerusalem; when the people are gathered together, and the kingdoms, to serve the Lord."

[38] Mr. Peck "was a man of note, as one of the early settlers of Illinois, and one of its first missionaries. He had labored for many years in that new country and in Missouri, and was now Editor of a paper devoted to Baptist principles." He had been summoned to Greene County by Mr. Dotson, who alerted Peck "that the 'Mormons' were about to take Green County," so "his immediate attendance" was requested. Pratt, *Autobiography,* 69.

[39] Peck's arguments, as recorded by Pratt, were primarily charges that the Book of Mormon could not be substantiated by archaeological proof. Pratt responded to these allegations at a later meeting and recorded his defense in his *Autobiography,* 69–70.

[40] This meeting was for the purpose of responding to Peck's charges. Pratt, *Autobiography,* 69.

[41] Jethro, the priest of Midian (Ex. 18:1), was the father-in-law of Moses. A revelation to Joseph Smith, given September 22–23, 1832, indicated that Moses received his priesthood authority from Jethro (D&C 84:6). Thus, McLellin is saying that the five or six priests whom he confronted lacked divine authority.

[42] See Pratt, *Autobiography,* 70–73.

[43] According to Parley P. Pratt, Calvin was an old farmer whom McLellin and Pratt met soon after entering Illinois. He had not attended a religious meeting for five years, but these missionaries gained his confidence and he "became a constant hearer, and opened his house" for their home. "He was very wealthy and bade [them] welcome to shoes, clothing or anything" they needed. Pratt, *Autobiography,* 67.

[44] Use of the Bible to prove Mormonism's claims was a standard strategy in early Mormon preaching.

[45] Zechariah 14:4 prophecies that the Lord's "feet shall stand in that day upon the mount of Olives," which will be split open from the east to the west, and 14:8 states that "in that day . . . living waters shall go out from Jerusalem." Mr. Peck interpreted this chapter as a prophecy concerning the destruction of Jerusalem by the Romans in A.D. 70, but Latter-day Saints and other Millennialists saw this text as a clear indication of events yet to come in preparation for the second advent of Christ. See, for example,

D&C 45:48. See generally Grant Underwood, *The Millenarian World of Early Mormonism* (Urbana: University of Illinois, 1993).

[46] According to Pratt, Peck believed that the prophetic portions of the Bible "were directly calculated to lead [people] into delusion and bewilderment; that the best way to read and understand prophecy was, to read it backwards—that is to say, after it is fulfilled; that it was never designed to be understood before it came to pass." Pratt, *Autobiography,* 69. Pratt, on the other hand, would write in the first chapter of *A Voice of Warning and Instruction to All People,* which went through multiple editions, that "the predictions of the prophets can be clearly understood, as much so as the almanac, when it foretells an eclipse." This idea of the inevitability of the fulfillment of prophecy is underscored in the motto that Pratt placed at the head of the second chapter of this often reprinted 1837 work: "What Is Prophecy but History Reversed?"

[47] Pratt had discussed Zechariah 14 in his remarks on April 15, 1833. He used this chapter to refute Peck's claim that the Millennium had already begun. Pratt, *Autobiography,* 72-73.

[48] This would have been Alexander Campbell. See note 13 above.

[49] Ridiculing the Book of Mormon by placing it in the context of fable was not uncommon. Also in 1833, C. S. Francis and Company publishing house (Boston and New York) issued *Mother Goose's Melodies,* the title page of which read as follows:

> Mother Goose's Melodies. The only Pure Edition. Containing all that have ever come to light of her memorable writings, together with those which have been discovered among the mss. of Herculaneum. *Likewise every one recently found in the same stone box which hold the Golden Plates of the Book of Mormon.* The whole compared, revised, and sanctioned, by one of the annotators of the Goose family. (Emphasis added)

We are grateful to Alfred L. Bush, curator of Western Americana in the Firestone Library, Princeton University, for bringing this publication to our attention.

[50] The Book of Mormon prophet Jacob described his motivation for sharing the gospel: "By laboring with our might their [the unrepentants'] blood might not come upon our garments; otherwise their blood would come upon our garments, and we would not be found spotless at the last day" (Jacob 1:19; also, 2:2).

[51] See Acts 3:21, a scripture commonly used as a prediction of the latter-day restoration of the gospel by Joseph Smith. This was a familiar theme in Pratt's preaching and writing about Mormonism. See, for example, Pratt, *A Voice of Warning,* chapter 1.

[52] About this meeting, Laura Russell, wife of John Russell, wrote to her husband on May 9, 1833:

Mormonism gains some they now have a church of 14 Members.
Mr. McLelin preached last sunday and did in a degree do away Mr.
Pecks Sermon. He said that the only substantial argument that had
been brought against the book of Mormon was the rite of sacrifices.
And contended that Lehi and Nephi had the same right to sacrifice that
Manoah, who was of the tribe of Dan, had and David and others
that did sacrifice and their offering was accepted of God. He made a
powerful appeal to the people asked them what testimony we had
that any church was accepted a true Church and owned of God when
there was no communication between earth and heaven, or in other
words has no seer and declared that there had not been any for many
hund. years. He said too that the book of Mormon and the Bible must
one prove the other or both fall together (A pretty bold assertion I
think.) Mrs Holden Mrs Simmons Mr Reed and Mr Jackson from the
Rainie joined them. They laid hands on them for the reception of
the Holy Ghost and administered the Sac. there was no visible
alteration attended them. If this is all deception it certainly is one of
the most cunningly devised things that ever entered the Human
heart. Now, my dear Husband, I wish you to read this to Mr. Peck and
ask him to give me an answer to it and help me out. I mean the part
alluding to the sacrifices. (Laura Russell to "My beloved Husband,"
May 9, 1833, 1–2, Russell Family Papers, Illinois State Historical
Library, Springfield)

We thank R. Steven Pratt for providing this letter and other material
concerning John Russell.

[53] Parley summarized this mission with McLellin in the following
words: "Hundreds of people were convinced of the truth, but the hearts of
many were too much set on the world to obey the gospel; we, therefore,
baptized only a few of the people, and organized a small society, and about
the first of June took leave and returned home." Pratt, *Autobiography,* 73.
This mission was noted by some nineteenth-century Illinois historians: "The
Mormon revival of 1830 to 1835 is well remembered. These were conducted by Elders McClellan and Parley P. Pratt in the west part of the county.
Considerable excitement grew out of these meetings and some converts
made." *History of Greene and Jersey Counties, Illinois* (Springfield, Ill.:
Continental Historical, 1885), 761–62.

[54] Three months earlier, on Feburary 27, 1833, in Kirtland, Joseph
Smith had received a revelation, now commonly called the Word of
Wisdom, which discouraged the drinking of hot drinks such as coffee
and tea (D&C 89:9). It is unlikely that McLellin was aware of this revelation,
since he left Independence on January 28, 1833, and was on this missionary
journey until May 24.

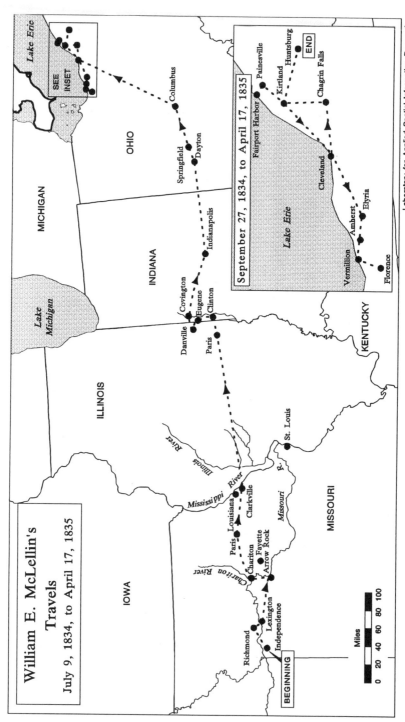

William E. McLellin's
Travels
July 9, 1834, to April 17, 1835

September 27, 1834, to April 17, 1835

Laboratory for Applied Spatial Information Research

MICHIGAN

Lake Erie

SEE
INSET

OHIO

Columbus

Springfield

Dayton

Indianapolis

INDIANA

Covington

Eugene

Clinton

Danville

Paris

Lake Michigan

ILLINOIS

Illinois River

St. Louis

Mississippi River

Clarkville

Louisiana

Paris

Missouri R.

MISSOURI

Clarkville

Chariton

Fayette

Arrow Rock

Chariton River

Richmond

Lexington

Independence

KENTUCKY

IOWA

BEGINNING

Miles

0   20   40   60   80   100

Painesville

Kirtland

Huntsburg

Chagrin Falls

END

Fairport Harbor

Lake Erie

Cleveland

Amherst

Elyria

Vermillion

Florence

William E. McLellin Journal IV
July 9, 1834–April 17, 1835

William E. McLelin's Journal commenced the 9th of July 1834 given between Zion & Kirtland[1]

————

After having three or four days to prepare; and being -called, chosen and appointed to go immediately to the East and assist in gathering up the **strength** of the Lord's house[2] on the 9th early in the morning I bid farewell to my companion and little babe[3] and started on horse back to discharge my duties and fulfil the will of God, but it was a more affecting parting than I ever had experienced with my Emiline because of our infant and because of the uncertainty of the length of time I should be gone. I passed on 10 [miles] to bro. T. Marsh's.[4] Br Joseph (and company) were there, a meeting had been appointed and bro. J was preaching. he spoke about an hour after I arrived to a large company of brethren and sisters and instructed them how they ought to live in order to the deliverance of Zion;[5] they seemed to be much affected and in the close He sealed them up unto everlasting life[6] and at the request of bro. J. Hitchcock bro. Joseph pronounced upon him the gift of utterance to perform the duties of his calling[7] so long as he lived if he were faithful—Thence 20 miles to a Mr Sanderson's and staid all night. he was a Tennesseean, He treated us very friendly. There were 19 of us in company[8] and in tolerable health. Thence 4 mls. to Richmond, thence 12 mls across the Misouri at Jack's old ferry to Lexington, Thence 13 mls and camped on a little prairie near old Mr

[*page 1*]
Journal July 1834
   By W. E. McLelin[9]

Tuesday the 22nd I took breakfast with Mr J. Jones in Paris Illinois, thenc[e] onward for Clinton but about 10 O'clock my fever rose again and I traveled in much pain until noon, when I told the brethren that I was so sick that I could not travel on. They offered to have some one stay with me but I thought it not best so they passed on and left me[10] and also one of their horses that was foundered with me at Mr McCown. Dr [Frederick G.] Williams[11] also left some medicine with me to take if I should continue sick. Mr & Mrs McCown used me very well and next morning would charge me nothing for their trouble and the[y] asked if I would not return when I recovered and preach in the neighbourhood——

Wednesday 23. I felt some better and in as much as I was only about 25 miles from the Eugene church[12] I thought I would try to get there. Consequently today I rode on about 15 miles and staid with a Mr L. French. he was very friendly and they treated me well and charged me nothing. He also was very anxious to have me preach.

But after breakfast I passed [on] and about 9 O'clock my fever rose again, but I still rode on and about noon I reached old brother Hubbard.[13] I was very sick and my fever was very high.—— Here I continued very sick until the 30th. My fever turned to the Ague[14] and I had two hard shakes—— [*page 2*] The brethren & Sisters were very kind to me and after the 30th I began to mend

and on Sunday 3t August I attended meeting with the brethren and preached about an hour and a half, We had a good meeting and the Saints seemed much stirred up and encouraged.

We app. another meeting for Tuesday 3.O[clock] with a request for all the members to turn out and they generally attended—— I preached to them on the rise and establishment of the church of the **Latter day** Saints and on the Covenants and Articles for about 2 hours: The brethren & sisters all manifested by rising their determination to double their diligence in the good cause—— Two persons also came forward and manifested their determinations to

serve the Lord and were received and immersed— (John Cooper
& Louisa Baily). I made two more app. one for Thursday 3 P.M.
at bro. Morris's about 5 mls off and one for Sunday at 11 A. M. at
bro. Hubbard's.

Thursday 7th I with 3 Elders (brothers Levi Jones, Lewis Sabriski
and James Johnson) attended my app. There was but a small congregation. I addressed them an hour and a half, first on some
parables that the saviour spoke to the Jews and then on the faith
of the ancient saints from 2 Peter 1.[15] &c. Those present paid very
good attention and I made another app. [f] at the same place for
next Wednesd[a]y 3 P. M.——

Friday 8th I wrote a letter at Sister Clark's and started it by mail
to Emiline with a five dollar bill in it.

Saturday morning Sis. Clark gave me a dollar to buy me a pocket
handkerchief with. I bought one and paid $1.25 for it. I also
bought little blank book for 12 1/2 cts to keep notes in. &C.

[*page 3*] **Sunday 10th** This morning I felt some what unwell. [♱]
But the congregation collected and seats were prepared in a grove
there not being room in the house. I opened meeting and addressed them for two hours on the Covenants the two places of
deliverance, The evidences of the book of Mormon, and the two
gatherings at Zion and Jerusalem.[16] &C &C. But the people were
[scattering] situated scattering and the wind rose which made it
extremely hard speaking. I dismissed. The church met again at
3 P. M. I addressed them about 20 minutes on 2 Peter 1·· 5 - 7[17] &C
then [open] we opened the door for members. Elizabeth Smith
(the wife of Eden) came forward, the church received her (she
had once been a member).[18] we immediately went to the river and
I immersed her— We then repaired to the house and again
address[ed] them on the nature of the laying on of hands &c and
also an exortation to the whole: We then united in prayr and while
brother Levi was praying I laid my hands on and confirmed those
who had been baptized— We then partook of the **'supper—'**[19]
and dismissed——

Monday 11th. This morning I felt some simptoms of the **flux**[20] which increased on me very fast until it became very painful—— In this situation I continued drinking teas and taking mild medicines until Saturday following. I took a dose of castor Oil which worked me very freely and next day I was some better——

Sunday 17th The brethren met and bro Levi exorted them from Rom[ans] 8.[21] &c. I was enabled to speak to them alittle [*page 4*] by holding to the bed post and I also interpreted for bro. Lewis Zabriskie who spoke some in '**Tongues**'[22] to the edification of the Church— I also spoke to them some and then exorted them to humble themselves and seek the gifts.[23] They appointed another mee for Wednesday 3. P. M.—— My disease declined and I gained strength, a little——

Wednesday 20th I attended the app. and after the meeting was opened I gave them a desertation of about an hour's length on the 12 Ch. of 1 Cor.[24] and closed with an Oration in the gift of tongues— The effect was tremendious on the congregation both believing and unbelieving—— Bro. N. Hubbard manifested also by speaking that he had received the gift of tongues, which I interpreted for him.

Friday I with bro. Lewis was called to visit Sister Susan Zabriskie (who had an unbelieving Husband) who had been taken with the bloody flux— we prayed with and laid hands on her.[25] She was healed. But the same evening a menial Doctor of the world who had been called came in and went to work. She became immediately worse and her case is doubtful——

Sunday 24th The brethren and sisters assembled again at bro. N. Hubbard's and I preached to them 2 hours on the Priesthood and on the Laws of Zion. We met again at 4 P. M. for Sacrament—— I did not expect to speak. But bro Levi being very sick and not able to attend and Lewis unwell I had to administer. We had a good meeting. [*page 5*] a door was opened for members and Harris Park arose and testified that he was willing to take upon him the name of Christ and was received, we immediately repaired to the river and I immersed him. Then dismissd the people, after appointing another meeting for next Wednesday 3 P. M.

Tuesday I was called to pray for old sister Mcman. She is between 70 and 80 years. She had the Phlhisis.[26] I laid hands on her and she experienced some relief——

Wednesday 27th Today a considerable congregation attended, and I read the 11th Ch of Isaiah[27] & addressed them for 2 hours on the gathering of the Jews to old Jerusalem and [and] the attendent consequenses: Then I exorted all present to be prepared for the coming of the Lord, which was soon at hand and I closed by repeating some of my exortation in an other tongue—— Then we gave a privilege to those who wished to join with us—— And three manifested their willingness to take upon them the name of the Lord— [They] (viz) Eden Smith,[28] Charles Curtis and Elizabeth Cady. They were received and we went to the water and I immersed them— then dismiss'd.

Last Monday brother Lewis Zabriskie called the Elders together with myself and expressed his intention and determination to lay down his license[29] and authority as an Elder in the church and stand as private member—— He said that he did not doubt the work, neither did he doubt but that God had called him and blessed him in the ministry, But he thought and felt as though it was an easier life to live a private member, and he believed that the Lord was willing to grant every man the desire of his own heart— Therefore [*page 6*] desired not to be a **mark** for the wicked but to stand behind the screne in the place of a member. Neither of the Elders seemed willing to his course. We reasoned with him until he agreed to keep his License and in a few days he came before the church and made his acknowledgements that he had been out of the way, and under the influence of and an evil power——, But was now determined to go his whole **length** in the cause——

Saturday 30th we had a confirmation meeting[30] at bro. L. Jones' at 4 P. M., there were none attended but the brothren and sisters and a few who seemed to be earnestly seeking the Kingdom. I spoke about one hour and a half on the rise and establishment of the church and on the nature and efficacy of its ordinances— Then I confirmed the three Who had been baptized—— we had some speaking in **tongues** & the Interpretation also—— Bro. Levi had been very sick but his health was somewhat improving—— Sister Jones who had been somewhat afflicted some years asked us to lay hands on her—— Bro. Lewis and I did so—— and she was healed.

Sunday 31st At eleven Oclock the house was filled— Bro Harris an Elder from over the Waubash opened the meeting by prayr. I then arose and addressed the people for 2 hours and a 1/2 on the Antiquity; validity and usefulness of the scriptures—— and then compared the evidences of the Bible those of the book of Mormon &C &C— At 4 P. M. the church assembled for sacrament and the house being again filled with people and the mee. being opened by bro Lewis, I again [*page 7*] arose and addressed them about an hour & 1/4 on the situation or **confusion** of the world and on the faith once delivered to the **saints** and exorted them to seek it— Then administered the Sac[rament] to the saints and opened a door for the reception of members— Elisha Hill and his wife Catrin (who had once belonged to the church but had been cut off) manifested in humility that they wished to return—— The church received them and we went immediately to the water and I immersed them. A few brethren and sisters assembled (about dark) at bro. Eden Smith's and I spoke to them again about an hour & 1/4 on charity and its effects and on the ordinance of laying on of hands, and then those two were confirmed by the laying on of my hands—— We also had some speaking in **tongues** & bro. Lewis received the **Interpretation** and interpreted partly what was said—— We made no farther app. for this week for I desired to rest and try to gain strength in order to go on my journey— But I read and studdied and wrote and visited among the brethren in order to strengthen them. &C. I and bro. Noah Hubbard were called upon to pray for sister Hubbard who was very sick. we prayed for and laid hands on her: She was healed and declared that she [was] had better in a few days than she had had in eleven years——

Sunday 7th September. We had a very large Congregation and I arose at 11 o'clock and addressed them for 1 hour & a 1/2 on the nature [of] and characters of false & true prophets, on the nature of the gathering to Zion—— and of the attendant results. &c. &c— The church assembled again at 4 P. M. Bro. Lewis opened the meeting and I addressed them by way of teaching and exortation about an hour— All the brethren and [*page 8*] Sisters who were then present, arose, one by one, and manifested their **faith** [and] **in** the book of Mormon and in the work of the Lord and also their fellowship with each other and their determinations to do good and keep all the Commandments—— I could not discover a jar in the feelings of any—— I again arose and expressed my joy at seeing their union, and went on to express my peculiar feelings in exortation, in as much as it was the last sacrament that I expected to administer to them on this visit. much feeling was manifest by the tears which flowed— The room seemed at once to be filled with Light and all hearts seemed to rejoice—— We all partook [partook] of the bread and wine in the bonds of union—— We then opened a door for the reception of members and Rachael Smith, Philip Curtis and Sally Curtis manifested their determinations before the church and were received (they had once been in the church). We went to the river and I immersed them. Some returned to the house and we had quite a good little meeting— the brethren and Sisters who had received the gift of Tongues manifested it and bro. Lewis Zabriskie interpreted for them very clearly—— Eight had received the gift while I was among them. We app. another met for next Wednesday 3 P. M.

Wednesday 10th The congregation collected. I opened the met and spoke to them about 2 hours. I first read Acts 20th[31] and spoke of the Apostles travels, Labours, afflictions and the way and manner they built up churches &C and then of the false religions of the day &C. I then read that part of the Covenants & Articles relating to our building up churches &C. Then I spoke particularly of of [*sic*] the duties of the various officers spoken of in the Covenants and set them plainly before the church so that I think they generally understood and rejoiced in the order of God. [*page 9*] We then gave liberty to any who wished to join us to manifest their feelings. Henry Bailey sen[ior]. expressed his feelings to the Church and was received & I immersed him and then we continued our meet until about midnight— Eden Smith was app. by the voice of the church and ordained an Elder under my hands. John Cooper was also app. and ordained a Teacher under my hands. Philip Curtis, Rachael Smith, Sally Curtis and Henry Bailey were confirmed by the laying on of my hands and all the Church expressed a desire to be blessed and they all kneeled in mighty but silent prayr and I went around among them and laid my hands on them and prayed for them and blessed them in the name of the Lord—— And some of them were really blessed while others did not experience so much. I then delivered to them an exortation (in which I bid them farewell) to live in peace and the God of love and peace should be with them—— Bro. Levi who had been so sick was at the meet and when hands were laid on him he was healed and expressed that he was well except weakness—— Four of the church received a recommend to go up to the Land of Missouri[32] (viz) Charles & Mary Ann Hubbard, and Charles & Sally Curtis,—— After having preached 18 times among the brethren and received and baptized 13 and after having some great blessings and good meets among them and after they were much strengthened and built up in the kno knowledge of the truth, I [tho] found it my privilege to leave them and pursue my journey to the East. The brethren and sisters while here were good to me as far as I needed both in afflictions and in [*page 10*] health. They gave me a **hat**, worth $6.00 and a pair of new **shoes** worth $2.00 and I had repairs to my ~~portmanteaus~~ saddle of $2.25 and a number of small gifts and presents and when I bid sister Jane Clark fare well she put $2 into my hand. &C—&C—— My horse did not get over his founder and I sold him to H. Bailey for $55.00 due the first of next May. I left the note with bro. Lewis Zabriskie and I borrowed of him $15 and sent it to Emiline by C. Hubbard. I swapped the horse that brother Joseph left with me to bro. E. Smith and got one to ride to the East——

Thursday 11th I started to the Danville Church. I staid with bro Jacob Morris all night. He gave me $2. to carry to the Editors of the Star.[33]

On Friday eve bro. Lewis and I reached bro. Saml Swinfords, the Elder who has the care of the Danville Church— The brethren seemed rejoiced to see us and three appts were [m] quickly circulated for Saturday eve 4 P. M. for Sunday 11 A. M. and 4 P M——

Saturday 13. only a few collected but they paid very good attention while I addresed them about 1 hour and a 1/2 on the confusion of the world and of the faith once delivered to the **saints** from 2 Peter 1^{34} &C.

Sunday 14. A few collected again at bro. J. Chandler's and bro. Lewis opened the meet and spoke a few minutes, I then spoke about 1 1/2 hours on the Testimonies of the book of Mormon on Covenants and Laws of the church &C— And at 4 P. M. I spoke again about 2 hours on the two places of deliverance and the two gatherings at Zion and Jerusalem as the preparatory work for the coming of the saviour &C &C. There seemed to be great interest felt in the subject and particularly among the few brethren and sisters. [*page 11*] After the ~~brethren~~ congregation were dismissed the brethren continued and we had quite an interesting time among ourselves— They seemed very much cheered and awakened to a sense of their duty. I hated to leave them——

Monday 15th I started to Kirtland. I crossed the Waubash at Covington, Fountain Co. Indiana. Thence to Indianopolis. Here I bought S. Whelpley's Compend[ium] of History for $1.25—Thence to Dayton Ohio. Thence [to] 5 miles to Watervliet a Shaker villags. here I stayed one day and two nights, learning the principles and practices of this singularly strange people^{35}—

Thence to Columbus—Thence to Cleveland—Thence ~~to~~ I reached Kirtland on ~~the~~ Saturday the 27 of Sept. I found the brethren generally well and my health had also very much improved— (I had only pr[e]ached once on the way on Friday eve the about 12 miles west of Dayton at Steels tavern.) Here I stayed intel

Sunday the 5th Oct This day [F] the brethren called on me to preach, and I delivered a discourse of about 1 1/4 hours on Luke

6-20-26³⁶ &C to general yea universal satisfaction to all— While here I had me a new cloke made that cost me about $14.00. This I did on credit——

Wednesday 8th [The/~~day~~/This morning] brother Joseph told that it was my duty to go to the Florence church and fill a promise that he had made for to go himself³⁷—— Accordingly I prepared & started with F[rederick] G. Williams who was going to Cleveland³⁸ in a Derbon.³⁹ We reached Cleveland in the afternoon which gave me sufficient time to visit the Lake shores and to view the scenery of the place——&c.

Thursday 9th I took a seat in the stage for [*page 12*] Elyria Lorain Co. I reached it in the afternoon. Thence on foot to the Amherst church⁴⁰—— They had app. a prayr meeting, but the eve being somewhat inclement only a few attended. brother A[lmon] Babbit opened the meeting by prayr. I then addressed them about an hour on various points, with exortation &c. The meeting was then dismissed- Two more meetings being app one for Saturday eve and one for Sunday. I found by enquiry of the Elders that the church was in a difficult situation on account of divisions among them, and Jealousies, &c. The Church consisted of 38 - members.

Friday & Saturday I spent in trying to get them to settle their differences and forgive each other— Though I believe I effected but little in consequence of the coldness and backwardness [f] among them— It was big **I** and little **u**. You are in fault but I a'n't &c. &C.

Saturday-evening quite a number collected & I addressed them from 2 Peter 1st Chapter⁴¹ &C for about 1 hour & 3/4— Though my spirit seemed somewhat bound in consequence of the dissensions among the brethren— But I laboured hard to stir them up.

Sunday, 1[~~3~~]2 a small congregation collected at a schoolhouse. Elder L[orin] Babbit opened by prayr. I then addressed them about 2 hours on the establishment of the Kingdom of Christ, on the evidences of the book of Mormon and on the evidinces and nature of the establishment of the Church of the 'latter day saints'[42] and closed by giving a desertation on the Covenants and Articles of the Church &C—— We did not break bread because there was such a general division in the Church.[43] We app. another mee. at Mr— [*page 13*] Barney's for candle light— I attended and spoke to them about 1 hour & 1/2 and I had great liberty and demonstration of the spirit in laying the Gospel and its ordinances open before them and also the confusion of the world with the traditions & commandments of men. We app. a meeting for the officers of the Church to receive instructions concerning the various points of their duty &C. on Monday eve also a prayr meetings for the Thursday eve's succeeding— and also a two days meeting for next Saturday and Sunday in Florence——

Monday 13th To day I became acquainted with a sister Eliza Byfield formerly E Daugherty—— Monday 13 in the evening the Elders Judea Griffeth, Lorin Babbit & Alman Babbit and Priests, Edson Barney and Teachers Leman Potter & (Hiram Griffeth (absent) Deacons Royal Barney & Duty Griffeth— all attended at bro. D. Griffeth's and I lectu[r]ed them in great plainness from the Covenants on their several duties as officers in the church of christ for about 2 hours— They seemed much edified and promised to try to do their duty—

Tuesday 14th I could not find a bro. but that was too much engaged to go and take me to Florence. consequently I traveled 14 miles on foot and having the night before taken cold and not being very well— I was very sore and tired— The brethren in Florence seemed to receive me joyfully and appointed a meeting for the next evening——

Wednsd 15. I was quite unwell but kept about— I visited brother Emer Harris who was very much afflicted with a rhuematic affection in his hip and thigh &C.—— [*page 14*] The Church in Florence[44] consisted of 50 members, 2 of whom were High-Priests, 4 Elders, 1 Priest, 1 Teacher— and 1 Deacon—— I found them rather low in spirits— only a few attended our meeting this evening and I was still quite unwell but I had prayed fervently unto the

Lord that I might be healed and that I might benefit and edify his children— I arose and adressed them 1 hour and 40 minutes on faith, hope, and charity and their good affects upon society—— My system was healed and I rejoiced much in my exortation to the brethren——They seemed cheered and somewhat animated—— The remainder of the week until Saturday I spent in reading and visiting among the brethren & sisters— in stir[r]ing them up &c.

Saturday 18th was a very disagreeable rainy day but notwithstanding a few of the brethren attended at the schoolhouse and I made a few observations to them and had pra[y]rs, &c.

Sunday 19th The day was fair but cold—— We assembled again at the schoolhouse and I preached to them about 1 hour and 40 minutes on the evidences of thruth, on the Kingdom of Jesus &c. We then broke bread and agreed to meet again at candle light at bro. Andersons——We met and the house was full. I arose and addressed them again 1.30. on the confusion on the earth—on the plainness of the Gospel and on the Authority which God has given to his church. I then exorted all to repent and turn to the Lord &c. bro. Milow Andrews delivered an exortation & prayr ~~good~~ &c which was very good on the occasion. [*page 15*] I appointed another meeting at the same place for [~~nex~~] the next Tuesday evening— one in Brownhelm for Wednesday eve and one in Amherst for Thursday eve and one in Florence schoolhouse for the next Sunday—

We met on Tuesday eve. The house was full composed of believers and unbeliev[e]rs. I addressed them about 1 hour and 1/2 -mainly on the Authority of the church of the 'Latter day Saints' and on the order and government of the church as laid down in the covenants in Com[mandments] 24-29-42.[45] All the brethren seemed to be pleased and well satisfied with the order of Messiah's Kingdom.

Wednesday evening (22) Bro. John Daily and myself attended in Brownhelm at George Ewings. among 20 or 30 brethren and sisters (as once was) only about a dozen attended—— and in all my ministry— all my traveling and all my preaching— I never was more difficulted to know what to say— But I arose trusting in God and spoke about 3/4 of an hour in which I presented to them their case, just as it was, having forgotten that they were purged from their old sins, without God and without hope in the world— In truth it did not seem to me that there were any brethren— true brethren here——

Thursday 23 I wasked [walked] about 7 mls to Amherst, there were considerable many considering the place turned out to our evening meeting— I was quite unwell with head-ache &C. notwithstanding which I arose and addressed them about one hour on the nature of the preparatory for the Millennium and the gathering of the righteous together to prepare the supper of the Lamb &C. Bro. Milow Andrews delivered an exortation to them to give heed &C. We app. a church meeting for next day at 9 O'clock in order to settle some existing difficulties among the [breth] Sisters here——

[*page 16*] **Friday 24th** We assembled and commenced business about 10 Oclock— I was appointed moderator by unanimous vote and I delivered some very appropriate remarks from Commandment 65 (meaning chapter) 10 - 15[46] on the nature of forgiving one another &C. The difficulty was between Emiline & Griffeth of the one part and   Barney the other— Elders present Judea Griffeth and Alman Babbit— Amherst and Moses Dailey & Milow Andress. [of] Florence, and Ezra Strong, Rockport— &c—— We set between 5 and 6 hours on close examination and after all had been said. we all as a conference concluded that it was the most little and pittiful thing that ever created so much trouble in a chu[r]ch—— We settled it to general satisfation of all except one woman and I returned with the brethren to Florence the same evening——

Saturday 25 It commenced raining this morning and rained pretty much all day. But yet the brethren had a church meeting and the most of them collected at Sister Patton's[47]—— Th[e]y had been dealing with some members who had been cold, indifferent and had not attended meetings— But they all either came forward or sent,

& (except one) and made satisfaction— There was considerable said by myself and others on the nature of church business &C— All seemed encouraged and cheered.

Sunday 26 It still continued to rain. But yet a number of brethren and sisters Collected again at sister Patton's room and I addressed them for about one hour & 30 minutes, respecting the Covenants of Abraham and Joseph and of the two places of deliverance in the last days &C. A number of the church then expressed their feelings by way of confessions & rejoicings &C, &C,—— We broke bread and then closed but [*page 17*]

[*The following text is in parentheses at the top of the page.*]

To Moses Daley
(An extract of a letter sent by me to the Florence Church and vicinity—— 'I have inquired at the hand of the Lord concerning this matter' 'and have engaged our bro. Wm E. McLelin to visit you who will teach you concerning the duty of the churches relative to Zion. I want therefore that you should receive him in the name of Lord, and uphold him by your prayr of faith, and in the name of the Lord of truth he will do you much good —Josep. Smith Jr)

appointed another or a prayr meeting at Brother J. Dailey's for candle light &c. I attended and took the lead of the meeting— Bro. M. Andress exorted some time, and then bro. Howard spoke and prayed and a number of others. I delivered a very animated discourse on the Ennity of Jew and Gentile—— and then of Gentile and Jew—— Short, but had much of the spirit and power of God— The brethren and sisters seemed much rejoiced and stirred up to a sence of duty——

Monday 27th I attended my app. this evening in Vermillion at bro. Stones— had quite a collection, and I addressed about two hours on the **faith** and usages of the ancient saints. Bro. J. Daley went with me (He is Preist in the Florence Church) and we tarried with a Mr Cleveland who was or said he was much pleased with the preaching——

Tuesday 28th This evening I attended our app. for prayr meeting at bro. M Daley's— Bro. Levi Hancock on his way from Missouri came in this afternoon and attended with us— The room was very much crowded—— I felt quite unwell— But yet— There were so ~~m~~ many who had come in who wished to [*page 18*] hear me preach— The brethren insisted ~~als~~ also— Finally I consented although I felt so much worn down— Bro. Levi opened the meeting by prayr, and I addressed the congregation about 2 hours on the various sectarion quotations of scripture— on the dealings of God with men, on the plainness of the Gospel and on the two Priesthoods[48] &C, &C,— But little more was said. We made another app. for prayr mee on Thursday eve. at brother Emer Harris's—

Wednesday 29th It was quite cold and snowed considerable. I had an app. at Amherst. The brethren furnished me with a horse and I started about 3. O' and reached there about dusk. The brethren and Sisters collected with a very few others— And brother Judea Griffeth opened the meeting by prayr and I addressed them about [~~1 hour~~] one hour and a 1/2 in comparing the Bible and the book of Mormon together and showing the happy results of the union of these two records in the work of the the [*sic*] gathering— In truth I believe I preached the greatest sermon for its length that I ever preached in life.

Thursday morning bro J. G[riffeth] presented me with this subscription with the money—— "We the members of the church of Christ in Amherst having considered the circumstances of our beloved brother Wm E. McLelin in as much as he has been labouring with us in the Gospel in Word and in Doctrine, for some time past; believe it to be our duty to assist him. We therefore subscribe t[hese] several sums annexed to our names for his benefit"——

	$ {cts}		$ {cts
Alman Babbit	{50 }	Emiline Cranney	{25
Almira Babbit	{50 }	Philander Cranney	{25

Royal Barney	{50 }	Edson Barney	{25
Duty Griffeth	{50 }	Jacob Chapman	{25
Leman Potter	{50 }	Mary Ann Griffeth	{25
Truman Jackson	{50 }	Judah Griffeth	{25
		Eliza Byfield	{13
	3{00 }		$1{63
	1{63 }		
	$4{63 }		

[*page 19*] Thursday 30th I returned to Florence but was quite unwell in consequence of fatigue &c.

Friday 31. This eve the most of the brethren met according to app, And I tried to get brother Harris or bro. Carter to take the lead of the meeting but no. Nothwithstanding my weakness across my breast, stomach, and bowels; I had still to go forward—— I was much blessed in exortation and was healed of my infirmity. We had a good meeting. A number of confessions were made of Coldness and a want of attention to prayrs &c.

November. Sunday 2. Florence.

This morning at 11 Oclock the church met at the schoolhouse—— And I addressed them about 2 hours in establishing the book of Mormon, not only from prophecy but also from reasonable circumstances &C—— We had intermition of 20 minutes and then came together again and I again addressed the congregation one hour on the 12 Ch. of 1 Cor[49] &c. We then broke bread among the saints & dismissd to come to gether again at candle lighting Br G. H. Carter preached about one hour and I again addressed them about one hour by way of a farewell— The saints appeared much animated and engaged in the cause of Christ——"

Tuesday 4 Moses Daley gave me this subscription——

John Daley	$ {1.25}		
Moses Daley	{1.00}	Gideon H. Carter	{ 25
Jared Starr	{ '50}	Phibe Ann Patton	{ 6 1/4
John Anderson	{ '50}	Celia Anderson	{ '5
Richard Howard	{ '30}	Elizabeth Wood	{ 12
Gideon D. Wood	{ 44}		{ 48 1/2

4{ 19} $4 - 37¹/2

{ 18}1/2⁵⁰

[*page 20*] **Tuesday 4th** This morning I bid all Farewell and left the Florence church and started for Kirtland— I got into the s[t]age in Amherst. Thence to Elyra, thence to Cleveland, thence to Chagrin, thence to Kirtland—about 65— It cost me $3-12¹/2 the trip——

Thursday— Friday & Saturday I spent in talking with the Heads &C——

Sunday 9. I went to meeting in a large schoolhouse—— It was supposed that there were about 500 persons present. Br Lyman Johnson opened the meeting and spoke about 3/4 of an hour on the 2 Chapter of 1 Corinthians⁵¹— He had but little Liberty. I then arose and addressed them one hour on the principles of "Going on to perfection"⁵² and after intermission I assisted old father John Smith in administering the sacrament—— The services of the day were closed by going to the water and bro. J. F. Boynton's baptizing a man, A number were heard to say 'It was the best meeting that I ever was at in Kirtland.' &C——

Monday 10. this day I wrote a letter to Emiline.

Tuesday I made preparations to start to the East on a preaching tour with a bro. NewCome— But I was called into the council chamber in connexion with bro. Boynton and it was decided that it was not wisdom for us to go so far— But that we must Labour in the regions round about—— Bro S[ydney] R[igdon] also gave me a most tremendious setting out about my awkward Jestures &C.[53] Our place of Labour was pointed out to be in Painesville and the regions round about——

[*page 21*] Wednesday [~~13~~] 12th Bro. John F. Boynton and I left Kirtland for Painesville by enquiry. without much trouble we obtained an app. in the Methodist Chapel[54] for Sat, eve;

Thursday we went to Fairport and we obtained an app. there for Sunday— thence to Richmond and we obtained an app. there for Friday evening— Here we found bro - E. Fuller and tarried with him.

Fri. eve, the we[a]ther was inclement, cold and rainy, only a few turned out— Bro. J. preached to them from Gal 1.. 6-10[55] about and hour. It was a fine discourse but he never mentioned the book of mormon once.

Saturday eve we attended our app in Painsv. a respectable congregation attended and I address[ed] them about one hour and a half on the nature of the Kingdom of Christ— I had good liberty. We made another app. at the same place for the next Tues. eve— [S] We spent our time for Study while here with bro. H. Kingsbury of this Place.

Sunday 16th We attended at F[air] P[ort] But there was great carelessness whether we preached or not— The congregation was small & scattering and inattentive— Bro. L. Johnson came from Kirt. and attended with us— I had expected bro. John to preach but he would not—— I arose and addressed them for about an hour or tried to, but it was poor preach—— We left no other app. for the place, but returned to bro. K[ingsbury]'s and took dinner—— This afternoon we went up to spend the evening with Sister Howe— Her husband was absent— The neighbours collected in to the amount of about 20 and we had quite a good

meeting. we spoke to them about an hour. They seemed interested— [~~They~~] We had their attention.

———

[*page 22*] Monday 17th This eve we attended at Richmond but the
would— be— holy Presbyterions— got the key to the schoolhouse; and would not let us in. consequently we did not preach;
but while here we found a quiet home with our bro. Fuller— Lord
have mercy on this wicked place.

Tuesday we returned to Painesvill and at eve attended our app.
The weather was rainy— only a few attend. bro. J[ohn] preached
to them one hour on the fall of the Jews and their scattering: also
their ingathering and the attendant results &c— I made a few
remarks—There were some who seemed to be willing to hear the
truth. We made no further app. for no person asked us to—

Wednesday 19. we returned through the rain and mud to Kirtland.
And I found a letter in the office from (my dear) little Emiline.
It contained much that filled me with Sorrow—— because of their
afflictions &c[56]— I read it to bro. Jos and his heart was much
affected because of the affliction of Zion— And he called a few of
the most faithful High-Priests together and we had a Solemn
meeting[57] and prayr that God might spare the innocent in Zion
and hasten their deliverance,, We had a very affecting time in-
deed= The brethren also while They were together choose Jos,
Sidney, Frederick and Oliver as trustees of the high school in Kirtland and they ingaged me for $18 per month to assist in instruct-
ing in s'd school[58]——

Monday 24th Nov. This morning I commenced boarding with bro.
Lyman Johnson and here I calculate to continue this winter—
reading, studying &C. I also wrote a letter to day to bro. Saml
Mc=[Lellin.]

December the 2nd I visited A. Blair.

Wednesday 3nd I visited A. Allen——

Painesville, Ohio, in 1846. These public buildings are typical of the halls in which McLellin and his companions preached to various congregations in this area. Drawn by Henry Howe. Courtesy Lake County Historical Society.

Main Street, Painesville, Ohio, 1850. Courtesy Lake County Historical Society.

Friday 5th This eve I attended my app. in Huntsburg.

In this town I continued until Saturday the 13th during which I preached 12 times and baptized 6 persons.[59]

Sunday 14 President Smith preached [*page 23*] three hours in Kirt during which he exposed the Methodist Dicipline in its black deformity[60] and called upon the Elders in the power of the spirit of God to expose the creeds & confessions of men—— His discourse was animated and Pointed, against all Creeds of men[61]——

Tuesday 16th I wrote a letter to Emiline.

Friday 19th This eve I attended my app. in Huntsburg at Mr Moss'. I had but little liberty and after I got through two campbellites made a very weak effort to oppose me but I made them ashamed of themselves before I got through with them—— I preached twice on Saturday, three times on Sunday and baptized two.

On Saturday 27th I re[c]d a letter—— from——Emiline.

On Monday 22nd The school commenced in Kirtland.[62] W[illiam] E. M[cLellin] & Elder Burdock teachers. J[oseph] S[mith,] S[idney] R[igdon,] F[rederick] G. W[illiams,] & O[liver] C[owdery] Trustees——[63]

Jan. 17. I & Elder D. Patten went to Huntsburg— Eld. P. preached Saturday and I baptized   Dudley and he preached again at night again on 1st Ch Eph.[64]

Sun. he preached again on John 14 - 2 -[65] and administ[er]d the bread and wine[66]——. And We then b[l]essed some children[67]—— and then went to the water and bap. R. Barker and then confirmed the two at T. Fonse's and ordained Noah Faunce Priest——

Jan 22nd I recd a letter from my brother—— Samuel McLellin——

[*page 24*] Jan 17th I again went to Huntsburg and preached five times, baptized two and retu[r]ned home the 20th and[68] on the 18th March I visited H[untsburgh] again and preach[e]d 4 times and recd a challenge from a Mr J. M. Tracy to hold a public discussion with him. I accepted it and we appointed Friday [and Satur] the 27 to meet.[69]

and on Monday the 23nd I returned to Kirtland and

on Thursday I in company with J[oseph] S[mith] Jr., L[yman] J[ohnson], D. W. P[atten], P[arley] P. P[ratt], (J[ohn] F. B[oynton]) and others others [*sic*] returned to H[untsburgh][70] and

on Friday & Saturday we spoke about 12 hours thirty minutes each alternately[71]——— And on Saturday eve I baptized Jotham Gardner who was about 88 years of age and his companion also———

Presdt J. S. preached about 3 hours on Sunday[72] and

on Monday morning we had a mee. and I immersed 4.[73] We returned home again

and on the 10 of April I and Elder J. F. Boynton went to H[untsburgh] again and staid till the 17 during which we preached 9 times and I bap. 4 more, Noah Faunce being ordained an Elder under my hand and Hiram Cory, Teacher.[74]

NOTES

[1] McLellin was in Missouri during the fourteen months that elapsed between the end of his missionary tour with Parley P. Pratt and the beginning of the tour described in Journal IV. This was a period of great trauma for the Saints who had gathered in Independence and its environs. The Missouri settlers who were not Mormon, apparently fearing that they would be overwhelmed by Joseph Smith's followers, attacked the Mormon leadership in July 1833, destroying the press that was publishing the *Evening and Morning Star,* causing the store that served the Saints to cease doing business, and subjecting Bishop Edward Partridge to the indignity of

being stripped, tarred, and feathered. Under extreme duress, church leaders were forced to sign an agreement that they would leave Jackson County by the end of the year. The situation, however, was so volatile that a brutal assault at the end of October put not only their leaders but the main body of Saints to flight. A bounty was offered for McLellin's capture, and he was imprisoned briefly under dreadful conditions and released upon agreement to leave Jackson County. Most of the Mormons, including McLellin, his wife Emeline, and infant daughter, then settled in Clay County.

When news of these outrages reached Kirtland, the Prophet's first response was to advise the injured Saints to seek legal redress. Joseph Smith instructed them "that it is not the will of the Lord for you to sell your lands in Zion, if means can possibly be procured for your sustenance without." Joseph Smith, Jr., *History of The Church of Jesus Christ of Latter-day Saints,* ed. B. H. Roberts, 2d ed. rev., 7 vols. (Salt Lake City: Deseret Book, 1971), 1:450 (hereafter cited as *HC*). However, McLellin sold thirty acres of his property "into the hands of the enemy, and [would have sold] seven acres more . . . to the enemy if a brother [Church member] had not come forward and purchased it and paid him his money" (*HC* 2:39). Despite this act, McLellin was part of the five-man committee responsible for representing the Mormons in negotiations with the Missourians (*HC* 2:99, 107). When the avenue of negotiation, however, appeared to be closed because Missouri authorities were in sympathy with the hostile non-Mormon residents of Jackson County, Joseph Smith received a revelation that "Zion shall not be moved out of her place, notwithstanding her children are scattered" (D&C 101:17). Received in mid-December 1833, and published on a broadside either sometime later that month or in January 1834, this revelation (D&C 101) contained a parable given "that you may know [the Lord's] will concerning the redemption of Zion" (D&C 101:43). Although expressed in the veiled language of parable, it called the Saints to "take all the strength of mine house, . . . my warriors, my young men, and they that are of middle age also among all my servants . . . [and] get ye straightway into my land; break down the walls of mine enemies; throw down the tower, and scatter their watchmen" (D&C 101:55-57). This revelation, along with one received on February 24, 1834 (D&C 103), became Smith's warrant to organize and lead an unofficial armed force, "Zion's Camp," out from Kirtland to "redeem Zion." Upon reaching Missouri, this para-military force, much weakened by dissent and cholera, failed to reclaim Mormon lands in Jackson County and was disbanded. See Lance D. Chase, "Zion's Camp," *Encyclopedia of Mormonism,* ed. Daniel H. Ludlow, 5 vols. (New York: Macmillan, 1992), 4:1627-29 (hereafter cited as *EM*).

During his brief stay in Missouri, Joseph Smith organized a Council of High Priests, June 23, 1834. In a subsequent meeting on July 3, the Prophet named the council's officers, a president, two assistant presidents, and twelve councilors, of which McLellin was one. On July 7, the council sustained the officers Joseph had chosen. At this same meeting, it was decided that McLellin should go to the East. See Donald Q. Cannon and Lyndon W. Cook, eds., *Far West Record* (Salt Lake City: Deseret Book, 1983), 68-73.

[2] Although the minutes of the High Priests Council meeting in which McLellin was assigned to go East do not include the wording of his appointment, ten of the Missouri brethren who had been called on June 23 to go to Kirtland to receive "their endowment . . . with power from on high" were also directed to "proclaim the everlasting Gospel and assist in gathering up the strength of the Lords house." Cannon and Cook, *Far West Record*, 68-69. See also *HC* 2:112-13. McLellin's use of the identical words suggests that this same phrase was used when he was called on the mission described in Journal IV. The phrase was also used in three revelations received by Joseph Smith in 1833 and 1834 in connection with Zion's Camp and the difficulties in Missouri (D&C 101:55; 103:22, 30; 105:16).

[3] William and Emeline's first child, Charles William McLellin. See page 303 below. Compare Susan Easton Black, *Membership of the Church of Jesus Christ of Latter-day Saints, 1830-1848*, 50 vols. (Provo, Utah: Religious Studies Center, Brigham Young University, 1989), 30:378.

[4] Thomas Marsh had a house in the eastern part of Clay County. *HC* 2:135.

[5] It is likely that this speech was based on the revelation the Prophet had received concerning the deliverance of Zion (D&C 105).

[6] This is a form of promissory benediction pronounced at the end of a sermon. See Mosiah 5:15 and D&C 68:12.

[7] Hitchcock's request refers to a revelation received by Joseph Smith in November 1831 which describes Orson Hyde's call and ordination to "proclaim the everlasting gospel, by the Spirit of the living God, from people to people, and from land to land . . . reasoning with and expounding all scriptures unto them" (D&C 68:1), using Hyde as an example for all ordained to the priesthood. This revelation (which came in response to an inquiry from McLellin, Luke and Lyman Johnson, and Hyde) defined the gift of "utterance" to those who are ordained as follows: "Whatsoever they shall speak when moved upon by the Holy Ghost shall be scripture, shall be the will of the Lord, shall be the mind of the Lord, shall be the word of the Lord, shall be the voice of the Lord, and the power of God unto salvation" (D&C 68:4). Hitchcock probably asked for the "gift of utterance to perform the duties of his calling" because he had not been ordained. He had been approved for the office of high priest on September 26, 1833, but was not ordained until August 7, 1834. Cannon and Cook, *Far West Record*, 66, 95.

[8] Joseph Smith wrote, "On the 9th I started for Kirtland, in company with my brother Hyrum, Frederick G. Williams, William E. M'Lellin and others, in a wagon." *HC* 2:135. Joseph described this trip to Kirtland as "a tedious journey from the midst of enemies; mobs, cholera, and excessively hot weather." *HC* 2:139.

⁹The words "Journal" and "By W. E. McLelin" are apparently in a different ink and hand than McLellin's.

¹⁰Joseph Smith also mentioned McLellin's illness: "I was obliged to leave . . . in Illinois, . . . Brother William E. M'Lellin, who was sick. We expect when he recovers that he will come to Kirtland. He was very humble, and I entertain no doubt as to his standing while he continues so." *HC* 2:146.

¹¹Frederick G. Williams, a member of the presidency of the Church, was a doctor; he practiced especially with herbal medicines. Lyndon W. Cook, *The Revelations of the Prophet Joseph Smith* (Salt Lake City: Deseret Book, 1985), 104; and Nancy Clement Williams, *After One Hundred Years* (Independence, Mo.: Zion's Printing and Publishing, 1951), 51.

¹²At about this time, the Eugene congregation consisted of fifty-five members and was presided over by Elder Levi Jones. Communication from John Murdock, *Messenger and Advocate* 1 (November 1834): 25.

¹³Noah Hubbard lived in Eugene, Indiana, on the Wabash River. John Murdock Journal, 16, on LDS Historical Library CD Rom, 2d ed. (Provo, Utah: Infobases, 1993).

¹⁴See note 37, Journal I above.

¹⁵2 Peter 1:1–4 reads as follows:

> Simon Peter, a servant and an apostle of Jesus Christ, to them that have obtained like precious faith with us through the righteousness of God and our Saviour Jesus Christ: Grace and peace be multiplied unto you through the knowledge of God, and of Jesus our Lord, According as his divine power hath given unto us all things that pertain unto life and godliness, through the knowledge of him that hath called us to glory and virtue: Whereby are given unto us exceeding great and precious promises: that by these ye might be partakers of the divine nature, having escaped the corruption that is in the world through lust.

¹⁶For more of McLellin's views concerning this topic, see McLellin's articles on "The Places of Gathering" and "The Covenant Lands" in McLellin, *Ensign of Liberty*, 24–29, 71–76. See also note 40, Journal I above.

¹⁷2 Peter 1:5–7 reads as follows: "And beside this, giving all diligence, add to your faith virtue; and to virtue knowledge; And to knowledge temperance; and to temperance patience; and to patience godliness; And to godliness brotherly kindness; and to brotherly kindness charity."

¹⁸John and Eden Smith, and thus probably Elizabeth, too, had recently clashed with the Kirtland-based church leadership. *HC* 1:370–71.

¹⁹The sacrament; the Lord's Supper.

²⁰A term for dysentery; this illness is characterized by diarrhea, nausea, chills, and the voiding of blood. At this time, it was treated by leeches attached to the abdomen, warm baths, and certain medicines, such as calomel-opium mixtures, castor oil, and salts. Robert Hooper, *Lexicon Medicum; or Medical Dictionary*, 2 vols. (New York: J. and J. Harper, 1829), 1:313.

[21] Romans 8 is a complex chapter. There is no way to determine on which part of it Levi Jones concentrated. Since he had been a member of Zion's Camp, it is quite possible that he used as the starting point of his exhortation verses 35–39:

> Who shall separate us from the love of Christ? shall tribulation, or distress, or persecution, or famine, or nakedness, or peril, or sword?. . . For I am persuaded, that neither death, nor life, nor angels, nor principalities, nor powers, nor things present, nor things to come, Nor height, nor depth, nor any other creature, shall be able to separate us from the love of God, which is in Christ Jesus our Lord.

But this chapter also contains other often-quoted verses: "If God be for us, who can be against us?" (v. 31); "All things work together for good to them that love God" (v. 28); and "For as many as are led by the Spirit of God, they are the sons of God" (v. 14), any of which could have been the focus of the exhortation. Moreover, the entire first section deals with the issue of the difference between the life of the flesh and the life of the spirit. In some new religious movements in the nineteenth century, Oneida, for example, and also in certain unconventional forms of Protestantism, verse 2 ("the Spirit of life in Christ Jesus hath made me free from the law of sin and death") was used to justify unusual sexual arrangements. It is even possible that this exhortation warned against such an interpretation.

[22] In chapter 10 of his *History of the Church,* John Whitmer wrote, "And it came to pass that in the fall of 1832, the disciples in Ohio received the gift of tongues, and in June, 1833, we received the gift of tongues in Zion [Missouri]." *HC* 1:297n. The gift of tongues, however, seems to have become an issue in the Eugene Branch where McLellin was at this time. A letter "To the Brethren in Zion," from Joseph Smith, Sidney Rigdon and F. G. Williams, speaks about this gift in the context of their being "engaged in writing a letter to Eugene respecting the two Smiths [John Smith and his son Eden]":

> As to the gift of tongues, all we can say is, that in this place, we have received it as the ancients did: we wish you, however, to be careful lest in this you be deceived. Guard against evils which may arise from any accounts given by women, or otherwise; be careful in all things lest any root of bitterness spring up among you, and thereby many be defiled. Satan will no doubt trouble you about the gift of tongues, unless you are careful; you cannot watch him too closely, nor pray too much. (*HC* 1:369)

McLellin himself spoke in tongues; see his journal entry for August 27, 1834, below.

[23] Gifts of the Spirit. Examples of manifestations of spiritual gifts in the early days of Mormonism are included in H. George Bickerstaff, "Gifts of the Spirit," *EM* 2:544–46.

[24] See note 17, Journal II above.

[25] The priesthood ordinance of the laying on of hands when persons are sick was introduced in an early 1831 revelation (D&C 42:43-44).

[26] Phthisis: pulmonary consumption, characterized by "emaciation, debility, cough, hectic fever, and purulent expectoration." Hooper, *Lexicon Medicum* 2:179.

[27] Isaiah 11:1-13 speaks of a rod coming out of the stem of Jesse, and prophesies that "a Branch shall grow out of his roots: And the spirit of the Lord shall rest upon him, the spirit of wisdom and understanding, the spirit of counsel and might, the spirit of knowledge and of the fear of the Lord." This event prepares the stage for the judgment of the world and the coming of the millennium: "The wolf also shall dwell with the lamb, and the leopard shall lie down with the kid. . . . They shall not hurt nor destroy in all my holy mountain: for the earth shall be full of the knowledge of the Lord." In this chapter, Isaiah prophesied of

> a root of Jesse, which shall stand for an ensign of the people; to it shall the Gentiles seek: and . . . the Lord shall set his hand again the second time to recover the remnant of his people . . . and shall assemble the outcasts of Israel, and gather together the dispersed of Judah from the four corners of the earth. The envy also of Ephraim shall depart, and the adversaries of Judah shall be cut off: Ephraim shall not envy Judah, and Judah shall not vex Ephraim.

This text was a very important scripture for early Mormons. In March 1838, Joseph Smith interpreted the meaning of the stem, the rod and the root spoken of by Isaiah in terms of the work of Christ and his priesthood holders in the last days (D&C 113:1-6).

[28] Like his wife, Elizabeth, Eden Smith had apparently been cut off from the Church and was now being brought back into fellowship. See note 18 above.

[29] Licenses were certificates which authorized priesthood holders to perform their duties (D&C 20:64; *HC* 2:403-4).

[30] A meeting held shortly after a baptism, for the purpose of confirming those who were baptized. The converts are confirmed members of the Church by the laying on of hands, and are given the gift of the Holy Ghost. See Rulon G. Craven, "Confirmation," *EM* 1:310-11.

[31] Acts 20:23-24 is one of the final testimonies given by the Apostle Paul: "The Holy Ghost witnesseth in every city, saying that bonds and afflictions abide me. But none of these things move me, neither count I my life dear unto myself, so that I might finish my course with joy, and the ministry, which I have received of the Lord Jesus, to testify the gospel of the grace of God." McLellin saw himself as following in the footsteps of Jesus' Apostles of old: bearing witness by the Holy Ghost from town to town, suffering afflictions, and fulfilling his missionary labors with joy.

[32] "All members removing from the church where they reside, if going to a church where they are not known, may take a letter certifying that they are regular members and in good standing" (D&C 20:84). "Let [those that travel to Zion] carry up unto the bishop a certificate from three elders of the church, or a certificate from the bishop; Otherwise he who shall go up unto the land of Zion shall not be accounted as a wise steward" (D&C 72:25-26).

[33] During the Jackson County persecutions, Church leaders decided to publish *The Evening and the Morning Star* in Kirtland until the difficulties were resolved and it could be reinstated in Independence. *HC* 1:409. Its first Kirtland publication was in December 1833. Milton V. Backman, Jr., *The Heavens Resound: A History of the Latter-day Saints in Ohio, 1830-1838* (Salt Lake City: Deseret Book, 1983), 281.

[34] See note 15 above.

[35] The Shakers (United Society of Believers in Christ's Second Appearing) accepted many doctrines which might have seemed strange to McLellin, including the belief that Ann Lee was the female manifestation of Christ. Shakers gathered into celibate societies where they lived a simple communal life. Practicing abstinence from pork was important to their understanding of what was required of God's people. See Stephen J. Stein, *The Shaker Experience in America* (New Haven: Yale University Press, 1992). The Mormons had previously had some experience in preaching among Shakers; as a result of this interaction, Joseph Smith received a revelation in 1831 which delineated differences between Mormon and Shaker doctrine (D&C 49).

[36] In Luke 6:20-26, the Lucan Beatitudes promise personal blessings to humble, righteous disciples; to the poor; to the hungry; to those who weep; and to those who are hated, rejected, and despised: "Rejoice ye in that day, and leap for joy: for, behold, your reward is great in heaven." This scripture conversely pronounces a woe upon the rich, the full, those who laugh, and the popular. McLellin was deeply attracted to the quiet Christian virtues, to building Zion with love and peace, establishing the kingdom out of the poor and plain of the earth, and enduring rejection and ridicule.

[37] Instead of traveling to Florence, Joseph Smith spent this time on a preaching trip to visit the members in Michigan. *HC* 2:168-69.

[38] Frederick G. Williams's beloved brother, William Wheeler Williams, lived in Cleveland, and F.G. Williams was possibly traveling to Cleveland to visit this family. Williams, *After One Hundred Years,* 81. Also, he had recently been spending time in Cleveland, working as a doctor, "administering to the [cholera victims], for the purpose of obtaining blessings for them, and for the glory of the Lord." Perhaps this trip with McLellin is another medicinal mission. *HC* 2:146.

[39] The exact meaning of this term is unknown.

[40] See note 29, Journal II above.

[41] See note 15 above.

[42] This is the first time McLellin used this name for the Church. Before May 3, 1834, the Church was known simply as the Church of Christ. However, because of the confusion which "developed because many religious communities in America and various local congregations also identified themselves as members of the Church of Christ or the Church of Jesus Christ," the Mormons agreed at a conference held on the aforementioned date to use the name "The Church of the Latter-day Saints." Backman, *Heavens Resound*, 257. The confusion between the churches organized by the followers of Joseph Smith and Alexander Campbell was particularly acute since both groups referred to their church as the "restored" Church of Christ. In 1838, Joseph Smith received a revelation (D&C 115) which modified this name to "The Church of Jesus Christ of Latter-day Saints." Susan Easton Black, "Name of the Church," *EM* 3:979. Later in his life, in an editorial and in an article entitled "The Name of the Church," McLellin wrote vehemently against the 1834 decision to change the name of the Church. See McLellin, *Ensign of Liberty*, 3, 20-24.

[43] The Book of Mormon instructs members not to partake of the sacramental bread and wine unworthily (3 Ne. 18:28-29). However, it never mentions cancelling the Lord's Supper altogether because of the unworthiness of the congregation. Apparently the strife was so strong in the Amherst branch at this time that the leaders felt the usual sacrament should be cancelled.

[44] This congregation was established in 1832, primarily through the influence of Orson Hyde. Hyde and Sidney Rigdon had been Campbellite missionaries in Florence and had baptized many people in 1829. In 1830, Hyde served as pastor of Florence and surrounding congregations. During this time, he met Mormon missionaries, became interested in the Book of Mormon, traveled to Kirtland, and was there baptized by Sidney Rigdon. See Brigham Young and others, "History of Brigham Young," *Millennial Star* 26 (November 26, 1864): 760-61. Following his conversion, Hyde returned as a missionary to Florence along with Hyrum Smith, where they "were the means of converting and baptizing many of [his] old Campbellite friends—[and] raised up and organized two or three Branches of the Church" in the vicinity. Brigham Young and others, "History of Brigham Young," 774.

[45] Book of Commandments, chapter 24, verses 29-42, is the 1833 printing of today's Doctrine and Covenants 20:37-60. This portion of the Church's initial Articles and Covenants prescribes the requirements for baptism and defines the duties of the elders, priests, teachers, and deacons.

[46] Book of Commandments, chapter 65, verses 10-15, is today's Doctrine and Covenants 64:8-13. These powerful verses require members of the Church to forgive all people and thus were particularly pertinent to the quarreling members of the Amherst branch.

[47] McLellin refers to the home as "Sister Patton's" because Phoebe Patten's husband, David W. Patten, was serving a mission in Tennessee at

this time. Lycurgus A. Wilson, *Life of David W. Patten* (Salt Lake City: Deseret News, 1904), 30. After McLellin left the Church, he was accused of plundering and robbing widow Patten's home in Missouri "under a pretense or color of law, on an order from General Clark." This happened in 1838 during the conflict known as the Missouri Mormon War. *HC* 3:215.

[48] The difference between the Aaronic and Melchizedek Priesthoods was particularly clarified on March 28, 1835, when Joseph Smith received the first fifty-eight verses of the revelation that is now Doctrine and Covenants 107. The remaining verses, which were revealed in 1831, deal with many of the same issues that figured in Doctrine and Covenants 68, likewise an 1831 revelation; it concerned Orson Hyde, Luke S. Johnson, Lyman E. Johnson, and McLellin. See Cook, *The Revelations of the Prophet Joseph Smith*, 109, 215-16; *HC* 2:209-17. Oliver Cowdery's letter about the restoration of the Aaronic Priesthood was published in *Messenger and Advocate* 1 (October 1834): 13-16.

[49] The first section of this chapter is concerned with the distribution of spiritual gifts among believers. See note 17, Journal II above. The chapter ends with a discussion of the distribution of responsibilities in the Church. In addition, 1 Cor. 12 includes a substantial discussion of how "by one Spirit are we all [church members] baptized into one body," (v. 13) all members being necessary to the health of the body. While determining which part of the chapter was the focus of McLellin's penultimate sermon to the Florence branch is impossible, it seems likely that, as there was a history of dissension in the branch, he might well have quoted the twenty-first verse which warns: "And the eye cannot say unto the hand, I have no need of thee: nor again the head to the feet, I have no need of you."

[50] McLellin was incorrect in some of his calculations.

[51] 1 Corinthians 2 describes how the Apostle Paul's preaching was not ornamented with learning but was, rather, straightforward testimony of "Christ, and him crucified" (v. 2). A key verse (13) states: "Which things also we speak, not in the words which man's wisdom teacheth, but which the Holy Ghost teacheth; comparing spiritual things with spiritual."

[52] This is apparently an allusion to Hebrews 6:1-2, setting forth the first principles and ordinances of the gospel of Jesus Christ: "Therefore leaving the principles of the doctrine of Christ, let us go on unto perfection; not laying again the foundation of repentance from dead works, and of faith toward God, Of the doctrine of baptisms, and of laying on of hands, and of resurrection of the dead, and of eternal judgment." Compare Article of Faith 4 and other related statements of basic LDS beliefs.

[53] The combination of McLellin's having preached two days before about "going on to perfection" and his being called down for using "awkward Jestures" suggests that McLellin was being influenced, although no doubt at second hand, by the prominent revivalist Charles Grandison Finney, whose fame had spread far and wide by the mid-1830s. Finney, who

preached a doctrine that came to be known as "perfectionism," formulated
what historian Martin E. Marty called "a theology of gesture." Believing that
"mere words will never express the full meaning of the gospel," Finney held
that a minister should "embody" the meaning of the biblical writers so that
his audience would understand the Bible as "a living reality." Along with
revival techniques such as the use of the anxious bench, the histrionic
gestures that Finney recommended as accompaniments to preaching became known as "new measures." Martin E. Marty, *Righteous Empire: The
Protestant Experience in America* (New York: Dial Press, 1970), 85-86.

[54] This is the building in which Joseph Smith and other LDS leaders
were brought to trial on several different occasions. Richard Neitzel
Holzapfel and T. Jeffery Cottle, *Old Mormon Kirtland and Missouri* (Santa
Ana, Calif.: Fieldbrook Productions, 1991), 112-13.

[55] Galatians 1:6-10 is a scripture commonly used by Mormons as
evidence of apostasy and, hence, the need for a restoration by angels of the
same gospel originally taught by Jesus and his Apostles:

> I marvel that ye are so soon removed from him that called you into the
> grace of Christ unto another gospel: Which is not another; but there be
> some that trouble you, and would pervert the gospel of Christ. But
> though we, or an angel from heaven, preach any other gospel unto you
> than that which we have preached unto you, let him be accursed. As we
> said before, so say I now again, If any man preach any other gospel unto
> you than that ye have received, let him be accursed. For do I now
> persuade men, or God? or do I seek to please men? for if I yet pleased
> men, I should not be the servant of Christ.

[56] Most of the Mormons who had been expelled from Jackson County,
including the McLellins, settled immediately to the north in Clay
County. McLellin rented a house in Liberty, the county seat. McLellin,
Ensign of Liberty 1:62. Although most of the residents in Clay County
displayed charity and tolerance, this was still a period of anxiety for the
dislocated Saints. The Church members did not know how long they
would remain in Clay County, as they were awaiting the restoration of
their Jackson County lands. Meanwhile, many found work constructing
buildings, teaching school, and working on farms. Despite the relative
freedom from persecution, the situation was so tense that Mormon public
meetings in Clay County were discouraged, missionaries were told not to
preach, and church members were instructed to administer the sacrament
only when convenient opportunities arose. Holzapfel and Cottle, *Old
Mormon Kirtland and Missouri,* 163, 166; James B. Allen and
Glen M. Leonard, *The Story of the Latter-day Saints* (Salt Lake City:
Deseret Book, 1976), 103-5.

[57] This meeting may have been a forerunner of the "solemn assembly,"
a conclave of profound spiritual significance in Mormonism first instituted

in March 1836 in connection with the dedication of the Kirtland Temple. See Richard E. Turley, Jr., "Solemn Assemblies," *EM* 3:1390-91.

[58] This institution was originally called the Kirtland School; "[it] was similar in many respects to the first high school organized in America (in Boston, twelve years earlier)." The Kirtland School is not to be confused with the School for the Elders, which had already begun its first term in November 1834. McLellin probably taught at the School for the Elders, as well as being the primary teacher at the Kirtland School. Unlike the School for the Elders, which instructed priesthood holders in doctrinal matters, the Kirtland School was attended by members of both sexes, and the curriculum was more basic, focusing primarily on geography, writing, arithmetic, and English grammar. Backman, *Heavens Resound,* 268-69, 272-73.

[59] Huntsburg is seventeen miles southeast of Kirtland. Although two other elders had previously preached in Huntsburg, no one had been baptized before McLellin came. Of this first visit, McLellin later wrote, "I preached sometimes, twice a day, and the truth took hold on the hearts of many, and six of the number came out and declared it openly by obedience." Of his subsequent visits to Huntsburg, McLellin wrote, "I always found that there were some who were honest in heart and ready to obey the truth." Of the many towns where McLellin preached the gospel, Huntsburg seems to be the one where he was most successful. By the end of his various stays there throughout 1834-35, he was responsible for establishing a congregation of twenty-seven members and "a number more believing and others seriously inquiring." Letter from McLellin to Oliver Cowdery, *Messenger and Advocate* 1 (April 1835): 102-3.

[60] While still a teenager, Joseph Smith said he had been "somewhat partial to the Methodist sect, and I felt some desire to be united with them." *HC* 1:3. One printer's apprentice at the *Palmyra Register* remembered that the future prophet had caught "'a spark of Methodism in the camp meeting, away down in the woods, on the Vienna Road.'" Another recalled that he had "joined the probationary class of the Palmyra Methodist Church." Joseph's wife Emma came from a Methodist family; one of her uncles was a lay minister and a brother-in law was a Methodist class leader in Harmony, Pennsylvania. No one knows whether it was to please his wife or at his own behest, but for over six months Joseph Smith's name was on the class roll in Harmony. Yet the future prophet said that a Methodist preacher expressed contempt when he told him about the spiritual experience that would become known as the "First Vision." Richard Bushman, *Joseph Smith and the Beginnings of Mormonism* (Urbana: University of Illinois Press, 1984), 54, 58, 94-95. Joseph believed that the Methodism of his wife's parents caused them to be hostile to him. Donna Hill, *Joseph Smith: The First Mormon* (Garden City, N.Y.: Doubleday, 1977), 62, 69, 73. In addition, among members of other Protestant groups, Methodists had been involved in the expulsion of the Mormons from Jackson County. *HC* 1:392.

McLellin's report of Joseph Smith's 1834 sermon indicates that Joseph's sentiments about Methodism had hardened into a combination of hostility and scorn. In an 1835 statement, he said that Methodists were "destitute of the spirit of righteousness." *HC* 2:319.

[61] Because strong opposition to all written creeds was present within Mormonism at this time, it is likely that McLellin believed that the Prophet was expressing opposition to the adoption of written creeds, a matter discussed in Peter Crawley, "The Passage of Mormon Primitivism," *Dialogue: A Journal of Mormon Thought* 13 (Winter 1980): 26–37. Since the Prophet and Sidney Rigdon were apparently working during the winter of 1834–35 on the "Lectures on Faith," which were intended to present in a "few words . . . the faith and principles of this society as a body" and which would be published in 1835, the discourse described here could have been an effort to make a clear distinction between "creeds" and descriptions of theology and doctrine. See Larry E. Dahl, "Lectures on Faith," *EM* 2:818–21. See also *HC* 6:57.

[62] The Kirtland School; see note 58 above. On this date, "a grammer school was organized and commenced in Kirtland, Ohio, taught by Sidney Rigdon and Wm. E. McLellin. It was held especially for the benefit of the young Elders of the Church, many of whom lacked the necessary education as representatives of the Church and missionaries to preach the gospel to the world." Andrew Jenson, Journal History of the Church, housed in LDS Church Archives, December 22, 1834 (hereafter cited as JH).

In a report written February 27, 1835, McLellin said that although students of all ages were accepted at first, the classes became so large that only those students who wished to study the sciences of penmanship, arithmetic, English grammar, and geography were allowed to attend. *HC* 2:200.

> Tuition and fees were comparable to those at other educational institutions in the area. Tuition for a term of English grammar (about six weeks) was one dollar, while the cost of studying other subjects ranged from two to four dollars. Young men and women living outside [Kirtland] obtained room and board with "respectable families" for one dollar or so per week. (Backman, *Heavens Resound,* 273)

A letter written by one of the students of this school shows the importance of this institution.

> Through childhood and early youth, my advantages, even for primary education, were the most meager. At seventeen, I attended the winter term of the grammar school taught by William E. McLellin, in Kirtland, and presided over by the Prophet; at the same time attending night lectures in geography. These were my greatest opportunities for schooling, and in them was finished my school education and if I have acquired in life anything further of worth, it has been snatched from the

wayside while on the run as a missionary, pioneer or while in Nature's great laboratory with the axe, plow, spade or garden implements.

Benjamin Johnson, letter to Gibbs, 1903, *LDS Historical Library CD Rom,* 2d ed. (Provo, Utah: Infobases, 1993).

[63] In the interim between this entry and the next on January 22, 1835, McLellin was part of a high council which met in the Kirtland schoolroom on December 28, 1834. Kirtland High Council minutes, 81, Archives Division, Church Historical Department, The Church of Jesus Christ of Latter-day Saints, Salt Lake City.

[64] Ephesians 1 contains many themes that have been important for Latter-day Saints from the beginning: foreordination from before the foundation of the world, the gathering together of all things into one during "the dispensation of the fulness of times," praise and glory in the atonement of Jesus Christ, the spirit of revelation and wisdom, and the inheritance of the Saints.

[65] John 14:2: "In my Father's house are many mansions: if it were not so, I would have told you. I go to prepare a place for you."

[66] At this time, wine was still used in the sacrament. Regarding the attitudes of church members toward the Word of Wisdom at this time, see Backman, *Heavens Resound,* 260.

[67] Verse 49 of the Articles and Covenants of the Church of Christ, published in 1833 as Chapter 24 of the Book of Commandments, reads: "Every member of this church of Christ having children is to bring them unto the elders before the church, who are to lay their hands upon them in the name of the Lord, and bless them in the name of Christ." Compare D&C 20:70.

[68] During the time that elapsed between McLellin's return from Huntsburg on January 17 and going back on March 18, 1835, the first Quorum of the Twelve Apostles, which included McLellin, was organized. The calling of the Twelve had been foretold sometime during the first half of June 1829, when the Prophet received a revelation which, among other things, directed Oliver Cowdery and David Whitmer, two of the Three Witnesses of the Book of Mormon, to "search out the Twelve" (D&C 18:37). The Apostles were called "to be especial messengers to bear the Gospel among the nations." *HC* 2:180. In a meeting held on February 14, 1835, the names of the Twelve were announced. McLellin was ordained to this position the following day; his specific blessing is recorded in *HC* 2:190-91. Among the others chosen to be apostles were McLellin's former mission companions Luke S. Johnson, Parley P. Pratt, David W. Patten, and John F. Boynton, and McLellin's Kirtland School student Heber C. Kimball.

On February 27, McLellin attended a meeting with eight of the Apostles, Joseph Smith, and other church leaders. During this meeting, the Prophet instructed the Apostles to keep detailed, careful minutes of all their apostolic meetings, especially those at which the Apostles would collectively make decisions in regard to policy or doctrine. In later meetings of the Twelve, McLellin and Orson Hyde served as clerks to record such minutes. *HC* 2:209, 219-22; and reports of the Twelve Apostles, *Messenger and Advocate* 1 (May 1835): 115-16 and 2 (October 1835): 204-7. Also at this meeting, McLellin played an active part in a discussion of the unique aspects of the apostolic calling. The conclusions reached by this discussion were as follows:

> They are the Twelve Apostles, who are called to the office of the Traveling High Council, who are to preside over the churches of the Saints, among the Gentiles, where there is a presidency established; and they are to travel and preach among the Gentiles, until the Lord shall command them to go to the Jews. They are to hold the keys of this ministry, to unlock the door of the Kingdom of heaven unto all nations, and to preach the Gospel to every creature. This is the power, authority, and virtue of their apostleship. (*HC* 2:198-200)

In March 1835, the Twelve met with Joseph Smith. McLellin reported that Joseph "proposed we [the Twelve] take our first mission through the Eastern States, to the Atlantic Ocean, and hold conferences in the vicinity of the several branches of the Church for the purpose of regulating all things necessary for their welfare. It was proposed that the Twelve leave Kirtland on the 4th day of May, which was unanimously agreed to." *HC* 2:209; and letter from Orson Hyde and McLellin to Oliver Cowdery, *Messenger and Advocate* 1 (March 1835): 90.

On March 13, the Elders' grammar school at Kirtland "closed to give the Elders an opportunity to go forth and proclaim the Gospel, preparatory to the endowment." Elder Evan M. Greene writes: "it was truly an affecting scene and all hearts seemed melted unto tenderness." JH, March 13, 1835.

[69] On April 16, 1835, McLellin described his March 18-23 visit to Huntsburg as follows:

> On the 21st of March I attended an appointment at the center of this town, in the midst of a society commonly called Campbellites, and the truth coming so near them it roused up thos [*sic*] whose craft was in danger, and I received a challenge to hold a public discussion with a Mr. J. M. Tracy, who, in his note to me, pledged himself to prove that "the book of Mormon was not a divine revelation." I have been informed that Mr. T. was formerly a Universalist preacher, but becoming tired of their principles or society, I know not which, latterly some of the Campbellites in Huntsburgh have hired him to preach for them. (McLellin to Oliver Cowdery, *Messenger and Advocate* 1 [April 1835]: 102)

This was not the first time a Campbellite had issued such a challenge; in early 1831, Thomas Campbell, one of the founders of the Disciples of Christ, had challenged Sidney Rigdon to a similar debate, one that allowed persons other than the principals to speak on either side. During that earlier debate, Campbell's son Alexander, also a Disciples founder, characterized the Book of Mormon as "Smith's fabrication," a book that contained "every error and almost every truth discussed in N. York for the last ten years." *Millennial Harbinger* 2 (February 1831): 85, as quoted in Klaus J. Hansen, *Mormonism and the American Experience*, 14; see also Bushman, *Joseph Smith and the Beginnings of Mormonism*, 125-26.

[70] McLellin's journal presents students of early Latter-day Saint history with a different chronology of—or at least a different location for—events surrounding the meeting in which the Twelve met with the Prophet "confessing their individual weaknesses and shortcomings, expressing repentance, and seeking the further guidance of the Lord," and Joseph's asking for and receiving the first fifty-eight verses of the revelation known as the "Revelation on Priesthood" (D&C 107). The heading of this section in the Doctrine and Covenants, the record signed by Orson Hyde and William McLellin that is printed in the *History of the Church* (2:209-10), and the record in the Kirtland High Council minutes, 1832-1837 (198) indicate that the meeting was held in Kirtland on March 28, 1835. Although the wording in these two records differs slightly, they both describe the same meeting. McLellin's name, along with that of Orson Hyde, is appended to both records.

McLellin, however, reports that on Thursday, March 26, he returned to Huntsburg in company with Joseph Smith, Lyman Johnson, D. W. Patten, Parley Pratt, John F. Boynton, and others. On Friday and Saturday, the 27th and 28th, he says that they (i.e., "we") engaged in debate with the Campbellite minister, "about eight hours each day." McLellin's description of the duration of each day's session of the debate is found in the letter he wrote to Oliver Cowdery two weeks later. See note 69 above.

Since Huntsburg is only seventeen miles away from Kirtland, it is possible that the Prophet and the Apostles returned to Kirtland after each day's debate was concluded. If that were the case, it would still have been possible for the meeting of the Prophet and the Twelve described above to have been held in Kirtland. McLellin's journal indicates, however, that he conducted the baptism of two persons in Huntsburg on the evening of the 28th, an event whose time and place is verified by an entry in *HC* 2:218. This would suggest that if the meeting was held in Kirtland, McLellin could not have attended, even though his name is appended to the meeting minutes. Since his journal indicates that McLellin and his fellows "returned home again" on Monday, which would have been March 30, it is also possible that this extremely significant meeting and Joseph's receipt of the "Revelation on Priesthood" occurred in Huntsburg rather than in Kirtland.

Cook, *Revelations of the Prophet Joseph Smith*, 215, accepts the March 28, 1835, date and concludes that the meeting was held on the late afternoon of that day. This conclusion would either argue for Huntsburg as the site or suggest that McLellin did not attend the meeting. What is not in doubt— or at least a point on which McLellin's journal and the *History of the Church* agree—is that President Joseph Smith preached in Huntsburg for three hours on Sunday, March 29, 1835.

[71] The outcome of the debate with the Campbellites in which the parties spoke alternately for thirty minutes for two full days is described in McLellin's April 16, 1835, letter to Cowdery:

> When the interview closed a majority of the congregation arose, by an anxious urgency on the part of Mr. T. to testify thereby that they did not believe in the divinity of the book of Mormon. But when I asked them if they had been convinced that it was false by Mr. Tracy's arguments, (if I might call them such,) there was not one to answer—"Yes."
>
> Whether good has resulted from that discusion [sic] can only be known by the effects produced. As soon as the debate closed I went immediately to the water and baptized two—it being Saturday.

[72] Joseph Smith also wrote about this sermon: "I preached about three hours, at Huntsburg—where William E. M'Lellin had been holding a public discussion, on a challenge from J. M. Tracy, a Campbellite preacher, the two days previous, on the divinity of the Book of Mormon—at the close of which two were baptized; and, on Monday, four more came forward for baptism." *HC* 2:218. See McLellin to Cowdery, 102.

[73] McLellin described this baptismal service in more detail in his letter dated April 16, 1835: "On Monday morning four more came forward and, 'were buried with Christ by baptism;' and were confirmed by the laying on of hands, in order that, 'they might put off the old man with his deeds and arise and walk in newness of life.'" In these lines, McLellin is quoting Romans 6:4 and Colossians 3:9.

[74] During this last known Huntsburg visit, the weather was very cold, accompanied by a heavy snowfall, "especially considering the season of the year," yet in his letter McLellin seems elated by his success, and full of spiritual conviction. He wrote:

> Since I have been here this time, more have been received into the church. Thus you see that *truth is powerful and will prevail.*
>
> I have for some time past been thoroughly convinced, that all that is wanting, is, to have the principles in which we believe, fairly, plainly and simply laid open to the minds of the honest in heart of this generation, in order to have the mild kingdom of the Redeemer spread and prevail over the commandments of men and the doctrines of devils. For many, even in this region, so near to Kirtland, I found when I first

came to this town, knew but little of our principles. They had heard much from rumor, 'tis true, but they seemed astonished when they come to hear our principles as we hold them, without exaggeration or misrepresentation. Said they, "these things are according to the scriptures, we believe they are true, and we want to obey them." When I see people thus willing to obey the *truth* as soon as they learn it, my heart cries, O! that the vineyard of the lord was filled with "the publishers of peace," that all the honest in heart might be prepared for the coming of the Lord, in power and great glory, and be ready to say, "even so come, Lord Jesus."

Then peace as in the garden of Eden will be restored to the earth, and then for a thousand years all kingdoms, nations and people from one end of heaven to the other, from the least to the greatest, will echo the sound "I know the Lord." For as Isaiah says, "all the people will be righteous." (McLellin to Cowdery, 102-3)

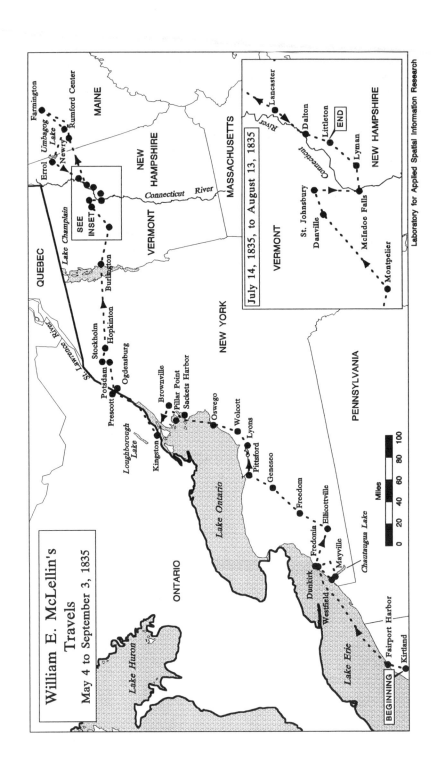

William E. McLellin's
Travels
May 4 to September 3, 1835

BEGINNING

ONTARIO

Lake Huron

Lake Erie

Fairport Harbor

Kirtland

Westfield

Dunkirk

Fredonia

Mayville

Chautauqua Lake

Ellicottville

Freedom

Geneseo

Pittsford

Lyons

Wolcott

Oswego

Lake Ontario

Sackets Harbor

Pillar Point

Brownville

Kingston

Loughborough Lake

Prescott

Ogdensburg

Potsdam

Stockholm

Hopkinton

St. Lawrence River

QUEBEC

Burlington

Lake Champlain

Errol

Umbagog Lake

Newry

Rumford Center

Farmington

MAINE

SEE INSET

NEW HAMPSHIRE

VERMONT

Connecticut River

NEW YORK

PENNSYLVANIA

MASSACHUSETTS

Miles

0   20   40   60   80   100

July 14, 1835, to August 13, 1835

VERMONT

St. Johnsbury

Danville

Montpelier

McIndoe Falls

Lyman

END

Littleton

Dalton

Lancaster

Connecticut River

NEW HAMPSHIRE

Laboratory for Applied Spatial Information Research

William E. McLellin Journal V
May 4, 1835–September 3, 1835

W. E. McLellin

1835

This book [The rest of this page is blank.]

W. E. M'Lellin's Journal giving
an account of his journeyings & preachings &c
in the year 1835, commencing May the 4th[1]

Monday morn. at 2 Oclock I in company with my friends the
twelve bid farewell to Kirtland and our brethren & sisters in order
to take a tour in the Eastern countries to preach the Gospel,
attend confirences and give council pertaining to the things of
God to our brethren in the churches abroad and to regulate the
things that are wanting.[2] Elders R. Orton & W. Bosley broug[h]t us
on a couple of waggons twelve miles to Fair Port. The steamboat
Sandusky was in port bound east— And we obtained a passage
and immediately set sail at about 6 oclock in the morn. This seemed
a great blessing of the Lord to us that we were not detained but
were so prospered in starting[3]— We were landed at Dunkirk at
about 4 oclock P.M. The same afternoon having sailed about 120
miles.[4] In this place we found a brother Russel Pemberton or one
who had been a brother, but who was now somewhat cast down
in his mind; with him we staid over night. Here we took council
among ourselves to seperate for a few days and preach the Gospel
in this region inasmuch as doors were opened to receive us

and the next morning being Tuesday the 5th I took Elder Luke
Johnson with me and started south inquiring by the way who

View of Grand River Shipyard, Fairport, Ohio, c. 1858. Courtesy Lake County Historical Society.

Fairport Harbor, Fairport, Ohio, c. 1858. McLellin and the other Apostles sailed from this harbor as they set out on their mission in 1835 to New York, New England, and Canada. Courtesy Lake County Historical Society.

was worthy or who would open their doors and and appoint a
meeting for us. We traveled about 4 ms. and came to the Village
of Freedonia where were three or four sectarion chapels. consequently the people were very self-righteous but some were willing
to hear us and an app. was circulated for us to preach in a schoolhouse at early candle light—— [*page 2*] The app. being circulated—We heard that there were some brethren living about two
miles distant and being anxious that they should hear of the mee.
we went to see them but Elders Orson Hyde and Lyman Johnson
had found them and were going to preach among them. We returned and attended our app. the schoolhouse was filled and I arose
and addressed them on the subject of the gospel from 1 Thes 1- 5[5]
for 1 hour and 1/2—They did not give very good attention but still
I think that some were seriously affected. One man named Brown
came and handed me 75 cents. But no person inviting us in the
village to stay with them we went about two miles and tarried
with a brother Fisher

and after we had taken breakfast We started south and traveled six
ms. and being weary we called at an Inn and took some little
refreshment and paid 25 cts and passed on about 7 mls. to a
Mr. Stephen Jones'. We called and told them that we were preachers of the—— church of the 'Latter Day Saints' and we would be
glad to be entertained for the night and also to get to preach in
the neighbourhood. They received us and entertained us hospitably and we found that [they] belonged to an order of religionists
called Christians. An app. also was circulated for next day at 4 P.M.
to be held in a schoolhouse in the little Village of St- Clairsville and
an other at candlelighting near Mr. Jones.

Thursday 7th This morning Elder L[uke] J[ohnson] heard of a
brother about 5 mls. distant and he left me in order to go and see
him— But I felt somewhat sore in consequence of walking and
I continued with Mr. Jones, reading, writing, studying and talking
&c— At 4 Oclock we attended in the village in order to fill our
app. but the schoolhouse was locked and only One person [which]
who was an old lady attended— consequently we left them shaking the dust from our feet as a testimony against them and We

returned to Mr Jones and att. our app. at eve—— a few att. of
some of whom were very wild, being boys, Elder J[ohnson] spoke
to them [*page 3*] about 3/4 of an hour— but some of them laughed
and talked so much that he quit— I arose and addressed them
about 3/4 of an hour longer and I succeeded in getting them still
or partly so and I had great liberty and preached to them the
Gospel and bore testimony of the truth to them— And we returned again and staid all night with Mr. Jones. He seemed quite
unbelieving but this lady seemed quite believing and inquired of
us with a great deal of anxiety to know the truth— We heard her
declare to her husband that 'she believed.'

Friday the 8th We took breakfast earley and then attended prayrs
with the family and left them feeling very solemn——The old lady
gave me one shilling in money and the old gentlemen paid us two
dollars for a book of Mormon for a young clerk in the village—We
started and walked on about 15 mls. to Mayvill which stands at the
head of the beautiful little Chatauqua Lake— Thence 5 mls. to a
bro. S. Foot's near Westfield &c— &c— Heres we staid and were
refreshed and rested until next morning— 'they seemed to be a
family of saints.'

Friday the 9th This morning at 10 oclock we met in Conference
at bro. Job Lewis'[6]—— All the twelve being present[7] we proceded
to business— Elder T. B. Marsh presiding[8]— The minutes of [the]
our— consultations are kept in our Apostolic record[9] therefore
I shall not insert any of [them] in this Journal——

Sunday the 10th A large assembly of peopl[10] assembled in bro.
Lewis' barn and Elder Marsh preached about two hours in the
forenoon on the covenants of God, &C— Elder Patten preached[11]
about one hour in the afternoon after reading the 11th Ch. of the
Hebrews[12]— The sacrament was administered by Elder Marsh—
A door was opened for members and We went to the water and
I baptized five individuals, viz Benja- Brown,[13] Rebeca Brown, Nancy
Snyder,   Some boys acted very wickedly at the
water's edge &c and finally one little fellow fell into the water——
At evening we had a confirmation meeting [*page 4*] and those

who had been immersed were confirmed by the laying on of my hands after I had spoken about 30 mts. from John 14 - 26[14] on the nature of the gift and power of the Holy Ghost &c. &c.

Monday 11th This morning the Church came together in order to consult about an appoint 'wise' men' to send up with their moneys to purchase lands in Zion and the regions round about[15] &C— &C— They did their business in the presence of the council and appointed Timt Foot. At 3 Oclock we had publick preaching by Elder B. Young. after reading a portion of the Saviour's teaching in the book of Mormon[16] he spoke about 1 1/2 hours contrasting the religions of the day with the **truth**. Thence we went immediately to the watter and Elder O. Hyde immersed 7 persons named as follows William Gould, Sally Ann Gould, Betsy Mapes, Fanny Wilton, Sabra Stringham, Hester Norton, Caroline L. Babcock——At evening we had another confirmation mee. and those baptized were confirmed by the laying on of hands and a number were blessed in order that they might be healed of infirmaties— We really had a good meeting and a powerful— It continued until about midnight with many good exortations.

Tuesday 12.th This morning 'the **twelve**' assembled in a room apa[r]t and after much conversation &C— We united in Solemn prayr to God to preserve us until we s[h]ould meet again at the Freedom Conference[17]— We then were saluted as brethren[18] by Elder Hyde— and seperated to [~~mant~~] travel through the regions in order to proclaim the Gospel, warn sinners and to gather up the deciples &C— &C— Elder O. Hyde and I joined in our ministry for the present in consequence of [~~some~~] our clerkship or our [*page 5*] Writing that we had to do as clerks of the council &C. Sylvester Norton came forward this morning and was received by the church[19] unto baptism and Elder Hyde and myself remained in order to attend to it. bro. O[rson] baptized him and confirmed him by the waters edge— and we spent the remainder of the day in writing[20] &C— &C—

Wednesday 13th This morning Elder O. Hyde and I left bro. Lewis' and the Westfield taking with us Lorenzo Lewis whom we ordained an Elder—— While here the brethren made a contribution for us and bro. B. Brown gave me—— $2.50 and in that had been given We recd $1.2 cts. each &C—— [W] Elder J. Gould brought us in his waggon about 8 mls. and we walked 7 to to Freedonia Vill. Here at 4 P.M. we att. an app. that I had left when I was here before. We had a very small congregation. I addressed them one hour and 30 mt from 1 Cor. 2 and 13[21] on the evidences, of truth, and Elder O. H[yde] spoke a few minutes and closed the mee. We made two more appts. one at a schoolhouse near bro. Brown's for Thursday eve and one at Leona for Sunday— We staid with bro. Fishers at Leona.

Thursday 14th This day we spent from 9 till 3. together in the woods in prayrs and contemplation endeavouring to obtain an open vision but we did not altho. we felt that we drew very near to God. At eve we att. our app. A few came in and Elder H. addressed them about one hour and [a] quarter from 2 Tim. 4[22] &C on the nature of the Priesthoods and of the coming forth of '**the book**' &c. I then arose and spoke about half an hour contrasting the religions of the day and telling them what I believed and what they might expect, of Judgements &c— &c— [*page 6*] Elder Hyde was invited by a Mr. Rood and I returned to bro. Brown's— His wife was somewhat believing, but yet, not entirely willing to obey the truth.

Friday 15th This morning bro. Brown handed me a $5.00 bill and told me that he felt happy so to do in order to help support the ministers who preached the things, that he Verily knew to be true. Take it, s'd he, for I give it to You in the name of a deciple'. ~~Saturday 16th We continued to write and finish that which we had to do and in the~~ and in the ~~afternoon~~ evening we attended an appointment about 3 miles south of Leona in Shumla. We had a small congregation who paid good attention but there were some out of the house round the windows who acted badly. I addressed the people about one hour and a quarter— from 2 Peter 1 and 1.[23] &c. We were invited and we staid with them till morning.

Saturday We returned to bro. Fishers and continued to write till afternoon and then we walked about 3 miles to bro. Bovce's and staid with them over night, A fine family (indeed)——

Sunday 17. We returned to Leona and at 10 Oclock the schoolhouse being filled, I arose and addressed them for 2 hours on the evidences of the book of Mormon— The people set seemingly astonished— At 2 Oclock we assembled again and Elder O. Hyde addressed the people on nature and power of the resurrection &C. and I administered the sacrament to the diciples present[24] after which I made known the nature of our cal[l]ings and of necesseties and the people donated $4.00 for our support— But none seemed willing to obey the truth.

Monday 18. We traveled about 15 miles [*page 7*] to Elder Nickerson's. here we found Elders B. Young & W. Smith who had been labouring in this church and region round about— They had a meeting this evening and Elder Young preached about an hour to them on the principles of our faith.

Tuesday We began again to wend our way easterly, we traveled about 19 miles and staid with a Mr. Drue, a lame man who treated us with the best that he had. [Undecipherable symbols]——

Wednesday 20. We proceeded on and took breakfast in little Valley with a Mr. Gray who was a cousin to Elder D. Elliott, thence to Ellecottvill thence to a Mr. Wissel's who received us to lodge with him during the night after we had been turned away from three or four houses and that too while it was raining quite hard— but they were quite poor——[a] About 24 mls.

Thursday 21. We passed on about a mile in the rain and called at a widow Loveless' and took breakfast and there seemed to be an anxiety to hear us preach insomuch that the neighbours soon gathered in and Elder Hyde preached to them 1 1/2 hours from Mark 13 - 21-22.[25] they seemed much affected and quite believing. After which we passed on about 10 miles and staid with a bro. till morning.

Friday 22. We passed on to Elder Cowdery's[26] and there we met with our brethren **the twelve** and found them all well and proceeded to business and opened our Conference,[27] Elder D. W.

Patten presiding and W. E. M'Lellin Clerk——See mints [minutes] much instruction was given respecting tongues &c.

Saturday commenced public preaching at 10 oclock in a large barn. Elder Kimball arose and read the 14 chap. of John[28] and spoke to the people about half an hour Very feelingly indeed [*page 8*] I then arose and spoke 1¼ hours from the same chap. on the nature and affects of the gift of the Holy Ghost. I had good liberty—— in the afternoon We met with the church in order to instruct them respecting the deliverence of Zion. Elders Hyde, M'Lellin and P. Pratt addressed them about 40 minutes each and the brethren seemed to receive our teachings and they s'd that they would obey or endeavour to at least. 'To appoint their wise men'[29] &c. Much was said also about superfluous dress and about the abuse of the gifts [of] in the Church &c &c.[30]

Sunday 24. A congregation of probably seven hundred assembled in a large barn and Elder O. Hyde preached to them a most plain and powerful discourse on the evidences of the book of Mormon for 1½ hours and at intermition he immersed 2 females who were received by the church unto baptism—— In the afternoon Elder P. Pratt preached about 1½ hours on life and immortality and then the sacrament was administered to the Saints by Elder Patten and a public collection taken up for the benefit of the twelve, which together with what we had all received since we had ~~received~~ parted at the last conference amounted to $2.00 and a few cents each. We ordained Loyd Lewis an Elder— and sent Elder J. Murdock and Lorenzo Lewis to pennsylvania to [s] Springevill to regulate that church and set in order the things that were wanting ther[e.]

Monday morning We in council laid hands on and set apart B. Young one of our number and J. P. Greene and [E] Amos Orton to go and introduce the Gospel among the Senecas of the remnants of Joseph[31] on the Allegany river[32]—— And after we had all prayed and sealed each other up until we should meet again at our next conference in Lyanstown[33]—— [*page 9*] After which we seperated each going his way in order to proclaim the truth— &C. I and Lyman

Johnson agreed to go together—And we attended an appointment
at Fairview corners about 5 miles distant. I addressed the people
in a schoolhouse for about 2 hours from Isa 8 and 20[34]— I spoke
on the effects [of] and evidences of truth, especially of the book
of Mormon &C— We staid over night with the bro. Wightmans
and we found them a very nice family indeed.

Tuesday 26. To day we attended an app. in the town of Hate. Elder
J[ohnson] had preached here two or three times last week, he
desired that I should address them and I arose and preached to
them about 2 hours from 2 Peter 1. 1.[35] I had great liberly [liberty]
and it was really an affecting time. Lyman exorted a while and
then invited all who wished to unite [to] with us to manifest it.
Joanna Swift an old Lady arose and said that she verily believed as
far as she understood. also Betsy Butterfield and Eliza Lyons a young
lady who was opposed by all her friends or nearly so— Elder J.
immersed them— We had a good time— The people generally
seemed to be affected. Elders H. Herryman & Willard Snow were
here with us— and Elder S. had preached here last Sunday afternoon—— We made a number more appointments for us during
the week——

Wednesday we attended our app. at a Mr. Chapman the brethren
in the region generally attended and I arose and the Covenants &
Articles and preached an hour and 3/4. the brethren & sisters
seemed to be strengthened and to rejoice much in the glorious
cause. I really felt happy. Elder Eaton's son (a methodist preacher
was present)

[*page 10*] Thursday 28th We attended an app about 5 miles distant
in the town of Linden. E[l]der J. preached about one hour on the
nature of the Kingdom of Christ and of faith &c——

Friday At 4 P.M. we attended our app. in the Swift settlement—
the house was crowded and L. J. preached one hour and a few
moments on Jer 31— - 31.[36] &C I then spoke about 30 minutes by
way of exortation and what I said was really by the power of the
spir[i]t of God— The people were melted down into tears— and

four went forward to the water and Elder J. immersed them. We then app two mee. for tomorrow and seperated. I staid with E. Eaton.

Saturday I att. my app. and preached on the Priesthoods for about one hour and 3/4 after which I immersed   Chapman—

Sunday 31. We held a meeting in bro. Wightman's barn commencing at 10 A.M. and it held till about 5 P.M. with 2 or 300 people. I spoke in the forenoon from John 5 and 30th[37] for one hour and 1/2 on the covenants of God and Evidences of the book of Mormon and at intermition I obtained 12 subscribers for the Mess[enger][38] In the afternoon Elder J. preached on faith &C We broke bread and confirmed those who had been baptized—but no more were immersed. We obtained about $5 donation from our friends.

Monday 1st of June. [✝] Bro. C. Wightman in a one hors[e] waggon brought us about 40 miles on our way to Lyons— as far as Mount Morris & then we walked on about 6 miles and put up with a Mr. Squires a little south of Gennessees and next morning we paid the 25 cents for supper and lodging &c——

[*page 11*] Tuesday 2. We passed on about 6 miles to the Gennessees Church, the most of whom had moved on to Kirtland &c, but an app was circulated for 4. P.M. and a few of the brethren assembled at Elder R. Hadlock's and I addressed them from Gen 17 - 1[39] for 11/4 hours. I had great liberty and the brethren seemed much encouraged. Here Elders P & O. Pratts L. Johnson & J. F. Boynton overtook us, &

MWednesday the 3. a bro. Granger brought us in a two horse waggon to within 5 miles of— Pittsford and there we took a canal boat about sunset for Lyons and rode smoothly on—— &c

Thursday morn about 10 A.M. we landed in Lyons, a flourishing county seat on the canal and then walked about 5 miles north to a bro Dixon's. Here Elder Patten preached in the evening and I made a few remarks following him. I should have told that my vest was worn out and bro J. Bosley in Gennessees bought me a pattern and trimmings for another and gave them to me.

Friday 5. This Morning at 10 A.M. 9 of the twelve assembled at Elder Colburn's in conference[40] according to previous app. Eldrs B. Young, William Smith and P. P. Pratt were absent— B. Y. [was] had not as yet returned from his mission to the Josephites.[41] Elder H. C. Kimball presided and after doing the business of the conference it was agreed that Elder— Hyde & Young should return to Kirtland for a little season according to requ[e]st from the Presidency[42] &c. conference dismissed about 4 P.M. and I and Elder Patten started together for Pillow Point[43] and walked on—— about five miles and were entertained by a Mr Griswould very hospitably— he had been a Methodist——

Saturday 6. This morning I forgot my Bible with Mr. G. and we traveled on about 10 miles [*page 12*] to the Village of Wolcott and after making ourselves known an app was circulated for us at sunset in a schoolhouse and we stopped with a Mr. Church 1/2 mile west of the Village. A little after sunset the people assembled and Elder P. preached to them about 1 1/2 hours on the subject of the vision.[44] the people were mostly Universalists in the Village. We gave another app. for Tomorrow 4 P.M.

Sunday 7. This morn. I attended a Baptist mee= and heard the speaker— But it was dull preach—— it was as much as I could do to keep from sleep— at twelve or at noon I att. a Presbyterian mee. in a Very fine chapel— the Priest read a pretty good sermon from his note book but it was a dry mess to me, but notwithstanding I suppose it seemed good to them for when he was through there was a donation made for him of $3.00. At 4 P.M. We attended our appointment at the schoolhouse and I had addressed the people about 20 minutes when a Methodist priest arose and said that he had an app. here at five o clock and he wished to fill it and he wanted to know if I would get through so as to give place. I told him that I did not know how long I should speak but I desired to speak until I should get through— However I told him that we would leave it to the people. A vote was called. Three or four voted for me to close and for him to speak but a majority Voted for me to continue— consequently I continued until I had spoken about two hours on the plain simplicity of the Gospel and its spiritual **gifts & powers**. After which Elder Patten called for a donation but not a man moved his tongue or his finger to help us. [*page 13*] consequently we left them believing that we had done our duty as to delivering our messsage and we wiped the dust off our feet and we also cle[a]nsed our feet in pure water as a testimony against them and we passed on toward old Oswego about 4 miles and put up with a Mr. Sears a Methodist man who received us in the name of deciples & entertained us very kindly and we talked with them much about what is on the earth and also what is coming, but I do not recollect to have ever felt more like mourning over the hardness of the hearts of this Generation———

Monday 8 We traveled about 20 miles, at eve we became quite weary and we tried at five or six different houses for entertainment but one had one excuse and another, another—— finally we came to a very poor man's dwelling and told him that we were preachers & that we were pennyless. he or rather She invited us in, being a Baptist by profession, but yet honest hearted. We were entertained hospitably, but they were Very [a]fraid of receiving a New revelation.

Tuesday we reached Oswego about 9 A.M. and the Steamer America was in, bound in a few minutes for Sackets Harbour. We got a passage on her by leaving a watch in pledge until we should pay $2. We sailed 60 miles and landed in the Harbour about 4. P. M- and bro. Childs living in the Village and in a few minutes we reached his house and found Elders Blakesly & Dutcher here who had an app about half mile distant at 5 Oclock We attended it and E. Patten preached from John 10th[45] and exorted a few minutes [*page 14*] The church here are 19 in number, a little enthusiastic and did not as a body pay any respect to the words of wisdom,[46] but seemed to be warm hearted and willing to learn from us the truth as it was. But even the Elders seemed to want almost every quality except Zeal and that they had abundantly— even to the saluting with a kiss[47]— &c.

Wednesday I wrote a letter for the office

and Thursday I attended an app. about six miles toward Watertown in a neighbourhood of the Christian Order and J. F. Boynton preached to a small cong[regation] on the plain simplicity of the Gospel and I think that I never heard a better discourse for its length—— it was forcible— here I left him and returned to the Harbour.— He made two or three app in this place—

Friday 12. This afternoon I preached in the Millcreek schoolhouse to the brethren and a few others. [on] My remarks were mostly concerning the book of Mormon and the rise of the Church—— These things seemed to give them great satisfaction and much instruction. They said that they [h] never had so heard before.

Saturday I wrote a letter to my brother S. M'Lellin and friends &c. at eve Elders Marsh & Ly[man]

Sunday 14. I preached in the forenoon in brother Luff's open barn for about 1½ hours on the 13 of th[e] 2 of 1 Cor.[48] but the unbelieving part of the congregation were very hard and took but little interest in it and some of them left me about the middle of my discourse. At 2 P.M. Elder Lyman J. preached in the schoolhouse from the 11th of Isa[49] on the literal gathering of the Jews and the meanes that God will use in their restitution &C [*page 15*] And at 6 Oclock the church met at bro Luffs and Elder Marsh administered the sacrament among them. We had quite a good meeting—

Monday there was a caravan of living animals exibited in Sackets, but the superstition of the brethren was such that I dare not go in to see them, however as they came into the Village I saw them and it was [a] grand sight to see sixty span of gray hosrs [horses] well rigged before nice waggons and carriages— drawing animals, birds and serpent &C. and Elephants seven or eight feet high, with a crown on his back with five musicians playing on their instruments and with poneys following them only 2 feet high— was novel. in the afternoon I went to Pillow Point— I rowed across the bay a little over a mile in a skift & blistered my right hand in only five or six places. At 5 oclock I attended Elder P. Pratt's app— only a few attended and I spoke to them about an hour although my head ached very badly——&c We went to a bro. Pratt's and tarried with him over night.

Tuesday 16. I returned to the Harbour thro[ugh] the rain and wind— I had a real merry ride; the waves rolled on the bay which was about 1¼ miles wide. I had an app. in the Village of Sackets Harbour at 5 oclock P.M. but it blowed and rained so that no persons attended and I was not sorry for I felt bad in consequence of the wickedness of those who called themselves deciples— they were most of them superstitious and very illitterate——

Wednesday I spent in visiting & counciling the brethern.

Thursday at [4] 5 Oclock I attended an app. at the schoolhouse at Mill creek and then had a number of brethren and sisters collected in, in order to attend the conference, I spoke on the covenants & Articles 1½ hours.

[*page 16*] Friday 19. Nine of the twelve met in conference on Pillow Point[50] and Elder Hyde whose turn it was to preside not being present I was called, of course, next. our business lasted till late in the afternoon.

Saturday morn we met again and continued business until about eleven oclock at which time Publick preaching was attended to by Elder Lyman Johnson on the Vision,[51] followed by Elder Boynton [for] with a few remarks & closed at ½ past 1. O[clock]. I thought best to have another meeting & I app. one at 5 Oclock supposing that the brethren would go home and take dinner and return, but the most of them tarried and stood round talking, waiting with anxiety for 5 to come. While I [was] had the Elders together instructing them in the duties of their office Elder P. Pratt came to me in company with others and said that he had something of the utmost importance to relate to me. I said to him to say on— and he observed that his feelings had not been so tried with any president since he had started on his mission and after I heard him

patiently I concluded that I would get the people immediately
together— for his greatest fault was that I had made an app. when
there was no need of one. I got the people together in the barn
and I desired that Elder Marsh should preach inasmuch as it was
his regular turn— But he declined. I was much grieved— because
I felt as though all the counsellors had forsaken me or at least they
thought that I had erred much in making the app. But I felt entirely clear and as tho I had done my duty and nothing more. And
finding that I had to conduct the meeting myself I went in and
opened the meeting and spoke about two hours on the Priests
Hoods to the general satisfaction and edification of all present
even to the brethren who had opposed me[52]——

[*page 17*] Sunday 21. This morning I called a council to know
whether Elder Marsh had lost his regular turn to preach or whether
I was wrong in doing what I did on yesterday— I[t] was decided
that I had done right and that he had lost his turn but it was
agreed that he and Elder Patten should conduct the meeting as it
mig[h]t seem them good. They did so and at intermition— Two
having come forward I went forward (it being their choice) and
immersed them at the edge of the great Lake Ontario. We had a
good meeting today ~~and~~ dismissed finally.

Monday morning Mrs. Eunice Lommery came to me and stated
that she wished to be baptized— I went immediately to the Lake
and immersed her and as we were coming up out of the water
David Colvin came to me with tears of contrition in his eyes and
to obey the commandments of the Lord. I immersed him and
confirmed them on the water's edge and they went their ways
rejoicing[53] and I crossed the bay to Sackits Harbour——

Tuesday 23. I walked out 7 miles to Brownville and back to see if
there was a letter in the office from my companion. But there was
none—— Elder Childs let me have Mahomets' Alcoran[54]— a book
that I had long desired to possess— and at 11 Oclock P. M. [~~We~~]
Elder T. B. Marsh, P. Pratt and myself took the steamer Oswego for
Kingston[55] (the others of the twelve not thinking that it would be
important for them to go, started easterly for the next conference)[56]

and we arrived in Kingstton about sunrise on—— Wednesday morning and we reached Elder F[rederich] Van Luwen's the same evening about 18 miles northerly——

[*page 18*] Thursday 25. In the afternoon the brethren attended [and] a meeting at bro. J[ohn] V[an] L[uwen] and Elder Pratt delivered a discourse to them of 2 hours length on the nature of the Kingdom of Christ &C—

Friday afternoon we had another meeting at bro. Boice's and Elder Marsh preached and I followed him with a few remarks and the spirit came upon me and I had great liberty and the brethren rejoiced much and some of them even shouted aloud——

Saturday I went to Kingston with Elder VanLuwen in a two horse waggon— A caravan of living animals being there I went in to see them and paid 25 cts. Here bro V. bought me some Casinett[57] for pantaloons, and I was thankful and as we returned home at Waterloo 3 mls. from the city Margaret Boice an acquaintance desired to to [*sic*] go with us to Loborough. we took her in and she rode on my lap and I became sorry for it was an uneasy ride for me and it also brought fresh to mind my younger days——

Sunday a large congregation collected in a barn and I addressed them on the evidences of the truth for about two hours in forenoon and in the afternoon Elder Marsh lectured them and others spoke and exorted and expressed their feelings &c— and just as we were about to dismiss Elder Hyde & Young arived from Kirtland[58] and brought me a letter— a little letter from my wife— it contained but little, but yet I loved it——

Monday We met with the church in conference.[59] Elder Pratt presided and the council gave the church much instruction on various points and we regulated the church[60] by appointing a presiding Elder[61] and then we appointed another meeting for tomorrow fore and afternoon——[62]

[*page 19*] Tuesday 30. In the forenoon Elder Young [and] preached and baptized three individuals and in the afternoon Elder Hyde

preached and administered the sacrament and we had a good time
with the Saints here and bid them Farewell.

Wednesday—— July 1st We seperated to meet again in [s]t Johnsbury V. T. [Vermont] the 17inst[63] [a] And I and Elder Young concluded to tarry a little while longer in Canada and we travel[e]d
about 18 miles and I preached at 5 Oclock in the afternoon at a
Mr. Daniel's (a son in Law to bro. Millet). Nothing important transpired only—— unbelief——

Thursday we went about 12 miles to Mr. Wm Myers' whose wife
was a good sister, they treated us kindly

and on [Thursday] Friday we went to a Tailor & engaged him to
make each of us a pair of pantaloons[64] and to have them finished
by [m] Monday night—— and in the evening we attended a prayr
meeting at a Mr Sniders' among a people who belonged to no
order of religionists but who professed to be very pious. They
invited & Elder Young spoke to them about an hour and I about
20 minutes. They gave good attention, but they felt or seemed to
feel as if they were sufficiently holy without any farther preparation but we knew that they were not prepared for the coming of
the Lord Therefore we appointed another meeting at the same
place for Sunday.

Saturday the 4th I spent (without any noise around) me writing
letters to my wife[65] and to the office and I sent them to Kirt by
Elder Wood——

Sunday we met quite a large congregation and I addressed them
1 1/2 hours from John 3 Chap[66] But while I was speaking I was
interrupted by a reformed Methodist preacher[67] but he was si-
lenced by the man of the house. [*page 20*] his name was Daniel
Perry and after I had ceased to speak, a man by the name of
Nathan Fellows arose and desired to ask me some questions, I
granted him the liberty and he read them from a paper that I
suppose he had written while I was speaking— I answered him

so that I supposed him satisfied— Elder Young spoke in the after-noon to but a small congregation and We offered to receive a donation to assist us to get to our next con[gregation] and we received almost 2 shillings in one of the wealthiest neighbourhoods in Canada———. We left them but we said in our hearts, the curses of God abide upon You— because you have rejected our testi-mony— You have rejected the truth— and have not administered to our necessities— And we cannot leave our blessing with You—

Tuesday 7 we received four dollars from brother Millet[t] and we left Mr. Myers' about 4 Oclock A.M. and we had fourteen miles to Kingston and we reached there about 9 A.M. and found the Steamer Comd. [Commodore] Barrie bound for Presscot— to start in a few moments and for one dollar each we were landed in Presscot 77 miles distance about 4 P.M. and we crossed over to Ogdensburg for one [monetary symbol] each and passed on about 3 miles and staid over night in the name of deciples,

and the next day we walked 28 miles and staid in Potsdam with a bro. Lamson

and next day a woman brought us on our way in a one horse waggon 10 miles to Elder Pine's in [s] Stocholm and the same eve Elder Fuller brought us 4 miles to bro Asahel Smith's and gave us also $2 in money

and the next day he brought early in the morning Elder Marsh overtook us and Elder F[uller] brougt us on 5 miles to Hopkinton and [*page 21*] and thence 2 mls. to Slab City or Sodom from which it was 75 miles to Port Kent on Lake Champlain and came on with us 7 mts. [miles] further to a tavern and thence we passed on traveling on a turnpike that was very sandy through a very poor lonely hilly rough country until we reached Port Kent on [S]

Sunday eve 12. But I should have said that on Saturday morn we call at a Mr M. Hawley who kept tavern and told him that we were preachers of the Gospel and we wanted some bread and milk for breakfast and we asked for it without money—— but he abused us and after we had born testimony to him we came to a little brook and clensed our feet as a testimony against him——At P[ort] Kent we had to tarry until——

Monday afternoon We crossed over the Lake 10 mls. to Burlington and on——

Tuesday morning 14th We took stage 12 miles from B. and rode 28 miles to Montpelier—— and thence   miles to Danville and thence 12 mls. to Elder Gardner Snow's in St Johnsbury and we reached here after a very fatiguing Journey and sore feet.

Thursday eve and on Friday we attended our conference.[68] Elder Luke Johnson presided and O. Hyde took the minutes.

And on Saturday Elder O. Hyde & Ly[man] Johnson preached to quite a large congregation.

Sunday I preached in the forenoon to about 1500 persons on the rise and government of the church of christ & & [*page 22*] P. Pratt preached in the afternoon on the Kingdom of christ, 9 were baptized during the meeting[69]

and on—— Monday 20, I wrote a letter for bro. William Smith to bro. Joseph.

and on——Tuesday 21. I wrote a letter to Emiline in the forenoon and preached in the afternoon at the Snow schoolhouse to a few from Gen. 17 - 1[70] on the nature of perfection

and on Wednesday I and Orson P were brought to Watterford lower Village by Elder Gardner Snow in a one horse waggon in order to meet Col. Miles' stage (but I should have mentioned that the brethrn in Johnsbury had two pair of boots made for and one pair was to[o] small and the other was too large so that I had to go without). We met the stage after going 10 mls and then went immediately down the connetticut river 12 miles to Mcadoes falls and staid over night with bro. Miles and in the morning his wife gave me two shirts (and I really needed them)

Thursday 23. Bro. Miles brought me up to Littleton about 14 mls. to brother D. Millen's

and on Friday afternoon I preached at his house to 9 persons for a congregation, I had not much liberty, I spoke about one hour,

Saturday 25. I preached at the school house to a small congregation from Gal. 1 - 8[71] for 1 3/4 hours. I had great liberty.

Sunday 26. I went on horseback 12 mls. to Dolton and preached in the forenoon to a large congregation from 2 Pet. 1 - 1.[72] I had good L[iberty] and in the afternoon I continued the same subject and broke bread among the Saints.

[*page 23*] Monday 27. This morning early I was called on by a Mr. Montgomery to go and pray for his infantchild who had fallen down celler the day previous and was hurt badly— The Doctor had been called but to no purpose. I went and prayed for the child & laid my hands upon [ħ] it but it did not seem to be healed immediately— And I betook myself to the woods and called mightily upon God and when I returned I found the child up and wanting to eat and to play. Its parents verily believed that it was healed by the power of God and so did I— And I felt to rejoice much——— In the afternoon I attended an app. in the Northern district of the town and preached & baptized 2 viz. Amelia Barrows & Ethan her son. They seemed to have a good understanding of the work—

Tuesday afternoon at 5 Oclock I preached at bro. Wilder's sC[hool] H[ouse] on the Priesthoods and tarried over night with Esqr Maxin.

We[n]dnesday 29. I rode about 16 miles and preached in the Parker schoolhouse in Lyman to quite a congregation, a part of whom seemed quite believing— and I made a number of other apps.

Thursday 30. I rode about 6 miles and preached to a small con[gregation] (mostly women) from the 37 Psalm & 37 verse[73] about 2 hours. I had great liberty especially in the latter part of my discourse. the Spirit was pourd out wonderfully, the people were melted down and the Lord gave me his spirit to speak in tongues (and it rolled powerfully) [*page 24*] But none felt willing at this time to take upon them the name of Christ. But there was a Mrs. Davis came forward and desired with great anxiety to be ~~heal~~ healed of infirmity. She had but little faith or humility— But by her earnest request, I knelt down and prayed for her, but she had not humility enough to kneell when I prayed and I did not lay hands on her. And she did not feel satisfied. consequently she followed me to where I put up over night at brother D. Mill[e]ns and at evening prayrs I prayed for her again and laid my hands on her but I had not any evidence that she would be healed unless she would go forward and embrace the Gospel of truth and I told her so.

Friday 31. I and bro. Millen rode about four miles and back and I preached in a schoolhouse to about a dozen hardhearted, unbelieving wicked creatures who cared but little for any thing else but the God of this world. I preached 3/4 of an hour.

August. Saturday 1st I went about 4 miles and preached [~~to~~] in a schoolhouse nearly filled with people who seemed to be quite believing and very friendly— It was in what was called Parker s[c]hool house I preached from Matt. 24— 3[74] for about 2 hours. I had great Liberty of speech and many were melted into tears. But none felt the importance of the subject enough to embrace the Lord by Baptism, consequently I left no more app. here——

Sunday 2. I [~~preached~~] was quite unwell but just able to go about, but yet [*page 25*] I [p] went about 4 miles, and preached in the forenoon and afternoon about 2 hours each on Paker hill in Lyman in the white chapel to a large congregation of various orders and opinions, first on the faith of the Saints and secondly on the truth of the book of Mormon. Some of the people seemed to be quite effected, but none seemed willing to obey the truth. I then told the congregation that some of my clothes were nearly worne out and if they felt disposed as they pa[s]sed out of the house when dismissed to put a donation into the hands of Bro. D. Millen. I would receive it thankfully— I received 60 cents. I suppose they did not expect it, and were not prepared.

Monday 3 To day I attended (tho still somewhat unwell) an app. at the Shoot's schoolhouse and the weather being Lowery at 1/2 past 4. the house was crowded and I preached to them about 2 hours from Mark 1 .. 15[75] on the nature of the kingdom of God and the plainness of the Gospel of truth. I then invited all to come forward and embrace it. Four manifested that they were willing to repent and they wished to be immersed for the remission of Their sins. They were received and another mee app. the next afternoon for the purpose of attending to the ordinances——

Tuesday 4 We met at Mr. Huntoon's and I preached 1 1/2 from Heb. 12 - 14[76] And I do not remember to have ever preached plainer. I showed the Authority that men have for acting in the name of Jesus (I thought) plainly. I then went to a little Lake and immersed Hiram Caffa & Betsy his wife, Polly Wright and Talitha Cumi Carter— and Confirmed them——

[*page 26*] Wednesday 5.th In the afternoon I met a schoolhouse full in Mr Briggs district and I preached one hour & 1/2— to them from Mark 13 & 21-22.[77] Many seemed to believe and one came forward and manifested a desire to join the church and was received so that he might obey the ordinances.

Thursday 6. At 8 Oclock A.M. I met a few at bro. Caffa's and talked to them some and immersed Albert Millen and Carter Huntoon and confirmed them on the waters edge. (Nothing special) A number of solicitations had come to me from the Carter settlement for me to go into that neighbourhood and preach and I sent an app. for Friday afternoon.

Friday 7[78] I went according to app. and preached from 8th Rom.[79] on the natur and effects of the Holy Ghost for 1 1/4 hours. & when done I walked into the yard and stood until all the congregation were gone with out ever receiving an invitation to go home with any one, to take supper or tarry ov[e]r night. consequently instead of feeling to bless them I felt to pity them & mourn over them. I returned about 2 miles to bro David Millens who made me as welcome as if I had been at home—And I really felt as though this was my home in this place.

Saturday 8. I went to the Shoot's schoolhouse again and preached with great liberty to the brethren and friends & conforted them.

Sunday 9. Bro. Millen brought me [*page 27*] in a waggon to Dolton and I preached in the forenoon to a large congregation on the second coming of christ and in the afternoon on the operation of the Spir[it] and on the evidences of the book of Mormon and in the evening I preached again on the principles of christian perfection and two manifested a desire to be baptized and we appointed a mee. for tomorrow.

Monday 10. At 5. P.M. We met at bro. Fisher's and I preached on the covenants, and Articles and then went to the water and immersed Fanny and Perces Athington and confirmed them on the water's edge— Here the brethren gave me a new pair of boots but they were poor things——

Tuesday 11. Elder Levi Wilder came and brought me on my way up the old connetticut river 27 miles and then I walked on 15 miles to Elder Isaac Aldrich's, Here I tarried with him until

Thursday 13. And then he brought me on my way a few miles and altho it rained very hard I passed on across a lone and dreary waste of mountains 22 miles to Priest Benj Sweat's in the town of Errol which seemed to be almost out of the world but yet I found good brethren here who were willing to hear the word of life

and I preached on Friday Saturday, Sunday twice and baptized **7** viz. James, Hezk. & N. Johnson, Charlotte Cone, Angeline Sweat, Sally Shattuck & Frederick Sweat, and on Monday I Administered the sacrament and con[*page 28*]firmed the believers and I and Elder Dan. Bean laid our hands upon and blessed their children— We had a heavenly time.

Tuesday 18. Elder Bean and I went to Letter B.[80] and I preached at 5 Oclock from 1 Thess. 1.5[81] for about 2 hours and I think that I hardly ever had such liberty in my life. All were astonished.

Wednesday. 19. I preached at Mr. Manuel's at 3 oclock from the 37th Psalm 37 vrse,[82] I had not very great Liberty.

Thursday 20. I went with Elder Bean 30 miles to Rumford Point and heard Elder Patten preach in a large Meeting house to a small congregation a 4 P. M Thence without [s] even a supper itself 6 mls to Priest Carter's and tarried ove[r] night after calling and taking supper at bro. Powers'.

Friday[83] I went about 6 mls and back at preached about 2 hours at 4 P.M. at a bro Cessions' and on the way I got tremendiously wet in a great hail storm.

Saturday I returned 36 mils to Letter B.

Sunday 23. I preached in the shoolhous in [Letter] B. on the second coming of Christ, and in the afernoon I met with the Church and broke bread, our services continued 4 hours and were very interesting indeed.

Monday I crossed Umbagog Lake 10 mls in a scow to Errol again

and Tuesday forenoon I wrote a letter to Emiline and in the afternoon while [*page 29*] picking Blue berries Elder Danl Bean came and brought me word that the Farmington conference would be held the ensueing Friday and the Twelve had sent word that they wished me to attend it. We immediately left for [Letter] B. and traveled the worst road that I ever see in all my life. night overtook us and it rained hard and we could see just as much (in passing ~~abou~~ about 3 miles through the wood) with the ends of

our fingers as with our eyes—— I shall never forget this night
Though I may travel ore the world.

Wednesday 26. I, Elder Bean and bro. S. Akers started to Farmington

and we arived Thursday afternoon (65) Mls. Here I continued with
the brethren until Monday morning.[84]

I preached on Saturday.

Monday 31 We parted to meet in Buffalo N.Y. the 24 Sept. Elder W. Smith
and I traveled together in a small waggon 47 miles to Newry.

Thence on Tuesday and Wednesday the 1 & 2 of September We
came to Dalton through Lancaster— 65. and thence on

Thursday 3. 12 miles to Littleton to brother D. Millen's.[85]
[*page 30 blank*]
[*page 31*]

Mandeville, Carroll Co., Mo.,
Nov. 11, 1884.

I received this book from the Express Office at Norborne,
Mo., yesterday, Nov. 10, 1884, as a present from Mrs. Emeline
McLellan, now at her son's in Troy, Mo.

J. L. Traughber, Jr.

[*page 32*]
Books that I want to purchase

Jones' Church History
Goodrich's Eclesiastical History
Dictionary of History
Ancient Geography & Atlas
Moshiem's Church History
Mahomat's X Koran (Bought)

[Đ] Creeds and Deciplines
Celcus History (Infidel)
Gahn's B. Archeology
All Religions, and ceremonies———X Bought
Fox Martyrs———X Bought
American Antiquities
"Clarks evidences of Religion"

[*page 33*]

Chronology[86]
———

Adam lived ~~lived~~ 246 years after the birth of Methuselah; Methuselah lived 100 years after the birth of shem; Shem outlived Abraham thirty five years— he lived until 110 years after the birth of Isaac, and fifty years after the birth of Jacob. Abraham, Isaac and Jacob were the direct progeny of Shem, through the line of the ~~line of the~~ eldest son— Shem of Methusalem and he of Adam. Hence we infer that Adam was acquainted with Methusalem, he with Shem and Shem with Abraham, Isaac and Jacob. These were the living Chronicles of **ancient** days, through whom were handed down to the <u>sacred</u> historian, the traditions of the events and institutions of those long ages, with undoubted accuracy. Six men were cotemporary with Adam & Noah and eight with Noah [Ȧ] and Abraham.

[*page 34 blank*]

NOTES

[1] On April 26, 1835, McLellin met with the Apostles and other church leaders in the unfinished Kirtland temple to receive from the Prophet "their charge and instructions . . . relating to their mission and duties." Joseph Smith, Jr., *History of The Church of Jesus Christ of Latter-day Saints,* ed. B. H. Roberts, 2d ed. rev., 7 vols. (Salt Lake City: Deseret Book, 1971), 2:218 (hereafter cited as *HC*). The Twelve gathered in the schoolroom two days later to plan the mission in which they would go forth to proclaim the

gospel. In this meeting, McLellin read the revelation which describes the calling of the Twelve (D&C 18), after which "it was voted that [the Twelve] forgive one another every wrong that has existed among [them] and that from [thenceforth] each one of the Twelve love his brother as himself, in temporal as well as in spiritual things." They also planned their departure, deciding to leave Kirtland at two o'clock A.M., May 4, 1835. *HC* 2:219. Then, on May 2, a general council of prominent priesthood members was held in Kirtland. At this council, for which McLellin served as clerk, Joseph Smith gave the Twelve further instructions concerning their duties and responsibilities. *HC* 2:219-22.

   [2]The succinct description of the purpose of this mission that McLellin gives here reflects both the Prophet's instruction to the Twelve and the overall makeup of Mormonism in this, the fifth year of the organization of the Church. By this time, the "tent of Zion" had organized stakes in Kirtland and Missouri, where the Mormons were creating *gathering centers* as they responded to the call to assemble "in unto one place upon the face of this land" (D&C 29:7-8). Both of these stakes had standing High Councils. In addition, small congregations of persons who had accepted the LDS message and had been baptized by missionaries like McLellin were spreading across the countryside. Led by local converts, these branches, as they were usually called, kept in touch with the center in two ways: they subscribed to the *Messenger and Advocate,* which was published by the Church in Kirtland; and they were visited periodically by elders sent from the gathering centers on preaching missions or assignments. President Smith's instructions to the Twelve regularized the overall structure of the Church by specifying that the Twelve "have no right to go into Zion [Missouri], or any of its stakes, and there undertake to regulate the affairs thereof; . . . but it is their duty to go abroad and regulate all matters relative to the different branches of the Church." *HC* 2:220.

   Branches in the several areas were to be called together in conferences in which the Apostles would inquire into the standing of all the elders in each conference and into the manner of their teaching, doctrines, and so on. At the same time, the Twelve were to inquire into the teaching, conduct, and faithfulness of all traveling elders (missionaries) who had recently labored within the boundaries of the various conferences. The former established a form of oversight over the scattered branches; the latter, a crucially important type of inquiry, allowed the Twelve, as representatives of the church President and familiar with recent revelations and other organizational developments, to determine what was being taught under the aegis of the Church. See "First Mission of the Twelve," a document signed by Orson Hyde, printed in *HC* 2:222-26.

   A suggestion that the role given to the Twelve to be a "traveling high council" was a part of a strategy to prevent Mormonism from becoming a victim of centrifugal forces as it moved ever further away from the gathering centers is found in the Kirtland High Council minutes of August 4, 1835. A copy of these minutes was clearly designed to be sent to the Twelve with a warning that if they had set themselves up as an independent council, subject to no authority of the Church, they would be outlaws. If they persisted in giving such an impression, it "would bring down the wrath and indignation of heaven on their heads." In other words, they needed always to keep in mind that they were representatives of and subject to the centralized authority of the Church.

For the most part, the history of this period in Mormonism has concentrated on the gathering centers, whose high councils kept careful records that have been preserved in the Kirtland High Council minutes, 1832-1837 (only available in the LDS Church Archives) and the *Far West Record: Minutes of The Church of Jesus Christ of Latter-day Saints, 1830-1844*, edited by Donald Q. Cannon and Lyndon W. Cook and published by Deseret Book in 1983. Descriptions of Mormonism in the countryside must be pieced together from the journals and letters of the elders whose missions carried them to the vicinities where branches were organized. For an extensive list of such records, see appendix II below. For further details about this "tour in the Eastern countries to preach the Gospel, attend conferences and give council pertaining to the things of God to our brethren in the churches abroad and to regulate the things that are wanting," see the accounts of the mission experiences of the other apostles recorded in Andrew Jenson, Journal History of the Church, housed in LDS Church Archives, September 26, 1835, 1-8 (hereafter cited as JH).

[3] Orson Pratt also described this fortuitous beginning in his journal: "[We] left Kirtland for Fairport, where we arrived a little after sunrise, and went immediately on board of a steam boat which left the port a few minutes after we got on board. Thus the Lord in his mercy provided a boat for us at the very moment we arrived which was according to our prayers." Elden J. Watson, comp., *The Orson Pratt Journals* (Salt Lake City: Elden J. Watson, 1975), 60.

[4] For a similar account of the journey to Dunkirk, see *HC* 2:222.

[5] 1 Thessalonians 1:5 reads: "For our gospel came not unto you in word only, but also in power, and in the Holy Ghost, and in much assurance; as ye know what manner of men we were among you for your sake."

[6] May 9 was Saturday. For more details about the proceedings of this Westfield conference, see *HC* 2:222-24; and "Report of the Twelve Apostles," *Messenger and Advocate* 1 (May 1835): 115-16.

[7] Before the Apostles left Kirtland, Joseph Smith told them that "when the Twelve are together, or a quorum of them, in any church, they will have authority to act independently, and make decisions, and those decisions will be valid. But where there is not a quorum, they will have to do business by the voice of the Church." *HC* 2:220.

[8] Before the Twelve began this mission, Joseph Smith said that "it would be the duty of the Twelve, when in council, to take their seats

together according to age, the oldest to be seated at the head, and preside in the first council, the next oldest in the second, and so on until the youngest had presided; and then begin at the oldest again." *HC* 2:219. Thomas B. Marsh was considered the eldest, so he presided at this first conference. At the following conference, the next oldest presided, and so on.

[9] Minutes of the conferences convened by the Twelve were usually kept by Orson Hyde, but sometimes by other apostles, including McLellin, who acted as clerk. Minutes from this eastern tour are reproduced in *HC* 2:222-26, 238, 241-42.

[10] The minutes kept by Orson Hyde indicate that about 500 people attended. *HC* 2:223.

[11] An article in the *Messenger and Advocate* said that Patten spoke about "the corruptions of the Gentile church." "Report of the Twelve Apostles," 116.

[12] Hebrews 11 is the most famous chapter in the New Testament on faith. Compare Alma 32 and Ether 12 in the Book of Mormon.

[13] Benjamin Brown later described his baptism:

> The second day of this conference, I, with four others, was baptized by Elder McLellin, and confirmed the same night. While undressing on the bank of the creek, preparing for the ordinance, Satan made a last effort to prevent my entering the church. A man coming along by the waterside came up to me and said, "I wish to speak to you for a few minutes before you go into the water." Thinking of course that he was a friend, or a member of the Church, who intended to give me some instruction as to my behavior when in the water, I listened to him, and, having got me to retire some rods off, he said, "Have you heard what has come out?" "No," I replied, "what about?" "Why," he continued, "concerning the Mormons, it has been discovered that it is all an imposture, a regular hoax to deceive the people. The affair has just come to light. If you wait only a little, you'll hear all about it." At first this completely stunned me, for I was listening very attentively, considering him one of the Church, and for a moment I began to question, but quickly recollecting the manifestations I had received, I told him he was a child of the devil, and I pushed past him to the water, and was baptized at once. (Benjamin Brown, *Testimonies for the Truth,* LDS Historical Library CD Rom, 2d ed. [Provo, Utah: Infobases, 1993], 5-6)

[14] John 14:26 is a key scripture regarding the functions of the Holy Ghost: "But the Comforter, which is the Holy Ghost, whom the Father will send in my name, he shall teach you all things, and bring all things to your remembrance, whatsoever I have said unto you." Just as Jesus promised his original disciples that they would enjoy the companionship of this spiritual comforter, McLellin and his brethren bestowed "the gift of the Holy Ghost" upon their converts, who thereafter sought and received many spiritual manifestations.

[15] McLellin was quoting a commandment given on December 16, 1833, after the Saints had been expelled from Jackson County but before the Prophet organized the Zion's Camp expedition. The revelation instructed the Saints

> to purchase all the lands with money, which can be purchased for money, in the region round about the land which I [the Lord] have appointed to be the land of Zion, for the beginning of the gathering of my saints; [purchase] all the the land which can be purchased in Jackson county, and the counties round about, and leave the residue in mine hand. Now, verily I say unto you, let all the churches gather together all their moneys; let these things be done in their time, but not in haste; and observe to have all things prepared before you. And let honorable men be appointed, even wise men, and send them to purchase these lands. And the churches in the eastern countries, when they are built up, if they will hearken unto this counsel they may buy lands and gather together upon them; and in this way they may establish Zion. (D&C 101:70-74)

[16] This is one of the few occasions in these journals that explicitly mention sermons being preached on texts from the Book of Mormon rather than the Bible. Third Nephi contains portions of the resurrected Savior's preaching during three days among the Nephites. The main text, a day-long sermon at the temple in the city of Bountiful, is found in 3 Nephi 11-18.

[17] This conference was scheduled for May 22. Orson Hyde and McLellin to Oliver Cowdery, *Messenger and Advocate* 1 (March 1835): 90.

[18] This practice of saluting as a custom to be observed in the School of the Prophets is based on instructions given in an 1832 revelation to Joseph Smith. The salute was made "with uplifted hands to heaven" (D&C 88:132; see 1 Kgs. 8:22). The revelation continued:

> And when any shall come in after him, let the teacher arise, and, with uplifted hands to heaven, yea, even directly, salute his brother or brethren with these words: Art thou a brother or brethren? I salute you in the name of the Lord Jesus Christ, in token or remembrance of the everlasting covenant, in which covenant I receive you to fellowship, in a determination that is fixed, immovable, and unchangeable, to be your friend and brother through the grace of God in the bonds of love, to walk in all the commandments of God blameless, in thanksgiving, forever and ever. Amen. (D&C 88:132-33)

[19] One of the problems in the branches had been outlined during the Westfield conference when some members made known a difficulty in their minds about the the baptism of one Lloyd L. Lewis, a brother who had been baptized by a traveling elder "without the church being called together to know if they would receive him to fellowship. The [Twelve] decided that if there was a fault, it was in the administrator, and not in the candidate."

HC 2:223. Therefore, when Sylvester Norton expressed his desire to be baptized just as nine of the Twelve were taking their leave, McLellin and Hyde called the church members in the branch together to prevent such a mistake from happening again. According to their report, after the members "prayed unto the Lord our Heavenly Father, in the name of Christ and [after] the Holy Spirit was shed forth upon us, and all were melted into humility and tears before the Lord," the candidate was accepted and McLellin and Hyde remained behind in order to baptize him. "Report of the Twelve Apostles," 116.

[20] One of the reasons they had remained after the other Apostles left was "to arrange the minutes of our conference and record them." "Report of the Twelve Apostles," 116.

[21] See note 51, Journal IV above.

[22] 2 Timothy gives direction to those who were performing pastoral functions in the early church. In a passage of the final chapter, Timothy is charged with preaching the word in and out of season, reproving, rebuking, and exhorting, because the time would come when the members would not endure sound doctrine. The fourth verse reads: "And they shall turn away their ears from the truth, and shall be turned unto fables." How Orson Hyde connected this text to the restoration of the Aaronic and Melchizedek Priesthoods and the coming forth of the Book of Mormon is not clear.

[23] 2 Peter 1:1 was a favorite scripture for McLellin: "Simon Peter, a servant and an apostle of Jesus Christ, to them that have obtained like precious faith with us through the righteousness of God and our Saviour Jesus Christ." Perhaps, as a modern apostle, he thought of himself as a modern Peter and found inspiration in the idea that servants and apostles had been called in his own day to preach the same faith that had been taught by Peter of old. If so, McLellin would have assured his listeners that they had received the same gospel that Peter had received through the righteousness of God and Jesus.

It is important to note that 2 Peter 1 also includes the verse in which the author assured his readers that God and Jesus had given to them "exceeding great and precious promises" by which they "might be partakers of the divine nature" (v. 4). Some early Saints connected this text to a doctrine that would later be called "eternal progression." While this doctrine was not fully disclosed until the Nauvoo period, an 1832 revelation to Joseph Smith and Sidney Rigdon (D&C 76) known as "The Vision" included a passage (vv. 51–59) that spelled out the promise to those who had "received the testimony of Jesus, and believed on his name and were baptized after the manner of his burial [by immersion]." Those who kept the commandments and "receive[d] the Holy Spirit by the laying on of the hands of him who is ordained and sealed unto his power" (v. 52), as McLellin believed that he was, became members of "the Church of the Firstborn":

> They are they into whose hands the Father has given all things—They are they who are priests and kings, who have received of his fulness, and of his glory; and are priests of the Most High, after the order of Melchizedek, which was after the order of Enoch, which was after the order of the Only Begotten Son. Wherefore, as it is written, they are gods, even the sons of God. (D&C 76:55-58)

[24] There were approximately twenty members in this town. "Report of the Twelve Apostles," 115.

[25] Mark 13:21-22 reads: "And then if any man shall say to you, Lo, here is Christ; or, lo, he is there; believe him not: For false Christs and false prophets shall rise, and shall shew signs and wonders, to seduce, if it were possible, even the elect." No doubt this text was used to assert that even those who thought they were chosen could be in error and to discredit ministers who were preaching different versions of the Christian gospel.

[26] This would have been Warren A. Cowdery, the presiding high priest of the congregation in Freedom (D&C 106), the brother of Oliver Cowdery.

[27] The Freedom conference was held from May 22-25; for details, see *HC* 2:224-25.

[28] Heber C. Kimball and McLellin both used John 14 as a text. This is the chapter that begins with the following familiar verses:

> Let not your heart be troubled: ye believe in God, believe also in me. In my Father's house are many mansions: if it were not so, I would have told you. I go to prepare a place for you. And if I go and prepare a place for you, I will come again, and receive you unto myself; that where I am, there ye may be also. (John 14:1-3)

The part of the chapter on which Kimball concentrated is not indicated, but McLellin seems to have focused on verse 26, a text he had used on May 10. See note 14 above.

[29] See note 15 above.

[30] The result of this day of preaching was favorable: "The church expressed their determination to put into practice the teachings we had given." *HC* 2:224.

[31] The Book of Mormon teaches that descendants of the biblical Joseph emigrated from Israel to the Americas centuries before the birth of Christ. Thus, the Book of Mormon refers to the pre-Columbian inhabitants of the Americas as the "remnant of Joseph." Furthermore, the book claims that someday the Lord will "bring a remnant of the seed of Joseph to the knowledge of the Lord their God" (3 Ne. 5:23). Brigham Young's special assignment to preach the gospel to the Native Americans had been announced and voted on in the general council of the priesthood held on

May 2, 1835, in Kirtland. He was to be accompanied by John P. Greene and Amos Orton. *HC* 2:222.

³² This reservation was one of eleven Seneca reservations established by the Treaty of 1797, consisting of forty-two square miles along both banks of the Allegheny River. By 1820, approximately half of the Seneca population was Christian. George H. J. Abrams, *The Seneca People* (Phoenix: Indian Tribal Series, 1976), 50–51, 58.

³³ The Lyonstown conference was scheduled for June 5, 1835. Hyde and McLellin to Cowdery, 90.

³⁴ Isaiah 8:20 reads as follows. "To the law and to the testimony: if they speak not according to this word, it is because there is no light in them." The themes of law (covenants and commandments) and testimony (by the Holy Ghost) are evident here.

³⁵ See note 23 above.

³⁶ Jeremiah 31:31–33 is a classic restoration scripture; it prophesies about the day when the Lord "will make a new covenant with the house of Israel, and with the house of Judah. . . . After those days, saith the Lord, I will put my law in their inward parts, and write it in their hearts; and will be their God, and they shall be my people."

³⁷ John 5:30 records these words of Jesus: "I can of mine own self do nothing: as I hear, I judge: and my judgment is just; because I seek not mine own will, but the will of the Father which hath sent me." While it is not possible to know how the early Mormons might have used this scripture, it could have been used to encourage all people to learn and do God's will, rather than to follow personal inclinations or the fashions of the world.

³⁸ In October 1834, the first number of the LDS periodical *Messenger and Advocate* was published in Kirtland, replacing the *Evening and Morning Star,* whose press had been destroyed when the Saints were driven from Independence, Missouri. While the *Star* had been published in quarto form, the *Messenger and Advocate* "was to be published in octavo form for greater convenience in binding and preserving." The name was changed to more clearly reflect the paper's goal of advocating the Church's "character and rights" before the accusations of the world. *HC* 2:167n. See J. Leroy Caldwell, *"Messenger and Advocate,"* in *Encyclopedia of Mormonism,* ed. Daniel H. Ludlow, 5 vols. (New York: Macmillan, 1992), 2:892. As indicated in note 2 above, one of the functions of this publication was keeping the Saints in the scattered branches in touch with those in the gathering centers.

³⁹ Genesis 17:1 says that when Abraham (Abram) was ninety-nine years old, God appeared and spoke to him. It is likely that the focus of McLellin's sermon was on God's words: "I am the Almighty God; walk before me, and be thou perfect" (Gen. 17:1). But it is also possible that McLellin selected this as a text because he wished to demonstrate that God could appear to mortals. If so, this choice could reflect his having heard Joseph Smith

describe the first of his visions. While this connection is obviously speculative, if other uses of this text by early Mormons are found, such uses could contribute to a circumstantial case that the Prophet was talking about his first vision earlier than has been assumed. See James B. Allen, "Emergence of a Fundamental: The Expanding Role of Joseph Smith's First Vision in Mormon Religious Thought," *Journal of Mormon History* 7 (1980): 43-61.

[40] The *History of the Church* indicates that there were so few members in the vicinity of Lyonstown (or the neighboring Rose), New York, that when the nine members of the Twelve who were in Lyonstown met, they decided that establishing a conference was unnecessary. *HC* 2:225. McLellin's account indicates that the Apostles met from 10 A.M. to 4 P.M., during which time the business of the conference was handled.

[41] The Seneca people. See note 31 above.

[42] At this time, Joseph Smith, Sidney Rigdon, and Frederick G. Williams made up the "Presidency" of the Church. Hyde and Young returned to Kirtland along with Apostle William Smith to serve as witnesses in a county court case wherein President Joseph Smith was a party. The *History of the Church* indicates that the Prophet "righteously triumphed over his enemies," but what the case was about is unknown. *HC* 2:225.

[43] Pillow [Pillar] Point, Jefferson County, New York, was to be the site of the next conference, scheduled for June 19. Hyde and McLellin to Cowdery, 90.

[44] As used here, "vision" was without doubt a reference to a vision that came to Joseph Smith and Sidney Rigdon when they encountered John 5:29 as they were working on a translation of the New Testament. Of major doctrinal importance, the content of this vision is described in Doctrine and Covenants 76. Cook, *Revelations of the Prophet Joseph Smith*, 157-66. Also see note 23 above.

[45] It is likely that Patten emphasized John 10:16: "And other sheep I have, which are not of this fold: them also I must bring, and they shall hear my voice." This use is likely because the Book of Mormon identified the "other sheep" as the Nephites and other people from the house of Israel to whom the Lord appeared after his resurrection (3 Ne. 15:16-16:3).

[46] The Word of Wisdom is the revelation now known as Doctrine and Covenants 89. The best-known portion of this revelation warns against the use of coffee, tea, alcohol, and tobacco. The nearby Pillow [Pillar] Point congregation "did not generally observe the Word of Wisdom." *HC* 2:225. This was probably true of the Sackets Harbor group as well.

[47] See 1 Cor. 16:20; 2 Cor. 13:12; and 1 Thes. 5:26. These New York members, and possibly McLellin as well, probably did not know that the translation of the Bible on which Joseph Smith and Sidney Rigdon worked for several years during the Saints' stay in Kirtland changed the word "kiss" to "salutation."

[48] See note 51, Journal IV above.

[49] See note 27, Journal IV above.

[50] For details of the Pillow [Pillar] Point conference, see *HC* 2:225–26.

[51] Orson Pratt mentioned in his journal that Lyman Johnson and he had previously preached about that particular vision. Watson, *Orson Pratt Journals*, 62. See notes 23 and 44 above.

[52] The opposition of his brethren to McLellin's actions is the first hint of conflict which would escalate as time passed. Yet McLellin's sermon was memorable enough for Orson Pratt to mention it in his journal. Watson, *Orson Pratt Journals*, 66.

[53] Orson Hyde's account of the Pillow [Pillar] Point conference indicates that three others were baptized on that day as well. *HC* 2:226.

[54] Muhammad's Qur'an.

[55] This concludes the New York segment of the mission. Of this period, McLellin and Hyde wrote:

> Our first labors, were in the State of New York, in which we continued about two months, and attended four conferences. Our exertions were crowned with as good success as we could reasonably expect considering the prejudices of the people, created by false and ridiculous statements, put in circulation by those who were first favored with the proclamation of the fulness of the everlasting gospel, contained in the book of Mormon: we had good reason to believe, that all the candid enquirers after truth, realized the force of the Savior's expression "A prophet is not without honor save in his own country." By our teaching and exhortations, the several branches of the church were strengthened and members were added; and of such, too, we hope, as will be saved. (Letter from the Twelve Apostles to John Whitmer, *Messenger and Advocate* 2 [October 1835]: 205)

[56] Originally, the next conference had been scheduled for June 29 at West Loborough, Ontario, Canada. Apparently, however, some of the Twelve decided not to attend this conference and went eastward to Vermont instead, where the next conference, appointed for July 17, was to be held in St. Johnsbury. Hyde and McLellin to Cowdery, 90.

[57] A lightweight twilled material for trousers, usually with cotton warp and wool filling.

[58] Hyde and Young had been to Kirtland to testify in a court case. See note 42 above.

[59] An account of this conference in *History of the Church* 2:235 indicates that the church in Loborough had twenty-five members. Not having had the same privilege of instruction as the branches in the United States, they were uninformed about many principles of the "new covenant," particularly with regard to recent revelations.

[60] The revelation on priesthood specified that the Twelve should "build up the church and regulate all the affairs of the same" (D&C 107:33). See Alma 45:21–22 for a Book of Mormon precedent for this practice.

In regulating the affairs of the Loborough congregation, the Twelve considered the case of Henry and Jacob Wood, who had been suspended from fellowship. The decision of the local brethren was upheld and the two were excommunicated. *HC* 2:235.

[61] Frederick M. Van Leuven was appointed to this position. *HC* 2:235.

[62] Of his experiences here, McLellin wrote:

> Thence we passed into Upper Canada and attended a conference on the 29th of June, not far from the source of the majestic St. Lawrence. Notwithstanding we had passed from the happy institution of our free republic into another realm, yet we could with propriety adopt the words of the presiding apostle and say, "God is no respecter of persons, but in every nation he that feareth God and worketh righteousness, is accepted of him:" for here we found a branch of the Saints who not only received us cordially, but also received our teachings with joy of heart. Some were added here also, by baptism, whom we expect to meet on the glorious morn of that day, when the dead in Christ shall rise and live. —May God grant that they may all be preserved, gathered to Zion and saved in the celestial kingdom.

By the time the Apostles left, McLellin added, the members had become "much encouraged." Twelve Apostles to John Whitmer, 205.

[63] This would be in keeping with the schedule set at the meeting of the Twelve on March 12, 1835. *HC* 2:209.

[64] See note 57 above.

[65] This is probably the letter to Emeline in which McLellin wrote: "You say that it will not be in your power to go to school this summer. I am glad that it is not, since Elder Hyde has returned and given me a description of the manner in which it is conducted; though we do not wish to cast any reflections." In any event, a letter from McLellin to Emeline that contained this statement fell into the hands of certain members of the the Kirtland High Council, which, in addition to President Joseph Smith, included Oliver Cowdery, Sidney Rigdon, Hyrum Smith, David Whitmer, John Whitmer, and others. Deeming Hyde's report concerning the school and McLellin's comment about it as libelous, the Kirtland High Council voted on August 4, 1835, to "withdraw . . . fellowship" from McLellin and Hyde "until they return and make satisfaction face to face." *HC* 2:240. The time when the outcome of this vote was communicated to McLellin is not known. Six weeks later, however, when the Twelve returned to Kirtland and met with the Church Presidency and members of the Council, this matter was considered. McLellin and Hyde "were found to be in fault, which they frankly confessed, and were forgiven." *HC* 2:283.

[66] John 3:3–5 is the classic New Testament scripture calling for adult conversion, baptism by immersion, and receiving the Holy Ghost:

> Jesus answered and said unto him, Verily, verily, I say unto thee, Except a man be born again, he cannot see the kingdom of God. Nicodemus

> saith unto him, How can a man be born when he is old? can he enter
> the second time into his mother's womb, and be born? Jesus answered,
> Verily, verily, I say unto thee, Except a man be born of water and of the
> Spirit, he cannot enter into the kingdom of God.

McLellin's missions to perform baptisms and bestow the gift of the Holy
Ghost were typical of Latter-day Saint proselyting from its commencement
in June 1829 forward.

[67] The nature of this interruption is not specified, but it is worth noting
that the Methodists used the traditional form of baptism common to
Catholic, Anglican, and Episcopal churches. This was a ritual in which
infants are brought into the church family—their brothers and sisters in
Christ—by being "christened," a liturgical rite in which a small amount of
water consecrated for the purpose is placed on the individual's head while
an ordained minister intones the words of the baptism ceremony. This same
ritual, which was derisively described by those who believed in baptism by
immersion as "sprinkling," was also used when an older child or an adult was
brought into the church.

[68] McLellin and Hyde described this conference: "Our next conference
was held in St. Johnsbury, the north eastern part of Vermont, where we
found many of the Saints, with whom we had a pleasant season of rejoicing,
and whose memory is fixed indelibly upon our heart, because of their firm
faith, and also their liberality in the support of the gospel." Twelve Apostles
to John Whitmer, 205. For more details concerning this conference, see
HC 2:238.

> [69] [This] public meeting was attended by a multitude of various classes,
> and orders, who generally gave good attention to the proclamation of
> the everlasting gospel of the Son of God. Intense anxiety seemed to
> sieze the minds of all the candid and honest in heart, and the Lord gave
> [the apostles] souls who were added to the number of the Saints, as
> seals of [the apostles'] ministry.

At the close of the Apostles' meetings in St. Johnsbury, "the twelve
separated, traveling in various directions, lifting up the standard of truth,
and proclaiming salvation to both old and young, rich and poor." Twelve
Apostles to John Whitmer, 205-6.

[70] This entry makes clear that in using Genesis 17:1, McLellin at this
point was focusing on God's command, "be thou perfect," and not on the
fact of his appearance to Abram. This focus would have been in keeping
with a generalized concern about perfectionism in American religion at this
time. Revivalist Charles Finney had developed a theology of perfectionism
that was having a profound effect on the revivals of the Second Great
Awakening. Stirrings generated by concern about perfection which eventually led to the "holiness" movement within Methodism were felt in Northeastern cities in the 1830s. John Humphrey Noyes, who would become the

leader of the Oneida "Perfectionists," was converted in 1831. And in Ohio, Asa Mahan, the major architect of what would become known as Oberlin perfectionism, became president of Oberlin College in 1835.

[71] Galatians 1:8 was undoubtedly used to affirm the restoration of the original gospel of Jesus Christ: "But though we, or an angel from heaven, preach any other gospel unto you than that which we have preached unto you, let him be accursed." Mormons, along with Christian primitivists, sought to practice Christianity as they understood it to have been defined and prescribed in the New Testament.

[72] See note 23 above.

[73] Psalms 37:37 reads: "Mark the perfect man, and behold the upright: for the end of that man is peace." This is another example of McLellin's attention to the question of perfection. Obviously, one of the dominant themes in McLellin's spiritual strivings was his belief that perfection and uprightness are essential for obtaining peace.

[74] Matthew 24:3 reports two questions asked by the disciples of Jesus concerning the last days: "When shall these things be? and what shall be the sign of thy coming, and of the end of the world?" Articulating the signs of the times was a common theme in McLellin's preaching, as in other early Mormon discourse; see Grant Underwood, *The Millenarian World of Early Mormonism* (Urbana: University of Illinois Press, 1993). Of the chapters modified by Joseph Smith in his inspired translation of the Bible, Matthew 24 is given singular treatment in the Pearl of Great Price, one of the LDS standard works. Regarding the signs of the times, see for example D&C 29:14; 39:23; 45:6-59; 58:64; 88:87-93. McLellin made particular use of D&C 45; see the discussion of his transcript of that revelation, pages 239-41 below.

[75] Mark 1:15 proclaims: "The time is fulfilled, and the kingdom of God is at hand: repent ye, and believe the gospel." To McLellin and his companions, who proclaimed the coming and the establishment of the kingdom of God in the last days, this scripture was immediately relevant to their message of repentance and faith in the newly restored gospel of Jesus Christ.

[76] Hebrews 12:14 reads: "Follow peace with all men, and holiness, without which no man shall see the Lord." Given McLellin's frequent emphasis on the themes of peace and holiness, this scripture was probably one of his favorites. Its concluding promise about seeing God may well have been understood in a realized sense, as well as millennially and eschatologically.

[77] See note 25 above.

[78] On this day, nine of the Twelve met in Bradford, Massachusetts, for the next conference on their calendar. *HC* 2:241-42. However, at this point the previously appointed schedule of conferences was changed; the Dover conference was cancelled due to lack of members, and the Saco and Farmington, Maine, conferences were rescheduled to a nearer date. *HC* 2:242.

[79] See note 21, Journal IV above, which refers to a sermon preached on this same text by Levi Jones.

[80] Also called "Sitter B." *HC* 2:253.

[81] See note 5 above.

[82] See note 73 above.

[83] On this day, seven of the other Twelve met to hold the Saco conference. *HC* 2:252-53.

[84] On Friday, August 28, the conference was held in Farmington, Maine. Of the Farmington conference, McLellin and Hyde wrote, "In this place, as well as in all others, where we had labored, we failed not to instruct the Saints in plainness, in all those matters relative to their present and eternal well-being." Twelve Apostles to John Whitmer, 206. For more details, see *HC* 2:253.

[85] Apostle Heber C. Kimball indicated that the Twelve met in Buffalo, New York, at the end of September. He wrote,

> We went on board the steamer "United States" and proceeded as far as Dunkirk, where she ran aground and sprung a leak, she made her way for Erie where she arrived with difficulty, but we were under the necessity of running upon a sand bar to save the boat from sinking, we reshipped and arrived at Fairport; we reached Kirtland the same evening, Sept. 27th. (JH, September 26, 1835, 7)

Most other sources report that the Twelve returned to Kirtland on the morning of September 26. *HC* 2:283.

[86] This sort of scriptural examination is performed in the "Lectures on Faith," which were taught at the School of the Elders during the previous winter. N. B. Lundwall, comp., *Lectures on Faith* (Salt Lake City: Bookcraft, n.d.), 19-22, 26-32.

The Kirtland Temple, dedicated March 27, 1836. McLellin was in Kirtland during the months when the temple was being completed. He participated in its ordinances and its dedication. His journals usually recorded accounts of his travels away from Kirtland and thus did not cover such events. From a set of stereoscopic photographs by Underwood and Underwood, 1904. Courtesy Rare Books and Manuscripts, Brigham Young University.

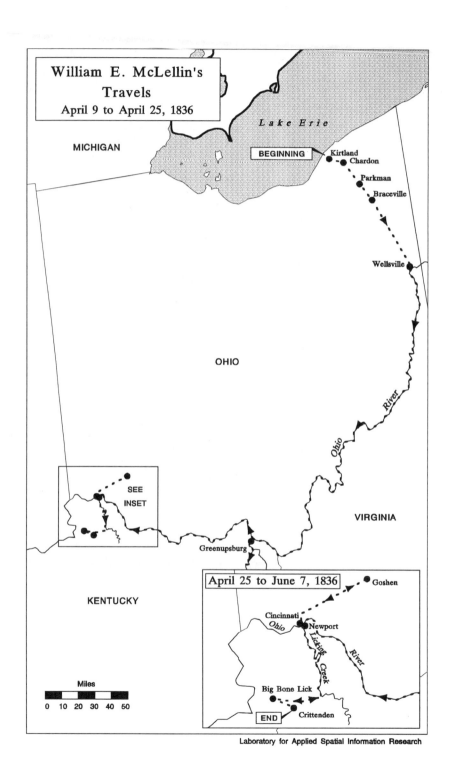

William E. McLellin's
Travels
April 9 to April 25, 1836

Lake Erie

MICHIGAN

BEGINNING

Kirtland
Chardon
Parkman
Braceville

Wellsville

OHIO

Ohio *River*

SEE
INSET

VIRGINIA

Greenupsburg

April 25 to June 7, 1836   Goshen

KENTUCKY

Cincinnati
Ohio   Newport
Licking Creek   *River*

Miles

Big Bone Lick

0 10 20 30 40 50

END   Crittenden

Laboratory for Applied Spatial Information Research

William E. McLellin Journal VI
April 9, 1836–June 7, 1836

**William E. McLellin's
Journal
1836——**

[page 3. Page 1 is a cover and page 2, its reverse, is blank.]

W. E. McLellin's Journal
Commencing April 9th 1836,[1]

Left home in Kirtland (after commending and dedicating my family to God and taking my leave of them) in order to journey and preach the [g] Gospel of the Son of God. Bishop Partridge and others[2] started to Zion and I started at the same time in order to journey with them as far as Wellsville on the Ohio river—— Saturday the 9. The day was unpleasand, it both rained and snowed— Bro. Joseph and six or seven others of the first brethren[3] accompanied us as far as Charidon and in consequence of the rain they continued with us over night *[page 4]* and we spent a very pleasant evening with them— Their society was really interesting—

Sunday 10. We took breakfast and then took a very affectionate farewell of our brethren after they had prayed with us and pronounced upon us their blessings. The ground was somewhat frozen and nearly covered with snow but notwithstanding we passed on as far as Parkman and called by the urgent request of a few brethren who remained there and tarried with them over night and held a meeting in the evening where I delivered a short discourse (3/4 of an hour) [on the] comparing the establishing of the religions of Moses, Jesus and Joseph followd by Elder J. Corrill with an exortation.

[*page 5*] Monday 11. We took our leave of the brethren early and pursued our course towards Wellsvill on the Ohio river and after a very laborious Journey (of 89 mls from Kirtland) throug snow rain and plenty of mud we reached Wellsville on Thursday afternoon. and the steam boat Detroit soon passing, called and took the brethren on so I had to [~~te~~] take my leave of them and they began to wend their way speedily toward their long absent homes and families——— But I found in the place a family of deciples (Saml Burwell & wife) whom I had baptized four or five years sinc[e] and some other friends with whom I consented to tarry a few days———

[*page 6*] On Friday evening bro. Burwell obtained an app. for me in the reformd Methodist chapel but in consequence of a dissatisfaction of the society we withdrew the app. to Bro. B[urwell]'s dwelling where I addressed those who assembled about 1 hour from John 14th 26⁴— The disturbence about the house was in consequence of a discourse deliverd in it about a week since by Elder D. W. Patten— The people's indignation was fired against him and also against the whole society—

Saturday I resested and studied.

Sunday 17th In the forenoon I attnded the Methodist preaching to hear Dr Rooter of Pittsburg——— He is called a great man——— (a Methodist).

[*page 7; the following is in parentheses at the top of the page.*] (Monday 18. I finished a letter and sent it immediately to my dear Emiline by bro. Jos. Ketting but I did not write to her where she might direct one to me)

In the afternoon at two oclock I attended my app. at Br. B's. A small congregation collected and I addressed them over two hours from Mark 1 - 14 . 15.⁵ They were [~~y~~] very attntive and some appeard to be somewhat believing—

Monday 18th To day I had determined to leave this **ungodly** Village— but my fri[e]nd D. Campbell (The **Mayor** of th place) with

whom I spent the most of my time— came to me and laid in such
a pressing request that I should not leave them for a few days
that I consented and an app. was circulated for candlelight for me
to speak in a gentleman's waggonshop— The people assembled
and I spoke to them [of] one hour 1/2 from Psalm 37 -37[6]——
[*page 8*] There was uncommon good attention and an increased
anxiety to hear me again and I promised to address them again on
Wednesday eve in the same pl[a]ce.

Tuesday I spent in reading and study of Hebrew and so forth.

Wednesday 21.[7] This forenoon I had an interview with M. Martin (A Campbellite Prie[s]t). I found him as the most of the same
order affraid to believe the **whole** truth— he seemed to be affraid
to believe—— In the eve I met a large congregation in A Roger's
waggonshop and I addressed them over one hour & a half on the
Evidences of the book of Mormon. I had very good attention
considering [the] it was in a Village— And I had a great deal
considerable of liberty—

Thursday 22. This morning there is to be seen in various parts of
the villag [*page 9*] men standing in groups and [these] their whole
converse was what they thought of me and of my preaching—
Some think me honest while others dishonest &C, &C. My friends
press me very hard to have me stay longer— and indeed there
seems to be quite an opening, but my feelings are to go on and
visit my relations— I left **home** for that purpose and it seems to
be my grand object— I feel sorry to leave my **friends here**—
It is true I have baptized none here but yet I believe that my bread
is cast upon the watters and I believe that some few Deciples will
be gathered out of this place— I could fain hope many— About
2 Oclock in the afternoon the Steamr Pittsburg called and I took
a passage for Greenupsburg for $3.00 but when I left Bro. B[urwell]
gave me 2. A. Campl 2 and the Mayor $5.00. This was well for me
[*page 10*] We had a prosperous and speedy trip and I landed at
Greenupsburg about dusk and I found my brotherinlaw & his wife
about 1/2 mile from the village who appeared quite glad to see me
and to entertain me. I found them very strongly settled in their

Universal religion—— Not willing to receive any reasoning or testimony in favour of the book of Mormon or my principles of faith or religion——

Saturday He and I started to go up Sandy about 20 miles to fill an appointmt of his on next day but we missed our way and after riding over the hills about 12 miles we found ourselves about as far from our app as when we started. consequently we turned about and returned home the same eve, quite fatigued— I however had a good oppertunity of conversing [*page 11*] with bro. Wadsworth—— But it all seemed to be to none effect only to discharge my duty.

Sunday 25. Bro. N[athan] W[adsworth] circulated an app for me for two Oclouck in the afternoon and I addressed a small congregation in the court-house for about one hour and a quarter— and as they had never heard one of our Elders before, I gave them a history of the work and the desighn of it as far as I was enabled to in one discourse. After I closed I was shaken very heartily by the hand and told that I had preached a very excellent discourse if I had only left out the new record—. I told them that that was all the glory of **it**— I took supper with my friends and then took the steamer Tuscumbia ~~and~~ [£] about 9 oclock in the eve and Landed in [*page 12*] Cincinnatti about noon the next day for $1.50. I took supper and tarried all night with a sister Nutting about a mile above the city— the sp[l]endid Cincinnatti. She treated me very well considering her circumstances— She is anxious to go to Zion— very—

Tuesday 27. I crossed the river and landed in K.Y. in Newport. thence I walked about 7 miles up the Licking to [~~Culb~~] Elder Robert Culbertson's. I found him at home and all the family well——

Wednesday 28. I spent the most of this day in visiting the brethren— And and [*sic*] app. being circulated for evening, I met with a large congregation considering the settlement and the short time of its circulation. I preached to them about 1 1/2 hours from 2 Tim. 3-16.[8] I had great liberty and the Saints were much comforted.

Another app. was given out [*page 13*] by Elder Culbertson for Friday evening.

Thursday I spent in reading and in writing a letter to my family——

Friday 30. I spent in conversation with inquirers and in reading and in the evening I reasoned with the congregation on the nature of the book of Mormon's being not a delusion but a true record about 2 hours— Some it pleased while others it made angry—as the **truth** always does——

Saturday I and Elder R. C[ulbertson] spent in reading and searching into various points of prophecy and doctrine of the scriptures.

Sunday 1. At eleven Oclock I preached at bro Geo. Youtsey's on the Divine authentic[it]y of my holy religion. I spoke 2¼ hours. I had tolerably good liberty at least so as to confound all the opposers present so that no one dared to cheap or raise his voice— [*page 14*] At 4 Oclock we had a meeting at Mrs. Betsy Culbertson— Elder R. C. opened the mee. and spoke a little while. I then spoke about one hour on the nature of the establishment of Christianity and then administered the sacrament to the Saints. The[n] being called upon we anointed,[9] prayed for and laid our hands upon A. Culbertson's sore leg— He seemed to be somewhat believing— I hope the Lord will heal him——

Monday 2. I came 7 miles to Cin[cinnati] my books not being finished (binding) I had to wait until 6 Olock which gave me a good oppertunity to wander over the city—— It is a sp[l]endid City. I tarried over night with a bro. Bull in Fulton. They treated me as saints ought, and entertained me gladly and cheerfully.

[*page 15*] Tues. 3. I walked 17 miles to a bro. McGee's in Newbury. They received me also joyfully

and I spent Wednisday also with them studying my [Hebrew] Bible, an app. was circulated and I addressed a small congregation at Br. Elston's from these words. "Let us as many as be perfect be thus minded" Phil. 3 - 15.[10] I had great liberty and all parties supposed it was a "great sermon"

Friday 6. I preached in the eve at bro. Char McGee's. I contrasted the churches of Moses, Peter and Joseph. I spoke about one hour.

Sunday 8. I had an app. at Eleven oclock, but the Methodist purposely made one at the same hour in the same village. I had notwithstanding a good turnout. I spoke in the forenoon from [*page 16*] John 5 - 39[11] on the nature and evidence of God's revelations— but the people seemed to be dumb to the voice of **truth**. At five Oclock I spoke again on the covenants and Articles of Our church.

Monday (9) eve I spoke again from 1 Thess. 1-5[12] and I spoke as though the Lord was speaking through me but yet the people seemed willing to go to Hell and determined so to do, for after the most powerful appeals to their heads, hearts and feelings none were willing to obey the Lord altho many said that they firmly believed.

Tuesday eve I preached in Goshen 5 miles north (it is quite a village and I had a schoolhouse full— I addressed them from 2 Tim 4 - 2[13] "Preach the word." I dwelt on the nature, Gift and power of the Holy spirit. I promised to address them again the next evening.

[*page 17*] [~~Tuesday~~] **Wes**day **11.** Today I had a long talk with a Doc. Meek who was an Infidel— He said he was verry sorry that I was so deluded but yet he could not tell me how to get out of it. Nay I got him into many difficulties that he could not get out of nor assign any reason why he remained in them. In the eve the little school house was filled again. I addressed them about one hour and a half respecting the book of Mormon and the nature and object of the establishment of the church of christ— but they came and went as though they were not interested in it, in the least. We lodged while here with a Mr Weston whose Lady belonged to the Saints. [~~We~~] I was well entertained indeed altho the old gentleman is called an Infidel. A young widow by the name of Roberts professed to believe but was not baptized.

[*page 18*] Thursday 12 Returned very early to Newbery and bro. McGee being sick called upon us to (bro. R Culbertson being with me) to pray for him, we did so, and he immediately arose took up his bed or pallet and put it away and declared that the Lord had healed him.[14] Mr. E. Holmes came with us to cincinnatti with a one horse waggon and we rode with him and thence across Ohio & walked up Licking 7 miles to the brethren.

Friday & Saturday I spent in visiting and strenghtening the saints and in studying Hebrew. Considernig the situation of things Elder Culbertson and I considered it unnecessary to hold a meeting.

Sunday 15. I walked about five miles over the Hills and hollows and held a meeting on Bank Lick Creek at a Campbell meeting house at 11 oclock—The con[*page 19*]gregation was so large that I had to prea[c]h in the open air, when I commenced speaking there was such a tickling seized me in my throat that it seemed impossible for me to address the people but I prevailed over it and spoke about 2 hours from Rom. 8 - 14.[15] when I was through no man either opposed me or asked me to preach again, consequently I made no farther app in the place—An old gentleman gave $1:38 for a book of Mormon and I left them. I returned with the brethren back to Licking after taking dinner with a Mr McLaughlin.

Monday 16. Bro. A. Hart and I went in a skift down to Cincinnati and he bought me a hat for $2.75 and we tried in a great many shoe stores to get me a pair of boots but we could not find a pair large enough for me except one and they were too large so that I had to go without— But the brethren gave me [*page 20*] $4.25 to assist me in getting a pair made.

Tuesday 17. I left the society of my brethren about ten oclock and started to Boon County. I walked about 20 miles [to] and staid over night with an old iron-sided Baptist[16] preacher, James Fennel. He treated me well, but he did not seem to have any more faith

Steamboats docked at Cincinnati, Ohio, 1848. McLellin sailed down the Ohio River on his final missionary journey. W. S. Porter. Courtesy of The Public Library of Cincinnati and Hamilton County.

Cincinnati Waterfront, 1848. McLellin stopped here in 1836 to shop for clothes and shoes. W. S. Porter. Courtesy of The Public Library of Cincinnati and Hamilton County.

in God or the Gospel [that] than the Devil. His father-in-law was there, a very old man and father to one of our brethren in Mo. He was very hard.

Wednesday morning I walked about two miles and took breakfast with old Mr. S. Emmett and appointed a mee. at G. Vest's one of his neighbour's for [Thur] next eve at [one] 6 oclock P.M. and then I walked about 5 miles to S. Stone's and made another for Friday noon in a schoolhouse near him—

[*page 21*] Thursday 19. I wa[l]ked about 6 miles and had a small cong[regation] rear [near] sunset and I commenced to address them but I had not spoken long before a cloud began to rise and the people became so uneasy that I quit speaking and dismissed them and they seemed to be glad that I had done so—

Friday 20. I walked about 5 miles and attended my app.— a small cong[regation] collected and I preached one hour on the second coming coming [*sic*] of Christ and I made two more app. for Sunday 22.

On Saturday there was a muster[17] and the people having to attend it I had no app. but I and J. G. Jinkenson rode about 5 miles to big Bone Lick and I saw some Mammoth bones,[18]

and on sunday at 11 I & Elder Culbertson (he came the evening previous) attended our app. & I preached about 2 hours on the [*page 22*] book of Mormon and the nature and power of the Gospel— Our meeting was in a new republican meeting house— I preached the first sermon that ever was preached in it and at 4 Oclock, after having taken dinner and walked 3 miles we met a large cong. at Mr. A. Hill's and after I had opened the meeting and talked to the young ladies for their ill manners, Elder Culbt. arose and spoke by way of reasoning about 3/4 of an hour and I also about as long— & I made two more app for mond. & Tues.

Monday 23. This morning bro. C[ulbertson] started **home**. And I attended my app. at B[rother] Hills. The house was full and

I spoke almost entirely about the book of Mormon giving them an explanation of it and of the rise of the Curch also— It thundered and rained and hailed quite hard while I was speaking.

[*page 23*] Tuesday 24. I met a house full at James Stone's and preched to them on the '**nature of the Gifts**' All that have attnded my meetings in this neighbourhood seemed to be confounded. in fact a number told me that they believed that I preached the truth but not one soul was willing to **obey the** thruth, therefore feeling that I had rid my garments of them[19] and that If they would not obey what they had heard it was useless to heap upon them[20] any more.

Therefore on Wednesday 25 I sit down and finished **a letter** to my Emiline and after taking dinner with Silas ~~Stone~~ Stone I set my face for a new place. I walked about six miles and put up for the night with a Mr. Webster, Father to Vardeman Webster who is a Baptist preacher and who I had understood disired to see a man of Our profession

[*page 24*] Thursday 26. Is a very rainy day— I left an app. at Mr. Webster's for Friday and then I walked 2 1/2 to Crittenden or (Pin Hook). There is a Campbelite meeting house in the place and I went to the proprietor of [~~the p~~] it and obtained the privilege of it to preach in it on Sunday at 11 oclock—— I went about two miles farther to see a methodist preacher ([~~Will S~~] William Secrets) but he was not at home, The circuit rider However came in and they invited me to tarry during the night. I did so. But Mr. Crawford the little priest was really of Baal— Light, vain, [~~Sassy~~] Saucy and even vulgar. [Friday 27] after taking breakfast I returned to Pinhook and I went to the school teacher and he promised to give out my app. I then returned through rain and mud back to Mr Webster's but very [*page 25*] few came to mee. in consequence of the weather but I preached to the few about an hour and gave out another app for next day.

Saturday 28. It rained continually all day without cesation so that I did [~~h~~] not have any meeting. I continued with Mr. Webster who treated me as a friend indeed

Sunday 29. I walked up to Crittenden and at half past 11. I commenced preaching to crowded house of respectable people. I spoke nearly 2 hours on the evidences of '**my religion**' and after I was through Mr Keys— a Campbellite— endeavoured to oppose what I had said but it was a very weak effort. He also called upon others to arise and cast in their might— A Mr Root (a Baptist priest) arose and said that he had taken notes and that he would answer my discourse on the next Sunday [*page 26*] A Dr. F. B. Webb invited me home with him. And I tarried until next day.

Monday A gentleman by the name of Barkshire sent for me and proposed that I should tarry until the next sunday and answer Mr. Root's argument for said he "I want you to have a fair shake." I consented to be there and gave out another app. for Wednesday eve— He offered ~~Monday~~ his house as a home for me freely if I would stay. Monday   I walked about 5 miles, to Mr S. Emmett's through the rain & mud. I [s]taid with him until Wednesday reading Campbell's and Owen's debate.[21] I ought to have observed that on Monday I put a **letter** in the office to my bro. Saml & also one to T. B. Marsh. It still continued to rain.

[*page 27*] **W**ednesday. I returned through the rain and mud to Crittenden and at early candle light I met a concourse of people in the meeting house and addressed them $1^1/2$ hours reasoning with them concerning the truths of my religion and removeing the obj[ections] of opposers. I then gave liberty to objectors and a Mr Roberts (a Campbellite Priest) arose and said 'that he hardly know what to say.' And I believed him— The truth was I had broke down his props. And in order to have something He asked me a number of questions which I answered freely. There was some confusion and lightness excited by his odd observations——

Thursday, F and Sat it rained almost continually so that I did not travel [~~much~~] any.

Sunday Morning— The appearance bid fair for a beautiful day——
[*page 28*] Before the usual hour the people began to assemble from all quarters seemingly— At the usual hour the house was

crowded to overflowing and there were many who could not get in who stood round the doors and windows. Mr Peak (a methodist) Mr. Root (a Baptist) and Mr K[e]yes (a Campbellite) took their seats in the stand, joining all their heads, powers and influences to oppose the truth— One prayed, another preached and the other exorted [to] all going to persuade the people to beware of me and of my religion. after they got through they tried to get the people dispersed—— But they almost unanimously voted to stay and hear me. They then had politeness enough to invite me into the stand—— I then proceeded to show their misrepresentations and to set [*page 29*] clearly our princi[p]les for about 1 1/2 hours. Intense anxiety seemed to pervade the assembly while I addressed them and after I was through, the Methodist priest arost [arose] to offer some objections but the people would not stay to hear him. In the afternoon the house where I was entertained was filled with visitors and I was asked a great many questions which gave me an oppertunity to set forth more fully many points of **truth**. After preaching I was taken with the sick head ache and until about midnight I suffered beyond discription.

Monday   I was not able to travel.

Tuesday   I bid farewell to Crittenden. I walked about five miles to my app and met a house full at 12 Oclock— I was not yet well but I addressed about one hour on the second coming of Messiah. [*pages 30–33 blank*]

[*page 34*]
    Subscribers[22]

Nathan Wadsworth, Greenupsburg, Ky. Pd.
Nathaniel Hughs, Mulberry, Clearmont Co. O[hio]. Pd.
Jos. B. Griffith Do—— Do——[23]
Wm Weston, Goshen, Ohio Pd.
(Isaac Elston for M[essenger] & A[dvocate] recd. Paid $1.00)
Silas Emmett, Gains Crossroads, Boon Co. Ky. Pd.
John G. Jinkenson— Do-Do Pd.
Silas [F] Stone— D——o——D——PD.

James E. Stone——PD.
(Nathnl Tanner— Fulton, Ohio, Paid $2.00)
William Finnel Do,Do.
Garret W. Barkshire (pd) Crittenden, Grant Ky
Robert Dyas Critt[enden], Grant Co. Ky Pd.
Elizabeth Barker Do——
William Crosby Centerville Montg[omery] Co. Ohio
Syvander Nutting paid $1.00——
Josiah Clark paid $2.00
[*page 35*] Saml Clark's paper to be changed from Martinsville to
Fulton Ohio

NOTES

[1] The Apostles, McLellin among them, had returned to Kirtland on September 26, 1835, from their mission to the East (described in Journal V). McLellin spent the fall and winter months in Kirtland, where, on January 21, 1836, Joseph Smith received a revelation in which he "beheld Elder M'Lellin in the south, standing upon a hill, surrounded by a vast multitude, preaching to them, and a lame man standing before him supported by his crutches; he threw them down at his word and leaped as a hart, by the mighty power of God." Joseph Smith, Jr., *History of The Church of Jesus Christ of Latter-day Saints,* ed. B. H. Roberts, 2d ed. rev., 7 vols. (Salt Lake City: Deseret Book, 1971), 2:381 (hereafter cited as *HC*). This revelation must have influenced McLellin's next mission call: a journey to the South, detailed in Journal VI. For further biographical details, see Larry Porter's essay below.

[2] In addition to Edward Partridge, the members of this group were Isaac Morley, John Corrill, and W. W. Phelps. They were returning to their homes in Missouri following the dedication of the Kirtland Temple. *HC* 2:436.

[3] At this time, the "first brethren" were the "principal heads of the Church." *HC* 2:436. These leaders would have included President Joseph Smith and his counselors, Sidney Rigdon and Frederick G. Williams; Hyrum Smith, the Prophet's brother; Oliver Cowdery and David Whitmer, two of the Three Witnesses to the Book of Mormon; John Whitmer, editor of the *Messenger and Advocate;* and possibly William Wines Phelps, who had made his home with Joseph Smith's family and assisted with the preparation of the Doctrine and Covenants for publication.

[4] See note 14, Journal V above.

[5] See note 75, Journal V above.

[6] See note 73, Journal V above.

[7] Wednesday was actually April 20. The journal dates are off by one day until May 1.

[8] More than likely, this verse was applied to the Book of Mormon. It reads: "All scripture is given by inspiration of God, and is profitable for doctrine, for reproof, for correction, for instruction in righteousness." See note 22, Journal V above.

[9] For an account of a similar ordinance performed in the early Christian church, see James 5:14. The use of this healing ritual in Mormonism is described in J. Elliot Cameron, "Priesthood Blessings," in *Encyclopedia of Mormonism,* ed. Daniel H. Ludlow, 5 vols. (New York: Macmillan, 1992), 3:1140–41.

[10] Philippians 3:15 sets the standard of perfection as the goal of the faithful and teaches that revelation is the path that opens the way to the perfecting of the Saints: "Let us therefore, as many as be perfect, be thus minded: and if in any thing ye be otherwise minded, God shall reveal even this unto you." An important theme in American religion at this time, the idea of perfection would be given expansive meanings by Joseph Smith, especially during the Nauvoo period. These meanings were foreshadowed, however, in the vision seen by Joseph Smith and Sidney Rigdon in February 1832, and would have been familiar to McLellin because he and several of his companions had preached on this topic during previous missionary tours. See note 70, Journal V above.

[11] John 5:39 has long been used as a proof text to exhort people to study the scriptures: "Search the scriptures; for in them ye think ye have eternal life: and they are they which testify of me." Mormons saw and used the Bible as a testimony not only of Jesus, but also of the restoration of the gospel by Joseph Smith and of the prophetic truth of the Book of Mormon. McLellin often challenged his audiences to compare the Bible and the Book of Mormon to find evidence of harmony between them.

[12] See note 5, Journal V above.

[13] See note 22, Journal V above.

[14] The gift of healing came to the fore while McLellin was in Newbury. A dozen days before, McLellin and others had anointed and given a priesthood blessing to A. Culbertson, who had a sore leg. In this instance, "bro. R. Culbertson" was present. McLellin's description of the event recalls Matthew 9:6–7 and Mark 2:11–12.

[15] Romans 8:14 reads: "For as many as are led by the Spirit of God, they are the sons of God."

[16] "Iron-sided Baptist" is a colloquial reference to the Primitive Baptists. They were anti-mission, anti-benevolent, anti-effort, strict Calvinists. Another term sometimes used for Baptists of the same theological persuasion was "iron-jacket Baptists."

[17] Calls to arms such as this muster were the last vestiges of the colonial militia system in the United States. Under the Uniform Militia Act of 1792, "militiamen (all men aged 18 to 45) were to arm and to equip themselves." However, the frequency of these musters and the training of these men was left to the decision of the state governments. Richard H. Kohn, "The Murder of the Militia System in the Aftermath of the American Revolution," in *In Defense of the Republic: Readings in American Military History,* ed. David Curtis Skaggs and Robert S. Browning III (Belmont, Calif.: Wadsworth Publishing, 1991), 79, first published in *The Military History of the Revolution: Proceedings of the Sixth Military History Symposium, USAF Academy 1974* (Washington, D.C.: Government Printing Office, 1976): 110–26.

[18] Big Bone Lick was one of the country's "outstanding prehistoric boneyards. Long ago the sulphur springs and salt formations of this valley attracted hordes of mastodons and other gigantic mammals." By the time of McLellin's visit, "specimens were still plentiful" despite numerous expeditions, including one by Thomas Jefferson, which had removed many of the bones. The bones have now been scattered to museums across Europe and America. Federal Writers' Project of the Work Projects Administration for the State of Kentucky, *Kentucky: A Guide to the Bluegrass State* (New York: Harcourt, Brace, 1939), 335.

[19] This is another reference to the idea that if those who had been consecrated as priests and teachers failed to teach people the word of God, their garments would not be found spotless at the day of judgment. See Jacob 1:19 in the Book of Mormon. See note 50, Journal III above.

[20] Perhaps McLellin was alluding to Proverbs 25:22 or Romans 12:20, verses that speak of heaping coals of fire on the heads of those who have been given bread to eat and water to drink.

[21] This is the famous 1829 debate in Cincinnati between Alexander Campbell and Robert Owen in which Owen attempted to prove that all religions have erroneous principles and are harmful to humanity. Following the debate, "the press heralded Alexander Campbell's supposed victory." For the best recent analysis of this debate, see Robert O. Fife, "In the Spirit of the Prophets: Alexander Campbell as a Social Thinker," in *Lectures in Honor of the Alexander Campbell Bicentennial, 1788-1988,* introduction by James M. Seale (Nashville: Disciples of Christ Historical Society, 1988). See also William E. Tucker and Lester G. McAllister, *Journey in Faith: A History of the Christian Church (Disciples of Christ)* (St. Louis: Bethany Press, 1975); and Richard William Leopold, *Robert Dale Owen: A Biography* (Cambridge: Harvard University Press, 1940; repub. New York: Octagon Books, 1969), 73.

[22] For the *Messenger and Advocate.*

[23] "Do—" was a nineteenth-century abbreviation meaning "ditto."

Letter of William E. McLellin
to the Quorum of the Twelve Apostles

Jan. 24th 1837[1]

My dear old Friends.

Your most excellent letter of Dec. 18. arived on yesterday, and I assure you it was received and read with a mixture of inexpressible Joy and regret.

It is just such a production as I might have expected from those with whom I had formed so intimate an acquaintance—and in whom I always have had the most implicit confidence. When I seated myself before my little fire side and read its contents,I seemed to enter into the tenderest part of your feelings and to sympathise with you. I saw with peculiar feelings the situation in which you had been placed by my leaving.

I imagined for a moment that I was one of You, and one of You in in [sic] my situation. O! with what feelings could I have written!! Not with better than You have written to me. I tell You Brethren I do not believe if the world was searched that there could be another band of men found who have warmer hearts than You. Your few lines brought fresh to my mind the many anxcious hours and the few happy ones we had spent and enjoyed together.

You say in your letter to me "when you left Kirtland, You left home. Come home, Come home." "If you will not come otherwise one or all of us will go after you."

You say farther, and what I did not expect to hear "Your place is yet vacant."——. Now Brethren, although you may have supposed that I was somewhat sceptical—Yet, let me say to You, I believe every word you say.And all that hinders me from quitting this state of retirement and <u>death</u> and speeding my way to your council chamber, to be a faithful partner with you in future in all your Joys and axieties in the sacred ministry which was confirmed upon us by the holy anointing which we have received—is, the <u>want</u> of means. My course I know has been novel in the history of the transactions of the anointed. The reasons of my conduct are <u>few</u> and I deem it unnecessary to make an attempt to asign them in this place. Suffice it to say, —I am sorry for the course that I have pursued.—

Can You, <u>Will</u> you forgive <u>me</u>?

Will Brother Joseph forgive me? And will the Church forgive me?

If so write to me immediately and let me <u>know</u> it. And please to obtain from President Smith my licence and send it to me, so that I may again feel that I have authority to lift up <u>my</u> voice in the midst of this generation.——

I have so <u>much</u> that I would be glad to communicate to <u>You</u> that I cannot on paper <u>begin</u> to express my feelings, nor relieve my mind. Therefore I will cease to write and I shall certainly wait in a state of anxious suspense the result of what I have written.

I am your distant and unfortunate brother

W. E. McLellin

"'Tis the voice of William E.
    To Brigham Young & Heber C.
Orson Hyde & Parley—P.
    Luke and William Orson P.
John and Lyman (all save three)."

We are enjoying evry good health and have been since ewe left K.

W. E. M.

[*on the envelope*]
Copy of a letter from Apostle William McLellen to his brethren in Kirtland Jan. 24th 1837. from the <u>original</u> which I've sent to the Historian's Off—

[letter transmitting original to Wilford Woodruff]
~~President~~ W. W. Woodruff

Dear brother
Having found this ~~relic~~ letter among my father's letters I send it to you, thinging you would like to preserve the original ~~copy~~ and maybe to publish it. ~~I have taken a copy to preserve as I prize it as a choice item of history.~~ Prizing it very highly I've retained a copy with this I also send a few others which I found in the same box—not knowing but they ~~might~~ would be so some value to you. Thought it best to send them.

Yours etc.
H. M. Whitney[2]

NOTES

Printed by permission of The Church of Jesus Christ of Latter-day Saints, Church Archives, Salt Lake City. In Helen Vilate Bourne Fleming (1884–1969) Collection, 1836–1963. Copy of original. Original apparently among letters to W. Woodruff in private hands.

[1] McLellin returned from his previous mission (detailed in Journal VI) in June 1836. Shortly thereafter, he became discontented with Church leadership. His 1872 recollections state:

In the spring of 1836 I took a mission south and returned the last of June; but only returned to find the Presidency to a great extent absorbed in temporal things. They had gone to New York and run into debt about forly [*sic*] thousand dollars for goods—which was never paid!!! They brought on a kind of stuff they called French Cordial. It would intoxicate. I myself saw [Joseph Smith] so much under its influence that he could not walk strait! You may doubt what I say, but it matters not. They formed a kind of an association and kept it up until they went into that swindling Kirtland banking concern, about which so many lies were prophesied. Popularity, and drinking, feasting and hilarity was the order of the day. The Presidency and leading men got up a ride to Cleve-land, some 15 couple. Fine dressing, fine carriages, fine harness and horses as the country produced were hired, and they set out. They drove into Cleveland and through the streets round and round to show Big. People inquired who is this? O its Joseph Smith—the Mormon Prophet! They put up at a first class hotel, called in the wine &c. Some of them became high, and smashed up things generally. Next morning their bill was over two hundred dollars. No matter we are Big-merchant-men of Kirtland. Next day on their way home they took dinner at Euclid, and imbibed so freely that when they started home they commenced running horses, turned over and smashed up one buggy so they had to haul it home in a wagon. But no confessions were ever required or made. All seemed to go swimingly!! But I sickened! I left!! I could tell much more. (William E. McLellin to Presidnt Joseph Smith, July 1872, RLDS Archives)

McLellin's loss of trust in Church leadership occurred during August 1836. Lyndon W. Cook, *The Revelations of the Prophet Joseph Smith* (Salt Lake City: Deseret Book, 1985), 107. As a result, he moved his family out of Kirtland.

[2] Helen Mar Kimball Whitney was a daughter of Heber C. and Vilate Kimball and wife of Horace K. Whitney (oldest son of Newel K. Whitney), and mother of Orson F. Whitney.

The McLellin Manuscripts of Doctrine and Covenants Sections 22 (RLDS 20), 45, 65, and 66

Students of the Doctrine and Covenants are beneficiaries of the William E. McLellin manuscripts, for they include copies of four revelations that are now Doctrine and Covenants sections 22 (RLDS 20), 45, 65, and 66. McLellin's copies of sections 45, 65, and 66 predate any publication of the same.[1] Since Joseph Smith and his associates edited the punctuation and wording of the revelations as they prepared them for publication, these early texts reflect essentially the state of these revelations in late 1831 or early 1832 when McLellin recorded or copied them. Moreover, since most of the handwritten copies of revelations that were used in publishing the 1833 Book of Commandments or the 1835 Doctrine and Covenants are no longer available, McLellin's manuscripts are all the more valuable.[2] They contribute to the data from which textual analysis can be done; they provide more precise information about the date on which each revelation was first given; and comments made by McLellin about these revelations add much to our understanding of why they were given.

In some cases, the manuscripts also reveal aspects of McLellin's personality. For instance, details of his copy of section 22 may suggest McLellin's temporary frustration with the way some revelations were worded. Certainly section 66 deals with some of McLellin's thoughts, feelings, and personal challenges that he seems to have been unwilling to write about otherwise in his journals.

In the following pages, McLellin's manuscripts of these four revelations are set in their historical contexts. Then each is analyzed for the contributions it makes and the questions it begets. Where significant differences occur between McLellin's manuscripts and the 1981 LDS edition of these revelations in the Doctrine and Covenants, the two have been placed side by side for ready comparison. Each manuscript adds new information to our knowledge.

Background to the McLellin Revelation Manuscripts

McLellin first arrived at Church headquarters in Kirtland, Ohio, on October 18, 1831. He spent three weeks in Ohio before he embarked on a mission with Samuel Smith. According to his own account in Journal I, he spent much of his time there "reading, learning and teaching." He desired to become acquainted with some of the church leaders, especially the Prophet Joseph Smith, about whom he had heard so much. That opportunity first arose for McLellin at a conference held in nearby Orange, Ohio, on October 25, 1831. "Here I first saw brother Joseph The Seer," William happily penned, "also brothers Oliver, John & Sidney and a great many other Elders."[3]

The proceedings of the conference strengthened McLellin's conviction that the true gospel had been restored. Many priesthood brethren bore witness of the truth of the work in which they were engaged. "This conference was attended by me with much spiritual edification & comfort to my heart," McLellin wrote in his journal.[4] The official minutes of the conference contain a report of McLellin's claim that "he had the greatest reason to rejoice of any present," and that he "would be subject to the will of God even unto death."[5] It was also at this conference that McLellin received his ordination to the high priesthood under the hands of Oliver Cowdery and thus became a member of the most trusted group of elders in the Church at that time.

After the conference, McLellin accompanied Joseph Smith to his home in Hiram, Ohio. McLellin's journal entry for October 29, 1831, tells us something of his own desires at that point as he writes, "This day the Lord condecended to hear my prayr and give me a revelation of his will, through his prophet or Seer (Joseph)—And these are the words which I wrote from his mouth."[6] McLellin then recorded the words to Doctrine and Covenants 66, a revelation directed specifically to himself and commanding him, among other things, to serve a mission in the eastern states.

The following day, back in Kirtland, McLellin wrote that he "read and copied revelations."[7] This is most likely when he copied sections 22 (RLDS 20), 45, and 65.[8] Like most missionaries of that early era, McLellin copied some of the revelations for personal study and for use in preaching.

During the next week another conference of elders convened, this time in Hiram, Ohio. The conference decided to prepare manuscripts of existing revelations and send them with Oliver Cowdery and John Whitmer to Independence, Missouri, for printing by W. W. Phelps. Even though McLellin attended this conference,[9] he did not make any comment about those manuscripts in his journal.

LDS Section 22, RLDS Section 20

Doctrine and Covenants section 22 (RLDS 20) deals with the covenant of baptism. McLellin's manuscript is distinctive because it dates the receipt of this revelation as April 16, 1830, just ten days after the Church's formal organization. Previously, all that was known about the date of this revelation was that it was received sometime in April 1830. If McLellin's date is correct, this revelation took place five days after six baptisms at Fayette and two days prior to seven more baptisms by Oliver Cowdery.

In 1873 Orson Pratt recalled the historical circumstances surrounding the receipt of this revelation:

> In the early days of this Church there were certain persons, belonging to the Baptist denomination, very moral and no doubt as good people as you could find anywhere, who came, saying they believed in the Book of Mormon, and that they had been baptized into the Baptist Church, and that they wished to come into our Church. The Prophet Joseph had not, at that time, particularly inquired in relation to this matter, but he did inquire, and received a revelation from the Lord. . . . These Baptists had to be re-baptized: there was no other way to get into this Church.[10]

At the time this revelation was given, Latter-day Saints and Baptists held in common the belief that faith and repentance followed by baptism by immersion brought about a remission of sins. The two churches differed, however, in that Joseph Smith taught that the authority to baptize had been lost from the earth, but that it had been restored in May 1829 by the heavenly messenger known in mortality as John the Baptist. The Baptists believed that the authority to baptize had been given by Christ to the primitive Church and had never been lost from the earth. Moreover, their prevailing view was that a pastor was authorized to perform baptisms simply by the consent of the congregation over which he ministered.[11] They believed that their baptisms would be recognized by God. Thus, when approached by Baptists, Joseph felt to inquire of the Lord whether they needed to be baptized anew in entering into the new and everlasting covenant.

LDS Doctrine and Covenants 22 was published at one point as one document together with LDS Doctrine and Covenants 20, and thus may have been part of what was known in the early days of the Church as the "Articles and Covenants of the Church of Christ." This compilation appeared in the Church's first periodical, the *Evening and the Morning Star,* in June 1832, and even earlier in the sometimes anti-Mormon newspaper, the *Painesville Telegraph,* on April 19, 1831.[12]

The 1981 LDS edition of Section 22 is here compared side by side with McLellin's manuscript, the differences bolded:

McLellin Manuscript	1981 Edition
A commandment to the church of Christ which was established in these last days in the year of our Lord 1830 on the fourth month and on the sixth day of the month which is called April—	
Behold I say unto you that all old covenants have I caused to be done away in this thing and this is a new and an everlasting covenant even **the same** which was from the beginning	1. Behold, I say unto you that all old covenants have I caused to be done away in this thing; and this is a new and an everlasting covenant, even that which was from the beginning.
Wherefore although a man should be baptized an hundred times it availeth him nothing for ye cannot enter in at the strait gate by the Law of Moses neither by your dead works	2. Wherefore, although a man should be baptized an hundred times it availeth him nothing, for you cannot enter in at the strait gate by the law of Moses, neither by your dead works.
for it is because of your dead works that I have caused this last Covenant ~~even that which was from the beginning~~ and this church to be built up unto me	3. For it is because of your dead works that I have caused this last covenant and this church to be built up unto me, **even as in days of old.**
wherefore enter ye in at the gate as I have commanded you and seek not to counsel your God. Amen. **April 16th 1830 Joseph Smith**	4. Wherefore, enter ye in at the gate, as I have commanded, and seek not to counsel your God. Amen.

The McLellin manuscript of LDS section 22 corresponds very closely with other known versions, including the 1981 LDS edition and the 1990 RLDS edition. Besides minor spelling and punctuation variations, the only significant difference is the wording "even as in days of old" (22:3), which in the modern editions describes the everlasting covenant and, importantly, the church that is to be built up. Instead of this wording, McLellin's manuscript originally read, "even that which was from the beginning," which repeats the phrase found in verse 1 and reaffirms the everlastingness of the covenant. The words "even that which was from the beginning" were then crossed out. No other manuscript of section 22 (RLDS 20) has this phrase. There are two other early versions of section 22, both of which agree with the modern edition.[13]

There are several possible explanations for McLellin's substitution of "even that which was from the beginning" in place of "even as in days of old" in verse 3. McLellin may have become confused and copied the phrase from verse 1 into verse 3, as sometimes happens when a copier's eyes are moving back and forth from the original to a copy. He may have simply assumed without checking that the covenant referred to in verse 3 would be described as "that which was from the beginning," since verse 1 used that language.[14]

On the other hand, McLellin may have purposely replaced "even as in days of old" with "even that which was from the beginning," and moved it to modify only the everlasting covenant. This seems possible because about the same time that he was most likely copying this section (late October–November 1831), McLellin was concerned that some of the language used in the revelations received by Joseph Smith could be better rendered. In November 1831, Joseph Smith received a revelation which discerned that McLellin and other elders had "sought in [their] hearts knowledge that [they] might express beyond [Joseph Smith's] language," and McLellin accepted the challenge to write a better revelation than those received by the Prophet (see D&C 67:4–9). He failed and was convinced that the revelations were from the Lord. Joseph Smith's history states:

> William E. McLellin, as the wisest man, in his own estimation, having more learning than sense, endeavored to write a commandment like

> unto one of the Lord's, but failed; it was an awful responsibility to write in the name of the Lord. The Elders all present that witnessed this vain attempt of a man to imitate the language of Jesus Christ, renewed their faith in the fullness of the Gospel, and in the truth of the command-ments and revelations which the Lord had given to the Church through my instrumentality; and the Elders all signified a willingness to bear testimony of the truth to all the world.[15]

McLellin's renewed faith in the revelations may have led him to cross out the phrase, "even that which was from the beginning." Either the inadvertent or the intentional substitution of this word-ing is possible.

The other early sources of section 22 are (1) a version found in *Evening and Morning Star* (*EMS*) 1, no. 1 (June 1832); and (2) the first entry in the "Book of Commandments, Laws, and Covenants, Book B" (*BLC*).[16] In addition to the features discussed above, McLellin alone capitalizes "Law" (v. 2) and includes the word "you" in verse 4, reading "as I have commanded *you.*"

BLC begins with an introduction like McLellin's: "A Command-ment unto the Church of Christ which was established in these last days A.D. 1830 in the fourth month & sixth day of the month which is called April."[17] Neither *EMS* nor any later source shares this same preface, although versions in the *Times and Seasons* and the *Millennial Star* have similar title statements:

> Revelation to the Church of Christ, which was established in these last days, in the year of our Lord One thousand eight hundred and thirty: Given at Manchester New York, April 1830, in consequence of some desiring to unite with the Church without rebaptism, who had previ-ously been baptized.[18]

BLC reads "even *the same* which was from the beginning" (v. 1). McLellin is the only other source that reads this way. All others read "*that.*"

Only McLellin and *BLC* use the spelling "strait" (v. 2). All other sources use "straight."[19]

McLellin and *EMS* use "ye" (v. 2); *BLC* uses "he." *BLC* reads "should*est* be baptized a" (v. 2) while McLellin reads like the other sources: "should be baptized." In verse 2, *BLC* spells *altho,* while McLellin spells *although,* as do all other sources.

Of these documents, the *Painesville Telegraph* publication is clearly older than the McLellin manuscript. Though the *BLC* version is very similar to the McLellin text, it can be dated only sometime before June 12, 1833, making it impossible to tell whether McLellin copied the *BLC* version or an earlier one.

Section 45

Doctrine and Covenants section 45 is one of the longest of all the recorded revelations of Joseph Smith. It deals with the signs of the latter days and the second coming of the Lord Jesus Christ, topics frequently spoken of by McLellin. This revelation was given on either March 6 or 7, 1831, one month after the Prophet Joseph Smith had arrived in Kirtland, Ohio, from New York. Joseph and his scribe, Sidney Rigdon, had begun work on an inspired translation of the Bible. As the translation progressed, Joseph often sought more knowledge from the Lord. Many of the present revelations in the Doctrine and Covenants came as direct answers to questions raised by the Prophet during his revision of the Bible.[20]

John Whitmer, the newly appointed church historian and close associate of the Prophet in Kirtland in 1831, gave some background to this revelation in his history: "In these days the Lord blessed his disciples greatly, and he gave revelation after revelation, which contained doctrine, instructions, and prophecies. The word of the Lord came to the Seer as follows."[21] Joseph Smith's own version of the excitement of those days is recorded in his history as follows:

> At this age of the church many false reports, lies, and fo[o]lish stories were published in the newspapers, and circulated in every direction, to prevent people from investigating the work, or embracing the faith. A great earthquake in China, which destroyed from one to two hundred thousand inhabitants, was burlesqued in some papers, as "Mormonism in China." But to the joy of the saints who had to struggle against every thing that prejudice and wickedness could invent, I received the following.[22]

William E. McLellin's manuscript of the revelation now known as section 45 is introduced as "A Prophecy of Joseph the Seer to the church of Christ delivered at Kirtland 6th March 1831."

Only the verses containing the two significant diffcrences between McLellin's manuscript and the 1981 edition have been arranged for comparison:

McLellin Manuscript

[verse 60] . . . and now behold I say unto you it shall not be given unto you to know any farther than this until the New testament shall be translated and in it all these things shall be made known.

[verses 72-75] . . . & now I say unto you keep these things from going abroa[d] unto the world that ye may accomplish this work in the eyes of your enemies that they may not know your works until ye have accomplished the thing which I have commanded you that when they shall know it. It may be terrible unto them. That fear may seize upon them and they shall stand afar off and tremble and all nations shall be affraid because of the terror of the Lord & the power of his might even so Amen.

1981 Edition

60. And now, behold, I say unto you, it shall not be given unto you to know any further concerning **this chapter,** until the New Testament shall be translated, and in it all these things shall be made known;

72. And now I say unto you, keep these things from going abroad unto the world **until it is expedient in me**, that ye may accomplish this work **in the eyes of the people, and** in the eyes of your enemies, that they may not know your works until ye have accomplished the thing which I have commanded you;

73. That when they shall know it, **that they may consider these things**.

74. **For when the Lord shall appear he shall** be terrible unto them, and they shall stand afar off and tremble.

75. And all nations shall be afraid because of the terror of the Lord, and the power of his might. Even so. Amen.

Only McLellin's copy and one other early manuscript in the handwriting of Edward Partridge give March 6, 1831, as the date of this revelation. All other sources, including the other 1831 version published in *EMS* in June 1832, give March 7 as the date. The difference is slight.

It is not known exactly when McLellin or Partridge copied their manuscripts; but if McLellin recorded his on October 30, 1831, it is the earliest known source of section 45. Circumstantial evidence corroborates that date, for the paper used for Journals I and II and for sections 22 and 45 are the same in size and quality.

Further evidence comes from McLellin's subsequent mission to the East with Samuel H. Smith. During this mission, he recorded in his journal the topics he preached, some of which suggest that he may have had a copy of section 45 with him. For example, McLellin's reference on November 18, 1831, reads, "I did so [ended preaching] after bearing testimony to the truth of the book of Mormon and to the judgement of God which would come upon them if they did not repent." This is perhaps an oblique reference to the instruction given in section 45 to the elders of the Church to "call upon the inhabitants to repent" (v. 64). The revelation declares the judgments that will fall upon those who do not repent. On December 2, 1831, McLellin "made some observations from prophecies," another possible reference to section 45, which he prefaced as "A prophecy of Joseph the Seer." An interesting reference to "Enoch's God" in McLellin's entry on October 30, 1831, also seems to indicate a familiarity with Doctrine and Covenants 45:11, which reads, "Wherefore, hearken ye together and let me show unto you even my wisdom—the wisdom of him whom ye say is the *God of Enoch,* and his brethren" (italics added). This reference to the God of Enoch is singular in the standard works of The Church of Jesus Christ of Latter-day Saints.

McLellin's manuscript of section 45 contains numerous minor differences in spelling, punctuation, and capitalization from other sources of Doctrine and Covenants 45. A good sampling of these differences can be seen in the lines included above. None of the differences is of any doctrinal significance.

Section 65

The background of Doctrine and Covenants 65 has long been a mystery to Latter-day Saints. All that is mentioned in the section heading of the 1981 LDS edition is that it is a "revelation given through Joseph Smith the Prophet, at Hiram, Ohio, October 1831," and that "the Prophet designates this revelation as a prayer." This information was taken from the history published in the *Times and Seasons.*[23] Found in the official *History of the Church* is the addition that the revelation was presumably given "in the forepart of October."[24]

Fortunately, William E. McLellin's manuscript of section 65 provides many new and useful insights.[25] When McLellin arrived in

Manuscript of the revelation of Joseph the Seer (D&C 65, actual size) on Matthew 6:10. Courtesy LDS Church Archives.

Kirtland in October 1831, he copied some of the revelations, probably including this brand new one. The text of the McLellin manuscript of section 65 follows:

> A revelation of Joseph the Seer 30 O^{ct}.. 1831 on the 6th Matthew 10 verse—
>
> Herken and lo a voice as one sent down from ~~Heaven~~ on high who is mighty and powerfu[l] whose going forth is unto the ends of the earth yea whose voice is unto all men prepare ye the way of the Lord make his paths strait. The keys of the kingdom of God is committed unto man on the earth and from thence shall the gospel roll forth unto the ends of the earth, as the stone which is hewn from the mountain without hands shall roll forth unti[l] it hath filled the whole earth. Yea a voice crying prepare ye the way of the Lord prepare ye the supper of the Lamb Make ready for the comeing of the bridegroom Pray unto the Lord. Call upon his holy name Make known his wonderful works among the people. Call upon the Lord that his kingdom may go forth upon the earth that the inhabitants thereof may receive it and be prepared for the days to come in the which the son of man shall come down in Heaven Clothed in the brightness of his glory to meet the kingdom of God which is set up on the earth. Wherefore may the kingdom of God go forth that the kingdom of heaven may come, that thou O God may be glorified in heaven so on earth that thine enemies may be subdued for thine is the honor, power and glory for ever and ever Amen. Jo^s. Smith Revelator

The most interesting detail about this document is in its heading where McLellin specifies that this is a revelation "on the 6th Matthew 10 verse." This information allows us to recognize for the first time that section 65 is not simply an ordinary or spontaneous prayer, but is deeply related to the Lord's Prayer, especially Matthew 6:10, "Thy kingdom come. Thy will be done in earth, as it is in heaven."

This insight provides readers with a valuable key to unlock and appreciate the meaning of this revelation. Several words in section 65 are, in fact, related to phrases in the Lord's Prayer. Following the introductory verses which invoke texts from Isaiah 40:3, Daniel 2:45, Matthew 3:3 and 22:2, and Revelation 19:9, the revelation focuses on Matthew 6:9–13. The revelation exhorts all people to "pray unto the Lord, call upon his holy name" (65:4); this acknowledgment of the holiness of God's name compares favorably with the initial instruction of the Lord's Prayer, "after this manner therefore pray ye: Our Father which art in heaven, Hallowed be thy

name" (Matt. 6:9). The revelation then pleads, "May the kingdom of
God go forth, that the kingdom of heaven may come, that thou,
O God, mayest be glorified in heaven so on earth" (65:6), which
echoes the main text mentioned in the McLellin heading (Matt. 6:10).
Much as the revelation expresses the hope "that thine enemies may
be subdued" (65:6), the Lord's Prayer asks for deliverance "from evil"
(Matt. 6:13). Finally, section 65 and the Lord's Prayer both conclude
with similar doxologies: "for thine is the honor, power and glory,
forever and ever. Amen" (65:6) and, "for thine is the kingdom, and
the power, and the glory, for ever. Amen" (Matt. 6:13). Identifying
these relationships between the Lord's Prayer and section 65 gives
both of these scriptures new meanings relevant to the modern
dispensation of the gospel of Jesus Christ.

While section 65 is clearly related to the Lord's Prayer, it is also
a separate text. It is neither a commentary on the Lord's Prayer
nor a new translation of it. The text of the McLellin version of
section 65 is very similar to the four other early manuscripts of this
revelation as well as the 1981 published version. Apart from
punctuation, heading, and acknowledgment of Joseph Smith as
revelator, the only differences between the 1981 edition and the
McLellin manuscript are these:

McLellin Manuscript	1981 Edition
Verse 1	
Herken and lo a voice as one sent down from on high . . . whose voice is unto **all** men prepare ye the way of the Lord make his paths **strait.**	Hearken, and lo, a voice as **of** one sent down from on high . . . whose voice is unto men—Prepare ye the way of the Lord, make his paths straight.
Verse 2	
keys . . . **is** committed	keys . . . are committed
the stone which is **hewn from** the mountain . . . until it **hath** filled	the stone which is cut out of the mountain . . . until it has filled
Verse 3	
Make ready for the **comeing of the** bridegroom.	make ready for the Bridegroom.
Verse 6	
that thou O God **may** be	that thou, O God, mayest be

The four other early sources of section 65 are (1) Manuscript #1 (RLDS), date unknown; (2) a copy found in the Kirtland Revelation Book (87), recorded before August 18, 1834; (3) a version published in *EMS* 1, no. 4 (September 1832), and (4) a reprint of the same in the Kirtland publication of *EMS* 1, no. 4 (April 1835). All these texts are similar to the newly found McLellin document in three ways. They all state that the revelation was received on October 30, 1831, whereas all later sources say only October 1831. In verse 1, all five use the spelling *strait.* In verse 6, all five read "That thou, O God, may."

Each early document, however, has its own peculiar points of agreement or disagreement with the McLellin text. In most sources, verse 1 reads "a voice as *of* one," but the McLellin document, Manuscript #1, and Kirtland Revelation Book all read "a voice as one." Likewise, the word *forever* appears as two words only in those three manuscripts.

Manuscript #1 often capitalizes words, such as Earth (vv. 1, 2, 5, and 6), Gospel (v. 2), Mountain (v. 2), and Clothed (v. 5), but these words are not capitalized in the McLellin document. Also, *and* is signified by *&* throughout Manuscript #1, while it is spelled out in McLellin. The writer of Manuscript #1 liked to double his l's: powerful is spelled *powerfull,* until is spelled *untill* (v. 2), and wonderful is spelled *wonderfull* (v. 4). Also, honor is spelled *honour* (v. 6). Manuscript #1 also contains the crossed-out word *kingdom* in the final verse.

The Kirtland Revelation Book reads "one sent down from ~~above~~ on high," where the McLellin document also has the words "on high," but they are written on top of the word "Heaven." Only the Kirtland Revelation Book and the McLellin document read "whose voice is unto *all* men" in verse 1, making the revelation more emphatically universal; all other sources lack the limitless *all.*

In verse 2, the Kirtland Revelation Book reads "hewed from," whereas McLellin and the *Evening and the Morning Star* publications read "hewn from." Most other sources read "cut out of," while Manuscript #1 reads "~~hewn from~~ cut out of." In verse 3, the Kirtland Revelation Book is the only other source to agree with McLellin's "coming of the bridegroom" and in not capitalizing "son of man" (v. 5).

In spite of several close similarities, the Kirtland Revelation Book also differs from McLellin in certain respects. In verses 1, 2, and 5, respectively, the Kirtland Revelation Book says "*and* make his paths," "committed unto *men*," and "set upon the earth." All other sources, including McLellin, do not have the "and," use man instead of the plural "men," and put a space between "up" and "on."

Finally, some aspects of the McLellin document are unique: It alone contains the information "on the 6th Matthew 10 verse," and uses the spelling "Herken" (v. 1). "Sent down" (v. 1) is not found in any of the four early sources, although it curiously appears in several later publications.[26] McLellin alone reads, "keys . . . *is* committed" (v. 2); likewise, the words "which is" (v. 2) are not found in any of the early sources, but first appear in the Manuscript History of the Church (1841–43). In verse 2, only McLellin reads "until it *hath* filled." All other sources use the word "has," although Manuscript #1 says "~~hath~~ has." In verse 5, "Heaven" is not capitalized in any source other than McLellin's.

In light of the fact that all of these manuscripts of section 65 have points at which they are similar to and different from each of the other sources, it is virtually impossible to determine which is earliest or which was copied from which. Thus, although the emergence of this manuscript adds to the pool of knowledge from which textual criticism of the Doctrine and Covenants can be done, it provides a sober reminder that textual history is an imprecise and uncertain science, often dealing with minute differences that have little effect on the meaning of the text.

Section 66

The main contribution of McLellin's journals to our understanding of section 66 is what they reveal about McLellin himself. The other revelations copied by McLellin had some significance to his missionary work, personal study, or both. But section 66 was revealed in direct response to McLellin's petition that Joseph Smith inquire of the Lord on his behalf. The emergence of the journals and the resulting study of McLellin's life and other papers make this revelation even more significant. Considerably more has been learned about McLellin's motivation to ask for a revelation concerning his standing before the Lord.

From thence I returned to Kirtland, but as I
caused old Father Smith to ride Tom and as I was [riding]
thing on I slipped off of a large log and strained
my ankle very badly— thence I rode; and just
as I was about to start to bed I asked brother
Joseph what he thought about my ankle's be=
ing healed. He immediately turned to me and
asked me if I believed in my heart that God
through his instrumentality would heal it.
I answered that I believed he would. He laid
hands on it and it was healed although
it was swelled much and had pained me se=
verely——— Thence I went home with him
on Saturday 29th Early in the morning we
reached there having staid Friday night in the
Nelson church— This day the Lord condescen=
ded to hear my prayer and give me a revelation of
his will, through his prophet or Seer (Joseph)
And these are the words which I wrote from his
mouth, Saying, Behold thus saith the Lord unto you
my servant William blessed are you, in as much as you have
turned away from your iniquities and have received my
truths, saith the Lord, your Redeemer, The Saviour of the
world; even of as many as believe on my name. Verily I
say unto you, blessed are you for receiving mine everlasting
Covenant, even the fulness of my Gospel sent forth unto the
children of men, that they might have life, and be made
partakers of the glories which are to be revealed in the last
days as it was written by the Prophets and Apostles in days of old.
Verily I say unto you my servant William that you are
clean but not all. Repent therefore of those things which
are not pleasing in my sight saith the Lord; for the Lord
will show them unto you. And now, verily I the Lord
will show unto you what I will concerning you: or
what is my will concerning you. Behold verily I say
unto you that it is my will that you should proclaim my
Gospel from land to land, and from city to city: yea in those
regions round about where it hath not been proclaimed.
Tarry not many days in this place. Go not up unto the land
Zion as yet; But in as much as you can send; Send.
Otherwise think not of thy property—

Page 21, Journal I (actual size). The text of the revelation given
by Joseph Smith to McLellin (D&C 66) begins at the middle of this
page and is written in smaller than usual script. Courtesy LDS
Church Archives.

In regard to this revelation, Joseph Smith's *History of the Church* simply states: "At the request of William E. McLellin, I received the following."[27] As the prophet's Nauvoo historians were compiling this information, they evidently concluded that McLellin's request took place at the conference on October 25, 1831, held at Orange, Ohio. Hence, the 1981 LDS edition of the Doctrine and Covenants says that this revelation was received on October 25, 1831, at Orange. McLellin's manuscript gives a new date: October 29, 1831. The journals also tell how McLellin went with Joseph from Orange to the Prophet's Hiram, Ohio, home where the revelation was given. Shortly after their arrival there on October 29, 1831, Joseph received the revelation on behalf of William E. McLellin. One very interesting detail is that McLellin served as Joseph's scribe in this endeavor. His journal entry for the day reads, "This day the Lord condecended to hear my prayr and give me a revelation of his will, through his prophet or Seer (Joseph)—And these are the words which I wrote from his mouth, saying" (then follows the text of the revelation).

Two additional sources date this revelation to October 29, 1831. An early manuscript in the handwriting of John Whitmer, housed in the RLDS archives reads: "A Revelation to Wm. E. McLelin rec d Oct 29th 1831."[28] The other document is an article by McLellin that appeared in 1848 in his short-lived periodical, the *Ensign of Liberty*. This agrees with Journal I by mentioning his attendance at a conference "in the town of Orange" on October 25. "From this conference I went home with the Prophet," McLellin continued, "and on Saturday, the 29th, I received through him, and wrote from his mouth a revelation concerning myself."[29]

In the same article McLellin wrote, "I had expected and believed that when I saw Joseph, I should receive . . . a revelation concerning myself."[30] According to his own account, that expectation included a special request of the Lord that was unknown to Joseph Smith. McLellin explained, "I went before the Lord in secret, and on my knees asked him to reveal the answer to five questions through his Prophet, and that too without his having any knowledge of my having made such a request."[31]

McLellin later acknowledged, both in his journals and in the *Ensign of Liberty*, that the revelation did indeed answer these questions. After McLellin had scribed the revelation into his journal, he ended the day's entry with this expression: "This revelation give great joy to my heart because some important questions were answered which had dwelt upon my mind with anxiety yet with uncertainty."[32] The *Ensign of Liberty* article, written more than ten years after McLellin had left the LDS Church, is even more insistent about the responses that came in the revelation. It describes the effect the revelation had on McLellin's conviction that Joseph Smith was indeed a prophet of God:

> I now testify in the fear of God, that every question which I thus lodged in the ears of the Lord of Sabbaoth, were answered to my full and entire satisfaction. I desired for a testimony of Joseph's inspiration. And I to this day consider it to me an evidence which I cannot refute.[33]

It is clear that McLellin believed, both while he was a member of the Church and ten years after he had become disaffected, that in 1831 Joseph Smith was a true prophet.

That McLellin himself insisted that this revelation specifically answered every one of the "five questions" that he revealed to no one but the Lord invites the inquiry, "What were the five questions?" McLellin left no list, probably because of the intensely personal nature of the questions. With the emergence of his journals and other papers, however, a careful reading of the answers in section 66 suggests likely possibilities:

Question 1   How does this little church that I have just joined, organized by Joseph Smith, fit into the religious world?

Answer   It represents mine everlasting covenant, even the fullness of my gospel, sent forth unto the children of men, that they might have life and be made partakers of glories which are to be revealed in the last days, as it was written by the prophets and apostles of old. (D&C 66:2)

Question 2   What is my spiritual standing?

Answer   You are clean, but not all; repent therefore of those things which are not pleasing in my sight, saith the Lord, for the Lord will show them unto you. (D&C 66:3)

Question 3   What is my role in the Church? I have closed my school
                and settled my affairs in Illinois. What am I to do now?

Answer   It is my will that you should proclaim my gospel,
                from land to land and from city to city. . . . Tarry not
                many days in this place [Ohio]; go not up unto the
                land of Zion [Missouri] as yet; but inasmuch as you
                can send, send; otherwise think not of property. . . .
                Go unto the eastern lands, bear testimony in every
                place . . . reasoning with the people. . . . Let my
                servant Samuel H. Smith go with you, and forsake
                him not. (D&C 66:5-8)

Question 4   I have seen and personally experienced the power to
                heal by both Joseph and Hyrum Smith. Will I be able
                to have this power?

Answer   Lay your hands upon the sick, and they shall recover.
                (D&C 66:9)

Question 5   How can I escape the temptation of adultery and
                other sins which have burdened me, especially since
                the recent death of my wife?

Answer   Be patient in affliction. Ask, and ye shall receive;
                knock and it shall be opened unto you. Seek not to be
                cumbered. Forsake all unrighteousness. Commit not
                adultery, a temptation with which thou hast been
                troubled. . . . Continue in these things even unto the
                end, and you shall have a crown of eternal life at
                the right hand of my Father who is full of grace and
                truth. (D&C 66:9, 10, 12)

Certainly any attempt to reconstruct McLellin's precise questions
is speculative at best. Perhaps they were quite different from those
posed above, but these possibilities seem reasonable. In any event, it
is clear that McLellin was seeking reassurance concerning his joining
the newly restored Church, including what possibilities the eternities
held for him. The revelation is indeed reassuring on those matters.

For years, McLellin has been best known as the man in Church
history who was "troubled" with the temptation to commit adultery

(D&C 66:10). Needless to say, the Lord's admonition to McLellin has provoked many questions concerning his fidelity, particularly since he became a noted apostate.

In his August 4, 1832, letter, McLellin spoke of his marriage to Cinthia Ann in 1829, and also of a later marriage to Emeline Miller on April 26, 1832.[34] Entries in Journal I now confirm that Cinthia and an infant had died and were buried near Charleston, Illinois, before the summer of 1831, suggesting that she may have died in childbirth.[35] From his tender feelings toward his deceased wife, it appears that William and Cinthia had enjoyed a fond marriage; this would indicate that his temptation to commit adultery came after her loss and not from any dissatisfaction in their marriage. Whatever influences led to the temptation, the mention of it with the commandment to repent of all his sins, followed by the promise of "a crown of eternal life at the right hand of my Father" (D&C 66:12), must have brought great comfort to McLellin.

The text of McLellin's manuscript of Doctrine and Covenants 66 is almost identical to the 1981 LDS edition. Beyond a number of capitalization and punctuation changes, the only differences are as follows: The McLellin manuscript reads, "unto *you* my servant Wm. McLellin," (v. 1) and "And now, verily I say," instead of "Behold, verily I say" (v. 5). The 1981 edition clarifies that Samuel (v. 8) is Samuel H. Smith, and has the plural word *hands* instead of the original singular (v. 9). Finally, whereas the McLellin manuscript admonishes him to "Keep these sayings true and faithful," the current edition reads, "Keep these sayings, *for they are* true and faithful" (v. 11).

Hearing and writing this revelation was a powerful experience in McLellin's life. It solidified his conviction that Joseph Smith was a true prophet and gave assurance that in spite of temptations, sins, and questions, McLellin could ask and receive, repent and become a candidate for "a crown of eternal life."

NOTES

The contributors to this chapter are Larry E. Dahl (D&C 66), Steven C. Harper (D&C 20 and 45), Trevor Packer and John W. Welch (D&C 65), and Bruce A. Van Orden (overview).

[1] A copy of Section 22 was published in the *Painesville Telegraph* [Ohio] on April 19, 1831.

[2] Oliver Cowdery and John Whitmer were commanded in Doctrine and Covenants 67 in early November 1831 to take the manuscripts of the revelations to Independence, Missouri, where W. W. Phelps would publish them as the Book of Commandments. Most of these handwritten manuscripts were probably destroyed by Jackson County mob action in July 1833 when the printing establishment was attacked.

[3] Journal I, October 25, 1831.

[4] Journal I, October 25, 1831.

[5] Donald Q. Cannon and Lyndon W. Cook, eds., *Far West Record* (Salt Lake City: Deseret Book, 1983): 21.

[6] Journal I, October 29, 1831.

[7] Journal I, October 30, 1831.

[8] In a letter of William E. McLellin to M. H. Forscutt, October 1870, RLDS Archives, published in *Saints' Herald* 19 (July 15, 1872): 436 are these words: "In 1831, I wrote off a number of the revelations as originally given, and have them now." McLellin may, however, have copied section 65 on February 25, 1831. His journal entry for that date says, "I wrote commandments and revelations at Father Smith's."

[9] *HC* 1:221-29 and D&C 68:7.

[10] Orson Pratt, "Distinguishing Characteristics between the Latter-day Saints and the Various Denominations of Christendom," *Journal of Discourses,* 26 vols. (Liverpool: Franklin D. Richards, 1856), 16:293-94; see also Lyndon W. Cook, *The Revelations of the Prophet Joseph Smith* (Provo, Utah: Seventies Mission Bookstore, 1981), 33. It may be that Orson Pratt himself was one of these Baptists. He was not baptized until his birthday in September 1830.

[11] See Daniel Merrill, *The Mode and Subjects of Baptism* (Raleigh, N.C.: Joseph Gales, 1807). Correspondence from Professor Bill J. Leonard of Samford University to Steven C. Harper, January 25, 1994.

[12] *Evening and Morning Star*, Independence, Mo., 1 (June 1832): 1-2; see generally Dean C. Jessee, *The Papers of Joseph Smith,* 2 vols. to date (Salt Lake City: Deseret Book, 1989-), 1:14n (hereafter cited as *PJS*); Cook, *Revelations*, 33, 125n, 126n.

[13] Additional early manuscripts are contained in the "Book of Commandments, Laws and Covenants, Book B," and *Evening and Morning Star* 1 (June 1832).

[14] McLellin may have been familiar with many of the scriptural passages that use the language "from the beginning," or "from the beginning of creation," to refer to the everlasting covenant. The 1981 edition of the LDS standard works uses this language approximately one hundred times in relation to the eternal nature of covenants or other aspects of the plan of salvation. These include Doctrine and Covenants 49:9: "Wherefore, I say

unto you that I have sent mine everlasting covenant, even that which was from the beginning."

[15] *PJS* 1:367-68; *HC* 1:220-29. Mark R. Grandstaff, "Having More Learning Than Sense: William E. McLellin and the Book of Commandments Revisited," *Dialogue* 26 (Winter 1993): 23-48, suggests that McLellin should not be castigated for his role in this episode. Instead, Grandstaff argues, this statement of Joseph Smith was dictated sometime in 1842 after McLellin apostatized and was therefore colored by later events. Grandstaff asserts that concern over the wording of revelations was not the only reason for the coming forth of D&C 67, and he sees little evidence that the elders were critical of the revelations, but in so doing he skirts D&C 67:5.

[16] For detailed information about these early documents, see Robert J. Woodford, "The Historical Development of the Doctrine and Covenants," 3 vols. (Ph.D. diss., Brigham Young University, 1974).

[17] McLellin's manuscript, however, does not capitalize "commandment" or "church." *BLC* maintains the basic trend of capitalizing, where McLellin does not. McLellin also spells out "the year of our Lord" instead of abbreviating A.D.

[18] *Millennial Star* 4 (December 1843): 116.

[19] This spelling may seem significant given the different meanings of "strait" and "straight." It is clear, however, that in 1831 the two spellings were interchangeable; see Noah Webster, *An American Dictionary of the English Language* (New York: Harper, 1844): 796. Also see section 65, where McLellin again uses "strait" in contrast with the 1981 edition's "straight" (D&C 65:1). The passage of the 1981 edition of the Book of Mormon to which section 22 seems to be referring, 2 Nephi 31:17-19, uses "strait." But the 1830 edition, which McLellin would have been familiar with, uses "straight." For analysis of the meanings of "straight" and "strait," see Daniel B. McKinlay, "Straight and Narrow," *Encyclopedia of Mormonism*, ed. Daniel Ludlow, 5 vols. (New York: Macmillan, 1992), 3:1419; John W. Welch, ed., "Getting Things Strai[gh]t," *Reexploring the Book of Mormon* (Salt Lake City: Deseret Book; and Provo, Utah: Foundation for Ancient Research and Mormon Studies, 1992), 260-62.

[20] Robert J. Matthews, *"A Plainer Translation": Joseph Smith's Translation of the Bible* (Provo: Brigham Young University Press, 1975), 256.

[21] Book of John Whitmer, 45-46, LDS Church Archives.

[22] *PJS* 1:350; *HC* 1:158.

[23] *Times and Seasons* 5 (April 1, 1844): 482.

[24] *HC* 1:218; *PJS* 1:365.

[25] See John W. Welch and Trevor Packer, "The Newly Found Manuscript of Doctrine and Covenants Section 65," *BYU Studies* 33 (1993): 331-36. For historical context regarding the allusions in D&C 65 to passages from the book of Daniel, see David J. Whittaker, "The Book of Daniel in Early

Mormon Thought," in John M. Lundquist and Stephen D. Ricks, eds., *By Study and Also By Faith,* 2 vols. (Salt Lake City: Deseret Book and F.A.R.M.S. 1990), 1:155-201.

[26] Various editions of the Doctrine and Covenants (1844-46, 1852-1920) and *Millennial Star* 5 (April 1845): 163.

[27] *HC* 1:220; and *PJS* 1:366.

[28] See Woodford, "The Historical Development of the Doctrine and Covenants," 1:841. RLDS Church Archivist Ronald E. Romig confirmed this information.

[29] *Ensign of Liberty of the Church of Christ* 1, no. 4 (January 1848): 61.

[30] *Ensign of Liberty* 1, no. 4 (January 1848): 61.

[31] *Ensign of Liberty* 1, no. 4 (January 1848): 61.

[32] Journal I, October 29, 1831.

[33] *Ensign of Liberty* 1, no. 4 (January 1848): 61.

[34] See above, pp. 82-83. This information negates Grandstaff's speculation that "McLellin may have failed to receive a divorce from his first wife, Cynthia Ann." Grandstaff, "Having More Learning Than Sense," 36n.

[35] Journal I, August 1 and September 22, 1831.

Part III: Supplemental Resources

William E. McLellin, c. 1870. Courtesy LDS Church Archives.

The Provenance of
William E. McLellin's Journals

Richard E. Turley, Jr.

The six journals of William E. McLellin have an interesting provenance.[1] After finishing Journal VI in 1836, McLellin lived in several places in the midwestern United States, ultimately moving to Independence, Missouri, in 1870. He died there on March 14, 1883, and his journals and other papers apparently passed into the possession of his widow, Emeline Miller McLellin.[2]

During the latter part of his life, William McLellin spent time discussing Mormon history with John L. Traughber, Jr., who was born in Missouri in 1854.[3] In 1889, Traughber wrote of McLellin, "I valued him very much. He and I were true friends[;] yet for the last two years of his life we were as far apart in religion as the poles of the earth."[4] According to a 1910 newspaper article, Traughber "was once a member of the Mormon church" but later apostatized.[5] Traughber corresponded with Joseph Smith III, president of the Reorganized Church of Jesus Christ of Latter Day Saints, in the 1870s.[6] A letter from Joseph III to Traughber dated July 14, 1879, suggests Traughber may have joined and later left the RLDS Church.[7]

Traughber received William E. McLellin's papers from the Norborne, Missouri, express office on November 10, 1884. They had been sent to him as a gift by Emeline McLellin, who was then staying with her son James in Troy, Missouri. The day after he received the items, Traughber penned notes describing how he got them.[8]

By 1901, Traughber was living in Mobile, Tyler County, Texas, and had become intrigued by the cellular cosmology of Cyrus Read Teed. He continued to discuss Mormonism with interested correspondents, however, including noted anti-Mormon Theodore Schroeder.[9] In a July 11, 1901, letter to Schroeder, Traughber mentioned he had one of William McLellin's two copies of the Book of Commandments

(1833), as well as a copy of McLellin's periodical *Ensign of Liberty*. Traughber also listed the titles of his own unpublished works about Mormonism. He expressed a willingness to sell all these materials and asked Schroeder to make him an offer for them.[10]

On July 29, Traughber wrote Schroeder again. He told Schroeder he wanted to move to Boise, Idaho, and hoped to get enough money from the sale of his Mormon materials to make the move possible.[11] On August 21, Traughber wrote Schroeder once more, this time revealing that he had in his possession some manuscripts written by McLellin, as well as McLellin's journal for parts of 1831 through 1836 and numerous letters. He offered to sell what he had if Schroeder could offer him enough to make the sale worthwhile to him.[12] The men apparently did not reach an agreement, and McLellin's papers remained in Traughber's hands.

By 1908, Traughber's health had begun to fail, and on January 13, he addressed a letter from Doucette, Texas, to the librarian of The Church of Jesus Christ of Latter-day Saints in Salt Lake City. The letter reached the office of the LDS Church president five days later. In the letter, Traughber told about the Book of Commandments in his possession and its provenance. He also described the incomplete journals and the manuscript books he received from McLellin's widow in 1884. "I want these things preserved," he wrote, "and as I am 53 years old, and not in the best of health, I may not be able to preserve them much longer. I am in straitened circumstances, and if the Church will pay me $50^{00} I will turn over to it these articles that I have described to you."[13]

The First Presidency of the LDS Church assigned Samuel O. Bennion, president of the Church's Central States Mission, to call on Traughber, examine the materials, and purchase them if they appeared authentic and valuable.[14] Bennion traveled to Doucette, where he acquired the materials from Traughber,[15] who died later that year.[16]

The persons who acquired McLellin's papers for the LDS Church passed away, and the existence of the papers in the Church's possession eventually was forgotten. In the 1980s, however, document dealer Mark W. Hofmann began claiming he had the opportunity to buy a group of materials known as "the McLellin Collection" from a private source. In June 1985, Hofmann offered to donate the collection to the LDS Church when he eventually acquired it. As later events would prove, however, Hofmann was a skilled forger who had made up the story about the McLellin Collection to defraud Salt Lake City coin dealer Alvin Rust and others. In an effort to keep his massive forgery and fraud scheme from being detected, Hofmann murdered two Latter-day Saints, Steven F. Christensen and Kathleen W. Sheets, in October 1985. The murders prompted an investigation that eventually landed Hofmann in prison with a recommendation that he never be released.

The Hofmann forgeries and murders catapulted McLellin's name into prominence after decades of relative obscurity. In March 1986, Dean C. Jessee of the Joseph Fielding Smith Institute for Church History at BYU informed Church Historical Department staff members about research notes he had made during his tenure as a department employee some years earlier. Following the lead provided by Jessee's notes, the staff located the uncatalogued 1908 correspondence between J. L. Traughber and LDS Church officials, together with related documents, which in turn led to the unexpected rediscovery of the long-lost McLellin journals and papers that had been in Church possession since they were acquired in 1908.[17]

Excerpts from these materials first appeared in the *Church News* in October 1992.[18] The McLellin journals are now published in their entirety, for the first time, in this volume.

Richard E. Turley, Jr., is Managing Director of the Historical Department of The Church of Jesus Christ of Latter-day Saints, Salt Lake City, Utah.

NOTES

[1] The originals of these journals are found in the Historical Department, The Church of Jesus Christ of Latter-day Saints, Salt Lake City (hereafter cited as LDS Church Archives), and are cataloged as MS 13538, fds. 1–6. I wish to thank RLDS Church Archivist Ronald E. Romig for bringing to my attention the sources in this article that relate to the RLDS Church.

[2] Lyndon W. Cook, *The Revelations of the Prophet Joseph Smith* (Salt Lake City: Deseret Book, 1985), 107; Andrew Jenson, *Latter-day Saint Biographical Encyclopedia,* 4 vols. (Salt Lake City: Andrew Jenson History Co., 1901–36), 1:83. Emeline was William's second wife, who Joseph F. Smith noted "was a cousin of Sister Nancy M. Hyde's." Joseph Fielding

Smith, *Life of Joseph F. Smith* (Salt Lake City: Deseret Book, 1969), 240; Cook, *Revelations of the Prophet Joseph,* 106. See further page 358 below.

[3] See, for example, Traughber's mention of an 1881 discussion with McLellin in J. L. Traughber [Jr.] to A. T. Schroeder, August 21, 1901, Theodore Schroeder Papers, Rare Books and Manuscripts Division, New York Public Library, Astor, Lenox, and Tilden Foundations (hereafter cited as Schroeder Papers), photo reproduction in MS 9030, fd. 4, LDS Church Archives. On the date of Traughber's birth, see Dawn Tracy, "'LDS Papers' Found in Houston," *Salt Lake Tribune,* December 2, 1985, A1, A3.

[4] Dawn Tracy, "Papers Seem Authentic, Expert Says," *Salt Lake Tribune,* December 3, 1985, A1, A3, citing note made by Traughber on February 27, 1889.

[5] "The Original Accessories," *Salt Lake Tribune,* May 2, 1910.

[6] Joseph Smith to J. L. Traughber, Jr., February 13, 1877, Joseph Smith III Letter Press Book, P6, book 1a, pp. 29–30, Reorganized Church of Jesus Christ of Latter Day Saints Library-Archives, Independence, Missouri (hereafter cited as RLDS Library-Archives); Joseph Smith to J. L. Traughber [Jr.], November 29, 1877, Joseph Smith III Letter Press Book, P6, book 1, pp. 243–44, RLDS Library-Archives.

[7] Joseph Smith to J. L. Traughber [Jr.], Joseph Smith III Letter Press Book, P6, book 2, pp. 264–69, RLDS Library-Archives.

[8] MS 13538, fd. 5, p. 16, and fd. 8, p. 134, LDS Church Archives; *History of Lincoln County, Missouri* (Chicago: Goodspeed, 1888), 571–72.

[9] J. L. Traughber [Jr.] to A. T. Schroeder, June 24, 1901, Schroeder Papers, photo reproduction in MS 9030, fd. 4, LDS Church Archives. For a summary of Schroeder's anti-Mormon activities, see A. Burt Horsley, "Theodore Schroeder Mormon Antagonist—Content and Significance of the Theodore Schroeder Collection, New York Public Library," in MS 9030, fd. 1, LDS Church Archives; Dennis L. Domayer, "Theodore Schroeder: A Biographical Sketch," in Ralph E. McCoy, comp., *Theodore Schroeder, A Cold Enthusiast,* Bibliographic Contributions, no. 8 (Carbondale, Ill.: The Libraries, Southern Illinois University, 1973), 1–4.

[10] J. L. Traughber [Jr.] to A. T. Schroeder, July 11, 1901, Schroeder Papers, photo reproduction in MS 9030, fd. 4, LDS Church Archives.

[11] J. L. Traughber [Jr.] to A. T. Schroeder, July 29, 1901, Schroeder Papers, photo reproduction in MS 9030, fd. 4, LDS Church Archives.

[12] J. L. Traughber [Jr.] to A. T. Schroeder, August 21, 1901, Schroeder Papers, photo reproduction in MS 9030, fd. 4, LDS Church Archives.

[13] J. L. Traughber [Jr.] to the Librarian of the Ch. of Jesus Christ of L. D. Sts., January 13, 1908, photocopy in MS 13539, #1, LDS Church Archives.

[14] Handwritten note attached to Traughber letter to Church Librarian; Joseph F. Smith, John R. Winder, and Anthon H. Lund to Samuel O. Bennion, January 18, 1908, photocopy in MS 13539, #2, LDS Church Archives.

[15] Central States Mission, Historical Record, LR 1562/11, vol. 1, pp. 222-29, LDS Church Archives; S. O. Bennion to Joseph F. Smith and Counselors, February 12, 1908, photocopy in MS 13539, #3, LDS Church Archives.

[16] Tracy, "'LDS Papers' Found In Houston"; Tracy, "Papers Seem Authentic, Expert Says."

[17] For an account of Hofmann's interactions with LDS Church officials, see Richard E. Turley, Jr., *Victims: The LDS Church and the Mark Hofmann Case* (Urbana: University of Illinois Press, 1992). A detailed description of the rediscovery of the papers appears on pages 248 to 251 of the book.

[18] "Excerpts from Journal and Writings of William E. McLellin, Early Apostle," *Church News,* October 24, 1992, 5, 13.

We dismissed. There were two Campbell
Preachers there who had come to contend with us
one of them arose and requested the privilege to
speak of the man of the house, he went on
though the people were not much attentive
I set and watched him till he was done I
then arose and removed the difficulties he
mentioned and I believe I gave general sat=
isfaction. — We attended our appointment
It was snowing considerable. And though we
had to break the ice I went down in
the watter and baptized the two sisters
who had joined There was a considerable con
gregation present, We appointed a prayr
meeting that night at friend Reeds
for the purpose of confirming those bap=
tized. The house was full Br Saml
opened the meeting and spoke about half
an hour I then rose and spoke about an
hour on the first establishment of Chris=
tianity then on the rise and progress of the
Church of Christ in these last days and the
importance of the ordinances of the gospel
but particularly that of the Laying on of the
hands for the reception of the Holy Ghost
I then prayed and laid my hands on them and
they said they rejoiced that they ever heard the
Plan of Salvation — I then exorted the people
to embrace the truth and Elizabeth Evershart com
forward and we repaired to the water and I
baptized her and as we came out of the
water Saml Buswell came to me and

Page 9, Journal II (actual size). This page reports the baptism of
two women in icy water. Courtesy LDS Church Archives.

The McLellin Journals and Early Mormon History

William G. Hartley

Like a sunken galleon filled with treasures, the recently recovered McLellin journals contain valuable historical insights. Historians, eager to compare McLellin's entries with existing facts and interpretations about early Mormon history, expect these important documents to corroborate much of what is already known, challenge parts of what has been held to be known, and offer new understandings never before known or considered. An initial search through the journals is in some respects disappointing—no blockbuster revelations or monumental disclosures here. (But the fact that they may disappoint some readers is a credit to the current state of LDS records and historical scholarship, particularly in the wake of Mark Hofmann's forgeries that one after another challenged what we thought we understood well.[1]) The journals also do not cover McLellin's better-known connections with LDS history: the episode regarding the attempt to write a more perfect revelation than Joseph Smith, his signing the preface to the Doctrine and Covenants, being called to the Twelve, experiencing pentecostal Kirtland Temple dedication days, and being excommunicated in 1838. Nevertheless, in terms of treasures, McLellin's journals contain a rich array of information.

Perhaps most importantly, these journals first walk modern readers into an early Latter-day Saint world devoid of stakes, wards, temples, the Doctrine and Covenants, hymnbooks, a Quorum of Twelve, baptismal fonts, women's organizations, Sunday Schools, tithing, and Articles of Faith. Less than two years old, the church that McLellin joined had no experienced leaders. The young Church was in a dynamic, emergent stage, constantly changing and restructuring—like a tree sprout newly burst from a seed, still forming its trunk and beginning to produce branches and leaves. When McLellin converted in mid-1831, the Book of Mormon had been published and sixty-two revelations in the present LDS Doctrine and Covenants had been received, but few of the revelations were widely accessible. By early 1833, some had been printed singly in the *Evening and Morning Star,* and a few hand-bound copies of the 1833 Book of Commandments were available. Present LDS Doctrine and Covenants sections 20 and 22 (at that time sometimes called the "Articles and Covenants"), along with section 42 (then known as "The Law"), were perhaps the most-used revelations among converts and missionaries like McLellin. When the Doctrine and Covenants became available in 1835, members eagerly obtained it.[2]

Historians are barely starting to assess the value of McLellin's journals to LDS history. At this early stage, several contributions can nevertheless be identified. What follows are preliminary probes to consider what new information the journals offer, first, about individual people, then about missionary activities, and finally, about early LDS Church practices and experiences.

Book of Mormon Witnesses

Although McLellin became disaffected from the LDS Church in 1838, he retained belief in the historicity and truthfulness of the Book of Mormon until his death. This tenacity of belief is now better understood because of McLellin's early, close contacts with Book of Mormon witnesses.[3] His journals contribute new, rich information about the following witnesses.

David Whitmer. One of the elders who helped convert McLellin was David Whitmer, one of the Three Witnesses, who said he had been shown the gold plates by the Angel Moroni. Whitmer, McLellin recorded on July 18, 1831, "bore testimony to having seen an Holy Angel who had made known the truth of this record to him." On August 3, McLellin bought the last Book of Mormon the elders had and began reading it. He determined to go to Independence before these missionaries did to "see if the testimony of the other witnesses would agree with theirs."

Martin Harris. When McLellin reached Independence, he inquired closely into the new faith. There he "met with David Whitmer & Martin Harris," two of the Three Witnesses, and rode with them ten miles westward.[4] The next day he talked with Hyrum Smith,[5] one of the Eight Witnesses, for four hours. They discussed, among other matters, "the testimonies given to him."[6] McLellin's careful conversations with these Book of Mormon witnesses convinced him that their testimonies were firm.

Hyrum Smith. When McLellin decided to be baptized, he asked Hyrum to baptize him. Newly baptized, McLellin left on August 25, 1831, for a preaching mission with Martin Harris, David Whitmer, Hyrum Smith, Harvey Whitlock, and Simeon Carter. Within a few days, the men separated, and McLellin became a preaching companion to Hyrum Smith. During their labors together, McLellin heard Hyrum testify several times as a witness of the Book of Mormon and other gospel matters. On September 1, for example, at the Chariton courthouse in Missouri, Hyrum bore testimony "respecting the truth of the book," after which McLellin "arose and read the testimony of the three witnesses." During this period of close contact and preaching labor with Hyrum, McLellin records only respect for and belief in Hyrum's convictions.

Hyrum and McLellin shared several previously unknown but notable experiences during their mission. For example, on September 10, many country people gathered to hear them preach in the Jacksonville, Illinois, courthouse. Once again, Hyrum became a public witness of the Book of Mormon, according to McLellin:

> I arose with confidence in Elijah's God and gave them a brief history of the book of Mormon, of its coming forth &c, Then reasoned upon and expounded prophecy after prophecy and scripture after scripture, which had reference to the book and to these days and after speaking with great liberty about 3 hours I concluded with a warning to them to flee from the wrath to come and gather themselves to Zion and prepare to meet the Lord at his second coming which was nigh at hand. Bro. H[yrum] Then arose and bore testimony to the truths which they had heard and gave them his evidence of the truth of the book.

On September 14, 1831, in Illinois, McLellin became ill with high fever and the ague. The following day, as the illness continued, McLellin realized that if God had called him to be a missionary, God should give him the requisite health. McLellin then received a blessing from Hyrum that healed him:

> I opened my mind to bro. H. We immediately bowed before the Lord and with all the faith which we had, we opened our hearts to him.

bro H. arose and laid his hands upon me. But marvelous for me to relate that I was instantly healed And arose and pursued my journey in health with vigour.

Hyrum and McLellin shared a heart-wrenching experience on September 22, 1831. That day McLellin visited his home town of Paris, Illinois, stopped at his wife's grave, and sorrowed. Then he and Hyrum met with others who were mourning the death of a daughter: "We gave them all the light that we could. Their minds were quite tender."

The two men began the month of October 1831 by exercising the gift of healing. After they preached in Stilesville, Indiana, a Christian preacher invited them "home with him; saying that his daughter's child was very sick." They all

> bowed before the great Jehovah and implored his mercy upon the child, we then arose and brother Hiram & I laid our hands upon it, and in a few minutes the little child got down from its mother's lap and went to play upon the floor. This caused them to rejoice and the old gentleman got down & prayed mightily, then arose & said that he believed that the Lord was there.[7]

Samuel H. Smith. In October 1831, McLellin was called to labor as a missionary with Samuel Smith east of Kirtland. "Elder McLellin failed to magnify this calling," Milton Backman asserts in his history of Kirtland, *The Heavens Resound*.[8] However, McLellin's journal shows that he labored busily to fill that calling for a month until poor health befell him and Joseph Smith seemed to approve his return to Kirtland. This labor made him well acquainted with Samuel, another of the Eight Witnesses of the Book of Mormon.

McLellin recorded a healing Samuel performed near Warren, Ohio. On December 15, McLellin recollects that a child was badly scalded. "Br Saml was there and laid his hands upon it and healed it in so much that it did not even so much as blister." Three days later, McLellin and Samuel blessed another child, surnamed Campbell, "who had a most remarkable sore face and next morning it was almost well."

On December 11, near Warren, Ohio, McLellin's preaching about evidences of the Book of Mormon set the stage for Samuel's testimony regarding the book. The duo's spirit and message won converts. On December 14, they conducted a through-the-ice baptism. Icy water and exposure took their toll on McLellin. The next day he became ill with diarrhea and "a violent cold." Still, he and Samuel preached in Youngstown, Austintown, and Weathersfield. On December 21, McLellin wrote, "my cold increased and my breast and lungs became so exceeding sore" that he was mostly confined to bed for a week. On December 27, Joseph and Hyrum Smith, Reynolds Cahoon, and Lyman Johnson visited him, and Joseph blessed and healed him and let him return to Kirtland.

Joseph Smith's Activities

Because McLellin spent time in and around Church headquarters in Kirtland, his journals contain both new and corroborative information concerning activities and personalities there, including Joseph Smith.[9] At a conference twenty miles from Kirtland on October 25, 1831, McLellin "first saw brother Joseph the Seer." During this conference, McLellin received "much spiritual edification & comfort to [his] heart" and was called to the high priesthood. McLellin thoroughly details many incidents not in the *History of the Church*.

McLellin recorded a healing blessing administered to him by Joseph Smith soon after the conference, an incident not mentioned in Joseph Smith's history. While returning to Kirtland with Father Smith, who was on horseback, McLellin "stepped off of a large log and strained [his] ankle very badly," so he got to ride the horse. Preparing for bed, "I asked brother Joseph what he thought about my ancle's being healed." After McLellin affirmed his faith in God, the Prophet "laid his hands on it [McLellin's ankle] and it was healed although It was swelled much and had pained me severely."[10]

McLellin and Joseph Smith left Kirtland on October 28, 1831, stayed overnight in "the Nelson church," and reached Hiram, Ohio, early the next day. Later that day McLellin scribed a revelation Joseph Smith received in McLellin's behalf (D&C 66).[11] The revelation, which McLellin was eager to receive, called him to repentance, called him on a mission to eastern lands with Samuel H. Smith, and promised him power to heal the sick. The revelation warned McLellin to be patient in affliction, not to go to Zion, not to think about his property, not to commit adultery, and not to return until commanded by the Lord to do so.

Joseph Smith's history skips from December 4, 1831, to January 8, 1832, but McLellin's journal provides new details about the young Prophet's activities during this time. For example, his visit to McLellin on December 27, 1831, when McLellin was suffering severely with a cold and sore lungs, was previously unknown. The next morning, after the Prophet had healed McLellin, the missionary arose and ate "breakfast and attended an ap[pointment]." That evening McLellin preached with Hyrum Smith and baptized Celia Burwell. Then, Joseph Smith "prayed & laid his hands upon sister Celia and she expressed great joy in the reception of the Holy spirit."

McLellin adds that the group then went to Hiram, Ohio, and had a prayer meeting on the evening of the 29th and on the 30th "held a council at father Whitmer's." The next day, McLellin went to Kirtland, while Joseph Smith apparently stayed in Hiram.

During January 1832, McLellin's journal mentions two more of Joseph Smith's noteworthy activities that are not in the Prophet's history.[12] At Kirtland on January 11, 1832, McLellin had a long talk with a Campbellite priest named Bennett and then on Friday brought him to Hiram, Ohio, to see Joseph Smith and Sidney Rigdon. The priest, McLellin said, "talked considerable with Br Joseph" that night. Then, after a revelation (D&C 75) called McLellin to labor with Luke Johnson in the South, he attended a meeting at Father Johnson's on January 29 "for a farewell to the brethren" who had also been called on missions.

On November 19, 1834, McLellin returned from a week's work near Painesville, Ohio, to Kirtland and found there a letter from his wife, Emeline, then in Missouri. After McLellin shared with the Prophet the "afflictions" that the letter described, Joseph Smith called a few high priests together for a "solemn meeting and prayr that God might spare the innocent in Zion and hasten their deliverance." McLellin concludes, "We had a very affecting time indeed."

McLellin wrote about a meeting on December 14, 1834, in Kirtland during which Joseph Smith openly criticized the Methodist beliefs, an episode not recorded anywhere else:

> President Smith preached three hours in Kirt during which he exposed the Methodist Dicipline in its black deformity and called upon the Elders in the power of the spirit of God to expose the creeds &

confessions of men——His discourse was animated and Pointed, against all Creeds of men.

While laboring in Huntsburg, near Kirtland, McLellin agreed to a public discussion on Friday and Saturday, March 27 and 28, 1835. Again, Joseph Smith's history does not mention this occasion, but Joseph, along with Lyman Johnson, David Patten, Parley P. Pratt, John Boynton, and others, went with McLellin. McLellin and J. M. Tracy, a local clergyman, talked alternately for more than twelve hours; following this debate, McLellin baptized two people. Then, on Sunday, the 29th, Joseph Smith preached for about three hours. The next day, McLellin baptized four more converts, and then the elders returned to Kirtland.

McLellin adds some detail to an activity mentioned in Joseph Smith's history for April 9, 1836. Accepting another missionary assignment, this time to the South, McLellin departed from Kirtland on April 9, 1836. He journeyed with Bishop Partridge, John Corrill, and others. Joseph Smith and a half-dozen of the "first brethren," as McLellin termed them, accompanied them to Chardon, where rains forced them all to stay the night together. "We spent a very pleasant evening with them," McLellin observed. "Their society was really interesting." The next morning, according to Joseph Smith's history, the Prophet "blessed them" and then headed back to Kirtland.[13] McLellin wrote that he and his traveling companions took a "very affectionate farewell" of Joseph Smith and the others "after they had prayed with us and pronounced upon us their blessings."

Other Mormon Associates

At the end of this volume is a biographical register that identifies the many people mentioned by McLellin. In many instances, he recorded otherwise unknown details about these people and their activities. For example, when McLellin, new in Independence, Missouri, felt tempted one night, branch president Newel Knight "after arising from prayr came and by the spirit of God was enabled to tell me the very secrets of my heart and in a degree to chase darkness from my mind."[14] Typically, his daily entries are peppered with names, many of which are nowhere else recorded in Church membership rolls or histories.

Biographical Information about McLellin

Of course, these journals also contain much new information about McLellin. His story, as unfolded in these journals, is that of a committed convert—from hearing the word preached to being baptized, becoming part of the Church's inner circle, and struggling to maintain faith during tests and trials of that faith. His entries provide key facts about his travels; information about his deceased wife, new wife, and other relatives; facts about his finances; a solid record of his many missionary labors and sacrifices to build up the Kingdom; and insights into his personality and his spiritual self, discussed in detail by Larry Porter, below.

Missionary Work, Methods, and Experiences

McLellin was a missionary, many times over. As a result, his journals contain useful detail about the nature of missionary work between 1831 and 1836. Historian Davis Bitton has profiled LDS missionary methods and practices for the 1830s, and McLellin's entries corroborate Bitton's conclusions. Bitton found that missionaries preached in courthouses, schools, churches, barns, private dwellings, and on street corners, though they preferred to preach in public meeting halls such as churches or courthouses. In such places, they often gave "liberty" to others, thus putting clergy in the audience on the spot. They held public debates at times. They knocked on doors of farmhouses along their route and took a day or two in villages and towns going from house to house. As recent converts, missionaries gave priority to preaching to relatives and personal friends. Their proselyting labors, Bitton observed, brought mixed success. Missionaries encountered much indifference and opposition. Clergy often vocally challenged them and blocked them from preaching. Sometimes the missionaries found interested listeners and baptized and confirmed many. As Bitton describes, McLellin preached in a variety of settings, receiving mixed responses.[15]

McLellin's journals, however, also contain new details about missionary work. For example, while working with Parley Pratt, McLellin carried his personal belongings in a "nap sack."[16] Music, McLellin shows, was part of some missionaries' methods.

In March 1833 in Illinois, McLellin recorded that at one meeting they "sung considerable, then opened by prayr and addressed them," and at the next day's meeting "we sung a number of songs."[17]

McLellin's journals underscore the fact that as church officers, missionaries in the 1830s felt free to take action as guided by the Spirit in branches they happened to enter. Missionaries were, in essence, traveling authorities who could regulate local matters on their own. McLellin and Hyrum Smith's travels brought them into a branch where two other elders had recently baptized several souls. Although the branch had priesthood officers serving in it, McLellin and Hyrum stayed there, preached, exhorted, strengthened the group, and then ordained a man to be a priest.[18]

McLellin's journals are one of the best contemporary sources for describing the fervent concerns of early Mormons that converts should move to Jackson County, Missouri. Only two days before McLellin heard the Mormon elders preach, on July 20, 1831, the Prophet had received a revelation designating Jackson County as a gathering place for the people of Zion and urging converts to buy lands there (D&C 57). McLellin's longing "to live among a people who were based upon pure principles and actuated by the Spirit of the Living God" was part of his desire for membership when he reached Jackson County.[19]

According to John Corrill, members at that time had become "quite enthusiastic," and "the church got crazy to go up to Zion."[20] The Zion attraction looms large in McLellin's journals. He taught that believers must head for Missouri, and he himself continually longed to settle there. On September 10, 1831, McLellin and Hyrum Smith preached and then "concluded with a warning to them to flee from the wrath to come and gather themselves to Zion and prepare to meet the Lord at his second coming which was nigh at hand." Similarly, on February 15, 1833, he and Parley P. Pratt urged Missouri listeners to read the Book of Mormon "and flee to Zion and save their souls."

After one strong preaching meeting, McLellin lamented that none came forward "as candidates for Zion."[21] McLellin's long labors in early 1833 converted a man named John Scott, whose response reflects the expectation that migration was required: "I am thoroughly convinced now of the truths which you preach and Just as soon as I can settle my business I shall remove to Zion," he told

McLellin.[22] In Ohio in 1834, McLellin recorded that four converts received recommends to go to Missouri.[23]

Unifying Fragmented Branches. Young branches of the early Church seemed to suffer from petty schisms and backsliding. McLellin's journals often describe his and other leaders' efforts to curb these forces. His experiences in Florence, Ohio, in October, 1834, give a good picture of a fledgling branch.

On October 7, 1834, Joseph Smith asked McLellin to substitute for him and work with the Florence, Ohio, branch that he had promised to visit. Joseph Smith gave McLellin a letter for President Moses Daley of the Florence branch, which said the word of the Lord was that McLellin should visit there and "teach you concerning the duty of the churches relative to Zion. I want therefore that you should receive him in the name of the Lord, and uphold him by your prayr of faith, and in the name of the Lord of truth he will do you much good." This Joseph Smith letter is found only in McLellin's journal. It is included at the top of McLellin's page 17 of Journal IV.

On his way to Florence, McLellin first worked with Saints at Amherst, where the thirty-eight member branch suffered from "divisions" and "jealousies."[24] For two days, he labored to have them "settle their differences and forgive each other," but "coldness and backwardness" blunted his efforts. At the Sunday meeting, McLellin carefully explained church government concepts taught in the Articles and Covenants, then he stopped the administering of the sacrament because of members' bad feelings. Monday night he lectured branch officers—three elders, a priest, a teacher, and two deacons— by interpreting the Articles and Covenants "in great plainness."[25]

McLellin then proceeded on foot fourteen miles to Florence, where "the brethren" received him "joyfully." Officers in the fifty-person Florence branch included two high priests, four elders, a priest, teacher, and deacon. On October 15, he found them "rather low in spirits." He preached and visited during the rest of the week, trying to stir the Saints up. That weekend and the next Tuesday, he held meetings and explained the government of the Church to them, and listeners seemed "well satisfied." McLellin spoke to twenty men and women in Brownhelm on Wednesday evening, but he discerned that there were not any "true brethren" in that group. On Thursday, October 23, McLellin walked to Amherst and conducted a hearing designed to help settle "some existing difficulties" among some sisters. The difficulty between the parties was presented. Two elders from Amherst, two from Florence, and one from Rockport sat for almost six hours "on close examination." When finished, "we all as a conference concluded that it was the most little and pittiful thing that ever created so much trouble" in a church. They settled the matter "to [the] general satisfaction of all except one woman."

At a Saturday meeting in Florence, McLellin was pleased by the good turnout. McLellin had been concerned about some members who had been "cold, indifferent and had not attended meetings." These souls came forward, except for one who sent a representative, who "made satisfaction" to the leaders. Teaching centered on church government principles, and "all seemed encouraged and cheered."[26] Sunday, a number of the Saints "expressed their feelings by way of confessions & rejoicings." The sacrament was then administered. At that evening's meeting, McLellin found that "the brethren and sisters seemed much rejoiced and stirred up to a sence of duty."

On Tuesday, October 28, McLellin preached at Florence. The next day, he met with the Amherst Saints and preached for about ninety minutes—the greatest sermon "for its length" that he "ever preached in life."

Amherst repairs completed, McLellin felt pleased when branch members presented him with money subscribed for his benefit. On October 30, he returned to Florence, where several members confessed to their coldness and lack of attention to prayers. During two Sunday meetings, November 2, McLellin spoke twice, the sacrament was administered, and that evening the Saints bid McLellin farewell. "The saints appeared much animated and engaged in the cause of Christ," he noted with satisfaction. McLellin left for Kirtland on November 4, carrying branch members' donations to help him travel.

1833 Mission with Parley P. Pratt. McLellin's journal for January 28 to May 24, 1833, is titled "A Journal of Wm E. McLelin & Parley Pratt." When compared with Pratt's account of this mission in his *Autobiography*, McLellin's is more detailed, shows how Pratt's memory later compacted some sequences, and describes several powerful experiences Pratt did not include.

For example, when the two started, McLellin noted that they would be traveling without money nor "two coats."[27] Therefore, he liked to record how lodging, meals, and ferry rides opened up for them. After meeting "carelesness now and indifference," the two men sought spiritual strengthening. On February 6, they retired to a high hill and read, meditated, and prayed mightily. But the next day, when they struggled to receive a great spiritual manifestation, it did not come. During a week's labor near Fayette, Missouri, they had encounters with a "noted Priest"[28] named Joel Haden. Then, working near Paris, Missouri, they were in contact with Mormons George Hinkle, Isaac Allred, and other members of the Salt River Branch.[29] On Sunday, February 24, 1833, McLellin explained the Articles and Covenants to members gathered at Isaac Allred's home. Later in the meeting, Parley preached on the testimony of Jesus. Afterwards, McLellin noted that Parley had not recollected "to have ever had more of the Spirit and Power of God upon him."

When McLellin and Pratt approached Clarksville, Missouri, by the Mississippi River, they again tried to obtain a spiritual manifestation. Pratt says only that they "cried mightily unto the Lord" to soften Clarksville residents' hearts,[30] but McLellin says they pleaded in fact for their own strength and obedience. When nearing a peak towering four hundred feet above them, Pratt saw it as "the place for contemplation." They "immediately ascended its tall summit" and sat on its peak. McLellin describes "five hours" of "meditation" and prayer. The missionaries hoped for "perfect obedience" and to "commune with the guardian Angel."[31]

McLellin corroborates and expands Pratt's abbreviated account of their encounter with a Baptist minister named Elizah Dodson. Pratt says Dodson argued against modern revelation and was perplexed when Pratt pointed out that Dodson's position meant that his own (Dodson's) call to the ministry by a voice from heaven was not legitimate. Dodson, Pratt noted, melted into tears when hearing the Book of Mormon read and opened his door and neighborhood to the elders. But then Dodson's heart hardened as he called in a Reverend Peck to stop the Mormons from taking the county.[32] McLellin says that on March 21, in a crowded schoolhouse, Pratt spoke with power for eighty minutes. Dodson took notes, finding some seventeen mistakes in Pratt's arguments, which he said he would explain the next day. On March 22, "friend Dodson" reasoned with the elders, after which Pratt read to him the Book of Mormon

account of Alma and Amulek's teachings and sufferings in Ammonihah. McLellin also fills in the details about Pratt's effect on the congregation. "His words were so powerful even to the cutting of those
to the heart who were present," and then McLellin "walked through
the room praising and blessing the name of the Lord." And the
missionaries' "once strong opposer" was "so affected that he did not
utter farewell but shaking us warmly by the hand we parted."

McLellin includes an incident which Pratt's account omits.
A week after Pratt's sermon, Dodson was again warning his neighbors about the elders and the Book of Mormon. Meetings were called
for March 30 and 31. Pratt and McLellin "betook ourselves to solemn
prayr that he [Dodson] might be confounded." That night the minister's arguments seemed to establish rather than undercut the Book
of Mormon, leading McLellin to affirm, "Here we realized the power
and efficacy of prayr." The next day two hundred to three hundred
people gathered in the schoolhouse, and that evening McLellin
"addressed them first on prayr and it was said that some kneeled who
were never seen so to do before." He asked those who believed to
stand, and to Dodson's dismay, about thirty men and women arose.
McLellin also mentions on April 9, 1833, that Pratt read from Enoch's
prophecy, giving yet another detail about this missionary journey
not previously known.

McLellin's account also details the "painful duty . . . of parting
with brother Parley" and the companionship's last baptisms.[33]
In May, McLellin returned to his home town of Paris, Illinois, and
Parley headed for Zion.

The Twelve's 1835 Mission. McLellin was called to be one of
the original twelve Apostles of the Restoration on February 14, 1835,
during a period when his journals are silent.[34] But McLellin's journal
contains many interesting and important details about the Twelve's
1835 mission eastward and northward and about individual Apostles.
Because he sometimes kept minutes when the quorum conferred
together, he told his journal that "the minutes of our consultations
are kept in our Apostolic record."[35]

At the start of the mission, McLellin felt the need for confirmation through a heavenly manifestation. So, with Elder Orson Hyde on
May 14, he "spent from 9 till 3. together in the woods in prayrs and

contemplation endeavouring to obtain an open vision but we did not altho. we felt that we drew very near to God."

Regarding the Twelve's conference in Freedom, New York, on May 22-24, McLellin recorded that Elder Heber C. Kimball spoke "very feelingly indeed," and that Elder Hyde preached "a most plain and powerful discourse on the evidences of the book of Mormon." McLellin notes that before Apostle Brigham Young, John P. Greene, and Amos Orton left to introduce the gospel among the Senecas, "we in council laid hands on and set apart" the trio. The Apostles "all prayed and sealed each other up until we should meet again at our next conference."[36] Later, on June 11, near Watertown, New York, McLellin noted that Elder Boynton preached to a small group "on the plain simplicity of the Gospel and I think that I never heard a better discourse for its length—— it was forcible."

During the mission, Elder McLellin was paired at times with Lyman Johnson, David Patten, and John Boynton. He worked with Thomas Marsh and Parley P. Pratt late in June, Brigham Young early in July, Orson Pratt in late July, and traveled with William Smith in September. While working with these Apostles, he constantly noted details about preaching activities, members, and branches. He was disappointed, for example, at the ignorance of members in the branch at Sackets Harbor, nineteen in number, that he encountered in early June. Of the members, he said that "they were most of them superstitious and very illitterate."[37]

As apostolic stories go, McLellin's rowing across the bay to Pillar Point and back is an unusual one. On June 15, he rowed a mile in a skiff, raising blisters on his right hand. Returning the next day, he called the trip "a real merry ride; the waves rolled on the bay."

McLellin recorded one petty incident. On June 19, Elder Hyde, "whose turn it was to preside," was not present, so McLellin took charge of a conference at Pillar Point. After a morning meeting the next day, he decided another meeting was needed and called one for 5 P.M. He expected his colleagues to go somewhere, take dinner, and return, but most of them stayed and waited at the meeting place during the long afternoon interval. Parley P. Pratt chastised McLellin because he saw no need for the extra meeting. When the meeting started, it was Thomas B. Marsh's "regular turn" to preach, but he refused to speak, so McLellin conducted the meeting himself and preached for two hours. Afterwards, however, McLellin felt that even the brethren "who had opposed me" felt satisfied with the service.[38] Then, trying to figure who was next in the rotation—had Marsh lost his regular turn to preach?—McLellin called a council of the Apostles. They decided that McLellin had acted properly and that Marsh had lost his turn. To smooth the troubled waters, they agreed that Marsh and Patten should together conduct the next meeting.

The standard study of the Quorum of the Twelve during this period is Ronald K. Esplin's dissertation. It states that the records he consulted do not make clear whether the presidency of the Twelve was rotational, as Joseph Smith had suggested, or was selected at each meeting. McLellin's journal makes clear that the Apostles adhered to the rotation system and showed some jealousy regarding it.

Late in July, Apostle McLellin had a personal spiritual experience. On July 27, an infant child surnamed Montgomery fell into a cellar and was badly hurt; a doctor did no good. McLellin prayed for the child and laid hands on it, but it did not seem to be healed immediately. So, "I betook myself to the woods and called mightily upon God and when I returned I found the child up and wanting to eat and to play. Its parents verily believed that it was healed by the power of God and so did I—And I felt to rejoice much." Three days later, at a meeting in Lyman, New Hampshire, the Spirit caused him to speak in tongues. "The Spirit was pourd out wonderfully, the people were melted down and the Lord gave me his spirit to speak in tongues (and it rolled powerfully)."

Church Practices, Procedures, and Customs

Being a new religion, Mormonism borrowed some practices from existing churches as well as created unique ordinances and customs during its foundation years. McLellin's journal entries occasionally note some of both.

The Sacrament. During McLellin's missionary travels, he often "broke bread among the diciples,"[39] something he did not find unusual. He mentions only wine—never water—although the August 1830 revelation stated "it mattereth not what ye shall eat or what ye shall drink" (D&C 27:2).

Meetings. As McLellin's journals corroborate, a typical meeting schedule for Mormons in the 1830s—one probably typical of some

other churches, too—was a Sunday morning or midday preaching
meeting and a Sunday afternoon or evening meeting at "candlelight."
At one of these meetings, the sacrament was administered. A mid-
week prayer meeting followed.[40] McLellin's entries allow modern
readers to reconstruct many previously unknown features of those
meetings, including much about the content of the preaching.[41]

The first Mormon meeting McLellin attended was a "family
prayr" the morning after he reached Independence. That evening
the Saints met in a prayer meeting. "Here I saw the manner of their
worship," McLellin wrote, where they "converse[d] freely upon the
things of religion,"[42] something he found unusual and refreshing.
On August 21, 1831, the day after being baptized, McLellin attended
a Sunday meeting. He termed this "a sacrament meeting," one of the
earliest recorded uses of that term. The meeting included a lecture
and then personal expressions—much like a modern LDS testimony
meeting. "A number of brethren and sisters spoke of the marvelous
works of God & of their willingness and determinations to serve
him," McLellin noted. That sisters bore witness is significant, this
being one of the earliest records showing that Mormon women
expressed themselves in such meetings. That evening William
attended a prayer meeting held in a schoolhouse. He was "much
disappointed" by this meeting, he said facetiously, because "instead
of shouting, screaming, jumping or shaking of hands in confusion,"
he found "peace, order, harmony and the spirit of God seemed to
cheer every heart, warm every bosom and animate every Tongue."
These people worshipped "in the beauty of Holiness." He "saw more
beauty in Christianity now than I ever had seen before."

According to his journals, McLellin participated in several
spiritual and more spirited meetings than were known of before.
On his mission with the Twelve in 1835, for example, he preached
in Kingston, Ontario, "and the spirit came upon me and I had great
liberty and the brethren rejoiced much and some of them even
shouted aloud."[43] At times the gift of tongues was manifested in meetings he attended. While laboring near his hometown in August 1834,
the gift appeared several times. At Sunday worship on August 17,
Lewis Zabriskie "spoke some in 'Tongues,'" and McLellin interpreted. Ten days later it happened again. McLellin preached to a
considerable congregation for two hours, then exhorted them to

prepare for the Lord's coming, "and I closed by repeating some of my exortation in an other tongue." When that meeting closed, he baptized three persons. At a meeting three days later, he confirmed the three, and "we had some speaking in tongues & the Interpretation also."[44] His notations show that he thought this spiritual exercise was highly unusual.

The next day was Sunday, August 31. At 11 A.M., McLellin spoke for more than two hours. Then at 4 P.M. the people reassembled for the sacrament. Two former Mormons asked for readmission, so "we went immediately to the water and I immersed them." At dark some Saints assembled at Eden Smith's home to confirm the two. McLellin spoke for more than an hour about the laying on of hands for the gift of the Holy Ghost and then "confirmed by the laying on of my hands." Some speaking in tongues followed, and Brother Lewis "interpreted partly what was said."

A week later McLellin spoke to a large congregation at 11 o'clock.[45] At the 4 P.M. sacrament meeting, McLellin exhorted for an hour, after which "all the brethren and Sisters who were then present, arose, one by one," and expressed faith in the Book of Mormon and the work of the Lord, feelings of fellowship, and determinations to do good and keep the commandments. This was McLellin's final sacrament meeting with these people, and emotions surfaced. The room seemed filled with light. Members then partook of the bread and wine "in the bonds of union." Three former Mormons asked for and received baptism. After the baptisms, the believers returned to the house, where "we had quite a good little meeting—the brethren and Sisters who had received the gift of Tongues manifested it and bro. Lewis Zabriskie interpreted for them very clearly."

Washing/Dusting of Feet. Responding to revelation (D&C 24:15) and following New Testament precedent (Matt. 10:14; Luke 9:5; Acts 13:51), McLellin and other missionaries occasionally washed or dusted off their feet as an act of testimony against towns or people who offensively rejected them. For example, on September 9, 1831, a Christian preacher charged him and Hyrum Smith with being false prophets. The man's "heart seemed so hard and wicked . . . but we left him raging and when we came to a brook Bro. H. washed his feet for a testimony against him." An instance of both dusting and washing the feet occurred on June 7, 1835, when David Patten and McLellin received no response to their preaching and no assistance with food or lodging. "We left them believing that we had done our duty as to delivering our message," he wrote, "and we wiped the dust off our feet and we also cle[a]nsed our feet in pure water as a testimony against them."

Baptism, Rebaptism, Confirmation, and Blessings. Several examples of these ordinances are cited earlier. Baptisms often occurred during meetings on any day of the week, not necessarily as part of special baptismal services. That people changed clothes when being baptized is clear, but McLellin's journals do not indicate that people donned white clothes or Sunday-best clothes for the immersion. Confirmations were performed at special meetings called for that purpose or at the next regularly scheduled meeting.

McLellin's journals are perhaps our only record that mentions three other unusual applications of the baptismal and confirmational ordinances—confirmations while another prayed, group baptisms of children, and rebaptisms of former Mormons.

Illustrative is a Wednesday evening meeting on September 10, 1834, where McLellin preached and then gave liberty to any who wanted to be baptized. Henry Bailey, Sr., volunteered and was baptized. The meeting then continued until midnight, featuring some priesthood ordinations and McLellin's confirming Henry Bailey, Sr., as well as three others who had been baptized three days earlier. But then, after McLellin confirmed them "by the laying on of my hands," the rest of the members desired to be blessed, too—as in some form of reconfirmation. McLellin complied: "They all kneeled in mighty but silent prayr and I went around among them and laid my hands on them and prayed for them and blessed them in the name of the Lord—— And some of them were really blessed while others did not experience so much."

Sometimes group baptisms were performed for children who were of baptismal age. On January 23, 1832, for example, McLellin went to a member's home for a morning meeting, after which he "baptized 9 children." McLellin's journal gives no evidence of any instruction or interviewing of the children prior to the ordinance.

On August 10, 1834, McLellin preached during a Sunday afternoon meeting, and then "opened the door for members," meaning for those wanting to be baptized. A woman came forward, who had once been a member. The Church members received her as a new member: "We immediately went to the river and I immersed her." Then the people returned from the water to the house for the confirmation. McLellin first preached and then exhorted, after which "we then united in prayr and while brother Levi [Jones] was praying I laid my hands on and confirmed those who had been baptized." Members then partook of the sacrament and the meeting ended. Clearly, according to McLellin's record, "inactive" or backslider Mormons could resume fellowship by being baptized again. He mentions several such souls but never identifies any as being excommunicants.

Priesthood Ordinations. It was not unusual in the early 1830s "for a man to hear Mormonism preached one day, be baptized the next, be ordained an elder on the following day and the day after that be out preaching Mormonism."[46] (However, by the late 1830s and early 1840s there was lag time of up to a year between many baptisms and ordinations.[47]) A guiding principle in early Mormonism was, "If ye have desires to serve God ye are called to the work" (D&C 4:3). McLellin's generation of new converts viewed that instruction as an obligation, not just an option.

According to the Articles and Covenants, the Church handbook of instructions of its day, men were to be "ordained according to the gifts and callings of God" unto that man and to be "ordained by the power of the Holy Ghost, which is in the one who ordains him" (D&C 20:60). Since ripe fields needed harvesters (D&C 14:3), there were pressures for the newly baptized to go out and preach. How could a new convert say he did not desire to serve God?

Thus, three days after McLellin's baptism, Simeon Carter and others told him "it was my duty to become an Elder in the church and go and preach the Gospel."[48] McLellin struggled with this idea of having to do missionary work immediately, so he solemnly prayed "respecting my ordination to the ministry," resigned himself to God's will, and in the next sacrament meeting offered to accept any calling that God inspired the leaders to give him. Hyrum Smith "immediately arose" and said he had received a "witness of the Spirit that I [McLellin] should be ordained an Elder." All present agreed, so Hyrum and Bishop Edward Partridge ordained him "to be an Elder in the Church of Christ." Thus McLellin was baptized on a Saturday and ordained an elder the next Wednesday.[49]

McLellin followed this basic pattern when baptizing converts himself. For example, early in October 1831, he and Hyrum Smith came to the neighborhood of Winchester, Indiana, where two elders had baptized several disciples. "Here we staid and preached and exorted and strengthened our brethren," McLellin wrote, "and ordained brother Jarvis Lee to be a Priest in the church."[50]

Priesthood Licenses. It is well known that men ordained to the ministry were required to carry with them licenses authorizing them as Mormon ministers, a common custom among Protestants. McLellin records a strange situation where an elder wanted to "retire" from his calling. A local elder, Lewis Zabriskie, met with McLellin and other local officers on August 25, 1834, and announced he was determined "to lay down his license and authority as an Elder in the church and stand as private member." Zabriskie "said that he did not doubt the work, neither did he doubt but that God had called him and blessed him in the ministry, But he thought and felt as though it was an easier life to live a private member." He desired "to stand behind the scene" as a member, not an officer. McLellin and others reasoned with him until he agreed to keep his license. A few days later, he came before the Church and "made his acknowledgements that he had been out of the way, and under the influence of and an evil power" but was now determined "to go his whole length in the cause."[51]

Blessing the Sick. The journals contain many accounts of McLellin's blessing the sick through the laying on of hands and of McLellin being the recipient of such blessings.[52] Typical is this entry: "I and bro. Noah Hubbard were called upon to pray for sister Hubbard who was very sick. we prayed for and laid hands on her: She was healed and declared that she [was] had better in a few days than she had had in eleven years."[53] It is notable, however, that McLellin's many accounts of blessing the sick fail to mention any anointings with oil prior to the laying on of hands.

McLellin recorded three healing encounters with mentally disturbed people. Near Carrollton, Illinois, Parley P. Pratt and he were called on to visit a "boy who had fitts and who some times raged and foamed like a mad man and who sometimes tried to kill his nearest friends." Although the boy was chained in an "outter house" and despite his "much impaired" intellect, he asked the elders to pray for him. Both elders united in prayer with the parents, and then the two men laid hands upon him and blessed him.[54]

Two weeks later they learned about "a young Lady in the neighbourhood who was afflicted with an evil Spirit even to fits & convultions." Relatives asked Pratt and McLellin to go and pray for her. She professed no religion, but her parents were Methodists "and quite believing," McLellin noted. They prayed with them and laid their hands on them.[55] Four days later, on April 6, 1833, they visited a man named Coon and prayed for "a fittyfied Girl." Apparently the elders' blessings were intended in part to relieve the recipient's afflictions, but McLellin makes no mention of any healing effects or improved condition.

High Priesthood and High Priests. Early references by McLellin to the high priesthood are especially significant. On June 3, 1831, at a conference in Kirtland, men were ordained for the first time to the "High Priesthood."[56] Gregory Prince's recent study of the historical development of LDS priesthood makes at least two assertions that McLellin's journal challenges. Prince states that in June 1831 men were ordained to a new order called both the Order of Melchizedek and the High Priesthood. However, he asserts, "this did not yet refer to the office of high priest which, though appearing in the Book of Mormon, was not yet applied to individuals in the Restoration," and it was not until November 1831 that a revelation (D&C 68) established for the first time the *office* of high priest. Second, Prince asserts that, prior to September 1832, the term "priesthood" was used "exclusively in conjunction with High Priesthood."[57]

McLellin, however, was one of several elders who were ordained to the High Priesthood on October 25, 1831, at a conference in Orange, Ohio.[58] Contrary to Prince's statement, McLellin's journal shows that he knew his ordination to the High Priesthood was to a particular office called high priest. It also establishes that the term "lesser priesthood" was indeed in use at that time. In an evening meeting on that date, McLellin noted, some elders "were ordained to the High-Priesthood of the Holy order of God among whom though I felt unworthy I was ordained and took upon me the high responsibility of that office." Note his use of the word "office." Then, he continues, "a number of others present were ordained to the lesser Priest-Hood."

Kirtland Area Mormon Activities. McLellin's entries about meetings and personalities in the Kirtland area add to the mosaic historians are piecing together.[59] His January 1832 entries, for example, reveal a busy schedule of conferences in Kirtland, which were "conducted with general harmony." Some councils dealt with "disobedient members"; others met "for the purpose of mutual edification." After a week of visiting members and holding meetings with Sidney and Mrs. Rigdon at Auburn, Warren, and Weathersfield, Ohio, McLellin returned to Kirtland and on Sunday, January 22, met with "the Kirtland brethren," preached about two hours, and administered the Lord's supper. That evening he attended a prayer meeting "at the flats."

In 1834, McLellin's journals again tell about activities not recorded elsewhere. On November 9, some five hundred people attended a meeting in Kirtland's large schoolhouse. Lyman Johnson opened the meeting, and McLellin preached. After intermission, McLellin "assisted old father John Smith in administering the sacrament." Services concluded with people "going to the water" and John Boynton baptizing a man. According to McLellin, many said that "it was the best meeting that I ever was at in Kirtland." Two days later, however, Sidney Rigdon humbled McLellin. McLellin was preparing to go on a preaching tour eastward but was called "into the council chamber," where it was decided that McLellin and John Boynton should labor in and near Painesville. Rigdon then proceeded to give McLellin "a most tremendious setting out about my awkward Jestures &C." This "setting out" may reflect early Mormonism's distaste for Charles Finney's "new measures" which were sweeping Evangelical Protestantism at the time and included dramatic gestures of the hands and arms.

As instructed, McLellin and Boynton spent a week in Painesville, Fairport, and Richmond. McLellin's journal measures the disregard which people near Kirtland felt towards their Mormon neighbors. On November 14, few came to the Richmond meeting. McLellin preached to a respectable congregation at Painesville on the 15th, to a small and inattentive one at Fairport on the 16th, and to about twenty who "seemed interested" that evening. McLellin and Boynton went to Richmond for their scheduled meeting on the 17th but found the Presbyterians had locked the schoolhouse and would not let them in. "Lord have mercy on this wicked place," McLellin wrote. The next day, they preached again to a few in Painesville, then returned to Kirtland on the 19th.

The American Scene

McLellin's entries also provide numerous unintentional glimpses into social realities that were part of his world. Because he occasionally used his journals to keep track of money matters, costs and prices are sometimes listed. For example, during his first trip to Missouri, he paid 25¢ to 50¢ for overnight lodging, about 25¢ for breakfast, 25¢ to 37¢ to feed himself and his horse, 50¢ for man and horse to cross the Mississippi River by ferry, and 25¢ to cross the Missouri River. He bought Hyrum Smith a horse for $35.00.

One entry, in which McLellin wrote about food he was offered, is memorable. On May 22, 1833, he was thirteen miles from Vandalia. "Being very hungry," he wrote, "I called for some dinner" at Mrs. Hodges's home. "But I assure you it was poor eat," he complained. "They gave me a little blue milk, cold fried me[at], and cold corn hoe cake, and it all appeared as though there was no respect to cleanliness while preparing it. But I shut my eyes and swallowed it down."

While at Sackets Harbor, New York, McLellin witnessed a strange "caravan of living animals" on its way to town. "But the superstition of the brethren was such that I dare not go in to see them," he wrote on June 15, 1835, suggesting perhaps that the people in charge were gypsies or persons considered to have devilish powers to charm the animals. But when the animal train paraded into the village, he caught a glimpse of the "grand sight" of "well rigged" wagons, elephants, birds, and serpents. Then on June 27 in Canada, he again saw "a caravan of living animals being there I went in to see them and paid 25 cts."

Questions and Leads for Further Research

McLellin's entries sometimes raise questions that, if answerable at all, can be answered only by research in sources other than these journals. On October 18, 1831, for example, he states that at Kirtland he "staid in the church" reading, learning, and teaching. Was this a church *building?* Did it contain sleeping quarters? Who else stayed there?

When McLellin traveled into some areas, he seemed to know where to find Saints who lived there. How did he obtain this information? His journals mention by name dozens of people. As the Biographical Register indicates, some we have information about, but many are only names until further research establishes who they were. One wonders what became of the people these missionaries converted.

McLellin recorded that he wrote letters to various relatives. Can reliable document collectors track down any of these letters? And how do McLellin's minutes of the Twelve Apostles' conferences during their 1835 mission compare with his contemporaneous journal entries? Further piquing our curiosity, McLellin mentioned other documents he encountered near Carrollton, Illinois, in 1833. He noted on April 21, 1833, that when Reverend Peck was attacking the Book of Mormon, Peck "also brought up E. Campbell's pamphlet written against it and then read a letter written by Samuel Sherwood." A week later, after McLellin finished a sermon, a Dr. Higgins "called the attention of the people while he read a copy of a letter written by Saml Sherwood, dated 25, Feb. in Independence, [Missouri] which was filled with falseties and exagerations." All these items seem worth searching for or exploring further.

Conclusion

Admittedly, this assessment of the worth of McLellin's journals is merely a beginning. What I have done here is to grab handfuls of historical treasures, wash them off a bit, and quite randomly hold them up to the light. McLellin's journals reveal the character of a dedicated, spiritually energetic convert and missionary. But perhaps more importantly for historians, the journals reveal myriad details about the world of early Mormonism. McLellin's journals also complete parts of our historical portrait of the era by including details not in the *History of the Church* or Parley P. Pratt's autobiography. Yet the journals also pose questions and open vistas that invite further research. Only such future studies will precisely calculate the value of the treasures of historical information scattered throughout the McLellin journals.

NOTES

[1] Of several books dealing with the Mark Hofmann forgeries, the most balanced are Richard E. Turley, Jr., *Victims: The LDS Church and the Mark Hofmann Case* (Urbana: University of Illinois Press, 1992) and Linda Sillitoe and Allen D. Roberts, *Salamander: The Story of the Mormon Forgery Murders* (Salt Lake City: Signature Books, 1988).

[2] Wilford Woodruff, for example, considered the Doctrine and Covenants to be "a Precious treasure A legacy from heaven." See Wilford Woodruff, *Wilford Woodruff's Journal, 1833-1898 Typescript*, ed. Scott G. Kenney, 9 vols. (Midvale, Utah: Signature Books, 1983-85), 1:42-43 (entries for September 3 and 24, 1835).

[3] Larry C. Porter, ed., "William E. McLellan's Testimony of the Book of Mormon," *BYU Studies* 10 (Summer 1970): 485-87.

[4] Journal I, August 18, 1831.

[5] A standard biography is Pearson H. Corbett, *Hyrum Smith—Patriarch* (Salt Lake City: Deseret Book, 1963). Corbett's narrative skims over Hyrum's activities in Independence. Hyrum arrived at an unspecified date and was there when Joseph Smith conducted a conference on August 9, 1831. Joseph left with the men, but Hyrum stayed. At another conference, Hyrum gave a discourse on Zion and the gathering of Saints there and read part of Psalm 102. Hyrum then departed with melted heart, reluctantly leaving behind a small cluster of Saints in precarious conditions (91-92).

[6] Journal I, August 19, 1831.

[7] Journal I, October 1, 1831.

[8] Milton V. Backman, Jr., *The Heavens Resound: A History of the Latter-day Saints in Ohio, 1830-1838* (Salt Lake City: Deseret Book, 1983), 106.

[9] Historical literature concerning Joseph Smith is voluminous. His official history is Joseph Smith, Jr., *History of The Church of Jesus Christ of Latter-day Saints*, ed. B. H. Roberts, 2d ed. rev., 7 vols. (Salt Lake City: Deseret Book, 1971) (hereafter cited as *HC*). For a history of his life, see Donna Hill, *Joseph Smith: The First Mormon* (New York: Doubleday, 1977). Dean C. Jessee has edited two volumes so far of Joseph Smith's papers: *The Papers of Joseph Smith, Volume I: Autobiographical and Historical Writings* (Salt Lake City: Deseret Book 1989), and *The Papers of Joseph Smith, Volume II: Journal, 1832-1842* (Salt Lake City: Deseret Book, 1992).

[10] Journal I, October 26, 1831.

[11] See further pp. 246-51.

[12] Joseph Smith's *History of the Church* gives little detail about his activities from January 10 to February 16, 1832, other than listing two revelations he received and stating that he was translating the Bible. See *HC* 1:241-45.

[13] *HC* 2:436.

[14] Journal I, August 20, 1831.

[15] Davis Bitton, "Kirtland as a Center of Missionary Activity, 1830-1838," *BYU Studies* 11 (Summer 1971): 502-4.

[16] Journal III, February 28, 1833.

[17] Journal III, March 11 and 12, 1833.

[18] Journal I, between October 6 and October 11, 1831.

[19] Journal I, August 20, 1831.

[20] John Corrill, *Brief History of The Church of Jesus Christ of Latter Day Saints (Commonly Called Mormons)* (St. Louis: John Corrill, 1839), 18-19.

[21] Journal III, April 9, 1833.

[22] Journal III, April 20, 1833.

[23] Journal IV, September 10, 1834.

[24] Journal IV, October 9, 1834.

[25] Journal IV, October 13, 1834.

[26] Journal IV, October 25, 1834.

[27] Journal III, January 28 and Feburary 2, 1833.

[28] Journal III, February 8, 1833.

[29] Journal III, February 16-25, 1833.

[30] Parley P. Pratt, Jr., ed., *The Autobiography of Parley Parker Pratt,* 4th ed. (Salt Lake City: Deseret Book, 1972), 83.

[31] Journal III, March 8, 1833.

[32] Pratt, *Autobiography,* 85-86.

[33] Journal III, May 6 and 5, 1833.

[34] An indispensable history of the LDS Twelve Apostles is Ronald K. Esplin, "The Emergence of Brigham Young and the Twelve to Mormon Leadership, 1830-1841" (Ph.D. diss., Brigham Young University, 1981).

[35] Journal V, May 9, 1835. This record is in the LDS Church Archives but is not generally available to researchers.

[36] Journal V, May 25, 1835.

[37] Journal V, June 16, 1835.

[38] Journal V, June 20, 1835.

[39] Journal III, May 19, 1833.

[40] William G. Hartley, "Mormon Sundays," *Ensign* 8 (January 1978): 19-25.

[41] See the introduction by John W. Welch, above, and the statistical analysis by Teresa Baer, below.

[42] Journal I, August 19, 1831.

[43] Journal V, June 26, 1835.

[44] Journal IV, August 30, 1834.

[45] Journal IV, September 7, 1834.

[46] Samuel George Ellsworth, "A History of Mormon Missions in the United States and Canada, 1830-1860" (Ph.D. diss., University of California, 1950), 38-39.

[47] Roger Launius, "A Survey of Priesthood Ordinations, 1830-1844," *Restoration Trail Forum* 9 (May 1983): 3-4, 6. Launius argues that it is a misconception that, between the years 1830 and 1844, men were ordained to a particular priesthood office and sent to preach within a very short time after baptism. Most men were not ordained for several months, his statistical analysis shows, and then it was usually to elder, although a third of his sampling became Aaronic Priesthood bearers first. However, Launius does not break down ordination time patterns by years, and it is my impression that in the early years ordinations followed baptisms quite closely.

[48] Journal I, August 23, 1831.

[49] Journal I, August 24, 1831.

[50] Journal I, October 11, 1831.

[51] Journal IV, August 27, 1834. For further information on priesthood licenses, see Donald Q. Cannon, "Licensing in the Early Church," *BYU Studies* 22 (Winter 1982): 96-105.

[52] James 5:14-15 urges Christians who are sick to call for the elders and be blessed by them. In July 1830 (D&C 24:13), modern revelation instructs Joseph Smith and Oliver Cowdery to heal the sick miraculously. A December 1830 revelation to Joseph Smith and Sidney Rigdon asserts that God will show great signs and miracles, including the healing of the sick by those having faith (D&C 35:8-9). Basic instructions are that two or more elders should pray for and lay hands on the sick in the Lord's name and bless them (D&C 42:44). By revelation, healing was to be one of McLellin's special gifts (D&C 66:9). In 1836, Joseph Smith saw in vision McLellin healing the sick; see *HC* 2:381.

[53] Journal IV, August 31, 1834.

[54] Journal III, March 21, 1833.

[55] Journal III, April 2, 1833.

[56] Donald Q. Cannon and Lyndon W. Cook, eds., *The Far West Record* (Salt Lake City: Deseret Book, 1983), 7-8.

[57] Gregory A. Prince, *Having Authority: The Origins and Development of Priesthood during the Ministry of Joseph Smith* (Independence, Mo.: John Whitmer Historical Association, 1993), 38-41, 51, 79-80.

[58] Cannon and Cook, *Far West Record*, 19.

[59] The standard one-volume history of the LDS Church in Kirtland is Backman, *Heavens Resound.*

William E. McLellin, c. 1875. Courtesy LDS Church Archives.

The Odyssey of
William Earl McLellin:
Man of Diversity, 1806–83

Larry C. Porter

Reconstructing a complete picture of the life and character of William E. McLellin is a challenge. His life took many turns, and at several important junctures the surviving historical records offer only snatches of information about his comings and goings, his thoughts and actions. In many ways, the years from 1831 to 1836 were McLellin's golden years, during which he rose to great heights of faith and service. But the loftiness of his desires and expectations also set the stage for his sharp reversals in 1838 and eventually led to his isolation from all groups of Latter-day Saints. But through his life also ran several continuous threads: his quest for peace, harmony, and egalitarian fellowship; his reliance on the ordinances of baptism and of the priesthood; his belief in the Book of Mormon; and his hopes for the establishment of Zion. Given the varied conditions and experiences in McLellin's life, sketching a coherent biography of his life is a daunting task.

In an 1880 letter to James T. Cobb of Salt Lake City, McLellin gave a brief description of himself that reveals much about his mind and character. He gave no quarter:

> I am *"opinionated."* When I thoroughly examine a subject and settle my mind, then higher evidence must be introduced before I change. I have set to my seal that the Book of Mormon is a true, divine record and it will require more evidence than I have ever seen to ever shake me relative to its purity I have read many "Exposes." I have seen all their arguments. But my evidences are above them all! . . . .
>
> When a man goes at the Book of M. he touches the apple of my eye. He fights against truth—against purity—against light—against the purist, or one of the truest, purist books on earth. I have more confidence in the Book of Mormon than any book of this wide earth![1]

At first reading, this statement seems enigmatic. How does one equate McLellin's sure defense of the Book of Mormon with his lengthy stance as one branded by many groups as apostate—an opposer of the Prophet Joseph Smith and his works? If there is anything absolutely consistent in the life-span of William E. McLellin, it is his tenacity and his perpetual adherence to the authenticity of the Book of Mormon. This characteristic is a regular feature of his 1831–36 journals, in which he mentions, or alludes to, the Book of Mormon approximately 230 times. Noticeably, he never faulted "The Book" or the revelations of Joseph Smith up to 1834, the year McLellin later concluded that Joseph had lost his prophetic mantle in the unsuccessful effort of Zion's Camp to deliver McLellin and the other Saints of Zion living in Missouri.[2] Many sources disclose the intricacies of this most interesting personality.

Family, Background, and Characteristics

William Earl McLellin was born on January 18, 1806, in Smith County, Tennessee.[3] His father, Charles McLellan, was born about 1766.[4] William makes no mention of his mother in any known source. She appears to have been either dead or out of the home during a substantial part of his life.[5]

The McLellin family located along Defeated Creek and Buffalo Creek near the eastern line between Smith County and Jackson County. A Charles McClanen (apparently William's father) lived in September 1803 by Defeated Creek on property adjoining the newly acquired land of Hugh McClanen (also McLelen and McLellan). McLellins were in the small communities of Donoho and Kempville, as well.[6] The site of the old Bagdad meetinghouse, Jackson County, where some of the McLellins worshiped, is still identifiable.[7]

While visiting with his father in April 1845, McLellin identified himself as "my Fathers 4th Son" and remarked that he then had "but two brothers and one sister living," one brother being older and the other younger than himself.[8] His brother Samuel was about nine years his senior, having been born about 1797.[9] On August 4, 1831, McLellin described a visit that he made to his younger brother Israel, born about 1810, who was then at their uncle William Moore's home six miles south of Springfield, Sangamon County, Illinois. McLellin was on his way to Jackson County, Missouri, to investigate Mormonism and shared with his brother and uncle the content of the Book of Mormon, which he had just purchased. During his return journey from Missouri, on September 13, 1831, he again called on his relatives only to find that his uncle William Moore had just left for Tennessee and that his brother Israel was also making plans to start for Tennessee in about a week. McLellin said, "I gave to him a book of Mormon to carry to my bro. Samuel,"[10] who in 1832 had a Carthage, Smith County, Tennessee postal address.[11] In 1850, Samuel; his wife, Elizabeth; and ten children were still living in Smith County.[12] The name of the missing brother is unaccounted for.

McLellin also held "a special meeting at my own natural sister's" home in the vicinity of Bagdad, Tennessee, on May 5, 1845. His sister was Nancy, born about 1803. She had married William Law (not the counselor to Joseph Smith).[13] No names were given by McLellin, however, when he visited a sister, brother-in-law, and their family in Greenupsburg [Greenup], Greenup County, Kentucky, on April 22, 1836.[14]

McLellin's boyhood and youth remain relatively obscure. Physically, he was strong and robust. When he attained his full stature, he measured 6 feet 3 inches. Tallness seems to have been a family trait. McLellin described his youngest brother as standing "six feet four inches and one half under the standard—in height, and weighs 224 lbs., without being fleshy—A kind of walking giant."[15] Throughout his life, McLellin was spoken of as a man of "perseverance and energy worthy of emulation."[16] He exhibited an obvious stamina in his ability to travel extensively and preach incessantly in meeting the requirements of innumerable appointments. He was an impressive orator with a strong physical bearing.

His personal characteristics both excited and exasperated his associates, their reactions running on a spectrum from total adoration to complete disdain. J. H. Newton of Philadelphia paid McLellin the ultimate tribute when he affirmed, "He has indeed enlisted my feelings to that extent, that I feel I could go to the death for him."[17] But James J. Strang of Voree, Wisconsin, denounced him: "O, William, arch-apostate! who can hereafter have the least confidence in such a perfidious monster of iniquity?"[18] Obviously, McLellin had a discernable impact on both his contemporaries and their institutions.

McLellin spoke of himself as being "opinionated." In a straight-forward manner, he informed Orson Pratt, "You sir, know me well enough to know, that it is my very nature to be frank and open in my intercourse with mankind." Robert M. Elvin said that William seemed "given to hospitality, and always willing to impart his religious opinions to all those who will hear him" but added, however, that "he enjoys the privilege to criticize, but receives criticism as persecution."[19] This latter trait cost him dearly in his interpersonal relationships.

William H. Kelley found McLellin to be a "man of thought, high aspirations, and a student."[20] McLellin had a propensity for books and an insatiable desire to learn. His journals show that he liked to acquire new books and to see that those volumes requiring binding received proper attention.[21] He enjoyed a "good flow of language," and this innate ability, coupled with the Spirit, often allowed him to sermon-ize with "great liberty" of expression for as much as three hours at a time.[22] His gift was facilitated by a loud voice, a distinct asset in that day. This capability was attested to with a note of humor by Vida E. Smith, who recalled:

> It was in Independence that William McLellin had loudly and with tremendous emphasis predicted the everlasting and unlimited smash of the church [RLDS]—but *he* was going to build a church that would stay for ever, and *he* was going to preach until he "would be heard for two miles." There was a twinkle in the blue eyes of my father [Alexander Hale Smith] then, as he mildly admitted the possibility of the latter part of the boast.[23]

John Nicholson remembered McLellin as "loud," "overbear-ing," and "bombastic" in voice and mannerisms during a courtroom scene in Nebraska City, Nebraska, during 1866.[24] His presence seems to have been generally known whenever he was in attendance.

McLellin grew up in an agrarian society and learned the farmer's trade in his father's family. However, from 1827 to 1835, as he stated, "I . . . taught school in five different States, and I . . . visited many schools in which I was not engaged, as teacher."[25] In July 1831, McLellin was residing in Paris, Edgar County, Illinois, where he was employed as a schoolteacher. He had between thirty and forty students, and, as he observed, "the people [were] generally satisfied with me as Teacher."[26] During March and April 1832, he "kept store" for Charles Sumner in Middlebury, Portage County, Ohio.[27] McLellin's skills as a teacher and writer afforded him frequent opportunities to serve as a clerk, author, and editor during his church ministries.

In the latter part of 1838, McLellin began making reference to his involvement in the practice of medicine, and he was subsequently identified by himself and others as "doctor." The physician of the period has been described as one who often

> developed a rare quickness of perception and self-reliance. A specialist was then unknown and he was called upon to treat every phase of bodily ailment, serving as physician, surgeon, oculist and dentist. His books were few and . . . his medicines were simple and carried on his person, and every preparation of pill or solution was the work of his own hands.[28]

His interest in medicine may have been spurred by the fact that he came to manifest the gift of healing as a young Mormon elder.

Concurrent with his work as a physician, McLellin became editor of two newspapers—the *Ensign,* printed in Buffalo, Scott County, Iowa Territory, from July through September 1844 (published with George M. Hinkle and representing the interests of The Church of Jesus Christ, the Bride of the Lamb's Wife); and *The Ensign of Liberty, of The Church of Christ,* Kirtland, Lake County, Ohio, published March 1847 through August 1849 on behalf of The Church of Christ.

On July 30, 1829, McLellin at age 23 married Cinthia Ann.[29] The young couple resided in the vicinity of Charleston, Clark County (later Coles County), Illinois, in 1830. Sadly, Cinthia died in that locality sometime after the 1830 census was taken but prior to August 1, 1831, when McLellin visited the grave of his "dearest friend and her blessed little infant."[30] Apparently, Cinthia died in childbirth, and she and her child were buried in or near Charleston.[31] McLellin lamented her loss when he mournfully exclaimed, "I was deprived of her most lovely endeavours to render me happy and agreeable, in consequence of which I spent many lonesome & sorrowful hours."[32]

McLellin's Conversion and Early Missionary Labors, 1831–32

McLellin's life was inexorably changed on July 14, 1831, shortly after the death of Cinthia Ann, when two Mormon missionaries appeared in Paris, Illinois. His biography from 1831 to 1836 soon became closely interwoven with many important developments in the early history of the LDS Church, and during these years, McLellin's abiding commitment to the principles of peace and brotherhood, the Book of Mormon, and the building of Zion took root in his soul.

McLellin "first heard the preaching" from Elders Samuel H. Smith and Reynolds Cahoon, who had stopped momentarily to preach in Paris while en route to Jackson County, Missouri.[33] The elders were able to secure an appointment for that evening in the Edgar County Courthouse in Paris. Only a few attended the meeting, McLellin among them. The hearers primarily "appeared hard hearted and wicked," but McLellin reflected, "When I heard it, I made up my mind that there was more in it than any religion I had ever before heard advocated."[34] After paying out their last money for a night's lodging, Elders Smith and Cahoon left Paris early the next morning and arrived in Independence, Missouri, on August 4, 1831.[35]

Only a few days later, Elders David Whitmer and Harvey Whitlock likewise came through Paris en route to Missouri in fulfillment of their mission call (D&C 52:25). McLellin learned about the elders' presence in the area on the morning of July 18, 1831. After tending to his school duties, he joined with others to hear them preach in a sugar grove 2 1/2 miles below the village. Each elder bore witness of the Book of Mormon. McLellin was especially impressed with the message of Whitlock, whom he later referred to as his "father in the gospel" and affirmed, "I never heard such preaching in all my life. The glory of God seemed to encircle the man and the wisdom of God to be displayed in his discourse."[36] David Whitmer's words on that occasion were similarly impressive and not forgotten fifty years later, when McLellin declared, "I saw him [Whitmer] June 1879, and heard him bear his solemn testimony to the truth of the book—as sincerely and solemnly as when he bore it to me in Paris, Ill. in July 1831."[37]

Determined to meet with the Prophet and translator of the Book of Mormon, McLellin closed his school in Paris on July 30, 1831, and by previous arrangement met Elders Whitmer and Whitlock at the residence of William White in Coles County. After paying their respects at the grave of Cinthia Ann, the new convert and his companions journeyed toward Jackson County, Missouri. On August 3, McLellin purchased a copy of the Book of Mormon from his friends, and they parted company.[38] McLellin privately confessed, "My object was to get to Independence before them and see if the testimony of the other witnesses would agree with theirs."[39]

At the Mount Pleasant ferry in Missouri, McLellin was greatly disappointed to learn that Joseph Smith and a company of elders had passed through there the previous day, August 14, and were now headed east to Kirtland, Ohio. William arrived in Independence on August 18, and with David Whitmer and Martin Harris went ten miles further west to Kaw Township, where they stayed with the Colesville Branch of the Church.[40] McLellin was especially impressed with the peace, order, harmony, spirit of God, and Christian beauty that he found among these people.

After a four-hour woodland discussion with Hyrum Smith, a lengthy session of secret prayer, and realizing that he "was bound as an honest man to acknowledge the truth and Validity of the book of Mormon," McLellin requested baptism. He stated, "I united with the Church of Christ on the 20th day of August, 1831, in Jackson Co., Mo., and I was administered to in baptism and confirmation by Elder Hyrum Smith, the brother of Joseph."[41]

At "a special conference of some fifteen elders" assembled in the Colesville Branch four days later, McLellin was ordained an elder by the laying on of hands by Hyrum Smith and Edward Partridge.[42] The following day, in company with Hyrum Smith, Martin Harris, David Whitmer, Harvey Whitlock, and Simeon Carter, the new elder left for Kirtland, Ohio. McLellin purchased a new Book of Mormon for the trip from Edward Partridge, at a cost of $1.25. On August 31, McLellin and his companion separated from the others, who were going through St. Louis, and preached along the way until they reached the home of McLellin's friend, William White, who lived near Charleston, Illinois.[43] There they kept a preaching appointment, purchased a horse for Hyrum Smith, and visited the grave of McLellin's deceased wife. At her burial site, McLellin once again reflected on "the uncertainty of all earthly Objects," before pressing on to Paris, Illinois, to settle final business affairs there. In Paris, Elder McLellin preached to friends and neighbors in his old schoolhouse.[44]

Departing the area of Paris, Illinois, the two missionaries reached the home of Joseph Smith, Sr., in Kirtland, Ohio, on October 12, 1831.[45] Because the Prophet was then residing in the home of John

John Johnson Farm, Hiram, Ohio, as it appeared sometime before 1874. Joseph Smith was residing here in 1831–32, when McLellin spent time in this home with the Prophet. Courtesy Western Reserve Historical Society.

Johnson in Hiram, Portage County, Ohio, McLellin did not meet him until he attended a conference of the Saints at the home of Sirenes Burnet in Cuyahoga County, Ohio. At that conference, McLellin and others were ordained to the office of high priest:

> On the 25th [October 1831] I attended a general conference in the town of Orange, about 20 miles distant. Here I first saw and formed an acquaintance with Joseph Smith, Jr., Oliver Cowdery, Sidney Rigdon, John Whitmer, &c. About 40 ministers attended the conference. During its sittings, I, with nine others were pointed out again by the spirit of revelation, as having the gifts and callings to the office of High Priest, and was ordained thereunto under the hands of Pres. Oliver Cowdery.[46]

McLellin accompanied Joseph Smith home to the John Johnson farm at Hiram. There his injured ankle was healed by the Prophet, and he remained three weeks absorbing all that he could from the words of Joseph. After praying for personal direction from the Lord, McLellin was privileged to write down the words of a revelation directed to himself through Joseph Smith (D&C 66). On October 29, he recorded in his personal journal the revelation which he had received, along with this additional note after the "Amen": "A revelation given to William E. McLelin a true descendant from Joseph who was sold into Egypt down through the loins of Ephraim his Son."[47] Highly pleased with this experience, McLellin wrote to his family: "I can truly say I believe him to be a man of God. A Prophet, a Seer and Revelater to the church of christ."[48]

A series of special conference sessions of the Church convened in Hiram on November 1–13, 1831. McLellin was an active participant and was named moderator of the final session.[49] The principal business centered on the publication of selected revelations. At the outset, the Prophet asked the elders present "what testimony they were willing to attach to these commandments." A number of the brethren said they would testify of their validity to the world. However, others confessed their inability to so testify without a satisfactory spiritual confirmation from within. Some also were concerned about the language employed in the revelations (D&C 67:5). Joseph was then given a revelation (D&C 67) to assist the brethren in their decision making. The Lord challenged anyone present to write a revelation equal to the least of those to be contained in the Book of Commandments.[50] McLellin was duly appointed to attempt the preparation of an authentic revelation. After his unsuccessful effort to do so, those who had been reticent now acceded, lending their support to the proposed publication and confirming their collective testimony thereto.[51]

Despite any initial reservations that McLellin may have experienced about the Book of Commandments, he continued to exhibit faith in these revelations of the Prophet. Immediately following the above-mentioned event, McLellin, Orson Hyde, Luke Johnson, and Lyman Johnson collectively sought the mind of the Lord, through Joseph Smith, relative to their future labors (D&C 68). McLellin was imbued with a desire to understand the nature of revelation as the means of obtaining the mind and will of the Lord. In later years, he was not hesitant to profess that he was the recipient of revelations both for himself and for others, notably in the Hinkle, Law, and Rigdon organizations.[52] This claim became particularly evident as he attempted to structure The Church of Christ in Kirtland from 1847 to 1849.[53]

McLellin and Samuel Smith had been called on October 29, 1831, to perform a mission in the "eastern lands." That same revelation contained a strong admonition and caution to McLellin: "Forsake all unrighteousness. Commit not adultery—a temptation with which thou hast been troubled" (D&C 66:7-8, 10).[54] The pair departed from Hiram on November 16, 1831. Their labors centered in eastern Ohio. On December 15, McLellin was taken with a violent cold, which settled in his lungs. He and his companion made their way to the home of Mr. John Edwards in Weathersfield by December 20, where McLellin was confined to bed. Samuel left his companion to recuperate and returned to Hiram, Ohio, on December 24. McLellin finally returned to Hiram on December 29, having baptized seven individuals during his 44-day sojourn.[55]

Commenting on their minimal term in the field, Elder Smith stated, "We went a short distance, but because of disobedience, our way was hedged up before us."[56] Samuel does not elucidate on the nature of that disobedience, but at the January 25, 1832, conference held at Amherst, Lorain County, Ohio, McLellin's commission to go to the "eastern countries" was revoked. Apparently, improprieties stemming form his recent labors in Portage and Trumbull counties were the cause. Orson Hyde was appointed in McLellin's stead to join Samuel Smith in his ministry to the "eastern countries" (D&C 75: 6, 13). With that same revocation, McLellin was severely chastened for the "murmurings of his heart" and for his having "sinned." Nevertheless, the Lord forgave him his errors and called him anew to undertake a proselyting mission to the "south countries" with Luke Johnson (D&C 75:7-9).

In the interim between McLellin's return from his mission with Samuel Smith on December 28, 1831, and the convening of the Amherst conference on January 25, 1832, he busied himself with a variety of tasks. Some twenty-two years later, McLellin shared with Orson Pratt a singular event which occurred to him on January 18, 1832, a day for which there is no entry in his journal. McLellin stated that he and the Prophet were alone in Joseph's translating room in the John Johnson home. William requested him to inquire of the Lord concerning an important matter. Joseph responded by saying, "Do you inquire of God and I will pray for you that you may obtain." Then William complied with the Prophet's directive and elatedly confirmed:

> I did receive and wrote it. And when I read it to him he shed tears of joy, and said to me, "Brother William, that is the mind and the will of God, and as much a revelation as I ever received in my life. You have written it by the true spirit of inspiration." But from this circumstance I never was vain enough to suppose that "I was planted in Joseph's stead," nor that it was my duty or privilege to receive by revelation laws or regulations for the whole church. I knew better. But at that time I saw, heard, and felt what I wrote. Tere [*sic*] and then I learned a principle, and was put in possession of a power that I never shall forget. I learned to know the voice of the Spirit of God clothed in words. And if I had heeded its voice from that day to this, I should have missed many—very many difficulties through which I have passed.[57]

This experience was considered by McLellin to be of great moment in uncovering his personal ability to seek and obtain the direction of the Lord. William performed ten baptisms in Kirtland during January 1832, among them that of Shadrach Roundy, who was visiting from New York.[58]

Leaving Hiram on February 2, 1832, McLellin and Luke Johnson commenced their mission to the "south." Initially their route closely paralleled that followed by McLellin and Samuel Smith the previous November and December. Their labors took them into eastern Ohio and across the state line into New Bedford, Pennsylvania. Retiring from the Keystone State, the missionaries recrossed into Ohio and preached to no avail at the home of Erastus Cowdery in Youngstown on February 20, 1832.[59] Taking leave of the "unbelieving" Cowdery, the companions visited the townships of Berlin in Trumbull County, and Springfield in Portage County. Advancing to the flourishing village of Middleberry, the brethren kept a preaching appointment and then retired for the evening at the country home of Charles Sumner on February 25. That night McLellin's mind was filled with doubts and he debated whether his call to preach was by man or by "the fountain of all wisdom." Unable to resolve his dilemma, the missionary determined that he would "cease proclaiming until I was satisfied in my own mind."[60] Obviously affected by the burden of his inner conflicts, he abruptly ceased making journal entries and did not resume them until January 28, 1833—eleven months later.[61]

Commenting on this sudden termination of their labors by his companion, Johnson stated, "Brother McLellin got a situation behind a counter to sell tapes, &c., and I, preferring not to proceed alone, returned to the town of Hiram, and the Prophet appointed Seymour Brunson in his stead, with whom I travelled through Ohio, Virginia and Kentucky."[62] In explanation of his actions, McLellin confided, "By traveling and labouring During such inclement weather, my health became impaired and I could not at that time exercise faith enough to be perfectly healed (neither could Timothy of old I T. 5,23) Consequently I stopped there [in Middleberry] and kept store for Col. [Charles] Sumner until the last of April [1832]."[63]

Marriage and Move to Zion

McLellin finally resolved not to continue his itinerant preaching but rather to find a wife and go to Zion in Independence, Missouri, where he thought that he could be most useful. Returning to Hiram from his employment with Col. Sumner in the latter part of April, McLellin immediately proposed marriage to Emeline Miller only four days after "first hinting" matrimony to her. The couple were married April 26, 1832, at Ravenna, Portage County, Ohio.[64] Although they experienced a whirlwind courtship, the pair had undoubtedly been acquainted for a period of several months. McLellin had lived at the John Johnson home for three weeks during October and November 1831.[65] Emeline was the niece of John and Elsa Jacobs

Johnson and was then living in Windham township. She had joined the LDS Church as early as April 1831 in Hiram and would have participated in the activities of the Saints which centered around the Johnson household—especially with the Prophet in that home from September 12, 1831, to April 1, 1832.[66]

Emeline was born to Martin and Rebecca Jacobs Miller, September 4, 1809, Pomfret, Windsor County, Vermont, the youngest of eight children. The Millers and the John Johnson family were close neighbors in Pomfret in 1810. William said that Emeline left Vermont and came to Ohio "when quite small," age eight. A company of some forty men, women, and children, left Pomfret and Hartford about January 23, 1818, headed for the Western Reserve of Ohio. The Miller and Johnson families were among them. Traveling by sled over a six-week period, they arrived in Hiram on March 4. The Millers settled on the west half of lot 36, and the Johnsons on the west ends of lots 22 and 39. The families still lived near one another in the 1830s.[67]

McLellin described his new bride as being twenty-two years old at the time of their marriage. She stood only 5 feet 1 inch as compared with his towering 6 feet 3 inches. She weighed between 110 and 120 pounds. In speaking of her attainments, William stated that "her education is common English. She has taught school some, though her principle business has been tailoring."[68] Between 1834 and 1848, they became the parents of six known children, four boys and two girls: Charles William, born April 14, 1834, in Liberty, Clay County, Missouri; Sarah Emeline, born January 5, 1836, at Kirtland, Ohio; James Martin, born February 22, 1838, probably while still at Far West; Helen Rebecca, born February 11, 1843, Hampton, Illinois; Albert Eugene, born June 2, 1845, in Scott County, Iowa; and Marcus Nelson, born February 9, 1848, at Kirtland, Ohio.[69]

Joseph Smith was attending a conference of the Church in Independence, Missouri, on April 26, the day that William and Emeline were married in Ravenna, Ohio. During his return to Ohio, the Prophet was detained in Greenville, Indiana, with Newel K. Whitney, who had suffered a broken leg and foot in a runaway-stage accident. Martin Harris arrived there from Kirtland to inform the Prophet of the condition of the Smith and Whitney families. He also notified Joseph of McLellin's activities in returning prematurely from his mission to the "south countries" and of his brief courtship and marriage.

The Prophet, upset with McLellin's failure to once again complete the assigned task and being acquainted with both parties in the marriage, assessed this turn of events in a letter which he wrote to his wife, Emma, in Kirtland, June 6, 1832.[70] Joseph observed:

> I am not pleased to hear that William Mclelin has come back and disobayed the voice of him who is altogether Lovely for a woman I am astonished at Sister Emaline yet I cannot believe she is not a worthy sister I hope She will [find] him true and kind to her but have no reason to expect it his Conduct merits the disapprobation of every true follower of Christ but this is a painful subject I hope you will excuse my warmth of feeling in mentioning this subject.[71]

While Joseph was coming overland from Missouri, mostly by stage, William and Emeline were en route to Independence. In company with about a hundred men, women, and children, primarily from Kirtland and from Nelson, Portage County, the pair left the Portage County area on May 2, 1832. Traveling to an Ohio River landing twenty miles south of Pittsburgh, the company boarded a steamboat that transported them to St. Louis in eight days and nights. At St. Louis the Saints purchased some oxen and with a caravan of fourteen wagons arrived in Independence on June 16, 1832.[72]

This emigrating company received a strong rebuke from the Prophet for their failure to observe the appropriate rules, which had been laid down in council for the removal of individuals and bodies of Saints to Zion. William E. McLellin was specifically cited. In a letter to W. W. Phelps, Joseph felt it his duty, "without sparing any," to state his reasons for the censure:

> Firstly making a mock of the profession of faith in the commandments by proceeding contrary thereto in not complying with the requirements of them in not obtaining reccomends &c seccondly, that the church should procede to receive Wm McLelin into there fellowship & communion on any other conditions, then the filling [of] his mission to the South countries according to the commandment of Jesus Christ, I cite your minds to this saying he that loveth Father or Mother wife & children more than me is not worthy of me thus saith the Lord Thirdly the unorganized & confused state in leaving here, and the evil surmisings which were among them & neglect of duty &c more than this I do not wish to mention, now therefore the buffitings of the advesary be upon all those among you who are eniquitous persons and rebelious, I would inform them they do not have my right hand of fellowship, but I will leave this subject for will not my God and Your God do right.[73]

Locally, McLellin's activity in a religious role seems not to have been inhibited in any fashion as he was a participant in a "special council" in the home of Bishop Edward Partridge in Independence and an ensuing conference there on July 3, 1832. In August and October, he acted as clerk of a conference in Kaw Township, Jackson County, clerk of another conference in Independence, and clerk of a council of high priests in that same community.[74]

By June 16, 1832, he had purchased two lots and a small cabin on Main Street in Independence. Between the time of his arrival in June 1832 and November 3, 1833, McLellin had acquired at least 37 acres of land in the area.[75] He said that he "o[b]tained a school here," and began teaching on July 8, 1832, for a period of three months. He reported that some thirty students were generally in attendance.[76]

Meanwhile, in Kirtland a council met on December 3, 1832. Not satisfied with certain unspecified activities of McLellin, they examined his case and excommunicated him. Paradoxically, on that very day, McLellin met with a council of high priests, transacting business in the home of Algernon Sidney Gilbert in Independence, Missouri.[77] As no minutes of the actual charges in the case appear to have been preserved, it is difficult to identify the causes associated with this action. However, his previous failure to complete his assigned mission to the "south countries" and unauthorized travel to Missouri may well have been the key factors, inasmuch as Joseph Smith was adamant in his statements concerning McLellin's neglect of duty and the withdrawal of his own fellowship.[78] The time and circumstances of McLellin's consequent reinstatement are not specified, but it coincides with his accepting another mission call in January, 1833, to the south.

Mission with Parley P. Pratt

Seemingly unaware of the proceedings against him in Ohio, McLellin fulfilled a protracted mission of four months with Parley P. Pratt early in 1833. On January 28, 1833, the pair left Independence and labored briefly in Liberty, Missouri, before returning to Independence to transact some unexpected business. The companions then crossed the state of Missouri, preaching in a variety of locations including Lafayette County; Mount Pleasant; Chariton; Fayette; and Paris, Missouri.[79]

Drawing near the Mississippi River, in the vicinity of Clarksville, Missouri, the missionaries were "walking together silently meditating on the works of God and the holiness of heart required of those who travel to proclaim the fulness of his gospel." Observing a tall mount, Pratt exclaimed, "There is the place for contemplation." Climbing up to its summit, McLellin reflected, "Here in this delightful place for meditation we recollected that it was recorded of Holy men of old that they sought Mountains and solitary places and there in exceeding high places they purified themselves and fasted and prayed and communed with their God." Though they prayed for some five hours, "the veil was not rent," as they had hoped.[80] Nevertheless, their wrestling in mighty prayer had the desirable effect of buoying up their spirits and preparing them for the task ahead. The missionaries had been warned that the community of Clarksville was filled with "a hardened and irreclaimable set of blasphemers and infidels." Elder Pratt further recorded, "[We] cried mightily unto the Lord that He would open our way, and move upon the hearts of the people to receive us and hear the Word."[81] The elders were treated with great hospitality and friendship and the next day ferried across the Mississippi River free of charge.

In Illinois they preached in Gilead, Calhoun County, and in the vicinity of Carrollton and Bluffdale, Greene County, their labors centering on western Illinois. Elder Pratt affirmed, "We tarried in the neighborhood some two months, and preached daily in all that region to vast multitudes, both in town and country, in the grove, and in school houses, barns and dwellings."[82] After experiencing some successes on May 6, 1833, Elder Pratt departed Illinois for a return journey to Jackson County. McLellin remained in the Carrollton area until May 20, when he too departed for Independence. His last journal entry for this period was made May 24, 1833, while still en route. He later stated that he finally reached home in the month of June 1833.[83]

Elder Pratt summarized their experience by saying, "Hundreds of the people were convinced of the truth, but the hearts of many were too much set on the world to obey the gospel; we, therefore, baptized only a few of the people and organized a small society."[84] During the four-month span of their mission, McLellin and Pratt combined their efforts in baptizing some fourteen persons.[85]

Trouble in Missouri

McLellin's blissful return to Independence was short lived. He said that in the month of July 1833, "I saw and passed through scenes which sickened my soul."[86] Having been away for so long, McLellin was asked to deliver a sermon at the Saints' meeting place on the Temple Lot in Independence. He said that a large number of local citizens with whom he had formed an acquaintance also turned out to hear him preach. He chose as his text for his two-hour sermon "The Gathering of the Last Days."[87]

McLellin declared that that very evening some of the principal men of the area met together and formulated the infamous document which was then circulated "pledg[ing] to each other, their property, their lives, and their sacred honors, to drive all the members of the Church of Christ, (whom they called Mormons,) from the county, peaceably if they could, but forcibly if they must."[88]

McLellin estimated the number of the mob who gathered on July 20, 1833, at the Jackson County courthouse in Independence at about five hundred men. Their revised declarations were presented to Bishop Edward Partridge and other Mormon leaders for a response. The mob's demand for the ultimate removal of the Mormons from Jackson County was initially refused by the Saints. McLellin said that to emphasize their determination to see their decree carried out, the mob then deliberately tore down the two-story brick building which served as both a printing office for the Latter-day Saints and a residence of W. W. Phelps. They then undertook to demolish the store of Algernon Sidney Gilbert and desisted only when Gilbert assured them that he would pack up his goods and cease his trading.[89]

McLellin said the mob then surrounded his home. However, he had seen them coming and "stepped a little out of the way" while they searched the premises for him. So anxious were these men to get their hands on McLellin and Oliver Cowdery that "they offered that if any man would catch us and deliver us up to them on the 23d [of July], they would pay $80 for either of us."[90] He and Oliver went into hiding in the woods and on occasion were able to secure a meal from their friends.

In order to avoid bloodshed, gain sufficient time to notify the Prophet, and investigate their legal options, the Mormons agreed to terms on July 23, 1833. The leaders of the Mormons were to be out of Jackson County on or before January 1, 1834. These leaders were to use their influence to persuade one-half of their followers to leave with them on January 1 and the others to remove by April 1, 1834. McLellin, Cowdery, and some others who had been forced into hiding were allowed to return home. McLellin now contented himself with his service as a member of the council of high priests, which regularly convened to transact important items of business among the Saints.[91] Evidently, McLellin thought the overall situation would ameliorate and the Saints could yet enjoy continued occupancy in Jackson County, for on August 15, 1833, he purchased an Independence town lot containing nearly seven acres.[92]

Because the Saints soon sought the aid of Governor Daniel Dunklin in Jefferson City and subsequently hired legal counsel to assist them in defending their civil rights in court, the mob cried "foul" and declared such actions a flagrant violation of their mutual agreement. Commencing in October, the "old citizens" began a series of attacks on Mormon communities in Jackson County.

During a November 1, 1833, raid by the mob on Independence, McLellin assisted other Saints in apprehending one of the attackers, Richard McCarty, when he was caught in the act of stoning the Algernon Sidney Gilbert store. McCarty was taken to Samuel Weston, Justice of the Peace, with the demand that a warrant be issued against him. Weston refused to make the arrest, and of necessity McCarty was released. Richard McCarty then obtained a warrant of his own, and on November 4, McLellin, A. S. Gilbert, Isaac Morley, John Corrill, and three or four other Saints were arrested for "Assault and Battery, and false imprisonment."[93]

McLellin said that he submitted to "a pretended civil authority . . . knowing that I had committed no offence." The brethren were taken to the Independence Courthouse about dark. While waiting for the court to be organized, they heard a disturbance at the door and a cry of, "Kill the d—d rascals, kill them." In order to give the prisoners some element of security, Samuel C. Owens proposed that they be put in jail until morning, when the trial could commence with some additional safety. McLellin said that "we consented, thinking that even a prison, would be a palace to us in preference to a court room where men like demons raged and foamed."[94]

The deep personal consternation of that moment was graphically described by McLellin when he related his being placed in the community's log jail:

> Two large men stepped up to me, and each clinched an arm, and thus gallanted me to the most horrid, soul harrowing, lonesome, loathsome place into which my feet ever entered, before or since. What! to be locked, chained, and barred within a little room in a jail, only twelve feet square!! And that, too, where felons, robbers, and murderers had dwelt, and there forced to remain during a dark, lonesome night; and that, too, without any certainty as to the future. O thou uneasy uncertainty! Thou horror-fed moment of prison life!! Surrounded by scores of beings "who feared not God, nor regarded the rights of man." The roar of musketry and the yells of more than heathen savages continually saluted our ears. The darkness of the night added to the fury of the scene.[95]

Early the next morning the jailor and a few others came to the prisoners and advised them that if they would leave the county immediately they would be released without standing trial. Recognizing the ferocity of the mob and the virtual impossibility of an impartial trial, the elders agreed to these unlawful demands. McLellin explained the immediacy of his forced departure from Jackson County: "Next morning early I was on the road with my family for Liberty, in Clay Co., where I hired a house and remained during the winter. The whole society, of some hundreds, immediately fled from Jackson county, as from a den of wolves."[96]

On December 5, 1833, the Prophet wrote to Bishop Edward Partridge in Clay County, Missouri, directing him that "the land [in Jackson County] should not be sold, but be held by the Saints, until the Lord in His wisdom shall open a way for your return."[97] The exiled Saints were not to sell their lands in Jackson County even under the exceptional conditions of extreme duress in which the mob had placed them. The people believed that a solution could be reached through the courts or other means by which they would be reinstated.

Despite the position of the leadership in this matter, McLellin offered his seven acres in Independence for sale. One of the Saints, James Newberry, purchased the same on December 14, 1833, in order to keep the property within the Church. When Parley P. Pratt and Lyman Wight, "representatives from Zion," reported the status of the Church in Missouri to the leading brethren in a Kirtland council meeting on February 24, 1834, they noted that

> none of their lands were sold into the hands of our enemies except a piece owned by bro. Wm. E. McLellin of thirty acres [unaccounted for] which he sold into the hands of the enemy, and seven acres more which he would have sold to the enemy if a brother [James Newberry] had not come forward & purchased it and paid him his money.[98]

It is difficult to determine whether McLellin's personal circumstances had become so desperate that he felt obliged to sell or whether the terrifying experience in the Independence courthouse and overnight incarceration in the jail had created a resolve never to return under existing conditions. In any event, the brethren reporting to the Kirtland council felt that he had served the enemy rather than the cause of the Saints with the sale. The personal situation of the McLellins was further complicated at this time when Emeline gave birth to their first child, Charles William McLellan, April 14, 1834, in Liberty, Missouri.[99]

Under the auspices of divine revelation (D&C 103), the Prophet marshalled a body of armed men known as Zion's Camp, which marched from Ohio and Michigan to Clay County, Missouri, during May and June 1834. Their avowed purpose was to reinstate the exiled Mormons to their Jackson County properties. On June 15, 1834, while situated on the west bank of the Chariton River, the camp was hailed by Bishop Edward Partridge, who had ridden out from Clay County to confer with them. He informed the Prophet that on the following day, June 16, a delegation of Saints were slated to meet with representatives of the old citizens of Jackson County in an effort to resolve their differences.[100] At the instigation of Governor Daniel Dunklin, Judge John F. Ryland had arranged the negotiations.[101]

Between 800 and 1,000 persons, including church leaders, met at the Clay County courthouse in Liberty on June 16. Representing the Mormons were William McLellin, W. W. Phelps, A. S. Gilbert, John Corrill, and Isaac Morley. The citizen's committee laid a dual proposition before the brethren. Either the Missourians would purchase from the Mormons all their land and improvements at 100 percent within a thirty-day period or conversely the Saints were to do the same thing for the old inhabitants.[102] Oliver Cowdery later editorialized on the issues involved, stating:

> It may be said, at first view, that the mob Committee have made a fair
> proposition to our friends in offering to buy their lands at 100 per cent.
> in 30 days, and of offering theirs on the same terms to our friends; but
> when it is understood that the mob hold possession of a large quantity
> of land more than our friends, and that they only offer 30 days for the
> payment of the same, it will be seen that they are only making a show
> to cover their past unlawful conduct.[103]

In their "answer" to the Jackson citizens, the Mormon arbitrators responded that they were not authorized to commit to a
course of action on behalf of their brethren without conferring
with them. They would call a gathering of the people and reply as
soon as "Saturday or Monday next," June 21 or 23, to Judge Joel T.
Turnham, chairman of the meeting. McLellin and the other agents
signed this written response.[104] However, negotiations broke
down and were not resumed, and the men of Zion's Camp were
ultimately discharged.[105]

For the rest of his life, McLellin harbored strong personal
resentment concerning the march of the Camp. How much he gave
vent to his feelings at the time is hard to ascertain. However, after his
separation from Mormonism, he had no qualms in attacking the
Prophet on the measures which Joseph had introduced in an attempt
to reclaim Zion. McLellin declared:

> After Joseph Smith had transgressed by imbibing and encouraging the
> spirit and practice of war by the church . . . then [he] set out at the head
> of the army and traveled one thousand miles, with the difficulties and
> transgressions of such a tour, which was prompted and carried out by
> the influence of a wrong spirit; we say if these things were not
> transgressions in a Seer, then we do not know what would be.[106]

In 1854, when he gave Orson Pratt a list of reasons for his separation
from Mormonism, McLellin's first rehearsal was a complaint about
Zion's Camp, saying:

> This doctrine was in 1833 "to renounce war and proclaim peace." This
> practice was in 1834, to proclaim war and gather up a troop, and travel
> from Kirtland, O. to Clay Co. Mo. with arms and munitions of war in
> hand. But it was a failure, so far as good was concerned. And in order
> to go to war they changed the name of the church, as well as spirit, and
> in doing so became a sect in all its bearings."[107]

Following the Fishing River revelation, in which the Lord announced
his "elders should wait for a little season for the redemption of Zion"
(D&C 105:9), the Prophet disbanded Zion's Camp.

On July 3, 1834, a conference was held in Clay County to organize a high council.[108] David Whitmer was ordained president of the new council with two counselors, W. W. Phelps and John Whitmer. McLellin was called as one of the twelve high priests comprising the council, being appointed on July 3 and confirmed on July 7.[109]

In succeeding years, this assembly was referred to a great many times by McLellin. He firmly contended that the Prophet Joseph Smith, having transgressed in the matter of Zion's Camp and in other temporal concerns, had negated his calling; and in the spirit of D&C 14:2 (1835 ed., now D&C 43:4)—"for if it be taken from [Joseph] he shall not have power, except to appoint another in his stead"—Joseph was literally transferring the keys of his calling to David Whitmer to act in his place. McLellin later steadfastly maintained that "Joseph had not power with God after he ordained David to be his successor."[110]

Labors in Kirtland, 1834

When the Prophet left Missouri on July 9, 1834, for his return journey to Kirtland, he was accompanied by McLellin and others who had been assigned to assist "in promoting the cause of Christ" in the east. McLellin recorded bidding farewell to his "companion and a little babe [Charles William]" and said that this "was a more affecting parting than I ever had experienced with my Emiline because of our infant and because of the uncertainty of the length of time I should be gone."[111]

McLellin indicated that there were nineteen in the Prophet's company as they passed through Missouri and across Illinois. On July 22, 1834, while traveling from his former home in Paris, Illinois, toward Clinton, Vermillion County, Indiana, McLellin became so ill that he could not proceed. While the Prophet and his companions continued, McLellin dropped off the trail to mend. During his recovery, he proselyted extensively in the vicinity of Eugene, Indiana, where a small branch of the Church had been organized.[112] Joseph Smith was pleased with McLellin's humility and entertained "no doubt as to his standing while he continues so."[113]

When he left the area to pursue his journey on September 15, 1834, Elder McLellin declared that he had "preached 18 times [one sermon ending in an oration in tongues, August 20, 1834] among the brethren and received and baptized 13." He reached Kirtland on September 27, 1834, with his health much improved.[114]

After filling numerous preaching appointments, completing some troubleshooting for the Prophet in the Florence Branch, and taking a short-term mission with John Boynton to the communities of Painesville, Fairport, and Richmond, Ohio, McLellin was engaged to assist in teaching the "high school" or "Kirtland School."[115] On November 19, 1834, McLellin was appointed an instructor by the trustees of the "Kirtland School," Joseph Smith, Jr., Sidney Rigdon, Frederick G. Williams and Oliver Cowdery. His wages were set at $18 per month. The teacher made arrangements to board with Lyman Johnson through the winter.[116]

McLellin had worked as a schoolteacher since 1827 and had taught in five states during that time; he was a welcome addition to the teaching staff. He shared a post with Brother Thomas Burdick. Heber C. Kimball, one of the students, also identified Sidney Rigdon as having given instruction in the school. Heber likewise stated that "nearly all of the elders and myself, and many of the sisters commenced going to school." Classes began on Monday, December 22, 1834. McLellin said that in 1835 he taught in the same building which housed the print shop and the Prophet's office. He explained, "I was teaching their High School in the lower room—the printing office being overhead. And I was often in Joseph's office." The printing office was the building situated on the lot immediately west of the Kirtland Temple.[117] McLellin later explained to Joseph Smith III that the Prophet was among those who attended his high school during the winter of 1834-35.[118]

Having been asked by the trustees to give a recapitulation of the school's progress, McLellin published his response on February 27, 1835:

> When the school first commenced, we received into it both large and small, but in about three weeks the classes became so large, and the house so crowded, that it was thought advisable to dismiss all the small students, and continue those only who wished to study the sciences of penmanship, arithmetic, English grammar and geography. Before we dismissed the small scholars, there were in all about 130 who attended. Since that time there have been, upon an average, about 100, the most of whom have received lectures upon English grammar; and for the last four weeks about 70 have been studying geography one half the day, and grammar and writing the other part.

T. Burdick's arithmetic, S. Kirkham's grammar and J. Olney's
geography have been used, with N. Webster's dictionary, as standard.[119]

In this survey of the school's activities, McLellin expressed the
regret that he would soon be leaving the institution but wished to see
it flourish; he had been called to the apostleship.

McLellin's Service in the Quorum of Twelve

A special meeting was called on February 14, 1835, of those
who had marched with Zion's Camp for the announced purpose of
giving a "Zion's blessing." The Presidency of the Church informed
the assemblage that the business of the gathering was to choose
twelve men to act as the Twelve Apostles or traveling high council.[120]
Twenty-nine-year-old McLellin was one of the Apostles chosen. After
McLellin and others expressed their personal feelings, the process of
ordination began. Each individual was called forward, and Oliver
Cowdery, David Whitmer, and Martin Harris laid hands on his head
and ordained him to the apostleship. At the same time, they also
predicted many things such as having "power to heal the sick, cast
out devils, raise the dead, give sight to the blind, have power to
remove mountains, and all things should be subject to [them]
through the name of Jesus Christ."[121] Still, the process of ordination
was not yet complete. Heber C. Kimball recalled that "after we had
been thus ordained by these brethren, the first presidency laid their
hands on us, and confirmed these blessings and ordination, and
likewise predicted many things which should come to pass."[122]

McLellin was ordained an apostle the next day, Sunday,
February 15, 1835, by David Whitmer, Martin Harris, and Oliver
Cowdery, who spoke the blessing. McLellin was assured that "in
the name of the Lord, Wisdom & intelligence shall be poured out
upon [you]," and the promise was given, "[You] shall be a prince
and a savior to Gods people."[123] McLellin asserted in 1870 that he
had been selected as clerk of the conference in which the Twelve
were first chosen and was named a scribe among them. He also
averred, "I now have our apostolic record, as we first made it up."[124]
At a meeting of the Twelve on February 27, 1835, the Prophet
counseled that body to make a record of their proceedings. Orson
Hyde and McLellin were appointed clerks and regularly performed
that service for the Twelve.[125]

From December 1834 through April of 1835, the new apostle repeatedly went to Huntsburg, Geauga County, Ohio, to fulfill appointments in that community. Many were responsive to his preaching in the midst of a strong Campbellite society, and at least eighteen individuals received baptism at his hand during this time period.[126]

McLellin observed, "The truth coming so near them it roused up those whose craft was in danger, and I received a challenge [March 18] to hold a public discussion with a Mr. J. M. Tracy." Mr. Tracy "pledged himself to prove that 'the book of Mormon was not a divine revelation.'"[127] McLellin was supported by an imposing array of brethren when he met Mr. Tracy and a large congregation of Campbellites on April 27 and 28, 1835. Joseph Smith, Lyman Johnson, David W. Patten, Parley P. Pratt, John F. Boynton, and others were in attendance. The two-day debate allowed the participants a total of some eight hours each, each speaking alternately for thirty minutes at a time. McLellin announced the results:

> When the interview closed a majority of the congregation arose, by an anxious urgency on the part of Mr. T. to testify thereby that they did not believe in the divinity of the book of Mormon. But when I asked them if they had been convinced that it was false by Mr. Tracy's arguments, (if I might call them such,) there was not one to answer—"Yes."[128]

Further results can perhaps be measured by Elder McLellin's baptizing two persons that evening. Also the Prophet spoke in the same meetinghouse on Sunday for three hours, and on Monday morning, four more persons came forward and "were buried with Christ by baptism" by Elder McLellin.[129]

While in council with the Twelve on March 12, 1835, President Joseph Smith proposed that the quorum take their first mission through the eastern states. It was further proposed that the Twelve take their leave from Kirtland on May 4, 1835. Many requests had been received from the eastern churches for conferences to be held in their particular localities. An itinerary was then voted on by the quorum.[130] Hyde and McLellin acted as clerks for this council meeting.[131]

At a March 28, 1835, meeting of the Twelve, a request was made that Joseph Smith petition the Lord on behalf of the quorum for a "great revelation" which would give them His mind and will concerning their forthcoming mission. In answer to the inquiry, what is termed the "Revelation on Priesthood" (D&C 107) was granted.[132] Further directions in preparation for their departure were received by both the Twelve and the Seventy as they met together in the unfinished Kirtland Temple on April 26, 1835; President Smith gave them a charge and instructions relating to their duties.[133] Finally, on May 2, in a general council of the priesthood and the first scheduled conference on their itinerary, the Prophet directed the Quorum of the Twelve Apostles to take their seats according to the chronological age of each member. Elder McLellin was seated sixth behind Thomas B. Marsh, David W. Patten, Brigham Young, Heber C. Kimball, and Orson Hyde.[134]

Rendezvousing at John Johnson's tavern at 2:00 A.M. on May 4, 1835, the Twelve and some others set out from Kirtland. Traveling to Fairport Harbor in two wagons, they boarded the steamboat *Sandusky*, which took them northeast on Lake Erie to Dunkirk, New York. Here they disembarked and commenced their labors in that sector in anticipation of their first New York conference at Westfield, Chautauqua County, on May 9.[135]

The specified conference day at Westfield was devoted primarily to business, which was followed by two days of public preaching, baptisms, confirmation meetings, and some additional business—a pattern followed generally throughout their tour of the east. At each location, the Brethren set in order the local branches and organized them into a conference. The entire Quorum of the Twelve was present at Westfield. Elder McLellin baptized five individuals on May 10, when "a door was opened for members," and addressed the Saints attending the confirmation meeting on the "nature of the gift and power of the Holy Ghost." Hyde and McLellin were clerks of the conference.[136]

McLellin attended the remaining New York conferences in Freedom, Lyonstown (Lyons township), and Pillar Point. Of the labors of the Twelve in the Empire State, he said:

> Our first labors, were in the State of New York, in which we continued about two months, and attended four conferences. Our exertions were crowned with as good success as we could reasonably expect, considering the prejudices of the people, created by false and ridiculous statements, put in circulation by those who were first favored with the proclamation of the fulness of the everlasting gospel, contained in the book

of Mormon: we had good reason to believe that all the candid enquirers after truth, realized the force of the Savior's expression "A prophet is not without honor save in his own country." By our teaching and exhortations, the several branches of the Church were strengthened and members were added; and of such, too, we hope, as will be saved.[137]

After attending conference in West Loughborough, Upper Canada (Ontario Province today), McLellin traveled eastward with Brigham Young, going by way of East Stockholm, St. Lawrence County, New York, where they visited Asael Smith, Jr., the Prophet's uncle.[138] The Twelve again met to conduct the St. Johnsbury, Vermont, conference, commencing on July 17, 1835. McLellin then missed the two succeeding conferences in Bradford, Massachusetts (on August 7, 1835), and Saco, Maine.[139]

McLellin did not explain why he had elected to forgo his attendance at these gatherings. Various of the Twelve had participated in some conferences and chosen not to attend others, depending on their individual situations.[140] Judging from the proselyting success McLellin had been enjoying in the communities of Dalton, Lyman, and Errol, New Hampshire, he appears to have been motivated by the press of ecclesiastical business.[141]

However, his presence was missed by the Brethren, and the Twelve sent a special message through Daniel Bean alerting him that the date of the final conference at Farmington, Maine, had been changed from October 2, to August 28, 1835, and that they wished him to be in attendance. He immediately left for Farmington on August 26, arriving the afternoon of the next day. McLellin preached at the conference on Saturday, August 29. On the following Monday, the Twelve separated, planning to meet next in Buffalo, New York, on September 24, for their return to Kirtland. McLellin began his journey west with William Smith.[142]

In Kirtland, clerks Hyde and McLellin posted a general report of the labors of the Twelve to the Saints in the *Messenger and Advocate*. In their closing statement, they confirmed that

the nature of our mission to the east was peculiar, and required us to spend most of our time among the various branches of the church; however, as we had opportunity we proclaimed the gospel in every place where there was an opening, and truly there is an effectual door opened for good and faithful laborers among the intelligent and liberal people of the east.[143]

The evening of the arrival of the Twelve in Kirtland, September 26, 1835, they convened in council with the Presidency of the Church. Elders McLellin and Hyde had returned to a strained situation in respect to "matters of difficulty" between themselves and President Rigdon. Their conduct had become an agenda item for the meeting.[144] While on his mission to the east, McLellin had received a letter from his wife, Emeline, stating that "it would not be within [her] power to go to school [Kirtland School] this summer." In response, McLellin had written, "I am glad that it is not [within her power to attend], since Elder Hyde has returned and given me a description of the manner in which it is conducted; though we do not wish to cast any reflections."[145] The reflections, nevertheless, impacted on Sidney Rigdon, who was in charge of the school.[146]

Having access to the letter, the Kirtland council concluded the attitude of McLellin and Hyde constituted an insult to the Presidency of the Church relative to the conduct of the school and proposed that action be taken on August 4, 1835. "The vote of the Council was: We hereby inform Elders M'Lellin and Hyde that we withdraw our fellowship from them until they return and make satisfaction face to face."[147] Now, on September 26, 1835, as the parties met "face to face" in council, the immediate situation was ameliorated with the simple recording in the minutes:

> An item contained in Elder Wm. E. McLelins letter to his wife expressing dissatisfaction with President Rigdon's school. Elder Orson Hyde was also designated with Elder McLelin, or blamed with him in the matter. In the same they were found to be in fault, which they frankly confessed and were forgiven.

Still, some personal feelings persisted.[148]

During the fall and winter of 1835-36, McLellin participated as a counselor on the Kirtland High Council.[149] A second child, Sarah Emeline McLellan, was born to the McLellins on January 5, 1836.[150] McLellin again associated with the School of the Elders, which was reorganized under the old name, the School of the Prophets in 1836. The school had commenced the study of Hebrew on their own, along with other subjects, but on January 4, 1836, the leaders split off the Hebrew school and created a separate unit. The Hebrew class met in the translating room or Presidency's room on the west end of the third floor of the Kirtland Temple.[151]

Originally, the brethren had thought to secure the service of a Dr. Daniel Piexotto, a professor at the Willoughby Medical College, but he delayed his coming to a point where it was determined advisable to move in another direction. McLellin and Hyde were sent to Hudson, Ohio, southwest of Kirtland, on January 4, 1836, to engage instead Professor Joshua Seixas.[152] The Prophet recorded that

> Elder McLellen returned from Hudson, and reported to the school that he had hired a Teacher, to teach us the term of 7. weeks for $320. that is 40. Schollars for that amount, to commence in about 15. days hence.—he is highly celebrated as a hebrew schollar, and proposes to give us sufficient knowledge in the above term of time to read and translate the language.[153]

After his arrival on January 26, 1836, Professor Seixas remained for almost three months, instructing an enrollment that grew to about 120 students. Three other classes were of necessity formed. Professor Seixas singled out a few of the brethren to participate in an advanced class after the first three weeks. McLellin was included in this number along with Joseph Smith, Oliver Cowdery, Sidney Rigdon, Orson Hyde, Orson Pratt, W. W. Phelps, Edward Partridge, and Sylvester Smith. Following the completion of the class, McLellin continued his individual Hebrew studies as opportunity presented itself.[154]

McLellin also took part in the Kirtland endowment, a special ritual or ordinance which had been promised to the Saints. The basic concept of this particular endowment is described in these terms:

> Joseph Smith taught that the endowment was a gift of knowledge derived from revelation, a gift of power emitting from God. This gift consisted of instructions relating to the laws of God, including the principle of obedience, and was partially designed to help missionaries to serve with greater power and to give them greater protection. The Prophet said that many would not comprehend the endowment, but that bearers of the priesthood should prepare for this gift by purifying themselves, by cleansing their hearts and their physical bodies. "You need an endowment, brethren," he said, "in order that you may be prepared and able to overcome all things."[155]

On January 21, 1836, the Prophet Joseph Smith was in the midst of introducing the ordinance of anointing and divulging key principles of the endowment to numbers of church leaders in the Kirtland Temple. In the President's room on the third floor at the west end, Joseph experienced an open vision of the celestial kingdom, or highest degree of heaven (D&C 137), and at the same time witnessed other scenes, one of which involved McLellin. He related:

> I also beheld Elder McLellen in the south, standing upon a hill surrounded with a vast multitude, preaching to them, and a lame man standing before him, supported by his crutches, he threw them down at his word, and leaped as an heart [hart], by the mighty power of God.[156]

We do not know of any sequel in which this scene was actually played out in the life of McLellin. Perhaps the vision represented a negated opportunity due to a variety of circumstances which followed.

McLellin attended the dedication of the Kirtland Temple on March 27, 1836. Stirred by their experience of the previous day and by a growing awareness of their responsibilities, the Twelve met together on March 28 for a time of "general confession." In the minutes kept by Elders Hyde and McLellin, they affirm the feeling of combined weakness and humility felt by the quorum:

> We have not realized the importance of our calling to that degree that we ought, we have been light minded and vain and in many things done *wrong, wrong.* For all these things we have asked forgiveness of our Heavenly Father, and wherein we have grieved or wounded the feelings of the Presidency we ask their forgiveness.[157]

McLellin participated in the Kirtland endowment in April 1836. Thinking that it would impart totally new knowledge, he felt it was not the experience which he had anticipated. He later described the event and his subsequent feelings:

> The next April [1836] was appointed for our endowment. We passed through it; but I, in all candor say, we were most egregiously mistaken or disappointed!
>
> In a few days I said to Joseph: "I am disappointed! I supposed— yes, I believed that during the endowment, I should get *knowledge;* but I have not."
>
> He said to me, "What do you want?"
>
> I said, "I want to *know* for *myself.*"
>
> He laid his hands upon my head, and prophesied thus: "If you will take a mission to the south, and pray fervently upon the hills and in the deep valleys, before you return you shall have your soul's desires."
>
> On the 9th of April I started on my southern tour, but did not realize what had been promised.[158]

Before the departure of the Twelve to their fields of labor in 1836, Joseph met with them on March 30 and gave them great latitude as to the areas in which they would serve that season. He explained, "The Twelve are at liberty to go wheresoever they will, and if any one will say, I wish to go to such a place, let all the rest say amen."[159] Most chose to go east, but McLellin chose to go south and to perform his labors ostensibly alone, save for periodic assistance from local brethren.

McLellin went as far as Wellsville on the Ohio River with a company of brethren who had participated in the building and dedication of the Kirtland Temple and had also been recipients of an endowment, namely Bishop Edward Partridge, Isaac Morley, John Corrill, and W. W. Phelps, who were now on their return journey to Missouri.[160] Separating from the Missouri brethren on April 11, 1836, McLellin concentrated his proselyting skills in a series of locations which took him both into Ohio and Kentucky. He said that he made his return to Kirtland in the latter part of June.[161]

Separation from the Saints

McLellin came back from his southern mission in a disconsolate mood. In his estimation, he had not received the particular witness that he was seeking relative to the endowment, and he said that he felt troubled with the transformation which was afflicting some of the Saints. McLellin later said, "I returned to Kirtland the last of June, but only returned to see speculation, pride and folly . . . by the leaders, &c, &c. I made up my mind to leave."[162]

In an 1847 rehearsal of the history of the rise of the Church signed by William E. McLellin, Leonard Rich, Jeremiah Knight, Alfred Bonney, Hiram L. Rounds, and Jacob Bump, the statement is made: "W. E. McLellin had, in August, 1836, ceased to be an active minister among that people because he verily believed that the course pursued by their Leaders would sooner or later bring inevitable destruction upon them and their followers."[163] To Jacob Cobb, William wrote in 1880:

I left the church in Aug. 1836, not because I disbelieved the Book or the (then) doctrines preached or held by the Church, but because *the Leading men* to a great extent left their religion and run into and after speculation, pride, and popularity! Just like the Israelites and the

Nephites often did. I quit because I could not uphold the Presidency as
men of God; and I never united with Joseph and party afterward!![164]

McLellin wrote a letter of withdrawal to the leadership in
August 1836. He later specified, "I peaceably withdrew from them;
merely writing back to them 'it was because I had lost confidence in
the HEADS of the church.'"[165] Whether or not his departure from
Kirtland was immediate, by November 7, 1836, McLellin had purchased property in Edgar County, Illinois, where he had many old
friends and acquaintances from his Paris schoolteaching days.[166] This
move was an apparent attempt to assuage his troubled feelings in
familiar surroundings.

In a concerted effort to retain McLellin's membership and
friendship in the quorum, the Twelve corresponded with him on
December 18, 1836. With sincere concern, they pled, "When you left
Kirtland, you left home. *Come home, Come home.* . . . If you will not
come otherwise one or *all* of us will go after you." And they unitedly
informed him, "Your place is yet vacant."[167] Demonstrating the
hoped-for response, McLellin answered his brethren, "I am sorry for
the course that I have pursued.—Can You, *Will* you forgive *me?*
Will Brother Joseph forgive me? And will the Church forgive me?"[168]

When the names of the licensed "Ministers of the Gospel" were
listed for the quarter in March 1837, McLellin's was among them.[169]
Whether or not it was a time of transition for the McLellin family in
their return to Kirtland, McLellin sold a parcel of land in Edgar
County, Illinois, on June 21, 1837.[170] At the conference of the Church
held in Kirtland on September 3, 1837, McLellin was among those
sustained to the Twelve.[171] He was with the Prophet and others in Far
West, Missouri, when affairs of the Church were regulated in that
region on November 7, 1837, and was again sustained as a member
of the Twelve in conference the following day. He accepted a
captain's commission in the 1st Company, 59th Regiment, 2nd Bri-
gade, 3rd Division of the Missouri state militia from Governor Boggs
on November 22, 1837. The oath was sworn before William W.
Phelps, presiding judge, Caldwell County Court.[172]

In later years, McLellin chose not to comment on this brief
interlude, when he again united with the faith and was for a season
once more in league with the Brethren. He preferred to recall only

that he had departed the faith in August 1836.[173] His wounded spirit had not yet healed sufficiently to withstand the tenor of the times. Difficulties associated with the rise and demise of the Kirtland Safety Society Anti-Banking Company in Kirtland and related events which followed from 1837 to 1838, caused tremors of apostasy at the highest levels of leadership:

> Between November 1837 and June 1838, possibly two or three hundred Kirtland Saints withdrew from the Church, representing 10 to 15 percent of the membership there. Many of the apostates had served in major positions of responsibility. During a nine-month period, almost one-third of the General Authorities were excommunicated, disfellowshipped, or removed from their Church callings.[174]

McLellin became concerned over what he termed "speculations," which he said continued on into the winter of 1837.[175] He allowed these feelings to again drive a wedge into his relations with the Prophet Joseph and the Church. David W. Patten took exception to the course that McLellin and some others were following and in the quarterly conference of the Church, held at Far West, Missouri, on April 7, 1838, "spake of William E. McLellin, Luke Johnson, Lyman Johnson, and John F. Boynton as being men whom he could not recommend to the Conference."[176]

On Friday, May 11, 1838, Joseph Smith said that he attended the trial of William E. McLellin for transgression before the bishop's court in Far West. The Prophet said that McLellin informed the court

> that he had no confidence in the heads of the Church, believing they had transgressed, and had got out of the way, consequently he quit praying and keeping the commandments of God, and indulged himself in his lustful desires, but when he heard that the First Presidency had made a general settlement, and acknowledged their sins, he began to pray again. When I interrogated him, he said he had seen nothing out of the way himself, but he judged from hearsay.[177]

While details are unknown, his dismissal definitely occurred in 1838.[178] Emeline McLellin stated that the whole time their family spent in Caldwell County was "only a few months." They then withdrew to Clay County, where they had lived at a previous time.[179] This had been an extremely trying season for Emeline, who gave birth to their third child, James Martin McLellan, on February 22, 1838, apparently while still at Far West.[180]

Before the excommunication of McLellin, action had similarly been taken against Oliver Cowdery, David Whitmer, John Whitmer, W. W. Phelps, and Lyman E. Johnson. Although McLellin took up residency twenty-five miles from Far West in Clay County, the other dissenters remained in Far West until June 19, 1838. On that day, with the exception of Phelps, who remained behind, they left Far West under some duress. Their apparent design was to go directly to Richmond, Ray County, Missouri, and await the arrival of their families who had been left behind.[181] However, McLellin said that their flight became more eventful than anticipated:

> Near sunset, David, Oliver, John and Lyman bid farewell to their youthful wives, and their little children, their homes and firesides. . . . But the darkness of night soon coming on, and being comparative strangers to the way, they directly lost their path. . . . But onward see those men wander, until the light of a new day broke in upon that part of the earth, and meeting a stranger, he points them to the road that will lead them to an old and tried friend's who lived about twenty-five miles from Far West. With joy, mixed with sorrow, he received them. Mrs. McLellin soon furnished them with a repast.[182]

The trio remained at the McLellin home for several days until they were joined by their families from Far West and passed on to Richmond. William remembered with great pleasure his opportunity to feed these men at his table.[183]

On July 13, 1838, President Joseph Smith and others convened to select replacements for "those of the twelve who had fallen away"—McLellin, Lyman Johnson, Luke Johnson, and John Boynton. Named in their stead were John E. Page, John Taylor, Wilford Woodruff, and Willard Richards.[184]

Expulsion of the Mormons from Missouri

Overt acts of mob violence against the Latter-day Saints commenced on August 6, 1838, at the "Election-day Battle" in Gallatin, Daviess County, Missouri. Ensuing troubles at nearby Adam-ondi-Ahman, Daviess County, then shifted to DeWitt in Carroll County, which was surrendered by the Mormons in October 1838. The illegal detention of three Saints in the camp of Missouri state militia under the command of Capt. Samuel Bogart consummated in the "Battle of Crooked River" in northwestern Ray County on October 25, 1838.

Emanating from reports of this armed conflict, the infamous "Order of Extermination" was issued by Missouri governor Lilburn W. Boggs at Jefferson City, October 27, 1838. A vicious attack by a mob force on the Mormon settlement of Haun's Mill in Caldwell County left seventeen men and boys dead and fifteen other persons wounded on October 30, 1838. Far West was surrounded by state militia, and Joseph Smith and other leading brethren were taken prisoner and conducted to the nearby camp of General Samuel D. Lucus, October 31, 1838.[185]

Timothy B. Foote, a Mormon elder living in Far West, visited the military camp. Though initially accosted and threatened in a very physical manner, he was allowed some latitude. He met McLellin among the troops and engaged him in conversation. Elder Foote explained:

> I walked around the entire guard, composed of about 200 men, who stood shoulder to shoulder around the prisoners, and was frequently saluted with terrible oaths and told to look for the last time on my Prophet, for his die was cast, &c. After passing around the guard, I passed on and met Wm. E. McLellan, formerly one of the Twelve Apostles. He was armed. I asked him to explain why he was there. He said "The Bible and all religion are matters of speculation and priestcraft from beginning to end, and 'Joe' is the biggest speculator of them all." I told him that I had heard him bear testimony that Joseph was a Prophet and that the Book of Mormon was true, and now he said to the contrary; and I asked him if he would tell me which time he lied! A crowd having gathered, McLellan slunk away, and I never saw him again.[186]

Parley P. Pratt, one of the prisoners with Joseph, also encountered McLellin in General Lucas's camp and described his conversation with him in these terms:

> While in this situation, Wm. E. McLellin, (who had once been intimate with me as a fellow laborer in the gospel, having deserted from the Church) came to me, (being one of the soldiers against us) and observed, "Well Parley, you have now got where you are certain never to escape; how do you feel as to the course you have taken in religion?" I replied that I had taken that course which I should take if I had my life to live over again. He seemed thoughtful for a moment, and then replied, "Well Parley, I think if I were you, I would die as I had lived: at any rate, I see no possibility of escape for you and your friends." This little interview gave us to understand that our doom was fixed in the minds of the people.[187]

McLellin likewise sought out Heber C. Kimball in Far West on November 1, 1838. He found Heber sitting on the ground, surrounded by Missourians and not having eaten for some twenty-four hours. Heber related:

> He came up to me and said "Bro. Heber what do you think of Joseph Smith the fallen prophet, now, has he not led you blindfolded long enough; look and see yourself poor, your family stripped and robbed, and your brethren in the same fix, are you satisfied with Joseph? I replied "Yes, I am more satisfied with him a hundred fold, than ever I was before, for I see you in the very position that he foretold you would be in; a Judas to betray your brethren, if you did not forsake your adultery, fornication, lying and abominations. Where are you? What are you about? you, and Hinkle, and scores of others; have you not betrayed Joseph and his brethren into the hands of the Mob, as Judas did Jesus? Yes, verily, you have; I tell you Mormonism is true, and Joseph is a true prophet of the living God, and you with all others that turn therefrom will be damned and go to hell, and Judas will rule over you.[188]

Ebenezer Page also met McLellin at Far West. He stated that "the redoubtable William was attached to Bogard's (Capt. Samuel Bogard's or Bogart's) company, and, harlequin like, decorated with red patches on his hat, shoulders, arms &c." Ebenezer reported that "William was the leader of a clan who went about from house to house, plundering the poor saints, and insulting both male and female." He credited McLellin with almost getting him shot and of singling him out to be included among the men who were marched to Richmond for the hearing held there.[189]

Joseph Smith had a succession of experiences with McLellin arising from the Mormon War. While the Prophet was attending the preliminary hearing trial at Richmond, conducted by Judge Austin A. King, November 12–28, 1838, William is reported to have asked the sheriff for the privilege of flogging Joseph. The sheriff was apparently willing if Joseph would fight. Joseph consented, providing that his irons be taken off. McLellin then asked for the additional assurance of a club to assist him, which request the sheriff refused because of the unfair advantage and would not allow any confrontation between the two.[190]

While the Prophet was incarcerated, witnesses prepared a sworn statement, which they presented to Col. Sterling Price, charging that

> William E McLellin is guilty of entering the house of Joseph Smith, Jun., in the city of Far West, and plundering it of the following articles, viz.— one roll of linen cloth, a quantity of valuable buttons, one piece of

cashmere, a number of very valuable books of great variety, a number
of vestings, with various other articles of value.

The witnesses also swore that McLellin had taken from Joseph's
stable a gig and harness and other articles.[191] John Lowe Butler was
likewise aware of McLellin's visit to the Smith home and gave added
information. He affirmed that McLellin had taken all the jewelry out
of Joseph's box and had also stolen a lot of bedclothes.[192]

During the April term of the Clay County Circuit Court in 1839,
Joseph Smith issued a complaint through his attorney, J. A. Gordon,
against McLellin to recover his property. McLellin was charged with
trespass in taking from him certain goods and chattels including a
library of books, specified yardages of broadcloth and calico, and
other articles valued at five hundred dollars. The accusation was
made that McLellin had failed to return these items "although often
requested so to do."[193]

At the instigation of Samuel Tillery, court clerk, the sheriff of
Clay County, Samuel Hadley, served a summons on McLellin on
March 22, 1839 (the summons was issued on March 6, 1839),
directing him to appear before the judge of the Clay Circuit Court on
April 15, 1839, to answer the "action of trespass."[194] On April 18,
1839, an answer to the complaint was entered on McLellin's behalf
by his attorney stating that he was not guilty of the charge. McLellin
and his attorney also petitioned the court requesting that the plaintiff "file a sufficient obligation with security for costs." The court
ordered the dismissal of the case "because said Plaintiff [Joseph
Smith] is wholly unable and without means or property to pay the
costs of this suit." Both parties in the suit had to be able to pay the
trial costs should the court rule against one or the other.[195]

Perhaps germane to the decision in the matter was the fact that
Joseph Smith was not present in Liberty or in court to propose any
alternative action. On April 18, he and others were in the process of
making their way out of Missouri, having escaped their captors while
on a change of venue from Gallatin to Columbia, Missouri.[196]

Anson Call stated that on January 15, 1839, he was invited to
the home of W. W. Phelps in Far West by Lyman Cowdery. In addition to Phelps and Cowdery, he found McLellin, David Whitmer,
Burr Riggs, and other apostates present. Cowdery was concerned
that Call had taken his brother Oliver Cowdery and David Whitmer

with a warrant for stealing certain goods belonging to Call and also items belonging to the Church while they were in transit between Kirtland and Far West. Lyman stated that Call had sworn falsely about goods which were not his and that he (Cowdery) had a bill in his pocket for their purchase in Cincinnati. He then intimidated him by explaining the punishment that hung over him. As a settlement in the matter, Cowdery proposed: "If you will go to the court with me at Richmond tomorrow and state that you did this [swore falsely concerning the identity of the goods] because Joe [Joseph Smith] told you so, that will then settle the matter and let the blame rest where it ought to." The attempt to find something against the Prophet by means of such coercion came to naught, however, when Anson Call refused to alter the oath he had taken in the matter.[197]

Activities in Iowa and Illinois

Emeline McLellin said, "We moved to Iowa from Clay Co." and specifically stipulated, "We never went to Nauvoo."[198] William McLellin later informed David Whitmer that "we lived near the mouth of Rock river, on the Mississippi, since 1839, until June, 1845."[199] Their removal to Iowa was probably some time following the April 1839 litigation involving Joseph Smith, Jr., and McLellin mentioned earlier. The family moved first to the area of Buffalo/Davenport, Scott County, Iowa. The McLellin family appears on the U.S. Census for Scott County in 1840. There were four children listed in the McLellin household as of June 1, 1840, which would have been Charles William, age six, Sarah Emeline, age four, James Martin, age 2, and an unknown female between fifteen and twenty months of age. McLellin practiced medicine there and reportedly attended Col. George L. Davenport and Antoine LeClaire, early proprietors of Davenport, Iowa. There is no confirmation of these events, and Dr. McLellin is not listed among the primary practitioners of Scott County in that period.[200]

It was said of McLellin that he "adopted the profession of medicine."[201] He makes periodic mention of his being "Doctor McLellin." He does not indicate where he acquired the skills of a medical doctor or with whom he may have trained. Nothing seems to have been said of his being a practicing physician prior to 1838.

However, he commented: "Dr. F. G. Williams practiced with me in Clay Co. Mo. during the latter part of 1838."[202] Possibly, he learned the art of medicine or at least expanded his skills through his association with Dr. Frederick G. Williams. Those who did not go to medical college acquired their professional knowledge in the offices of established practitioners. Williams had been a practicing physician for many years. He followed the eclectic system, borrowing methods from both the botanical and the more traditional medical systems. Oliver Cowdery referred to Williams as an "eminent and skillful man" and a "botanic physician—which course of practice is generally approved by us."[203] Even if Dr. Williams were not McLellin's mentor, certainly McLellin would have observed the techniques of his highly experienced colleague. As to his own method of practice, Dr. McLellin speaks of attending a "Botanico Medico Convention" in Kirtland in August 1846. In 1847 he assured his friend and medical colleague, Dr. John C. Bennett, that he had "a good stock of most of the Botanic remedies on hand" and in 1850 indentified himself as a "botanic physician."[204]

In 1844, McLellin explained to Sidney Rigdon that in 1840 he had moved into the little village of Hampton, Rock Island County, Illinois, living in a home that cost him nearly $1,000.[205] Land records confirm his purchase of two lots in the town of Hampton on March 2, 1841.[206] McLellin was now situated on the Illinois side of the Mississippi, a short distance from Scott County, Iowa Territory. A fifth child, Helen Rebecca McLellan, was introduced into the household during this transitory period, born in Hampton on February 11, 1843.[207]

At some time between his disaffection towards Joseph and the Church in Missouri and his forthcoming association with George M. Hinkle in Iowa, McLellin allegedly affiliated briefly with the Methodist faith, the circumstances of which remain vague.[208]

In the November 1839 issue of the *Times and Seasons,* members of the Twelve in Commerce (later Nauvoo), Illinois, warned the Saints, "We have heard that a man by the name of George M. Hinkle is preaching in the Iowa Territory, we would remark to the public, that we have withdrawn our fellowship from him, and will not stand accountable for any doctrines held forth by him."[209] The Brethren had excommunicated Hinkle on March 17, 1839, at Quincy, Illinois, for betraying Joseph Smith and other church leaders at Far West and turning them over to the Missouri state militia during the height of the Mormon War, October–November 1838.[210]

On June 24, 1840, Hinkle organized The Church of Jesus Christ, the Bride, the Lamb's Wife. The first conference was held in Moscow, Muscatine County, Iowa, on November 30, 1842, and the next four conferences were at the same location. At the fifth conference, which met at the home of Daniel Henderson in Moscow on September 16, 1843, the motion was made and seconded that

> William E. McLellin be ordained to the ministry in this church, and be united with elder Hinkle in bearing the glad tidings of salvation to the world. Carried unanimously, and he was duly set apart, by the laying on of hands, and straight way preached this to be the true, the only true church of God now on the earth.[211]

William and Emeline were again identified as being residents of Scott County, Iowa, on August 31, 1843, when he sold a fifteen-acre parcel of land in Rock Island County, Illinois.[212] McLellin next purchased property in Scott County, bordering on the Mississippi River on March 18, 1844.[213] These activities are indicative of an increased activity with George M. Hinkle in Buffalo, Scott County.

In the wake of the well-known *Nauvoo Expositor* incident on June 7, 1844, William Law, Wilson Law, Robert D. Foster, Austin Cowles, and James Blakeslee—who had been excommunicated on April 7 and had commenced publications opposing Joseph Smith—left Nauvoo with their families and traveled to Burlington, Iowa. William Law, formerly second counselor to Joseph Smith, wrote that on June 17, James Blakeslee, a counselor to Law in his church organization, set out from Burlington "for West Buffalo to visit Mr. McClellin and Mr. Hinkle, that we might know what they were about."[214]

When the sixth conference was held at Buffalo on June 24, 1844, McLellin was appointed secretary, and he also addressed the congregation on the subject of the apostleship. He "strongly urged the essential importance of the apostolic office in this church." Hinkle then addressed the church and from the scriptures spoke of the propriety of that office being established. Upon Hinkle's favorable response, the conference sanctioned the ordination of both Hinkle and McLellin to the high priesthood. The two men were then set apart as the first apostles in the church under the "apostolic plan of ministry." Next McLellin was called to join Elder Shortridge (previously named) as one of the two counselors in the presidency of the church.[215] A "long and warm debate" then ensued between Hinkle, McLellin, and others over whether the presiding authority should continue as it had been with Hinkle the presiding elder and the other two as counselors or, as McLellin wished, whether the three members of the presidency should "preside jointly and equally, one having no preeminence over the others." The conference voted that it be "left as they found it," until further examination at the October conference. McLellin had introduced an element of competition or vying for leadership which caused Hinkle to recoil.[216]

At Buffalo on July 15, 1844, Hinkle and McLellin became the publishers of a periodical entitled the *Ensign*. The *Ensign* was devoted to the "religious principles and views of 'The Church of Jesus Christ, the Bride the Lamb's Wife.'" Its "pole-star" was to be "religion—pure and undefiled religion." McLellin served as editor of the paper until October 1844, when the ongoing dispute with Hinkle over the plan of government caused his resignation. William's "Farewell Address" from the editorship appears in the October issue.[217]

The residue of the June 1844 conference debate over the functioning of the presidency continued to fester at the conference held on October 7, 1844, in the Liberty schoolhouse in Louisa County, Iowa. McLellin's proposal for a three-man, rotating presidency, each taking a turn at presiding, "was not relished by the church." Recognizing that his plan was not in favor, McLellin "withdrew all his motions on the subject" and "exhorted the church to remain under the old order of ministry." He confessed his error in attempting the change of the presidency, requested their pardon, and returned home.[218]

Within a matter of days, the disenchanted McLellin left Buffalo for Hampton, Illinois, where he still had a residence on lots one and two. He had very nearly lost this property through an 1843 sheriff's sale but was able to redeem the same through the appropriate legal channels by 1844.[219] In Hampton he met with William Law and his counselors, Austin Cowles and James Blakeslee, who had chosen that community in which to live for the present. What influence McLellin may have had in their selection is an open question. While strengthening ties with these men, he also came in contact with Wilson Law, Robert D. Foster, Charles A. Foster, and John C. Bennett, all of whom had located in Hampton. After returning to Buffalo and engaging in a heated argument with Hinkle, McLellin severed his association with the Hinkle organization and established himself at Hampton. By December 18, 1844, he had sold his Scott County, Iowa property.[220]

Meanwhile, the martyred Prophet's two former counselors, Sidney Rigdon and William Law, had been exchanging serious correspondence concerning the ultimate interests of the two organizations which they now represented. In the midst of these entreaties, McLellin wrote to Rigdon on December 23, 1844:

> With feelings of no ordinary character I seat myself to address a few lines to you. . . . The first bright beam of sunshine—PERMANENT ray of hope which I have been enabled to discover, since the people of God in the last days began to apostatise . . . has now made its appearance in the separation of two of the first presidency with their friends, from the great body of that people, who work iniquity. . . .
>
> The Lord has shown to me that by a union of President Law and yourself, together with each, your friends, that all the honest in heart among the Latter Day Saints and throughout the world will UNITE. . . . I have seen all the communications between you and pres. Law, and I am pleased with the spirit that they breathe. My word for it that Wm. Law and his brethren who are here with him, are men of inestimable value in the things of God. . . .
>
> We are in daily expectation of your answer to Pres. W. Law's last letter to you. I do not know (as yet) whether it is my duty to wait till the northern wind ceases to freeze before I speed my way to you. One thing certain I shall move as directed.[221]

Association with Sidney Rigdon

At Hampton, McLellin professed to have received a revelation on January 7, 1845, directing him to "go with MY SERVANT WILLIAM LAW [to Pittsburgh, Pennsylvania, for consultation with Sidney Rigdon and his fellows], and stand by each other in all right principles, and even in perils if need be; for with him I the Lord am well pleased." He reported the additional admonishment, "Yea, I say unto you again, go with him, and go speedily unto the east, where you can unite with my servants who are willing to forsake all for Christ's truth."[222]

Beginning with a January 19, 1845, entry, James Blakeslee chronicles in his journal the next strategic move:

And now, as the Lord had made known to us our Duty concerning his people immediately Elders Wm Law & WE McLellin made the nessesary [*sic*] preparation, and Being Recommended by the ~~Church~~ <Brethren> at Hampton, started for Pittsburgh PA. January the 30th 1845, in a buggy wagon drawn by two horses, and we who were left behind continued to hold meetings as usual.[223]

Soon after their March arrival in Pittsburgh, William Law was invited by Sidney Rigdon to preach to his congregation; he addressed them "concerning the sins of Nauvoo."[224] Their presence in Pittsburgh was timed to coincide with the conference announced by Rigdon for April 6 to 11. While awaiting the forthcoming sessions, McLellin made use of his time by directing a letter on March 15 to the editor of Rigdon's *Messenger and Advocate*. In it he outlined the rise of the Church from 1830 and stated his views as to the person or persons to whom "the first Authority or first presidency of the church of Christ, rightly and legally belongs, since the death of Joseph Smith." In conclusion, McLellin asked the questions, "What man now living has had the most extensive knowledge and experience in the church of Christ, since the year 1830?—The year of its birth. Who is it that has presided jointly—shall I say equally with Joseph Smith in all its councils, in all its general assemblies?" And in response to his own query, McLellin declared, "I answer distinctly and emphatically that that man is President Sidney Rigdon. I feel my interest identified with his, and I feel also to stand by him in all righteousness before God while he stands as a man of God, to plead with the world."[225]

A conference of Rigdon's church commenced on April 6, 1845, in their hall at 201 Liberty Street, Pittsburg. During the Monday, April 7, session, it was proposed and carried that Sidney Rigdon be the "first president of this kingdom and church, and to stand as prophet, seer, revelator and translator, to this church and kingdom of Christ of the last days." McLellin "then stepped forward in obedience to the word of the Lord to him in a vision, and took the president by the hand, and declared his determination to stand by him and his family in all righteousness before God until the time of the end." McLellin was named as one of the clerks of the conference along with Joseph M. Cole and George W. Robinson.[226] McLellin was also appointed to the apostleship.[227]

As the conference session opened on April 8, it was moved and seconded that the organization presently called The Church of Jesus Christ of Latter Day Saints be known simply as The Church of Christ. During the course of that day, it became increasingly apparent that the unification correspondence and discussions between the churches sponsored by Sidney Rigdon and William Law had opened doors for members of Law's church to be integrated into the Rigdonite organization.[228]

McLellin bid Sidney Rigdon farewell at the wharf in Pittsburgh on April 14, 1845, as McLellin boarded the steamboat *Yucatan* and headed down the Ohio. He traveled west with Hinkle and Samuel James. McLellin was given liberty to address the passengers. Half way through the sermon, a cabin boy about twelve years old fell overboard. Despite efforts to save him, he "sank to rise and breath no more until the 'sound of the last trump.'" This sad event broke up the sermon.[229]

At Louisville, Kentucky, McLellin separated from his companions and journeyed to Tennessee. He said that he had not originally intended to do so but that he had been moved by the Spirit, which revealed to him that if he went to visit his father, Charles McLellan, that he would have the privilege of baptizing him into The Church of Christ and would then receive a father's blessing at his hands. William first called on his older brother Samuel and then traveled some twenty-five miles to the home of his younger brother Israel with whom his father resided in the vicinity of northeastern Smith County, Tennessee.[230]

William likened himself to the prodigal son, now returning after an absence of sixteen years to call on his seventy-nine-year-old father, whom he had not seen since 1829. His older brother Samuel was a local Methodist preacher, his younger brother Israel professed no religion, and his sister, Nancy McLellan Law, belonged to what William termed "the Christian order" or The Church of Christ, which met in the old Bagdad meetinghouse just across the line in Jackson County. McLellin was able to secure the Methodist meetinghouse for a Sunday appointment and there addressed the people "among whom I had been born and brought up."[231]

That afternoon, May 4, 1845, Charles McLellan confessed that he believed with all his heart what had been taught and that he wished to be baptized by his son. William and his father, with some other family members, went to the Cumberland River, where the ordinance was performed. Reflecting on that moment, McLellin elatedly exclaimed, "My Father in the flesh is in the kingdom of the Lord O my soul!" The following day, at the home of his sister, McLellin confirmed his father and ordained him to the higher priesthood. He then had the privilege of receiving a blessing under the hands of his parent, just as the Spirit had whispered to him while on the Ohio River.[232]

On May 6, before leaving for Hampton, Illinois, McLellin presented a copy of the Book of Mormon to his father. One of his oldest brother's sons, John P., age twenty-two, accompanied him on his return home, traveling by way of Nashville to St. Louis. On May 16 at Nauvoo, they found that the Saints were putting up the rafters of the temple. The pair finally arrived in Hampton on May 17.[233]

After only a moment's respite, McLellin, accompanied by Austin Cowles, set out on May 20, 1845, for West Buffalo, Iowa. There they joined with Hinkle and Blakeslee in conducting a conference. Through the combined efforts of these men, nearly one hundred persons accepted baptism under the Rigdonite covenant.[234] Among those baptized was Harvey Whitlock, who had come some fifty miles from his home in Cedar County, Iowa. Whitlock was the man who, with David Whitmer, had first introduced Mormonism to McLellin at Paris, Illinois, in July 1831. McLellin performed the ordinance in the Mississippi River. Relative to this singular moment, McLellin reported to Sidney Rigdon, "My father in the flesh, and my father in the gospel, are both in this kingdom; and I have been privileged to introduce them since I last saw you." McLellin and Blakeslee continued ministering in the region until May 29, 1845.[235]

McLellin informed Rigdon that he and his family intended to move from Hampton, Illinois, to Pittsburgh, Pennsylvania, in mid-June 1845. Emeline gave birth to their sixth child, Albert Eugene McLellan, on June 2, 1845 in Scott County, Iowa.[236] McLellin was in Buffalo, Iowa, on June 15 and assisted Blakeslee in confirming Blakeslee's wife following her baptism. And on June 16, McLellin participated in the washing and anointing of fourteen priesthood-bearers during a conference held in a West Buffalo home. On June 17, he and Austin Cowles bade a fond farewell to the Saints in Buffalo.

Blakeslee called it "a melting time in deed not an eye in the whole congregation but that was bathed in tears." McLellin and Cowles then returned to Hampton for the final days before their move to Pennsylvania. At last, James Blakeslee stated, on June 24, "at the Break of day Br. W.E. Mclellin and family stoped [*sic*] at Buffalo on his way to pittsburgh, on the steamer, Fortune, all well and in good spirits."[237]

In July 1845, Benjamin Winchester, who had been called as one of the Rigdonite Twelve in The Church of Christ, entreated Sidney Rigdon to send McLellin to Philadelphia to assist in combating the likes of Parley P. Pratt and a "flare up among the twelvites" in that city.[238] McLellin left Pittsburgh with Rigdon on August 1, 1845 "to visit some of the interior counties" of Pennsylvania and perhaps some of the eastern cities.[239] Although not much is recorded concerning their journey, it is evident that it included a visit to the Cumberland Valley and "Adventure Farm," about one and one-half miles west of the village of Greencastle, Franklin County, Pennsylvania, some fifty-nine miles southwest of Harrisburgh. This area was soon to be the designated gathering place for the The Church of Christ. McLellin bore strong testimony of its virtues in a later item of correspondence to Bishop William Richards.[240]

While Rigdon returned to Pittsburgh, McLellin boarded the train at Chambersburgh for the trip to Philadelphia on August 12. The wonder of modern engineering caused McLellin to comment, "We rolled on something at the rate of 2 miles in four minutes. This thought I as we trunnelled along is next to flying."[241] In the "city of brotherly love," McLellin sought to correct some problems of internal dissention which were tearing the branch apart. McLellin reported to Rigdon, "We had an appointment for the church to come together; they came, and with but little difficulty we buried the hatchet so deep that we lost sight of the end of the handle. Fellowship and peace are restored to the saints here."[242]

Working out of Philadelphia, McLellin visited other eastern branches. He was in Woodstown, New Jersey, the latter part of August 1845, where he baptized two people. McLellin then returned to Philadelphia and baptized four on September 4. He next arrived in New York City on September 5, where he proselyted for a time.[243] McLellin was again in Philadelphia for a conference of The Church of Christ on October 6-8, 1845. Sidney Rigdon and other primary leaders were present. McLellin took his seat as one of the secretaries of the conference. Among the items of business was the elevation of George M. Hinkle to the Rigdonite Quorum of the Twelve, replacing J. M. Cole.[244]

Separation from the Rigdonites

Once again, William E. McLellin's life took a dramatic turn. In the Philadelphia conference of October 1845, he had borne a testimony of "faith and confidence in the truth of the work."[245] However, by December he was again cut adrift, casting about for answers arising from a new crisis. At a meeting of the Grand Council held in Pittsburgh on December 9, 1845, Benjamin Winchester and Richard Savary were charged by Josiah Ells with transgression. On examination it was found that the charges were not brought according to the laws of the quorum. The meeting was adjourned until Saturday, December 13, when the cases would be heard according to law. But Winchester, one of the Rigdonite Twelve, and Savary, a member of the Grand Council, voluntarily withdrew rather than be tried by that body.[246]

McLellin, a personal friend of Benjamin Winchester, had taken strong exception to the rebuke of these two men by Rigdon. When the Grand Council met on December 13, McLellin was not seated, as he had been suspended for transgression by the First Presidency until the next April conference. President Rigdon then presented his suspension of McLellin to the council in the form of a proposition:

> I am now about to put a question around this council, therefore raise your hearts to the Lord, that you may be prepared to act in righteousness before him—I say, I did the will of the Lord in the case of suspending brother M'Lellin? Passed in the affirmative. It is known, that in this house an attempt was made to injure me, because I had rebuked two men. Now the question I wish to ask this council, (in whose presence this attempt was made,) is this, If the statements, made by those men had been true, would they, in your estimation militate against my character as a prophet? To which every member of the council replied, in his place, "they would not."[247]

McLellin put in a personal appearance at the Grand Council meeting on December 30, 1845. He "came forward and refused to stand his trial, and vacated his seat." Without hesitation the Council then proposed and passed on the name of William Bickerton of

West Elizabeth, Pennsylvania, to fill his seat in the Grand Council. McLellin's position in the Quorum of the Rigdonite Twelve was later filled by the appointment of Algernon S. Rigdon in the April 1846 conference.[248]

Sidney Rigdon printed a powerfully worded denunciation of McLellin in the February 1846 issue of the *Messenger and Advocate*.[249] In the March issue, Rigdon again took William to task for his February correspondence to Leonard Soby in which he tried to convince Soby that the true place of gathering should be Kirtland, Ohio, and not the Cumberland Valley in south central Pennsylvania, as designated by Rigdon.[250]

In defining his own position in relation to Rigdon, McLellin later affirmed to David Whitmer, "At the death of Joseph Smith, I looked around and reflected, and I finally hoped that S. Rigdon had reformed, as he said, and that he would assist in carrying out the original design of God in raising up his church." William then explained to his friend, "I united with him, and remained about six months. But I found in him (after a little trial) hypocrisy, dishonesty and fanaticism. I saw that with him I could have no hope of future prosperity, so as to bring in 'the rest of God.' I quit him."[251]

McLellin reportedly combined with his friend Austin W. Cowles in an attempt to form the nucleus of an organization. However, their association was but momentary, each choosing to go in a different direction.[252]

Return to Ohio and Encounter with the Strangites

McLellin moved Emeline and the children from Pittsburgh to the township of Shalersville, Portage County, Ohio (immediately north of Ravenna), where they arrived on April 12, 1846. Here he again established his medical practice. In an August 14, 1846, letter to his friend Dr. John C. Bennett (in Voree, Wisconsin), he remarked, "I have engaged in my old profession of medicine. I have secured already a very considerable ride, and my business is increasing as the people become more and more acquainted with me."[253] Enlarging on his medical experiences in the area, he informed Bennett:

> I reached home last night about 11, P. M., from Kirtland, where I have been attending a Botanico Medico convention. Some fifteen or twenty

> Dr.'s were present, and we had a very good and interesting time. Dr. Tilletson [also Tillotson], from Thompson, lectured in the afternoon of the 12th on the history of the different modes of practice, and was very ingenious, amusing and interesting. By unanimous vote I was requested to lecture in the evening. I consented, and for two hours I guess the walls of that superb edifice, "the Temple of God," re-echoed with the sound of "m[e]rcury, m[e]rcury, and the m[e]rcury dealers." J. J. Strang, from Voree, was one of my audience.[254]

McLellin concluded his letter to Dr. Bennett with the query, "How would you like to have a partner?" He assured Bennett that if he thought there was room for two he would spend the winter practicing with him. He stated, "I have a good stock of most of the Botanic remedies on hand. I have a good horse, buggy and cutter, all of which I could bring."[255] The proposed partnership never reached fruition.

James J. Strang and William Smith had arrived in Kirtland on August 7, 1846, from Voree, Wisconsin for a four-day conference of Strang's adherents in the area. Strang organized a stake of Zion there with Leonard Rich as stake president; Jacob Bump as bishop; and Martin Harris called as a missionary to England.[256] James J. Strang conversed with McLellin freely while the two were in Kirtland and then visited McLellin at his home in Shalersville on August 17, 1846. McLellin later reported that Strang

> laid siege to me in order to have me unite with him in his organization. I gave him some encouragement, and took the matter under advisement, but the more I prayed and reflected, the more I have doubted his claims. He has published my name as one of THE TWELVE, but he did so entirely contrary to my will or wish.[257]

McLellin's "encouragement" appears to have had some substance. On September 30, 1846, he again wrote from Shalersville to John C. Bennett, counselor to Strang, stating, "Would to God that this morning I was wending my way (instead of writing this) to Voree, in order to attend the conference to be holden there on the 6th proximo . . . but, the Lord preserving my life, it will only be a few months. . . . Before I will be among you."[258] Apparently McLellin's conversations with Strang plus such entreaties as this were sufficient for Strang to suppose he had drawn William into the net. However, it should be noted that in a later debate with Strang, McLellin stoutly denied ever having written "any such letters as he [Strang] has pretended to publish" and likewise denied that Strang had ever

ordained him to the apostleship or that he had joined with him
at all.[259] But Strang countered in that same debate by introducing to the moderator and audience actual letters sent both to
himself and to Bennett in McLellin's own handwriting and signed
by him. The letters give substantive evidence of McLellin's affiliation with the Strangites and certainly implied his having priesthood in the organization.[260]

Jacob Bump and others who were initial adherents to the
Strangite movement certainly felt that McLellin was making definite overtures and had written to Strang from Kirtland in October
1846 saying:

> Br. Wm. E. mcClenlan came to this place came in to [our] thursday
> Evening meeting and gave us a good Lecture he thinks of going to
> voree to do that which the [Lord] has for him to do and we think
> Br Strang that he may and will do much good for the Saints, he is a
> strong man tryed and faithful, will go his whole soul for that wich is
> right he is a deserning person and . . . has suffered much by matter
> presented to him & the Church that was not of God.[261]

The McLellins moved to Kirtland from Shalersville on October 29, 1846, in order to be nearer to a small nucleus of the "church
of Christ" with whom McLellin felt compatible, the members of
which were then imbued with the teachings of James J. Strang. They
numbered about one hundred persons and were presided over by
Leonard Rich. This body met in the Kirtland Temple at least four
times weekly.[262] Besides Jacob Bump and Martin Harris, others
affiliating with that congregation were Jeremiah Knight, Hazen
Aldrich, Alfred Bonney, and Miss Mary E. Bond. Still later, J. P. Noble,
Isaac Dudley, and Cornelius Davis united with them.[263]

Whatever alliances McLellin may have previously formed with
Strang, he severed his ties with that organization, as did a majority
of the members of the Strangite stake in Kirtland. McLellin's
withdrawal brought a stinging rebuke from the editor of *Zion's
Reveille*: "[McLellin] returned to the true church under the prophet
James, and has now A-P-O-S-T-A-T-I-Z-E-D again, because he could not
be one of the first Presidency. . . . O, William, arch-apostate! who can
hereafter have the least confidence in such a perfidious monster of
iniquity? Cease to pervert the right ways of the Lord, and utterly
forsake your adulterous propensities."[264] This rebuff was followed in

succeeding issues by a series of attacks on McLellin's integrity, backed by reported documentation of his duplicity in the matter.[265] McLellin made a retort of his own in April 1847 relative to the validity of Strang's foundational claims.[266]

Seeking the "Old Foundation"

After months of personal struggle and contemplation over the course to be taken in aligning himself with the true church of the restoration, McLellin wrote to David Whitmer on December 2, 1846. He informed David that for more than three years he had been trying to "get back on the old foundation," but that he had now "been shown that the church would prosper, if David [Whitmer] and Oliver [Cowdery] would step forward into her front rank, and occupy their proper places before the Lord, their brethren, and the world."[267] He reminded David that in July of 1834, following the march of Zion's Camp, Joseph Smith had laid hands on Whitmer's head and ordained him to succeed him as seer. And by the Lord's own words that should Joseph transgress he (Joseph) "should not have power except to appoint another." McLellin insisted that Joseph had transgressed and thus the Lord had appointed Whitmer to lead and he must not shrink from his duty.[268]

McLellin explained that "Kirtland . . . is the very place where God designs to build up his kingdom, and to establish his saints, that the pure in heart may gather here from all the world."[269] If Whitmer would but consent to come to Kirtland, an announcement would be made of a June 1847 conference to be held in the house of the Lord. There the church would be reorganized "upon her old foundation." Jacob Bump offered to "fit up" a house for David to live in. McLellin expressed the desire that both David and Oliver make Kirtland their home.[270]

McLellin and the Kirtland congregation waited in vain for a communication from Richmond, Missouri. Neither Whitmer nor Cowdery ever came to take their station. The Kirtland membership continued to organize with continued anticipation, however. The *Ensign of Liberty, of The Church of Christ* was published under the editorship of William E. McLellin commencing with the March 1847 issue. On May 26, 1847, McLellin left Kirtland for Pittsburgh, where he both preached and met with such old friends as Benjamin

Winchester. Then he returned home for the June 21 conference of
The Church of Christ.[271]

McLellin was authorized by the conference to take a tour
through the western states, ostensibly to travel to Richmond where
he could meet face to face with David Whitmer and procure a
response to their inquiry. McLellin left Kirtland on July 6, and did not
return until November 3, 1847. He first journeyed to Voree, Wisconsin, where he was successful in organizing a branch of The Church
of Christ numbering between forty and fifty persons, right in the
heart of the Strangite movement.[272]

He also made an important call at the home of Oliver
Cowdery in Elkhorn, Walworth County, Wisconsin, to solicit
Oliver's participation in the movement and to ask him to exert his
influence in causing David Whitmer's acceptance of the presidency. Following McLellin's visit, Oliver wrote to David concerning the situation:

> So far as I understand his labor, it has simply been directed to one great
> object—to wit: in preparing, or endeavoring to prepare the way for the
> old ship to unhitch her cables and again sail forth. . . .
>
> We may not live to see the day, but we have the authority, and
> do hold the keys. It is important should we not be permitted to act in
> that authority, that we confer them upon some man or men, whom God
> may appoint, that this priesthood be not taken again from the earth till
> the earth be sanctified. I want to see you much on this great matter.
>
> That our brother william has been directed and influenced in
> what he has been doing by the Holy Spirit, I need not say to you I fully
> believe. I do not say that every thing he has done has been done by
> inspiration—it would be strange if it were so. But that God has touched
> his heart, that he might begin to prepare the way, I have no doubt. In
> this doing he has done well, and he will in no wise lose his reward. . . .
>
> You will talk this matter all over, and make all the necessary
> enquiry, and I will only say that when the time comes, I am ready! But
> I am not persuaded that it has yet fully come.[273]

McLellin next traveled south into Illinois, where he organized
a small branch at the "head of Plum River, Jo Davis County," in
August. McLellin was in Nauvoo, Illinois, by August 28 and visited
with Emma Smith Bidamon. He asked Emma what confidence she
had in the Book of Mormon and the work of the last days. McLellin
said, "Her answer was prompt—'I have all confidence in that spirit

of intelligence by which the book of Mormon was translated, and by which the revelations were given to the church in the beginning.'"[274]

Moving directly to Richmond, Missouri, McLellin arrived on September 4 and lodged with David Whitmer. They sat up until one o'clock in the morning conversing. Two days later, David Whitmer, Jacob Whitmer, Hiram Page, and McLellin drove to Far West, where they conferred with John Whitmer for two days and nights. McLellin reported to them a revelation received in Kirtland on February 10, 1847, relative to the rebaptism and the reordination of all adherents to The Church of Christ. The revelation was read, approved, and acted upon. McLellin rebaptized Whitmer and the others in a nearby stream; he then confirmed each of them. This was followed by a succession of re-ordinations of all present. Whitmer was re-ordained "to all the gifts and callings to which he had been appointed through Joseph Smith, in the general assembly of the inhabitants of Zion, in July 1834."[275]

David Whitmer received a revelation that McLellin was to build up the church in the land of Kirtland. But the voice to the others specified, "A commandment I give unto you my servant David, and also my servants John, and Hiram, and Jacob, that you must remain until I command you, and then you shall only be permitted to visit the faithful in my kingdom. For now ye do hold the right of this, the consecrated land of Zion."[276] John Whitmer and Oliver Cowdery were appointed counselors to David Whitmer in the presidency. David appointed McLellin "president to stand in relation to me as [Oliver] stood to Joseph," with responsibilities "to build up the church of Christ in Kirtland." Jacob Whitmer and Hiram Page were ordained high priests.[277]

McLellin had supposed that Kirtland would become the home of David Whitmer, "the Lord's Prophet," and was greatly disap-pointed that Whitmer was unwilling to make that commitment. But at least he left with what was then considered to be a clear mandate from David to continue his labors in Ohio. However, the approbation of the Whitmers, Oliver Cowdery, and Hiram Page would later change. McLellin visited Independence briefly and then again passed through Nauvoo, where he saw "that superb structure, 'the Nauvoo Temple,'" and visited with Lucy Smith, mother of the Prophet, commenting that, "Her faith and confidence in her religion, seemed only to have gathered strength by the varying vicissitudes through which she had passed during a long life."[278]

He attended the "Hinklite" conference in Mercer County, Illinois, on October 6, 1847. There he found Samuel James, formerly a counselor to Sidney Rigdon, and George Hinkle, previously a member of the Rigdonite Twelve, who had also departed the faith and were now organizing anew. McLellin said, "We saw and heard strange things."[279] McLellin also visited Voree, Wisconsin, where he and James J. Strang locked horns in a lengthy public debate.[280] After preaching in Voree and holding a brief meeting with Oliver Cowdery in Elkhorn, McLellin was again in Kirtland on November 3, 1847.[281]

As the year 1848 dawned on The Church of Christ in Kirtland, the congregation numbered forty-two, "all at peace and fellowship among themselves." Marcus Nelson McLellan, a seventh child, was welcomed into the home, February 9, 1848.[282] If harmony existed in the ranks of The Church of Christ, McLellin could not find the same among another Kirtland group by the same name, commonly known as the Brewsterites. He attended their conference in Kirtland in June 1848. On the third day, their small membership split into two factions, one going with Austin Cowles, the other with Hazen Aldrich. McLellin commented, "I was present when Pres. Aldrich dismissed his general assembly—but it only consisted of himself and two others, and I as spectator—Poor thing, thought I, let it die!"[283]

McLellin was perhaps unknowingly echoing his own demise. Symptomatic of the decline was the irregularity of the publication of the *Ensign of Liberty*. Fifteen months slipped away from the May 1848 issue to the August 1849 number because of a lack of promised financial support. McLellin hastened to assure his readers, in what proved to be the last printing, that "the want of means to publish our paper has not prevented the church of Christ in this place from holding their meetings punctually."[284]

The death knell may well have been sounded from an unexpected quarter. On behalf of David Whitmer, Hiram Page prepared a lengthy and carefully worded letter "to all the saints scattered abroad," in which a number of key elements of "brother William's" organization and doctrine were soundly denounced. The letter, dated from Richmond, Missouri, June 24, 1849, declared:

> In 1847 brother William commenced vindicating our characters as honest men; in that he done well. In September 1848, he made us a visit and professed to have been moved upon by the same spirit of God that led him to do us justice by vindicating our characters, moved upon him to come here and have us organize ourselves in a church capacity; but it must come through him, which would give a sanction to all that he had done, which would give a more speedy rise to the cause than anything else could. . . .
>
> But we had not as yet come to an understanding, but consented to the organization after three days of successive entreaties. Now we acknowledge that the organization was not in accordance with the order of the Gospel Church. As we observed that we had not come to an understanding, it infers that we now have, or we think we have come to understanding, and the understanding which we have received is as follows.[285]

Hiram Page then enumerated the criteria by which the church should be governed, among which were:

> 1. That the office of High Priest does not belong to the church of Christ under the gospel dispensation, and that all offices filled exclusively by High Priests are null and void.
>
> 2. The office of a Seer is not, nor never has been the means by which the Lord intended his church should be governed. . . .
>
> 3. That the gathering dispensation has not come, and every effort of men to bring about the gathering of the saints into bodies, is only sowing the seeds of discord, and is heaping upon the innocent many calamities which might be avoided.[286]

At the conclusion of his declaration, Hiram Page observed, "It is evident that the way is not opened for us to organize as we should; but when the way is opened, we shall organize according to the Apostolic order."[287]

After this repudiation by David Whitmer—the very source of his projected authority—of these and other basic tenets, McLellin sought vindication. The August number of the *Ensign of Liberty* was devoted to a moment-by-moment description of his course of action while with the Whitmers and of their responses at the time. McLellin felt that these men had in no way been overly persuaded and their actions, tempered by revelation from the Lord, had been measured enough to make a solid decision.[288]

The Church of Christ in Kirtland, under McLellin's tutelage, did not withstand the rude blast. The Brewsterites, who in 1848 had labeled McLellin as their "most violent opposer," took satisfaction in June 1850 from the fact that his once-flourishing organization had "been completely disorganized" and had "passed out of existence."[289]

"Not an L.D. Saint of Any Click or Party"

McLellin purchased land in Chester township in the western limits of Geauga County, Ohio, on March 18, 1853.[290] McLellin is reported to have served as postmaster at Chester Cross Roads, Chester Township. He also practiced medicine in the community. Among his patients was Nancy Young Kent, sister of Brigham Young.[291]

From "Chester + Roads," McLellin addressed a lengthy letter to his former yokemate, Orson Pratt, dated April 29, 1854, in response to correspondence which Orson had directed to McLellin from Baltimore on April 21. Orson had given him a warm, personal invitation "to go to Salt Lake City, and throw [himself] and energies into the bosom of *that church.*" Pratt also affirmed that "I most earnestly desire to see *you repent,* if repentance is for you; of this, I cannot judge."[292]

Though somewhat genial, McLellin explained that he need not go "all the tedious way to Utah to learn the will of God concerning himself." He had "learned to know the voice of the spirit of God clothed in words," through visions and revelations which he had received since his initial experience with Joseph Smith. "Hence," he observed, "I know I am not cast off forever." He maintained that on an individual basis, "I only need to bring my heart right before God, and exercise great faith in him, and humble prayer before him, (which is my high privilege) in order to obtain 'Wisdom from God, and knowledge from heaven.'"[293]

As for repentance, McLellin concluded,

> I care not for the judgement that men pass upon *me* in this matter. But I have not in this letter called upon You, or upon *that Church* to repent. For I do not believe that they as a people can repent. Even though they, like Ninevah, should sit in sack-cloth and ashes; or like Esau, should see it earnestly and carefully with tears. For they have polluted every holy thing ever committed to their charge and have committed all manner of abominations in the sight of the Heavens.[294]

In the communication, McLellin unfolded item for item what he considered to be the excesses of Mormonism from 1834 (before which, he believed, the Prophet had acted rightly) to the present. Included in the doctrines and practices which he considered repugnant to his faith were the practice of war in 1834 with the march of Zion's Camp; changing the name of the Church, likewise in 1834; the failure of the sought-for endowment of 1836; and the disastrous merchandizing, speculation, and pride and the development of "ruinous-rotten banking" associated with the Kirtland Safety Society. He further renounced

> the Tithing of the members of one tenth of all their property. Their baptisms for the dead. . . . Their popishly combining the spiritual and temporal power in the Head of the Church. Their doctrine of the generation of spirits. Their system of plurality of Gods-and God making. Their doctrine of polygamy-the plurality of wives and concubines, and their exaltations consequent upon the foregoing.[295]

After McLellin had meticulously laid out for Orson Pratt the practices which he abhorred, he enjoined, "Hence you see your home among the mountains would be no *home* to me. Your people could not be my people nor your God my God."

In settling some old affairs, McLellin gave a quitclaim deed to F. F. Allen for his Kirtland City property on July 17, 1854, and still later, while in the process of moving to Michigan, William sold his Kirtland township acreage to Hiram Dixon, on September 28, 1859.[296]

The McLellins moved to Genesee County, Michigan, in 1859.[297] While living there, their daughter Helen married Lafayette W. Clarke on December 9, 1863. The young couple had two children during the family's stay in Genesee County: Grace in 1864 and Sidney Burdette in 1866.[298] McLellin was a prodigious letter writer. It is by scraps of surviving correspondence that we occasionally catch a glimpse of his whereabouts and activities during another transitory period in his life. Writing from Linden, Genesee County, Michigan, on January 10, 1861, McLellin addressed the newly identified head of the Reorganized Church of Jesus Christ of Latter Day Saints, Joseph Smith III, giving a brief history of his experience with Smith's father to more recent times. He explained that "for some dozen years past I have been retired from all religious organizations—following my professional business [that of medicine]."[299]

McLellin felt it his "solemn duty" to lay certain items before the Prophet's son. McLellin reminded him that at Amboy, Illinois, in April 1860, Smith had spoken of the Prophet and said, "I believe my Father was a good man." In that speech, he had also condemned the practice of polygamy. McLellin explained that the two statements were incompatible. The Prophet could not be called a "good man" because he participated in that "diabolical" principle. McLellin said to him, "I do not wish to say hard things to You of your Father, but Joseph, if You will only go to your own dear Mother, she can tell You that he believed in Polygamy and practiced it long before his violent death! That he delivered a revelation sanctioning, regulating, and establishing it." McLellin then begged Joseph, "Take not your own dear Father for a pattern in your religious career. Altho he might have had some good traits, Yet in all that constitutes pure-God-like goodness he was woefully lacking! If you have determined to be Great in the eyes of God, then do carve out your own course, but not pattern after his."[300] McLellin was relentless in his disparagement of the Prophet Joseph Smith's character and of his activities in the period after 1833.

Though dropping out of the limelight as a religious leader, McLellin commenced a line of correspondence with Granville Hedrick in 1864. McLellin said that he received more than a dozen letters from him in that exchange.[301] Hedrick was then living one and one-half miles west of Washburn, Illinois, and headed the Church of Jesus Christ of Latter Day Saints (Hedrickite). In the October 1864 issue of that denomination's publication, *The Truth Teller*, Hedrick published one of McLellin's letters, which was postmarked Union Corners, Genesee County, Michigan. The substance of the letter was a doctrinal treatise on the "one universal, immutable *Law* existing and governing the whole in all ages of man, on this earth . . . both God and man's right to direct intercourse. The Lord's right to speak, and men's right to hear and his duty to obey."[302]

A tragic aftermath of the Civil War period visited the McLellin household on May 6, 1865, with the death of their son, Albert Eugene, age nineteen. Albert had enlisted as a private in Company C, 16th Michigan Infantry, on January 15, 1862. He was honorably discharged on April 18 or 21, 1862, because of a disability. However, Albert was again recruited in Munday Township, Genesee County,

Michigan, and enlisted in Detroit on April 19, 1864. He was assigned as a private to the 27th Infantry Regiment, Michigan Volunteers, Company A. As recorded in the regimental roll, Albert Eugene McLellan was "wounded severely [in action] 7/30/64 before Gettysburg [Pa.], [in] Va., Absent since." Albert returned to his Michigan home but regrettably "died May 6, 1865 of an accidental shot." He was buried in the Gage Cemetery, Fenton Township, Genesee County, Michigan.[303]

There were those who recognized the potential that was curtailed during McLellin's self-imposed exile from direct association with organized religion. Emma Smith Bidamon spoke positively of McLellin to her son Joseph Smith III in a communication from Nauvoo on February 2, 1866, as she observed,

> I hope that Wm. E. McLellen will unearth his long burried talents, and get them into circulation before it is everlastingly too late for his own good as well as for the benefit of others, for he is certainly a talented man.[304]

McLellin never chose to affiliate with the Reorganization because of philosophical and doctrinal differences, attempting only to lend his advisory talents through correspondence and conversation—wherever accepted.

Return to the West

At least some members of the McLellin family were again on the move in 1865, this time back to Missouri. James M. McLellan, a son, purchased land in the town of Troy, Lincoln County, Missouri, on November 25, 1865.[305] When James M. McLellan and his wife Martha A. and Lafayette W. Clark and his wife Helen R. McLellan signed a deed of trust for lands in Saline County, Missouri, on December 1, 1866, they were listed as being from Lincoln County, Missouri, where they had established previous residency.[306] McLellin may well have traveled to Missouri in concert with some of his children in 1865. However, one biography times his arrival in 1866. McLellin definitely purchased properties in Brownsville, Salt Pond township, Saline County, Missouri, on January 26, 1867, and February 26, 1867.[307]

An interesting interlude in McLellin's life was charted by an English convert, John Nicholson, who was emigrating to Utah in this pivotal 1866 period. On July 14, 1866, Nicholson landed in Wyoming, Nebraska, where emigrant companies were being organized prior to crossing the plains to Salt Lake City. At the request of the local brethren, he remained for several weeks to assist in the business of outfitting. In this situation, he became a party to a lawsuit involving William McLellin.

Years before, the Church had had some transactions in Kirtland, Ohio, with a man named McIntosh which were never satisfied. Now, McIntosh was working through his representatives, William E. McLellin and five Nebraska City lawyers, and had "obtained an attachment to seize all the property that could be found belonging to any of the parties who acted for the Church in the business matter alluded to."[308] Among those named in the action were Brigham Young, Orson Hyde, and Heber C. Kimball.

A law officer hunted over the outfitting grounds and legally attached items addressed to Brigham Young and Heber C. Kimball, including wire for the Deseret Telegraph line shipped in the name of President Young and two boxes made out to Heber C. Kimball. The latter actually contained property belonging to David P. Kimball and John Nicholson. A lawsuit, *Kimball and Nicholson v. McIntosh,* was commenced to recover possession of the property, and the hearing was held in nearby Nebraska City, Nebraska.[309] In describing the trial scene, John Nicholson observed:

> The witnesses in the case were required to sit upon a little box, in front of the justice and close to McLellin, who took the lead in examining them in behalf of McIntosh. Brother Horton Haight informed me that this man was W. E. McLellin, formerly one of the Twelve Apostles, who apostatized. . . .
>
> Brothers Isaac Bullock and Collins M. Gillet were placed on the witness stand, and the way to which McLellin bullied these brethren did not increase my respect for him.
>
> When the time came for me to give evidence . . . I was close to McLellin. He commenced with me, as with the other witnesses, to shout in a loud and overbearing voice. In fact, he almost yelled his questions. . . . After my examination was concluded, McLellin made a speech. He spoke very loud for a while, but there did not appear to be much point to his remarks. . . . After speaking a few minutes, in a bombastic manner, he came to an abrupt stop without any apparent cause. . . .
>
> He grossly misrepresented my testimony, crediting me as having made statements I never uttered. This made me somewhat indignant

that a man should be so wilfully untruthful, so I exclaimed, "I never said any such thing."[310]

Nicholson's lawyer, a Mr. Miner, "turned upon McLellin with intense ferocity, and denounced him as an apostate 'Mormon' a man who had turned traitor once, he said, could not safely any more be trusted. McLellin appeared to think he had got enough of that, so he arose and left the room." The twelve man jury ruled in favor of Kimball and Nicholson.[311] Amidst the emotions of litigation is perhaps some insight into McLellin's courtroom manner when he served as the inquisitor. William appears to have been operating out of Missouri when this incident occurred.

From his Brownsville, Missouri, residence in July 1869, McLellin gives us a significant glimpse into the religious tenor of his family. He was personally excited about his recent conversion to the Hedrickite faith and his anticipated return and that of some members of the immediate family to Independence, Jackson County. To trusted friends, he confided:

> [Emeline] has seen so many start ups [restoration movements begin] that she is discouraged. She is not very pious, or spiritual minded. But is willing to go with me to Zion. Mr Clark—Helen's husband [Lafayette W. Clarke] will move with us. . . . He is an entire unbeliever in any thing, but rather a noble hearted fellow. . . . All our children are entire unbelievers. But I dont believe that any of my blood will still remain in unbelief. My faith is that they will all come in finally—altho it may be by judgements—some judgement! C Wm [Charles William McLellan] still lives in one part of our house. But is as near an infidel as may be.[312]

For McLellin, who had thought to pursue a course of spiritual understanding over the period of his life, it must have been disconcerting to be unable to witness similar convictions in his own household at this stage of his life.

While living in Brownsville, McLellin traveled to Independence to attend the June conference of The Church of Christ (Temple Lot) or Hedrickites. While there, he was baptized into that faith on June 5, 1869.[313] McLellin said that his conversion came as a result of a number of prophecies which Granville Hedrick had delivered which came true. He cited one prediction that some of the faithful should return to Zion in 1867, which occurred, and a second that the Lamanites should begin to receive the gospel in

1868. This latter prophecy he believed was fulfilled when two elders labored among the Creeks and were successful in raising up a branch of forty members. However, the key to his affiliation may be found in his affirmation that:

> They go back on the original principles as taught at first in 1830 and up to 1834 when they declare Joseph fell. Dont You know that I published in the "Ensign" in 1847 that Jos. fell in 1834. Please read on page 77. We sit aside all extras as doctrine and principle which cannot be sustained by the New Testament, and that *inestimable inspired* book of Mormon.[314]

He further asserted,

> On the 5th I stated to them precisely my position, that I was willing to believe Hedrick was a Prophet, and the church had chosen him to preside over the whole church, and I was willing to take him to preside . . . hence I united with them. . . . But mind you, I did not say that I believed him a Seer or Translator. He has never given proof of having those gifts in his possession.

McLellin went to Richmond, Missouri, and personally reported his affiliation with the Hedrickites to David Whitmer. McLellin said, "David was perfectly satisfied with my course, and even justified it. . . . I tell you I have as much confidence in David, as in any man in this wide world." While in Richmond, McLellin said, he received a revelation through David, but he did not specify the substance.[315]

Final Years in Independence

McLellin was anxious to be among his brothers and sisters in Zion. The day following his baptism, he had been called to preach to the Independence congregation, and Granville Hedrick himself caught him by the shoulders and said, "We did not know there was so much in you." McLellin sold his home in Brownsville, Missouri, for $1,700 cash. He then purchased a frame home in Independence for $1,500. His two-story frame residence was on Lot 69, on the west side of Main Street, just one and one-half blocks south of the town square and between Lexington and Kansas streets.[316] Vida E. Smith described the place as a "low-ceiled, quaint, old home," which was kept "scrupulously neat" by Emeline.[317] McLellin sold his Brownsville property to his son Charles William in September 1869.[318]

Despite receiving opportunities to preach and participate among the Hedrickites, McLellin soon waned in his fervor for their cause and separated from them on November 3, 1869, after just four months.[319] Twenty days later, in a letter to D. H. Bays, he denounced "Brigham-ism, Young Joseph-ism [and] G. Hedrick-ism," saying that he had no use for them.[320]

McLellin was preoccupied with writing a book on early Mor-monism and associated doctrines in 1870. In his correspondence to friends, he expressed, "I have been reading and writing most of the summer and fall so far I have quite a book of manuscript, I expect to publish it some day but shall not until I get spiritual minded brethren around me to read and scan each treatise. I want it to contain pure truth and nothing else."[321] By February 1872 he was still doing little but writing and felt that the book was almost completed. However, he lamented that he had no means to print it.[322]

The growing mortality among his children took its toll in the midst of his writings. Sarah Emeline passed away at age thirty-seven, October 29, 1873. Sarah had married a Mr. Gilmore and left a young son, Burdett Gilmore. Burdett was later cared for by Emeline McLellin for two years in Independence, where he attended school.[323]

Evidently, McLellin continued to prepare his manuscript over succeeding years and was still producing chapters in 1878. Of the surviving manuscripts in possession of the LDS Church, dated titles include, "The Gospel" (1876), "The Bible: Queries Respecting It" (1877), "The Blood of Adam and of Christ" (1877), "Some of My Thoughts in 1878. Why I Am not an L.D. Saint of Any Click or Party," and undated manuscripts entitled "Priesthood" and "Spiritual Gifts and Powers."[324]

What the intended continuity of the existing materials is or what manuscripts are now missing from the contemplated whole remains a matter of conjecture. In 1901, President Joseph F. Smith commented on his visit, in company with Orson Pratt, to McLellin in 1878. President Smith observed, "He stated that he was writing a book about his early connection with the Church, but I have never learned that he completed it."[325] The book was never finished, and its components have scattered in disarray since his demise.

In 1875–76, David Whitmer formed a church and performed baptisms. The emphasis of the new organization was a return to "original Mormonism."[326] Following a visit with McLellin in 1878, Orson Pratt stated that McLellin had informed him that David Whitmer "has organized a church or society of his own, of about 30 members: they profess to believe in the Bible and Book of Mormon, but reject all other revelations."[327] The long-anticipated Church of Christ with Whitmer at its head had lost some of its luster for McLellin now that it was finally a reality. Joseph F. Smith said that McLellin made these observations about a visit to Whitmer:

> David had started out in a new organization, his grandson, George Schweich, is a "seer," possessing a "peepstone," and is to be the "coming man" to bring forth the hidden plates and translate them. David has ordained his grandson an elder and authorized him to perfect his great and wonderful mission.

However, Orson Pratt said that "McLellin believes this is a species of spiritualism and denounces it as from the devil. On this point he and David Whitmer split."[328] McLellin seems not to have had any integral part to play in the formation of the new Church of Christ, outside of being an observer.

Following his visit with Elders Orson Pratt and Joseph F. Smith in Independence, Missouri, during early September 1878, McLellin established a rather regular exchange of correspondence with Joseph F. Smith, which extended virtually to the day of McLellin's death. Copies of twelve letters, dated from December 5, 1878, to January 30, 1883, written to McLellin by Smith, still exist.[329] None of the McLellin letters to Salt Lake City have been found. However, the extant letters show that both men were adamant in their respective stands on the issues discussed. Many contemporary subjects as well as items from the past were addressed by the two men. At the request of McLellin, certain pamphlets were forwarded to Independence by Joseph F. Smith and a subscription to the *Deseret News* was extended annually until William's death. The men likewise discussed the availability of key publications and periodicals of Mormonism from the early period which McLellin was anxious to procure. In March 1879, Joseph F. Smith could not refrain from inviting McLellin to come west on a visit and to consider locating again with the Saints; he entreated:

> I should be very much pleased to see you out here on a visit, and the facilities there now are for travelling would make the Journey a pleasure

trip, for you, of only a few days absence from home. For my own feelings I should like you to came and dwell with us, but that might not suit you at all. We have a good country. God has blessed it since we came here, so that verdure abounds in the desert.[330]

Similarly in April 1881, having just named those who had returned to the Church after being estranged, Joseph F. Smith expressed the personal hope that

> I should be most heartily pleased to see the two remaining ones [actually there were three of the original apostles still living apart from the Church, i.e., McLellin, William B. Smith, and John F. Boynton] also return to the fold, that their last moments might be numbered and their last efforts identified with the people and the Great Cause they espoused in their youth.[331]

McLellin did not exhibit a detectable interest in a visit nor a return to the fold.

Death and Eulogy

The sudden death on November 11, 1880, of their eldest son, Charles William, at age forty-six, must have been heart-wrenching for the McLellins. And one can only imagine the attendant grief which followed when their youngest son, Marcus Nelson, also expired at only age thirty-two on February 5, 1881.[332]

W. H. Kelley of the RLDS faith had an opportunity to assess the state of McLellin's physical condition and demeanor on a visit to Independence on September 13, 1881. Kelley observed:

> Our short acquaintance with the Doctor while there led us to believe that he is not a very bad man after all. He is now advanced in years and strong and vigorous, and shows to have been a man of thought, high aspirations, and a student. To our surprise had nothing to say, really, against the faith. We rather enjoyed his acquaintance. He has led a rather of a strange career, but if he has any hope in God at all, it is in connection with the work revealed through the Seer. In spite of himself, he warms up towards the Saints. He is sour, however, and possesses a happy faculty of quoting the past and placing incidents and emphasizing to match, in order to make out a plausible case of his own.[333]

William E. McLellin passed away in Independence, Missouri, on March 14, 1883, at the age of seventy-seven. Word of his demise was immediately forwarded to the *Saints' Herald* in

Tombstone of William E. McLellin, in Woodlawn Cemetery, Independence, Missouri. Its text reads: "William Earl McLellan Born in Smith Co. Tenn. Jan. 13. 1806 Died in Independence Mo. Mar. 14, 1883." Courtesy of Ronald E. Romig and RLDS Church Archives.

Lamoni, Iowa, by F. C. Warnky. The paper editorialized his death with these observations:

> Dr. Wm. E. McLellin was an old man full of years, and in many respects a remarkable man of some attainments, and a fertile brain, active temperament, loose attachments, and strong and persistent enmities; which most likely gives the key to his estrangement from the men of the Church in the rise of it. He was a strong believer in the Book of Mormon, and probably in the mission of Joseph Smith up to a certain date, which he fixed somewhere in 1834; but discarded much or all the work after that date.[334]

Vida E. Smith, daughter of Alexander Hale Smith, son of the Prophet Joseph Smith, attended the viewing of William E. McLellin with her mother Agnus. She confided:

> We were there out of respect to the quick-moving, gentle mannered little widow, who stood by the coffined dead of her husband, William E. McLellin. Some were there in sheer curiosity and some to pay a conventional duty to this citizen of such magnificent physical proportions; such powerful voice and peculiar temperament, who had come first into their city in the thirties with a band of Mormon missionaries, one who came later to make his home with them, when the fire of his early religious zeal was burned out, and he was an alien from the gospel faith of his early manhood.[335]

Vida also spoke of a tall, dark, and rather distinguished man who stood close to "the delicately formed little widow and called her mother." This would have been their lawyer son, James Martin McLellan of Troy, Missouri. Vida E. Smith and her mother rode in the carriage with Emeline, which "followed the one-time apostle of Latter Day Saint doctrine to the open grave in that beautiful old cemetery [Woodlawn Cemetery]." Vida lamented the crowding in of the houses that have since "filled that place of peace to the gates."[336] The unobtrusive snow-white marble headstone simply reads, "William Earl McLellan, Born in Smith Co. Tenn. January 18, 1806, Died in Independence, Mo. March 14, 1883."[337]

After a pleasant visit with McLellin in Independence on September 13, 1881, W. H. Kelley made a telling observation as he remarked, "Judging by putting this and that together, and one would be apt to think that the Doctor is something of a monument of defeated ambition. Everybody has a story and a side."[338]

As one probes the story of McLellin, one becomes acutely aware of the intricacies of his character. Outwardly, he was a man of exceptional diversity, displaying the talents of a schoolteacher, evangelist, apostle, editor, doctor of medicine, and husband and father. Inwardly the complexities of his mind raced along a gambit of thought as he tried to bring the realities of personal communion with his maker in league with an earthly institution which would bear His final approbation. Whatever solace he enjoyed with the Eternal, his personal ambition to be a leading figure in the successful establishment of Christ's institutionalized church on earth was a perpetually fleeting objective which eluded him to the last.

Emeline Miller McLellan continued her residence in Independence for several years, joining the Reorganized Church of Jesus Christ of Latter Day Saints on July 1, 1888. She was baptized by Frederick G. Pitt and confirmed by Isaac N. White and Frederick G. Pitt.[339] Emeline sold some of her holdings in Independence on July 14, 1891, but apparently still retained some rental property there in 1892. She was living with her daughter, Helen Rebecca McLellan Clarke in Denison, Texas, as of April 24, 1892.[340] Emeline died in Denison, on November 1, 1907, at the age of 98. She is buried in the Clarke family cemetery, which Betty Clark Heller describes as then being on farmland west of Denison but surrounded by growth today.[341] Emeline is spoken of as having a "self sacrificing spirit which animated this remarkable woman all her life." She was likewise recognized as one who had spent many years "on the border of civilization where courage of the highest order was needed and she had it, both physical and moral."[342]

NOTES

[1] William E. McLellin to James T. Cobb, Independence, Missouri, August 14, 1880, Manuscripts Collection, New York Public Library. For a description of James T. Cobb and the complete text of the McLellin letter, see Larry C. Porter, "William E. McLellan's Testimony of the Book of Mormon," *BYU Studies* 10 (Summer 1970): 485-87.

[2] *Ensign of Liberty*, Kirtland, Ohio, 1 (April 1847): 17-18; and 1 (December 1847): 46-47.

[3] William E. McLellin's gravestone inscription, Woodlawn Cemetery, Independence, Missouri. Upon the author's request for information, Ronald E. Romig and Annette Curtis of the Missouri Mormon Frontier Foundation, Jackson County, Missouri, found the headstone and forwarded the

inscription. Ronald E. Romig to Larry C. Porter, February 18, 1994; the author personally visited McLellin's burial site and inspected the tombstone April 14, 1994.

[4] When McLellin met with his father on April 26, 1845, he stated that the aged gentleman was seventy-nine years of age. *Messenger and Advocate of The Church of Christ,* Pittsburgh, Pennsylvania, 1 (July 1, 1845): 252.

[5] Some references have incorrectly listed Cinthia Ann as his mother when in fact she was his first wife.

[6] The original Bagdad post office, which serviced the district where the McLellins lived, was set up in Smith County from 1832 to 1892, when it was moved to nearby Jackson County. *The History of Smith County Tennessee* (Dallas, Tex.: Smith County Homecoming '86, Heritage Committee, 1987), 132-33, 155-57, 231-32, 463-64. Smith County, Tennessee, Deeds 1800-1807, vol. 1, pp. 230-31, September 26, 1803. McLellin left Tennessee in 1829.

[7] McLellin directed an April 1845 letter to his father, addressing it to Bagdad, Tennessee. While visiting his father in that vicinity on April 27, 1845, he stated that he gave out a preaching appointment to the people "among whom I had been born and brought up." See *Messenger and Advocate of The Church of Christ* 1 (July 1, 1845): 253; and Daniel Haskel and J. Calvin Smith, *A Complete Descriptive and Statistical Gazetteer of the United States of America* (New York: Sherman and Smith, 1843), 45. The site of Bagdad is just inside the western border of Jackson County, Tennessee, northwest of "Bagdad Church." See Frank R. Abate, ed., *Omni Gazetteer of the United States of America,* 11 vols. (Detroit: Omnigraphics, 1991), 4:842; and United States Geological Survey, Granville, Tennessee, Quadrangle, 7.5 Minute Series, 1968. Bagdad is 10.5 miles northeast of Carthage, the county seat of Smith County, and 64 miles northeast of Nashville.

[8] *Messenger and Advocate of The Church of Christ* 1 (July 1, 1845): 252-53.

[9] 1850 Census, Tennessee, 4:254.

[10] Journal I, August 4-6, and September 13-14, 1831.

[11] McLellin to Beloved Relatives, August 4, 1832, in this volume.

[12] 1850 U.S. Census of Smith County, Tennessee.

[13] *Messenger and Advocate of The Church of Christ* 1 (July 1, 1845): 253. Nancy McLellan Law is identified in Last Will and Testament of William E. McLellan, Record of Wills, Jackson County, Missouri, Book O, 47-48. McLellin left his niece Tabitha $200 for taking such good care of her mother Nancy; see also William Law (Nancy, Tabitha, etc.), U.S. 1860 Census of Tennessee.

[14] Journal VI, April 22, 1836.

[15] Joseph Fielding Smith, comp., *Life of President Joseph F. Smith, Sixth President of The Church of Jesus Christ of Latter-day Saints* (Salt Lake City: Deseret News Press, 1938), 238-39; and *Messenger and Advocate of The Church of Christ* 1 (July 1, 1845): 252.

[16] *Saints' Herald* 26 (May 15, 1879): 147.

[17] *Messenger and Advocate* 1 (September 1, 1845): 315-16.

[18] *Zion's Reveille* 2 (January 14, 1847): 3.

[19] McLellin to Cobb, August 14, 1880; McLellin to Orson Pratt, Chester Cross Roads, Ohio, April 29, 1854, Archives Division, Church Historical Department, The Church of Jesus Christ of Latter-day Saints, Salt Lake City (hereafter cited as LDS Church Archives); and *Saints' Herald* 26 (May 15, 1879): 147.

[20] *Saints' Herald* 29 (March 1, 1882): 67.

[21] See McLellin Journals IV-VI, September 15, 1834; June 23, 1835; and May 2, 1836. In 1885, John W. Brackenbury, who had acquired a number of books which had belonged to William E. McLellin, offered them to the RLDS Church for the selective perusal of Pres. Joseph Smith III. See *Saints' Herald* 32 (May 9, 1885): 296.

[22] Journal I, September 10, 1831; and *Millennial Star* 26 (December 17, 1864): 808-9.

[23] *Journal of History* 5 (April 1912): 215.

[24] *Juvenile Instructor* 18 (May 15, 1883): 158-59.

[25] *Messenger and Advocate* 1 (February 1835): 80.

[26] McLellin to Beloved Relatives, August 4, 1832.

[27] Journal II, February 25, 1832; and *Millennial Star* 26 (December 17, 1864): 835.

[28] William E. McLellin to Joseph Smith [III], Independence, Missouri, July 1872, RLDS Church Archives, Independence, Missouri; Harry E. Downer, *History of Davenport and Scott County, Iowa*, 2 vols. (Chicago: S. J. Clarke, 1910), 1:495.

[29] McLellin to Beloved Relatives, August 4, 1832.

[30] Journal I, August 1, 1831; and 1830 Census for Clark County, Illinois. Coles County was created from Clark County in 1830. The 1840 Illinois Census lists the people who were the McLellin neighbors in Clark County—Jesse Fuller, John Price, and William White—as now being in Coles County.

[31] Charleston was first laid out in 1831 and identified as the county seat of the newly created Coles County. Journal I, September 20-22, 1831; and J. M. Peck, *A Gazetteer of Illinois* (Philadelphia: Grigg and Elliot, 1837), 179.

[32] McLellin to Beloved Relatives, August 4, 1832.

[33] In response to revelation (D&C 52:30), Samuel H. Smith and Reynolds Cahoon commenced their journey from Kirtland, Ohio, to Jackson County, Missouri on June 9, 1831, arriving in Paris, Illinois, on July 14, 1831. Andrew Jenson, *Journal History of the Church*, housed in LDS Church Archives, June 9, 1831 (hereafter cited as JH); and Diaries of Reynolds Cahoon, 1831-1832, pp. 1-7, LDS Church Archives.

[34] JH, June 9, 1831; Diaries of Reynolds Cahoon, 1831-1832, p. 7; William E. McLellin to Beloved Relatives, August 4, 1832; and *Ensign of Liberty* 1 (January 1848): 60.

³⁵ Diaries of Reynolds Cahoon, 1831-1832, August 4, 1831, p. 10. For a different description of this meeting by Lucy Mack Smith, see her *History of Joseph Smith by His Mother* (Salt Lake City: Bookcraft, 1958), 209-10. See also *HC* 7:218.

³⁶ Journal I, Sunday, July 24, 1831. An interesting paradox occurred in 1845 relative to these two men. Both McLellin and Whitlock had left the LDS Church. McLellin joined with the Rigdonites and went to Buffalo, Iowa, to preach at a Church of Christ conference. Harvey Whitlock came fifty miles to attend. McLellin said:

> It was my privilege to introduce him [Whitlock] by baptism and ordination into the "Church of Christ". . . . I led that man down and immersed him in the great Mississippi. . . . He can again lift up his voice, and publish the principles of salvation to all who may hear, with those thrills of eloquence, that are seldom heard except from gifted minds and voices like his. (*Messenger and Advocate* 1 [July 15, 1845]: 269)

³⁷ McLellin to Cobb, August 14, 1880.

³⁸ Elders Whitmer and Whitlock pursued a course through St. Louis, and McLellin went by way of Springfield.

³⁹ Journal I, July 30-August 3, 1831.

⁴⁰ Journal I, August 15-18, 1831.

⁴¹ Journal I, August 19-20, 1831; and *Ensign of Liberty* 1 (January 1848): 60.

⁴² Journal I, August 24, 1831; William E. McLellin to Elder D. H. Bays, November 23, 1869, in *Saints' Herald,* 17 (May 15, 1870): 290-91. The "Far West Record" does not record the activities of that "special conference."

⁴³ Journal I, August 31-September 19, 1831.

⁴⁴ Journal I, September 21-23, 1831.

⁴⁵ Journal I, September 29-October 12, 1831.

⁴⁶ *Ensign of Liberty* (January 1848): 61; and Donald Q. Cannon and Lyndon W. Cook, eds., *Far West Record* (Salt Lake City: Deseret Book, 1983), 19, 21, 24, 25. At the end of his life, McLellin would argue against the legitimacy of the ecclesiastical office of high priest.

⁴⁷ Journal I, October 29, 1831. For a discussion of the differences in date and place cited in the McLellin Journal and the current headnote to Doctrine and Covenants 66, see pages 248-49 above.

⁴⁸ McLellin to Beloved Relatives, August 4, 1832.

⁴⁹ The other elders present were Joseph Smith, Oliver Cowdery, Sidney Rigdon, David Whitmer, John Whitmer, Peter Whitmer, Jr., Christian Whitmer (not listed until November 8), Orson Hyde, Luke Johnson, and Lyman Johnson. Cannon and Cook, *Far West Record,* 26-33.

⁵⁰ Robert J. Woodford, "The Historical Development of the Doctrine and Covenants," 3 vols. (Ph.D. diss., Brigham Young University, 1974), 1:21-23.

[51] Joseph Smith, Jr., *History of The Church of Jesus Christ of Latter-day Saints,* ed. B. H. Roberts, 2d ed. rev., 7 vols. (Salt Lake City: Deseret Book, 1971), 1:224-26 (hereafter cited as *HC*); for an alternative discussion of McLellin's participation in this incident, see Mark R. Grandstaff, "Having More Learning Than Sense: William E. McLellin and the Book of Commandments Revisited," *Dialogue: A Journal of Mormon Thought* 26 (Winter 1993): 23-48.

[52] McLellin to Pratt, April 29, 1854; *The Ensign,* Scott County, Iowa Territory, 1 (November 1844): 78; *Gospel Herald* 2 (November 4, 1847): 142; and *Messenger and Advocate* 1 (April 15, 1845): 169; 1 (July 1, 1845): 251-52.

[53] *Ensign of Liberty* 1 (March 1847): 13; 1 (April 1847): 17-18; and 1 (August 1949): 99-104.

[54] Journal I, October 29, 1831.

[55] Journal I, November 27-December 28, 1831. See appendix III for the names of those baptized.

[56] Journal I, November 16-December 29, 1831; also JH, November 16, 1831; Samuel H. Smith Journal, 1831-33, LDS Church Archives.

[57] McLellin to Pratt, April 29, 1854.

[58] Journal II, January 30, 1832.

[59] Journal II, February 2-20, 1832.

[60] Journal II, February 20-25, 1832.

[61] Although McLellin may have recorded some journal entries for this period, there is currently no evidence that he continued the practice until the latter part of January 1833.

[62] *Millennial Star* 26 (December 31, 1864): 835.

[63] Journal II, February 25, 1832; and McLellin to Beloved Relatives, August 4, 1832.

[64] McLellin to Beloved Relatives, August 4, 1832. The marriage license lists Emeline as being from Windham, Portage County. They were married by Almon Babcock, justice of the peace. Portage County Marriage Licenses, 3 (1817-36): 715; and Marriage Records 1 (1808-40): 749. In the letter of John M. McLellan to Larry C. Porter, May 19, 1994, a brief biography of "Emeline McLellan" places the marriage in Ravenna, Portage County.

[65] Journal I, October 29-November 16, 1831.

[66] Emeline McLellan to D. L. Kelley, April 24, 1892; and Emeline McLellan to editors of *The Saints' Herald,* December 1899, see *Saints' Herald* 47 (January 10, 1900): 26; and *HC* 1:215, 265. Her brother Charles also joined about this time. Letter of Franklin Miller, Jr., to Larry C. Porter, Gambier, Ohio, August 3, 1994.

[67] John M. McLellan to Porter; Franklin Miller, Jr., to Porter; Susan Easton Black, comp., *Early Members of the Reorganized Church of Jesus Christ of Latter Day Saints,* 6 vols. (Provo: Religious Studies Center, Brigham Young University, 1993), 4:371-72; Martin Miller (c. 1763) Family

Group Record; U.S. Census, Pomfret, Vermont, 1810; U.S. Census, Hiram, Ohio, 1820 and 1830; McLellin to Beloved Relatives, August 4, 1832. *History of Portage County, Ohio* (Chicago: Warner, Beers, 1885), 470-71; Gertrude Van Rensselaer Wickham, ed., *Memorial to the Pioneer Women of the Western Reserve* (Cleveland: J. B. Savage, 1896), 157.

[68] McLellin to Beloved Relatives, August 4, 1832.

[69] John M. McLellan, a great-grandson of James Martin McLellan, telephone interview with Porter, May 18, 1994; McLellan to Porter, May 19, 1994; and William McClelin household, 1860 Census of Mundy Township, Genesee County, Michigan; see setting of individual births in this biography.

[70] Cannon and Cook, *Far West Record*, 43; *HC* 1:271; and Joseph Smith to Emma Smith, in Dean C. Jessee, *The Personal Writings of Joseph Smith* (Salt Lake City: Deseret Book, 1984), 238-39.

[71] Jessee, *Personal Writings of Joseph Smith*, 239, 669.

[72] *HC* 1:271-72; Joseph Smith to W. W. Phelps, July 31, 1832, in Jessee, *Personal Writings of Joseph Smith*, 244; and McLellin to Beloved Relatives, August 4, 1832.

[73] Smith to Phelps, in Jessee, *Personal Writings of Joseph Smith*, 244-45.

[74] Cannon and Cook, *Far West Record*, 53, 55-57; and JH, October 2, 1832.

[75] McLellin to Beloved Relatives, August 4, 1832; Kirtland Council Minute Book, February 24, 1834, typescript, 42; and *HC* 2:39.

[76] McLellin to Beloved Relatives, August 4, 1832. During the rest of 1832, McLellin remained in Missouri and served as clerk at conferences held on August 24 and October 2 and was present at councils held on July 3, October 5, October 25, and December 3. Cannon and Cook, *Far West Record*, 50-51, 53, 55-58.

[77] Dean C. Jessee, *The Papers of Joseph Smith*, 2 vols. to date (Salt Lake City: Deseret Book, 1989-), 2:4; Cannon and Cook, *Far West Record*, 57-58.

[78] On July 31, 1832, Joseph Smith instructed the Saints in Missouri not to receive McLellin into fellowship except on the condition of "the filling [of] his mission to the South countries according to the commandment of Jesus Christ," citing Matt. 10:27. Jessee, *Personal Writings of Joseph Smith*, 244.

[79] Journal III, February 28-March 7, 1833.

[80] Journal III, March 8, 1833.

[81] Parley P. Pratt, *Autobiography of Parley P. Pratt* (Salt Lake City: Deseret Book, 1938), 83.

[82] Pratt, *Autobiography of Parley P. Pratt*, 84.

[83] Journal III, March 9-May 24, 1833; and *Ensign of Liberty* 1 (January 1848): 61, specified his return to Independence in June 1833.

[84] Pratt, *Autobiography of Parley P. Pratt*, 91.

[85] See appendix III for a list of the baptisms.

[86] *Ensign of Liberty* 1 (January 1848): 61.

[87] *Ensign of Liberty* 1 (January 1848): 61.

[88] *Ensign of Liberty* 1 (January 1848): 61.

[89] *Ensign of Liberty* 1 (January 1848): 61.

[90] *Ensign of Liberty* 1 (January 1848): 61.

[91] *Evening and the Morning Star* 2 (January 1834): 124; and Cannon and Cook, *Far West Record*, 62-67.

[92] Jackson County, Missouri Land Deed Record Book B, 328-29.

[93] *Evening and the Morning Star* 2 (January 1834): 124-25; and *Times and Seasons* 1 (December 1839): 20. For an excellent description of the log jail in which William E. McLellin and the other brethren were placed, see Pearl Wilcox, *Jackson County Pioneers* (Independence: Pearl Wilcox, 1975), 430-31.

[94] *Ensign of Liberty* 1 (January 1848): 61-62.

[95] McLellin also wrote, "One thought, however, kept our hearts from sinking. It occasionally visited my mind during that long night, as a bee would its hive, to leave its sweets, and then go in search for more; and that was, 'I am innocent of their charge—I am suffering for Christ and truth's sake, and I shall get my reward either in life or at the resurrection of the just.' A voice too, as of a ministering angel, would occasionally speak to my mind and to my heart, and its voice was as calm as the zephyr of a summer's morning, saying, 'Be still, and trust in me, and I the Lord will be your deliverer.'" *Ensign of Liberty* 1 (January 1848): 62.

[96] Another account of McLellin's release from jail describes Lieutenant Governor Lilburn W. Boggs coming to the prisoners early in the morning of November 5, warning them to flee for their lives. For accounts of experiences similar to those of McLellin during the Jackson County persecutions, see Chapman Duncan, autobiography, in *Miscellaneous Mormon Diaries*, 15:3-4, 31, Special Collections, Harold B. Lee Library, Brigham Young University, Provo, Utah; Newel Knight, journal, in *Scraps of Biography*, Tenth Book of the Faith-Promoting Series (Salt Lake City: Juvenile Instructor Office, 1883), 82, 85-86; *HC* 1:394-95, 432; and letter from John Corrill to Oliver Cowdery, *Evening and Morning Star* 2 (January 1834): 125. *Ensign of Liberty* 1 (January 1848): 62.

[97] *HC* 1:451

[98] Jackson County, Missouri Land Deed Record Book C, 34-35; and Kirtland High Council minutes, February 24, 1834.

[99] McLellan, telephone interview.

[100] James L. Bradley, *Zion's Camp 1834: Prelude to the Civil War* (Salt Lake City: Publishers Press, 1990), 159-62.

[101] Writing from Richmond, Missouri, on June 10, 1834, Judge Ryland addressed his correspondence to A. S. Gilbert in Clay County, requesting that the respective parties meet in Liberty, Missouri, on June 16. The delegates were invited to sit down together with himself as moderator and

work out a compromise in this dangerous situation. John Corrill and A. S. Gilbert responded for the Church on June 14, stipulating that the Saints would be present.*Times and Seasons* 6 (January 15, 1846): 1088-89.

[102] *Times and Seasons* 6 (January 15, 1846): 1089-90; and *Evening and the Morning Star* 2 (July 1834): 175.

[103] *Evening and the Morning Star* 2 (July 1834): 175.

[104] *Evening and the Morning Star* 2 (July 1834): 175.

[105] Several reasons have been suggested for the cessation: the accusation that the Mormons had something to do with the sinking of a ferryboat carrying some of the arbitrators back to Jackson County from the June 16, meeting; the attack of the mob on Zion's Camp at the forks of the Little and Big Fishing Rivers; the high probability that the citizens of Jackson County had no actual intention of selling their lands to the Saints; and the inability of the Mormons to give up their Zion. Roger D. Launius, *Zion's Camp* (Independence: Herald House, 1984), 133-36.

[106] *Ensign of Liberty* 2 (December 1847): 46.

[107] McLellin to Pratt, April 29, 1854.

[108] The conference convened at the home of Lyman Wight on the property of Col. Michael Arthur.

[109] *HC* 2:122-26.

[110] *Ensign of Liberty* 1 (December 1847): 46-47; see also 1 (April 1847): 17-18.

[111] Journal IV, July 9, 1834; Cannon and Cook, *Far West Record*, 71-73; and *HC* 2:124-26.

[112] Journal IV, July 9-July 22, 1834.

[113] August 16, 1834; and Jessee, *Personal Writings of Joseph Smith*, 331.

[114] Journal IV, July 22-September 11, 1834; and *The Indiana Gazetteer* (Indianapolis: E. Chamberlain, 1849), 197, 218; see appendix III for list of baptisms.

[115] Journal IV, October 5-November 19, 1834. During the winter of 1834-35, the Church initiated two institutions of learning in Kirtland: one was called the School for the Elders (replacing the School of the Prophets), and the other was named the Kirtland School. Milton V. Backman, Jr., *The Heavens Resound* (Salt Lake City: Deseret Book, 1983), 268.

[116] Journal IV, November 19-24, 1834; and *Messenger and Advocate*, Kirtland, Ohio, 1 (February 1835): 80.

[117] Journal IV, December 22, 1834; *Messenger and Advocate* 1 (February 1835): 80; *Saints' Herald* 17 (September 15, 1870): 556; *Times and Seasons* 6 (April 15, 1845): 868; and Backman, *Heavens Resound*, 78, 156.

[118] McLellin to Smith [III], July 1872. For a description by McLellin of the school, see *Times and Seasons* 6 (April 15, 1845): 868.

[119] *Messenger and Advocate* 1 (February 1835): 80 (immediately below the McLellin article is a notice of the commencement of spring term

on April 20, 1835, and an invitation to young gentlemen and ladies living at a distance to take board with respectable families for $1.00 to $1.25 per week.

[120] Oliver Cowdery, David Whitmer, and Martin Harris, in accordance with revelation and acting in conjunction with the First Presidency, called the following brethren to the Quorum of the Twelve Apostles (in order as first chosen): Lyman Johnson, Brigham Young, Heber C. Kimball, David W. Patten, Luke Johnson, William E. McLellin, Orson Hyde, William Smith, John F. Boynton, Orson Pratt, Thomas B. Marsh, and Parley P. Pratt. *Times and Seasons* 6 (April 15, 1845): 868.

[121] *Times and Seasons* 6 (April 15, 1845): 868.

[122] *Times and Seasons* 6 (April 15, 1845): 868.

[123] Kirtland Council Minute Book, February 15, 1835, typescript 151-53.

[124] *Saints' Herald* 17 (September 15, 1870): 553.

[125] Kirtland High Council minutes, February 27, 1835. McLellin later stated, "On the 27th of the same month [February 1835], in a conference Orson Hyde and myself were chosen to act as secretaries of that quorum, and we were required to keep a record of the most important matters touching the ministry &c. of those Apostles," *Messenger and Advocate* 1 (March 15, 1845): 149.

[126] Journal IV, December 5, 1834, to March 30, 1835; see appendix III for list of baptisms.

[127] William E. McLellin to Oliver Cowdery, April 16, 1835, in *Messenger and Advocate* 1 (April 1835): 102-3.

[128] McLellin to Cowdery, April 16, 1835, 102.

[129] McLellin to Cowdery, April 16, 1835, 102; and Journal IV, March 27-30, 1835; see appendix III for list of baptisms.

[130] The itinerary established the first conference in Kirtland, May 2; Westfield, New York, May 9; Freedom, New York, May 22; Lyonstown, New York, June 5; at Pillow [Pillar] Point, New York, June 10; West Loboro (West Loughborough), Upper Canada, June 29; in Johnsbury (St. Johnsbury), Vermont, July 17; Bradford, Massachusetts, August 7; Dover, New Hampshire, September 4; Saco, Maine, September 18; and Farmington, Maine, October 2.

[131] *HC* 2:209-17; and *Messenger and Advocate* 1 (March 1835): 90. For an additional analysis of this first combined mission of the Twelve, see Ronald K. Esplin, "The Emergence of Brigham Young and the Twelve to Mormon Leadership, 1830-1841" (Ph.D. diss., Brigham Young University, 1981), 161-74.

[132] *HC* 2:209-17.

[133] *HC* 2:218-19.

[134] *HC* 2:219-20. After this first arrangement by age, the brethren were to hold their place in the quorum according to seniority of ordination.

135 Journal V, May 4, 1835; and *HC* 2:222.

136 Journal V, May 9-12, 1835; *Messenger and Advocate* 1 (March 1835): 90; and *Messenger and Advocate* 1 (May 1835): 115-16; see appendix III.

137 *Messenger and Advocate* 2 (October 1835): 205.

138 Journal V, July 9, 1835.

139 The Bradford and Saco conferences had been rescheduled from September 18 to August 21, 1835. The intervening Dover, New Hampshire, conference, originally scheduled for September 4, 1835, had been canceled altogether.

140 For instance, McLellin recorded only five apostles out of twelve attended the conference in West Loughborough, Upper Canada (now Ontario Province), i.e., Thomas B. Marsh, Brigham Young, Orson Hyde, Parley P. Pratt, and himself (Journal V, June 23-July 1, 1835). However, John F. Boynton is also said to have been present; see *Millennial Star* 27 (February 18, 1865): 102.

141 Journal V, July 26-August 26, 1835; see appendix III for list of baptisms.

142 Journal V, August 25-August 31, 1835.

143 *Messenger and Advocate* 2 (October 1835): 204-7.

144 Kirtland High Council minutes, September 26, 1835.

145 *HC* 2:240; Orson Hyde had returned to Kirtland from his eastern mission to testify in a court case involving the Prophet Joseph Smith. Orson rejoined McLellin in Upper Canada on June 29, 1835. He bore a letter to McLellin from Emeline, but it is by no means certain that this was the letter in question (see "History of Brigham Young," ms. no. 3, LDS Church Archives; and Journal V, June 5 and 28, 1835).

146 *HC* 2:283.

147 *HC* 2:239-40.

148 Kirtland Council Minutes, September 26, 1835. For further discussion of this incident, see also the Joseph Smith diary entry of January 16, 1836, in Jessee, *Personal Writings of Joseph Smith*, 135-39.

149 Kirtland High Council Minutes.

150 McLellan, telephone interview.

151 Backman, *Heavens Resound*, 270.

152 Backman, *Heavens Resound*, 270.

153 Jessee, *Personal Writings of Joseph Smith*, 124.

154 Backman, *Heavens Resound*, 271-72. Evidences of his continued personal studies of Hebrew can be found in his journal entries for Journal IV, April 19, 1836; May 4, 1836; and May 13-14, 1836.

155 Backman, *Heavens Resound*, 285.

156 Jessee, *Personal Writings of Joseph Smith*, 146.

157 Council of the Twelve Meeting, Kirtland High Council minutes, March 28, 1836.

[158] *Saints' Herald* 17 (September 15, 1870): 554. McLellin also expressed to Orson Pratt, "In 1836 they sought an endowment from on high. But . . . they made a perfect failure." McLellin to Pratt, April 29, 1854.

[159] *HC* 2:432.

[160] Journal VI, April 9-11, 1836; and *HC* 2:436.

[161] Journal VI, April 11-June 7, 1836. Though his journal records events only to June 7, he later specified that he arrived back in Kirtland "the last of June"; see *Saints' Herald* 17 (September 15, 1870): 554.

[162] *Saints' Herald* 17 (September 15, 1870): 554.

[163] *Ensign of Liberty* 1 (January 1847): 9, 13.

[164] McLellin to Cobb, August 14, 1880.

[165] *Saints' Herald* 17 (May 15, 1870), 291.

[166] Edgar County, Illinois Land Deed Records, book 3, 271.

[167] William E. McLellin to the Quorum of the Twelve Apostles (Apostles in Kirtland, Ohio), January 24, 1837, copy in LDS Church Archives.

[168] McLellin to Quorum of the Twelve, January 24, 1837.

[169] *Messenger and Advocate* 3 (March 1837): 472.

[170] Edgar County, Illinois Land Deed Records, book 3, 323. However, this is not the same parcel of land acquired by McLellin in that county on November 7, 1836 (book 3, 291).

[171] Kirtland High Council minutes, September 3, 1837.

[172] Cannon and Cook, *Far West Record,* 123; and *Elders' Journal* 1 (November 1837): 29-30; and Franklin Miller, Jr., to Larry C. Porter, Gambier, Ohio, August 3, 1994, copy of oath enclosed.

[173] McLellin affirmed, "I remained with the church until August, 1836, . . . [and] I have never operated with Joseph Smith or his party from that day to this!!" *Saints' Herald* 17 (May 15, 1870): 291.

[174] Backman, *Heavens Resound,* 328, also asserted that "almost half of those who were excommunicated, disfellowshipped, or dropped from their positions of responsibility in 1837 or 1838 later repented and returned to the Church."

[175] *Saints' Herald* 17 (September 15, 1870): 554.

[176] Cannon and Cook, *Far West Record,* 160.

[177] *HC* 3:31.

[178] The minutes of the court are not presently available for an assessment of what action was taken against McLellin on this occasion. Nothing is recorded in the *Far West Record* as to the disposition of the court. The date of May 11, 1838, is most often ascribed as being the day of his excommunication. Andrew Jenson stated that McLellin was cut off on May 11, 1838, for "unbelief and apostasy." Andrew Jenson, *Latter-day Saint Biographical Encyclopedia* (Salt Lake City: Deseret News, 1901-36), 83; see also *HC* 3:31n; *Millennial Star* 26 (December 17, 1864): 808.

[179] McLellan to Kelley, April 24, 1892.

[180] McLellan, telephone interview.

[181] Leland Homer Gentry, "A History of the Latter-day Saints in Northern Missouri from 1836 to 1839" (Ph.D. diss., Brigham Young University, 1965), 132-68; and *Ensign of Liberty* 1 (March 1847): 9.

[182] *Ensign of Liberty* 1 (March 1847): 9.

[183] *Ensign of Liberty* 1 (March 1847): 9.

[184] Doctrine and Covenants 118; Thomas B. Marsh to Wilford Woodruff, July 14, 1838, in Wilford Woodruff, *Wilford Woodruff's Journal, 1833-1898 Typescript*, ed. Scott G. Kenney, 9 vols. (Midvale, Utah: Signature Books, 1983-84), 1:276-77.

[185] Gentry, "History of the Latter-day Saints in Northern Missouri," 247-484.

[186] *Deseret Evening News*, June 4, 1868, 2, col. 4.

[187] Parley P. Pratt, *History of the Late Persecution Inflicted by the State of Missouri upon the Mormons* (Detroit: Dawson and Bates, Printers, 1839), 41.

[188] Heber C. Kimball Journal, book 94C, November 1, 1838, LDS Church Archives.

[189] *Zion's Reveille* 1 (April 15, 1847): 55-56.

[190] *Millennial Star* 26 (December 17, 1864): 808.

[191] The statement was signed by Caroline Clark, James Mulholland, Mrs. Sally Hinkle, and Joanna Carter. *HC* 3:286-88. The witnesses said that McLellin was assisted by Harvey Green, Burr Riggs, and Harlow Redfield. Harlow Redfield was later vindicated of wrongdoing, however. *HC* 3:287.

[192] According to Butler, this latter theft caused some initial problems for Joseph who had sent home for bedding to ward off the winter cold during his imprisonment. Butler's wife, Caroline, told Emma Smith to send what bedding she had to Joseph and her friends in Far West would see that she and her family were supplied with the necessary coverings. "Autobiography of John Lowe Butler, 1808-1861," typescript, 16, LDS Church Archives.

[193] Richard L. Anderson shared copies of four Clay County Court documents with the writer, the first of which is a complaint filed by the attorney for the plaintiff, J. A. Gordon, in the Clay County Circuit Court, April term 1839, "Joseph Smith Jr complains of William E. McCleland," in Clay County Courthouse, Liberty, Missouri. Apparently, Joseph Smith's attorney erroneously listed the trespass as having occurred in September 1838 rather than in the month of November.

[194] Summons issued by Samuel Tillery, Circuit Court Clerk, through Samuel Hadley, Sheriff of Clay County, Missouri, to William E. McCleland, dated March 6, 1839, in Clay County Courthouse, Liberty Missouri, copy in possession of Richard L. Anderson.

[195] Answer to the complaint and dismissal action, April 18, 1839, Clay County Courthouse, Liberty, Missouri, copies in possession of Richard L. Anderson.

[196] Hyrum Smith stated that Sheriff William Morgan allowed the prisoners to escape and gave them direct assistance in doing so. Gentry, "History of the Latter-day Saints in Northern Missouri," 586-91.

[197] Anson Call, "Autobiography of Anson Call," 16-17, typescript, BYU Special Collections.

[198] McLellin to Kelley, April 24, 1892.

[199] William E. McLellin to David Whitmer, December 2, 1846, in *Ensign of Liberty* 1 (April 1847): 17. Geographically, both communities are near the Rock River's mouth as it empties into the Mississippi.

[200] 1840 U.S. Census, Scott County, Iowa; McLellan, letter to author, cites Davenport as a place of residence for the McLellin family at one juncture; and Downer, *History of Davenport and Scott County, Iowa,* 1:495-515.

[201] *Millennial Star* 26 (December 17, 1864): 809.

[202] McLellin to Smith [III], July 1872.

[203] Frederick G. Williams, "Frederick Granger Williams of the First Presidency of the Church," *BYU Studies* 12 (Spring 1972): 244-45, 251. The author of this article is a grandson twice removed of Frederick Granger Williams.

[204] *Gospel Herald,* Voree, Wisconsin, 2 (December 2, 1847): 164; and Census Record (Kirtland District 85, Lake County), 1850.

[205] William E. McLellin to Sidney Rigdon, December 23, 1844, in *Messenger and Advocate* 1 (January 1, 1845): 91-93.

[206] Land Deed Records, Rock Island County, Illinois, book D, 346.

[207] John M. McLellan to Porter.

[208] *Zion's Reveille,* Voree, Wisconsin, 2 (January 28, 1847): 12.

[209] *Times and Seasons* 1 (November 1839): 15.

[210] *HC* 3:283-84; and statement of Hyrum Smith, *Times and Seasons,* 1 (November 1839): 21.

[211] *Ensign* 1 (October 1844): 61-62.

[212] Rock Island County, Deed Record Book E, 388-89.

[213] Deed Record Lands, Scott County, Iowa Book D, 115-16.

[214] Lyndon W. Cook, *William Law* (Orem, Utah: Grandin Book, 1994), 56-58.

[215] *Ensign* 1 (October 1844): 61-63.

[216] *Ensign* 1 (October 1844): 63.

[217] *Ensign* 1 (October 1844): 58-59.

[218] P. Matteson, October 23, 1844, in JH, October 23, 1844; and *Ensign* 1 (November 1844): 71-72.

[219] Rock Island County Deed Record, book F, 63. Action against McLellin commenced September 16, 1843, and was resolved in his favor June 10, 1844.

[220] P. Matteson, October 24, 1844; *Messenger and Advocate* 1 (January 15, 1845): 92; and Scott County, Iowa Deed Record Lands, December 18, 1844, book D, 250-51.

²²¹*Messenger and Advocate* 1 (January 15, 1845): 91-92. Announcement had been made in Nauvoo in November that "Sidney Rigdon Esq.,— has resuscitated the 'Latter-day Saints Messenger and Advocate,' at Pittsburgh, Pa. We understand that through this medium the accessories to the murder of Joseph and Hyrum Smith, with John C. Bennett as the ne plus ultra, will form a union of all the excommunicated members from the church of Jesus Christ of Latter-day Saints." *Times and Seasons* 5 (November 1, 1844): 697. Overtures of unification were certainly in progress among certain of those who had been excommunicated by the LDS.

²²²*Gospel Herald* 2 (November 4, 1847): 142. A second revelation of encouragement is recorded on the same page, reportedly given from Hampton on January 18, 1845.

²²³James Blakeslee Journal, January 19, 1845, in Ronald E. Romig to Larry C. Porter, June 7, 1994.

²²⁴F. Mark McKiernan, *The Voice of One Crying in the Wilderness: Sidney Rigdon, Religious Reformer, 1793-1876* (Lawrence, Kan.: Coronado Press, 1971), 142.

²²⁵William E. McLellin to Samuel Bennett, March 15, 1845, in *Messenger and Advocate* 1 (March 15, 1845): 149-51.

²²⁶*Messenger and Advocate* 1 (April 15, 1845): 168-69.

²²⁷James Blakeslee, a counselor to William Law, was named one of Rigdon's twelve apostles. Austin Cowles, another counselor to Law, was called as president of the high priests' quorum. *Messenger and Advocate* 1 (April 15, 1845): 171-72. These brethren were likewise ordained "prophets, priests and kings, unto God," and became part of the "quorum of seventy-three," a decision-making body within the church. Interestingly, George M. Hinkle was present from Buffalo, Iowa, and was similarly ordained to this latter quorum. He was there for the purpose of forming a union between himself and Rigdon. Hinkle was appointed an evangelist to "Iowa and the West." In his own publication, *Ensign* 1 (March 1845): 133, Hinkle had foreshadowed his own alliance with Rigdon by stating, "We are glad to hear that all, who really deserve the name of 'Latter day Saints,' are flocking to his [Rigdon's] standard, and deserting the unholy clique at Nauvoo." In *Ensign* 1 (April 1845): 154-55, Hinkle announced "The Reason Why" he had formed a union with Rigdon at the Pittsburgh conference; *Messenger and Advocate* 1 (April 15, 1845): 168-73; and *Messenger and Advocate* 1 (June 15, 1845): 231-32.

²²⁸William Law was not present at the conference, nor was he a factor in the proceedings, only diminishing in such authority as he once held among his very small group of adherents. McLellin later gave his assessment of the expired organization: "Law's ism was a short-lived thing. It never spread beyond its first movers. It is only now remembered as an ism which in its operations and results proved the death of Joseph and Hyrum Smith." *Ensign of Liberty* 1 (December 1847): 45.

²²⁹ William E. McLellin to Sidney Rigdon and Ebenezer Robinson, May 28, 1845, in *Messenger and Advocate* 1 (July 1, 1845): 251-53.

²³⁰ *Messenger and Advocate* 1 (July 1, 1845): 251-52. The 1850 Census for Smith County, Tennessee, identifies Israel's wife as Frances, and in 1850 there were five children in the household.

²³¹ *Messenger and Advocate* 1 (July 1845): 252-53. Nancy McLellan Law and certain other relatives are named on the list of the membership of The Church of Christ; see *The History of Smith County Tennessee*, 113-14.

²³² *Messenger and Advocate* 1 (July 1845): 253.

²³³ *Messenger and Advocate* 1 (July 1845): 253. In this same correspondence, McLellin said that his older brother's son would also accompany him and his family to Pittsburgh in order to go to school. McLellin had already made plans to move from Hampton to Pittsburgh. The name of the son, John P., is derived from the Samuel McLellan household in the 1850 Census of Smith County, Tennessee.

²³⁴ *Messenger and Advocate* 1 (July 1, 1845): 253; and 1 (July 15, 1845): 267-68, 270-71.

²³⁵ *Messenger and Advocate* 1 (July 15, 1845): 267-68. The 1840 Iowa Census lists Whitlock's residence as Cedar County, Iowa; and James Blakeslee Journal, May 29, 1845, RLDS Archives, in Romig to Porter, June 7, 1994.

²³⁶ The 1860 U.S. Census for Genesee County, Michigan, lists Albert's birth place as Iowa and not Illinois, though McLellin was still operating out of Hampton, Illinois.

²³⁷ *Messenger and Advocate* 1 (July 1, 1845): 254; their June 1845 move was noted by McLellin in *Ensign of Liberty* 1 (April 1847): 17; McLellan, telephone interview, confirmed Albert's birth date; James Blakeslee Journal, June 15-24, 1845, in Romig to Porter, June 7, 1994; and *Messenger and Advocate* 1 (July 15, 1845): 263-64.

²³⁸ *Messenger and Advocate* 1 (July 15, 1845): 272.

²³⁹ *Messenger and Advocate* 1 (August 1, 1845): 273.

²⁴⁰ *Messenger and Advocate* 2 (March 1846): 464; see also 2 (June 1846): 471-73; and 2 (August 1846): 505.

²⁴¹ *Messenger and Advocate* 1 (August 15, 1845): 302.

²⁴² *Messenger and Advocate* 1 (August 15, 1845): 302. McLellin's accomplishments while in Philadelphia were highly lauded; see *Messenger and Advocate* 1 (August 15, 1845): 300; and 1 (September 1, 1845): 315-16.

²⁴³ *Messenger and Advocate* 1 (September 15, 1845): 333.

²⁴⁴ *Messenger and Advocate* 1 (November 1845): 392-400. Conference was held in the Hall of the Sons of Temperance at the corner of Sixth and Haines Streets.

²⁴⁵ *Messenger and Advocate* 1 (November 1845): 398.

²⁴⁶ *Messenger and Advocate* 2 (January 1846): 425.

[247] *Messenger and Advocate* 2 (January 1845): 425-27. When George M. Hinkle learned of McLellin's suspension, he immediately responded from West Buffalo, Iowa, on December 20, 1845:

> We here, are not the least surprised at the downfall of Dr. M'Lellin; it fulfills the prediction of many of our best members. You may not fear his influence with the church here, for he has none. I do not rejoice at his downfall, but it will be a benefit to the cause in this country, if he is never again placed as one of your council. (*Messenger and Advocate* 2 [February 1846]: 447)

[248] *Messenger and Advocate* 2 (January 1846): 427; and 2 (June 1846): 470; George M. Hinkle nominated Algernon S. Rigdon for the appointment in McLellin's place.

[249] *Messenger and Advocate* 2 (February 1846): 437. In the Grand Council meeting of February 20, 1846, it was announced that Austin Cowles had resigned; see *Messenger and Advocate* 2 (March 1846): 456.

[250] *Messenger and Advocate* 2 (March 1846): 463-64.

[251] William E. McLellin to David Whitmer, December 2, 1846, in *Ensign of Liberty* 1 (April 1847): 17.

[252] Cowles subsequently became the editor of the Brewsterite (James Collin Brewster) publication, *The Olive Branch*, Kirtland. *Zion's Reveille* 2 (January 28, 1847): 12; and *Olive Branch* 1 (August 1848): 1, 7.

[253] *Ensign of Liberty* 1 (April 1847): 17; and *Gospel Herald* 2 (December 2, 1847): 164.

[254] *Gospel Herald* 2 (December 2, 1847): 164.

[255] *Gospel Herald* 2 (December 2, 1847): 164.

[256] Roger Van Noord, *King of Beaver Island, The Life and Assassination of James Jesse Strang* (Urbana: University of Illinois Press, 1988), 51; *Ensign of Liberty* 1 (April 1847): 17; and *Gospel Herald* 2 (December 2, 1847): 164.

[257] *Ensign of Liberty* 1 (April 1847): 17.

[258] *Zion's Reveille* 1 (November 1846): 2.

[259] *Gospel Herald* 2 (November 25, 1847): 155.

[260] *Gospel Herald* 2 (December 2, 1847): 164-66.

[261] Jacob Bump, Leonard Rich, Amos Babcock, and S. B. Stoddard to James J. Strang, Kirtland, Ohio, October 15, 1846, LDS Church Archives.

[262] *Ensign of Liberty* 1 (April 1847): 17. The Kirtland congregation was numbered at forty-two in January 1848; see *Ensign of Liberty* 1 (January 1848): 54.

[263] *Ensign of Liberty* 1 (March 1847): 13; 1 (April 1847): 20; and 1 (December 1847): 36; see also Reuben McBride to Brigham Young, Kirtland, Ohio, November 1, 1848, LDS Church Archives. *Gospel Herald* 2 (December 2, 1847): 164.

[264] *Zion's Reveille* 2 (January 14, 1847): 3.

[265] *Zion's Reveille* 2 (January 21, 1847): 6; 2 (January 28, 1847): 11–12; and *Gospel Herald* 2 (December 2, 1847): 164–66.

[266] *Ensign of Liberty* 1 (April 1847): 29–32; see also the McLellin/Strang debate in Voree in which McLellin declared, "All this stuff about my character and my letters and Dr. Bennett is flummery!" *Gospel Herald* 2 (November 25, 1847): 155.

[267] *Ensign of Liberty* 1 (April 1847): 17–18.

[268] *Ensign of Liberty* 1 (April 1847): 17–18; compare Doctrine and Covenants 43:4.

[269] *Ensign of Liberty* 1 (April 1847): 19.

[270] *Ensign of Liberty* 1 (April 1847): 17–20.

[271] *Ensign of Liberty* 1 (December 1847): 33.

[272] *Ensign of Liberty* 1 (December 1847): 33–34.

[273] Oliver Cowdery to David Whitmer, July 28, 1847, in *Ensign of Liberty* 1 (May 1848): 91–93.

[274] *Ensign of Liberty* 1 (December 1847): 34.

[275] *Ensign of Liberty* 1 (December 1847): 34; and 1 (August 1849): 99–105.

[276] *Ensign of Liberty* 1 (August 1849): 102–3.

[277] *Ensign of Liberty* 1 (August 1849): 103–4; and David Whitmer to Oliver Cowdery, September 8, 1847, in *Ensign of Liberty* 1 (May 1848): 93.

[278] *Ensign of Liberty* 1 (December 1847): 34–35.

[279] *Ensign of Liberty* 1 (December 1847): 35. McLellin later remarked:

> Samuel James and George M. Hinkle, during '47, found their way from the death-groans of Rigdonism in the [Cumberland] valley, to the fertile plains of Illinois, and there tried to resurrect and again rear up the fallen kingdom; but a late letter from a valued friend in that region, has this laconic saying in relation to them: "There is nothing more of James and his man George—their ism has breathed its last." (*Ensign of Liberty* 1 [May 1848]: 90)

[280] For example, *Zion's Reveille* 2 (October 28, 1847): 129–31; 2 (November 4, 1847): 140–42; 2 (November 25, 1847): 153–58; 2 (December 2, 1847): 164–66.

[281] *Ensign of Liberty* 1 (December 1847): 32–36.

[282] *Ensign of Liberty* 1 (January 1848): 54; and McLellan, telephone interview, for birth of Marcus Nelson McLellan.

[283] *Ensign of Liberty* 1 (January 1848): 63.

[284] *Ensign of Liberty* 1 (August 1849): 97.

[285] Hiram Page to Alfred Bonny, Isaac N. Aldrich, and M. C. Ishem June 24, 1849, in *Olive Branch,* Springfield, Ilinois, 2 (August 1849): 27–29; David later reported that in 1848 he recognized the displeasure of the Lord relative to the ordination of high priests. See David Whitmer, *An Address to All Believers in Christ* (Richmond, Mo.: David Whitmer, 1887), 65.

David Whitmer and others renounced the "errors of McLellinism" in *The Return,* Davis City, Iowa, 1 (January 1889): 10.

[286] *Olive Branch* 2 (August 1849): 28-29.

[287] *Olive Branch* 2 (August 1849): 29.

[288] *Ensign of Liberty* 1 (August 1849): 99-105.

[289] *Olive Branch* 2 (August 1849): 30; and 2 (June 1850): 190.

[290] Geauga County, Ohio, Deed Record no. 47, 269-70.

[291] Richard L. McClellan (no relation to William E. McLellin), telephone interview,Chesterland, Ohio, June 10, 1994.

[292] McLellin to Pratt, April 29, 1854; see also *The 1833 Ohio Gazetteer* (Columbus: Scott and Wright, 1833), 123.

[293] McLellin to Pratt, April 29, 1854.

[294] McLellin to Pratt, April 29, 1854.

[295] McLellin to Pratt, April 29, 1854.

[296] Lake County, Ohio Land Deed Record, vol. L, 56; Lake County, Ohio Land Deed Record, vol. R, 171-72.

[297] McLellan, letter to author.

[298] Ken L. Clark, Jr., telephone interview, May 18, 1994. Grace Clarke was born November 2, 1864, and Burdette Sidney Clarke on August 15, 1866. The two families stayed together, and the birth of the children are an index to the continued presence of the McLellins in Michigan.

[299] William E. McLellin to Joseph Smith [III], January 10, 1861, RLDS Church Archives; Linden, Michigan, is in Fenton township, Genesee County, and is sixty miles northwest of Detroit; see L. De Colange, *The National Gazetteer* (London: Hamilton, Adams, 1884), 570.

[300] McLellin to Smith [III], January 10, 1861.

[301] William E. McLellin to "Our very dear friends," July 12, 1869, RLDS Church Archives. In the letter, Emeline sent her "love to Mrs Bond and Mary." "Our very dear friends" appear to be Ira Bond, Charlotte W. Bond, and their daughter Mary W. Bond in Kirtland, Ohio; see Black, comp., *Early Members of the Reorganized Church* 1:516-18; see also Granville Hedrick to William E. McLellan, March 9, 1866, The Church of Christ (Temple Lot) Archives, Independence, Missouri.

[302] *The Truth Teller,* Bloomington, Illinois, 1 (October 1864): 57-58.

[303] John M. McLellan to Porter; there is a family note which states, "One son was killed during the war at Bowling Green, Kentucky." However, this is inaccurate; see "Descriptive Roll, Twenty Seventh Infantry Regiment, Michigan Volunteers, 1861-1866," vol. 27, page 9, Family and History Library, Salt Lake City, film no. 0915044, which lists him as being wounded in Virginia prior to the battle of Gettysburg, Pennsylvania; see also *Michigan, Civil War Centennial Observance Commission. Committee on Civil War Graves Registration. Graves Registration Records: Genesee County,* Film # 0914817, item #855; and Merle Perry, Jr., *Genesee County, Michigan Cemeteries,* 22 vols. (Flint, Michigan: Flint Genealogical Society, 1991), 21:79.

[304] Emma Smith Bidamon to Joseph Smith [III], February 2, 1866, RLDS Church Archives.

[305] Land Record Book S, Lincoln County, Mo., 179-80; and McLellan, letter to author.

[306] Saline County, Missouri, Deed of Trust Record Book 2, 119-21; see also Saline County, Missouri, Land Deed Record Book 5:575-76. In an 1869 indenture, James M. McLellan is named as a resident of Troy, Lincoln County, Missouri; see Saline County, Missouri, Land Deed Records Book O, 280-81.

[307] McLellan, letter to author; Saline County, Missouri, Land Deed Record Book 8, 13-14, 417.

[308] *Juvenile Instructor* 18 (May 15, 1883): 158.

[309] *Juvenile Instructor* 18 (May 15, 1883): 158.

[310] *Juvenile Instructor* 18 (May 15, 1883): 158-59.

[311] *Juvenile Instructor* 18 (May 15, 1883): 159.

[312] McLellin to "Our very dear friends," July 12, 1869.

[313] McLellin to "Our very dear friends," July 12, 1869; "Old Record," Church of Christ (Temple Lot), 28, cited in biographical notes of the late Inez Smith Davis, RLDS Church Archives; see *Saints' Herald* 121 (July 1974): 42, 450.

[314] McLellin to "Our very dear friends," July 12, 1869.

[315] McLellin to "Our very dear friends," July 12, 1869.

[316] McLellin to "Our very dear friends," July 12, 1869; Land Deed Records, Jackson Co., Missouri, Book 68:380; O. B. and Joanne Chiles Eakin, *Record of Original Entries to Lands in Jackson County Missouri* (Independence: O. B. and Joanne C. Eakin, 1985), 28.

[317] *Journal of History* 5 (April 1912): 214.

[318] Saline County, Missouri, Land Deed Records Book 11, 320.

[319] Church of Christ (Temple Lot), "Old Record Church of Christ," 28, in Inez Smith Davis, *The Story of the Church* (Independence: Herald Publishing House, 1964), 123n.

[320] McLellin to Bays, November 23, 1869, 291-92.

[321] William E. McLellin to "My dear old friends," October 21, 1870, RLDS Church Archives.

[322] William E. McLellin to "My old friends," February 22, 1872, RLDS Church Archives.

[323] McLellan, telephone interview; and John M. McLellan to Porter.

[324] The McLellin collection acquired by the LDS Church in 1908 contained, in addition to McLellin's six journals from the 1830s, six essays and one set of notes evidently written by McLellin around 1876-1877. Although they are late-in-life reflections, the notes usually address topics that attracted McLellin's attention almost half a century earlier. These materials sometimes advance views that differ from or contradict his earlier

positions, but McLellin never acknowledges those differences. The collection includes six papers, which are briefly summarized as follows.

"The Gospel" is a response to an October 1876 sermon. McLellin argues that Adam, Enoch, Noah, and others knew about the gospel, the mortal condescension of God in Christ, and the infinite atonement. He explains that the purpose of the gospel in its fullness is to allow all believers to commune directly with heaven and to be delivered both in body and spirit.

"The Blood of Adam and of Christ" is a January 1877 discussion of blood as the vehicle through which the fall of Adam came and, reciprocally, through which the atonement of Christ will be efficacious in at least fifteen enumerated ways. McLellin argues for an elevated status for Adam before the Fall and promotes many LDS doctrines, for example translated beings, celestial glory, and the understanding of the Fall found in the Book of Mormon.

"Priesthood" is a short undated essay about the orders of priesthood—patriarchal, Melchizedek, Aaronic, Christian—revealed by God in different eras. Contrary to his preaching in the 1830s about two priesthoods, McLellin here argues that only one priesthood order can exist on earth at a time.

"Spiritual Gifts and Powers" is an undated explication of the gifts of wisdom, knowledge, faith, healing, miracles, prophecy, discerning spirits, speaking in tongues (which he here claims should be used only if persons present do not understand the tongue spoken), and beholding angels. McLellin emphasizes the need for direct ministration of the Father, the Son, the Holy Spirit, or other intelligences in heaven.

"The Bible: Queries Respecting It" is a lengthy 1877 essay about the inspiration, composition, compilation, and translation of the Bible, blaming uninspired scribes and copyists for the many omissions, errors, and discrepancies in this sacred volume of scripture.

"Why I Am Not an L.D. Saint of Any Click or Party or Some Principles and Practices of the Church of Christ" is an 1878 statement that accepts Joseph Smith's gift to translate the Book of Mormon but objects to several aspects of Joseph Smith's ordination, titles, and prominence in the organization of the Church in 1830. Criticizes Zion's Camp for renouncing peace, and rejects the plurality of Gods, two priesthoods, baptism for the dead, tithing, and the restoration of the priesthood by John the Baptist.

In addition, McLellin wrote extensive notes on the "Ruins of Central America and Yucatan," copied verbatim and without comment from a book about some early travels in that area.

[325] *Deseret News,* December 21, 1901, 57.

[326] Steven L. Shields, *Divergent Paths of the Restoration* (Los Angeles: Restoration Research, 1990), 102.

[327] Orson Pratt to Marian Stevens House, September 18, 1878, in *Heart Throbs of the West,* comp. Kate B. Carter, 12 vols. (Salt Lake City: Daughters

of Utah Pioneers, 1939-51), 5:417; see also "Report of Elders Orson Pratt and Joseph F. Smith," *Millennial Star* 49 (December 9, 1878): 769-70.

[328] Joseph Fielding Smith, *Life of Joseph F. Smith* (Salt Lake City: Deseret Book, 1938), 238-40.

[329] Twelve letters of Joseph F. Smith to William E. McLellin, from December 5, 1878, to January 30, 1883, LDS Church Archives.

[330] Joseph F. Smith to William E. McLellan, March 7, 1879, LDS Church Archives.

[331] Joseph F. Smith to William E. McLellan, April 10, 1881, LDS Church Archives.

[332] McLellan, letter to author.

[333] *Saints' Herald* 29 (March 1, 1882): 67.

[334] *Saints' Herald* 30 (March 31, 1883): 194.

[335] *Journal of History* 5 (April 1912): 214-15.

[336] *Journal of History* 5 (April 1912): 215.

[337] Romig to Porter, February 18, 1994. My personal thanks to Ronald E. Romig and Annette Curtis of Missouri Mormon Frontier Foundation for locating the grave of William E. McLellin in February 1994. The Woodlawn Cemetery is situated on Noland Road in Independence, Missouri, between Pacific and Sea Streets. William E. McLellin is buried in lot 1, block 14, subdivision 1, section 2. The grave can best be reached by passing through the north entrance from Pacific Street on to High Street Drive in the cemetery. Turn left or east on the second street, which is Pine Avenue. The grave is on the south edge of Pine Avenue just forty-five yards west of the next intersection, which is Ever Green Way. There are no other headstones visible in Lot 1, and the records for individual lots were destroyed by fire. The lot is in the name of "Mrs. Emeline McLellan." However, Emeline is buried in Denison, Texas.

[338] *Saints' Herald* 29 (March 1, 1882): 67.

[339] RLDS Deceased Files; Early Reorganization Minutes, 1872-1905, Book D, in Black, *Early Members of the Reorganized Church* 4:371-72; and E. McLellin to Editors, December 1899, *Saints' Herald* 47 (1900): 26-27.

[340] Jackson County Deed Record Book 176, 585; McLellan to Kelley, April 24, 1892.

[341] Black, *Early Members of the Reorganized Church* 4:371-72; *Salt Lake Tribune,* January 3, 1986, Sec. B., 1; and Betty Clark Heller, telephone interview, Memphis, Tennessee, May 18, 1994.

[342] John M. McLellan to Porter.

Charting the Missionary Work of William E. McLellin: A Content Analysis

M. Teresa Baer

The Mormon missionary journals of William E. McLellin convey to readers an America much different from today.[1] For example, the harshness of 1830s life pulsates in McLellin's instances of frequently recurring illnesses without the comfort of qualified physicians. Descriptions of fording creeks at high water, being exiled for lengths of time by bitter cold or excessively rainy weather, traveling to exhaustion through overwhelming heat with only rancid food and water for sustenance, all add to a picture of the difficulty of early American life.

A bounty of idyllic snapshots shine through as well, though: the peacefulness of sitting atop a high hill overlooking the Mississippi River as it flows past log cabins and smoking chimneys; the amazement at encountering circuses for the first time in Canada and New York; the exhilaration of visiting Cincinnati, the western hub famous for its growing culture and enterprise; the wonder of trekking to a corner of Kentucky where mammoth bones had recently been discovered. These sights, too, project an authentic picture of America in the 1830s.

More importantly, McLellin's journals testify sincerely about converts to the Mormon Church in its earliest period. In Journal I, McLellin expresses his awe on first hearing about Mormonism from David Whitmer and Harvey Whitlock. Awe transforms into joy as McLellin accepts a vital role for a people whom he perceives as having inherited, at last, the true meaning of religion. Hundreds of Americans join in McLellin's spiritual conversion as he and other missionaries traverse the states, many as a result of being deeply touched by McLellin's strongly emotional convictions.

Throughout his missionary journals, McLellin also portrays the agonizing struggles which ensue in his heart and mind: times when he believes that the devil is fighting for his soul and times when he doubts the righteousness of his own discourse. Clearly, these journals compose a very thoughtful and personal reckoning of a schoolteacher become Mormon elder.

The journals also form a meticulous accounting of Mormon missionary preaching in the 1830s, for McLellin is a fine record keeper. The daily entries in his journals describe 434 appointments during which McLellin and other Mormon missionaries delivered orations or counseled individuals. The day, date, geographic location, and purpose of the meeting are always available or are easily discernible. More often than not, McLellin also provides information regarding time of day, setting, identity of the preacher, topics of discussion, and responses of the audience. For almost half the appointments, he relates details of audience size, societal or occupational status, and religious backgrounds, as well. All these details are statistically analyzed below in order to determine what McLellin's journals reveal about early Mormon missionary work.

Methodology

A specialist helped to design a database for analyzing the wealth of information in the six journals.[2] The database divides information about the preaching appointments into three categories: description of time, place, and setting; identification of the preachers and the topics of their exhortations; and description of the audiences and their responses to the Mormon preaching. Each category is then cross-referenced against all others for a complete internal comparison of the data. In most cases, sufficient data exists to render cross-tabulation useful. Of course, if less than 100 percent about either cross-indexed category is known, even less can be ascertained about them together. Tables and charts are then derived from these cross-referenced sets. The main results of this analysis will be summarized throughout the report.

In addition, a database-fields list follows in an addendum to this chapter. The list includes each category of data outlined below and its constituent parts. The fields list is a complete rendition of what was employed in the analysis and thus is an inclusive listing of the abundant and varied minutiae documented so faithfully by William McLellin.

Mormon Preachers

In each of the appointments that McLellin describes in his six journals, he indicates that one or more Mormons preached sermons, and he names 80 percent (n = 495) of them. Of these, McLellin names himself as preacher nearly two-thirds (n = 319) of the time. Another 12 percent (n = 57) of the time, he records that Parley Pratt lectured. Twenty-six other Mormons are mentioned less frequently. Their names follow in descending order according to how many times they delivered orations in the six journals: Hyrum Smith, Samuel Smith, David Patten, Joseph Smith, Jr., Lyman Johnson, Harvey Whitlock, Orson Hyde, Thomas Marsh, John Boynton, Brigham Young, David Whitmer, Lewis Zabriskie, Joseph Coe, Luke Johnson, Milo Andrus, Sidney Rigdon, Robert Culbertson, John Corrill, Brother Daniel (full name unknown), Frederick Williams, Gideon Carter, Heber Kimball, Levi Jones, Newel Knight, Reuben Fields, and Simeon Carter.

Attendance

McLellin records approximate audience size for 43 percent (n = 188) of the appointments. For almost two-thirds (n = 124) of these, small groups of 12 or fewer were present. Audiences for the remaining appointments were almost equally divided between medium-sized groups of 13 to 49 (n = 31) and large groups of 50 or more people (n = 33).

Small audiences attended almost evenly throughout the week: slightly more on Mondays, slightly less on Tuesdays. Diverging from this pattern, over one-fourth (n = 8) of the medium-sized audiences gathered on Sundays, none on Mondays, and very few on Fridays. The rest of the medium-sized groups assembled equally on Tuesdays, Thursdays, and Saturdays. As might be expected, over one-third (n = 13) of the large audiences collected at appointments on Sundays. Another third (n = 11) met on Mondays and Saturdays. The rest attended Tuesdays through Fridays.

Over time, audience size grew. In Journals I and II, 81 percent
(n = 13) and 82 percent (n = 23), respectively, of known audience
sizes are small. In Journal I, another 6 percent (n = 1) are medium
sized, and in Journal II, 11 percent (n = 3) are also medium-sized.
Twenty-two percent (n = 15) of the audiences in Journal III are
medium sized, and another 18 percent (n = 12) are large. By Journal
IV, almost one-third (n = 8) of the audiences are medium sized, and
7 percent (n = 2) are large. Close to one-fourth (n = 34) of the
audiences in Journal V are large, and 12 percent (n = 4) are medium
sized. Finally, 36 percent of the audiences in Journal VI are large.
Viewed from a different perspective, the data show that nearly three-
fourths (n = 23) of all medium-sized groups appear in the middle two
journals; and 82 percent (n = 28) of the large audiences surface in the
third, fifth, and sixth journals. Obviously, the Mormon Church was
attracting increasing attention.[3]

Preaching Topic Distribution

McLellin mentions 603 separate topics used for oratorical or
counseling purposes but describes only 71 percent (n = 566) in any
detail. These are divided into seven categories according to their
subject matter: distinctively Mormon topics, Mormon Church business, Mormon sacraments, general religious topics, general Christian
topics, Bible verses, and millennial topics.

Figure 1 depicts the distribution of the preaching topic categories.[4] Over one-fourth (n = 153) of all known topics and other
missionary activities relate specifically to Mormonism. Those themes
classified under distinctively Mormon topics mentioned most often
were exhortation, evidences of the Book of Mormon, and the Doctrine and Covenants. Almost 20 percent (n = 110) of the meetings
that McLellin and the other Mormon missionaries conducted were
for Mormon Church business or administering Mormon sacraments.[5]

The rest of the categories may or may not have involved
characteristically Mormon discourse. Although probably most
preaching by Mormon missionaries supported the developing
Mormon belief system, content analysis captures only that which
McLellin directly states. No assumptions about underlying Mormon
themes have been made in this study.

Figure 1: Distribution of Preaching Topics

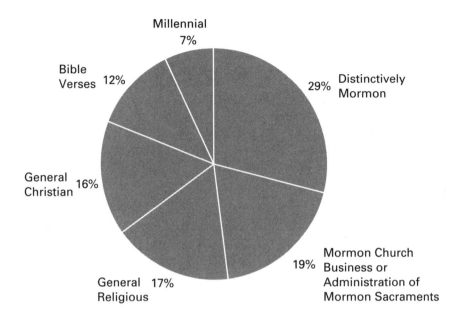

Seventeen percent (n = 96) of all topics and activities under-taken were generally religious. Besides a miscellaneous category of 38 one-time, specific discussions regarding particular situations at hand, the general religious themes most often reported are requests for donations for Mormon missionaries, support for the previous preacher's sermon, and personal counseling.

Another 16 percent (n = 93) of all topics pertain to Christianity in general. Laying on of hands, the Gospel, and the kingdom of Christ are the general Christian topics employed most often. General Christian and general religious topics together compose one-third (n = 189) of all topics.

Specific Bible verses total about 12 percent (n = 66) of all topics. The books quoted the most often include the Gospel of John, the First Epistle to the Corinthians, and the Second Epistle of Peter.

Almost 7 percent (n = 38) of all topics are about the Millennium. Those used most were the Judgment Day, the deliverance of Zion and/or Jerusalem, and the signs of the times.

McLellin provides attendance information in connection with 40 percent (n = 225) of the preaching topics. General religious topics were discussed 39 percent (n = 35) of the time in small groups. General Christian topics were also presented in over one-fourth (n = 24) of the time in small groups. Thus, general Christian topics were addressed over half the time (n = 24). While distinctively Mormon topics compose about one-fourth (n = 23) of all topics discussed in small gatherings, they were addressed an almost equal number of times regardless of audience size.

Mormonism was also the lecture subject nearly half the time (n = 18) with medium-sized groups. General Christian topics supplied another 23 percent (n = 9). Interestingly, the Millennium was almost never discussed in medium-sized gatherings. On the other hand, 63 percent (n = 5) of the time that the Millennium was the subject of a sermon, large audiences were present. Furthermore, half (n = 10) of the Bible verses that were quoted were quoted for large audiences. Large audiences heard specifically about Mormonism 40 percent (n = 23) of the time. Over half (n = 30) the time, they heard about general religious and general Christian topics and explications of Bible verses in almost equal amounts.

Geographic Location

The eleven states in which preaching appointments occur have been separated into three natural geographic categories: Missouri, the sparsely populated western frontier of the 1830s United States; the Midwest, referred to as "the West" during this period; and the Northeast, in and around New England. Using these divisions, nearly two-thirds (n = 284) of all appointments occurred in the Midwest, mainly in Ohio and Illinois. Another 22 percent (n = 94) transpired in the Northeast, and 13 percent (n = 56) were made in Missouri, mainly in the north and central parts of the state close to the Missouri River.

Mormon missionary meetings in Missouri were attended by much smaller audiences than those held in the Midwest or Northeast. All but one of the large audiences McLellin records met outside of Missouri, and only 19 percent (n = 6) of medium-sized audiences gathered there.

McLellin describes the time of day in which the meetings transpire for 65 percent (n = 282) of the appointments, but he rarely specifies the exact hour. In general, meetings on Mondays through Saturdays convened in the morning only 15 percent (n = 31) of the time, while 35 percent (n = 25) of all Sunday appointments started in the morning.

In Missouri, appointments were held in the afternoon or evening 91 percent (n = 30) of the time. Eighty-three percent (n = 148) of the appointments in the Midwest also met in the afternoon. The Northeast deviates somewhat from this standard. Only two-thirds (n = 47) of the appointments there occurred in the afternoon or evening.

Figure 2 cross-references preaching topics and geographic location. In the Midwest and the Northeast, general religious and general Christian topics compose close to 40 percent (n = 122; n = 38, respectively) of all topics preached about in the region. However, in the Northeast, sermons were preached on Bible verses almost one-third (n = 30) of the time. This number represents nearly three times the frequency of sermons about the Bible that McLellin records for the Midwest. On the other hand, millennial topics were used twice as frequently in the Midwest as in the Northeast. Additionally, distinctively Mormon topics were discussed slightly more often in the Midwest than in the Northeast.

Figure 2: Percent of Preaching Topics per Geographic Location

Topic Categories	Missouri [N = 47]	Midwest[1] [N = 305]	Northeast[2] [N = 104]
General Religious	49	18	16
General Christian	13	22	20
Bible Verses	6	11	29
Millennial	6	10	5
Distinctively Mormon	26	39	30

[1] Midwest: Illinois, Indiana, Kentucky, and Ohio.
[2] Northeast: Maine, New Hampshire, New York, Ontario, and Vermont.

Lecture material was much more conservative in Missouri than in the Midwest or Northeast. Of the topics utilized in Missouri, 62 percent (n = 29) are categorized as either general religious or general Christian. Neither topics dealing with the Bible nor with the Millennium were mentioned frequently here. Moreover, only about one-fourth (n = 12) of the topics pertained specifically to Mormon issues or beliefs. Obviously, Mormon missionaries preached a radically different message to the western-most United States citizens than they conveyed to more mainstream Americans.[6]

Setting

McLellin specifies the setting for two-thirds (n = 291) of the appointments. Of these, 62 percent (n = 181) are in private homes. However, as McLellin and the other Mormon missionaries traveled from west to east, more meetings were held in public settings, probably a reflection of the greater availability of public structures in the Northeast. On the Missouri frontier, 78 percent (n = 35) of the meetings occurred in homes. In the Midwest, 65 percent (n = 123) of the meetings transpired in homes (except in Kentucky where only 53 percent (n = 9) were held in houses). But schoolhouses were also popular, and on several occasions courthouses, churches, and the countryside served as meeting places in Missouri and in the Midwest. Rarely, however, were meetings in Missouri held in schoolhouses. In the more settled Northeast, however, 59 percent (n = 33) of the meetings were held in public settings, usually in schoolhouses but quite often in barns.

Figure 3: Percent of Preaching Topics per Setting

Topic Categories	Public Settings[1]	Private Settings[2]
General Religious [N = 159]	30	70
General Christian [N = 68]	41	59
Bible Verses [N = 39]	67	33
Millennial [N = 24]	63	38
Distinctively Mormon [N = 114]	52	48

[1] Public Settings: Barn, church, courthouse, countryside, meetinghouse, mill, school, and tavern.
[2] Private Settings: House.

Naturally, 86 percent (n = 102) of all appointments with small or medium-sized audiences were held in private homes, and 94 percent (n = 30) of meetings with large audiences met in public settings. On Saturdays and Sundays, meetings occurred equally in private and public settings, but on weekdays, meetings were held more often in private homes (average 69 percent, average n = 24).

Figure 3 indicates that far more general religious and general Christian topics were addressed in private rather than in public settings. Conversely, Bible verses and millennial topics occurred far more often in public settings than in houses. Distinctively Mormon topics were utilized about equally in both settings.

Preaching across Time

Figure 4 represents the sermon topics found in each journal. The number increases steadily from Journal I to Journal V. Nearly half (n = 207) of all topics appear in Journals IV and V. In Journal VI,

Figure 4: Total Missionary Discourse Topics across Time

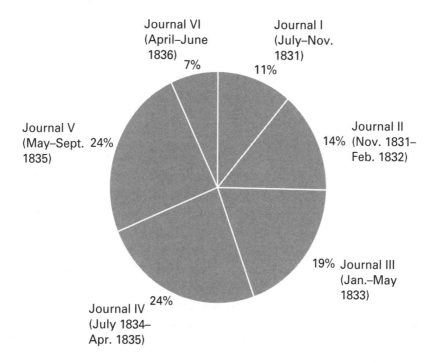

when William McLellin traveled alone to southern Ohio and northern Kentucky, sermonizing drops off dramatically. This decline in McLellin's missionary preaching preceded his upcoming resignation as a Mormon Apostle, and, therefore, is perhaps an augury of that notable event.[7]

Figure 5 portrays the distribution of preaching topic categories across time. General religious and general Christian topics increase in the years 1831–33 from 36 to 57 percent (n = 20, n = 51, respectively), then decrease steadily to 29 percent (n = 12) by 1836. At the same time, accounts of directly quoting the Bible increase from zero in 1831 to 29 percent (n = 30) of all topics in 1835, when the elders journeyed to the Northeast, and then decrease to 22 percent (n = 9) in 1836. In a reverse development, the use of millennial topics declines over time. Starting out as 16 percent (n = 9) of all preaching topics in 1831, the Millennium was employed less than one-third as often (n = 2) by 1836.

The extent to which distinctively Mormon topics were the focus of sermons appears more erratic when compared across time. Specific Mormon topics were addressed an average of 44 percent of the time in the first (n = 26), second (n = 28), fourth (n = 40), and sixth (n = 18) journals. Topics categorized as distinctively Mormon were mentioned less often in the fifth journal and rarely throughout the third journal. This phenomenon will be considered together with information regarding attendance, geographic location, and meeting purposes in the following section.

Purpose of Meetings

The purposes for all 434 appointments form five categories: Mormon Church meetings, Mormon sacrament meetings, Mormon business meetings, missionary preaching, and individual encounters.

Over one-half (n = 14) of all Mormon business meetings occurred on Mondays and Fridays. The rest transpired equally throughout the week except on Sundays, when almost none were held. In contrast, 42 percent (n = 37) of Mormon Church meetings (including those where baptisms and sacraments were performed) met on Sundays and another 19 percent (n = 17) on Wednesdays. The rest occurred fairly equally through the week.

Figure 5: Percent of Preaching Topics per Time Period

Topic Categories	Journal I July–Nov. 1831 [N = 55]	Journal II Nov. 1831–Feb. 1832 [N = 63]	Journal III Jan.–May 1833 [N = 90]	Journal IV July 1834–April 1835 [N = 103]	Journal V May–Sept. 1835 [N = 104]	Journal VI April–June 1836 [N = 41]
General Religious	18	16	38	18	16	17
General Christian	18	29	19	21	20	12
Bible Verses	0	2	11	16	29	22
Millennial	16	10	10	7	5	5
Distinctively Mormon	47	44	21	39	30	44

Thirty percent (n = 73) of the missionary preaching sessions transpired on Sundays and 16 percent (n = 38) on Fridays. The rest ranged fairly evenly throughout the week, the least being on Mondays. As the reader would anticipate, individual encounters arose every day of the week.

As noted, nearly two-thirds of the meeting times are known. Of the timing known for Mormon business meetings, over half (n = 7) were conducted in the morning, usually at 10 A.M. In contrast, more than four-fifths of Mormon Church and sacrament meetings (n = 57) and missionary preaching sessions (n = 127) met in the afternoon or evening. Three-fourths (n = 35) of the individual encounters also happened in the latter part of the day.

Of settings known, homes were employed almost exclusively for Mormon business meetings (90 percent, n = 9). Additionally, 83 percent (n = 54) of all individual encounters took place in homes, as did 77 percent (n = 41) of all Mormon Church meetings. In contrast, over half (n = 86) of all missionary preaching was conducted in public settings.

Of known attendance, all Mormon business meetings and almost all individual encounters involved small groups of people. Mormon Church meetings (including sacraments) also tended to be small: 63 percent (n = 17) had small audiences and 33 percent (n = 9) medium-sized audiences. Contrasting sharply with the other types of meetings, 44 percent (n = 32) of the missionary preaching sessions attracted large crowds, and 29 percent (n = 21) drew medium-sized audiences.

Figure 6 shows the distribution of preaching topic categories according to the purpose of the meeting. Interesting to note here is that the distribution of topic categories for meetings of Mormon Church members is almost equal to that for missionary preaching, including ample use of specific Mormon topics. Topics broached in individual encounters deviate markedly from those addressed for other meeting types. Twenty-seven percent (n = 21) of all individual encounters involved healings. Accordingly, almost one-third (n = 18) of all topics mentioned during one-on-one meetings involved laying on of hands which is classified in this analysis under general Christian topics. Therefore, supplemented heavily by activities regarding healing, general religious and general Christian topics compose three-fourths (n = 43) of all topics mentioned during personal meetings. Topics included in the categories of Bible verses and the Millennium are almost nonexistent, and distinctively Mormon topics (excluding sacraments and business themes) form less than one-fourth (n = 13) of the discussion topics for individual encounters.

The remainder of the charts show the cross-referenced distribution of McLellin's perceptions regarding preaching topic categories and audience responses. Overall, McLellin articulates his interpretation of audience responses for about 82 percent (n = 563) of the responses he appears to have encountered. For the comparison, negative and neutral responses are combined into unfavorable responses. The most common unfavorable responses are nothing gained, questioning, and disbelief. The most common favorable responses are new appointments, generally positive reactions, and baptism.

Seventy-three percent (n = 409) of all responses that McLellin describes are favorable. Favorable responses are slightly higher for private settings than for public ones. They are highest for New Hampshire (82 percent, n = 23) and lowest for Kentucky and Canada (61 percent, n = 17; and 62 percent, n = 8, respectively).

Figure 6: Percent of Preaching Topics per Purpose of Meeting

Topic Categories	Meetings of Church Members[1] [N = 97]	Missionary Preaching[2] [N = 264]	Individual Encounters[3] [N = 57]
General Religious	18	16	42
General Christian	20	19	33
Bible Verses	17	18	0
Millennial	7	11	2
Distinctively Mormon	39	36	23

[1] Meetings of Church Members: Mormon Church meetings and prayer meetings.
[2] Missionary Preaching: General preaching sessions and social occasions upon which Mormons preached.
[3] Individual Encounters: Individual meetings with Mormon preachers and healing sessions.

Figure 7 summarizes the overall audience responses to the preaching topic categories. Most favored were general Christian topics at 85 percent (n = 87), and Bible verses at 83 percent (n = 72). Listeners responded favorably to distinctively Mormon topics 78 percent (n = 173) of the time. Surprisingly, general religious topics were less well-received at 75 percent (n = 87). The Millennium was least-favored at 67 percent (n = 37). In fact, a much-used topic in this last category, the signs of the times, was the least favored overall.

Figure 8 shows that the message of the Saints was favored 95 percent (n = 72) of the time in Mormon Church meetings (excluding sacrament and business meetings). Favorable responses drop considerably for missionary preaching to 69 percent (n = 234) and even more for individual encounters. This last statistic is particularly interesting because it reveals the extent to which Americans disagreed about worship practices and general religious ideas even when members of the same church consulted among themselves—such as the Mormons were doing in almost half of the individual encounters.

The following kinds of meetings were called: 6 percent (n = 26) were Mormon business meetings, 20 percent (n = 88) Mormon Church meetings and Mormon sacrament meetings, 56 percent (n = 242) missionary preaching, and 18 percent (n = 78) individual encounters.

Forty-five percent (n = 35) of the individual encounters happened with fellow Mormons and the rest with non-Mormons (n = 43). If these two numbers are added appropriately to data about Mormon Church and sacrament meetings or to missionary preaching sessions, they reveal that the overall emphasis of the missionary journeys was approximately one-third (n = 149) to administer to Mormon churches and two-thirds (n = 285) to do missionary preaching.

Furthermore, apparently each missionary journey may have had an explicit goal—either to primarily minister to Mormon congregations, to primarily convert new members, or to do both. If all individual encounters are excluded as happenings which could not be planned in advance and all Mormon meetings are combined, a comparison of Mormon meetings versus missionary preaching sessions reveals that the journeys in Journals I, III, and VI were assumed primarily for missionary preaching (84 percent, n = 38; 86 percent,

Figure 7: Favorable Response per Preaching Topics

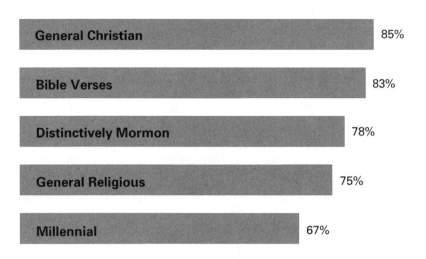

General Christian — 85%

Bible Verses — 83%

Distinctively Mormon — 78%

General Religious — 75%

Millennial — 67%

Figure 8: Favorable Response per Purpose of Meeting

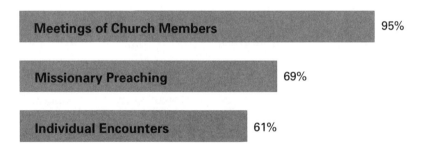

Meetings of Church Members — 95%

Missionary Preaching — 69%

Individual Encounters — 61%

n = 66; and 100 percent, n = 30, respectively); the journeys in Journal IV were predominantly for the administration of the Mormon Church (70 percent, n = 49); and the trips in Journal II were undertaken for a combination of purposes (45 percent Mormon Church, n = 21; and 55 percent missionary preaching, n = 26). What this analysis discloses about the purpose of the journey to the Northeast which McLellin describes in Journal V is misleading. Statistically, this trip served primarily the purpose of proselyting (70 percent, n = 61). In fact, however, this journey was a mission undertaken by the Council of the Twelve to hold local conferences with Mormon congregations throughout the Northeast. Therefore, many of the meetings that arc categorized as missionary preaching sessions were local conferences attended by a mixed audience of Mormons and non-Mormons.

Adding this information on purpose to the findings on attendance reveals that as the 1830s progressed, the Mormon missionaries attracted more people to their meetings whether they were ministering to Mormon congregations or working to increase membership. This pattern corroborates the well-known portrayal of the early Mormon Church as growing in renown and increasing in membership during this period. But two previous sections of this report relate that distinctively Mormon topics appear to have been avoided in certain places or during particular time periods. This suggests that the increasing renown was not always positive for the new church.

Combining comparisons between meeting purposes, geographic locations, preaching topics, and time periods demonstrates that the percentage of times when McLellin and his companions lectured specifically upon Mormon topics was quite high in Journals I, II, IV, and VI. During these tours, the Mormon missionaries traveled mainly in Ohio, northern Kentucky, and along the Illinois–Indiana border, where they often preached to Mormon congregations. Although McLellin describes topics which could be classified as singularly Mormon (e.g., the Book of Mormon, establishment of the Mormon Church, or Doctrine and Covenants) less than one-third of the time in Journal V, this was a tour, as indicated above, in which the Twelve were holding conferences with and speaking to congregations of Saints throughout the Northeast.

In Journal III, McLellin reports that distinctively Mormon topics were discussed only 21 percent of the time. On this tour from January to May 1833, McLellin and Parley Pratt visited central Missouri and worked in western Illinois along the Missouri–Illinois border to convert new members. During this period, the Mormon missionaries preached to some of their largest crowds, yet they seem to have avoided talking directly about Mormonism. The incongruity of these findings raises the possibility that preaching about Mormonism was not as welcomed or accepted in the "far west" as elsewhere in 1833. If this inference is correct, it supports the Mormons' accounts of the existence of hatred of the Saints and therewith foreshadows the impending persecution of the Mormons in Missouri.

Types of Audience Members

Sixty-two percent (n = 370) of the time, McLellin supplies some information regarding the social status and/or occupation of those in the audience. Excluding the incidence of Mormon elders and preachers as audience members (n= 49), 78 percent (n = 250) of the audience types are categorized as villagers. This category usually refers to people that McLellin portrays as residing in small settlements or towns but for whom he designates no occupations. However, 10 percent (n = 25) of those classified as villagers were farmers, and several were children and service industry personnel. Another 13 percent (n = 40) of the audience members McLellin describes were non-Mormon ministers, and 10 percent (n = 31) were professionals. About half (n = 16) of the audiences in which professionals are counted were those in which McLellin was an audience member before he began his missionary career. Of the remaining audience members classified as professionals, almost half (n = 7) were military personnel and just over half (n = 8) were doctors and lawyers.[8]

The reader should not view the breakdown of audience types or audience religions in the next section as gauges of how many people from each social, occupational or religious grouping were in attendance at a given time or place. First, McLellin tells us only what he knows—which is often very little. In the larger crowds, it would be almost impossible to list the social status, occupation, or religion of everyone in attendance. Nor was this part of his mission. Furthermore, each count of a social status, occupation, or religion may represent one or any number of people from the same grouping. These data cannot determine, for example, whether there were more professionals at Mormon missionary meetings in the Midwest or in the Northeast.

The area of audience religions is particularly problematic. While the purpose of a great deal of the preaching described in the journals was to convert new members, 73 percent (n = 202) of all the audiences where religion is specified are Mormon. One reason that more Mormons than members of other religious faiths appear in this analysis is that the religious affiliation of Mormons is easier to discern than that of others—McLellin often calls Mormons by characteristically Mormon titles such as *brother, sister,* and *elder*. Likewise, most of those whom McLellin designates as professionals and farmers lived in the Midwest—the area in which McLellin and several of his family members resided. The research cannot determine whether more people from these occupational groups lived in the underpopulated Midwest or whether McLellin was just more familiar with the people there. The latter must surely be true. Hence, the reliability of some of the statistical information for types of audience and audience religion is questionable.

Of known types of audience groups, professionals attended missionary preaching sessions 59 percent (n = 10) and individual encounters 29 percent (n = 5) of the time. Non-Mormon ministers appeared at missionary preaching sessions 63 percent (n = 25) and conversed individually with the missionaries 38 percent (n = 15) of the time. Villagers also came to missionary preaching 63 percent of the time (n = 156), but they also gathered at Mormon Church meetings (including sacraments) almost one-fourth of the time (n = 57).

Figure 9 compares preaching topics per type of audience. General topics compose almost one-half (n = 23) of all preaching topics for audiences including non-Mormon ministers, 41 percent (n = 11) of the topics when professionals are in attendance (including all incidences of McLellin as an audience member), but only 36 percent (n = 101) of topics if villagers are in the audience. Bible verses constitute only 4 percent (n = 1) of discussion topics for professionals; they form 8 percent of the topics (n = 4) for non-Mormon ministers and 16 percent (n = 46) for villagers. In contrast, frequency of use of the Millennium is highest for professionals and lowest for villagers. Distinctively Mormon topics, while lowest for non-Mormon ministers, compose close to 40 percent of topics utilized for all groups (professionals, n = 12; non-Mormon ministers, n = 19; and villagers, n = 115).

Figure 10 represents the favorable responses for types of audience groups. In order to correspond directly with figure 9, all incidences of McLellin's representation of the professionals category are included. As might be expected, villagers were the most favorably disposed to the message of the Saints, professionals less so, and non-Mormon ministers the least favorably inclined.

Figure 9: Percent of Preaching Topics
per Types of Audience

Topic Categories	Profes-sionals[1] [N = 27]	Non-Mormon Ministers[2] [N = 50]	Villagers[3] [N = 280]
General Religious	37	36	17
General Christian	4	10	19
Bible Verses	4	8	16
Millennial	11	10	6
Distinctively Mormon	44	36	41

[1] Professionals: Civil servants, doctors, lawyers, politicians, and military officers.
[2] Non-Mormon Ministers: Non-Mormon priests, preachers, and circuit riders.
[3] Villagers: Farmers, children, service industry personnel, and town dwellers of no specified occupation.

Figure 10: Favorable Response per Type of Audience

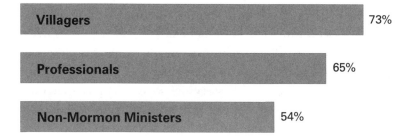

Villagers 73%

Professionals 65%

Non-Mormon Ministers 54%

Audience Religion

McLellin supplies information about audience religion approximately 46 percent (n = 278) of the time. Of those times, 73 percent (n = 202) are categorized as Mormons, 13 percent (n = 37) attendees from established religions, 9 percent (n = 26) Campbellite-Christians, and 5 percent (n = 13) those with unconventional beliefs. This breakdown does not, however, necessarily represent the religious affiliations of the audience population.

People with unconventional beliefs attended missionary preaching appointments or conversed individually with the Mormon missionaries most often on Sundays, Thursdays, and Fridays (69 percent, n = 9, divided equally). Members of established religions appeared on Sundays almost one-fourth (n = 9) of the time. Campbellite–Christians attended nearly one-fourth (n = 6) of the time on Wednesdays and 39 percent (n = 10) on Fridays and Saturdays. Mormons attended almost one-third (n = 62) of the time at Sunday meetings and 17 percent (n = 34) more on Wednesdays.

About three-fourths of the Mormon missionary meetings that Mormons and Campbellite–Christians attended were held in private homes (n = 90, n = 12, respectively). People of unconventional beliefs came to meetings at houses less often (two-thirds, n = 8). Those of established religions, however, attended only 56 percent (n = 19) of the time in private homes.

McLellin supplies information regarding attendance 45 percent (n = 124) of the time that he supplies information regarding audience religion. Audiences containing people of established religions comprise the biggest group in the large audience category (38 percent, n = 6). Audiences with Mormons in them constitute about one-third (n = 4) of large audiences. The medium-sized audience category is comprised primarily of audiences with Mormons (59 percent, n = 13), the rest divided almost equally between audiences containing members of established religions and/or Campbellite–Christians. The small-audience category includes even more audiences with Mormons in them (two-thirds, n = 60), and audiences including people from established religions make up 16 percent (n = 14) of these groups. Interestingly, the unconventional religionists that McLellin mentions attended only meetings of small audiences.

Not surprisingly, 99 percent (n = 129) of those religious groups known to have been at Mormon business or Church meetings (including sacraments) are Mormons. Mormon meetings compose 65 percent (n = 129) of the appointments that Mormons attended. Another one-fourth (n = 49) of the appointments involving audiences with Mormons are missionary preaching sessions. All other audience religion groups went to missionary preaching sessions between 54–65 percent (n = 7, n = 17) or had individual encounters almost all the rest of the time that they attended Mormon meetings.

Figure 11 compares preaching topics to audience religion. As this figure depicts, almost a third of the time those with unconventional beliefs, as well as Mormon Church members, heard a message that was either about general religious or general Christian topics; nearly one-half of the time, they heard about distinctively Mormon topics. On the other hand, Campbellite–Christians and those of established religions, both of whom were in competition with the rising Mormon Church, listened to a message that was general about one-half of the time. Both groups also learned about the Millennium approximately one-eighth of the time.

Mormons and those from established religions listened to considerably more explications of specific Bible verses than the other groups. Also, Campbellite–Christians, themselves members of a new religious organization, heard about distinctively Mormon topics with 17 percent more frequency than those from established religions who learned of them the least.

As figure 12 illustrates, audiences with Mormons in attendance showed the highest incidence of favorable responses at 92 percent (n = 202). Surprisingly, audiences including established religions responded with the next highest rate of favorable responses, but this figure is still 36 percent lower than for audiences containing Mormons.

Audiences encompassing people with unconventional beliefs and/or Campbellite–Christians were less favorably impressed. For these groups, McLellin records a near fifty-fifty split between favorable and unfavorable responses (favorable responses—unconventional, n = 10; Campbellite–Christian, n = 24).

Conclusions

Several patterns of early Mormon preaching emerge from the analysis of William McLellin's journals. The initial Mormons often competed with strongly opposed religious groups—those long established and those, like the Campbellites, that were newly arising alongside the Mormon Church. Mormonism, like the other American religions, was firmly grounded in Christianity. The fervor of the audience responses indicates, however, that the message of the Saints was unique—springing not only from Christianity, but also from a new vision, wondrous and controversial, about life and God.

Figure 11: Percent of Preaching Topics per Audience Religion

Topic Categories	Unconventional Beliefs[1] [N = 11]	Church Members[2] [N = 178]	Campbellite-Christians[3] [N = 43]	Established Religions[4] [N = 44]
General Religious	9	6	26	32
General Christian	18	25	21	21
Bible Verses	0	17	2	11
Millennial	18	6	12	14
Distinctively Mormon	55	47	40	23

[1] Unconventional Beliefs: Deists, Universalists, people who professed no faith, and one man who believed that God created a different "Adam" for each of the human races.

[2] Church Members: Mormon church members and new converts to Mormonism.

[3] Campbellite-Christians: These represented one newly emerging religion.

[4] Established Religions: Baptists, Methodists, Presbyterians, and Catholics.

Figure 12: Favorable Response per Audience Religion

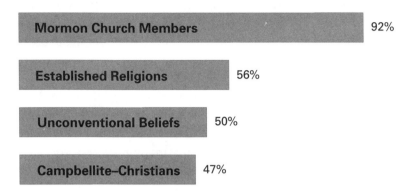

Mormon Church Members	92%
Established Religions	56%
Unconventional Beliefs	50%
Campbellite–Christians	47%

Although not in a manner that can be quantified, this intense scrutiny of William McLellin's journals reveals that the developing Mormon belief system played a vital part in the search by early Americans for spiritual truths equal to the extraordinary experiences they were encountering in the American wilderness-paradise. Mormon teachings garnered the curiosity of bold inquirers and captured hundreds of their hearts and intellects. Like William McLellin, these converts were profoundly touched by the Mormon message because it quenched their thirst for meaning and belongingness within the singular American republic.

The journals also tell us quite clearly that the purpose of the early Mormon missionary journeys was to increase membership as well as to minister to existing congregations. This pattern resembled the circuit-riding traditions of early American religious groups. Moreover, these journals also indicate that at the outset in the countryside the difference between Mormon worship patterns and those of other Christians was not as great as has sometimes been supposed. For example, Mormon meetings were most often held on Sundays and Wednesdays—the usual schedule for other Christian groups. Additionally, Mormons, like other Christians, often acted as faith healers.

But these traditional patterns within Mormonism existed alongside increasing efforts to set the Mormons apart from conventional Christian groups by "gathering the Saints together in Zion." McLellin comments very little about this latter movement, although it is obvious from the journals that he and his family dwelt with gathering multitudes of newly converted Mormons first in Independence, Missouri, and later in Kirtland, Ohio. Moreover, for a time, McLellin played an important role in Mormonism as it was developing in these gathering centers. The part he played at the center is not reflected in these journals, however.

The rediscovery and subsequent research of the six William McLellin journals tells a story of Mormonism in the countryside that had never been fully known. At the same time, they elucidate McLellin's great contribution to the inauguration of the Mormon missionary tradition. He was among the first converts and among the first of the Apostles, as well. His faith and dedication advanced the growth of The Church of Jesus Christ of Latter-day Saints, both with membership and with ideology. Now that his journals have been analyzed, McLellin once more augments the spiritual depth and growth of the Church. Indeed, McLellin's richly-detailed and sensitive accounts of early Mormon missionary work constitute invaluable primary sources for the history of the first half-decade of the Mormon Church and for the history of early nineteenth-century American religion, as well.

Addendum: Database Fields List

Journal Number: Journal I; Journal II; Journal III; Journal IV; Journal V; Journal VI.

Day of Week: Sunday; Monday; Tuesday; Wednesday; Thursday; Friday; Saturday.

Time: 8 A.M.; 9 A.M.; 10 A.M.; 11 A.M.; 12 P.M.; 1 P.M.; 2 P.M.; 3 P.M.; 4 P.M.; 5 P.M.; 6 P.M.; A.M. Exact time unknown; P.M. Exact time unknown; Not Available; Not Clear.

State: Missouri; *Midwest:* Illinois, Indiana, Kentucky, Ohio, Pennsylvania; *Northeast:* Canada (Ontario), Maine, New Hampshire, New York, Vermont; *Other:* Tennessee.

Setting: *Private:* House, Cabin, Dwelling; *Public:* Barn, Church, Courthouse, Countryside, Meetinghouse, Mill/Artisan Shop/etc., School, Tavern, Various (moved from one setting to another during appointment).

Meeting Type: *Mormon Church Business:* Mormon Church Business, Council of the Twelve; *Mormon Sacrament Meetings:* Baptism, Confirmation, Ordination, Sacrament/Communion; *Mormon Church Meetings:*

Mormon Church Meeting, Prayer Meeting; *Missionary Preaching:* Preaching session to convert new members, Social gathering; *Individual Encounters:* Healing; Individual Encounter.

Attendance: *Small:* One individual, Few/one dozen or less; *Medium:* Small group (13-24 people), 25-50 people/a house full; *Large:* Big group (50-100 people, meetinghouse full), Over 100 people/barn full.

Types of Audience: *Professionals:* Civil Servants (Sheriff, City Administrators, Teachers, etc.), Military Personnel, Politicians, Professional people (Doctors, Lawyers, Judges, etc.); *Non-Mormon Ministers:* Non-Mormon Ministers, Preachers, Priests, etc.; *Villagers:* Farmers/Rural Dwellers, Children/Adolescents, Service Industry Personnel (Ferrymen, Innkeepers, Shopkeepers, etc.), Villagers/Undescribed Townspeople.

Audience Religions: *Unconventional Beliefs:* Belief in many different "Adams," Deist, Professors of no religion, Shaker, Universalist; *Mormons:* Mormon, and those newly baptized Mormon; *Campbellite-Christians:* Campbellite, Christian; *Established Religions:* Baptist, Catholic, Methodist, Presbyterian.

Preachers: Bro. Coe (probably Joseph); Brigham Young; Bro. Daniel (last name uncertain); David Whitmer; David Patten; Frederick Williams; Gideon Carter; Heber Kimball; Hyrum Smith; Harvey Whitlock; John Corrill; John Boynton; Joseph Smith, Jr.; Levi Jones; Luke Johnson; Lyman Johnson; Lewis Zabriskie; Milo Andrus; Newell Knight; Orson Hyde; Reuben Fields; Robert Culbertson; Simeon Carter; Samuel Smith; Sidney Rigdon; Thomas Marsh; Various preachers, known or unknown; William McLellin.

Topics: *General Religious Topics: Other:* Charity; Spiritual counseling/ Consolation; Defame creeds of men; Donation requested for Mormon preachers; Faith; False religions; Forgiveness; Farewell to congregations; Glories of heaven; Humility; Lord's Prayer; Preaching about prayer; Praise to the Lord; The priesthood; Refute opposing preacher's antagonism; Singing; Support/Testimony for previous preacher's preaching; Miscellaneous, one-time discussions; Trust in God, not man; World confusion.

 General Christian Topics: General Scriptures: Authority to act in name of Jesus Christ; Early Christianity; Evidences of truth; Fall of Jews; Faith of the Saints; Gentiles and Jews; Relations/Actions of God to man; Nature of gifts/Gifts; "Gospel"; Laying on of hands; Holy Spirit; Jesus Christ; Kingdom of Christ; Life/Immortality; Principles of perfection; Prophecies; False/True Prophets; Resurrection; "Scriptures"; Sectarian quotes of scripture; Bearing testimony.

 Bible Verses: Bible: Communion/Last Supper; Gospels (Matthew, Mark, Luke, and John); New Testament; Old Testament; Parables; Specific biblical text; Acts 20, no verse given; 1 Corinthians 2, no verse given; 1 Corinthians 12, no verse given; 1 Corinthians 13, no verse given; 1 Corinthians 13:2;

Ephesians 1, no verse given; Ezekiel 6, no verse given; Galatians 1, no verse given; Galatians 1:6; Galatians 1:8; Galatians 5:19; Genesis 17:1; Hebrews 11, no verse given; Hebrews 12:14; Isaiah 8:20; Isaiah 11, no verse given; Isaiah 49, no verse given; Jeremiah 31:31; John 3, no verse given; John 5:30; John 5:39; John 10, no verse given; John 14, no verse given; John 14:2; John 14:26; Luke 6:20; Mark 1:14; Mark 1:15; Mark 13:21; Matthew 24:3; 2 Peter 1, no verse given; 2 Peter 1:1; 2 Peter 1:5; Philemon:3; Psalm 37:37; Psalm 102:1; Romans 8, no verse given; Romans 8:14; 1 Thessalonians 1:5; 2 Timothy 3:16; 2 Timothy 4, no verse given; 2 Timothy 4:2.

Millennial Topics: Millennium: Book of Revelation; Deliverance of Zion and/or Jerusalem; Gathering of Jews and/or Indians; Glories of millennial reign; Judgment Day; Plan of salvation; Signs of times.

Mormon Church Business: Mormonism: Church business.

Mormon Sacraments: Mormonism: Baptism; Confirmation; Invitation to join Mormon Church; Ordination; Sacrament/Communion.

Distinctively Mormon Topics: Compare Bible and Book of Mormon: Covenants of Abraham and Joseph, Crosscheck, Establishment of religions, Two priesthoods, Religions (Old and New Testaments and Book of Mormon); *Mormonism:* Alma and Amulek, Authority of Mormon Church, Book of Mormon, Doctrine and Covenants, Establishment of Mormon Church, Evidences of Book of Mormon, Exhortation, Gifts of the Mormon Church, Interpreting what was spoken in tongues, Joseph Smith's revelations, Mormon Church laws, Difference between Mormonism and contemporary religions, Difference between Mormonism and world confusion, Principles of Mormon religion, Sinning/Abuse of gifts of Mormon Church, Speaking in tongues, Testimony for Mormonism, Gathering at Zion, Specific Book of Mormon text, Testimony of Three Witnesses.

Responses: *Favorable Responses: Positive:* New appointment(s); Attentiveness; Baptism; Belief; Purchase/Borrow Book of Mormon; Invitation to supper/board; Commitment to obey Mormon Church laws, God's will, or elder's advice; Confession; Contribution (money, clothing, etc.); General [generally positive]; Healing(s); Interpreting what was spoken in tongues; Joyousness; Solemnity/Seriousness; Speaking in tongues; Subscription to *Star* or *Messenger & Advocate;* Tears; Audience votes for Mormons to preach/preach longer; Received witness from God.

Unfavorable Responses: Negative: Anger; Specific challenges to particular doctrinal elements; Disbelief; Deliberate disruptive activities; General [generally negative]; Inattentiveness, general disorder; Indifference; General antagonistic opposition; General rejection; Complete silence; Rudeness.

Neutral: Compare Bible and Book of Mormon; Nothing gained; Questioning.

Miscellaneous Codes: Information not available; Information not clear (blotted, stricken out, left blank, coded).

NOTES

[1]The author would like to gratefully acknowledge the assistance of Tere Hogue, School of Liberal Arts Writing Center (IUPUI).

[2]The database specialist, William Stuckey, is the Coordinator of Technical Services for the School of Liberal Arts (IUPUI).

[3]See the meeting purpose section of this article.

[4]All percentages listed in the text and the figures are rounded off.

[5]Combined here, these two categories are included only when pertinent to a comparison. They will be identified throughout this report when involved in cross-tabulations.

[6]See the meeting purpose section of this article.

[7]McLellin was reconciled to the Mormon Church in 1837 only to be excommunicated in 1838. See letter of McLellin to the Quorum of the Twelve Apostles, *HC* 3:31.

[8]Unless stated otherwise, except for the first two meetings that McLellin attended before he left his home to follow the Mormons, accounts describing his attendance while he was still a teacher have been dropped from the analysis concerning types of audiences.

Appendix I: Articles in Early LDS Periodicals on Subjects of Preaching in McLellin's Journals

The following topics correspond with preaching subjects mentioned in the McLellin journals. These topics are also the subject of articles that appeared in the *Evening and Morning Star* (Independence, Missouri, and Kirtland, Ohio, June 1832–Sept. 1834):

The Articles and Covenants (D&C 20) and laws of the Church (June, July, Oct. 1832; Jan., Mar., June 1833); baptism and laying on of hands (Apr. 1833); Book of Mormon (June, Aug., Nov., Dec. 1832; Jan., Feb., June, July 1833); Christianity (Sept., Oct., Nov. 1832); Church government (Oct. 1832); duties of elders (July, Nov. 1832; Jan. 1833); the ensign to the nations (June 1832); errors of the Bible (July 1833); faith of the Saints (Feb., Apr.-Sept. 1834, and continued in the *Messenger and Advocate,* Nov. 1834 to Aug. 1837); false prophets (July 1833); false religions of the day (July 1833); gathering of the Saints (June, July, Aug., Dec. 1832, Jan., June, July 1833); gospel of Jesus Christ (Apr. 1833; Aug., Sept. 1834, and continued in the *Messenger and Advocate,* Nov. 1834 to May 1837); Jews and Gentiles (Feb. 1833); judgment day (Oct. 1832); kingdom of God (Jan. 1833); millennium (Dec. 1832; Sept. 1833; Jan., Feb., Apr.-Aug. 1834, and continued in the *Messenger and Advocate,* Nov. 1834 to May 1835); prayer (Sept. 1832; Mar. 1833); priesthood (Jan. 1833); prophecy (Jan. 1834); restoration of the Jews (Aug., Dec. 1832; June, July 1833); resurrection (Dec. 1832); revelation (Sept. 1832); rise and establishment of the Church (Mar., Apr., June, July 1833; May 1834); scripture (July, Aug. 1832; May 1833); errors of the Bible (July 1833); second coming of Jesus Christ (June, Sept. 1832; June 1833); signs of the times and the works of God in the last days (Aug., Oct. 1832; Jan., Feb., Mar., Apr., June, July, Dec. 1833; Sept. 1834); two places of gathering (Dec. 1832); and Zion (Dec. 1832).

For similar articles from the *Messenger and Advocate* (Kirtland, Ohio, Oct. 1834 through Sept. 1837) that likewise correspond with topics found in the McLellin journals, see, for example, the following titles:

"Anniversary of the Church of Latter Day Saints," 3, no. 7 (Apr. 1837): 486-89

"Beware of Delusion," 2, no. 4 (Jan. 1836): 250-52

"Delusion," 1, no. 6 (Mar. 1835): 90-93, on internal evidences for the Book of Mormon

"Evidences of the Book of Mormon," 3, no. 4 (Jan. 1837): 433-35

"Faith of the Church," a series that ran from 1834 to 1836

"Let Every Man Learn His Duty," 2, no. 4 (Jan. 1836): 248-50

"Order of the New Testament Church. No. I," 2, no. 2 (Nov. 1835): 212-14

"Perfection," 2, no. 8 (May 1836): 310-12; and 3, no. 2 (Nov. 1836): 406-8

"The Ancient Order of Things," 1, no. 12 (Sept. 1835): 183-86

"The Record of the Nephites," 2, no. 1 (Oct. 1835): 203-4

"The Saints and the World," 3, no. 3 (Dec. 1836): 417-23

"The Saints of the Last Days," 2, no. 8 (May 1836): 307-12

"To the Saints," 2, no. 2 (Nov. 1835): 219-20

"The Gospel," a series that ran from 1834 through 1837

"Millennium," a series from 1834 to 1835

"Latter Day Glory," regarding the Restoration of the Gospel, 3, no. 2 (Nov. 1836): 401-4

Revelation, in "Latter Day Saints," 2, no. 8 (May 1836): 315-16

"Prayer," 1, no. 11 (Aug. 1835): 168-70

"Prophetic Warning," 2, no. 10 (July 1836): 342-46

"Is the End Near?" 1, no. 10 (July 1835): 149-50

"Lo, the Days Come, &c." 1, no. 11 (Aug. 1835): 166

Zion, in "To the Elders of the Church of Latter Day Saints," 1, no. 12 (Sept. 1835): 179-82; 2, no. 2 (Nov. 1835): 209-12; and 2, no. 3 (Dec. 1835): 225.

In addition, several letters from Oliver Cowdery, W. W. Phelps, Sidney Rigdon, Warren Cowdery, and others published in the *Messenger and Advocate* regularly mention such topics as the Book of Mormon, revelation, the rise and establishment of the Church, priesthood authority, spiritual gifts, the gathering of Zion, signs of the times, and the millennium. Especially relevant to these topics is the running correspondence between Oliver Cowdery and W. W. Phelps.

Appendix II: Other Early Mormon Missionary Journals and Accounts

In addition to the McLellin Journals, the following missionary journals or accounts from the 1830s are housed in the LDS Church Archives:

Aldrich, Hazen. Three one-page synopses of missionary labors in Illinois and Ohio with Willard Snow, Oct. 1834–Feb. 1835; traveling east from Kirtland, Ohio, to New Hampshire and Maine, partly in company with Darwin Richardson, June–Dec. 1835; and in New York, Vermont, and lower Canada, May–Oct. 1836.

Barnes, Lorenzo Dow. Reminiscences and diaries, 1834–39, include an account of missionary journeys in Ohio, Virginia, Kentucky, and Pennsylvania.

Burket, George. This 97-page manuscript contains an account of missionary travels through Illinois during March and April 1836 and travel to Clay County, Missouri, Apr.–May 1836. The volume begins with a copy of a December 1833 revelation later published as section 101 of the Doctrine and Covenants.

Cahoon, Reynolds. Two journals from June–Sept. 1831 and Jan.–Aug. 1832, giving an account of his missionary travels through Ohio, Indiana, and Illinois on his way to Independence, Missouri, and return journey to Ohio. Includes references to his association with Hyrum Smith, William E. McLellin, and other early church leaders.

Carter, Gideon Haden. A 43-page account of his missionary travels in New York and Vermont with Sylvester Smith, Apr.–Dec. 1832.

Carter, Jared. A 189-page manuscript including missionary journeys through Vermont, New York, and Michigan in 1833.

Carter, John Simms. This 94-page journal covering Dec. 1831–Sept. 1833 describes missionary activities in Vermont and New York and includes an extract from a revelation found in section 88 of the Doctrine and Covenants.

Carter, Simeon. Two-page synopsis of his missionary labors, in company with others, primarily in Illinois and Indiana, beginning in Nov. 1834.

Coe, Joseph. A short missionary report given March 7, 1832 of labors primarily in Ohio and New York.

Coltrin, Zebedee. Three volumes include accounts of several missionary journeys in Missouri, Ohio, Pennsylvania, and New York, 1832–34. Includes a copy of Doctrine and Covenants, sections 20 and 42, as recorded by John Whitmer.

Cowen, Horace. A record of meetings and baptisms, Mar. 1833–Jan. 1834, in Pennsylvania, New York, New Hampshire, Vermont, Maine, Massachusetts, and lower Canada.

Gates, Jacob. One-volume account of his 1836 missionary travels to Illinois and Indiana.

Grant, Jedediah Morgan. Includes an account of his missionary travels from Kirtland to New York, mainly from Apr. 1836 to Aug. 1837. The diary of Harvey Stanley, Grant's missionary companion in 1835, is in the same 42-page volume.

Greene, Evan M[o]lbourne. Four volumes of his missionary travels in northeastern Ohio, Jan.–Mar. 1833; New York, Massachusetts, and Maine, Apr. 1833–Sept. 1834; south of Kirtland, Oct.–Dec. 1834; and in New York, July–Oct. 1835.

Greene, John Portineus. Eleven-leaf diary, Sept.–Oct. 1833. Account of his missionary travels in Chautaugua and Erie counties in New York, mentions a meeting with Joseph Smith and Sidney Rigdon on their way to Canada.

Hancock, Solomon. A brief missionary report of labors in Missouri and Illinois between Jan. and Apr. 1835, en route from Missouri to Ohio, with companion, Charles W. Patten.

Holmes, Milton. Three-page missionary report covers missionary efforts between Dec. 1834 and Mar. 1836, mostly in Tennessee and Illinois.

Hutchings, Elias. A 30-page summary of missionary travels in Ohio, Dec. 1834–Feb. 1835 and 1836.

Hyde, Orson. This 94-page journal is an account of missionary experiences with Samuel H. Smith in New York, Massachusetts, and in the East from Feb.–Dec. 1832.

Johnson, Joel Hills. Volume briefly recounts his missionary travels in east central Ohio, Aug.–Sept. 1835, part of the time in company with Ezra Thornton. This same account is recopied in another volume.

Lyman, Amasa. Four volumes include missionary travels in Virginia, Ohio, and Pennsylvania in 1833; New York, New Hampshire, and Vermont in 1834; Ohio, Pennsylvania, and New York in 1835; and New York in 1836.

Martin, Moses. Entries from May–Nov. 1834 include an account of missionary travels in Ohio.

Morley, Isaac. A brief, April 19, 1835, report by Isaac Morley and Calvin Beebe, summarizing their missionary activities in Missouri, Illinois, Indiana, and Ohio.

Murdock, John. One volume includes a copy of daily entries for his missionary travels in Missouri, Ohio, and New York. Nine-page diary details his missionary journey through Missouri, Feb.–June 1832, in company with Parley P. Pratt, Lyman Wight, and Levi Hancock.

Partridge, Edward. Two reports from 1835 and a one-volume diary summarize his missionary travels with Thomas B. Marsh, Feb.–Apr. 1835, in Missouri, Illinois, Indiana, and Ohio. Also his mission to the east with Isaac Morley, June–Oct. 1835.

Patten, David Wyman. 57-page journal from July 1832–July 1834 includes missionary activities in Michigan, Ohio, Tennessee, and other states.

Post, Stephen. Journal contains an account of his missionary activities beginning in March 1836 in Ohio, Pennsylvania, and New York.

Pratt, Orson. Volumes span June 1833–June 1834 and Feb. 1835–Nov. 1837. Accounts of various missionary travels in Ohio, Canada, New Hampshire, New York, Vermont, and Pennsylvania.

Rathbun, Robert. A brief 1833 report recounts missionary activities while traveling from Missouri, through Illinois and Indiana, to Ohio, between August and October in an unnamed year.

Rich, Charles Coulson. Five volumes contain accounts of his journey from Missouri to Illinois in July 1834; a trip to Eugene, Indiana, to attend a conference with Solomon Wixom, Oct.–Nov. 1834; missionary travels in Illinois, Apr.–June and Sept.–Nov. 1835; missionary travels in Illinois, Indiana, Kentucky, and Ohio; mission with Lyman Wight to purchase land for the Church in Missouri, Oct.–Dec. 1836.

Robbins, Lewis. Brief missionary report given Feb. 24, 1834. A synopsis of his missionary travels from Missouri, through Illinois and Indiana, to Kirtland, Oct. 1834–Jan. 1835.

Smith, Eden. A 15-page journal from Sept. 1831–Aug. 1832 records a number of brief preaching tours in Ohio, during which he performed baptisms and other ordinances.

Smith, Hyrum. Brief entries in two volumes describe his travels to preach and visit Latter-day Saint congregations in Ohio, Dec. 1831–Jan. 1832, and to preach to his Smith uncles in New York with David Whitmer, Aug.–Sept. 1835.

Smith, John. Diary covers May 1831–Aug. 1832 and includes an account of missionary travels near his home in Portage County, Ohio, including one journey with Joseph Smith, Sr.

Smith, John. Two volumes include entries regarding missionary labors in and around Potsdam, New York, where he resided, Jan.–May 1833. Also his missionary travels in New York and New Hampshire, 1836, in company with his brother, Joseph Smith, Sr.

Smith, Samuel Harrison. Missionary report of labors in company with William E. McLellin in eastern Ohio, Nov.–Dec. 1831. Diary from Feb. 1832–May 1833 recounts missionary activities with Orson Hyde, traveling eastward through Ohio, Pennsylvania, New York, and New England.

Smoot, Abraham. Entries describe his missionary travels in Tennessee and Kentucky during 1836, with Wilford Woodruff, David W. Patten, Warren Parrish, and others.

Snow, Erastus. Lengthy journal and abridgement describe missionary activities in and around his hometown of St. Johnsbury, Vermont, and in New Hampshire. Also travel to Kirtland, Nov.–Dec. 1835; and missionary travels in Pennsylvania, Apr.–Dec. 1836.

Snow, Willard. Brief missionary report mentions missionary travels with Hazen Aldrich, Oct. 1834–Feb. 1835 in Missouri, Illinois, Indiana, and Ohio.

Snow, William. Journal includes local missionary work, July 1832–Jan. 1833.

Stanley, Harvey. His 49-page journal covers May–Oct. 1835 and records missionary travels with Jedediah M. Grant in New York. A journal of Jedediah M. Grant, dated 1836–1839, is located in the same volume.

Stephens, Daniel. Missionary report briefly reviews preaching in New York and Pennsylvania and missionary activity while traveling east between Missouri and Kirtland.

Waite, Truman. A 5-page, 1833 missionary report mentions two brief missions in Ohio, Mar.–Sept. 1833, one with Jenkins Salisbury and the other with Milo Andrus. A one-page account written in 1835 summarizes his activities, Aug. 1834–Aug. 1835, including missionary labors in Ohio and New York.

West, Nathan. A two-page missionary report written in 1835 recounts missionary labors in Indiana and Ohio with Levi Hancock and later with Zebedee Coltrin.

Whitmer, Peter, Jr. Brief synopsis of his mission to the Lamanites, 1830-31, with Oliver Cowdery, Parley P. Pratt, and Ziba Peterson.

Willes, Thomas L. This Apr.-Oct. 1833 diary recounts missionary travels in Pennsylvania and New York.

Wixom, Solomon. Diary includes brief entries referring to his missionary travels in Missouri, 1835, and in Illinois, 1835-36, with Charles C. Rich as one of his companions.

Woodruff, Wilford. Two journals record his proselyting activities in Arkansas, Tennessee, and Kentucky, 1835-36. His missionary companions included Warren Parrish, David W. Patten, Thomas B. Marsh, and Abraham O. Smoot.

Young, Brigham. Several small journals document missionary travels in western New York, 1832; missionary labors in Mendon, New York, and Canada, 1833; travels with members of the Twelve through the eastern states, May-Sept. 1835.

We express appreciation to Steve Sorensen of the LDS Church Archives for supplying the data about these early missionary journals.

In the archives of the RLDS Church, a journal of this general type by James A. Blakeslee can be found; it contains 227 small pages, covering events from 1837-46; also, a personal history by James Marvin Adams, 19 large pages, ending in 1844.

Appendix III: Baptism Register

LDS baptisms performed by William E. McLellin:

1.	Reuben Fields	11/27/1831	Warren, OH
2.	Mrs. Reuben Fields	11/27/1831	" "
3.	Mother C. Reed	12/14/1831	Weathersfield, OH
4.	Sarah St. John	12/14/1831	" "
5.	Elizabeth Everhart	12/14/1831	" "
6.	Samuel Burwell	12/14/1831	" "
7.	Celia Burwell	12/28/1831	" "
8-16.	Nine children	1/23/1832	Kirtland, OH
17.	Shadrick Roundy	1/30/1832	" "
18.	Robert McCord	3/6/1833	Eastern MO
19.	James H. Reed	5/5/1833	Bluffdale, IL
20.	Joseph Jackson	5/5/1833	" "
21.	Katharine Holden	5/5/1833	" "
22.	Nancy Simmons	5/5/1833	" "
23.	John Cooper	8/5/1834	Eugene, IN
24.	Louisa Baily	8/5/1834	" "
25.	Elizabeth Smith	8/10/1834	" "
26.	Harris Park	8/24/1834	" "
27.	Eden Smith	8/27/1834	" "
28.	Charles Curtis	8/27/1834	" "
29.	Elizabeth Cady	8/27/1834	" "
30.	Elisha Hill	8/31/1834	" "
31.	Catrin Hill	8/31/1834	" "
32.	Rachael Smith	9/7/1834	" "
33.	Philip Curtis	9/7/1834	" "
34.	Sally Curtis	9/7/1834	" "
35.	Henry Bailey, Sr.	9/10/1834	" "
36-41.	Six people	12/5/1834	Huntsburgh, OH
42.	Dudley	1/17/1835	" "
43-44.	Two people	1/17/1835	" "
45.	Jotham Gardner	3/28/1835	" "
46.	Mrs. Gardner	3/28/1835	" "

47-50.	Four people	3/30/1835	Huntsburgh, OH
51.	Benjamin Brown	5/10/1835	Westfield, NY
52.	Rebecca Brown	5/10/1835	" "
53.	Nancy Snyder	5/10/1835	" "
54-55.	Two people	5/10/1835	" "
56.	Chapman	5/30/1835	Hate, NY
57-58.	Two Unknown	6/21/1835	Pillar Point, NY
59.	Eunice Lommery	6/22/1835	" "
60.	David Colvin	6/22/1835	" "
61.	Amelia Barrows	7/27/1835	Dalton, NH
62.	Ethan Barrows	7/27/1835	" "
63-66.	Four people	8/3/1835	Lyman, NH
67.	Hiram Caffa	8/4/1835	" "
68.	Betsy Caffa	8/4/1835	" "
69.	Polly Wright	8/4/1835	" "
70.	Talitha Cumi Carter	8/4/1835	" "
71.	Unknown	8/5/1835	" "
72.	Albert Millen	8/6/1835	" "
73.	Carter Huntoon	8/6/1835	" "
74.	Fanny Athington	8/10/1835	Dalton, NH
75.	Perces Athington	8/10/1835	" "
76.	James Johnson	8/14-16/1835	Errol, NH
77.	Hezk. Johnson	8/14-16/1835	" "
78.	N. Johnson	8/14-16/1835	" "
79.	Charlotte Cone	8/14-16/1835	" "
80.	Angeline Sweat	8/14-16/1835	" "
81.	Sally Shattuck	8/14-16/1835	" "
82.	Frederick Sweat	8/14-16/1835	" "

LDS baptisms performed either by McLellin or his companions:

1.	Aaron Holden	4/15/1833	Bluffdale, IL
2.	James White	4/15/1833	" "
3.	Sophia White	4/15/1833	" "
4.	Susannah Campbell	4/21/1833	" "
5.	Elizabeth Reed	4/21/1833	" "
6.	Mandana Campbell	4/23/1833	Near Bluffdale, IL
7.	Mary Ann Clark	4/23/1833	" "
8.	Levi Merick	5/1/1833	" "
9.	R. Barker	1/18/1835	Huntsburgh, OH

Biographical Register

This biographical register lists every personal name that McLellin mentions in his journals. Each entry begins with the surname as McLellin wrote it. When McLellin spells a name both correctly and incorrectly, his incorrect spelling is in parentheses. If McLellin uses two equally possible variations, both spellings are listed in capital letters, connected by *or*. If available, the birth and death dates of each person are listed in parentheses following the name. Biographical information in the register focuses on events in the 1830s. Only correct spellings of place names are used here; variations are covered in the Gazetteer. We were unable to identify many of the people McLellin mentions. When several options are possible, we list them and give information on likely candidates. Entries for the names for which we could find no outside information only reflect the roles of these people in the journals. Full citations of sources abbreviated in brackets at the end of each entry are given in the bibliography at the end of this register. The subject index in this volume can be used to locate the page number in the journals on which these individuals are mentioned by McLellin.

AKERS, S., traveled with McLellin and Elder Bean from Errol, New Hampshire, to the Farmington conference in Farmington, Maine, in Aug. 1835. Probably Samuel Akers (1793–1870), born in Bradford, New Hampshire, on Mar. 3, 1793, to John Akers and Esther Buck. Married Sarah Whittimore. Died on Dec. 30, 1870. His heir is listed as Perrigrine Sessions. [TIB.]

ALDRICH, Isaac (d. 1882), was ordained a priest by Lyman E. Johnson on July 24, 1833, at a conference held in Charleston, Vermont. Orson Pratt records he was ordained an elder on Sept. 28, 1833. Hosted McLellin for two nights in Aug. 1835 while living fifteen miles from the Connecticut River. Possibly the same Isaac Aldrich who was born on Mar. 11, 1817, in Fitzwilliam, New Hampshire, to Isaac and Abigail Aldrich. Married Abigail Ann Everett on Aug. 29, 1839, and died on July 30, 1882. [JH, July 24, Sept. 28, 1833; and TIB.]

ALLEN, A., was living in Kirtland, Ohio, when McLellin visited him on Dec. 3, 1834. Possibly Andrew Lee Allen, born in Nov. of 1791 or 1794 in New Hampshire to Elijah Allen and Mehitable Hall. Married Clarinda Kapp on Dec. 11, 1824, in Cattaraugus County, New York, and they had ten children. Eventually married two other women. Baptized in Sept. 1833.

Was ordained an elder. Was a counselor in the Coonville, Iowa, branch presidency in 1848. Died on Aug. 14, 1870, in Provo, Utah. In addition, an Achmond Allen is listed in Willoughby, Ohio in1840. [CR, Lake County, Ohio, 1840; *MR-L* 1:479-82.]

ALLRED?, Daniel, hosted meetings for McLellin on Mar. 3 and 4, 1833. Was baptized on Mar. 6, 1833 and became a member of the Salt River Branch, Monroe County, Missouri. Possibly the son of Isaac Allred.

ALLRED?, Hannah, was possibly Hannah Caroline Allred, born on Sept. 20, 1808, in the town of Ohio, Kentucky, to James Allred and Elizabeth Warren. Attended McLellin's meeting on Mar. 6, 1833. Received a patriarchal blessing from Hyrum Smith in 1843 and died on Feb. 23, 1850. [*MR-L* 2:174-76.]

ALLRED, Isaac (1813-59), was born on June 28, 1813, in Tennessee to James Allred and Elizabeth Warren. Was baptized on Sept. 10, 1832. Married Julia Ann Taylor on Oct. 11, 1832, and they had ten children. Hosted two meetings in Feb. 1833 while living in Fayette, Missouri. Marched with Zion's Camp in 1834 and was subsequently ordained a seventy. Served a mission to Great Britain, 1851-55. Assaulted and killed by Thomas Ivie over a misunderstanding concerning sheep Allred was tending on May 12, 1859. [*MR-L* 2:180-84.]

ALLRED, James (1784-1876), was born on Jan. 22, 1784, in Randolph, North Carolina, to William Allred and Elizabeth Thrasher. Married Elizabeth Warren on Nov. 14, 1803, and they had twelve children. Was baptized on Sept. 9, 1832. Hosted McLellin in Feb. 1833 while living in Fayette, Missouri. Marched with Zion's Camp in 1834. Was ordained a high priest by Joseph Smith, Jr., and served as a body guard to the Prophet. Became the high constable and supervisor of streets in Nauvoo. Went to Utah in 1851 where he acted as the presiding elder of the Allred settlement, now known as Spring City, until he died in 1876. [*MR-L* 2:185-89.]

ANDERSON, Celia, donated money to McLellin in Florence, Ohio, in Nov. 1834.

ANDERSON, John, was probably born on Mar. 9, 1796, in Windham, Connecticut, to Lemuel Anderson and Rachel Hall. Married Lydia Kellog. Donated money to McLellin in Nov. 1834. Hosted an appointment in Florence, Ohio, on Oct. 19, 1834. At an 1837 conference in Far West, Missouri, he objected to the nomination of Lyman Wight to the Missouri High Council. Played in the Nauvoo band and may have served as a stone-cutter for the Nauvoo Temple. Joined the Reorganized Church and became their representative to Salt Lake City in 1869; died in Nauvoo, Illinois. [*HC* 2:523-24; JH, Dec. 31, 1844; *MR-L* 2:338-39; and *MR-R* 1:113-14.]

ANDRESS, Milow. *See* Andrews, Milow.

ANDREWS or ANDRESS, Milow, is Milo Andrus (1814-93), born on Mar. 6, 1814, in Wilmington, New York, to Ruluf Andress and Azuba Smith. Was baptized on Mar. 12, 1832. Married Abigail Jane Daley on Feb. 14, 1833. Marched in Zion's Camp in 1834. Spoke on several occasions at meetings McLellin was holding; living in Florence, Ohio, in Oct. 1834. Appointed president of the Florence Branch in 1836. Moved to Missouri in 1837 and then to Illinois in 1838. Served a mission to England, 1848-50. Moved to Utah by 1855. Died in Oxford, Idaho, on June 19, 1893. [AF; Andrus, autobiography, 5; and Bitton, *Guide to Mormon Diaries,* 11.]

ANDRUS, Milo. *See* Andrews, Milow.

ARTERBERRY and his family were not at home in Missouri when McLellin tried to stop there on Feb. 18, 1833.

ATHINGTON, Fanny, is Fanny Atherton, born in Dalton, New Hampshire, to Samuel Atherton and Molly Brown. Baptized by McLellin on Aug. 10, 1835, in Dalton, New Hampshire. Married Harvey Redfield on Oct. 26, 1837. [*MR-L* 2:708.]

ATHINGTON, Perces, is Perces Atherton (1820-1906), born on May 27, 1820, in Dalton, New Hampshire, to Samuel Atherton and Molly Brown. Baptized by McLellin on Aug. 10, 1835, in Dalton, New Hampshire. Married Aaron Freeman Farr in Jan. 1844. Moved to Utah in 1847. Died on Dec. 31, 1906, in Logan, Utah. [*Church Chronology,* Dec. 31, 1906; and *MR-L* 2:714-15.]

AVERY was living near the center of Braceville, Ohio, when McLellin and Samuel Smith visited and then stayed with him on Nov. 30, 1831. Possibly Barton F. Avery (1796-1857), born on Sept. 16, 1796, in Aurora, New York, to Dudley Avery and Hannah Morgan. Raised by his uncle, Daniel Avery. Married Betsy Brown on Sept. 23, 1817. Kept a temperance house and then began a hotel business in 1842. Served as an associate judge in Ohio prior to 1848. Possibly the same Baptist minister who was baptized by Don Carlos Smith. Died in Chardon, Ohio, on Apr. 12, 1857. [*History of Geauga,* 23, 94-95; and McConkie, *Doctrines of Salvation* 3:110.]

BABBIT, Alman (Almon) (1813-56), was born in 1813 in Massachusetts to Ira Babbitt and Nancy Crosier. Married Julia Ann Johnson on Nov. 23, 1833, and they had six children. Probably was baptized in 1833. Marched with Zion's Camp in 1834. Was an elder when he attended and participated in the meetings McLellin held in Amherst, Ohio, during Oct. 1834. Donated money to McLellin. Was ordained a seventy by Joseph Smith on Feb. 28, 1835, and later was ordained a high priest. Served a mission to Ontario,

Canada, 1837-38. President of the Kirtland Stake, 1841-43. Practiced law and frequently defended the Mormon right to Nauvoo. Signed treaty surrendering Nauvoo. Disfellowshipped in 1839, 1841, 1843, and 1851, each time quickly resolving his transgressions. Moved to Utah by 1855 and became active in politics there until he was attacked and killed by Cheyenne Indians in the fall of 1856. [*MR-L* 3:1-5.]

BABBIT, Almira (1810-45), is Almira Castle born on Feb. 6, 1810, in Pompey, New York, to Horace and Susan Castle. Married Lorin Whiting Babbit, and they had five children. Donated money to McLellin in Amherst, Ohio, in Oct. 1834. Baptized before 1836. Died Aug. 8, 1845, in Nauvoo. [*MR-L* 9:143-44; and *PK,* 3.]

BABBIT, Lorin Whiting (1806-83), was born in Sept. 1806 in New Marlborough, Massachusetts, to William Babbit and Lydia Bishop. Married Almira Castle, and they had five children. Was an elder who attended and participated in the meetings McLellin held in Amherst, Ohio, during Oct. 1834. Was ordained a seventy and served a mission to Ohio in 1844. Shareholder in the Kirtland Safety Society and member of the Second Quorum of the Seventy in Kirtland. Served as a probate judge in Beaver, Utah. Joined the Reorganized Church in Apr. 1863. Died on Aug. 22, 1883, in Stewartsville, Missouri. [*MR-L* 3:23-25; and *MR-R* 1:203-4.]

BABCOCK, Caroline L., was baptized and confirmed on May 11, 1835, by Orson Hyde near Westfield, New York.

BAILEY, Henry, Sr., was baptized and confirmed by McLellin on Sept. 10, 1834. According to census records, he and his family of three were living in Eugene, Indiana by 1830. [CR, Vermillion County, Indiana, 1830.]

BAILY, Louisa, was baptized by McLellin on Aug. 5, 1834, in Eugene, Indiana.

BAIRD, Samuel, was a cousin to McLellin who sent him a letter from Canterville, Missouri, which McLellin received on May 17, 1833.

BAKER is Colonel Edward D. Baker (1811-61), born in London, England. Came to Illinois in 1815. Admitted to the bar in Carrollton, Illinois, 1830. Married Mary Ann Lee, 1831. Became a Campbellite, 1831. Never became a formal minister but did become a very popular speaker. Active in the Black Hawk War, 1832. Hosted McLellin and Parley Pratt on Mar. 20, 1833. They attended a meeting at which Baker preached in Greene County, Illinois. Moved to Springfield, Illinois, and became close friends with Abraham Lincoln, 1835. Elected to the Illinois House of Representatives, 1837. Elected to the Illinois Senate, 1840. Defeated Abraham Lincoln, who named his son after Baker, for the Whig nomination to Congress, 1844. Active in the

Mexican War. Moved to Galena to allow Lincoln a political chance, 1848. Served as superintendent of the Construction of the Panama Railroad, 1851. Died in Balls Bluff, Virginia, during the Civil War, Oct. 21, 1861. Marble statue entitled *Baker* stands in the United States White House. There are two Mr. Bakers listed in Carrollton, Illinois, in 1830. [CR, Greene County, Illinois, 1830;Haynes, *History of the Disciples*, 465-69.]

BARKER, Elizabeth, is listed as a subscriber to the *Messenger and Advocate* in 1836. Located in Ohio, possibly Fulton, Ohio.

BARKER, R., was baptized by McLellin on Jan. 18, 1835, in Huntsburg, Ohio.

BARKSHIRE, Garret W., encouraged McLellin to stay in Crittenden, Kentucky, to answer the opposition's claims in 1836. Listed as a subscriber to the *Messenger and Advocate* in Crittenden. [CR, Grant County, Kentucky, 1830.]

BARNEY, Edson (1806-1905), was born June 30, 1806, in Ellisburg, New York, to Royal Barney and Rachel Marsh. Married Lillis Ballow on Jan. 1, 1831, and they had seven children. Baptized in May 1831 by Simeon Carter. Was ordained a teacher in 1832 and a priest in 1833. Marched in Zion's Camp in 1834. Donated money to McLellin in Amherst, Ohio, in Oct. 1834. Was ordained a seventy in 1835. Worked as a carpenter on the Kirtland Temple and was a stockholder in the Kirtland Safety Society. Served as a captain in the Nauvoo Legion. Served a mission to the eastern states in 1844 and three other missions by 1861 to the western territories. Came to Utah in 1851 where he died on Feb. 2, 1905. [*MR-L* 3:716-20.]

BARNEY, Royal, Jr. (1808-90), was born in Dec. 1808 in Ellisburgh, New York, to Royal Barney and Rachel Marsh. Married Sarah Bowen Esterbrook on Nov. 4, 1829, and they had six children. Baptized in May 1831 by Simeon Carter. Was a deacon who lived in Amherst, Ohio, 1830-38, where he donated money to McLellin. Marched with Zion's Camp in 1834 and was ordained a member of the First Quorum of Seventy in Apr. 1835. Farmer. Lived in Freeport, Indiana, 1840-43. Migrated to Utah in 1852 where he died in 1890. [Bradley, *Zion's Camp*, xxiii; and *MR-L* 3:758-62.]

BARNUM hosted McLellin and Samuel Smith while living in Braceville, Ohio, Nov. 1831. After they preached in his home, his daughter, Irene, wished to join the new church but he would not allow this; he became angry and bitter toward McLellin and Smith. Possibly Samuel Barnum. [CR, Trumbull County, Ohio, 1830; JH, Nov. 16, 1831.]

BARNUM, Irene, converted by McLellin and Samuel Smith's sermon in Nov. 1831. Was the daughter of the Mr. Barnum whom McLellin met on Nov. 21, 1831. [JH, Nov. 16, 1831, 1.]

BARROWS, Amelia, is Amelia (Emily) Waterman (b. 1782), who was born on Nov. 17, 1782, in Norwich, Vermont, to Daniel Waterman and Phebe House. Married Jacob Barrows on May 27, 1814. Baptized by McLellin on July 27, 1835, in Dalton, New Hampshire. Mother of Ethan Barrows. [TIB.]

BARROWS, Ethan (1817-1904), was born on Jan. 12, 1817, in Dalton, New Hampshire, to Jacob Barrows and Amelia (Emily) Waterman. Baptized by McLellin on July 27, 1835, in Dalton, New Hampshire. Labored as a merchant and married Lorena Covey. Was ordained a seventy in Dec. 1840. Signed the 1843 Scroll Petition for Missouri redress. Died in Apr. 1904 in Salt Lake City. [*MR-L* 4:13-14; and TIB.]

BEAN, Daniel, was baptized and was ordained an elder by Horace Cowan in Letter B, Maine, on Mar. 23, 1833. Blessed children with McLellin in Errol, New Hampshire, Aug. 17, 1835. Traveled with McLellin and attended the Farmington Conference in New Hampshire, Aug. 1835. At a conference in Maine, in Aug. 1836, he was appointed clerk and also represented the Errol, New Hampshire, and Newry, Maine, branches. [JH, Mar. 23, 1833; Aug. 14, 1836.]

BEEBE, Calvin (1800-61), was born on July 1, 1800, in Paris, New York. Married Submit Starr on Nov. 19, 1823, in Ohio. Moved to Jackson County, Missouri, by 1831 and Clay County, Missouri, by 1833. Held a meeting with Peter Whitmer in Missouri at George Seely's prior to McLellin's arrival on Mar. 1, 1833. Was ordained a high priest on Oct. 5, 1832, in Independence, Missouri, and began a mission with Daniel Cathcart to Illinois, Indiana, Michigan, and Ohio. Served as clerk in a conference held on Sept. 26, 1833. Traveled with Isaac Morley from Missouri to Ohio. Served as member of the Far West High Council. Operated a mercantile business, 1837-38. Excommunicated and joined the Reorganized Church. Died on July 12, 1861. [*MR-L* 4:510-11; and *MR-R* 1:367-68.]

BELLEW hosted two appointments while living in Greene County, Illinois, May 1833.

BENNETT was a Campbellite Priest with whom McLellin spent time talking in Jan. 1832. McLellin took him to visit the Prophet. Located in Kirtland, Ohio.

BENNETT, Esquire William T., fed dinner to McLellin and others in Shelby County, Illinois, Aug. 3, 1831. Possibly William Bennett, who was a supervisor for Ash Grove in Shelby County, Illinois, 1860-61. [CR, Shelby County, Illinois, 1830; Bateman, *History of Shelby County*, 645.]

BERCH. *See* Birch.

BILLINGS, Titus (1793-1866), was born in Mar. 1793 in Greenfield, Massachusetts, to Ebeneezer Billings and Joyce Esther. Married Diantha Morley on Feb. 16, 1817, and they had nine children. Was baptized in Kirtland on Nov. 15, 1830, and was ordained a deacon in Oct. 1831. Hosted meetings in Kirtland, Ohio, Jan. 1832. Immigrated to Missouri early in the spring of 1832. Was ordained an elder by Thomas B. Marsh on Mar. 10, 1832, and a high priest by Edward Partridge and Isaac Morley on Aug. 1, 1837. Delivered a message to McLellin and Parley Pratt to return to Independence, Missouri, in Jan. 1833. Served as counselor to Bishop Partridge and as bishop at Far West. Fought in the 1838 Battle of Crooked River, Missouri, and later served as an officer in the Nauvoo Legion. Worked as a stone mason, carpenter, and musician. Moved to Utah where he died in Provo on Feb. 6, 1866. [*HC* 1:266; and *MR-L* 5:303-7.]

BIRCH (Berch), James H., hosted McLellin and Parley Pratt while living near the court house in Fayette, Missouri, Feb. 1833. Subscribed to the *Star*. [CR, Howard County, Missouri, 1840.]

BIRCH (Berch), Mrs., hosted McLellin and Parley Pratt in Fayette, Missouri, Feb. 1833. Bought a Book of Mormon. Married James H. Berch.

BLAIR, A., was an agricultural worker living in Kirtland, Ohio, when McLellin visited him on Dec. 2, 1834. [CR, Lake County, Ohio, 1840.]

BLAKESLY is James Blakeslee (1802-66), born on July 18, 1802, in Milton, Vermont. Baptized on July 19, 1833, by David W. Patten. Was ordained a priest in July 1833. Was ordained an elder in the spring of 1834 by Thomas Dutcher and a seventy in 1840 by Brigham Young. Served missions in New York and Canada in the 1830s. Was preaching with Elder Dutcher in Sackets Harbor, New York, when McLellin attended their appointment in June 1835. Presided over meetings in Booneville, New York, and was present at a conference held in Sackets Harbor, New York. Presided over branch in Ontario, Canada, in 1837. Sent several letters to church leaders about the success he was seeing. Excommunicated on May 18, 1844, and joined Sidney Rigdon's church. Became affiliated with James Strang and was eventually baptized into the Reorganized Church on Apr. 8, 1859, and remained an active member until his death on Dec. 18, 1866, in Batavia, Illinois. [JH, May 18, July 2, Aug. 1, 1835; Sept. 18, June 11-12, Aug. 20, 1837; July 18, 19, 29, 1840; *MR-L* 49:343, 348; and *MR-R* 1:486-87.]

BLEDSOE hosted McLellin and Parley Pratt in Greene County, Illinois, Mar. 19, 1833. Could be M. O. Bledsoe or Moses Bledsoe. [CR, Greene County, Illinois 1830 and 1840.]

BOICE hosted an appointment for McLellin in Loughborough, Ontario, Canada on June 26, 1835.

BOICE, Margaret, rode on McLellin's lap to Loughborough, Canada, on June 27, 1835.

BONDURANT, Captain, hosted McLellin in Missouri, Feb. 28, 1833. Two Bondurants are listed in 1830 and 1840 censuses. [CR, Pike County, Missouri, 1830 and 1840.]

BONHAM, Mr., hosted McLellin in Missouri, on Sept. 6, 1831, and Feb. 27, 1833. He believed that a number of Adams existed in the creation and also that the Book of Mormon was a "good moral and rule of life." Possibly Jerrimiah Bonhime. [CR, Pike County, Missouri, 1830.]

BONHAM, Mrs., hosted McLellin in Sept. 1831 and Feb. 1833.

BOOSINGER, George (1784-1861), was born in Tennessee. While living near Middlebury, Ohio, he hosted McLellin in Feb. 1832. He was also living there in 1840. Farmer. Filed a petition on Jan. 20, 1840, in Illinois against Ray County, Missouri, for damages. Possibly lived a short while in Ray County, Missouri, during 1836 but was ordained a high priest in Kirtland in 1836 while helping to satisfy the temporal needs of those working on the Kirtland Temple. Performed at least two baptisms in Middlebury, Ohio, which Orson Hyde recorded. [Jessee, *Personal Writings of Joseph Smith,* 181; JH, May 4, 1836; *MR-L* 6:135; and *PJS* 2:528.]

BOSLEY, J., purchased a vest pattern and trimmings for McLellin in Geneseo, New York. A John Bosley is found in the Geneseo, New York, 1830 census. [CR, Livingston County, New York, 1830.]

BOSLEY, William Bull (1818-42), was born on June 13, 1818, in Lovinia, New York, to Edmund Bosley and Ann Kelly. Helped transport the Twelve from Kirtland to Fairport, Ohio, in May 1835. Was ordained a member of the Second Quorum of Seventy. Married Eleanor (Ellen) Pack on Feb. 22, 1838. Signed Kirtland Camp Constitution in July 1838. Died on June 5, 1842, in Nauvoo. [Backman, *Heavens Resound,* 385; *PK,* 8; and Young, *Organization of the Seventies,* 4.]

BOUCE hosted McLellin near Laona, New York, on May 16, 1835.

BOVCE. *See* Bouce.

BOYNTON, John Farnum (1811-90), was born on Sept. 20, 1811, in Massachusetts to Eliphalet Boynton and Susannah Nichols. Was baptized in Sept. 1832 and ordained an elder that same year. Was McLellin's missionary companion to Painesville, Ohio, in Nov. 1834. Was ordained an apostle on Feb. 15, 1835. Married Susannah Lowell on Jan. 20, 1836, and they had five children. Served as a missionary with Zebedee Coltrin. Apostatized; was disfellowshipped from the Quorum of Twelve on Sept. 3, 1837. Employed in the invention of torpedoes and other wartime inventions, and by 1886 he had thirty-six patents in the national patent office. Died in Syracuse, New York, on Oct. 20, 1890. [*MR-L* 6:425-28; and *PK,* 8.]

BRADLEY, Father S., was preaching when McLellin and Parley Pratt arrived, and he asked them to address his audience near Fayette, Missouri, Feb. 9 [actually Feb. 10], 1833.

BRIGGS, Mr., was probably a civic figure who lived between Lyman and Dalton, New Hampshire, Aug. 5, 1835. Censuses list several Briggses. [CR, Grafton County, New Hampshire, 1830 and 1840.]

BROCKMAN, S. or L., hosted McLellin overnight in Randolph County, Missouri, Aug. 14, 1831. Possibly Stephen H. or Lindsey E. Brockman. [CR, Randolph County, Missouri, 1840.]

BROWN, Mr., gave McLellin $.75 in Fredonia, New York, May 5, 1835.

BROWN, Mrs., seemed to believe McLellin's message but was unwilling to be baptized on May 14, 1835.

BROWN, Benjamin (1794-1878), was born on Sept. 30, 1794, in Queensbury, New York, to Asa Brown and Sarah Moon. Married Sarah Mumford on Sept. 12, 1819, and they had five children. After delaying baptism a year to wait for his wife, he was baptized on May 10, 1835, by McLellin in Westfield, New York, and later hosted and donated money to him. Was ordained a high priest. Attended the Kirtland Temple dedication. Said to have been visited by two of the three Nephites. Served several missions. Bishop in Far West and Salt Lake City. Emigrated to Utah in 1848 where he died in Salt Lake City on May 22, 1878. [*CHC,* 2:21, 3:149; and *MR-L* 7:32-36.]

BROWN, Rebecca, was baptized by McLellin on May 10, 1835, in Westfield, New York.

BULL hosted McLellin on May 2, 1836, in Fulton, Ohio.

BURASUS or BURRASE was living near Bluffdale, Illinois, when he hosted an appointment, Apr. 1833. Could be William Burriss or John Burruss in Greene County. [CR, Greene County, Illinois, 1830 and 1840; *HGC,* 141, 315, 317, 323-27.]

BURDOCK is probably Thomas Burdick (b. 1795), born on Nov. 17, 1795, in Canajoharie, New York, to Gideon Burdick and Catherine Robertson. Taught with McLellin at the Kirtland School. Married Anna Higley. Became a membership license clerk in 1836 in Kirtland and county clerk in Pottawatomie, Iowa, in 1840. Was ordained bishop in Kirtland in 1841. [Backman, *Heavens Resound,* 369; and *MR-L* 7:522-23.]

BURNETT, Edmund Jr., hosted McLellin in Hubbard Town, Ohio, Feb. 1832. [CR, Trumbull County, Ohio, 1830.]

BURNETT, Silas, was a Baptist living near Hubbard Town, Ohio, Feb. 17, 1832. [CR, Trumbull County, Ohio 1830 and 1840.]

BURRASE. *See* Burasus.

BURWELL, Celia, was baptized by McLellin and confirmed by Joseph Smith on Dec. 28, 1831, in Weathersfield, Ohio. Married Samuel Burwell. McLellin revisited the Burwells in Wellsville, Ohio, in Apr. 1836.

BURWELL, Samuel, was baptized by McLellin on Dec. 14, 1831, in Weathersfield, Ohio. Hosted appointments in Wellsville, Ohio, Apr. 1836. Donated money to McLellin, Apr. 21, 1836.

BUTTERFIELD, Betsy, was baptized by Lyman Johnson on May 26, 1835, in Hate, New York.

BYFIELD, Eliza, formerly Eliza Daugherty, became acquainted with McLellin and donated money to him in Oct. 1834 in Amherst, Ohio.

CADY, Elizabeth, was baptized by McLellin on Aug. 27, 1834, in Eugene, Indiana. She is possibly Elizabeth Harris who married William Cady on Feb. 12, 1816. [Graham, *Ohio Marriages,* 34.]

CAFFA, Betsy, was baptized by McLellin on Aug. 4, 1835, near Lyman, New Hampshire. Wife of Hiram Caffa.

CAFFA, Hiram, was baptized and confirmed by McLellin on Aug. 4, 1835, near Lyman, New Hampshire. Hosted an appointment on Aug. 6, 1835.

CAHOON, Reynolds (1790-1861), was born on Apr. 30, 1790, in New York to William Cahoon and Mehitabel Hodges. Married Theresa Stiles on Dec. 11, 1810. Fought in the War of 1812. Was probably baptized on Oct. 11 or 12, 1830, by Parley Pratt. Details of Cahoon's conversion are unknown. Was ordained an elder by Sidney Rigdon on June 3, 1831, and was ordained a high priest by Joseph Smith. Appointed on Oct. 11, 1830, to obtain money to assist Joseph Smith in finishing the inspired translation of the Bible. Served as a missionary with Samuel Smith in Ohio, Indiana, Illinois, and Missouri in 1831, and they introduced McLellin to Mormonism. Went with Joseph and Hyrum Smith and Sidney Rigdon to visit McLellin when he was sick on Dec. 27, 1831, and hosted a council of elders while living in Kirtland, Ohio. Worked on the Kirtland Temple on Jan. 5, 1832, and served as counselor to Bishop Whitney. Helped lead the Saints west as captain of the sixth company and died in Salt Lake City in 1861. [Backman, *Heavens Resound,* 96, 146; and *MR-L* 8:215-21.]

CALVIN, J., fed dinner to McLellin and Parley Pratt in Greene County, Illinois, May 5, 1833. Possibly J. W. Calvin, who was a member of the General Committee from the Bluffdale precinct for the Agricultural and Mechanical Association. A Jordan Calvin also lived in Greene County. [CR, Greene County, Illinois, 1840; *HGC,* 323.]

CALVIN. *See* Beebe, Calvin.

CAMPBELL had a child with a sore face that McLellin and Samuel Smith administered to and healed near Niles, Ohio, Dec. 18, 1831. Possibly John Campbell, who served as a state senator from 1818–19. Several Campbells are listed in Trumbull County. [CR, Trumbull County, Ohio, 1830 and 1840; *History of Geauga,* 23.]

CAMPBELL, A., gave $2 to McLellin in Wellsville, Ohio, May 21, 1836. Possibly Andrew Campbell, who married Sarah Archer on Aug. 31, 1769, in Portsmouth, New Hampshire. More likely an Alex Campbell, who is also listed. [CR, Columbiana County, Ohio, 1840; Oesterlin, *New Hampshire Marriage Licenses,* 36.]

CAMPBELL, D., the mayor of Wellsville, Ohio, convinced McLellin to stay and preach there in Apr. 1836. Later, donated $5 to McLellin. [CR, Columbiana County, Ohio, 1840.]

CAMPBELL, E., probably Alexander Campbell, wrote an anti-Mormon pamplet which Reverend Peck read at a meeting in Carrollton, Illinois, on Apr. 21, 1833, in an attempt to disprove McLellin.

CAMPBELL, I. C., was a member of the Christian Order (Campbellite?) who hosted McLellin in Greene County, Illinois, in Apr. 1833. Possibly J. C. Campbell, a Presbyterian minister who preached in Edgar County, Illinois. [*History of Edgar County,* 659.]

CAMPBELL, Mandana, was baptized by McLellin on Apr. 23, 1833, in Bluffdale, Illinois.

CAMPBELL, Susannah, was baptized on Apr. 21, 1833, in Greene County, Illinois. Probably related to Mandana Campbell. Probably Susannah Staples before marrying John Campbell by 1810. Possibly widowed by 1835. May have been baptized again on July 6, 1835, by John Greene in Elmira, New York. [Jackman, "Autobiography," 7; JH, July 6, 1835; and TIB.]

CARTER, hosted McLellin and Daniel Bean near Rumford Point, Maine, Aug. 20, 1835. Probably Daniel Carter (1803–87), born on Aug. 28, 1803, in Benson, Vermont, to Jabez Carter and Rebecca Dowd. Married Clarissa Amelia Foster on Sept. 26, 1829, and they had four children. Married three more wives. Was baptized in 1833. Was ordained a priest by Orson Pratt on

June 8, 1833, in Bath, New Hampshire. Died on Apr. 10, 1887, in Bountiful, Vermont. In addition, Ephriam Carter is listed in census records. [CR, Oxford County, Maine, 1830 and 1840; *MR-L* 8:760-63; and *Orson Pratt Journals,* 16.]

CARTER, Gideon H. (1798-1838), was born in 1798 to Gideon Carter and Johanna Sims. Married Hilda Burwell in 1822, and they had seven children. Was baptized on Oct. 25, 1831, by Joseph Smith and confirmed by Sidney Rigdon. Was ordained a priest that same day and an elder on Jan. 25, 1832. Served a mission to Vermont in 1832. Hilda died in 1832, and he married Charlotte Woods on Dec. 31, 1833. They had three children. Preached with McLellin at a meeting in Florence, Ohio, in Nov. 1834. Member of the Kirtland High Council in 1837. Killed in the Battle of Crooked River on Oct. 25, 1838. [*BE* 3:615; and *MR-L* 8:782-86.]

CARTER, Simeon (1793-1869), was born on June 7, 1793, in Killingsworth, Connecticut, to Gideon Carter and Johannah Sims. Married Lydia Kenyon on Dec. 2, 1818, and they had three children. Was baptized in Feb. 1831. Was ordained a deacon, elder, and high priest by June 1831. Told McLellin he should become an elder, and they began serving a mission as companions in Aug. 1831. Marched in Zion's Camp. Served a mission to England, 1846-49. Crossed plains in Orson Hyde's company and in 1851 founded Brigham City, where he died on Feb. 3, 1869. [*MR-L* 9:61-65.]

CARTER, Talitha Cumi, was baptized and confirmed by McLellin on Aug. 4, 1835, near Lyman, New Hampshire.

CESSIONS is Perrigrine Sessions (1814-93). Born on June 15, 1814, in Newry, Maine, to David Sessions and Patty Bartlett. Married Julia Ann Kilgore on Sept. 21, 1834, and they had two children. Was baptized on Sept. 17, 1835. Hosted one of McLellin's appointments in New Hampshire, Aug. 21, 1835. Was ordained a seventy on Apr. 26, 1839, and a high priest in 1858. Served missions to Maine in 1843 and England in 1852-54. Farmer and stockraiser. Died on June 3, 1893, in Bountiful, Utah. [*MR-L* 38:738-49.]

CHANDLER, J., hosted a meeting McLellin organized on Sept. 14, 1834, in Danville, Ohio.

CHAPMAN hosted an appointment for McLellin in Hate, New York, on May 27, 1835. Was baptized by McLellin on May 30, 1835.

CHAPMAN, Jacob (b. 1803), was born on Mar. 12, 1803, in Palmyra, New York, and later married Julia. Marched in Zion's Camp. Donated money to McLellin in Amherst, Ohio, in Oct., 1834. Was ordained a member of the First Quorum of Seventy. Received patriarchal blessing from Joseph Smith, Sr., in Kirtland, Ohio, 1836. [Bradley, *Zion's Camp,* xxiv; and *MR-L* 9:289.]

CHILDS was living in Sacketts Harbor, New York, when McLellin visited him and received the Koran as a gift from him in June 1835. Is probably Alfred B. Childs (1796–1852), born in New York to March Anthony Childs and Hannah Bennedict. Married Sally (Polly) Barber on Mar. 19, 1817, and they had twelve children. Signed the agreement to leave Missouri in 1839 and later posted claims against the state. Moved to Iowa in 1841, where he became the postmaster. Was ordained a seventy before 1845. Moved to Utah, where he ran a sawmill and died on Dec. 22, 1852, in Ogden, Utah. [JH, Jan. 29, Nov. 29, 1839; and *MR-L* 9:592–601.]

CHURCH hosted McLellin on June 6, 1835, outside the village of Wolcott while McLellin was on his way to Jefferson County, New York. Possibly Hiram Church. [CR, Wayne County, New York, 1840.]

CLARK, Jane, allowed McLellin to write a letter at her home and gave him money for a handkerchief in Aug. 1834. Gave him more money in Sept. 1834. Possibly marched with members of Zion's Camp. [JH, Oct. 10, 1864.]

CLARK, Josiah, listed as a subscriber to the *Messenger and Advocate* in 1836. [CR, Boone County, Kentucky, 1830.]

CLARK, Mary Ann, was baptized in Bluffdale, Illinois, on Apr. 23, 1833.

CLARK, Samuel, listed as a subscriber to the *Messenger and Advocate* who changed his address from Martinsville to Fulton, Ohio, in 1836. Several Samuel Clarks lived in Hamilton and Clinton Counties. [CR, Clinton County, Ohio, 1830; CR, Hamilton County, Ohio, 1840.]

CLENDENON hosted an appointment in Bluffdale, Illinois, Apr. 17, 1833. Possibly H. Perry Clendennen, who arrived in Greene County in 1819. Became a member of the Old Settlers Association and at one point served as the precinct vice president for Woodville. The 1830 census also lists a George Clenden. [CR, Greene County, Illinois, 1830; *HGC,* 315, 317.]

CLEVELAND hosted McLellin and John Daley in Vermilion, Ohio, Oct. 27, 1834.

COE, Joseph (1784–1854), was born on Nov. 12, 1784, in New York to Joel Coe and Huldah Horton. Married Pallas Wales in 1816. Was baptized early in 1831 and was ordained a high priest that same year. Served a mission with the Prophet Joseph to Missouri in 1831, and then served with Ezra Thayre in New York. Hosted McLellin and participated in meetings while living in Kirtland, Ohio. Called as land agent for the Church and helped lay the cornerstone for the Kirtland Temple in 1833. Member of the Kirtland High Council in 1836 but apostatized in 1837. Died in Kirtland in 1854. [Backman, *Heavens Resound,* 67, 73, 115, 144, 289, 327; and *MR-L* 10:653–55.]

COLBURN, Thomas (1801–87), was born on Aug. 3, 1801, in New York to Jonathan Colburn and Hannah Hamilton. Married Sarah Bower on Aug. 11, 1825, and they had six children. Was baptized on Apr. 15, 1833, and marched with Zion's Camp in 1834. Hosted a conference of the Quorum of the Twelve in June 1835 in Lyons, Wayne County, New York. Eventually was ordained a high priest. Served missions to Germany and England. Came to Utah with Heber C. Kimball and died in Salt Lake City on Jan. 19, 1887. [*MR-L* 10:692–95; and *PK*, 17.]

COLTRIN, Zebedee (1804–87), was born in Ovid, New York, to John and Sarah Coltrin. Married Julia Ann Jennings. Was baptized on Jan. 9, 1831, by Lyman Wight and was ordained an elder on Jan. 21, 1831, by John Whitmer. Appointed to travel to Missouri with Levi W. Hancock on June 6, 1831. Established a large branch of the Church in Winchester, Indiana, in 1831. Preached in Winchester, Indiana, with Levi Hancock prior to McLellin's arrival in Oct. 1831. Member of Zion's Camp and was afterward ordained a seventy in 1835. Served as a counselor in the Kirtland Stake presidency in 1841. Appointed to campaign for Joseph Smith for president of the United States. Died in Utah in July 1887. [*BE* 1:190; and *MR-L* 11:210–15.]

COLVIN, David (1815–80), was born in Dec. 1815 to William Colvin and Lydia Sherman. Baptized by McLellin on June 22, 1835, in Lake Ontario near Pillow [Pillar] Point, Jefferson County, New York. Married Harriet Ann Dullabaugh in 1843. Farmer. Moved to Utah by 1850, where he was rebaptized in 1857 and died on July 31, 1880. [*MR-L* 11:220–22.]

CONE, Charlotte, was baptized by McLellin in Errol, New Hampshire, Aug. 1835.

COON had McLellin and Parley Pratt come to his house and pray for a sick girl near Bluffdale, Illinois, Apr. 6, 1833. Censuses list several Coons in the area. [CR, Greene County, Illinois, 1830 and 1840.]

COON, I., hosted McLellin and Parley Pratt in Greene County, Illinois, Apr. 5, 1833.

COOPER, John (1803–71), was born on Sept. 15, 1803, in Washington, Ohio, to Jeremiah and Elizabeth Cooper. Married Rhoda Clark. Baptized by McLellin on Aug. 5, 1834, in Eugene, Indiana. Was ordained a teacher in the Aaronic Priesthood by McLellin on Sept. 10, 1834. Was ordained a high priest on Oct. 8, 1837, and served as a presiding elder in Rochester, Ohio. Became affiliated with the Reorganized Church by 1856, which he remained with until his death in Santa Rosa, California, on May 23, 1871. [JH, Oct. 8, 28, 1837; *MR-L* 11:538; and *MR-R* 2:304.]

CORRILL, John (b. 1794), was born on Sept. 17, 1794, in Bone, Massachusetts. Married a woman named Margaret, and they had five children. Was baptized on Jan. 10, 1831. Was ordained an elder and then served a mission with Solomon Hancock until June 3, 1831, when he was ordained a high priest and second counselor to Bishop Partridge in Kirtland. McLellin first met him in Independence, Missouri, on Aug. 18, 1831. In 1833 he remained in Independence to complete the Saints' business and later spent time in jail. Became overseer of the Kirtland Temple and then in 1836 attended the dedication. Served as keeper of the Lord's storehouse beginning in 1837. Called as Church historian in 1838 but apostatized later that year. Excommunicated on Mar. 17, 1839, and became a bitter enemy to the Church until his death. [*BE* 1:241; and *MR-L* 11:718-21.]

CORY, Hiram, was born in Pinckney, New York, in 1819. Married Fanny Spencer. Was ordained a teacher on Apr. 10, 1835, by McLellin in Huntsburg, Ohio. Member of the Kirtland Safety Society. [JH, Jan. 2, 1837; and *MR-L* 11:644.]

COWAN, Thomas, hosted McLellin and Luke Johnson as they began their mission to the South, Feb. 1832. Was living in Garrettsville, Ohio.

COWDERY, Erastus (1796-1833), was born on Aug. 13, 1796, in Wells, Vermont, to William Cowdery and Rebecca Fuller. Older brother of Oliver Cowdery. Hosted McLellin in Youngstown, Ohio, Feb. 20, 1832. Died without marrying on June 16, 1833. [AF; CR, Trumbull County, Ohio, 1830.]

COWDERY, Oliver (1806-50), was born on Oct. 3, 1806, in Wells, Vermont. He met Joseph Smith and became his scribe while translating the gold plates in Apr. 1829. Received the Aaronic and Melchizedek Priesthoods with the Prophet Joseph in 1829. One of the Three Witnesses of the Book of Mormon. Charter member of the Church when it was organized and served a Lamanite mission to Missouri in 1830. Sidney Rigdon ordained him a high priest. Serving as Second Elder of the Church when McLellin encountered him. Married Elizabeth Ann Whitmer in 1832, and they had six children. In 1834 he administered church affairs in Joseph's absence from Kirtland. Appointed one of the trustees of the Kirtland School. Excommunicated from the Church for apostasy in Apr. 1838 and began practicing law in Ohio and Wisconsin. In 1848 he ran unsuccessfully for the state legislature in Wisconsin. Orson Hyde rebaptized him in 1848. Died in Richmond, Missouri, in 1850. [*BE* 1:246-51; and *MR-L* 12:109-12.]

COWDERY, Warren A. (1788-1851), was born in Oct. 1788 in Poultney, Vermont, to William Cowdery and Rebecca Fuller. Married Patience Simmonds (Simmons) on Sept. 22, 1814, in Pawlet, Vermont, and they had eleven children. Was a physician in Pawlet. Lived in Freedom, New York, by 1816. Ran an apothecary business. Postmaster of Freedom in 1824. Called to be the presiding high priest of Freedom on Nov. 25, 1834. Lived in Kirtland, Ohio, 1836-51. In 1836, he helped write the dedicatory prayer of the Kirtland Temple. Called to be on the Kirtland High Council in May 1837. Edited the *Messenger and Advocate* from July to Sept. 1837. Died on Feb. 23, 1851. [*MR-L* 12:117–19.]

COWIN, Mrs., spent some time in conversation with McLellin and Samuel Smith in Garrettsville, Ohio, Nov. 17 [actually Nov. 18], 1831.

CRANNEY, Emiline, donated money to McLellin while living in Amherst, Ohio. Probably the Emiline involved in an out-of-hand petty disagreement which McLellin mediated, also in Amherst.

CRANNEY, Philander, donated money to McLellin while living in Amherst, Ohio. Possibly became deputy sheriff in Cache Valley, Utah, by 1869. [JH, Feb. 2, 1869.]

CRAWFORD was a Methodist circuit rider who met McLellin in Crittenden, Kentucky, May 26, 1836. Possibly one of several Jno. Crawfords listed in census records. [CR, Boone County, Kentucky, 1830 and 1840; CR, Campbell County, Kentucky, 1830.]

CRIGLER hosted an appointment near Chariton, Missouri, Feb. 9, 1833. Censuses list several Criglers in Howard County. [CR, Howard County, Missouri, 1830 and 1840.]

CROSBY, William, listed as a subscriber to the *Messenger and Advocate*. Located in Centerville, Ohio, in 1836.

CULBERTSON, A., was administered to by McLellin and his father, Robert Culbertson, on May 1, 1836, in Newport, Kentucky.

CULBERTSON, Betsy, hosted one of McLellin's appointments in Newport, Kentucky, May 1, 1836. Married Robert Culbertson.

CULBERTSON, Robert, was probably baptized in early 1834 by Simeon Carter. Headed missionary work and led branch where he was living near Newport, Kentucky. Hosted McLellin in Apr. and May 1836. Was ordained a seventy in 1836 and was living in Caldwell, Missouri, by 1838. Resident of Nauvoo by 1842. [JH, May 2, 1834; and Young, *Organization of the Seventies,* 2–4.]

CURTIS, Charles, was baptized in Eugene, Indiana, by McLellin on Aug. 27, 1834. Received recommend to move to Zion with his wife, Sally, on Sept. 10, 1834.

CURTIS, Philip, was apparently a former member whom McLellin rebaptized on Sept. 7, 1834, in Eugene, Indiana. Listed on 1830 census in Vermillion County, Indiana. Possibly became the presiding elder in Hornerstown, New Jersey, by 1855. [CR, Vermillion County, Indiana, 1830; and JH, Oct. 7, 1855.]

CURTIS, Sally, was apparently a former member whom McLellin rebaptized on Sept. 7, 1834. Received recommend to go to Zion on Sept. 10, 1834. Married Charles Curtis.

DAILEY, John. *See* Daley, John.

DALEY (Daily), John (1780-1841), was born in 1780 to John Daley and Amy Mapes. Married Elizabeth Ennis, and they had nine children. Was a priest in the Florence church who accompanied McLellin to Brownhelm and Vermillion, Ohio, in Oct. 1834. Hosted a prayer meeting on Oct. 26, 1834. Left Ohio in 1837, probably for Missouri. Petitioned Missouri for redress and is mentioned in Nauvoo Conference Minutes in 1839. Died in 1841. [*MR-L* 13:73-74; and JH, Oct. 5 and Nov. 29, 1839.]

DALEY (Daily), Moses (1794-1865), was born Apr. 16, 1794, in Walkill, New York, to John Daley and Amy Mapes. Married Almira Barber on Jan. 22, 1819, and they had eleven children. Apparently the presiding elder of the Florence, Ohio, church that McLellin visited. Was ordained a high priest and was appointed to purchase lands in Kirtland. Wrote a Missouri petition. Died on Dec. 9, 1865, in Riverside, California. [*MR-L* 13:81-84.]

DANIEL. *See* Allred?, Daniel.

DANIELS hosted a meeting near Loughborough, Ontario, Canada, July 1, 1835. Son-in-law to Arthur Millet.

DATON hosted an appointment in western Illinois, Mar. 16, 1833.

DAVIS, Esquire, requested and hosted a meeting on Sept. 3, 1831. Lived at the head of the Salt River in Missouri.

DAVIS, Mrs., wanted an instant healing from McLellin in the vicinity of Lyman and Dalton, New Hampshire, July 30, 1835. Several Davises are listed in local censuses. [CR, Coos County, New Hampshire, 1830 and 1840; CR, Grafton County, New Hampshire, 1830 and 1840.]

DEMOSS hosted McLellin 152 mi. west of Louisiana, Missouri, Aug. 1831. Possibly John or William Demoss of Saline County, Missouri. [CR, Saline County, Missouri, 1830 and 1840.]

DEWITT hosted McLellin in Jacksonville, Illinois, Sept. 1831. Possibly A. B. Dewitt. [CR, Morgan County, Illinois, 1830.]

DIXON hosted an appointment in Lyons, New York, in June 1835. Possibly Christopher Flintoff Dixon (1815-1905), born on May 6, 1815, in New Brunswick, Canada, to Charles Dixon and Elizabeth Humphrey. Married Jane Elizabeth Wightman on Sept. 1, 1834, in Kirtland. Died on Sept. 12, 1905. Possibly David Dixon, who signed a petition to Governor Lilburn Boggs of Missouri in 1838. [JH, Sept. 22, 1838; and *PK,* 14.]

DODDS, A., is Asa Dodds (b. 1793), born in New York. Was baptized and received the priesthood by Jan. 1832. Served mission with Orson Pratt to Ohio in Oct. 1831. Called to serve a mission with Calves Wilson in 1832. Was ordained a high priest by Hyrum Smith on Feb. 2, 1832. Had problems with his eyes for which he requested a priesthood blessing in Fayette, Missouri, in Feb. 1833. By 1850 he was residing in Farmington, Ohio. [Cook, *Revelations of the Prophet,* 154.]

DODSON, Reverend Elizah, was the son of Major and Amy Dodson. Was the first Baptist minister at the Carrollton Church estabished in 1827. Continually and openly opposed the remarks of McLellin and Parley Pratt while near Carrollton, Illinois, 1833. Became the Baptist minister to the White Hall Church built in 1838. He also served as a pastor in Scott County. By 1853 he was located in Woodburn, Illinois. He frequently opposed the Mormon preachers. His father is likely McLellin's "old Mr. Dodson." [*American Baptist Register,* 84-85; CR, Greene County, Illinois, 1830; *HGC,* 307-9; Pratt, *Autobiography of Parley P. Pratt,* 84-85.]

DODSON, Mrs., seemed sympathetic to message when visited by Parley P. Pratt and McLellin in Mar. 1833. Married Elizah Dodson.

DOLSON possibly owned a tavern near Shelby County, Illinois, where McLellin obtained food in 1831. Hosted a meeting in Sept. 1831.

DRUE was a lame man who hosted McLellin near Ellicottville, New York, May 19, 1835. Could be one of several Drews in the area. [CR, Cattaraugus County, New York, 1830 and 1840.]

DUDLEY was baptized by McLellin on Jan. 17, 1835, in Huntsburg, Ohio.

DUTCHER accompanied Elder Blakeslee to an appointment near Sacketts Harbor, New York. Probably Thomas Dutcher, who had ordained James Blakeslee an elder. [*MR-L* 49:348.]

DYAS, Robert, is Robertson J. Dyas. Listed as a subscriber to the *Messenger and Advocate.* Located in Grant County, Kentucky in 1836. Married Mary Jane Henderson on Nov. 2, 1837. [Craig, *Grant County Marriages,* 9.]

EASTER or ESTER hosted McLellin and a meeting within 16 mi. of Lafayette County, Missouri, on Aug. 27, 1831. When McLellin stopped by again seventeen months later, on Feb. 5, 1833, they had lost the faith. Possibly Little Burg Ester. [CR, Lafayette County, Missouri, 1830.]

EATIN, Esquire Daniel, was a hardened Deist who hosted McLellin and Samuel Smith near Warren, Ohio, Dec. 1831 through Feb. 1832. Possibly Daniel Eaton who earlier hosted McLellin and Samuel Smith also in Weathersfield. [CR, Trumbull County, Ohio, 1830 and 1840; JH, Nov. 16, 1831.]

EATON, Daniel. *See* Eatin, Esquire Daniel.

EATON, E., hosted McLellin on May 29, 1835, near Linden, New York.

EATON, son of Elder Eaton. The son was a Methodist preacher. Heard McLellin and Lyman Johnson preach near Linden, New York on May 27, 1835.

EDWARDS, John, hosted McLellin and appointments in Weathersfield, Ohio in Dec. 1831 and Feb. 1832. [CR, Trumbull County, Ohio, 1830.]

EDWARDS, Mother, had a vision revealing the divinity of the Book of Mormon. Was administered to and healed of palsy in Weathersfield, Ohio, Feb. 13, 1832. May have been married to John Edwards. {CR, Trumbull County, Ohio, 1830.]

ELLIOTT, D., was a cousin to Mr. Gray of Little Valley, New York. Probably David Elliott (1799-1855), born in Nov. 1799 in Charleston, New York, to Peter and Phoebe Elliott. Married Mary Cahoon on May 21, 1831, and they had three children. Baptized on June 2, 1831, and marched in Zion's Camp in 1834. Was ordained a seventy in Feb. 1835. Moved to Missouri in 1838. Died on Dec. 2, 1855, in Salt Lake City. [*MR-L* 15:354-56; and *PJS* 2:543.]

ELSTON, Isaac, hosted an appointment on May 4, 1836, in Newberry, Ohio. Listed as a subscriber to the *Messenger and Advocate,* 1836. More than one Isaac Elston may have lived in Clermont County. [CR, Clermont County, 1830 and 1840.]

EMMETT, Silas (b. 1780), was born around 1780 in Frederick, Virginia, to John Emmett and Mary Stephens. Married Elizabeth Trowbridge on May 5, 1801, and they had three children. Hosted McLellin in May 1836, and was listed as a subscriber to the *Messenger and Advocate* in Gains Crossroads, Kentucky, 1836. [AF; and Craig, Marriage Records, 6.]

ESTER. *See* Easter.

EVANS fed McLellin breakfast in Carlinville, Illinois, May 21, 1833. Possibly Abram V. Evans. [CR, Macoupin County, Illinois, 1840.]

EVERHART, Elizabeth, was either John Everhart's mother, wife, or daughter. Baptized in Weathersfield, Ohio on Dec. 14, 1831, by McLellin. Was healed by Luke Johnson, Feb. 13, 1832. [JH, Nov. 16, 1831.]

EVERHART, Father, living in Weathersfield, Ohio. Probably John Everhart, who was scalped and killed by Indians in Missouri on July 30, 1857. [CR, Trumball County, Ohio, 1830; and JH, Aug. 12, 1857.]

EWING, George, hosted a meeting for McLellin on Oct. 22, 1834, in Brownhelm, Ohio.

FAUNCE, Noah, was ordained a priest on Jan. 18, 1835. Was ordained an elder by McLellin on Apr. 10, 1835, in Huntsburg, Ohio.

FELLOWS, Nathan, addressed questions to McLellin at the conclusion of a meeting in Ontario, Canada, July 5, 1835.

FENNEL, James, was a Baptist preacher in Boone County, Kentucky, who hosted McLellin on May 17, 1836.

FIELDS, Mrs., baptized by McLellin on Nov. 27, 1831, in Warren, Ohio. Married to Reuben Fields.

FIELDS, Reuben, lived in Warren, Ohio, when he was baptized by McLellin on Nov. 27, 1831. By Feb. 1832 he began to doubt. McLellin restored his faith, and Reuben said he would visit the Prophet Joseph. Member of the Kirtland Safety Society in 1837 and resided in Kirtland, 1836-38. Was ordained an elder on Oct. 8, 1837.

FINNEL, William, was listed as a subscriber to the *Messenger and Advocate*. Located in Fulton, Ohio in 1836.

FISHER hosted McLellin on May 4 and 13, 1835, in Laona, New York. Possibly Edmund Fisher, born on July 7, 1803, in Wrentham, Massachusetts, to Pliny Fisher and Sally Cook. Married Cornelia Jane Sherman. Marched with Zion's Camp and subsequently was ordained a seventy. Died on Sept. 5, 1872. [*PK, 22.*]

FISHER hosted McLellin in Aug. 1835 in Dalton, New Hampshire.

FLEENER, Colonel, hosted an election which McLellin attended in or near Coles County, Illinois, Aug. 1, 1831. Possibly L. B. Fleenor. [CR, Coles County, Illinois, 1840.]

FLETCHER was the sherriff of Lafayette County, Missouri, who hosted McLellin and Parley Pratt, Feb. 4, 1833. Possibly James Fletcher, who was a member of the first Lafayette County jury in 1821. Several other Fletchers also lived in Lafayette County. [CR, Lafayette, County, Missouri, 1830 and 1840; Young, *History of Lafayette County,* 1:51.]

FONSE, T., hosted a meeting where McLellin performed confirmations and ordinations in Huntsburg, Ohio.

FOOT, S., hosted McLellin when he stopped near Westfield, New York, in May 1835.

FOOT, Timothy (1799-1886), was born on Dec. 29, 1799, in Oswegatchie, New York, to Stephen Foote and Rhoda Hand. Married Jane Ann Russell in 1823. Was baptized in Sept. 1833. Was appointed on May 11, 1835, to be an agent for the Westfield, New York Saints to purchase land in Zion. Was ordained a seventy and in Mar. 1849 was ordained a high priest by John Murdock and J. L. Heywood. Died on Apr. 18, 1886, in Nephi, Utah. [*MR-L* 16:628–30.]

FOSTER, G. S., fed McLellin and his horse at his establishment in or near Howard County, Missouri, Aug. 15, 1831. Probably George S. Foster. [CR, Howard County, Missouri, 1830.]

FRANCIS, D., was from Kirtland. McLellin visited Francis's sister, the wife of Mr. Osburn in Greene County, Illinois in 1833.

FRENCH, L., hosted McLellin near Eugene, Indiana, July 23, 1834. Many French families lived in the area. [CR, Clark County, Illinois, 1840; CR, Edgar County, Illinois, 1840; Vermillion County, Indiana, 1830.]

FULKERSON hosted McLellin overnight near Lexington, Missouri, Aug. 16, 1831. Possibly Fredrick Fulkerson or Rubin Fulkerson, who was named sherriff of Lone Jack, Jackson County in 1845. [CR, Lafayette County, Missouri, 1830 and 1840; Wilcox, *Jackson Pioneers,* 96.]

FULLER, Elder, gave McLellin $2.00 and a ride on July 9, 1835, in St. Lawrence County, New York.

FULLER, E., is Edward Meeks Fuller (b. 1792), born on Jan. 26, 1792, in Clifton Park, New York, to Isaiah Fuller and Catherine Smith. Married Hannah Elizabeth Eldridge in 1814. Was ordained a high priest. Hosted McLellin and John Boynton in Richmond, Ohio, in Nov. 1834. [*MR-L,* 17:411.]

FULLER, Jesse, arrived and settled in Pleasant Grove Township in 1828 from Virginia. He and his family were good friends of McLellin in Coles County, Illinois. [Bateman, *History of Coles County,* 640; CR, Coles County, Illinois, 1840; CR, Clark County, Illinois, 1830.]

FULLER, Mrs., a friend whom McLellin visited in Aug. and Sept. 1831 and May 1833. Married Jesse Fuller.

GANNAWAY, John & Aunt Betsy, were good friends whom McLellin visited in Effingham County, Illinois in May 1833. Probably John Ganaway. [CR, Clark County, Illinois, 1830; CR, Effingham County, Illinois, 1840.]

GARDNER, Jotham, was born in 1747 in Hanover, New Jersey, to Mary and Thomas Gardner. Married Hannah Russell on June 20, 1762. On Jan. 28, 1835, at age eighty-eight, he was baptized by McLellin in Huntsburg, Ohio. [TIB.]

GARDNER, Mrs., is Hannah Russell who was born in 1749 in Harvard, Massachusetts, to Jason and Elizabeth Russell. Married Jotham Gardner on

June 20, 1762. Was baptized on the same day as her husband in Huntsburg, Ohio, on Jan. 28, 1835. [TIB.]

GATES, Esquire, hosted appointments in Mar.–May 1833. Located in Greene County, Illinois.

GOFF is James Goff (1808–87), born in 1808 in McMinnville, Tennessee, to Daniel Goff and Sarah Simpson. Married Mary Elizabeth Kimbrough on May 2, 1830, and they had ten children. Baptized on Mar. 1, 1832, and was ordained a seventy in June 1839. Moved to Utah in 1850, where he died Aug. 4, 1887, in Provo, Utah. [*MR-L* 18:592–95.]

GOFF is Mary Elizabeth Kimbrough Goff (b. 1811), born on Oct. 16, 1811, in Rowan County, North Carolina, to Aaron Kimbrough and Nancy Steward. Married James Goff on May 2, 1830. Baptized by George Hinkle prior to McLellin's arrival in Fayette, Missouri, in Feb. 1833. [*MR-L* 26:697–99.]

GOULD, J., was an elder who transported McLellin to Fredonia Village, New York, in May 1835. Probably John Gould (1808–51), born on May 11, 1808, in Ontario, Canada, to Seth E. Gould. Married Olivia Abigail Harrington. Named special messenger from Kirtland to Missouri with Orson Hyde in Oct. 1833. Was ordained one of the first seven Presidents of the First Quorum of Seventy on Apr. 6, 1837. Was ordained a high priest and began mission to Illinois in Apr. 1844. Died on May 9, 1851, in Iowa. [*PK,* 29; and McCune, *Personalities,* 45.]

GOULD, Sally Ann (b. 1812), was born on July 25, 1812. Married William Gould. Baptized by Orson Hyde on May 11, 1835, near Westfield, New York. [*PK,* 29.]

GOULD, William (b. 1808), was born on May 17, 1808. Married Sally Ann. Baptized by Orson Hyde on May 11, 1835, near Westfield, New York. Signed a statement stating he would leave Missouri. Was ordained a seventy by 1836. [*PK,* 29; and JH, Dec. 31, 1836; Jan. 29, 1839.]

GRANGER transported McLellin and others to the vicinity of Pittsford, New York, in June 1835. Probably Oliver Granger (1794–1841), born on Feb. 7, 1794, in Phelps, New York, to Pierce Granger and Clarissa Trumble. Married Lydia Dibble on Sept. 8, 1818, and they had three children. Mostly blind from exposure in 1827. Was ordained an elder by Brigham Young and Joseph Smith. Was ordained a high priest on Apr. 29, 1836. Worked on Kirtland Temple and served as member of the Kirtland High Council. Served as Church land agent in 1839. Served mission to several eastern states. Died on Aug. 25, 1841, in Kirtland. [*MR-L* 18:843–45; and McCune, *Personalities,* 45.]

GRAY fed Hyde, Lewis, and McLellin breakfast in Little Valley, New York, May 20, 1835. Cousin to David Elliott. Many Gray families lived throughout the area. [CR, Cattaraugus County, New York, 1830 and 1840.]

GREEN, J. P., is John Portineus Greene (1793-1844), born on Sept. 3, 1793, in Herkimer, New York, to John C. Greene and Ann Chapman. Married Rhoda Young on Feb. 11, 1813. Served mission to eastern states in 1833. Was called to serve a mission to the Senecas with Amos Orton in May 1835. Member of Kirtland High Council in 1836. Branch president in New York City in 1839. Member of Nauvoo City Council in 1841 and served as city marshal in 1843. Died in Nauvoo on Sept. 10, 1844. [*PK,* 30; and *PJS* 2:549.]

GRIFFETH, Duty (1782-1872), was born on Mar. 31, 1782, in Canaan, New York, to Samuel J. Griffeth and Fear Greene. Married Barbara Ann Overacker in 1805. Was a deacon who donated money to McLellin in Amherst, Ohio. Died on Dec. 18, 1872. [TIB.]

GRIFFETH, Jos. B., was listed as a subscriber to the *Messenger and Advocate.* Possibly located in Mulberry, Ohio, in 1836. Several Joseph Griffeths lived in the area. [CR, Butler County, Ohio, 1830 and 1840; CR, Clermont County, Ohio, 1840; Hamilton County, Ohio, 1830 and 1840.]

GRIFFETH, Judea or Judah (1795-1880), was born on May 23, 1795, in New York to Samuel J. Griffeth and Fear Greene. Married Mariah Rockwell on Oct. 13, 1822. Was an elder in Amherst, Ohio, in Oct. 1834. Died on Mar. 31, 1880. [TIB.]

GRIFFETH (Griffith), Hiram (d.1845), was a member of a teacher's quorum in Amherst, Ohio. He married Mary Ann Griffith and was a member of the Kirtland Poor Camp in 1837 and died in 1845 in Nauvoo. [*HC* 3:93; *PK,* 30.]

GRIFFITH, Mary Ann, donated money to McLellin's missionary efforts. Possibly born on Dec. 27, 1792, in Burke County, Georgia. Married to Hiram Griffith. [*MR-L* 19:334; and *PK,* 30.]

GRISWOULD, Mr., possibly Adonijah Griswold, born in 1772. Collected contributions then hosted meetings for McLellin in Mar. and Apr. 1833 in Greene County, Illinois. Many Griswolds lived in Greene County. [*A Census of Pensioners,* 187; CR, Greene County, Illinois, 1830 and 1840.]

GRISWOULD, Mrs., hosted McLellin in Mar. and Apr. 1833. Seemed unbelieving.

GRISWOULD was a former Methodist who hosted McLellin and Patten in June 1835 near Lyons, New York. Several Griswolds lived in Wayne County, New York. [CR, Wayne County, New York, 1830 and 1840.]

HADEN, Joel H., was a Christian priest who hosted McLellin and Parley Pratt for a while near Chariton, Missouri, Feb. 1833. Invited them to preach and then openly opposed them. [CR, Howard County, Missouri, 1830.]

HADLOCK, R., is Reuben Hedlock (b. 1801), born in 1801. Married Susan Wheeler in 1827. Hosted an appointment in Geneseo, New York, in June 1835. Became president of the elders quorum in Kirtland and a member of the Kirtland Safety Society in 1837. Moved to Missouri in 1838, served mission to England in 1840, and moved to Nauvoo in 1841. Prepared engravings for facsimiles in the book of Abraham and worked on the *Times and Seasons* in 1842. Served as president of the England Mission, 1843-45. Carpenter. [JH, Jan. 2, 1837; Feb. 23, 1842; and *PJS* 2:551.]

HAMBRIGHT, Colonel, is John W. Hambright (b. 1806), born on Jan. 29, 1806, in Kentucky. Hosted McLellin and Parley Pratt overnight in his cabin near Mount Ephraim, Missouri, Feb. 2, 1833. Married Lewis Hudspeth in 1833. Built the "Prairie House," a halfway station between Independence and Lexington and two miles southeast of Sibley. Served as constable of Fort Osage Township in 1836. Later became the postmaster of Sibley. Guests often stayed at his home. Known as a horse doctor. Always referred to as Colonel Hambright although there is no record of having been in the military. [CR, Jackson County, Missouri,1840; Wilcox, *Jackson Pioneers,* 56-58; and Young, *History of Jackson County, Missouri,* 112.]

HANCOCK, Levi (1803-82), was born on Apr. 7, 1803, in Springfield, Massachusetts, to Thomas Hancock and Amy Ward. Was baptized Nov. 16, 1830, in Kirtland by Parley Pratt. Was ordained an elder by Oliver Cowdery and a president of the Seventy by Joseph Smith. Served a mission to Jackson County, Missouri, in June 1831 with Zebedee Coltrin, and they preached in Winchester, Indiana, establishing a large branch of the Church there prior to McLellin's arrival in Oct. 1831. Married Clarissa Reed on Mar. 29, 1833, and they had eight children. Marched with Zion's Camp in 1834. Participated in one of McLellin's appointments in Florence, Ohio, while on his way from Missouri in Oct. 1834. Contributed to the Kirtland Temple. Served as a Nauvoo police officer, in the Nauvoo Legion, and as musician and religious leader in the Mormon Battalion Company E. Died in Utah on June 10, 1882. [*BE* 1:188; and *MR-L* 20:497-506.]

HANCOCK, Solomon (1793-1847), was born in Aug. 1793 in Springfield, Massachusetts, to Thomas Hancock and Amy Ward. Married Alta Adams on Mar. 12, 1815, and they had ten children. Was baptized on Nov. 16, 1830, in Ohio. Was ordained an elder in 1831 and later was ordained a high priest. Served a mission to Missouri in 1831 with Simeon Carter. Became a member of the high council in Missouri. Alta died. Married Phoebe Adams on June 28, 1836, and they had five children. Moved to Illinois in 1839 and then to Iowa in 1846. Died on Dec. 2, 1847. [*MR-L* 20:524-28.]

HANNAH. *See* Allred?, Hannah.

HANSON, Esquire G. M., is Reverend George M. Hanson, who came to Wabash Point and Dry Grove from Virginia in 1828 as a Methodist preacher. Drafted, circulated, and then carried to the state capitol the petition to create Coles County. He obtained passage of the bill. Obtained the establishment of a post office. Became its first postmaster on Feb. 18, 1830. Gave dinner to McLellin in Coles County, Illinois, Aug. 2, 1831. Served as a member of the First Board of County Commission. Representative in the legislature, 1842–46; senator, 1846–48. [Bateman, *History of Coles County*, 641–45; CR, Clark County, Illinois, 1830 and 1840.]

HARPER and his family hosted McLellin and Parley Pratt near Bluffdale, Illinois, Mar. 24 [actually Mar. 23], 1833. Possibly Ephraim or Carlton Harper. [CR, Greene County, Illinois, 1830 and 1840.]

HARRIS, Emer (1781–1869), was born May 29, 1781, in Cambridge, New York, to Nathan Harris and Rhoda Lapham. Brother of Martin Harris. Married Roxana Peas on July 22, 1802, and they had six children. After her death, he married Deborah Lott on June 16, 1819, and they had four children. After her death, he married Parna Chapell on Mar. 29, 1826, and they had four children. Obtained the first bound copy of the Book of Mormon. Was baptized in Feb. 10, 1831, and was ordained an elder and a high priest that same year. Preached with Simeon Carter. Afflicted with rheumatism in his hip. McLellin visited him in Florence, Ohio. Carpenter. Died in Utah in 1869. [*MR-L* 21:17–23.]

HARRIS, Martin (1783–1875), was born on May 18, 1783, in Easttown, New York, to Nathan Harris and Rhoda Lapham. Served as scribe early in the translation of the Book of Mormon and became one of the Three Witnesses in 1829. Contributed financially to the publication. Baptized on Apr. 6, 1830, by Oliver Cowdery and thereafter was ordained a priest. McLellin traveled with Martin, David Whitmer, and Hyrum Smith a while after he was ordained an elder in Aug. 1831. Served as a member of the Kirtland High Council and marched with Zion's Camp. Assisted in choosing the first Quorum of the Twelve in 1835. Excommunicated in Dec. 1837 and rebaptized in 1842. Estranged again until he was rebaptized in Salt Lake City in Sept. 1870. Died in 1875 in Clarkston, Utah. [*MR-L* 21:84–89.]

HARRISON. *See* Smith, Samuel Harrison.

HART, A., traveled with McLellin to Cincinnati, where he bought McLellin a hat in May 1836. Possibly Adna Hart, uncle to Wilford Woodruff, Sr. [JH, Aug. 20, 1837.]

HARVEY or HARVY, J., was upset that so many people were responding to McLellin's teachings in Greene County, Illinois, 1833. Gave the closing prayer at one of John Mason Peck's meetings on Apr. 20, 1833. Lived near Apple Creek Prairie, Illinois, 1833. Was possibly a member of Brigham Young's company in 1847 during the move west and served in the militia operations in Utah against Johnston's Army in 1857-58 and in the 1865-68 Black Hawk War. [*HC* 7:626; *MR-L* 21:426-31.]

HAWLEY, M., owned a tavern near Hopkinton, New York. Refused to give food and drink to McLellin and his fellow travelers on July 11, 1835. Possibly Milo Hawley. [CR, Franklin County, New York, 1830.]

HEAD, Anthony, hosted McLellin in Missouri in Feb. 1833. He and his family appeared to believe McLellin's message.

HEATON, Benjamin, read 138 pages of the Book of Mormon and subscribed to the *Star* in Calhoun or Pike County, Illinois, Mar. 1833.

HEATON, Mrs., believed Book of Mormon after borrowing copy from McLellin. Married Benjamin Heaton.

HENDERSON was a Christian priest. McLellin attended some of his meetings and became friends with him in Apple Creek Prairie, Illinois, Apr. 1833. Possibly D. P. Henderson, who was actively associated with these Christians. Served fifty years as a pastor, evangelist, and leader in the cooperative missionary work and Christian education. Was a writer, editor, and clerk of the court in Jacksonville. Several other Hendersons are also listed in the area. [CR, Greene County, Illinois, 1830 and 1840; Haynes, *History of the Disciples*, 529.]

HERRYMAN, H., was an elder who apparently served a mission with Willard Snow in May 1835. Probably Henry Harriman (1804-91), born in Rowley, Massachusetts, to Enock Harriman and Sarah Fowler. Was baptized in 1832 by Orson Hyde. Marched with Zion's Camp. Was ordained a seventy in 1835 and one of the first seven Presidents of Seventy in 1838, in which calling he continued for the remainder of his life. Traveled to Utah in 1848. Served missions to Great Britain in 1857 and Dixie in 1862. Died in Huntington, Utah, on May 17, 1891. [*BE* 1:191-94; and *CHC* 4:21.]

HETTY. *See* Milton.

HICKLIN, Mrs., hosted McLellin and others in Paris, Illinois, in July and Sept. 1831. Seemed to believe their message. Married T. Hicklin.

HICKLIN, T., hosted McLellin, Harvey Whitlock, and David Whitmer in Paris, Illinois, in July 1831 while McLellin began his investigation of Mormonism. In July and Sept. 1831, he hosted McLellin and Hyrum Smith and allowed them to preach in his home. Showed interest in Mormonism. Possibly Thomas Hicklin, who arrived in the Pike Precinct of Edgar County from Kentucky in 1824. [Bateman, *History of Edgar County,* 637; CR, Edgar County, Illinois, 1830.]

HIGGINS, Doctor, read anti-Mormon literature at an appointment in Greene County, Illinois on Apr. 28, 1833. Possibly Harrison Higgins, who was the District 3 superintendent of elections in 1821 although several other Higginses also lived in the area. [CR, Greene County, Illinois, 1830 and 1840; *HGC,* 257.]

HILL hosted McLellin overnight between Hillsboro and Vandalia, Illinois, May 21, 1833. [CR, Bond County, Illinois, 1830 and 1840; CR, Fayette County, Illinois, 1830 and 1840; Montgomery County, Illinois, 1830 and 1840.]

HILL, A., hosted appointments in Boone County, Kentucky, May 22, 1836. Probably Abner Hill. [CR, Boone County, Kentucky, 1830 and 1840.]

HILL, Elisha and Catrin, were rebaptized into the Church on Aug. 31, 1834. Lived in Missouri, and later petitioned that state for redress. Elisha was ordained a seventy in Utah. [*MR-L* 22:915; and JH, Apr. 2, 1856.]

HINCLE. *See* Hinkle.

HINKLE, George M. (1801-61), was born on Nov. 13, 1801, in Jefferson, Kentucky. Was baptized in 1832. Lived and did missionary work in Missouri. Assigned on Feb. 25, 1833, to visit churches in Illinois and Indiana. Operated store in Far West. Served on Missouri High Council in 1836. Commanded the militia defending Far West in 1838. Eventually apostatized; was excommunicated on Mar. 17, 1838. On Oct. 31, 1838, he turned Joseph Smith and other leaders over to General Lucas. Died in Iowa in 1861. [*MR-L* 23:182-83; and *PJS* 2:553.]

HITCHCOCK, J., is probably Jesse Hitchcock (1801-46), who was born on Aug. 10, 1801, in Ash County, North Carolina. Was baptized on July 20, 1831. Was ordained an elder before July 1832 and a high priest on Sept. 26, 1833, in Clay County, Missouri. Appointed to labor with John Killian. Given a blessing by Joseph Smith in Zion on July 9, 1834. Member of the Missouri High Council in 1836. Served as the acting scribe for Joseph Smith in 1836. Served a mission to Illinois in 1843. Died in Iowa while crossing the plains in 1846. [JH, July 2, 1832; Sept. 26, 1833; *MR-L* 23:238-39; and *PJS* 2:553-54.]

HODGES, Mrs., fed McLellin in Fayette County, Illinois, May 22, 1833. Possibly Elizabeth Hodge, head of household. [CR, Fayette County, Illinois, 1840.]

HOLDEN, Aaron, was baptized by McLellin on Apr. 15, 1833, in Bluffdale, Illinois. Still living in Greene County, Illinois, in 1835. Wrote from Carthage, Illinois, to have missionaries sent there in 1837. [Jackman, "Autobiography," 6; and JH, May 21, 1837.]

HOLDEN, Katharine, was baptized by McLellin on May 5, 1833.

HOLMES, E., is probably Erastus Holmes (1801–63), born in Pennsylvania. Settled in Newbury, Ohio. Traveled with McLellin from Newbury to Cincinnatti, Ohio, May 12, 1836. Never joined the LDS Church although he was friendly to the Saints. Served as the postmaster of Mulberry from 1839–47. Living in Cincinatti by 1850. He died in Milford, Ohio, in 1863. [CR, Clermont County, Ohio, 1830 and 1840; *PJS* 1:491.]

HORTON invited McLellin to make an appointment south of Carrollton, Illinois, on Mar. 22, 1833, but McLellin declined. Could be any of the Hortons listed in Greene County. [CR, Greene County, Illinois, 1830 and 1840.]

HOWARD, Richard, was possibly born in 1814 in Royalton, Vermont. Attended a conference in Far West, Missouri. Member of the high council in Iowa. Donated money to McLellin in Florence, Ohio. [*MR-L* 24:120; and JH, Apr. 26, Oct. 5, 1839.]

HOWE, Sister, hosted McLellin in Florence, Ohio, while her husband was away in Nov. 1834. Probably Harriet Howe (1804–79), born in Friendship, New York, in 1879. Was baptized before 1834. Made clothing for workers of the Kirtland Temple. Worked on the curtains of the Kirtland Temple. [*PJS* 2:555; and Jessee, *Personal Writings of Joseph Smith,* 655n.]

HUBBARD, Charles Wesley (1810–1903), was born on Feb. 7, 1810, in Sheffield, Massachusetts, to Noah Hubbard and Cynthia Clark. Married Mary Ann Bosworth in Aug. 1832, and they had twelve children. Was baptized in Nov. 1833 and rebaptized on July 7, 1877. Given recommend to move to Zion with his wife in Sept. 1834 while living in Eugene, Indiana. Came to Utah in 1848 with the Heber C. Kimball Company and served as a bishop there. Served a mission to Great Britain 1856–58. Colonized southeast Nevada. Died on Dec. 19, 1903, in Utah. [*MR-L* 24:275–84.]

HUBBARD, Cynthia Clark (1785–1866), was born on Oct. 22, 1785, in Sheffield, Massachusetts, to David Clark and Prudence Kellogg. Married Noah Hubbard on Sept. 21, 1806, and they had eleven children. Healed by McLellin and her husband. Given recommend to go to Zion in Sept. 1834 while living in Eugene, Indiana. Died on Jan. 8, 1866, in New Richmond, Indiana. [*MR-L* 9:770–72.]

HUBBARD, Mary Ann Bosworth (1816–1908), was born on Aug. 12, 1816, in Salisbury, Connecticut, to Jared Bosworth and Lucy Hubbard. Married Charles Wesley Hubbard in Aug. 1832, and they had twelve children. Was baptized in Nov. 1833. Came to Utah in 1848 with the Heber C. Kimball Company where she died on Nov. 29, 1908. [*MR-L* 6:254–56.]

HUBBARD, Noah (1778-1846), was born on Oct. 20, 1778, in Sheffield, Massachusetts. Married Cynthia Clark in Sept. 1806, and they had eleven children. Resided in Eugene, Indiana. Cared for McLellin when he was sick. Hosted appointments. Received the gift of tongues. He and McLellin administered to his wife Cynthia, who was sick. Resided in Nauvoo, Illinois. Died in Council Bluffs, Iowa, on Aug. 26, 1846. [*MR-L* 24:312-14.]

HUFF invited McLellin and Pratt to stay in his home near Gilead, Illinois, Mar. 13, 1833. Possibly John. [CR, Calhoun County, Illinois, 1830.]

HUGHS, Nathaniel, was listed as a subscriber to the *Messenger and Advocate* in Mulberry, Ohio, in 1836. [CR, Clermont County, Ohio, 1830.]

HUNTOON, Carter, hosted an appointment on Aug. 4, 1835. Was baptized by McLellin near Lyman, New Hampshire, on Aug. 6, 1835.

HYDE, Orson (1805-78), was born on Jan. 8, 1805, in Oxford, Connecticut, to Nathan Hyde and Sarah (Sally) Thorpe. Served as a Campbellite minister under Sidney Rigdon until he heard Mormon preachers. Was baptized on Oct. 2, 1831, by Sidney Rigdon. Was ordained a high priest on Oct. 25, 1831. Married Marinda (Nancy) Johnson on Sept. 4, 1834, and they had eleven children. Marched in Zion's Camp in 1834. Became an apostle on Feb. 15, 1835, and served a mission with the Twelve that same year. Served as McLellin's companion during May 1835. Preached and baptized in several places during the summer of 1835. From 1837-38 he served with Heber C. Kimball in England. Visited Jerusalem in 1841 and dedicated Palestine for the gathering of the Jews. Apostatized in Oct. 1838 for short while. Died on Nov. 28, 1878, in Spring City, Utah. [*MR-L* 24:957-64.]

IVEVTTS, possibly Everetts, ran or owned a ferry near Independence on the Missouri River where McLellin and Parley Pratt crossed for free on Jan. 28, 1833.

IVEY (IVY), Mr. and Mrs., hosted McLellin and a meeting in Missouri in Aug. and Sept., 1831. Several Ivey families lived in Ralls and Monroe counties, Missouri. [CR, Monroe County, Missouri, 1840; CR Ralls County, Missouri, 1830.]

JACKSON, Joseph, was baptized by McLellin on May 5, 1833.

JACKSON, Truman, was born in New York around 1801. Donated money to McLellin in Amherst, Ohio. Member of the Kirtland elders quorum, 1836. Was ordained a seventy by Hazen Aldrich in 1837. Married Ann Brown in 1837. [*PJS* 2:558.]

JENNINGS was located near Jackson County, Missouri. Hosted McLellin and others on Aug. 26, 1831. Many Jennings families lived in the area. [CR, Lafayette County, Missouri, 1830 and 1840.]

JINKENSON, John G., went with McLellin to see some mammoth bones on May 21, 1836. Listed as a subscriber to the *Messenger and Advocate*. May have been located in Gains Crossroads, Kentucky, 1836. Probably John Jinkerson, who was listed on the 1830 census of Boone County as married with six children. [CR, Boone County, Kentucky, 1830; Lawson, *Boone County, Kentucky*.]

JOHNSON, Hezk., was baptized by McLellin in Errol, New Hampshire Aug. 1835.

JOHNSON, J., is John Johnson (1778-1843), born on Apr. 11, 1778, in Chesterfield, New Hampshire, to Israel Johnson and Abigail Higgins. Married Elsa Mary Jacobs on June 22, 1800, and they had fifteen children. Was baptized during the spring of 1831. Joseph Smith and his family lived in his home, 1831-32. Hosted church meetings in Hiram, Ohio. Was ordained an elder and later a high priest in 1833. In 1837 he was rejected as a high councilor and consequently withdrew from the Church in 1838. Died in Kirtland on July 30, 1843. [*MR-L* 25:613-16; and Cook, *Revelations of the Prophet*, 199.]

JOHNSON, James (d. 1859), was present at a conference in Far West, Missouri, Oct. 2, 1832. Was an elder who accompanied McLellin to his appointment in Eugene, Indiana, on Aug. 7, 1834. Property owner in Caldwell County, Missouri, 1837. Became a seventy in 1852. Shot by Delos M. Gibson in Salt Lake City because Johnson knew Gibson was a horse thief. Died on May 28, 1859. [JH, May 26, 1852, and May 27-28, 1859; and *MR-L* 25:586.]

JOHNSON, James, was baptized by McLellin in Errol, New Hampshire, Aug. 1835.

JOHNSON, Luke Samuel (1807-61), was born in Nov. 1807 in Pomfret, Vermont, to John Johnson and Elsa Mary Jacobs. Baptized on May 10, 1831, by Joseph Smith. Was ordained a priest, elder, and high priest by Oct. 1831. Served several missions to the eastern states between 1831 and 1836. Served a mission to the South with McLellin beginning in Feb. 1832. Married Susan Armelda Poteet on Nov. 1, 1833, and they had six children. Marched in Zion's Camp. Was ordained an apostle in Feb. 1835. Attended Hebrew school, 1835-36. Disfellowshipped in 1837; apostatized and was excommunicated on Apr. 13, 1838. Helped the Prophet Joseph escape from jail in 1838. He was rebaptized on Mar. 8, 1846. Went to Salt Lake City in 1847; served as a bishop in Tooele. Died on Dec. 9, 1861, in Salt Lake City. [*MR-L* 25:649-56.]

JOHNSON, Lyman (1811-56), was born on Oct. 24, 1811, in Pomfret, Vermont, to John Johnson and Elsa Mary Jacobs. Baptized in 1831 by Sidney

Rigdon. Was ordained an elder on Oct. 25, 1831, by Oliver Cowdery and was ordained a high priest on Nov. 1, 1831, by Sidney Rigdon. Attended the School of the Prophets. Married Sarah Long (Lang) on Sept. 4, 1834, and they had two children. Marched in Zion's Camp. Allowed McLellin to board at his home in Kirtland during the winter of 1834. Was ordained an apostle on Feb. 14, 1835. Preached with McLellin, May through July 1835. Charter member of the Kirtland Safety Society in 1837, in which he lost money. Charged Joseph Smith with slander and lying in May 1837. Disfellowshipped on Sept. 3, 1837, and subsequently excommunicated for apostasy on Apr. 13, 1838. Drowned in the Mississippi on Dec. 20, 1856. [*MR-L* 25:657–60; and *PJS* 2:560.]

JOHNSON, N., was baptized by McLellin in Errol, New Hampshire, Aug. 1835.

JONES, Esquire, hosted McLellin on Mar. 9, 1833, in Calhoun or Pike County, Illinois. Possibly John Jones. [CR, Calhoun County, Illinois, 1840.]

JONES, J., is possibly Jacob Jones (d. 1857), who was one of the earliest settlers in the Paris, Illinois, region in the early 1820s. He came from Whitehall, New York. The marriage of his daughter, Narissa, was the first performed in the area. Owned the first store. Fed breakfast to McLellin, July 22, 1834. Merchant, prominent citizen, and he served for a time as the county treasurer. Died in 1857. A James Jones also lived in the area. [CR, Edgar County, Illinois, 1840; *The History of Edgar County Illinois,* 264 303, 314, 580.]

JONES, Levi (b. 1816), was born on Aug. 22, 1816, in Cortland, New York, to Peter and Eunice Jones. Married Sarah Zolide Reed. Marched in Zion's Camp, 1834. As an elder, accompanied McLellin to an appointment in Eugene, Indiana, on Aug. 7, 1834, and preached there. Baptismal date recorded as 1841. [*MR-L* 26:5.]

JONES, Major, fed McLellin and Parley Pratt breakfast east of Howard County, Missouri, Feb. 16, 1833. Numerous Joneses are listed in the area. [CR, Howard County, Missouri, 1830 and 1840.]

JONES, Mrs. Stephen, hosted McLellin in May 1835. Believed gospel message and donated money to McLellin.

JONES, Sister, is probably Sarah Zolide Reed Jones, wife of Levi Jones. Had been sick for years and was healed by the priesthood.

JONES, Stephen, hosted McLellin and Luke Johnson in St. Clairesville, New York, in May 1835. [CR, Chautauqua County, New York, 1830 and 1840.]

KETTING, Jos., carried a letter from McLellin to his wife in Apr. 1836.

KEYES. *See* Keys.

KEYS (Keyes) was a Campbellite who banded with other denominations' preachers to oppose McLellin in Crittenden, Grant County, Kentucky, May and June 1836. Possibly William or John Keys. [CR, Campbell County, Kentucky, 1830 and 1840.]

KIMBALL, Heber Chase (1801-68), was born on June 14, 1801, in Sheldon, Vermont, to Solomon Farnham Kimball and Ann(a) Spaulding. Married Vilate Murray on Nov. 22, 1822, and they had ten children. Was baptized on Apr. 15, 1832. Was ordained an elder in 1832. Presided at a conference of the Twelve in Geneseo, New York. Marched with Zion's Camp. Attended Sidney Rigdon and McLellin's grammar school, 1834-35. Was ordained one of the original Twelve Apostles on Feb. 14, 1835. Served missions to Canada and the eastern states. Served as head of the first mission to England in 1837, which he returned to in 1840. Arrived in Salt Lake in 1847. Served as Brigham Young's first counselor. Became active in Utah government. Helped lay and consecrate the southeast cornerstone of the Salt Lake Temple. [*MR-L* 26:623-54.]

KINGSBURY, H., is Horace Kingsbury (1748-1853), born in 1798 in Litchfield, Connecticut. Married Diantha Stiles in 1826. Moved to Painesville, Ohio, in 1827. Hosted McLellin and John Boynton there in Nov. 1834. Wrote a letter proclaiming the integrity of Joseph Smith and Oliver Granger to the Prophet's debtors. Jeweler and silversmith. Became mayor of Painesville in 1848. Died on Mar. 12, 1853, in Painesville, Ohio. [JH, Oct. 26, 1838; *MR-L* 26:851; and *PJS* 2:563.]

KNIGHT, Newel (1800-1847), was born on Sept. 13, 1800, in Marlboro, Vermont, to Joseph Knight and Polly Peck. Married Sally Colburn on June 7, 1825, and they had one child. Baptized by David Whitmer in May 1830. Was ordained a priest on Sept. 26, 1830, an elder before June 1831, and a high priest before July 3, 1832. Helped ease McLellin's mind concerning Mormonism after his conversion. Sally died on Sept. 15, 1834. Married Lydia Goldthwaite on Nov. 24, 1835, and they had seven children. Participated in the Kirtland Temple dedication. Was the subject of this dispensation's first miracle when he was relieved of evil spirits by Joseph Smith. Served a mission to western New York. Died in Nebraska on Jan. 11, 1847. [*MR-L* 27:24-29; and Cook, *Revelations of the Prophet*, 79.]

LAMSON hosted McLellin in Potsdam, New York, July 1835.

LANE, Nathaniel, was a Universalist who hosted McLellin and spread word of an appointment in Braceville, Ohio, in Nov. 1831. [CR, Trumbull County, Ohio, 1830; JH, Nov. 16, 1831, 1.]

LANTERMAN, Peter, hosted an appointment in Austintown, Ohio, Dec. 17 [actually Dec. 18], 1831. [CR, Trumbull County, Ohio, 1830.]

LEE, Jarvis, was ordained to the office of priest in Winchester, Indiana, by McLellin and Hyrum Smith in Oct. 1831.

LESSLEY hosted McLellin and Parley Pratt in or near Howard County, Missouri, Feb. 15, 1833. Three Lesleys are listed in Randolph County, which borders Howard County. [CR, Randolph County, Missouri, 1840.]

LEWIS, Job, owned a tavern in Westfield, New York. Hosted a conference of the Church, May 1835. Joseph Smith stayed with him while recruiting men for Zion's Camp in Mar. 1834. Married a woman named Margaret. Excommunicated in 1836. [Bradley, *Zion's Camp,* 10; and *PJS* 2:565.]

LEWIS, Joshua (1795-1835), was baptized in the winter of 1830-31. Hosted McLellin while he investigated the Church. Hosted the first conference in Zion while living in Jackson County, Missouri. A deathly ill John Murdock stayed with him and his family for two to three months in 1831. Sent to acquire a peace warrant for the Saints in 1833. Died in Clay County, Missouri, 1835. [*MR-L* 28:69; and JH, June 14 and Aug. 4, 1831; Nov. 3, 1833.]

LEWIS, Lloyd, was baptized in 1835 in Westfield, New York, and was ordained an elder on May 24, 1835. Left the Church by Nov. 1835. [JH, May 10, May 22, and Nov. 19, 1835.]

LEWIS, Lorenzo, ordained an elder by McLellin and Orson Hyde in May 1835. Traveled with them until he was sent with John Murdock to Springville, Pennsylvania, in May 1835. Excommunicated on Sept. 28, 1835. [JH, Sept. 28, 1835.]

LOMMERY, Eunice, was baptized by McLellin on June 22, 1835, in Lake Ontario near Pillow [Pillar] Point, New York.

LOVELESS, Widow, fed McLellin breakfast and hosted an appointment northeast of Ellicottville, New York, May 21, 1835.

LUFF hosted appointments in Millcreek, New York, in June 1835.

LYONS, Eliza, was baptized on May 26, 1835, by Lyman Johnson in Hate, New York. Possibly the Sister Lyon that Almon Babbitt sent a letter by to President Young in Winter Quarters during Apr. 1847. Joseph Smith records that he visited her minutes after her infant died on Christmas Eve, 1842. [JH, Apr. 5, 1847; Dec. 24, 1842.]

MACKEY hosted McLellin and Parley Pratt in eastern Missouri, probably Pike County, Mar. 7, 1833. Several Mackeys are listed in the records of Pike County. [CR, Pike County, Missouri, 1830 and 1840.]

MANUEL hosted an appointment in Letter B, Maine, Aug. 19, 1835. Possibly John Manuel. [CR, Oxford County, Maine, 1830.]

MAPES, Betsy, was baptized by Orson Hyde on May 11, 1835, in Westfield, Chautauqua County, New York.

MARSH, Thomas B. (1799–1866), was born on Nov. 1, 1799, in Acton, Massachusetts, to James Marsh and Mary Law. Married Elizabeth Godkin in Nov. 1820. Sought Joseph out after hearing about the "golden book" in 1829. Was baptized on Sept. 3, 1830, in Cayuga Lake near Fayette, New York. Was ordained an elder that same day. Called to preach with Ezra Thayre in Missouri, 1831–32, and later he served in New York. Was ordained an apostle in 1835. Preached with McLellin and others of the Twelve in 1835. Apostatized in 1838 but was later rebaptized. Died in Ogden, Utah, in Jan. 1866. [*MR-L* 29:466–72.]

MARTIN, M., was a Campbellite priest who met with McLellin in Wellsville, Ohio on Apr. 21 [actually Apr. 20], 1836. [CR, Columbiana County, Ohio, 1840.]

MAXIN, Esquire, hosted McLellin near Dalton, New Hampshire in July 1835.

MCCAFFERTY, Widow, hosted McLellin in or near Saline County, Missouri, Aug. 15, 1831, and Feb. 5 [actually Feb. 6], 1833. Possibly Catherine McCafferty. [CR, Saline County, Missouri, 1830.]

MCCORD, Mother, said she believed, but would not be baptized due to fear of the cold water in eastern Missouri, Mar. 1833.

MCCORD, Robert, was baptized by McLellin on Mar. 6, 1833, in eastern Missouri. Son of Mother McCord. Marched in Zion's Camp and contracted cholera. Died as a result in Missouri. [JH, June 30, 1834.]

MCCOWN, Doctor, hosted McLellin while he was sick near Paris, Illinois, July 22, 1834. Possibly Scipio McCowin, or Jonathan McCown who was a prominent early settler of Edgar County. [Bateman, *History of Edgar County,* 625; CR, Vigo County, Indiana, 1830.]

MCCOWN, Mrs., hosted McLellin while he was sick in July 1834.

MCCUNE, Esquire, hosted McLellin in Pike County, Missouri, Aug. 12, 1831. Possibly William McCune or McClure. [CR, Pike County, Missouri, 1830.]

MCGEE, Char., hosted McLellin and an appointment in May 1836 in Newberry, Ohio. Was administered to by Robert Culbertson and McLellin on May 12, 1836.

MCLAUGHLIN fed McLellin dinner on Bank Lick Creek, Kentucky, May 15, 1836. Possibly Thomas McLaughlin. [CR, Kenton County, Kentucky, 1840.]

MCLELLIN, Cinthia Ann, was the first wife of McLellin. Died shortly before the commencement of the McLellin journals in 1831 and was buried next to her deceased infant in Coles County, Illinois.

MCLELLIN, Emeline Miller (1809-1907), was born on Sept. 4, 1809, in Vermont. Became William McLellin's second wife on Apr. 26, 1832, and they had six children. Baptized into the Reorganized Church on July 1, 1888. Died on Nov. 1, 1907, in Texas. [*MR-R* 4:371-72.]

MCLELLIN, Israel, was McLellin's brother. They discussed Mormonism while Israel was staying with their uncle south of Springfield, Illinois, in Aug. 1831. Israel carried a Book of Mormon to Samuel McLellin in Tennesee in Sept. 1831.

MCLELLIN, Samuel, was a brother to and frequent correspondent with McLellin. Located in Tennessee.

MCMAN, Sister, was sick with phethisis, and McLellin administered to her.

MEAD or MEED hosted an appointment for McLellin and Parley Pratt on Mar. 11, 1833, and then he housed the Methodist circuit rider. Possibly Isaac Mead of Calhoun County, Illinois. [CR, Calhoun County, Illinois, 1830.]

MEED. *See* Mead.

MEEK, Doc., and McLellin discussed Mormonism in Goshen, Ohio, May 11, 1836. Possibly Samuel G. Meek. [CR, Clermont County, Ohio, 1830.]

MERICK was baptized by McLellin on May 1, 1833. Probably wife of Levi Merick.

MERICK, Levi, was baptized by McLellin on Apr. 30,1833. He and his wife were living in Carrollton, Illinois, in 1835. Killed during the Haun's Mill Massacre on Oct. 30, 1838. [Dyer, *The Refiner's Fire,* 90; and Jackman, "Autobiography," 6.]

MILES, Col., hosted McLellin and Orson Pratt in McIndoe Falls, New Hampshire, July 22, 1835. His wife gave McLellin two shirts. Possibly Albert Miles, born on Jan. 22, 1812, in New York to Thomas Miles and Sally Seger. Married Margaret Mariah Veets in 1833, and they had six children. Was ordained a seventy. Likely received the title colonel when he served in the Indian War. He also served as a member of the Utah Militia. He is listed as being rebaptized in 1886. Emigrated to Salt Lake City in 1848, where he died on May 12, 1886. [*MR-L* 30:880-84.]

MILLEN, Albert, was baptized by McLellin on Aug. 6, 1835, near Lyman, Grafton County, New Hampshire.

MILLEN, David, hosted McLellin in Lyman, New Hampshire, 1835. Possibly David Rudisill Miller (1793–1874), born on Dec. 13, 1793, in York, Pennsylvania, to John Miller and Mary Magdalena Rudisill. Married Barbara Henry on Nov. 18, 1817. Was ordained a seventy. Died on Sept. 18, 1874. [*MR-L* 30:977–79.]

MILLER hosted McLellin on several occasions in Braceville, Ohio. Probably Eleazer Miller (1795–1876), born Nov. 4, 1795, in Coeymans, New York, to John Miller and Sabra Bradway. Married Rebecca Rathbone in 1816, and they had eight children. Was baptized in 1831 by Levi Gifford. Baptized Brigham Young. Marched with Zion's Camp in 1834. Served on the committee to expedite the removal of the Illinois Saints. Moved to Utah in 1848, where he ran the Church farm. Was ordained a seventy on Jan. 5, 1851. Died in Salt Lake City on Apr. 12, 1876. [*MR-L* 30:971–76.]

MILLER, G., was a Campbellite/Universalist who hosted McLellin overnight near Braceville, Ohio, Feb. 3, 1832. Possibly Guryon or George Miller. [CR, Trumbull County, Ohio, 1830 and 1840.]

MILLET donated money to McLellin in Canada.

MILLIGIN served McLellin dinner 78 mi. west of Louisana, Missouri, Aug. 14, 1831. Census records include a J. G. C. Milligan. [CR, Monroe County, Missouri, 1840.]

Milton and Hetty (last name unknown), friends of McLellin whose daughter, Mary Ann, died while he was away in 1831 investigating the Church. They lived in Paris, Illinois.

MITCHEL, Mr., was at the legislature when McLellin and Parley Pratt stopped at his home near Lafayette County, Missouri, Feb. 4, 1833. Probably N. C. Mitchell, who served as a state representative from 1832–34 although several other Mitchels lived in the area.. [CR, Clay County, 1830 and 1840; CR, Lafayette County, Missouri, 1830 and 1840; Ray County, Missouri, 1830 and 1840; Young, *History of Lafayette County,* 71.]

MITCHEL, Mrs., fed McLellin and Parley Pratt breakfast on Feb. 4, 1833, near Lafayette County, Missouri.

MITCHEL, Doctor S., was McLellin's uncle who hosted McLellin one evening in Indianapolis, Indiana, on Oct. 4, 1831.

MITCHEL, J. or I., was an uncle to McLellin who spent the evening with him at Dr. Mitchel's home in Indianapolis, Indiana, Oct. 4, 1831.

MONTGOMERY called on McLellin to administer to his child who was healed in Dalton, New Hampshire, July 27, 1835. Possibly James Montgomery. [CR, Coos County, New Hampshire, 1840.]

MOORE, Uncle William, was an uncle to McLellin who hosted him in Aug. 1831 near Springfield, Illinois. Discussed Mormonism with McLellin and desired to know the truth. When McLellin stopped again in Sept. 1831, Moore had gone to Tennessee. [CR, Sangamon County, Illinois, 1830.]

MOREDOCK. *See* Murdock.

MORLEY, Isaac (1786-1865), was born Mar. 11, 1786, in Montague, Massachusetts. Married Lucy Gunn in June 1812. After baptism on Nov. 15, 1830, he donated his large farm to the Church. Served as first counselor to Bishop Partridge, 1831-40. Served a mission to Missouri with Ezra Booth in June 1831 and a mission to the eastern states in 1835 with Edward Partridge. McLellin met him in Independence, Missouri, in Aug. 1831. Attended dedication of the Kirtland Temple. Was ordained a patriarch in Nov. 1837. Arrested shortly thereafter by mobs but was exonerated. Moved to Nauvoo in 1845 and to Utah in 1849. Appointed as a presiding member of the Salt Lake High Council. Colonized Manti, Utah. Died in Fairview, Utah, on June 24, 1865. [Cook, *Revelations of the Prophet,* 79-80; and *MR-L* 31:621-29.]

MORRIS, Jacob, hosted an appointment on July 7, 1834, and hosted McLellin near Danville, Ohio, on Sept. 11, 1836. Gave money to the *Star.*

MOSS hosted an appointment in Huntsburg, Ohio, Dec. 19, 1834. Possibly part of the Betsey Moss household. [CR, Geauga County, Ohio, 1840.]

MUN, B., was a former Methodist preacher who hosted McLellin and Parley Pratt in Calhoun or Pike County, Illinois, Mar. 1833. Subscribed to the *Star.* Possibly Benjamin Munn. [CR, Calhoun County, Illinois, 1830.]

MUN, Mrs., appeared to believe McLellin's message. Married to B. Mun.

MURDOCK, John (1792-1871), was born on July 15, 1792, in Kortwright, New York. Was baptized in Ohio on Nov. 5, 1830. Served a mission to Missouri with Hyrum Smith, 1830-32. Marched with Zion's Camp in 1834. Sent with Lorenzo Lewis to Springville, Pennsylvania, in 1835. Moved to Missouri in July 1836 and then to Nauvoo in 1841. Settled in the Salt Lake Valley on Sept. 24, 1847, where he died on Dec. 23, 1871. [*MR-L* 32:20-29.]

MYERS, William, hosted McLellin in Ontario, Canada, July 1835.

NAIL, hosted McLellin for tea in Bluffdale, Illinois, on Mar. 21, 1833. Possibly Daniel Nail, born around 1804. Member of the Old Settlers Association for Greene County. [*HGC,* 315.]

NEGUS, R. S., subscribed to the *Star* in Carrollton, Illinois, Mar. 25, 1833. Possibly Robert S. Negus. [CR, Greene County, Illinois, 1830.]

NEWCOME was possibly Samuel Newcomb, born Jan. 8, 1794, died Aug. 13, 1879. Went on a mission to the eastern states with Oliver Granger in 1833. Planned to go on a "preaching tour" with McLellin, but McLellin travelled instead with John F. Boynton. [*HC* 4:408; *PK,* 50.]

NICKERSON, Freeman (1778-1847), was born in South Dennis, Massachusetts, Feb. 5, 1778. In 1800 he emigrated to Vermont, where he met and married Huldah Chapman. They had nine children. Was a commissioned lieutenant in the War of 1812. Joined the Church in Apr. 1833 and served a mission to Ohio later that year. In Oct. 1833, he accompanied Joseph Smith and Sidney Rigdon on a mission to Canada. In May 1835, he hosted Brigham Young and William Smith in his home at Leona, New York.

NORTON, Hester, was baptized by Orson Hyde on May 11, 1835, in Westfield, New York.

NORTON, Sylvester, was baptized and confirmed by Orson Hyde on May 12, 1835, in Westfield, New York.

NUNALLY, N. W., lived in Paris, Illinois. Hosted Harvey Whitlock and David Whitmer, who introduced Mormonism to McLellin. Probably Major Nelson W. Nunnally (1801-69), born in Buckingham County, Virginia, in 1801. Married Letitia S. Hicklin, and they had nine children. Resided much of his life in Paris, Illinois. Died in 1869. [AF; CR, Edgar County, Illinois, 1830; 1840; and Jackman, "Autobiography," 17.]

NUTTING, Sister, hosted McLellin in Cincinnati, Ohio, Apr. 25, 1836. She was very anxious to go to Zion. Probably Syvander.

NUTTING, Syvander, was listed as subscribing to the *Messenger and Advocate* in 1836.

ODEL, Jacob, married McLellin's second cousin, Lucinda White. Located in Macoupin County, Illinois, May 15, 1833.

ODEL, Lucinda White, was McLellin's second cousin. Located in Macoupin County, Illinois, May 15, 1833.

ORTON, Amos (1792-1847), was born in 1792 in Tyringham, Massachusetts. Moved to New York by 1830. Accompanied Joseph Smith and others to Michigan in Oct. 1834. Sent with J. P. Green on a mission to the Senecas in May 1835. Was ordained a seventy in Kirtland in 1836. Married a woman named Elizabeth, who died in 1837. Married Dorcas Sekins (Seekings) on Aug. 23, 1837. Served a mission with Brigham Young to the Indians. Served a mission to New York. Excommunicated in 1838. Died in 1847. [*MR-L* 33:206; and *PJS* 2:576.]

ORTON, R., is Roger Orton (1799–1851), born in 1799 in New York. Brother of Amos Orton. Married Clarissa Bicknell around 1822. Was baptized in the early 1830s. Marched in Zion's Camp in 1834. Accompanied Joseph Smith and others to Michigan in Oct. 1834. As an elder, transported the Twelve to Fairport, Ohio, in May 1835. Served on Kirtland High Council in 1835. Saw an angel during the 1836 Kirtland Temple dedication. Became one of the seven presidents of the Seventy in 1845. Died in Lee County, Iowa, in 1851. [Backman, *Heavens Resound,* 195, 292; *MR-L* 33:213; and *PJS* 2:576.]

OSBURN was a Baptist priest. McLellin heard him preach near Bluffdale, Illinois, Apr. 6, 1833. [CR, Greene County, Illinois, 1830 and 1840.]

OSBURN, Mr., hosted McLellin near Carrollton, Illinois, Mar. 22, 1833. He had been a Methodist preacher. [CR, Greene County, Illinois, 1830 and 1840.]

OSBURN, Mrs., a Reformed Methodist and sister of a D. Francis who lived in Independence, Missouri. Hosted McLellin near Carrollton, Illinois. [CR, Greene County, Illinois, 1830 and 1840.]

PARK, Harris, was baptized by McLellin on Aug. 24, 1834, in Eugene, Indiana. Assigned to do missionary work on Aug. 18, 1844, in Tazewell, Virginia. [*HC* 7:260.]

PARTRIDGE, Edward (1793–1840), was born on Aug. 27, 1793, in Pittsfield, Massachusetts. Owned a hatting business in Ohio, 1819. Married Lydia Clisbee in 1819. Member of the Campbellites until he listened to Mormon missionaries. Traveled with Sidney Rigdon to New York in 1830 to see Joseph Smith. Was subsequently baptized on Dec. 11, 1830, and was ordained an elder. Visited relatives in Massachusetts to share Mormonism. Called in 1831 as the first bishop in Missouri. Met McLellin in Aug. 1831 near Independence, Missouri. Responsible for allocation of inheritances in Jackson County, Missouri. Served a mission to the eastern states, 1835. Attended the Kirtland Temple dedication in 1836. Arrested for treason in 1838 but found innocent. Died in Nauvoo in May 1840 as a result of weakening from persecution. [*BE* 1:218–22; and *MR-L* 34:11–17.]

PATTEN, David Wyman (1799–1838), was born Nov. 14, 1799, in Theresa, New York, to Benonio Patten and Edith (Abigail) Cole. Married Phoebe Ann Babcock in 1828. Was baptized on June 15, 1832, by his brother John Patten. Was ordained an elder that same day by Elisha H. Groves. Was ordained a high priest on Sept. 2, 1832, by Hyrum Smith. Was ordained an apostle by Oliver Cowdery on Feb. 15, 1835, in Kirtland. Traveled and preached with McLellin and other members of the Twelve in 1835. Served several missions to the eastern states and Canada. Was the captain who led the Mormons at the Battle of Crooked River, where he was killed on Oct. 25, 1838. [Cowley, *Prophets and Patriarchs,* 177-83; and *MR-L* 34:80-84.]

PATTON hosted McLellin in Jackson or Lafayette County, Missouri, Aug. 1831. Several Pattons and Pattens lived in the area. [CR, Jackson County, Missouri, 1830 and 1840; CR, Lafayette County, Missouri, 1840; CR, Ray County, Missouri, 1830.]

PATTON, Phibe Ann, is Phoebe Anne Babcock (1807-41), born around 1807. Married David Wyman Patton (Patten) in 1828. Hosted a meeting in her home in Florence, Ohio on Oct. 25, 1834. Died Jan. 5, 1841, in Nauvoo. [*MR-L* 3:56.]

PEAK was a Methodist who joined with other denominations' preachers to oppose McLellin in Crittenden, Kentucky, June 5, 1836. Possibly Willis Peak of Gallatin County (on the west side of Grant County). [CR, Gallatin County, Kentucky, 1840.]

PECK, Reverend, is J. M. Peck, who was one of the earliest settlers of Greene County and one of the first Baptist ministers when he arrived in 1820. Attended McLellin's appointments and preached against him in Greene County Illinois, Apr. 1833. Served as the preacher at Bethel Church in Madison County, Illinois. Served as editor of a paper devoted to Baptist principles. Resided in Rock Springs. A Henry Peck is also listed. [*American Baptist Register,* 84, 86; *HGC,* 321; CR, Greene County, Illinois, 1840; and Pratt, *Autobiography of Parley P. Pratt,* 86.]

PEMBERTON, Russel, was living in Dunkirk, Ohio, in May 1835 as a member but was losing his faith. Member of the Kirtland Safety Society. [JH, Jan. 2, 1837.]

PERRY, Daniel, Reformed Methodist preacher; attended an appointment in Ontario, Canada, July 5, 1835.

PETER. *See* Whitmer, Peter.

PHELPS, William W. (1792-1872), was born on Feb. 17, 1792, in Hanover, New Jersey, to Enon Phelps and Mehitable Goldsmith. Married Sally Waterman on Apr. 28, 1815, and they had eleven children. Was baptized in Kirtland on June 10, 1831. Was ordained an elder in June 1831 and was later ordained a high priest in Nauvoo. Sent a letter to Parley Pratt and McLellin from Zion. Was a school teacher, printer, justice of the peace, notary public, and editor of the *Western Courier.* Served as a member of a presidency of the Church in Missouri, 1834-38. Helped found Far West. Excommunicated on Mar. 10, 1838. Rebaptized in 1840. Came to Utah in 1848, where he served as Speaker of the House of Representatives in the state legislature. Died in Salt Lake City in 1872. [*MR-L* 34:787-93; and *PJS* 2:580.]

PINE hosted McLellin in Stockholm, New York, July 9, 1835. Possibly Joseph Pine, born on July 11, 1794. Was ordained a high priest. Married a woman named Adelia. Counselor in Kirtland elders quorum. Member of the Kirtland Camp. [*MR-L* 35:6; Backman, *Heavens Resound,* 369; and *HC* 3:92.]

POOL, L. or S., hosted McLellin and Pratt overnight near Paris, Missouri, Feb. 18, 1833. Possibly Samuel. [CR, Monroe County, Missouri, 1840.]

POTTER, Leman, was a teacher who donated money to McLellin's missionary efforts while living in Amherst, Ohio.

POWERS fed dinner to McLellin near Rumford Point, Maine, on Aug. 20, 1835. Possibly John Milton Powers, born on Jan. 39, 1815, in Butler County, Ohio, to Aaron and Martha Powers. Was ordained a seventy. Preached in Ohio. Campaigned for Joseph Smith's presidential race. [*HC* 6:339, 340; and *MR-L* 35:495.]

PRATT, Orson (1811-81), was born on Sept. 19, 1811, in Hartford, New York, to Jared Pratt and Charity Dickenson. Baptized on Sept. 19, 1830, by Parley Pratt. Was ordained an elder on Dec. 1, 1830, a high priest on Feb. 2, 1832, and an apostle on Apr. 26, 1835. Married Sarah Marinda Bates on July 4, 1836, and they had twelve children. Editor of the *Millennial Star.* Excommunicated in 1842; rebaptized in 1843. Came to Utah on July 21, 1847, where he became a member of the state legislature and Speaker of the House of Representatives. Crossed the ocean sixteen times on missions and became the last survivor of the original Quorum of the Twelve still in the Church. Died in Salt Lake City on Oct. 3, 1881. [*MR-L* 35:550-66.]

PRATT, Parley Parker (1807-57), was born in Burlington, New York, in 1807 to Jared Pratt and Charity Dickenson. Married Thankful Halsey (1797-1837) in 1827. Served a mission to the Lamanites in 1830. Immigrated to Missouri with his wife during the summer of 1832, and settled in the western portion of Jackson County. Served many missions during his lifetime, including one with McLellin to Missouri and Illinois beginning in Jan. 1833. Marched with Zion's Camp in 1834. Became an apostle in 1835. Participated in the Twelve's 1835 mission to Canada and the northeastern United States. Traveled to Utah in 1847. Killed in Van Buren, Arkansas, in 1857. [*MR-L* 35:568-82.]

PRICE, John, and his neighbors gathered to listen to Harvey Whitlock speak in or near Coles County, Illinois, Aug. 2, 1831. Possibly the John Price at whose residence in Ash Grove Township, Illinois, Hyrum Smith preached in the late 1830s or early 1840s. Other John Prices are also listed. [Bateman, *History of Shelby County,* 645; CR, Clark County, Illinois, 1830; CR, Shelby County Illinois, 1830 and 1840.]

REED or READ, Mr., hosted appointments in Weathersfield, Ohio, Dec. 1831 and Jan. 1832. His wife was a Roman Catholic. Census records list two Reed families. [CR, Trumbull County, Ohio, 1830.]

REED or READ, Mrs., hosted McLellin in Dec. 1831 and Jan. 1832. A Roman Catholic.

REED, Elizabeth, is apparently Elizabeth Cumming Reid. Married James H. Reid. Baptized by McLellin on Apr. 21, 1833, in Greene County, Illinois. Possibly went west in 1856 with a handcart. [AF; JH, June 11, 1856; and *MR-L* 36:367–68.]

REED, James H. is James H. Reid (1816–86). Born on Jan. 12, 1816, in Scotland to John Reid and Mary Murray. Married Elizabeth Cumming. Baptized by McLellin on May 5, 1833, in Greene County, Illinois. Died on Jan. 12, 1886. [*MR-L* 36:367–68.]

REED, Mother C., was baptized by McLellin on Dec. 14, 1831, in Weathersfield, Ohio. Several older women named Reed lived in the area. [CR, Trumbull County, Ohio, 1830 and 1840.]

REEVES, Mr. and Mrs., hosted an ill McLellin in Morgan County, Illinois, Aug. 6, 1831. Several Reeve families lived in the area. [CR, Morgan County, Illinois, 1830 and 1840.]

RENICK, Widow, and her two sons hosted McLellin and Parley Pratt overnight and fed them dinner on Feb. 3, 1833. However, they would not allow them to talk religion. Located near Mount Ephraim, Missouri. Several Renick families in the area were headed by females. [CR, Jackson County, Missouri, 1840; CR, Lafayette County, Missouri, 1830 and 1840.]

RICHARDS, G., hosted an appointment in Greene County, Illinois, Apr. 1833.

RICHARDS, Mr. and Mrs., spent time talking with McLellin and Samuel Smith in Garrettsville, Ohio, Nov. 18, 1831. Censuses list two Richards households. [CR, Portage County, Ohio, 1830.]

RIGDON, Phoebe Brook, traveled with McLellin and Sidney Rigdon in Jan. 1832. Married Sidney Rigdon.

RIGDON, Sidney (1793–1876), was born on Feb. 19, 1793, in Pennsylvania to William and Nancy Rigdon. Married Phoebe Brook on June 12, 1820, and they had eleven children. Joined Alexander Campbell and others in founding the Disciples of Christ or Campbellite faith. Taught by Parley Pratt, Oliver Cowdery, and others in 1830 and was baptized in Nov. of that same year. In Dec. he traveled with Edward Partridge to see Joseph Smith and became the Prophet's scribe for the inspired translation of the Bible

Was ordained one of the Presidency of the High Priesthood in Mar. 1832. Traveled with McLellin in Jan. 1832. Was set apart as first counselor to Joseph Smith in Mar. 1833. Served a mission to Ontario, Canada that same year. Trustee of the Kirtland school. Helped arrange the Doctrine and Covenants in 1835. Among those church leaders betrayed by George M. Hinkle in 1838. Helped found Nauvoo and served on its city council. Took the Saints' Missouri grievances to Washington, D.C. Joined the Masonic order. Became Joseph Smith's running mate in the 1844 U.S. presidential race. Claimed guardianship of the Church upon Joseph's death and was subsequently excommunicated. Organized his own church and later published a paper in the Pittsburgh area. Died in Friendship, New York, in 1876. [*BE* 1:31–34; and *MR-L* 36:894–99.]

ROBERTS was the Campbellite priest who tried to challenge McLellin in Crittenden, Kentucky, June 1, 1836. Many Robertses are listed in the area. [CR, Boone County, Kentucky, 1830 and 1840; CR, Campbell County, Kentucky, 1830 and 1840; CR, Grant County, Kentucky, 1840.]

ROBERTS, Major, was the sheriff of Calhoun County, Illinois, who advertised an appointment for McLellin and Parley Pratt in Gilead, Illinois, Mar. 11, 1833. Possibly Levi or David Roberts. [CR, Calhoun County, Illinois, 1830 and 1840.]

ROBERTS, Widow, She professed to believe but was not baptized. Was taught by McLellin in Goshen, Ohio, May 11, 1836.

ROBLEY, Henry, hosted McLellin and Parley Pratt in Apple Creek Prairie, Illinois, in Mar. and Apr. 1833. Married Caroline Griswould of Carlinville, Illinois. Census records list a Henry Robley in the area. Possibly also Harry A. Robley, who was born around 1814 to Captain Richard Robley and Desire Griswould. [CR, Greene County, Illinois, 1830 and 1840; Miner, *Past and Present,* 606–8.]

ROGERS was possibly Isaac Rogers who was born on Apr. 29, 1794. Married Susan Milles. Other Rogerses are listed in the area. In 1833, let McLellin use his horse between Carrollton, Illinois, and Vandalia, Illinois. Died on Apr. 30, 1861. [CR, Greene County, Illinois, 1830 and 1840; *MR-L* 37:516–17; and *PK,* 59.]

ROGERS hosted McLellin on Aug. 12, 1831, 43 mi. west of Louisiana, Pike County, Missouri. Several Rodgerses and Rogerses are listed in the area. [CR, Monroe County, Missouri, 1840; CR, Ralls County, Missouri, 1830 and 1840.]

ROGERS, A., hosted a meeting in his wagon shop on Apr. 21 [actually Apr. 20], 1836 in Wellsville, Ohio. Possibly Alex Rogers. [CR, Columbiana County, Ohio, 1840.]

ROOD hosted Orson Hyde in Laona, New York, May 14, 1835. Possibly Joseph Rood, although other Rood and Rudd families lived in the area. [CR, Chautauqua County, New York, 1830 and 1840.]

ROOT was a Baptist minister who preached against McLellin in Crittenden, Grant County, Kentucky, May and June 1836.

ROOTER, Dr., was a Methodist from Pittsburgh, Pennsylvania, whom McLellin heard on Apr. 17, 1836, in Wellsville, Ohio. Censuses list a Ruter and a Rutter. [CR, Allegheny County, Pennsylvania, 1840.]

ROUNDY, Shadrick or Shadrach (1788-1872), was born on Jan. 1, 1788, in Rockingham, Vermont, to Uriah Roundy and Lucretia Needham. Married Betsy Quimby on June 22, 1814, and they had ten children. Baptized by McLellin on Jan. 30, 1832. Was ordained an elder by Orson Hyde and Samuel H. Smith on May 16, 1832. Was ordained a seventy and a high priest in Kirtland. Served as Joseph Smith's bodyguard, as a member of the Nauvoo Legion, and as captain of the Nauvoo police force. Initiated into Masonry in 1842. Moved west in 1847. Assisted in bringing poor migrants from the Midwest to the Salt Lake Valley. Died in July 1872 in Salt Lake City. [*BE* 1:642-43; and *MR-L* 37:795-803.]

RUNKLE was a tavern keeper who hosted an appointment for McLellin and Parley Pratt in Clarksville, Missouri, Mar. 8, 1833.

RUSSELL, John (1793-1865), was born on July 31, 1793, to John Russell and Lucretia Preston. Became a reputable writer. Married Laura Ann Spencer on Oct. 25, 1818. One of the earliest settlers of Greene County. Became the postmaster and as such gave Bluffdale its name. Was a farmer, educator, writer, and preacher of the Bluffdale Baptist church organized in 1832. Obtained a Baptist preacher license on Feb. 6, 1833 in Bluffdale, but remained unordained. Hosted McLellin and Parley Pratt near Carrollton, Illinois, in Mar. and May 1833. Several years later, he sheltered Sidney Rigdon and Parley P. Pratt when they escaped from Missouri. Pratt said that Russell was a "very learned and influential man." When the first public school opened in fall 1851, he was the professor in charge. He had a long career as a writer for periodicals. Was the editor of the newspaper, the *Back Woodsman,* begun in 1837. One of his short stories, "The Mormoness; or Trials of Mary Maverick, a Narrative of Real Events," was based on the experiences of Levi Merrick, who was baptized by McLellin in Carrolton on Apr. 30, 1833. This tale of Mormon suffering was "probably one of the first fictionized treatments of the Mormon theme." Died on Jan. 21, 1865. [CR, Greene County, Illinois, 1830 and 1840; Flanagan, "John Russel"; *HGC,* 297, 309, 340, 321; and Pratt, *Autobiography of Parley P. Pratt,* 84.]

RUSSELL, Sister, was Laura Ann Spencer, wife of John Russell. [Flanagan, "John Russel."]

SABRISKI, Lewis. *See* Zabriski, Lewis.

SAMUEL. *See* Smith, Samuel Harrison.

SANDERSON was originally from Tennessee but lived 4 miles from Ray County, Missouri when he hosted McLellin, July 9, 1834. Possibly Edward Sanderson. [CR, Ray County, Missouri, 1840.]

SCOTT, Colonel John, a Deist who hosted McLellin and Pratt as well as several appointments in Greene County, Illinois, Mar.–May 1833. Possibly John W. Scott. [CR, Greene County, Illinois, 1830 and 1840.]

SCOTT, R., hosted McLellin overnight near Carrollton, Illinois, on Apr. 24, 1833. Possibly Robert J. Scott, who arrived from Ohio in 1825 and settled land north of Brouilletts Creek. An R. B. Scott is also listed. [CR, Greene County, Illinois, 1830 and 1840; Bateman, *History of Edgar County,* 636.]

SEARS was a Methodist who hosted McLellin and David Patten near Wolcott, New York, June 7, 1835. Several Sears families are listed. [CR, Cayuga County, New York, 1830; CR, Wayne County, 1840.]

SECRETS, William, was a Methodist preacher living near Crittenden, Kentucky, May 26, 1836. Married Sally Ann Jones on Dec. 8, 1829. [CR, Grant County, Kentucky, 1830; Craig, *Grant County Marriages,* 5.]

SEELY, George, hosted a meeting and subscribed to the *Star* in Missouri, Mar. 1833. [CR, Pike County, Missouri, 1840.]

SHATTUCK, Sally, was baptized by McLellin in Errol, New Hampshire, Aug. 1835.

SHELLEDY, Lawyer, helped McLellin settle his affairs in Paris, Illinois.

SHERWOOD, Samuel, wrote a letter against Mormonism dated Feb. 25, (probably 1833) from Independence, Missouri, which was read on Apr. 21, 1833, by Rev. Peck at an appointment for McLellin and Parley Pratt in Greene County, Illinois. A copy of the letter was again read at an appointment of McLellin's and Pratt's on Apr. 28, 1833, by a Doctor Higgins at the home of a Mr. Wilson, Greene County, Illinois.

SIMMONS, Nancy, was a Methodist widow who hosted McLellin overnight in Greene County, Illinois, Apr. 3, 1833. Was baptized on May 5, 1833, by McLellin near Bluffdale. She wrote two weeks later to tell him that she had returned to the Methodist faith. [CR, Greene County, Illinois, 1840.]

SLOVER, Jacob, fed McLellin dinner in Effingham or Coles County, Illinois, May 23, 1833. Possibly the Mr. Slover who ran a mercantile in Coles County, Illinois. [Bateman, *History of Coles County,* 649; CR, Clark County, Illinois, 1830.]

SMITH, Asael, Jr. (1773-1848), was born May 21, 1773, in Windham, New Hampshire, to Asael Smith and Mary Duty. Married Elizabeth Schellenger on Mar. 21, 1802, and they had eight children. Baptized in June 1835 by Lyman E. Johnson. Hosted McLellin near Stockholm, New York, July 9, 1835. Was ordained a high priest. Was called as the fourth presiding patriarch of the Church although he did not act in this office because of poor health. Died in Iowaville, Iowa, en route to the west in July 1848. [*BE* 1:182; and *MR-L* 39:695.]

SMITH, Eden (1806-51), was born in Indiana in 1806 to John Smith. Married a woman named Elizabeth. Was ordained a priest on Sept. 11, 1831, by Joseph Coe. Was ordained an elder on Nov. 17, 1831, by Reynolds Cahoon. Disfellowshipped on July 2, 1833. Rebaptized in Eugene, Indiana, by McLellin on Aug. 27, 1834. Was reordained an elder on Sept. 10, 1834, by McLellin. Served a mission to Pennsylvania. Died in Vermillion County, Indiana, on Dec. 7, 1851. [*MR-L* 39:763-65.]

SMITH, Elias (1804-88), was born on Sept. 6, 1804, in Royalton, Vermont, to Asael Smith and Elizabeth Schellenger. Swapped horses with McLellin in Eugene, Indiana. Baptized on Aug. 27, 1835, by Hyrum Smith and was ordained an elder the next day. Was ordained a high priest by Joseph Smith. Died on June 24, 1888, in Salt Lake City. [*MR-L* 39:771-78.]

SMITH, Elizabeth, was rebaptized by McLellin on Aug. 10, 1834, in Eugene, Indiana. Wife of Eden Smith.

SMITH, Hyrum (1800-1844), was born on Feb. 9, 1800, in Tunbridge, Vermont, to Joseph Smith, Sr., and Lucy Mack and was an elder brother to the Prophet Joseph. Married Jerusha Barden on Nov. 2, 1826, and had six children. Was baptized in June 1829. Became one of the Eight Witnesses to the Book of Mormon and a charter member of the Church. Served a mission to Missouri with John Murdock in 1831. Talked with McLellin about the Church and then baptized him. He proposed that McLellin be ordained an elder. Preached in various areas in company with various members of the Twelve. After Jerusha's death in 1837, he married Mary Fielding and had two children. Served as second counselor to President Joseph Smith, 1837-41. Served as Assistant President, patriarch of the Church, and member of the Nauvoo Legion until his martyrdom with Joseph on June 27, 1844. [*BE* 1:52-53; and *MR-L* 39:880-87.]

SMITH, John (1781-1840), was born on July 16, 1781, in Hillsborough, New Hampshire. Married Clarissa Lyman in 1815. Baptized by his nephew, Joseph Smith, Jr., on Jan. 9, 1832. Passed the sacrament with McLellin on Nov. 9, 1834. Served missions with his brother, Joseph Smith, Sr., in 1832 and 1836. Was a member of the Kirtland High Council, stake president in Nauvoo, and the presiding patriarch. [*MR-L* 39:944-52.]

SMITH, Joseph, Jr. (1805–44), was born on Dec. 23, 1805, in Sharon, Vermont, to Joseph Smith and Lucy Mack. Received the First Vision of this dispensation in 1820 and subsequently became the first Prophet of this dispensation. Married Emma Hale on Jan. 18, 1827 Received Gold Plates on Sept. 22, 1827, from Moroni and translated them in 1829 into the Book of Mormon. Received the Aaronic Priesthood from John the Baptist on May 15, 1829. Baptized with Oliver Cowdery that same day. Received the Melchizedek Priesthood from Peter, James, and John. Published the Book of Mormon in 1830. Organized The Church of Jesus Christ of Latter-day Saints on Apr. 6, 1830. Moved to Kirtland and began translating the Bible in Jan. 1831. Subject to persecution and numerous attempts on his life. McLellin first saw him at a conference near Kirtland on Oct. 25, 1831. Organized the first high council on Feb. 17, 1834, and that month began recruiting for Zion's Camp. Trustee of the Kirtland School. Organized the Quorum of the Twelve Apostles in Feb. 1835. That year he also received the papyrus scrolls which he translated into the Book of Abraham. Dedicated the Kirtland Temple in 1836. Incarcerated several times and was martyred in Carthage Jail on June 27, 1844. [*BE* 1:1–8; and *MR-L* 40:25–29.]

SMITH, Joseph, Sr. (1771–1840), was born July 12, 1771, in Topsfield, Massachusetts to Asael Smith and Mary Duty. Was baptized Apr. 6, 1830. Was ordained a high priest on June 3, 1831, by Lyman Wight. Moved with his family to Kirtland in 1831. Was ordained patriarch on Dec. 18, 1833. Served a mission to the eastern states in 1836 with his brother. Became one of the founders of Nauvoo. Died of tuberculosis on Sept. 14, 1840. McLellin's references to "Father Smith" and "old Father Smith" could also refer to Joseph Smith's Sr.'s brother John Smith. [*BE* 1:181–82; and *MR-L* 40:16–22.]

SMITH, Mrs., was healed by McLellin in Dec. 1831 near Niles, Ohio. Censuses list dozens of Smiths in Trumbull County, Ohio. [CR, Trumbull, County, Ohio, 1830 and 1840.]

SMITH, Rachael, was baptized on Sept. 7, 1834, in Eugene, Indiana by McLellin. Possibly the Rachel Smith born on Nov. 29, 1813, in Stratford County, New Hampshire. Married Howard S. Smith. Joined the RLDS Church on Oct. 7, 1862, in Galland's Grove, Iowa. Possibly the Rachel Smith who was married to Elder Nathan Tanner by Amasa Lyman in Apr. 1836. [JH, Apr. 5, 1836.; *MR-R* 5:494.]

SMITH, Samuel Harrison (1808–44), was born on Mar. 13, 1808, in Tunbridge, Vermont, to Joseph Smith, Sr., and Lucy Mack. Baptized on May 25, 1829. One of the Eight Witnesses to the Book of Mormon. Was ordained an elder in June 1830. Was an early missionary for the Church. Subsequently served several missions and baptized many. Served with McLellin on a mission to the East. Married Mary Bailey on Aug. 13, 1834. In Nauvoo he served as a member of the Presiding Bishopric, bishop of a Nauvoo ward, alderman, and a member of the Nauvoo Legion. Died one month after the martyrdom of his brothers in 1844. [*BE* 1:278-82; and *MR-L* 40:212-18.]

SMITH, William (1811-94), was born on Mar. 13, 1811, in Royalton, Vermont, to Joseph Smith, Sr., and Lucy Mack. Baptized on June 9, 1830, by David Whitmer. Was ordained a teacher in 1830, a priest in 1831, an elder in 1832, a high priest in 1833, an apostle in 1835, and Church patriarch in 1845. Married Caroline Amanda Grant on Feb. 14, 1833, and they had two children. Marched in Zion's Camp in 1834. McLellin wrote a letter for William to Joseph Smith on July 20, 1835. Traveled with McLellin at the end of Aug. and beginning of Sept. 1835. Excommunicated on Oct. 12, 1845. William associated with James Strang until 1847. Joined the RLDS Church in 1878. Died on Nov. 13, 1894. [*MR-L* 40:371-78.]

SNIDERS hosted a prayer meeting of a religious group in Ontario, Canada, July 2, 1835.

SNOW, Gardner (1793-1889), was born in Chesterfield, New Hampshire, to James Snow and Abigail Farr. Married Sarah Sawyer Hastings on Nov. 30, 1814, and they had nine children. Was baptized on June 18, 1833. Hosted McLellin and fellow travelers in St. Johnsbury, Vermont, July 1835. Transported McLellin and Orson Pratt to Waterford, Vermont in July 1835. Sometime before 1850, he emigrated to Utah where he died in Manti in Nov. 1889. [*MR-L* 40:545-48.]

SNOW, Willard (1811-53), was born on May 6, 1811, in St. Johnsbury, Vermont, to Levi Snow and Lucina Streeter. Was baptized on June 18, 1833, by Orson Pratt. Marched with Zion's Camp. Was ordained a seventy in 1835. Apparently served a mission with H. Herryman in May 1835. Married Melvina Harvey on May 14, 1837, and they had eight children. Married Susan Harvey in 1846, and they had one child. Also married Mary Bingham. In 1847, moved to Utah where he became a member of the state legislature. Served a mission to Scandinavia and died on Aug. 21, 1853, at sea on the way home. [*BE* 4:374; and *MR-L* 40:634-39.]

SNYDER, Nancy, was baptized by McLellin on May 10, 1835, in Westfield, New York.

SOUTH, Widow, hosted McLellin overnight near Shelbyville, Illinois, Aug. 3, 1831. Census lists several Souths. [CR, Shelby County, Illinois, 1830.]

SQUIRES hosted McLellin for $.25 south of Geneseo, New York, June 1, 1835. Multiple Squiers and Squires are listed in the area. [CR, Livingston County, New York, 1830 and 1840.]

ST. JOHN, James, was located near Warren, Ohio. Hosted meetings Dec. 1831-Feb. 1832. [CR, Trumbull County, Ohio, 1830; JH, Nov. 16, 1831]

ST. JOHN, Sarah. On Dec. 10, 1831, her baby was badly burned and Samuel Smith healed it. Was baptized by McLellin on Dec. 14, 1831, in Trumbull County, Ohio. [CR, Trumbull County, Ohio, 1830; JH, Nov. 16, 1831.]

STARS (STARR), Jared (1791-1855), was born on Jan. 13, 1791, in Groton, Connecticut, to William Stars and Freelove Bailey. Married Eunice Burdick on Nov. 21, 1814, and they had nine children. Was baptized in Mar. 1832. Died in July 1855 in Salt Lake City. [*MR-L* 41:278-80.]

STONE hosted an appointment on Oct. 27, 1834, in Vermilion, Ohio.

STONE, James E., hosted an appointment and subscribed to the *Messenger and Advocate*. Located in Boone County, Kentucky, 1836. [CR, Boone County, Kentucky, 1830.]

STONE, Silas, hosted an appointment and later fed McLellin dinner in Boone County, Kentucky, May 1836. Subscribed to *Messenger and Advocate*. [CR, Boone County, Kentucky, 1830 and 1840.]

STRINGHAM, Sabra (1821-1909), was born on Sept. 1, 1821, in Colesville, New York, to George Stringham and Polly Hendrickson. Baptized by Orson Hyde on May 11, 1835, in Westfield, New York. Married John Balser Heki on May 16, 1841. Died on Apr. 1, 1909. [*MR-L* 42:142.]

STRONG, Ezra (1788-1877), was born on June 26, 1788, in Albany, New York, to Deacon Ezra Strong and Nancy Gates. Married Olive Lowell on Nov. 19, 1814, and they had ten children. Was an elder in Rockport, Ohio. Was ordained a high priest in 1836. Farmer. Died on Apr. 12, 1877. [*MR-L* 42:154-56.]

SUMNER, Esquire Charles, hosted McLellin overnight at his country home in Middlebury, Ohio, Feb. 25, 1832. Served as an associate judge from Feb. 1834 through Feb. 1840 on the Court of Common Pleas. [CR, Portage County, Ohio, 1830; *History of Portage County,* 332.]

SUSE, W., was a Deist who hosted McLellin and Samuel Smith overnight near Warren, Ohio, Dec. 1, 1831. Refused to believe their message unless they performed a sign.

SWEAT, Angeline, was baptized by McLellin in Errol, New Hampshire, Aug. 13, 1835.

SWEAT, Benjamin, was a priest who hosted McLellin in Errol, New Hampshire, Aug. 13, 1835. Several Sweats and Swetts are listed by census records. [CR, Coos County, New Hampshire, 1830 and 1840.]

SWEAT, Frederick, was baptized by McLellin in Errol, New Hampshire, Aug. 13, 1835. Represented the Northbridge Branch at a conference in Salem, Massachusetts, in 1842. [JH, Sept. 11, 1842.]

SWIFT, Joanna, was born in Sharon, Connecticut. Baptized on May 26, 1835, by Lyman Johnson in Hate, New York. Received patriarchal blessing on May 23, 1836, from Joseph Smith, Sr. [*MR-L* 42:376.]

SWINFORD, Samuel, led the Church in Danville, Illinois, in 1834.

TANNER, Nathaniel, was listed as a subscriber to the *Messenger and Advocate.* In Fulton, Ohio, 1836. [CR, Hamilton County, Ohio, 1830 and 1840.]

TERRILL hosted an appointment in Fowler, Ohio, Feb. 11, 1832. Census records list five Terrells. [CR, Trumbull County, Ohio, 1830.]

THAYER or THAIR, Ezra is Ezra Thayer (1791–1856). Born on Oct. 14, 1791, in Randolph, Vermont, to Ezra Thayer and Charlotte French. Married Polly Wales in 1810. Operated a tannery in Kirtland. Served as land agent in 1833. In 1834, marched with Zion's Camp, where he contracted cholera. Died in Randoph, Massachusetts, in 1856. [Backman, *Heavens Resound,* 73, 194; *MR-L* 43:76–78; and *PJS* 2:598.]

THORNTON directed McLellin to where Harvey Whitlock, David Whitmer, and Hyrum Smith went, Aug. 15, 1831. McLellin visited him again Feb. 6 [actually Feb. 7], 1833. Located in Chariton County, Missouri. Several Thorntons lived in the area. [CR, Saline County, Missouri, 1830 and 1840.]

THORNTON, Colonel, was located near Liberty, Missouri. When McLellin and Parley Pratt stopped by, he had gone to the legislature on Jan. 28, 1833. The governor appointed Thornton as aid to the Missouri Militia and gave him the task of serving as an informant on the Mormons. In June 1836, chaired a committee in a public meeting in Liberty, Missouri, to draft resolutions against the Mormons. Became extremely anti-Mormon. [CR, Clay County, Missouri, 1830 and 1840; Young, *History of Jackson County,* 261.]

THORNTON, Mrs., wife of Colonel Thornton, fed McLellin and Parley Pratt on Jan. 28, 1833.

THRASH hosted McLellin in Aug. and Sept. 1831 in Chariton County, Missouri. Hosted an appointment when McLellin revisited him in Feb. 1833. Possibly Andrew Thrash. [CR, Chariton County, Missouri, 1830 and 1840.]

TILLERY hosted McLellin and Parley Pratt overnight in Liberty, Missouri, Jan. 29, 1833. Several Tillery families are listed. [CR, Clay County, Missouri, 1830 and 1840.]

TRACY, J. M., challenged McLellin to a public discussion in Huntsburg, Ohio, Mar. 18, 1835. Possibly John M. Tracy. Myron Tracy is also listed as one of the officiating clergyman of the Congregational Church which was organized on Feb. 15, 1834, in Chardon. [CR, Geauga County, Ohio, 1840; *History of Geauga,* 116.]

TROTTER was a Methodist circuit rider for Calhoun County, Illinois, Mar. 1833.

TURNER (Turney), Thomas, married Betsy Bishop. Baptized by Parley Pratt on May 13, 1833, and then hosted an appointment in Bluffdale, Illinois. Died in Far West, Missouri. [*PK,* 73.]

VAN LUWEN, F., is Frederick Matthew Van Leuven, born on Feb. 14, 1808, in Nine Partners, Dutchess County, New York to John VanLeuven, Sr. and Mary Ann Pulver. Married Lydia Draper on Feb. 14, 1827, had ten children, and died on Nov. 3, 1876, in San Bernardino, California. Hosted a meeting for McLellin on June 25, 1835, and bought him cloth for new pants. Was ordained a high priest, seventy, and Presiding Elder. [*HC* 2:233, 235; 3:30, 92; and *MR-L* 44:284–90.]

VAN LUWEN, J., is John Van Leuven, Jr. (1801–89), born on Aug. 10, 1801, in Dutchess County, New York, to John Van Leuven, Sr., and Mary Ann Pulver. Married Fanny Draper. Was baptized in 1834 by Brigham Young. Hosted meeting in Loughborough, Canada, on June 25, 1835. Member of Kirtland Camp. Later affiliated with the Reorganized Church in Iowa. Died on Apr. 28, 1889, in Atchison County, Missouri. [*MR-L* 44:293; and *MR-R* 6:19.]

VEST, G., hosted an appointment in Boone County, Kentucky, May 18, 1836. Possibly one of two George Vests in the area. [CR, Boone County, Kentucky, 1830 and 1840.]

WADSWORTH, Nathan, arranged a meeting for McLellin on Apr. 25, 1836, in Greenupsburg, Kentucky; McLellin's brother-in-law.

WALKER, Esquire, hosted appointments near Bluffdale, Greene County, Illinois, Apr. 1833. Possibly J. E. Walker, who was the first settler of Walkerville, Greene County, Illinois. Settled that town in 1835. It flourished but eventually died out. In Carrollton, he lost the 1849 election for trustee but won the 1850 election. Censuses also list several other Walkers. [CR, Greene County, Illinois, 1830 and 1840; *HGC,* 337.]

WATSON hosted McLellin and appointments in or near Greene County, Illinois, in Mar. and May 1833. Possibly William Watson, born around 1800. One of the earliest settlers of Greene County. Moved there from Kentucky. Mercantilist and worked in real estate. Later in his life, he moved to Calhoun County, Illinois. Censuses also list other Watson families. [CR, Greene County, Illinois, 1830 and 1840; CR, Jersey County, Illinois, 1840; and *Portrait and Biographical Album,* 331.]

WATTERMAN was living in Vandalia, Illinois, when McLellin delivered Mr. Rogers's horse to him, May 22, 1833. Possibly H. C. Waterman. [CR, Fayette County, Illinois, 1840.]

WEBB, Dr. F. B., hosted McLellin overnight in Crittenden, Kentucky, on May 29, 1836.

WEBSTER hosted McLellin and an appointment. Possibly Cornelius Webster. Father to Vardeman Webster. Other Websters are listed. Located in Boone County, Kentucky, May 1836. [CR, Boone County, Kentucky, 1830 and 1840.]

WEBSTER, Vardeman or Vardiman, Baptist preacher in Boone County, Kentucky, May 25, 1836. [CR, Boone County, Kentucky, 1840 and 1850.]

WESTON, William, hosted McLellin in Goshen, Ohio, May 11, 1836. His wife was LDS. Subscribed to *Messenger and Advocate* in 1836.

WHITE, James, was baptized with his wife Sophia by McLellin on Apr. 15, 1833, in Bluffdale, Illinois. Later hosted meetings in his home in May 1833. Possibly the man who led a faction to England, 1844. The group's name was Jarael and later changed to House of Israel. [Crary, *Kirtland,* 57.]

WHITE, Sophia, was baptized by McLellin on Apr. 15, 1833, in Bluffdale, Illinois. Married James White.

WHITE, William, hosted McLellin and appointments in Coles County, Illinois, in July and Sept. 1831. Censuses list several William Whites. [CR Clark County, Illinois, 1830; and CR, Coles County, Illinois 1840.]

WHITLOCK, Harvey Gilman (1809-74), was born in Massachusetts. Was baptized in 1831. Was ordained a high priest on June 3, 1831. One of the LDS preachers McLellin heard in Paris, Illinois, in July 1831. Excommunicated in 1835; rebaptized in 1836. Left the Church again in 1838. In 1864, moved from Utah to California where he joined the RLDS Church. Excommunicated from the RLDS Church in 1868. Died in California in 1874. [*MR-L* 45:873-75; and *PJS* 2:602.]

WHITLOCK, Minerva (b. 1810), was born in Litchfield County, Connecticut, on July 3, 1810. Married Harvey G. Whitlock by 1830, and they had eight children. Arrived in Zion in Aug. 1831. [*MR-L* 45:882-83.]

WHITMER, Father, is Peter Whitmer, Sr. (1773-1854), born on Apr. 14, 1773, in Pennsylvania. Married Mary Musselman, and they had eight children. Strict Presbyterian until converted to Mormonism. The Church was organized on Apr. 6, 1830, at his farm in Fayette, New York. Was baptized on Apr. 18, 1830, by Oliver Cowdery. Moved to Kirtland in 1831.

Living in Hiram, Ohio, by Dec. 1831. Hosted a council of elders on Dec. 30, 1831. Moved to Jackson County in 1832. Held a meeting in Missouri at George Seeley's prior to McLellin's arrival on Mar. 1, 1833. Turned away from the Church by 1838. Died on Aug. 12, 1854, in Richmond, Missouri. [*BE* 1:282-83; and *MR-L* 45:918-20.]

WHITMER, David (1805-88), was born on Jan. 7, 1805, in Pennsylvania. Was baptized by Joseph Smith in June 1829. One of the Three Witnesses of the Book of Mormon. Was ordained an elder on Apr. 6, 1830. Moved to Kirtland by June 1831. One of the LDS preachers McLellin heard in Paris, Illinois, in July 1831. Living in Jackson County, Missouri, in Oct. 1831 but returned to Kirtland by Sept. 1834. Returned to Missouri and was rejected by the Saints there as a president of the Caldwell Stake on Feb. 5, 1838. Excommunicated on Apr. 13, 1838, in Far West, Missouri. Moved to Richmond, Missouri, where he upheld his testimony of the Book of Mormon until his death on Jan. 25, 1888. [*BE* 1:263-70; and *MR-L* 45:899-902.]

WHITMER, John (1802-1878), was born on Aug. 27, 1802, in Fayette, New York, to Peter Whitmer and Mary Musselman. Married Sarah Jackson on Feb. 10, 1833, and they had five children. Baptized in June 1829; ordained an elder in 1830, and a high pirest in 1831. One of the Eight Witnesses of the Book of Mormon. Served several brief missions. Called to be the first Church Historian. Excommunicated in 1838, but never denied his testimony of the Book of Mormon. Died July 11, 1878.

WHITNEY, Newel Kimball (1795-1850), was born on Feb. 5, 1795, in Marlborough, Vermont, to Samuel Whitney and Susannah Kimball. Married Elizabeth Ann Smith on Oct. 20, 1822. Campbellite until baptism in Nov. 1830. Operated a store in Kirtland. Called to raise funds for building Zion and called as bishop in Kirtland in 1831. Participated in laying the Kirtland Temple cornerstone. One of the founders of Nauvoo. Succeeded Bishop Partridge as Presiding Bishop. Died in Salt Lake City on Sept. 23, 1850. [*BE* 1:222-27; and *MR-L* 45:963-71.]

WIGHTMAN, C., hosted McLellin and Lyman Johnson as well as appointments in Fairview Corners, New York, in May and June 1835. Possibly Charles Wightman, who was ordained an elder in Kirtland in 1836 and a seventy in Kirtland on Jan. 10, 1837. [*PJS* 2:179; and JH, Jan. 10, 1837.]

WILDER, Levi B. (1806-83), was born on June 25, 1806, in Concord, Vermont, to Nathan Wilder and Mercy May. Married Caroline Osgood on June 11, 1829. Transported McLellin up the Connecticut River on Aug. 11, 1835. Was ordained a seventy on Jan. 10, 1837. Died on Sept. 9, 1883. [*MR-L* 46:263-64.]

WILHITE hosted McLellin the night he left Paris, Illinois, for Jackson County, Missouri, July 30, 1831.

WILLIAMS, Frederick Granger (1787-1842), was born in 1787 in Suffield, Connecticut, to Warren Wheeler Williams and Ruth Granger. Married Rebecca Swain around 1815. Was baptized in Oct. 1830. Was ordained a high priest in Oct. 1831. Served a mission to the Lamanites with Oliver Cowdery, Parley Pratt, and others, 1830-31. Marched in Zion's Camp in 1834. One of the trustees of the Kirtland School. A farmer, medical doctor, and justice of the peace. Served as scribe to Joseph Smith beginning in 1832. Served as Second Counselor in the First Presidency until he was rejected and later excommunicated in 1839. Rebaptized in 1840. Died in Quincy, Illinois, in 1842. [*BE* 1:51-52; and *MR-L* 46:516-20.]

WILLS, Mrs., gave McLellin dinner and suggested he set up an appointment. Married Thomas Wills. [CR, Ralls County, Missouri, 1830.]

WILLS (Will), Thos., gave McLellin dinner and hosted a meeting on Feb. 26, 1833, near Paris, Missouri. [CR, Ralls County, Missouri, 1830.]

WILSON hosted an appointment in Greene County, Illinois, Apr. 26, 1833.

WILTON, Fanny, was baptized by Orson Hyde on May 11, 1835, in Westfield, New York.

WINSHIP hosted an appointment near Gilead, Illinois, Mar. 12, 1833. Census records list three Winships. [CR, Calhoun County, Illinois, 1830.]

WISSEL was a poor man who hosted McLellin and Orson Hyde near Ellicottville, New York, May 20, 1835. Possibly David Wisel. [CR, Cattaraugus County, New York, 1830.]

WOOD carried letters from McLellin to Kirtland on July 4, 1835, while McLellin was preaching with Brigham Young. Probably Jacob Wood, born on Nov. 4, 1804, in Ernestown, Canada, to Henry Wood and Elizabeth Demelt. Married Rebecca Simpkins. Attended a conference held in Kirtland on July 13, 1833, upon the return of Brigham Young from Canada with Canadian brethren. Excommunicated in 1835 in Loughborough, Ontario Canada. [*HC* 1:289, 2:235; and TIB.]

WOOD, Elizabeth, donated money to McLellin in Florence, Ohio, in Nov. 1834.

WOOD, Father, was a Christian preacher near Stilesville, Indiana. Invited McLellin and missionaries to attend a preachers' conference. Afterward, McLellin and his companions healed Wood's grandson on Oct. 1, 1831. Possibly James Wood. [CR, Hendricks, County, Indiana, 1830.]

WOOD, Gideon Durfey (1808-90), was born on June 30, 1808, in Hartwick, New York, to Jabez Wood and Lydia Stephens. Married Hannah Daley in Dec. 1830, and they had five children. Baptized either in Feb. 1832 or 1834 by Orson Hyde. Donated money to McLellin in Florence, Ohio, in Nov. 1834. Was ordained a seventy by Joseph Young, Feb. 1846. Farmer and school teacher. Died on Sept. 9, 1890, in Springville, Utah. [*MR-L* 47:278-81.]

WOOD, Uncle Nathan, uncle to McLellin. He fed breakfast to McLellin and showed interest in the missionaries. Probably located in Coles County, Illinois, Aug. 1, 1831.

WRIGHT, Polly, was baptized by McLellin on Aug. 4, 1835, near Lyman, New Hampshire.

YOUNG, Brigham (1801-77), was born on June 1, 1801, in Whitingham, Vermont, to John Young and Abigail (Nabby) Howe. Married Miriam Works on Oct. 8, 1824, and they had two children. After her death, he married Mary Ann Angel on Feb. 18, 1834, and they had six children. Was baptized and was ordained an elder on Apr. 14, 1832, by Eleazer Miller after two years of studying Mormonism. Marched with Zion's Camp in 1834. Served a mission to Canada in 1832 and in 1835, missions to the eastern states in 1835-37, and missions to England in 1839-41. Became an apostle on Feb. 14, 1835. Attended the Hebrew School, 1835-36. Became the second prophet and President of the Church on Dec. 5, 1847. Led the Saints to Utah. Died on Aug. 29, 1877, in Salt Lake City. [*MR-L* 48:38-67.]

YOUTSEY, Geo., hosted an appointment on May 1, 1836, near Newport, Kentucky.

ZABRISKIE, Lewis, spoke in and interpreted tongues at various meetings in Vermillion County, Indiana. Possibly the Lewis Zabriskie (1796-1884), who was born on Mar. 8, 1796, in Northhampton, Pennsylvania, to Christian Zabriskie and Elizabeth Morgan. Married Amelia Burton on Sept. 9, 1822, and they had six children. After her death, he married Jane Porter Reed on Sept. 3, 1835, and they had nine children. Baptized by George Hinkle in May 1832. Was rebaptized on Mar. 8, 1857, by Dominicus Carter. Came to Utah in 1849. Died in McCloud, Kansas, on Apr. 4, 1884. [*MR-L* 48:307-11.] Possibly the Lewis Zabriskie (1817-72) who was born on Sept. 17, 1817, in Hamilton, Ohio, to Henry and Eleanor Zabriskie. Was baptized in Apr. 1836. Married Mary Keziah Highbee on Apr. 13, 1839, and they had six children. Was ordained a seventy on Oct. 9, 1845. Farmer and harness maker. Died in Spring City, Utah, in Nov. 1872. [*MR-L* 48:312-16.]

ZABRISKIE, Susan, was healed by the priesthood and then worsened when a doctor treated her in Ohio.

BIBLIOGRAPHY

AF. LDS Ancestral File.

A Census of Pensioners for Revolutionary War of Military Services; with their Names, Ages, and Places of Residence . . . Washington, D.C.: Blair and Rives, 1841.

American Baptist Register. Philadelphia: American Baptist Publication Society, 1853.

Anderson, Karl Ricks. *Joseph Smith's Kirtland: Eyewitness Accounts.* Salt Lake City: Deseret Book, 1989.

Andrus, Milo, autobiography, Special Collections, Harold B. Lee Library, Brigham Young University, Provo, Utah.

BE. Andrew Jenson. *Latter-day Saint Biographical Encyclopedia,* 4 vols. Salt Lake City: Deseret News, 1901-1936.

Backman, Milton V. Jr. *The Heavens Resound: A History of the Latter-day Saints in Ohio, 1830-1838.* Salt Lake City: Deseret Book, 1983.

Baptist Clergy Census Directory, 1840-1849, 1850-1852. Edited by Ronald Vern Jackson and others. North Salt Lake, Utah: Accelerated Indexing Systems International, 1988.

Bateman, Newton, Paul Selby, and George D. Chafee, eds. *Historical Encyclopedia of Illinois and History of Shelby County.* Chicago: Munsell, 1910.

Bateman, Newton, Paul Selby, and H. Van Sellar, eds. *Historical Encyclopedia of Illinois and History of Edgar County.* Chicago: Munsell Publishing, 1905. Microfilm.

Bateman, Newton, Paul Selby, and Richard V. Carpenter, eds. *Historical Encyclopedia of Illinois and History of Boone County.* Chicago: Munsell Publishing, 1909.

———. *Historical Encyclopedia of Illinois and History of Coles County.* Chicago: Munsell, 1906.

Bitton, Davis. *Guide to Mormon Diaries and Autobiographies.* Provo, Utah: Brigham Young University Press, 1977.

Bradley, James L. *Zion's Camp 1834: Prelude to the Civil War.* Salt Lake City: Publishers Press, 1990.

Brown, John Thomas. *Church of Christ: A Historical, Biographical, and Pictorial History of Churches of Christ in the United States, Australasia, England and Canada.* Louisville, Kentucky: J. P. Morton, 1904.

CHC. B. H. Roberts. *A Comprehensive History of The Church of Jesus Christ of Latter-day Saints, Century One* 6 vols. Provo, Utah: The Church of Jesus Christ of Latter-day Saints, 1965.

CR. United States Census Records.

Campbell, Alexander. *Autobiography of Alexander Campbell.* Watertown, New York: Post Printing House, 1883.

Carter, N. F. *Native Ministry of New Hampshire.* Concord, New Hampshire: Rumford Printing, 1906.

Church, Leslie Frederic. *The Early Methodist People.* London: Epworth Press, 1949.

Church Chronology. Andrew Jenson, comp., *Church Chronology: A Record of Important Events Pertaining to the History of the Church of Jesus Christ of Latter-day Saints.* Salt Lake City: Deseret News, 1914.

Complete Regular Army Register of the United States: For One Hundred Years, (1779 to 1879). Compiled by Thomas H. S. Hamersly. Washington D.C.: T. H. S. Hamersly, 1880.

Cook, Lyndon W. *Revelations of the Prophet Joseph Smith.* Provo, Utah: Seventy's Mission Bookstore, 1981.

County by County in Ohio Genealogy. Columbus, Ohio: State Library of Ohio, 1978.

Cowley, Matthias F. *Prophets and Patriarchs.* Chattanooga, Tennessee: Ben E. Rich, 1902.

Craig, Robert D., comp. *Grant County, Kentucky, Marriages: 1820-1850.* n.p., 1968.

Craig, Robert D., comp. Marriage Records: Boone County, Kentucky: 1798-1818. n.p, n.d.

Crary, Christopher G. *Kirtland: Personal and Pioneer Reminiscences.* Marshalltown, Iowa: Marshall Printing, 1893.

Dill, R. S. *History of Fayette County, Ohio Together with Historic Notes on the Northwest, and the State of Ohio.* Dayton, Ohio: Odell and Mayer, 1881.

Documentary History of Vandalia, Illinois. Vandalia, Illinois: Vandalia Chamber of Commerce, 1954.

Dyer, Alvin R. *The Refiner's Fire: Historical Highlights of Missouri.* Salt Lake City: Deseret Book, 1960.

1812 Ancestor Index. Compiled and Edited by Eleanor Stevens Galvin. Norcross, Georgia: Harper Printing, 1970.

Enumeration of Youth and Partial Census for School Districts in Portage County, Ohio, 1832-1838: Includes a Census of Youth and Parents for Akron in 1838. Kent, Ohio: American History Research Center, Kent State University Library, 1982.

Flanagan, John T. "John Russel of Bluffdale," *Journal of the Illinois State Historical Society* 42 (Sept. 1949): 272-84.

Graham, Bernice, comp. *Washington County, Ohio Marriages, 1789-1840.* Baltimore, Maryland: Genealogical Publishing Company, 1989.

Greene County, 1803-1908. Xenia, Ohio: Aldine, 1908.

HC. Joseph Smith, Jr. *History of The Church of Jesus Christ of Latter-day Saints,* B. H. Roberts, ed., 7 vols. Salt Lake City: Deseret Book, 1964.

HGC. *History of Greene County, Illinois: Its Past and Present.* Chicago: Donnelley, Gassette, and Lloyd, 1879.

Hamersly, Thomas H. S. *Complete Regular Army Register of the United States for One Hundred Years 1779-1879.* Washington, D.C.: T. M. S. Hamersly, 1880.

Haynes, Nathaniel Smith. *History of the Disciples of Christ in Illinois, 1819-1914.* Cincinnati: Standard Publishing, 1915.

Heitman, Francis B. *Historical Register and Dictionary of the U. S. Army, from its organization, Sept. 29, 1789 to Mar. 2, 1903.* Washington D.C.: Government Printing Office, 1903.

The History of Edgar County Illinois. Chicago: William Lebaron, Jr., 1979.

History of Knox County, Ohio: Its Past and Present. N. N. Hill, Jr., comp. Mt. Vernon, Ohio: A. A. Graham, 1881.

History of Geauga and Lake Counties, Ohio, with Illustrations and Biographical Sketches of its Pioneers and Most Prominent Men. Evansville, Indiana: Unigraphic, 1973.

History of Montgomery County, Ohio. Chicago: W. H. Beers, 1882.

History of Portage County, Ohio. Chicago: Warner, Beers, 1885.

Hurlin, William. *The Baptists of New Hampshire.* Manchester, New Hampshire: John B. Clarke, 1902.

Index Cards of Congregations and Pastors in the United States 1807-1953. Salt Lake City: Filmed by Genealogical Society of Utah, 1987.

Index to the War of 1812 Pension Application Files. Washington, D.C.: The National Archives, National Archives and Records Service, General Services Administration, 1960.

Index to War of 1812 Pension Files. Transcribed by Virgil D. White. 3 vols. Waynesboro, Tennessee: National Historical Publishing, 1989.

JH. Jenson, Andrew. Journal History of the Church. Notebooks of type-written transcriptions and printed documents maintained in the LDS Church Archives, Salt Lake City:

Jackman, Levi. "Autobiography of Levi Jackman." Special Collections, Harold B. Lee Library, Brigham Young University, Provo, Utah.

Jessee, Dean C., ed. *The Personal Writings of Joseph Smith.* Salt Lake City: Deseret Book, 1984.

Lawrence, Robert F. *The New Hampshire Churches.* N.p.: Claremont Manufacturing, 1856.

Lawson, Rowena, trans. *Boone County, Kentucky 1810-1840 Censuses.* Bowie, Md.: Heritage Books, 1986.

List of Officers of the Army of the United States from 1779-1900. Compiled by Colonel William H. Powell. New York: L. R. Hamersly, 1900.

The Lives of Early Methodist Preachers. London: Wesleyan Conference Office, 1871-1872.

MR-L. Susan Easton Black, comp. *Membership of The Church of Jesus Christ of Latter-day Saints, 1830-1848,* 50 vols. Provo, Utah: Religious Studies Center, Brigham Young University, 1989.

MR-R. Susan Easton Black, comp. *Early Members of the Reorganized Church of Jesus Christ of Latter Day Saints,* 6 vols. Provo, Utah: Religious Studies Center, Brigham Young University, 1993.

McConkie, Bruce R., comp. *Doctrines of Salvation: Sermons and Writings of Joseph Fielding Smith.* Salt Lake City: Bookcraft, 1955.

McCune, George M., ed. and comp. *Personalities in the Doctrine and Covenants and Joseph Smith History.* Salt Lake City: Hawkes Publishing, 1991.

Methodist Ministers Card Index: All Ohio Conferences, 1797-1981. Columbus, Ohio: Ohio Historical Society, 1982.

Miner, Edward. *Past and Present of Greene County, Illinois.* Chicago: S. J. Clarke, 1905.

Minutes of the Beaver Baptist Association, Convened at Warren, Trumbull County, Ohio, 1813. New Lisbon, Ohio: William D. Lepper, 1813.

Missouri Cemetery Records Volume 1. Kansas City, Missouri: Heart of America Genealogical Society and Library, 1981.

Missouri Marriages before 1850. 3 vols. St. Louis: Ingmire Publishing, 1983.

Missouri Marriages before 1840. Baltimore: Genealogical Publishing, 1982.

Norton, Anthony B. *A History of Knox County, Ohio From 1779 to 1862 Inclusive.* Columbus: Richard Nevins, 1862.

Oesterlin, Pauline Johnson. *New Hampshire Marriage Licenses and Intention: 1709-1961.* Bowie, Maryland: Heritage Books, 1991.

Official Register of Missouri Troops for 1862. St. Louis: Adjutant General's Office, 1863.

Ohio Cemetery Records. Baltimore, Maryland: Genealogical Publishing, 1984.

Old War Index to Pension Files, 1815-1926. Washington D.C.: The National Archives, National Archives and Records Service, General Services Administration, 1959.

PJS. Dean C. Jessee, ed. *The Papers of Joseph Smith.* 2 vols. to date. Salt Lake City: Deseret Book, 1989—.

PK. Milton V. Backman and others, comps. *A Profile of Latter-day Saints of Kirtland, Ohio and Members of Zion's Camp, 1830-1839: Vital Statistics and Sources.* Provo, Utah: Brigham Young University, 1983.

The Past and Present of Boone County, Illinois. Chicago: H. F. Kett, 1877. Facsimile reprint. Bowie, Maryland: Heritage Books, 1989.

Portage County, Ohio Newspaper Obituary Abstracts 1825-1870. Compiled and edited by Michael Barren Clegg. Vol. 2. N.p., 1982.

Portrait and Biographical Album of Coles County, Illinois. Chicago: Chapman Brothers, 1887.

Portrait and Biographical Album of Knox County, Illinois. Chicago: Biographical Publishing, 1886.

Portrait and Biographical Album of Vermillion and Edgar Counties. Chicago: Biographical Publishing, 1881.

Portrait and Biographical Record of Shelby and Moultrie Counties. Chicago: Biographical Publishing, 1891.

Powell, Colonel William H. *List of Officers of the Army of the United States From 1779-1900.* New York: L. R. Hamersly, 1900.

Pratt, Parley P., Jr., ed. *Autobiography of Parley P. Pratt.* 3d ed. Salt Lake City: Deseret Book, 1938.

Putnam, Rufus. *Pioneer Record and Reminiscences of the Early Settlements of Fayette County, Ohio.* Cincinnati: Applegate, Pounsford, 1872.

Record of the Services of Illinois Soldiers. Springfield, Illinois: H. W. Rokker, 1882.

Sells, Grace R. *The History of Braceville Township, Trumbull County, Ohio.* N.p., 1976.

Stone, Barton Warren. *History of the Christian Church in the West.* Lexington, Kentucky: College of the Bible, 1956.

TIB. The Church of Jesus Christ of Latter-day Saints Temple Index Bureau.

Wilcox, Pearl. *Jackson County Pioneers.* Independence, Missouri: n.p., 1975.

Young, Joseph, Sr. *History of the Organization of the Seventies.* Salt Lake City: Deseret News, 1878.

Young, William. *History of Jackson County, Missouri.* 1881; Kansas City, Missouri: Union Historical, 1966.

Young, William. *Young's History of Lafayette County, Missouri.* 2 vols. Indianapolis, Indiana: B. F. Bowen, 1910.

Gazetteer

Not surprisingly, the many changes in the American landscape since the 1830s have made it difficult to locate on modern maps many of the place-names mentioned by McLellin. For example, places named by McLellin may no longer exist, or the places still exist but their names have been changed. Although most place-names have been located on historic or modern maps, or both, a few names seem to have disappeared entirely. However, careful comparisons between historical and highly detailed modern maps indicate that some locations mentioned by McLellin may have been mere crossroads or a small grouping of homes or farms. In a few instances (e.g., Weathersfield, Trumbull County, Ohio, and "Letter B," Oxford County, Maine), no town exists today, but *townships* (normally six-mile-square territorial divisions) do exist in the appropriate locale that have names mentioned by McLellin. Readers are reminded that, more often than not, LDS missionaries of this period labored in rural districts, districts that to this day have very small population densities. See, for example, modern maps of the locales east of Potsdam, New York; northwest of Rumford, Maine; or at the mouth of the Chariton River, Missouri, where the town Chariton, mentioned often by early Mormons, and shown on maps of the 1830s period, no longer exists.

In most instances the place-names given by McLellin in the journals serve as main entries for the gazetteer. Known changes (e.g., changes owing to county redistricting) are indicated (often with such modifiers as "now" or "present-day") inside parentheses immediately following the place-name in question. Place-names probably misspelled by McLellin are corrected, again inside parentheses immediately following the place-name in question. Locations of places mentioned by McLellin that do not appear on modern maps— or appear but only in subtle form (e.g., township names)—have been determined through the following means: (1) researching historical atlases and gazetteers (see the accompanying bibliography); (2) using the logic of following McLellin's movements across the map in accordance with the type of transportation he used for each phase of his journeys; and (3) consulting census data. Place-names that cannot be completely verified are indicated by using modifiers "possibly," "probably," or "very likely."

Distances given by McLellin in the journals are repeated in this gazetteer unless they appear to be significantly in error. McLellin's distances tend to be long—as would be expected of a person who mostly traveled on foot or horseback—often under poor conditions of weather, visibility (he often traveled at night), or road surface. Distances added by the editors have been estimated using maps and gazetteers that were published as near to McLellin's time as could be found. Since road routes have also changed over time, in most instances these distances are straight-line ("as the crow flies") approximations.

ILLINOIS

Apple Creek, flows southwestward from Sangamon County, cuts across the southeastern corner of Morgan County and the northwestern corner of Macoupin County, crosses Greene County, and empties into the Illinois River

Atlas, Pike County, 25 mi. northwest of Carrollton

Bluffdale, Greene County, 10 mi. west of Carrollton above the east bank of the Illinois River

Carlinville, Macoupin County, 38 mi. southwest of Springfield

Carrollton, Greene County, 28 mi. west of Carlinville

Charleston, Coles County, 27 mi. southwest of Paris

Clark County

Coghorn's Grove, very likely Cochran's Grove, Shelby County, just inside the eastern boundary, 13 mi. west of Paris

Danville, Vermilion County, 9 mi. east of the Wabash River and 62 mi. northwest of Indianapolis, Indiana

Gilead, Calhoun County, 8 mi. southwest of Carrollton

Hillsboro, Montgomery County, 24 mi. southeast of Carlinville

Illinois River, from its origin at the confluence of the Des Plaines and Kankakee Rivers southwest of Chicago, flows southwestward through Illinois; specifically, as pertains to the journals, forms the northwestern boundary of Morgan County, divides Pike and Calhoun Counties on the west from Scott and Greene Counties (and present-day Jersey County) on the east, then empties into the Mississippi River north of St. Louis, Missouri

Jacksonville, Morgan County, 31 mi. west of Springville

Macoupin River (now Macoupin Creek), from its origin in northwestern Montgomery County, flows southwestward across Macoupin County, generally along the southern boundary of Greene County (and the northern boundary of present-day Jersey County), and empties into the Illinois River

Monroe County

National Road, In Illinois and Indiana. Present-day U.S. 40 and Interstate 70 follow generally the same trace

Paris, Edgar County, 10 mi. west of the Illinois–Indiana boundary and 18 mi. northwest of Terre Haute, Indiana

Philip's Ferry, Scott County, per journal description, ferry crossing of the Illinois River west of Winchester

Randolph County

Scott County

Shlbyville (Shelbyville), Shelby County, 63 mi. southwest of Paris

Smith's Ferry (Landing), Calhoun County, ferry crossing of the Illinois River, 3 mi. southeast of Gilead

Springfield, Sangamon County, 54 mi. northwest of Shelbyville

Vandalia, Fayette County, 24 mi. southeast of Hillsboro

INDIANA

Bellville (Belleville), Hendricks County, on National Road 8 mi. northeast of Stilesville

Clinton, Vermillion County, on the west bank of the Wabash River 15 mi. north of Terre Haute

Covington, Fountain County, on the east bank of the Wabash River 12 mi. east of Danville, Illinois

Eugene, Vermillion County, on the west bank of the Wabash River just east of the Indiana–Illinois boundary, 20 mi. north of Clinton

Indianopolis (Indianapolis), Marion County

Stilesville, Hendricks County, on the National Road 17 mi. southwest of Indianapolis

Terre-Haute (Terre Haute), Vigo County

Wabash River, from its origin just east of the Illinois–Ohio boundary, flows generally westward across east central Indiana, bends southwest at Logansport, passes Lafayette, then bends south, flowing past Clinton to and just beyond Terre Haute, where it becomes the boundary between Indiana and Illinois, passes Vincennes, and flows on southward and empties into the Ohio River at the southwest corner of the state

Winchester, Randolph County, 8 mi. west of the Indiana–Ohio boundary and 69 mi. northeast of Indianapolis

KENTUCKY

Bank Lick Creek, Kenton County, flows eastward through northern Kenton County and empties into the Licking River 3 mi. south of Newport

Big Bone Lick, Boone County, 17 mi. southwest of Newport (now a state park)

Crittenden, Grant County, 21 mi. southwest of Newport

Gains Crossroads, Boone County, 13 mi. southwest of Newport

Greenupsburg (now Greenup), Greenup County, on the south bank of the Ohio River 22 mi. northwest of Huntington, West Virginia

Licking River, from its origin in southeast Kentucky, flows northwest through Pendleton County, forms the boundary between Kenton and Campbell Counties, and empties into the Ohio River across from Cincinnati, Ohio

Little Sandy River, from its origin in Elliott County in northeastern Kentucky, flows northeastward and empties into the Ohio River at Greenup

Newport, Campbell County, immediately southeast of the confluence of the Licking and Ohio Rivers, across from Cincinnati, Ohio

MAINE

Farmington, Franklin County, 21 mi. northeast of Rumford

Letter B, Oxford County, per journal description, in the vicinity east of Umbagog Lake. Modern maps show that a 6-by-8 mi. rectangular township plat immediately east of Umbagog Lake is designated Upton "B"

Newry, Oxford County, 14 mi. west of Rumford

Rumford Point, Oxford County, just west of Rumford

Umbagog Lake, on the boundary between Maine and New Hampshire northwest of Rumford

MISSOURI

Arrow Rock, Saline County, on the west bank of the Missouri River 15 mi. southwest of Fayette

Big Sny (Sni-A-Bar or Sniabar Creek, or River), flows north then east through Jackson and Lafayette Counties and empties into the Missouri River near Winchester

Charitin (Chariton), Chariton County, at the confluence of the Chariton and Missouri Rivers

Chariton River, from its origin in south central Iowa, flows south through Adair, Macon, and Chariton Counties, where it empties into the Missouri River southwest of Salisbury

Clarksville, Pike County, on the Mississippi River 10 mi. southeast of Louisiana, Missouri

Fayette, Howard County, 95 mi. east of Independence

Independence, Jackson County

Ivevtts ferry, probably Everett's Ferry, per journal description, ferry crossing of the Missouri River 3 mi. from Independence, probably north in the direction of Liberty

Jack's old ferry, per journal description, ferry crossing of the Missouri River at Lexington

Kaw Township, west of Independence, center of present-day Kansas City

Lexington, Lafayette County, on the south bank of the Missouri River, 31 mi. east of Independence

Liberty, Clay County, 12 mi. north of Independence

Lick Creek, Ralls County, 17 mi. southeast of Paris

Little Blue Creek (or River), Jackson County, flows north just east of Independence and empties into the Missouri River

Louisiana, Pike County, on the Mississippi River 72 mi. northwest of St. Louis

Missouri River, forming the northwest boundary of the state, bends eastward at Kansas City and flows through north central Missouri and empties into the Mississippi River just north of St. Louis; specifically, as pertains to the journals, forms the boundary between Clay, Ray, Carroll, Chariton, and Howard Counties on the north, and Jackson, Lafayette, and Saline Counties on the south

Mount Ephraim, per journal descriptions, in Jackson County between Little Blue and Sni-A-Bar Creeks

Mount Pleasant, ferry crossing on the Missouri River 1 mi. from Chariton, Chariton County

Paris, Monroe County, 46 mi. northeast of Fayette

Prairie Creek (Fire Prairie Creek), 10 mi. east of Independence

Randolph County

Richmond, Ray County, 25 mi. east of Liberty

St. Louis, St. Louis County

Saline County

Salt River, from its origin (as the North Fork of the Salt) in Schuyler County, flows southeastward through Adair, Knox, Shelby, and Monroe Counties, then, joined by the Middle and South Forks of the Salt, meanders eastward through Ralls County and empties into the Mississippi River just north of Louisiana, Missouri. The Salt River Branch (principally the Winkles, Allreds, and Ivies), was near present-day Florida, Monroe County, at the confluence of the North and Middle Forks of the Salt River 13 mi. east of Paris

Zion, name given by revelation (via Joseph Smith) to a vast city that was to have its center at Independence, Jackson County

NEW HAMPSHIRE

Carter Settlement, per journal description, 2 mi. from Littleton, Grafton County

Connecticut River

Dolton (Dalton), Coos County, on east bank of the Connecticut River 8 mi. northeast of Littleton

Errol, Coos County, 4 mi. west of the boundary between New Hampshire and Maine at Umbagog Lake

Lancaster, Coos County, just east of the Connecticut River, 17 mi. northeast of Littleton

Littleton, Grafton County, 14 mi. southeast of St. Johnsbury, Vermont

Lyman, Grafton County, 10 mi. southwest of Littleton

NEW YORK

Brownville, Jefferson County, 9 mi. northeast of Sackets Harbor

Buffalo, Erie County

Chautauqua Lake, Chautauqua County, at the western extremity of the state

Dunkirk, Chautauqua County, on the east shore of Lake Erie

Ellicottvill (Ellicottville), Cattaraugus County, 38 mi. southeast of Dunkirk

Fairview Corners (Fairview), Cattaraugus County, 4 mi. southeast of Freedom

Freedonia, or **Freedonia Village** (Fredonia), Chautauqua County, 3 mi. south of Dunkirk

Freedom, Cattaraugus County, 26 mi. northeast of Ellicottville

Gennessees, very likely Geneseo, Livingston County, 34 mi. northeast of Freedom

Hate, probably Haight, Allegany County, 15 mi. southeast of Freedom

Hopkinton, St. Lawrence County, 14 mi. east of Potsdam and 20 mi. southeast of the St. Lawrence River

Lake Champlain

Lake Ontario

Leona (Laona), Chautauqua County, 4 mi. south of Dunkirk

Linden, probably Lyndon Township, Cattaraugus County, 13 mi. south of Freedom

Little Valley, Cattaraugus County, 7 mi. southwest of Ellicottville

Lyons, Wayne County, on the Erie Canal 12 mi. east of Palmyra

Mayvill (Mayville), Chautauqua County, at the northwest tip of Chautauqua Lake

Mill Creek, Jefferson County, 3 mi. east of Sackets Harbor

Mount Morris, Livingston County, 28 mi. northeast of Freedom

Ogdensburg, St. Lawrence County, on the south bank of the St. Lawrence River

Oswego, Oswego County, on the southeast shore of Lake Ontario

Pillow Point (Pillar Point), Jefferson County, directly north across the bay from Sackets Harbor

Pittsford, Monroe County, 6 mi. southeast of Rochester

Port Kent, Essex County, on the west shore of Lake Champlain

Potsdam, St. Lawrence County

Sackets Harbor, Jefferson County, at the eastern extremity of Lake Ontario

St. Clairsville, possibly Sinclairville, Chautauqua County, 16 mi. southeast of Dunkirk

Shumla, Chautauqua County, 7 mi. south of Dunkirk

Slab City, or **Sodom,** probably present-day Nicholville, St. Lawerence County, 2 mi. east of Hopkinton

Stockholm, St. Lawrence County, 9 mi. northeast of Potsdam

Swift Settlement, per journal description, near Freedom

Watertown, Jefferson County, 11 mi. east of Sackets Harbor

Westfield, Chautauqua County, 17 mi. southwest of Dunkirk

Wolcott, Wayne County, 14 mi. northeast of Lyons

OHIO

Amherst, Lorain County, 7 mi. northwest of Elyria

Auburn, Geauga County, 9 mi. northwest of Hiram

Austentown (Austintown), Trumbull (now Mahoning) County, 4 mi. west of Youngstown

Berlin, probably present-day Berlin Center, Trumbull (now Mahoning) County, on the northeast shore of Berlin Lake 18 mi. southwest of Youngstown

Braceville, Trumbull County, 7 mi. west of Warren

Brownhelm, Lorain County, 10 mi. northwest of Elyria

Centerville, Montgomery County, 9 mi. south of Dayton

Chagrin (Chagrin Falls), Cuyahoga County, 13 mi. south of Kirtland

Chardon, Geauga County, 8 mi. southeast of Kirtland

Cincinnati, Hamilton County

Cleveland, Cuyahoga County

Columbus, Franklin County

Dayton, Montgomery County

Elyria, Lorain County, 22 mi. southwest of Cleveland

Fairport, or **Fair Port,** Geauga (now Lake) County, on the south shore of Lake Erie 10 mi. northeast of Kirtland

Florence, Huron (now Erie) County, 10 mi. southwest of Amherst

Fowler, Trumbull County, 10 mi. northeast of Warren

Fulton, Hamilton County, on Ohio River 2 mi. east of Cincinnati City Center, now absorbed by that city

Garrettsvill (Garrettsville), Portage County, 3 mi. southeast of Hiram

Goshen, Clermont County, 20 mi. northeast of Cincinnati

Heatin's Mill, probably absorbed by Niles, Trumbull County, between Warren and Youngstown

Hiram, or **Hiram Township,** Portage County, 24 mi. southeast of Kirtland

Howland, Trumbull County, absorbed by present-day Warren

Hubbard Town (Hubbard), Trumbull County, 16 mi. southeast of Warren

Huntsburg, Geauga County, 17 mi. southeast of Kirtland

Kirtland, Geauga (now Lake) County

Lake Erie

Lorane Co W. Reserve (Lorain County), west of Cleveland

Middleberry village, or **Middlebury,** very likely Middlebury, Portage County, since absorbed by Akron

Nelson, Portage County, 5 mi. east of Hiram

Newbury (probably now Mulberry), Clermont County, 17 mi. northeast of Cincinnati

Ohio River

Orange, Cuyahoga County, 14 mi. southwest of Kirtland

Painesville, Geauga (now Lake) County; 8 mi. northeast of Kirtland

Parkman, Geauga County, 6 mi. northeast of Hiram

Richmond, Geauga (now Lake) County, just west of Fairport

Rockport, Cuyahoga County, on Rocky River 7 mi. west of Cleveland

Springfield, Portage (now Summit) County, near Akron; possibly North Springfield, 9 mi. southeast of Akron, or Springfield Township, southeast of Akron

Vermilion, Erie County, on the south shore of Lake Erie 14 mi. northwest of Elyria

Warren, Trumbull County, 39 mi. southeast of Kirtland

Watervliet, Montgomery County, 5 mi. southeast of Dayton City Center, now absorbed by that city

Weathersfield, probably absorbed by Niles, Trumbull County. Niles is in the center of Weathersfield Township.

Wellsville, Columbiana County, on the north bank of the Ohio River 37 mi. northwest of Pittsburg, Pennsylvania

Western Reserve, O. Once claimed by Connecticut, the Western Reserve was a tract south of Lake Erie and north of the 41st Parallel that extended from the Ohio–Pennsylvania boundary west to the western boundaries of present-day Erie and Huron Counties

Windham, Portage County, 5 mi. south of Nelson

Youngstown, Trumbull (now Mahoning) County

ONTARIO, CANADA

Kingston, at the origin of the St. Lawrence River on Lake Ontario

Loborough (Loughborough), very likely 9 mi. north of Kingston near Loughborough Lake

Presscot (Prescott), on north bank of the St. Lawrence River across from Ogdensburg, New York

Waterloo, per journal description, 3 mi. from Kingston (not to be confused with Waterloo, Ontario, northwest of Toronto)

PENNSYLVANIA

New Bedford, Lawrence County, just across the Pennsylvania–Ohio boundary 7 mi. east of Youngstown

Pittsburgh, Allegheny County

VERMONT

Burlington, Chittenden County, on the east shore of Lake Champlain

Connecticut River

Danville, Caledonia County, possibly West Danville, 7 mi. west of St. Johnsbury

McAdoes Falls, very likely McIndoe Falls, Caledonia County, on the west bank of the Connecticut River 12 mi. south of St. Johnsbury

Montpelier, Washington County

St. Johnsbury, Caledonia County

Watterford Lower Village (Lower Waterford), Caledonia County, on the west bank of the Connecticut River 7 mi. southeast of St. Johnsbury

Gazetteer Bibliography

AAA. *Northwest Ohio.* Falls Church, Virginia, 1982 ed.

The American Heritage Pictorial Atlas of United States History. Ed. Hilde Hennkagan and others. New York: American Heritage Publishing, 1966.

Bartholomew, John. "Patterns on the Land" and "S. C. Atkinson Map, 1837." In *Historical Maps of Kentucky.* Ed. Thomas D. Clark. Lexington: University Press of Kentucky, 1979.

French, J. H. *Gazetteer of the State of New York . . . .* Syracuse, N.Y.: R. P. Smith, 1860.

Gordon, Thomas F. *Gazetteer of the State of New York . . . .* Philadelphia, pub. by author, 1836.

Mitchell, S. Augustus. *A Tourist's Pocket Map of Ohio.* Columbus: Ohio Historical Society, 1835.

Paullin, Charles O. "Chapin Map, 1839." In *Atlas of the Historical Geography of the United States.* Ed. John K. Wright. Baltimore: Carnegie Institution of Washington and the American Geographical Society of New York, 1932.

Rand McNally 1991. *Commercial Atlas and Marketing Guide.* 122d ed. Chicago: Rand McNally, 1991.

Rand McNally Road Atlas: United States. Canada. Mexico. Chicago: Rand McNally, 1992.

Smith, Thomas H. *The Mapping of Ohio.* Kent, Ohio: Kent State University Press, 1977.

Tanner, H. S. *A New Map of Illinois.* Philadelphia, 1833.

Tanner, H. S. *A New Map of Ohio.* Philadelphia, 1833.

Writer's Program, WPA in Ohio. *The Ohio Guide.* New York: Oxford University Press, 1940.

health. They gave one a hat worth $6.00 and a pair of new shoes worth $2.00 and I had repairs to my ~~boots saddle~~ of $2.25 and a number of small gifts and presents and when I bid sister Nancy Clark fare well she put $2 into my hand. ☞

My horse did not get over his founder and I sold him to H. Bailey for $55.00 due the first of next May. I left the note with bro. Lewis Zabreskie and ~~I borrowed~~ of him $15 and sent it to Emiline by C. Hubbard I swapped the horse that brother Joseph left with me to bro. E. Smith and got one to ride to the East ——

Thursday 11th I started to the Danville Church I staid with bro. Jacob Morris all night. He gave me $2. to carry to the Editors of the star. On Friday eve bro. Lewis and I reached bro. Sam Swinford, the Elder who has the care of the Danville Church. The brethren seemed rejoiced to see us and three app'ts were quickly circulated for Saturday eve 4 P.M. for Sunday 11 A.M. and 4 P.M. ——

Saturday 13. only a few collected but they paid very good attention while I addressed them about 1 hour and a½ on the confusion of the world and of the faith once delivered to the saints from 2 Peter 1.4. Sunday 14. A few collected again at bro. J. Chandler's and bro. Lewis opened the met. and spoke a few minutes, I then spoke about 1½ hour on the Testimonies of the book of Mormon on Covenants and Laws of the church &c —— And at 4 P.M. I spoke again about 2 hours on the two places of deliverance and the two gatherings at Zion and Jerusalem as the preparatory work for the coming of the saviour &c &c There seemed to be great interest felt in the subject and particularly among the few brethren and sisters.

Page 10, Journal IV (actual size). The contrasting entries on this page, with equal flourish, range from mundane concerns about shoes, promissory notes, and horses, to sermons on perfection, Zion, and the coming of the Savior.

Scripture Index

Page numbers in *italics* refer to scriptures found in the McLellin Journals. Page numbers in roman type refer to citations in editorial notes and essays.

Bible	14-16, 21, 25, 78, *83, 106, 116,* 127, *136, 145,* 227	49	21, 26, *108,* 126, 404
		54:17	126
Old Testament	*110*	Jeremiah	
		31:31	180, 404
		31:31-33	204
Genesis 17:1	25, *181, 190,* 204, 208, 404	Ezekiel	
		6	404
		6-9	21, 26, *109,* 126
Exodus 18:1	127	Daniel 2:45	243
1 Kings 8:22	201	Zechariah	
		14	*116,* 128
Psalms	22	14:4	127
37:37	19, 25, *192, 195,* 209, *215,* 404	New Testament	20, *83, 110*
102	21, 26, *113*	Matthew	
102:1	404	3:3	243
102:12-28	126	6:10	243, 244
102:16-22	126	6:13	244
		6:31-34	124
Song of Solomon	*112,* 126	6:9	244
		6:9-13	243
Isaiah	169	9:6-7	227
2:3	*83*	10:14	54, 279
6:10	124	10:9-10	123
8:20	25, *180,* 204, 404	13:15	124
		22:2	243
11	25, *135, 184,* 404	24:3	25, *192,* 209, 404
11:1-13	158	Mark	
31:31	26	1:14	404
40:3	243	1:14-15	25, *214*

Mark, cont.
1:15	404
2:11-12	227
1:15	7, *193*, 209
4:12	124
13:21	404
13:21-22	25, *178*, *193*, 203
16:17	54
16:17-18	54

Luke
6:20	404
6:20-26	25, *139-40*, 159
9:5	54, 279
10:4	123
22:35	123

John
	383
3	25, *188*, 404
3:3-5	207
4	59, *61*
4:14	59
4:22	59
4:24	59
5:29	205
5:30	*181*, 204, 404
5:30, 39	25
5:39	*218*, 227, 404
10	26, *183*, 404
10:16	205
12:40	124
14	*179*, 404
14:1-3	203
14:2	26, *152*, 165, 404
14:26	25, 200, *214*, 404

Acts
	13-18, 24
1:11	15
2:4	16
2:16	25
2:17	25
2:19	25
2:25	25
2:38	25
2:39	25
2:42	16
2:47	25

3:1-11	16
3:14-15	25
3:21	128
4	25
4:32	17
5	17
5:12	25
5:16	16
5:41	18
6-7	25
8	25
8:17	25
9:34, 36-43	25
10:34	25
10:44-46	16
12	25
13:51	54, 279
14:1-7	17
15:5	18
16-20	17
16:16-18	25
19:11-12	25
20	25, *137*, 403
20:23-24	158
28:27	124

Romans
6:4	168
8	26, *134*, 157, 404
8:2	157
8:14	25, 157, *219*, 404
8:28	157
8:31	157
8:35-39	157
10	*64*
10:4	74
10:10	74
10:13	74

1 Corinthians
2	26, *147*, 403
2:2	161
2:13	25, 161, *177*, *184*
12	19, 25, 26, 54, *65*, *134*, *146*, 403
12:1-11	75
12:10	52

1 Corinthians, cont.
12:13   161
13   403
13:2   403
16:20   205

2 Corinthians
12:1-2   *84*
13:12   205

Galatians   *107*
1   20, *34*, 404
1:6   404
1:6-10   26, 53, *148*, 162
1:8   25, *191*, 209,
              404
1:12   53
5:19   404
5:19-21   125

Ephesians 1   26, *152*, 165,
              404

Philippians 3:15   25, *218*, 227

Colossians 3:9   168

1 Thessalonians
1:5   25, *174*, *195*,
              199, *218*,
              404
5:26   205

1 Timothy 5:23   *82*, 302

2 Timothy   202
3:16   *216*, 404
4   26, *177*, 404
4:2   25, *218*, 404

Philemon 3   404

Hebrews
6:1-2   161
11   26, *175*, 200,
              404
12:14   25, *193*, 209,
              404

James 5:14   227

2 Peter   383
1   7, 19, 21, *133*,
              140, 404
1:1   *177*, *180*, *191*,
              202, 404
1:1-4   156
1:1-7   25
1:4   202
1:5   404
1:5-7   *133*, 156

Bible—Joseph
Smith Translation 55, 78, 126

Revelations
4:1   *84*
19:9   243

Book of Mormon   3, 6-7, 8, 11,
              19-23, 25-26,
              29, *33*, *36*, *37*,
              39, *42*, *43*, *44*,
              49, 54, *61*, *62*,
              64, *65*, *71*, *72*,
              78, *79*, *80*, *81*,
              83, *94*, *103*,
              104, *106*, *107*,
              108, *109*, *110*,
              111, *112*, *115*,
              118, 124, *136*,
              137, *139*, *140*,
              145, *146*, 165,
              167, 168, *178*,
              179, *181*, *184*,
              192, *194*, *215*,
              217, *218*, *219*,
              222, *223*, 227

1 Nephi
21:1-26   126
22:26   74

2 Nephi
10:9-10   126
16:10   124
31:17-19   253

Jacob   125
1:19   128, 228
2:2   128

Enos 1:2–3, 10	125
Mosiah 5:15	155
Alma	
9–16	21, 26, 125–126
32	200
45:21–22	206
3 Nephi	22, 26
5:23	203
11–18	21, 201
11–28	126
13:31–34	124
15:16–16:3	205
18:28–29	160
20:29–33	55
21:23	48
22:17	126
Ether	
12	200
13:6	55
12:22–40	125
Book of Com-	
mandments	57, 58
24	165
24:29–42	*142,* 160
65:10–15	*143,* 160
Articles and Cove-	
nants (D&C 20)	*96, 110, 119,*
	137, 141, 160,
	180, 185, 194,
	272, 274, 281
v. 49	165
Doctrine and	
Covenants	24, 226
4:3	281
14:3	281
18	198
18:37	165
20	264
20:37–60	160
20:60	281
20:64	158
20:70	165
20:84	159

20:75	53
22	235–39, 264
22:2	238
22:3	237
24:15	54, 279
24:18	123
27:2	277
28:9	48
29:7–8	198
29:11	74
29:14	209
39:23	209
42	264
42:43–44	158
43:4	312, 374
45	239–41
45:6–59	209
45:11	241
45:26–47	49
45:43–44, 66–71	48
45:48	128
45:58	74
45:60	240
45:64	241
45:64–69	55
45:72–75	240
46	20, 75
49	159
49:9	252
52	48, 49
52:30	360
52:3	50
52:10	48
55	49
56:8–9	76
57	271
58:58–59	50
58:63	53
58:64	209
60:1–17	50
60:14	53
60:14–15	54
62:5	53
64:8–13	160
65	126, 241–46
65:1	244, 253
65:2	244
65:3	244
65:4	243
65:6	244

Doctrine and Covenants, cont.

66	234, 246–51, 267, 299, 361
66:2	249
66:3	249
66:5–8	250
66:7–8, 10	300
66:9	250
66:9, 10, 12	250
66:10	251
66:12	251
67	57, 299
67:4–9	237
67:5	253, 299
67:6–8	57
68	161, 283, 300
68:1	155
68:4	155
68:7	252
68:8	58
68:12	155
69:6	123
72	76
72:25–26	159
73:1–2	76
73:4	76
75	77, 268
75:1–5	77
75:6, 13	301
75:6–12	77
75:7–9	301
75:14	78
75:19–20	77
76	20, 22, 26, 205
76:51–59	202
76:52	202–3
76:55–58	203
84:6	127
84:77–81	123
84:78	123
84:84	124
88:87–93	209
88:132	201
88:132–33	201
89	205
89:9	129
101:17	154
101:43	154
101:55	155
101:55–57	154
101:70–74	201
103	154, 310
103:22	155
103:30	155
105	155
105:9	311
105:16	155
106	203
107	161, 167, 316
107:33	206
113:1–6	158
115	160
118	369
137	320
Moses 7	126
Joseph Smith— Matthew	209
Articles of Faith 4	161

Tues. 3 I walked 17 miles to ¹⁵ a bro. McGee's in Newbury. They received me also joyfully and spent Wednesday also with them studying my ✡️ Bible, an app. was circulated and I addressed a small congregation at Br. Elston's from these words. "Let us as many as be perfect be thus minded" Phil. 3. 15: I had great liberty and all parties supposed it was a "great sermon."

Friday 6. I preached in the eve at bro. Cha. McGee's. I contrasted the churches of Moses, Peter and Joseph I spoke about one hour.

Sunday 8. I had an app. at Eleven oclock, but the Methodist purposely made one at the same hour in the same village. I had notwithstanding a good turnout. I spoke in the forenoon from

Page 15, Journal VI (actual size). These brief lines reflect McLellin's interests in studying Hebrew, in comparing the churches led by Moses, Peter, and Joseph Smith, and in preaching despite opposition from other groups.

Subject Index

A

Abominations of flesh, 107

Abraham, covenants of, 144

Acts, book of
and McLellin journals compared, 13–18
spiritual outpourings in, 16

Adams, Bonham's belief in multiple, 38, 97

Adultery, McLellin tempted to engage in, 46, 250-51, 254

Ague, McLellin suffers from, 40, 132

Akers, S., travels with McLellin, 196, 415

Aldrich, Hazen, 344

Aldrich, Isaac, 194, 415

Allen, A., 149, 415

Allred?, Daniel, 99, 100, 416
counseled to preach in Illinois and Indiana, 97

Allred?, Hannah, 100, 416

Allred, Isaac, 96, 274, 416

Allred, James, 97, 416

Allred family, 124

Amherst, Ohio, 130, 482

Amherst Branch, divisions in, 140

Ammonihah, 107, 125-26

Ancient Christianity, 13-18, 66
restoration of, 63

Ancient church, 20, 63, 407. *See also* Christianity; Church of Christ; Church of God
faith of, 133
persecution of, 17, 81

Ancient faith, McLellin on, 43

Anderson, Celia, 147, 416

Anderson, John, 142, 147, 416

Andrews or Andress or Andrus, Milow, 142, 143, 144, 381, 417

Angel Moroni, 29, 79, 80
and David Whitmer, 264

Angels
God speaks through, 93
McLellin seeks, 92, 101

Animals, caravan of, 184, 187

Anointing, for healing, 217

Anti-Mormon pamphlets, 117-18, 286

Apostles, ancient, McLellin on, 137

Apple Creek, Illinois, 28, 88, 476

Arrow Rock, Missouri, 28, 130, 479

Arterberry, Mr., 95, 417

Articles and Covenants, 110, 119, 132, 141, 406. *See also* the scripture index
beauty of, 96
on duties of officers, 137
McLellin on, 141, 180, 185, 194, 218

Athington, Fanny, 414, 417
baptized and confirmed by McLellin, 194

Athington, Perces, 414, 417
baptized and confirmed by McLellin, 194

Atlas, Illinois, 28, 476

Attendance, at missionary meetings, 381-82

Auburn, Ohio, 60, 482

Audience, at preaching appointments
members, types of, 395-97
religion of, 397-99
responses of, 391-94
size, 381-82

Austentown (Austintown), Ohio, 60, 482

Authority
given to Church, 142
McLellin on, 193

Avery, Mr., 63, 417

B

Babbit, Alman [Almon], 140, 141, 143, 417
  donation of, to McLellin, 145
Babbit, Almira, 418
  donation of, to McLellin, 145
Babbit, Lorin Whiting, 141, 418
Babcock, Caroline L., 418
  baptized and confirmed, 176
Bailey, Henry, Sr., 280, 413, 418
  baptized, 138
  buys McLellin's horse, 138
  confirmed, 138
Baily, Louisa, 413, 418
  baptized, 132-33
Baird, Samuel, 418
  McLellin receives letter from, 121
Baker, Edward D., 418
  dry preaching of, 106
Baldwin, Wheeler, 49
Bank Lick Creek, Kentucky, 478
Baptism, 66, 83, 95, 406. *See also* Rebaptism
  of believers prevented, 121
  christening as, 208
  early Mormon, 280-81
  of former members, 135, 279, 281
  group, 280
  invitation to, 62
  need for, 235-36
  of new converts, 63, 70, 100, 115, 117, 119-20, 129, 132-33, 135, 136, 137, 138, 193, 279
  people unwilling to accept, 192
Baptisms, register of, 413-14
Baptist minister, 274-75
Baptists, 72, 98, 103, 108, 115, 120, 219, 224, 227
Barker, Elizabeth, 419
  subscribes to *Messenger and Advocate,* 226
Barker, R., 414, 419
  baptized, 152
Barkshire, Garret W., 224, 419
  subscribes to *Messenger and Advocate,* 226
Barney, Sis., 143

Barney, Edson, 141, 419
  donation of, to McLellin, 146
Barney, Royal, 141, 419
  donation of, to McLellin, 146
Barnum, Mr., 62, 74, 419
Barnum, Irene, 74, 419
  baptism of, 62
Barrows, Amelia, 414, 420
  baptized by McLellin, 191
Barrows, Ethan, 414, 420
  baptized by McLellin, 191
Bean, Daniel, 420
  blesses children, 195
  travels with McLellin, 195-96
Beauty of regulations, 96
Beebe, Calvin, 98, 420
Bellew, Mr., 118, 120, 420
Bellville (Belleville), Indiana, 28, 477
Bennett, Mr., 69, 268, 420
Bennett, John C., 329, 332, 339, 371
Bennett, William T., 31, 420
Bennion, Samuel O., and McLellin journals, 258
Berlin, Ohio, 60, 482
Bible, 16, 21, 25, 383. *See also* the scripture index
  compared to Book of Mormon, 136, 145
  and early Mormonism, 14
  errors of, 377, 406
  evidences of, 106
  McLellin's testimony of, 83
  McLellin's use of, 16
  plainness of gospel in, 108
Bible, Hebrew, McLellin studies, 217
Bickerton, William, 337
Big Bone Lick, Kentucky, 212, 228, 478
Big Sny (Sni-A-Bar or Sniabar Creek or River), Missouri, 479
Billings, Titus, 68, 70, 76, 89, 421
Birch, Mrs., 421
  buys Book of Mormon, 94
Birch, James H., 421
  subscribes to *Evening and Morning Star,* 94
Bishop, responsibilities of, 51-52
Blair, A., 149, 421

Blakeslee, James, 183, 330, 333, 335-36, 371, 421
Bledsoe, Mr., 105, 421
Blessing, 280, 282. *See also* Healing
    of children, 152, 195
    of congregation, 138
    of mentally disturbed, 283
    mode of, in early Church, 283
    of one possessed, 283
    of the sick, 282-83
Blood, of Adam and Christ, 377
Bluffdale, Illinois, 88, 104-17, 476
Boggs, Lilburn W., 325, 364
Boice, Bro., 187, 421
Boice, Margaret, 187, 422
Bondurant, Capt., 98, 422
Bonham, Mr., 422
    belief in multiple Adams, 38, 97
    opinion of Book of Mormon, 98
Book of Commandments, 299-300. *See also* the scripture index
    compilation of, 57
    covenants in, 142
    McLellin's copies of, 257
Book of Mormon, 20-21, 85, 111, 118, 148, 176, 201, 264, 406. *See also* the scripture index
    attacks against, 286
    attempts to disprove, 94, 109, 115
    coming forth of, 4, 39, 43, 177
    compared to Bible, 106, 136, 145, 227
    copies sold, 36
    evidences of, 65, 80, 105, 106, 108, 136, 140, 178, 179, 180, 181, 194, 215, 266, 377, 382, 406
    as glory of Church, 216
    history of, 64
    importance of, in early Mormonism, 6-7
    improper grammar of, 103
    McLellin buys his first, 31
    McLellin explains, 223
    McLellin first hears of, 29
    McLellin gains testimony of, 33-34
    McLellin gives to brother, 81
    McLellin on, 184, 218, 222
    McLellin preaches without, 112
    McLellin sells, 219

McLellin sells his, 32
McLellin's emphasis on, 22
McLellin's testimony of, 80, 83, 107, 291-92, 296-97
members' faith in, 137
origins of, 79
Parley P. Pratt reads, to congregation, 103, 110
as preaching topic, 201, 275, 394
prophecies of, 105, 106
prophecy and reasonable circumstances of, 146
prophecy and scripture concerning, 39
reconciled with Bible, 145
as a sign of the times, 49
supported by Bible, 227
testified of, 29, 37, 39, 42, 47, 49, 54, 61, 105, 107, 139, 217, 264, 265
as true record, 192, 217
utility of, 62
vision of truth of, 71
witnesses of, 80, 264-67
Boosinger, George, 73, 422
Booth, Ezra, 50, 51
Bosley, J., 422
    buys a vest for McLellin, 182
Bosley, William Bull, 171, 422
Bouce, Bro., 177, 422
Boynton, John F., 22, 153, 165, 167, 181, 185, 269, 276, 284, 315, 323, 366, 381, 422
    baptizes, 147
    called on mission with McLellin, 147-48
    refuses to preach, 148
    on simplicity of the gospel, 184
Braceville, Ohio, 28, 60, 212, 482
Bradley, S., 93, 423
Branches, outlying, strengthening of, 272-73
Brewsterites, 344-45
Briggs, Mr., 193, 423
Brockman, S., 32, 423
Brown, Mr. and Mrs., 423
    give McLellin money, 174
Brown, Sis., 423
    believes McLellin's message, 177

Brown, Benjamin, 414, 423
  baptism of, 175, 200
  donation of, to McLellin, 177
Brown, Rebecca, 414, 423
  baptized, 175
Brownhelm, Ohio, 482
Brownville, New York, 170, 481
Buffalo, New York, 481
Bull, Bro., 217, 423
Bump, Jacob, 339-41
Burasus, Mr., 113, 114, 423
Burdick, Thomas, 313-14
Burdock, Bro., 423
  as teacher in Kirtland high school,
    152
Burlington, Vermont, 170, 484
Burnett, Edmund, Jr., 72, 424
Burnett, Silas, 72, 424
Burrase. *See* Burasus
Burwell, Celia, 214, 268, 413, 424
  baptized, 67
Burwell, Samuel, 67, 214, 413, 424
  baptized, 66
  donation of, to McLellin, 215
Bushman, Richard, and publication of
    McLellin journals, xiii
Butterfield, Betsy, baptized, 180, 424
Byfield, Eliza, 141, 424
  donation of, to McLellin, 146

C

Cady, Elizabeth, 413, 424
  baptized, 135
  confirmed, 136
Caffa, Betsy, 414, 424
  baptized and confirmed by McLellin,
    193
Caffa, Hiram, 414, 424
  baptized and confirmed by McLellin,
    193
Cahoon, Reynolds, 14, 24, 50, 59, 67, 75,
    267, 296, 424
Call, Anson, 327-28
Calvin, J., 115, 120, 127, 425
Campbell, Mr., 66, 425
Campbell, A., 425
  gives money to McLellin, 215

Campbell, Alexander, 117, 124, 128,
    160, 228, 286
  McLellin reads debate of, 224
Campbell, D., 425
  gives money to McLellin, 215
  persuades McLellin to stay in
    Wellsville, Ohio, 214-15
Campbell, I. C., 112, 425
Campbell, Mandana, 414, 425
  baptized, 117
Campbell, Susannah, 414, 425
  baptized by McLellin, 117
  commits to be baptized, 115
Campbell, Thomas, debates Sidney
    Rigdon, 167
Campbellites, 152, 160, 167-68, 224
  in audience, 397-401
  contend with missionaries, 65-66
  criticize Mormonism, 124
  encounters with, 47, 59, 61, 64, 69,
    70, 72, 74, 105-6
  meetinghouse of, 223
  oppose McLellin, 225
  priest of, 215, 224, 268
Carlinville, Illinois, 88, 476
Carrollton, Illinois, 88, 476
Carter, Bro., 195, 425
Carter, Gideon H., 381, 426
  donation of, to McLellin, 147
  refuses request from McLellin, 146
Carter, Simeon, 32, 36, 50, 76, 265, 281,
    297, 381, 426
  leaves Independence for mission to
    East, 36
  tells McLellin to become an elder, 34-
    35
Carter, Talitha Cumi, 414, 426
  baptized and confirmed by McLellin,
    193
Carter, William, 49
Carter Settlement, New Hampshire, 480
Centerville, Ohio, 482
Cessions, Bro., 195, 426
Chagrin (Chagrin Falls), Ohio, 130, 482
Chandler, J., 139, 426
Chapman, Bro., 180-81, 414, 426
Chapman, Jacob, 426
  donation of, to McLellin, 146

Chardon, Ohio, 212, 482

Charitin (Chariton), Missouri, 28, 88, 130, 479

Chariton River, Missouri, 28, 88, 130, 479

Charity, 136

   effects of, on society, 142

Charleston, Illinois, 28, 88, 476

Chautauqua Lake, New York, 170, 481

Cherry, Mr., 74

Children

   blessed, 152

   loss of, 41-42

Childs, Elder, 183, 186, 427

Christ. *See* Jesus Christ

Christianity, 383, 406. *See also* Ancient Church; Church of Christ; Church of God

   ancient, 13-18

   establishment of, 217

   origins of, 66

   true, 64

   and unity, 16-17

Christians

   becoming true, 64

   persecution of, 17

Chronology, of Old Testament, 197

Church, Mr., 182, 427

Church of Christ

   establishment and nature of, 218

   McLellin on, 190

Church officers, duties of, 137

Church of God

   differences from the world, 64

   distinguishing qualities of, 69

Church of Jesus Christ of Latter-day Saints, The

   authority of, 142

   early identity of, 5-6, 8-9

   early practices of, 277-83

   and family prayer, 278

   history of, McLellin on, 216, 263-83

   in last days, 63, 66

   McLellin investigates, 29-34

   meetings of, 278-80

      confirmation, 63, 66, 120, 135-36, 158, 175-76

      prayer, 268, 278

      sacrament, 34, 99, 117, 120, 121, 278, 279

      testimony, 279

   members of

      dedication to Church of, 34

      determination of, to keep commandments, 137

      disagreements between, 143

      division among, 273

      love and peace of, 33

      solemnity of prayers of, 35

      Spirit of God with, 34

      unity of, 137

   name of, 11, 160

   rebaptism in, 280-81

   regulation of, 187

   rise and establishment of, 132, 136, 141, 406, 407

   rise and progress of, 66

   rise of, 63, 184, 223, 406, 408

   unifying branches of, 272-73

   worship practices of, 277-83

Cincinnati, Ohio, 212, 482

Circuit rider, 223

Clark, Jane, 427

   gives McLellin money, 133, 138

Clark, Josiah, 427

   subscribes to *Messenger and Advocate,* 226

Clark, Mary Ann, 414, 427

   baptized, 117

Clark, Samuel, 427

   subscribes to *Messenger and Advocate,* 226

Clarksville, Missouri, 88, 130, 479

Clendenon, Mr., 116, 427

Cleveland, Mr., 144, 427

Cleveland, Ohio, 60, 130, 482

Clinton, Indiana, 130, 477

Coe, Joseph, 50, 68-69, 381, 427

Coghorn's Grove, Illinois, 476

Colburn, Thomas, 428

   hosts conference of Twelve, 182

Coltrin, Zebedee, 44, 55, 428

Columbus, Ohio, 130, 482

Colvin, David, 414, 428

   baptized and confirmed by McLellin, 186

Comfort, of gospel to Saints, 216
Commandments, members'
    determination to keep, 137
Communion, nature of, 122
Cone, Charlotte, 414, 428
    baptized by McLellin, 194
    confirmed by McLellin, 195
Conference, 81
    of Church, 187-88
    of Twelve, 190
Confirmation, 63, 66, 83, 100, 120, 129,
    133, 138, 181, 193, 195, 279-81
    of McLellin, 34
Confirmation meeting, 63, 66, 135-36,
    158, 175-76
Confusion of the world, 139, 141, 142
Connecticut River, New Hampshire, 170,
    480
Contention, among the Twelve, 276-77
Coon, Mr., 112, 428
Coon, I., 112, 428
Cooper, John, 413, 428
    baptized, 132-33
    ordained a teacher, 138
Corrill, John, 33, 34, 52, 226, 269, 271,
    308, 310, 321, 365, 381, 428
    preaches with McLellin, 213
Cory, Hiram, 429
    ordained a teacher, 153
Council
    of elders, 68, 90
    meeting, 147-48
Covenant lands, 121
Covenants, 62, 65, 71
    of Abraham and Joseph, 144
    of God, 181
    McLellin speaks on, 133
Covenants and Articles. *See* Articles and
    Covenants
Covenants and laws, 119
    of the Church, 139
Covington, Indiana, 130, 477
Cowan, Thomas, 70, 429
Cowdery, Erastus, 72, 429
Cowdery, Lyman, 328
Cowdery, Oliver, 32, 46, 50, 56, 58, 165,
    207, 226, 299, 308, 313-14, 319,
    329, 341, 343-44, 366, 429

appointed trustee of Kirtland high
    school, 149
    shown gold plates, 49
Cowdery, Warren, 203, 429
    hosts conference of Twelve, 178
Cowens, Bro., 73
Cowin, Mrs., 59, 430
Cowles, Austin, 330, 336, 338, 344, 371
Cranney, Emiline, 430
    donation of, to McLellin, 145
Cranney, Philander, 430
    donation of, to McLellin, 145
Crawford, Mr., 223, 430
Crigler, Mr., 93, 430
Crittenden, Kentucky, 212, 478
Crops, in Independence, Missouri, 83
Crosby, William, 430
    subscribes to *Messenger and
    Advocate,* 226
Culbertson, A., 227, 430
    anointed for healing, 217
Culbertson, Betsy, 217, 430
Culbertson, Robert, 227, 381, 430
    heals sick man, 219
    preaches with McLellin, 216-17, 219,
    222
Cumorah, 79
Curse, by McLellin and Brigham Young
    on unbelievers, 189
Curtis, Charles, 413, 430
    baptized, 135
    confirmed, 136
    receives recommend to go to Zion,
    138
Curtis, Philip, 413, 430
    confirmed, 138
    rebaptized, 137
Curtis, Sally, 413, 431
    confirmed, 138
    rebaptized, 137
    receives recommend to go to Zion,
    138

D

Dailey, Moses. *See* Daley, Moses
Daily, John. *See* Daley, John
Daley, John, 142, 144, 431
    donation of, to McLellin, 147

Daley, Moses, 143-45, 273, 431
   donation of, to McLellin, 146-47
Daniel, Mr., 188, 381, 431
Daniel, book of, 253
Danville, Illinois, 130, 476
Danville, Vermont, 170, 484
Daton, Mr., 104-5, 431
Davis, Mr., 38, 431
Davis, Mrs., 431
   asks to be healed, 192
Dayton, Ohio, 130, 482
Dedication, of McLellin's family to God,
   213
Deism, 62, 63, 71, 72, 106, 116
Deliverance
   two places of, 133, 144
   of Zion, 131, 155
Demoss, Mr., 32, 36, 431
Dewitt, Mr., 39, 431
Discernment, power of
   gift of, 52
   by Newel Knight, 34, 269
   of spirits, 33, 84
Dispensations, compared, 213, 218
Division, among members of Church,
   273
Dixon, Bro., 181, 431
Doctrine and Covenants. *See also* the
   scripture index
   manuscripts of
      section 22, 235-39
      section 45, 239-41
      section 65, 241-46
      section 66, 246-51
   section 65, relation to Lord's Prayer,
      243-44
   section 66, 45-46
      answers McLellin's questions,
         249-50
      recording of, 234
Dodds, A., 96-97, 432
Dodson, Rev. Elizah, 105-10, 113-14,
   127, 275, 432
   confounded, 109
   congregation of, converted to
      Mormonism, 276
   lists mistakes in McLellin's sermon,
      106-7

   overcome by Spirit, 107
   preached against Mormonism, 106-7,
      109, 120-21
   sorrowed by missionaries' success,
      110
Dodson, Mrs. Rev. Elizah, 108, 432
Dolson, Mr., 31, 40, 432
Dolton (Dalton), New Hampshire, 170,
   480
Donations
   community refuses to give, 183
   McLellin and Lyman Johnson receive,
      181
   McLellin and Orson Hyde receive,
      178
   McLellin given boots, 190
   McLellin given shirts, 191
   of members to McLellin, 138, 145-46
   poor quality of, 194
   received by McLellin and Young, 189
   refused, 189-90
   sparseness of, 193
   the Twelve share, 179
Dream, prophetic, by McLellin, 31
Dress, superfluous, 179
Drue, Mr., 178, 432
Dudley, Bro., 413, 432
   baptized, 152
Dunkirk, New York, 170, 481
Dunklin, Daniel, 308, 310
Dusting of feet, 61, 72, 174, 279-80
   against Campbellites, 47
   against Christian preacher, 39
   against M. Hawley, 189-90
   by Patten and McLellin, 183
   scriptures concerning, 54
Dutcher, Elder, 183, 432
Dyas, Robert, 432
   subscribes to *Messenger and
      Advocate,* 226
Dysentery, McLellin suffers from, 134

E

Early Mormonism, characteristics of,
   263-89
Early Mormons, persecution against, 81
Easter, Mr., 36
Eatin, Daniel, 63-64, 71, 433

Eaton, Mr., 180, 433
Eaton, E., 181, 433
Edwards, Mrs., 433
    healed by McLellin and Luke Johnson,
        71
    vision of truth of Book of Mormon, 71
Edwards, John, 64, 66-67, 69, 71, 74,
    433
Elders, 80, 83
    called to expose creeds, 152
    conference of, 82
    council of, 68, 90
    duties of, 406
    meeting of, 35-36, 45, 47
Ellicottvill (Ellicottville), New York, 170,
    481
Elliott, David, 178, 433
Elston, Isaac, 217, 433
    subscribes to *Messenger and
        Advocate,* 225
Elyria, Ohio, 60, 130, 483
Emmett, Silas, 222, 224, 433
    subscribes to *Messenger and
        Advocate,* 225
Endowment, 319-21, 347
Enoch
    God of, 241
    prophecy of, 113, 275
Ensign, 295, 331
*Ensign of Liberty, of the Church of
    Christ,* 258, 295, 341, 344-45, 374
Errol, New Hampshire, 170, 480
Esters, Mr., 91, 433
Eugene, Indiana, 130, 477
Evans, Mr., 122, 433
Evening and Morning Star, 99, 103,
    109, 118, 138, 264
    goals of, 86
    McLellin sends copy to relatives, 84
    McLellin solicits subscriptions for, 84
    topics in, 406-7
Evening prayers, 192
Everhart, Mr., 71, 433
Everhart, Elizabeth, 413, 433
    baptized, 66
    healed by Luke Johnson, 71
Evil power, influence of, 135

Evil spirits
    affliction by, 111
    casting out of, 111
Ewing, George, 142, 433
Excommunication
    of disobedient members, 68
    of McLellin in 1832, 78, 85, 305
    of McLellin in 1838, 323-24
Excuses, of congregation, 98
Extravagance, Mormon dislike of, 285

F

Fairport, Ohio, 170, 483
Fairview Corners (Fairview), New York,
    481
Faith, 72, 407
    of ancient church, 133
    of ancient saints, 144
    effects on society of, 142
    Lyman Johnson preaches on, 180-81
    McLellin's lack of, 82
    of members, 137, 406
    once delivered to the Saints, 104,
        111, 112, 136, 139
    tests of, 270
Faithfulness, blessings conditional upon,
    131
Family prayer, effect on McLellin, 33
Farmington, Maine, 170, 478
Faunce, Noah, 434
    ordained an elder, 153
    ordained a priest, 152
Fayette, Missouri, 88, 130, 479
Fellows, Nathan, 188, 434
Fellowship, of members, 137
Fennel, James, hardness of, 219-22, 434
Fields, Reuben, 63, 70, 74, 381, 413, 434
    baptism of, 62
Fields, Mrs. Reuben, 413, 434
    baptism of, 63
Finnel, William, 434
    subscribes to *Messenger and
        Advocate,* 226
Finney, Charles Grandison, 161-62, 285
Fisher, Bro., 174, 194, 434
Fleener, Col., 30, 434
Flesh, abominations of, 107
Fletcher, Mr., 91, 434

Florence, Ohio, 130, 141–45, 272, 483
Flux, McLellin suffers from, 134
Fonse, T., 152, 434
Foot, S., 175, 434
Foot, Timothy, 434
    appointed to repurchase land in Zion,
        176
Forgiveness, McLellin on, 143
Foster, Charles, 332
Foster, G. S., 32, 435
Foster, Robert, 330, 332
Fowler, Ohio, 483
Freedom, New York, 170, 481
Freedonia or Freedonia Village
        (Fredonia), New York, 170, 481
French, L., 132, 435
Fulkerson, Mr., 32, 435
Fuller, Elder, 189
Fuller, Mrs., 41, 435
Fuller, E., 148, 149, 435
Fuller, Edson, 49
Fuller, Jesse, 30, 123, 435
Fulness of gospel
    believe and obey, 70
    new covenant of, 71
Fulton, Ohio, 483

G

Gains Crossroads, Kentucky, 478
Gannaway, Betsy, 123, 435
Gannaway, John, 123, 435
Gardner, Mrs., 413, 435
Gardner, Jotham, 413, 435
    baptized, 153
Garments, rid of blood of, 223
Garrettsvill (Garrettsville), Ohio, 28, 60,
        483
Gates, Mr., 104, 116, 119, 436
Gather, McLellin called to encourage
        people to, 46
Gathering, 198–99, 407
    in Bible and Book of Mormon, 145
    centers of, 8
    of Church of Christ, 119
    effects of, 121
    fervor to, 272
    to flee God's wrath, 39
    of Jews, 43–44, 135, 184

of Jews and Native Americans, 108
McLellin on, 43–44, 137
modes of travel for, 83
as preparation for Millennium, 143
as preparation for Second Coming,
        39, 139
results of, 137
of Saints, 43, 288
two places of, 55, 65, 106, 121, 133,
        139, 406
Gennessees, New York, 170, 481
Gentiles
    enmity with Jews, 144
    God's dealings with, 114
Gestures, Mormon dislike of, 284
Gift of the Holy Ghost, 268
    nature and effects of, 179
Gift of tongues, 157
    McLellin on, 134
    members manifest, 134, 136, 137
Gift of utterance, 131, 155
Gifts of the Spirit, 43, 84, 157, 266, 278–
        79, 407. *See also* Discernment,
        power of; Healing
    defined, 75
    in early Mormonism, 11
    in McLellin journals, 16
    McLellin on, 116, 377
    nature of, 223
    tongues, 16, 134, 135, 136, 137, 157,
        278
    utterance, 44, 131, 155
Gilbert, Algernon Sidney, 305, 307–8,
        310, 365
Gilbert, Sidney, 50
Gilead, Illinois, 88, 476
Gloom, of unbelievers, 38
Glory
    of gospel, 65
    of heaven and Zion, 65
    of Millennium, 62, 65
God. *See also* Spirit of God
    and dealings with men, 145
    fills McLellin's mind with truth, 37
    glory of, encircles Harvy Whitlock, 30
    judgments of, 38, 44, 47, 61
    McLellin resigns will to, 35
    members on marvelous works of, 34

God, cont.
nature of, 83–84
people exhorted to trust in, 107
protects missionaries, 40
requirements of, 43
revelations of, 57
revelations to McLellin, 45–46, 77
sweetness of members' communion with, 35
works of, in last days, 42, 72
wrath of, 39
Goff, James, 436
baptized by George Hinkle, 95
Goff, Mary Elizabeth, 436
baptized by George Hinkle, 95
Gold plates, description of, 79
Goshen, Ohio, 212, 483
Gospel, 174, 406, 407
bonds of, 120
comforts Saints, 216
glories of, 65
Hyrum Smith on, 36
McLellin on, 47, 62, 64, 377
nature and power of, 222
plainness of, 108, 111, 142, 145, 183, 184, 193
Gould, J., 177, 436
Gould, Sally Ann, 436
baptized and confirmed, 176
Gould, William, 436
baptized and confirmed, 176
Granger, Bro., 181, 436
Gray, Mr., 178, 437
Greene, John P., 204, 437
mission to the Senecas, 179, 276
Greenupsburg (now Greenup), Kentucky, 212, 478
Griffeth, Duty, 141, 437
donation of, to McLellin, 146
Griffeth, Hiram, 141, 437
Griffeth, Joseph B., 437
subscribes to *Messenger and Advocate*, 225
Griffeth, Judea, 141, 143, 437
donation of, to McLellin, 146
presents McLellin with donations, 145

Griffeth, Mary Ann, 437
donation of, to McLellin, 146
Griswould, Mr., 111, 113, 114, 182, 437
illness of, 108
passes hat for donations, 107
Griswould, Mrs., 108, 437
Guidance
of missionaries, 274
by the Spirit, 272

H

Haden, Joel H., 124, 274, 438
on falseness of Book of Mormon, 94
preaches against modern revelation, 93
Hadlock, R., 181, 438
Hambright, Col., 90, 438
Hancock, Levi, 44, 55, 438
preaches with McLellin, 145
Hancock, Solomon, 32, 50, 438
Hanson, Mr. G. M., 30, 439
Hardheartedness, of Christian preacher, 39
Harper, Mr., 108, 439
Harris, Bro., 136
refuses request from McLellin, 146
Harris, Emer, 439
McLellin visits, 141
Harris, Martin, 51, 265, 297, 314, 339, 366, 439
leaves Independence for mission to East, 36
shown golden plates, 49
testimony of, 264
travels with McLellin, 33, 37
Hart, A., 439
donates hat to McLellin, 219
Harvey, John, 110, 116, 439–40
Hate, New York, 481
Hawley, M., 440
elders dust feet against, 189–90
Head, Anthony, 95, 440
Healing, 136, 176, 283
in book of Acts, 16
of child, 43, 66–67, 191, 266, 277
of congregation, 72
of Cynthia Hubbard, 136
of Elizabeth Everhart, 71

Healing, cont.
from evil spirits, 111
gift of, 266
impossible without faith, 192
of McLellin, 40, 96, 141–42, 265
of McLellin by Joseph Smith, 45, 67,
  267, 268, 299
McLellin given power of, 46
in McLellin journals, 16
McLellin prays for power of, 191
of leg, 217
of Levi Jones, 138
power of, 250
by prayer, 96
of sick, 84
of Sister Jones, 136
Heatin's Mill, Ohio, 483
Heaton, Benjamin, 440
reads Book of Mormon, 103
Heaven
glories of, 65
veil of, 92, 102
Hebrew, McLellin studies, 215, 217, 219
Hedrick, Granville, 348, 352
Hedrickites, 348, 351–53
Henderson, Mr., 112, 440
Herryman, H., 180, 440
Hetty, 440
loss of daughter of, 42
Hicklin, T., 42, 440
Higgins, Dr., 286, 441
reads anti-Mormon tract at meeting,
  118
High priests
council of, 154–55
meeting for deliverance of Zion, 149
office of, earliest reference to, 55–56,
  283
Hill, Mr., 122, 441
Hill, A., 222, 441
Hill, Catrin, 413, 441
rebaptized, 136
Hill, Elisha, 413, 441
rebaptized, 136
Hillsboro, Illinois, 88, 476
Hinkle, George M., 95, 96, 124, 274, 295,
  330–32, 334–35, 337, 344, 371,
  373–74, 441

counseled to go to Illinois and
  Indiana, 97
Hiram, Ohio, 28, 45–47, 60, 483
Historiography of Mormonism, 4–5, 9–10
History, Compendium of, McLellin buys
  S. Whelpley's, 139
Hitchcock, J., 441
given gift of utterance, 131
Hodges, Mrs., 441
feeds McLellin, 122, 285
Hofmann, Mark W., 263, 287
and McLellin journals, 3, 258
Holden, Mrs., 129
Holden, Aaron, 414, 441
baptized, 115
Holden, Katherine, 442
baptized, 119–20
Holmes, E., 219, 442
Holy Ghost, 200–201
gift and power of, 176, 179
laying on of hands to receive, 66
nature and effects of, 193
Hope
effects on society of, 142
lack of, in members, 143
Hopkinton, New York, 170, 481
Horton, Mr., 107, 442
Howard, Richard, 144, 442
donation of, to McLellin, 147
Howe, Sis., 148, 442
Howland, Ohio, 483
Hubbard, Charles Wesley, 442
receives recommend to go to Zion,
  138
Hubbard, Cynthia, 138, 442
healed, 136
Hubbard, Mary Ann, 442
receives recommend to go to Zion,
  138
Hubbard, Noah, 132, 156, 282, 443
heals wife, 136
speaks in tongues, 134
Hubbard Town (Hubbard), Ohio, 60, 483
Huff, Mr., 104, 443
Hughs, Nathaniel, 443
subscribes to *Messenger and
  Advocate,* 225

Huntoon, Carter, 414, 443
    baptized and confirmed by McLellin, 193
Huntsburg, Ohio, 130, 163, 483
Hyde, Orson, 45, 160, 161, 174, 187, 190, 200, 202, 205, 207, 208, 210, 276, 300-301, 316, 319, 350, 366-67, 381, 443
    absent from meeting of Twelve, 185
    assigned to return to Kirtland, 182
    baptizes, 176, 179
    missionary work of, 206
    preaches, 70, 179
    salutes the Twelve, 176
    travels with McLellin, 176-78
Hymns, in meeting, 103, 104

I

Ignorance, of members, 276
Illinois River, 476-77
Independence, Missouri, 28, 79-86, 88, 130, 287, 402, 479
    description of, 50-51, 83
Indianopolis (Indianapolis), Indiana, 130, 477
Indifference, of congregation, 102
Interpretation of tongues, 134, 136, 279
    by Lewis Zabriskie, 137
Ivevtts, Mr., 89, 443
Ivevtts ferry, Missouri, 89, 479
Ivey, Mr. and Mrs., 32, 38, 443
Ivie, John, 124
Ivie, William, 50

J

Jack's old ferry, Missouri, 479
Jackson, Mr., 129
Jackson, Joseph, 121, 413, 443
    baptized, 119-20
Jackson, Truman, 443
    donation of, to McLellin, 146
Jackson County, Missouri, 30. *See also* Zion
    persecution in, 153-54
    purchase of land in, 201
Jacksonville, Illinois, 28, 477
Jennings, Mr., 36, 443

Jerusalem, gathering in, 44, 65, 133, 135, 139
Jesus Christ. *See also* Second Coming
    appearance on American continent, 110
    baptism according to commandments of, 34
    in Book of Mormon, 176
    cause of, 146
    kingdom of, 140, 142, 148
    living church of, 34
    name and gospel of, 120
    parables and preaching of, 133
    Parley P. Pratt testifies of, 97
    preaches to Jews, 133
Jethro, father-in-law of Moses, 115
Jews, 406
    enmity with Gentiles, 144
    fall of, 149
    gathering of, 106, 108, 121, 184
    gathering to Jerusalem, 44, 65, 133, 135, 139
    God's dealings with, 114
    Savior preaches to, 133
Jinkenson, John G., 222, 444
    subscribes to *Messenger and Advocate,* 225
John, Gospel of, 32, 47, 119
John (the Revelator), 84
Johnson, Hezk., 414, 444
    baptized by McLellin, 194
    confirmed by McLellin, 195
Johnson, James, 133, 414, 444
Johnson, John, 46, 56, 68, 70, 73, 78, 268, 299, 301, 303, 444
Johnson, Luke S., 70-73, 77, 78, 161, 165, 181, 268, 300, 323-24, 366, 381, 444
    appointed to mission to South with McLellin, 70
    heals Mother Edwards with McLellin, 71
    presides over conference of Twelve, 190
    serves mission with McLellin, 301-2
    travels with McLellin, 171-74
Johnson, Lyman, 67, 72, 147, 149, 153, 161, 167, 174, 184, 206, 267, 269,

Johnson, Lyman, cont.
  276, 284, 300, 313, 315, 323-24,
   366, 381, 444
  attends meeting with McLellin, 148
  baptizes, 181
  on the gathering of the Jews, 184
  preaches at conference of Twelve,
   190
  travels with McLellin, 179-81
Johnson, N., 414, 445
  baptized by McLellin, 194
  confirmed by McLellin, 195
Jones, Mr., 95, 102, 445
Jones, Sis., 445
  believes gospel, 175
  donation of, to McLellin, 175
  healed, 136
Jones, J., 132, 445
Jones, Levi, 133, 134, 135, 156, 157, 281,
   381, 445
  healed, 138
  health of, 136
  prays while McLellin confirms new
   member, 133
Jones, Stephen, 174-75, 445
  buys Book of Mormon, 175
Joseph, covenants of, 144
Joy, of McLellin, 137
Judgment Day, 383, 406
Judgments of God
  on unrepentant, 61
  on world at Second Coming, 38, 39,
   44, 48, 63, 177

K

Kaw Township, Missouri, 479
Ketting, Joseph, 445
  carries letter for McLellin, 214
Keys, Mr., 446
  opposes McLellin, 224-25
Kimball, Heber C., 165, 179, 203, 210,
   232, 276, 313-14, 316, 325-26,
   350, 366, 381, 446
  presides over conference of Twelve,
   182
Kimball, Vilate, 232
Kingdom of Christ (of God)
  establishment of, 110, 140

  nature of, 112, 148, 180, 187, 193,
   406
  order of, 142
  Parley P. Pratt on, 190
Kingsbury, H., 148, 446
Kingston, Ontario, Canada, 170, 484
Kirtland, Ohio, 7, 8, 11, 28, 44-45, 60,
   130, 170, 212, 341, 402, 483
  activities in, 284-85
  apostasy in, 323
  McLellin in, 68-70, 82, 139, 229
Kirtland Safety Society, 323, 347
Kirtland School, 163, 164, 313-14, 318,
   365
  commencement of, 152
  McLellin on, 207
  organization of, 149
Knight, Newel, 50, 381, 446
  discerns heart of McLellin, 34
  gift of discernment, 269
  travels with McLellin, 52
Koran, McLellin borrows, 186

L

Lamson, Bro., 189, 446
Lancaster, New Hampshire, 170, 480
Lane, Nathaniel, 48, 61-62, 446
Lanterman, Peter, 67, 447
Last days, 80, 407
  gathering in, 65
  God's works in, 42, 72
  God's wrath in, 63
  signs of, 239
Law, William, 330, 332, 334, 371
Law, Wilson, 330, 332
Laws of Zion, 134
Laying on of hands, 83, 136, 158, 176,
   383, 390, 406
  for blessing, 138, 283
  for blessing of children, 195
  to cast out evil spirits, 111
  for confirmation, 34, 63, 68, 117,
   120, 138, 176, 195
  effect of, 136, 138
  for healing, 40, 43, 45, 46, 66, 71, 72,
   136, 138, 176, 191, 192, 217, 283
  for Holy Ghost, 100, 268
  importance of, 66

Laying on of hands, cont.
  by Joseph Smith Jr., 67–68, 260
  McLellin on, 133
  to set apart, 179, 276
Lee, Jarvis, 282, 447
  ordained as priest, 44
Leona (Laona), New York, 481
Lessley, Mr., 94, 447
Letter B, Maine, 478
Levitical priests, 56
Lewis, Job, 447
  hosts conference of Twelve, 175–76
Lewis, Joshua, 33–34, 52, 447
Lewis, Lloyd, 201, 447
  ordained an elder, 179
Lewis, Lorenzo, 447
  mission to Pennsylvania, 179
  ordained an elder, 176–77
Lexington, Missouri, 28, 88, 130, 479
Liberty
  God grants to McLellin, 41
  McLellin speaks with, 39
  in speaking, 278
Liberty, Missouri, 88, 479
License to preach, 135, 158, 159, 282
Lick Creek, Missouri, 479
Licking River, Kentucky, 212, 478
Light, room filled with, 137
Light and glory, of Spirit of God, 47
Linden, New York, 481
Little Blue Creek (or River), Missouri, 479
Little Sandy River, Kentucky, 478
Littleton, New Hampshire, 170, 480
Little Valley, New York, 481
Loborough (probably Loughborough), Ontario, Canada, 484
Lommery, Eunice, 414, 447
  baptized and confirmed by McLellin, 186
Lorane County Western Reserve (Lorain County), Ohio, 483
Lord's Prayer
  propriety of, 110
  relation to D&C 65, 243–44
Louisiana, Missouri, 28, 130, 479
Loveless, Mrs., 178, 447
Luff, Bro., 184, 447

Lyman, New Hampshire, 170, 480
Lyons, Eliza, 447
  baptized, 180
Lyons, New York, 170, 481

M

Mackey, Mr., 100, 447
Macoupin River, Illinois, 28, 88, 477
Madness, of boy, 106
Mammoth bones, McLellin sees, 222
Manuel, Mr., 195, 448
Mapes, Betsy, baptized and confirmed, 176, 448
Marsh, Thomas B., 68, 75, 131, 155, 184, 186, 200, 276–77, 316, 366, 381, 448
  on the covenants of God, 175
  McLellin writes to, 224
  preaches, 187
  presides over conference of Quorum of Twelve, 175
  travels with McLellin and Brigham Young, 189
Martin, M., 215, 448
Mayvill (Mayville), New York, 170, 481
McAdoes Falls, Vermont, 170, 485
McCafferty, Mrs., 32, 91, 448
McCord, Mrs., 99, 448
  afraid to be baptized in cold water, 100
McCord, Robert, 413, 448
  baptized and confirmed, 100
  reasons with Parley P. Pratt and McLellin, 99
McCown, Mr. and Mrs., 448
  care for McLellin when ill, 132
McCune, Mr., 32, 448
McGee, Char., 217–18, 219, 448
  healed, 219
McLaughlin, Mr., 219, 448
McLellin, Cinthia Ann, 295, 297, 449
  death of, 251, 254
  grave visited by McLellin, 30, 41
  McLellin longs for, 82
McLellin, Emeline Miller, 78, 84, 116, 120, 122, 131, 133, 138, 147, 152, 155, 207, 268, 310, 312, 318, 324, 328, 357–58, 449

McLellin, Emeline Miller, cont.
  correspondence with McLellin, 105, 115, 116, 119, 120, 122
  description of, 82
  desire to meet McLellin's relatives, 85
  marriage of, 82, 251, 302-3
  McLellin receives book from, 196
  McLellin receives letter from, 149, 152, 187
  McLellin's enjoyment of, 83
  McLellin writes to, 188, 190, 195, 214, 223
  shortness of courtship of, 82
McLellin, Helen, 155
McLellin, Israel, 80, 81, 85, 449
  visited by McLellin, 31, 40
McLellin, Samuel, 85, 117, 449
  McLellin gives Book of Mormon to, 40
  McLellin receives letter from, 152
  McLellin writes to, 84-85, 149, 184, 224
McLellin, William E.
  admonitions to, 46
  on Americans, 81
  ancestry of, 46
  as Apostle, 388, 402
  arrangement of personal affairs, 42
  asks forgiveness of Church, 230
  asks for new missionary license, 230
  asks for visitation from angel, 92, 101-2
  asks to flog Joseph Smith, 326-27
  to assist in gathering, 131
  association with Strangite church, 339-41
  attempts to convert relatives, 84
  attempts to write a revelation, 57-58, 237-38, 253, 300
  baptism of, 34, 297
  baptizes, 70, 136, 137, 138
  begins first mission, 35-36
  biography of, 291-378
  blessed with power of healing, 46
  blesses congregation, 138
  and Book of Mormon witnesses, 264-67
  brings converts to Rigdonite church, 334-35

  buys first Book of Mormon, 31
  buys horse for Hyrum Smith, 41
  called as teacher in Kirtland School, 149
  called on mission, 46, 267, 281
  called to Quorum of Twelve, 275-76
  called to repentance, 46
  changing preaching topics of, 19-23
  children of, 131, 303, 310, 312, 318, 323, 328-29, 335, 347, 349, 353, 355, 357
  clerk at conference of Twelve, 175-76, 179
  concerned with language in the revelations, 237
  confirmation of, 34
  confirms new members, 133
  conflict with Sidney Rigdon, 318
  confounds opposition, 107, 217
  content analysis of missionary work of, 379-405
  conversion of, 79-80, 296-97
  converts candidates for Zion, 65
  conviction that Joseph Smith was a prophet, 251
  copies revelations, 47, 234
  correspondence with Emeline McLellin, 105, 115, 116, 119, 120, 122
  correspondence with Joseph F. Smith, 354-55
  correspondence with Orson Pratt, 346
  court case against LDS Church leaders, 350-51
  death and eulogy, 355-58
  death of Cinthia Ann, 82
  debates clergyman, 269
  debates J. M. Tracy over validity of Book of Mormon, 315
  debates James Strang, 344
  decides to stop preaching, 73
  dedicates family to God, 213
  describes origins of Mormonism, 79-80
  desire to have garments clean of blood, 117
  desire to settle down, 83

McLellin, William E., cont.
    determined to keep the
        commandments, 89
    difficulty leaving family, 131
    difficulty speaking, 142–43
    discontent with Church, 231
    disfellowshipped, 318
    doubts his call, 73
    dreams of journey to Independence,
        31
    dusts feet, 61, 72
    early impressions of Mormonism, 29–
        35, 79–84
    and emphasis on the Book of
        Mormon, 22
    endowment and, 319–21, 347
    estrangement from Mormonism of,
        23, 26
    on excesses of Mormonism, 347
    excommunications of, 78, 85, 305,
        323–24, 368
    faith of, tested, 270
    family background and characteristics
        of, 292–95
    fatigue and thirst of, 123
    fed poorly, 122
    fighting the devil, 380
    filled with Spirit, 65
    finances of, 138
    finds and returns pocketbook, 95
    finds horse to cross creek, 90
    finds true meaning of religion, 379
    first encounter of, with Joseph Smith,
        45
    first journey of, to Independence, 30–
        33
    first missions of, 300–302
    first sermon of, 36
    frustration of, with people, 91–92,
        113–14
    generosity toward, 285
    gets new shoes, 111
    gift of healing of, 289
    greatest sermon of, 120
    healed by Hyrum Smith, 40, 265
    healed by Joseph Smith Jr., 67, 267,
        268, 299
    healed by Parley P. Pratt, 96

    healed by Samuel Smith, 67
    healed through prayer, 142
    healing power of, 226
    heals child, 43, 266, 277
    heals Mother Edwards, 66
    heals Mrs. Smith, 66
    hears of Joseph Smith, 30
    hopes for letter from Emeline, 186
    illness of, 31, 40, 66–67, 80, 82, 84,
        96, 114, 122, 141, 145–46, 156,
        225
    imagines Lamanite wandering the
        land, 101
    imprisoned, 308–9
    inability to preach, 270
    inspiration of, while preaching, 36,
        38, 39
    interprets tongues, 134
    introduction to Mormonism, 29–30
    joins Hedrickites, 351–52
    joins Hinkle's church, 330
    joins Rigdon's church, 333
    as Joseph's scribe for D&C 66, 45–46,
        248
    in Kirtland and vicinity, 68–70, 139–
        40, 284–85
    leaves Hinkle's church, 332
    leaves Paris, Illinois, 30
    leaves Rigdon's church, 337–38
    leaves the Hedrickites, 353
    leaves the LDS Church, 321–24
    letters written by, 79–85, 229–32,
        286
    list of, of books to buy, 196–97
    loneliness of, 83
    longs for relatives, 84–85
    Lord speaks through, 218
    Lord's will concerning, 46
    with Luke Johnson, 70–73, 78
    man takes, over creek, 91
    marriages of, 85, 295, 302–3
    marriage to Emeline Miller, 82
    medical practice of, 295, 328
    meditation and prayer of, 35, 92,
        101–2
    mission call of, revoked, 301
    mission of, to East, 131–69

McLellin, William E., cont.

missions of, personal description of, 80, 82

mission with Hyrum Smith, 36-44, 265-66, 282

mission with Parley P. Pratt, 89-129, 305-6

mission with Samuel Smith, 61-78, 266-67

mourns wickedness of members, 185

moves to Zion, 304-5

and music in preaching, 271

on need to prepare for Second Coming, 83, 92, 110, 111, 188

nervous about preaching, 46

not to go to Zion, 46

ordained an elder, 35, 80, 281, 297

plainness of preaching of, 48

on plainness of the gospel, 111

plunders Joseph Smith's home, 326-27, 369

poverty of, 84

praises Quorum of Twelve, 229

praises Lord, 107

prayers of, 41

prays for girl, 111, 112

prays for mad boy, 106

prays for man's sore eyes, 96

prays for missionary success, 92

prays opposition will be confounded, 109

prays to know truth of Church and Book of Mormon, 33-34

preaches without Book of Mormon, 112

preaches with power, 113

preaches with Spirit of God, 180

preaching topics of, 18-23

preparation for mission of, 47

presides over conference of Twelve, 185-86

pride of, 41

public opinion of, 215

purchases land in Independence, 83

questions mission call, 302

reads scripture, 137

receives donations from members, 138, 145-47

receives revelation, 301

register of baptisms by, 413-14

relatives of, 79

reliance on God, 41

on revelation, 346

revelation received for, 45-46, 57, 77, 267, 299, 300

Rigdon, conflict with, 318

with Samuel Smith, 47-48, 61-67

as scribe to Joseph Smith, 56, 70

seeks spiritual manifestation, 274

seeks to establish "old foundation" of church, 341-46

sees caravan of animals, 184, 187, 285

sells land in Zion, 309-10

sends money to wife, 138

separates from Parley P. Pratt, 120

sermons of, 18-24

service in Quorum of Twelve, 314-21

settles differences in Amherst, 140

shortness of courtship, 82

speaks by the Spirit, 187

speaks in tongues, 135, 278

spends night with Joseph Smith Jr., 45

spiritual confirmation of, of truth of Mormonism, 35

spiritual gifts of, 270-71

sprains ankle, 45

stops preaching, 82

struggle of, to be obedient, 101

struggles with Satan, 34, 100-101

success of, in proselyting, 65-66, 413-14

teaches school, 83, 305

temptations of, 70, 269

testifies of prayer, 109

testimony of, of Book of Mormon, 265, 291-92, 296-97

testimony of, of Joseph Smith, 81-82, 84

travels without purse or scrip, 89, 90

unable to preach, 41

visits grave of Cinthia Ann McLellin, 30, 41, 297

visits Lucy Mack Smith, 343-44

wives of, 82-83

McLellin, William E., cont.
  writes papers on Mormonism, 353,
    376-77
  writes to Emeline, 133
  and Zion's Camp, 310-12, 347, 377
McLellin journals
  acquisition of, by LDS Church, 258-
    59
  compared to Acts, 13-18
  description of, xv-xvi
  editorial procedures for, xvi-xx
  initial expectations of, 3
  preaching topics in, 23, 382-84
  provenance of, 257-61
  publication history of, xiii-xv
  religious content of, 16
McLellin letters, 79-85, 229-31
McMan, Sis., administered to by
    McLellin, 135, 449
Mead, Mr., 103, 449
Medicines and remedies, 134
Meditation, 275
Meed. *See* Mead
Meek, Dr., 218, 449
Meetings, of The Church of Jesus Christ
    of Latter-day Saints, 277-79
  Bishop's council, 69
  confirmation, 63, 66, 135, 158
  council, 147-48
  elder's council, 68
  for deliverance of Zion, 149
  high priest council, 154-55
  prayer, 33, 34, 66, 68, 70, 141, 145,
    188, 268, 278
  sacrament, 134, 136, 142, 144, 146,
    147, 160
  Sunday, 68, 70
Men, dealings of God with, 145
Merick, Levi, 118, 121, 414, 449
  baptized, 119
Messenger and Advocate
  McLellin gets subscriptions for, 181
  subscribers to, 225-26
  topics in, 407
Methodism, 152, 182, 183
  and Joseph Smith, 163-64, 268
Methodist, 72, 73, 93, 108, 111, 214
  believes missionaries' testimony, 108

opposition to missionaries, 43, 103,
    225
priest/preacher, 223
  attempts to poison McLellin, 37
  encounters with, 103, 182
  gives dinner to McLellin, 30-31
  interrupts McLellin's sermon,
    188
  opposition of, 37, 42
schedules meeting to conflict with
    McLellin's, 218
unreasonableness of, 111
Middleberry or Middlebury, Ohio, 483
Miles, Col., gives McLellin a ride, 190,
    449
Mill Creek, New York, 481
Millen, Albert, 414, 449
  baptized and confirmed by McLellin,
    193
Millen, David, 192, 193, 194, 196, 450
Millennialism, in McLellin's journals, 15
Millennium, 80, 383, 406, 407
  glories of, 62, 65
  preparation for, 143
Miller, Bro., 48, 61, 70, 450
Miller, Emeline. *See* McLellin, Emeline
    Miller
Miller, G., 70, 450
Millet, Bro., 188, 450
  gives money to McLellin and Brigham
    Young, 189
Milligin, Mr., 32, 450
Milton (last name unknown), 450
  loss of daughter of, 42
Ministers, as sermon audience, 395-97
Miracles, in McLellin journals, 16
Missionaries
  baptisms by, 413-14
  called in the early Church, 282
  commanded to travel in pairs, 82
  God's protection of, 40
  hardships of, 18
  meetings of
    geographic location of, 384-87
    purpose of, 388-94
  methods of, 271
  opposition to, 61, 72, 105

Missionaries, cont.
  preaching topics of, 18-26
    Articles and Covenants, 19
    Book of Mormon, 19-23, 25
    gathering, 19
    gifts of the Spirit, 19
    God's judgments, 19
    gospel, 19
    judgments of God, 19
    laying on of hands, 19
    Second Coming of Christ, 19
  without purse or scrip, 89, 90
  way opened for, 90-91, 274
Missouri, troubles in, 307-12, 325-28
Missouri River, 479-80
Mitchel, Mr., 91, 450
Mitchel, J., 44, 450
Mitchel, Dr. S., 44, 450
Montgomery, Mr., McLellin heals child
  of, 191, 450
Montpelier, Vermont, 170, 485
Moore, William, 31, 40, 80, 81, 451
Morley, Isaac, 33, 52, 226, 308, 310, 321,
  451
Mormon, origin of the term, 80
Mormon historiography, 4-5, 9-10, 286
Mormonism
  coming forth of, 158, 213
  description of doctrines of, 83-84
  divine authenticity of, 217
  early, 7-9, 11
    and the Bible, 14
    converts to, 8
    growth of, 13, 17, 198-99
    and McLellin journals, 14
    preaching topics of, 18-23, 25
    rise of, 13-14
    spirituality of, 14
  evidences of, 224
  gifts of the Spirit in, 7, 11. *See also*
    Gifts of the Spirit
  organization of, 198-99
  in outlying areas, 7-10
  plainness of, 29
  as preaching topic, 384
  principles of, 225
  prophecies concerning, 158
  truth of, 224

Mormons, persecution of, 17, 153-54
Moroni. *See* Angel Moroni
Moronihah. *See* Ammonihah
Morris, Jacob, 451
  gives money to *Evening and*
    Morning Star, 138
  McLellin preaches at place of, 133
Moss, Mr., 152, 451
Mount Ephraim, Missouri, 480
Mount Morris, New York, 481
Mount Pleasant, Missouri, 480
Mun, B., 102-3, 451
Murdock, John, 32, 50, 451
  mission to Pennsylvania, 179
Music, with preaching, 104, 270-71
Myers, William, 188, 189, 451

N

Nail, Mr., 106, 451
National Road, Illinois, 88, 477
Native Americans
  gathering of, 108
  missions to, 179, 352
  and Mormonism, 203-4
Nature, spiritual experiences in, 35, 92,
  100-102, 119, 275-76
Nauvoo Expositor, 330
Nelson, Ohio, 28, 60, 483
New Bedford, Pennsylvania, 60, 484
Newbury (probably now Mulberry),
  Ohio, 483
Newcome, Bro., 452
  called on mission with McLellin, 147
Newport, Kentucky, 212, 478
Newry, Maine, 170, 478
New Testament, church of, 20, 407
Nicholson, John, 294, 350-51
Nickerson, Elder, 178, 452
Nineteenth century, religious fervor in,
  5-6
Norton, Hester, baptized and confirmed,
  176, 452
Norton, Sylvester, 202, 452
  baptized and confirmed, 176
Nunally, N. W., 29, 452
Nutting, Sis., 216, 452
Nutting, Syvander, 452
  subscribes to *Messenger and*
    Advocate, 226

O

Obedience, McLellin on, 65
Odel, Jacob, 121, 452
Odel, Lucinda White, 452
    second cousin to McLellin, 121
Officers, of Church, duties of, 137
Ogdensburg, New York, 170, 481
Opposition, to missionary work, 37, 41, 43, 47, 61
Orange, Ohio, 483
Ordinances, 70, 193. *See also* Baptism; Blessing; Laying on of hands; Sacrament; Confirmation
    importance of, 66
    McLellin on, 15, 141
    nature and efficacy of, 136
    of the priesthood, 283
Ordinations, 80, 138, 153, 280-83, 289. *See also* Baptism; Blessing; Confirmation
    to high and lesser priesthoods, 45
    method of, 281-82
    as priest, 44
    rebaptism, 133, 135, 137, 279, 280-81
Orton, Amos, 204, 452
    mission to Senecas, 179, 276
Orton, R., 171, 453
Osburn, Mr., 453
    preaches from Song of Solomon, 112
Osburn, Mr. and Mrs., 108, 453
Oswego, New York, 170, 481
Owens, Robert, McLellin reads debate of, 224

P

Page, Hiram, 343, 345
Painesville, Ohio, 130, 483
Parables, 119, 133
Paris, Illinois, 28-30, 41, 79-80, 130, 477
    McLellin returns to, 81
Paris, Missouri, 28, 88, 130, 480
Park, Harris, 413, 453
    baptized by McLellin, 134-35
Parkman, Ohio, 212, 483
Partridge, Edward, 33, 36, 69, 75, 76, 226, 269, 297, 305, 307, 310, 319, 321, 453

as bishop, 51-52
    ordains McLellin an elder, 35, 281
    tarred and feathered, 153-54
    travels with McLellin, 213
Patten, David W., 153, 160, 165, 167, 200, 269, 277, 280, 315-16, 323, 366, 381, 453
    administers sacrament, 179
    people's indignation toward, 214
    preaches, 181, 195
    preaches at conference of Twelve, 175
    presides over conference of Twelve, 178-79
    travels with McLellin, 152
Patton, Mr., 33, 36, 454
Patton, Phibe Ann, 143, 160, 454
    donation of, to McLellin, 147
Paul, Apostle, 107
Peace
    members admonished to live in, 138
    at Mormon conference, 81
    of Mormon meetings, 34, 68
    of Mormons, 33
Peck, Rev., 116-17, 127-29, 274, 286, 454
    anti-Mormon sermons of, 114-17
    interferes with baptism, 115
    opposes McLellin, 225, 454
Pemberton, Russel, 454
    cast down in mind, 171
Perfection, 69, 227, 407
    going on to, 147
    McLellin on, 217-18
    nature of, 190
    principles of, 194
Perfectionism, in American religion, 208-9
Perry, Daniel, 454
    defends McLellin, 188
Persecution
    of Mormons, 17, 153-54
    of truth, 81
Phelps, W. W., 50, 226, 310, 312, 319, 321, 324, 327, 454
    on *Evening and Morning Star,* 86
    McLellin and Pratt receive letter from, 119

Philip's Ferry, Illinois, 477
Phlhisis, 135
Pillow Point (Pillar Point), New York, 170, 481
Pittsburgh, Pennsylvania, 484
Pittsford, New York, 170, 482
Pity, on unbelievers, 194
Plainness
    of gospel, 108, 111, 183, 184, 193
    of Hyrum Smith's preaching, 44
    of McLellin's preaching, 48, 95, 102
    of Parley Pratt's preaching, 94, 100, 108
    of truths of Mormonism, 29
Plan of redemption, 83, 119
Plan of salvation
    McLellin on, 62
    people rejoice in, 66
Polygamy, 348
Pool, L., 95, 455
Port Kent, New York, 482
Potsdam, New York, 170, 482
Potter, Leman, 141, 455
    donation of, to McLellin, 146
Powers, Bro., 195, 455
Prairie Creek (Fire Prairie Creek), Missouri, 480
Pratt, Orson, 72, 181, 190, 199, 206, 294, 301, 319, 346, 353-54, 366, 455
    recalls circumstances of D&C 22, 235
Pratt, Parley P., 76, 123, 125-29, 153, 165, 167, 181, 185, 186, 269, 271, 273-76, 282, 286, 309-10, 315, 325, 336, 366, 381, 394, 455
    absent from conference of Twelve, 182
    appoints presiding elder, 187
    asks for visitation from angel, 92, 101-2
    on Book of Mormon, 105, 271
    on creation, 96
    criticizes McLellin, 185-86, 276
    desire to have garments clear of blood, 117
    determined to keep commandments, 89
    finds horse to cross creek, 90
    on gathering of Jews, 108
    on kingdom of Christ, 187
    lays hands on McLellin, 96
    man takes, over creek, 91
    meditation and prayer of, 92, 101-2
    and music in preaching, 270-71
    on nature of revelation, 110-11
    obtains ferry passage without fee, 89, 125
    power of God on, while preaching, 97
    prays for afflicted people, 96, 106, 111, 283
    prays for missionary success, 92
    prays opposition will be confounded, 109
    preaches, 179
    preaching topics of, 21
    presides over conference of Church, 187
    on prophecy, 128
    on Second Coming, 97
    separates from McLellin, 120
    serves mission with McLellin, 21, 89-129, 305-6, 394
    struggles to be obedient, 101
    struggles with Satan, 100-101
    testifies of Christ, 97
    travels without purse or scrip, 89
    words cut to hearts of listeners, 107
Prayer, 275, 278, 281, 282, 406, 407
    family, 33, 278
    in groups, 281
    McLellin on, 110
    of members, solemnity of, 35
    power and efficacy of, 109
    for spiritual manifestation, 274
    of Twelve Apostles, 276
Prayer meeting, 33, 34, 66, 68, 70, 141, 145, 188, 268, 278
Preaching, in McLellin journals
    topic distribution of, 382-84
    topics, 5, 18-26
Presbyterians, 72, 149
    McLellin attends meeting of, 182
    opposition from, 284-85
Presscot (Prescott), Ontario, Canada, 170, 484
Price, John, 31, 455

Prices, in the 1830s, 285
Pride, of McLellin, 41
Priesthood, 134, 406, 407. *See also*
    Ordinances; Ordination; High
    priest; Levitical priests
    blessings by, 96, 282-83
    duties of, 96, 141
    licenses, 282
    McLellin on, 122, 145, 181, 186, 191,
        377
    McLellin ordained to, 45, 80
    meeting, 141
    method of ordination to, 281-82
    nature of, 177
    offices of, 137-38, 283
    orders of, 45, 56, 161, 283
    ordination to, 138, 153, 281, 282,
        283, 289
Professionals, as sermon audience, 395-
    97
Prophecies, 44, 64, 69, 71, 80
    of Book of Mormon, 106
    fulfilled, 109
    of gathering, 106
Prophecy, 406. *See also* Dreams
    of Book of Mormon, 39
    McLellin on, 73, 75
Prophets, character and nature of true
    and false, 137, 406
Proselyting, methods of, 270-71
Provenance, of McLellin journals, 257-59

Q

Quorum of the Twelve Apostles. *See*
    Twelve, Quorum of

R

Read. *See* Reed, Mr. and Mrs.
Rebaptism, 133, 137, 280-81
    of inactive members, 281
Recommend, to go to Zion, 138
Reed, Mr. and Mrs., 64, 66, 67, 69, 456
Reed, Mrs. C., 413, 456
    baptized and confirmed, 65-66
Reed, Elizabeth, 414, 456
    baptized by McLellin, 117
Reed, James H., 413, 456
    baptized, 119-20
    confirmed, 129

Reeves, Mr. and Mrs., 31, 456
Reformed Egyptian, xviii, 79
Religion, principles of, 216
Religions
    contrasted, 177
    false, 137, 406
Religious marketplace in 1830s, 5
Renick, Mrs., 90, 456
Reorganized Church of Jesus Christ of
    Latter Day Saints, 257, 347-49,
    355
Repentance, 83
    admonitions about, 92, 93
    for baptism, 193
    McLellin on, 61, 142
    of members, 143-44
Restitution of all things, 119
Restoration of ancient church, 63
Resurrection, 406
    nature and power of, 178
Revelations, 70, 233-51, 406, 407
    divine authority of, 84
    fear of, 183
    of Joseph Smith Jr.
        to McLellin, 45-46
        McLellin copies, 47
    McLellin reads, 68
    nature and evidences of, 108, 111,
        218
    new, 62
    transcript of, 45-46
Revivalism, 161-62
Richards, Mr. and Mrs., 59, 456
Richards, G., 114, 456
Richmond, Missouri, 130, 480
Richmond, Ohio, 483
Rigdon, Phoebe Brook, 69, 284, 456
Rigdon, Sidney, 32, 50, 51, 53, 56, 76,
    81, 157, 160, 164, 167, 205, 207,
    226, 268, 284, 289, 299, 313, 318-
    19, 329, 332-34, 336, 338, 371,
    381, 456
    appointed trustee of Kirtland high
        school, 149
    censures McLellin, 284
    McLellin chastised by, 148
    McLellin's first encounter with, 44-45
    preaches with McLellin, 69

Riggs, Burr, 327
Roberts, Maj., 103, 457
Roberts, Mr., 457
    challenges McLellin, 224
Roberts, Mrs., 219, 457
Robley, H., 108, 110, 111, 113-14, 457
    buys Book of Mormon, 118
Rockport, Ohio, 483
Rogers, Mr., 32, 457
    lends horse to McLellin, 122
Rogers, A., 215, 457
Roman Catholic, 64
Rood, Mr., 177, 458
Root, Mr., 224, 458
    opposes McLellin, 225
Rooter, Dr., McLellin attends sermon of,
    214, 458
Roundy, Shadrach, 70, 78, 301, 413, 458
Rumford Point, Maine, 479
Runkle, Mr., 102, 458
Russel, Sis., 128-29, 458
    believes testimony of Parley P. Pratt
      and McLellin, 107
    gives postage to McLellin, 122
Russel, John, 109, 111, 125, 128-29, 458
    disbelief in Book of Mormon, 104-5
    solicits donations for Parley P. Pratt
      and McLellin, 107
Ryland, John F., 310

S

Sabriskie, Lewis. *See* Zabriskie, Lewis
Sackets Harbor, New York, 170, 482
Sacrament, 70, 99, 117, 120, 122, 129,
    133, 134, 136, 142, 144, 146, 147,
    152, 160, 178, 181, 184, 188, 191,
    195, 217, 273, 277-79, 281, 284
    at conference of Twelve, 175
    at elders' meeting, 35
    McLellin administers, 137
    meeting, 34, 134, 136, 142, 144, 146,
      147, 160, 279
    of non-Mormons, 44
    not administered because of
      disagreements, 141, 160
Saints, faith of, 192
Salt River, Missouri, 480
Salt River Branch, 274

Sanderson, Mr., 131, 459
Satan
    seals hearts and minds, 91
    spirit of, in Methodist priest, 37
    temptations of, 100-101
    tries to deceive McLellin, 34
Savior. *See* Jesus Christ
School, in Independence, 83. *See also*
    Kirtland School
School of the Prophets, 201, 318, 365
Schroeder, Theodore, and McLellin
    journals, 257
Scott, Jacob, 49
Scott, John, 271
Scott, Col. John, 105, 106, 107, 109, 120,
    121, 459
    plans to move to Zion, 116
Scott, R., 117, 459
Scriptures, 406
    antiquity and validity of, 136
    creation of, 197
    index of, 487-91
    McLellin studies, 62, 68
    sectarian quotation of, 145
    usefulness of, 136
    wresting of, 116
Sealing, unto everlasting life, 131
Sears, Mr., 183, 459
Second Coming, 271, 406
    gathering as preparation for, 39, 139
    imminence of, 42, 135
    importance of, in early Mormonism, 7
    McLellin on, 194-95, 222, 225
    people admonished to prepare for,
      92, 110, 111
    people unprepared for, 188
    preparation for, 83, 135, 279
    signs of, 239
Secrets, William, 223, 459
Seely, George, 98, 99, 459
Seixas, Joshua, 319
Senecas, missionaries sent to, 179
Sessions. *See* Cessions
Shakers, 159
    McLellin visits, 139
Shattuck, Sally, 414, 459
    baptized by McLellin, 194
    confirmed by McLellin, 195

Shelledy (lawyer), 81, 459
Sherwood, Samuel, 286, 459
    anti-Mormon tracts of, 117, 118
Shipps, Jan, and publication of McLellin
    journals, xiii
Shlbyville (Shelbyville), Illinois, 28, 477
Shumla, New York, 482
Signseeking, 63
Signs of the times, 16, 113, 383, 406,
    407
    Harvy Whitlock on, 29
    preceding Second Coming, 49, 239
Simmons, Nancy, 111, 413, 459
    baptized, 119-20, 129
    returns to Methodists, 122
    temptation and faith of, 121
Slab City or Sodom, New York, 482
Slover, Jacob, 123, 459
Smith, Mrs., healed by McLellin, 66, 461
Smith, Asael, 189, 460
Smith, Eden, 133, 138, 156, 157, 158,
    413, 460
    ordained an elder, 138
    rebaptized, 135
    reconfirmed, 136
Smith, Elias, 460
Smith, Elizabeth, 156, 158, 413, 460
    rebaptized, 133
Smith, Emma Hale, 78, 85, 349
    and Methodism, 163
Smith, Hyrum, 32-44, 50, 52, 54, 59, 68,
    75, 80-81, 155, 207, 226, 265-66,
    267, 268, 271, 279, 282, 287, 297,
    381, 460
    baptizes McLellin, 34
    discussion of, with McLellin, 33
    dusts feet, 39
    heals a child, 43, 266
    heals McLellin of ague, 40
    illness of, 37
    McLellin buys horse for, 41
    mission of, with McLellin, 36-44
    ordains McLellin as elder, 35
    plainness of preaching of, 44
    preaches, 37, 39, 40, 41, 44, 45, 67
    testimony of, of Book of Mormon, 37,
        39, 265
Smith, John, 147, 156, 157, 284, 460

Smith, Joseph, Jr., 14, 20, 23, 32, 33, 47,
    49, 50, 52, 53-54, 55, 56, 61, 70,
    75, 76, 78, 154-55, 156, 158, 159,
    162, 164, 190, 205, 207, 263, 272,
    287, 301, 302, 303, 305, 312, 317,
    319, 322-24, 328, 330, 343, 346,
    347, 367, 381, 461
    activities of, 267-69
    appointed trustee of Kirtland high
        school, 149
    blesses McLellin, 269
    confirms Celia Burwell, 67-68, 268
    death of, 338
    on the deliverance of Zion, 131, 154
    denounces creeds, 152
    discusses gospel with Campbellite
        priest, 69
    elder's testimony of, 80
    on the endowment, 319
    on gifts of the Spirit, 52, 75, 157
    heals McLellin, 45, 67, 267, 268, 299
    instructions of, to Quorum of Twelve,
        197-200, 314
    and Kirtland School, 164, 313
    letter of, to members in Florence, 144
    McLellin asks forgiveness of, 230
    McLellin first hears of, 30
    McLellin plunders house of, 326-27
    McLellin's criticism of, 231-32, 311-
        12, 322, 325, 348, 377
    McLellin's first encounter with, 45,
        81-82, 296-99
    on McLellin's marriage, 85, 304
    McLellin's testimony of, 82, 84
    and Methodism, 163-64, 268
    Missourians' opinions of, 33
    ordained to First Presidency, 77
    ordains David Whitmer, 341
    persecution of, 81
    and polygamy, 348
    preaches, 131, 148, 153, 168, 269,
        315
    preaches against Methodism, 268
    pronounces gift of utterance, 131
    as Prophet, 56, 82, 84
    and Quorum of Twelve, 165-66, 167-
        68, 315, 321
    rebukes McLellin, 304

Smith, Joseph, Jr., cont.
    receives revelation, 48, 50, 51, 54, 57, 75, 76, 77, 126, 154, 155, 159, 160, 161, 167, 226, 289, 299-300, 315-16, 319-20
    receives revelation for McLellin, 45-46, 57, 58, 77, 234, 268, 299, 319-20
    revelations of, 20, 57, 58, 84, 287, 299
    seals members up unto everlasting life, 131
    as seer, 82, 84
    sees gold plates, 79
    and temple lot, 50, 51
    travels with McLellin, 213
    vision of, of McLellin, 226, 289, 320
    visions of, 204-5, 319-20
    visited by Moroni, 79
    on Zion, 48, 50
    and Zion's Camp, 21, 310-12
Smith, Joseph, Sr., 44, 45, 70, 81, 267, 297, 461
Smith, Joseph, III, 348-49
    and McLellin journals, 257
Smith, Joseph F., 353-55
Smith, Lucy Mack, 343-44
Smith, Rachael, 413, 461
    confirmed, 138
    rebaptized, 137
Smith, Samuel H., 50, 52, 59, 73, 74, 75, 267, 296, 381, 461
    dusts feet, 47, 61
    heals child, 66
    heals McLellin, 67
    mission of, with McLellin, 47-48, 61-67
    serves mission with McLellin, 300-301
    testifies of Book of Mormon, 65
    testimony of, 266-67
Smith, Sylvester, 319
Smith, William, 178, 190, 205, 276, 317, 339, 462
    absent from conference of Twelve, 182
    travels with McLellin, 196
Sniders, Mr., 188, 462

Snow, Gardner, 190, 462
    gives McLellin and Orson Pratt a ride, 190
Snow, Willard, 180, 462
Snyder, Nancy, 414, 462
    baptized, 175
South, Mrs., 31, 462
Speaking in tongues, 134, 136. *See also* Gifts of the Spirit, tongues
Spirit of God, 122. *See also* Holy Ghost
    allows discernment, 34
    fills room with light, 137
    guidance by, 100, 271, 278
    helps McLellin preach, 36, 43-44, 47, 187, 192
    light and glory of, 47
    and McLellin journals, 16
    McLellin loses, 41
    among members, 34, 297
    nature, gift, and power of, 218
    operation of, 194
    upon Parley Pratt, 97
    when McLellin preaches, 180
Spirits
    evil, 111
    power of discerning, 33
Spiritual gifts, of gospel, 183. *See* Gifts of the Spirit
Springfield, Illinois, 28, 477
Springfield, Ohio, 130, 483
Squires, Mr., 181, 462
St. Clairsville, New York, 482
St. John, James, 64, 71, 74, 75, 462
St. John, Sarah, 413, 463
    baptized, 65-66
    confirmed, 66
St. Johnsbury, Vermont, 170, 485
St. Louis, Missouri, 130, 480
Starr, Jared, 463
    donation of, to McLellin, 147
Steel's Tavern, 139
Stilesville, Indiana, 28, 478
Stockholm, New York, 170, 482
Stone, Bro., 144
Stone, James E., 223, 463
    subscribes to *Messenger and Advocate*, 226

Stone, Silas, 223, 463
  subscribes to *Messenger and Advocate,* 225
Strait, spelling of term, 238, 245
Strang, James J., 293, 339–41, 344
Stringham, Sabra, 463
  baptized and confirmed, 176
Strong, Ezra, 143, 463
Sumner, Charles, 73, 82, 302, 463
Superstitions, of disciples, 185
Supper of the Lamb, 143
Suse, W., 63, 463
Sweat, Angeline, 414, 463
  baptized by McLellin, 194
  confirmed by McLellin, 195
Sweat, Benjamin, 194, 463
Sweat, Frederick, 414, 463
  baptized by McLellin, 194
  confirmed by McLellin, 195
Swift, Joanna, baptized, 180, 464
Swift Settlement, New York, 482
Swinford, Samuel, 139, 464

T

Tanner, Nathaniel, 464
  subscribes to *Messenger and Advocate,* 226
Terre-Haute (Terre Haute), Indiana, 28, 478
Terrill, Mr., 71, 464
Testimony meeting, 278–79
Thair, Ezra. *See* Thayer, Ezra
Thayer, Ezra, 49, 76, 464
  council concerning, 69
Thornton, Col., 89, 464
  unbelief of, 91–92
Thornton, Mr., 32, 464
Thrash, Mr., 37, 464
  unbelief of, 91–92
Three Witnesses, testimony of, 37
Tillery, Mr., 89–90, 464
Timothy, the Apostle, 82
Tongues, gift of, 157, 279. *See also* Gifts of the Spirit, tongues; Interpretation of tongues
  at conference of Twelve, 179
  McLellin on, 279
  speaking in, by McLellin, 192, 278

Tracy, J. M., 168, 269, 464
  challenges McLellin to debate, 153
  debates validity of Book of Mormon with McLellin, 315
Traughber, John L., Jr., and McLellin journals, 257–61
Travel, modes of, 83
Trotter, Mr., 465
  interrupts McLellin's sermon, 104
  opposition from, 103
Trust in God, 107
Truth, 114
  of Book of Mormon, 34, 192
  evidences of, 142, 177, 180, 187
  McLellin filled with, 37
  members' zeal for, 61
  of Mormonism, 224
  opened to McLellin, 36
  people admonished to receive, 92
  people unwilling to obey, 223
  pleases and angers, 217
  versus religion, 176
Turner, Thomas, 120, 121, 465
  baptized, 119
Twelve, Quorum of, 17, 314–21
  called on mission, 315–18
  conference of, 178, 185–86, 190, 195–96
  contention among, 277
  correspondence of, with McLellin, 322
  disagreement among, 185–86
  1835 mission of, 166, 171–210, 276
  invite McLellin to return, 229
  McLellin praises, 229
  McLellin's letter to, 229–30
  meeting of, 175
  oppose Hinkle's church, 330
  organization of, 165
  prayer meeting of, 176
  rotational presiding of, 186, 277

U

Umbagog Lake, Maine, 170, 479
Universalism, 48, 62, 70
Universalists, 182
  unwilling to believe, 216

V

Vandalia, Illinois, 88, 477
Van Luven, Frederick M., 207, 465
Van Luwen, John, 465
 buys cloth for McLellin, 187
Vermilion, Ohio, 130, 484
Vest, G., 222, 465
Villagers, as audience, 395-97
Vision, 26, 84, 185. *See also* Dreams
 of Joseph Smith, 226, 227
 McLellin and Hyde seek for, 177
 McLellin seeks, 276
 of truth of Book of Mormon, 71

W

Wabash River, Indiana, 88, 478
Wadsworth, Nathan, 216, 465
 subscribes to *Messenger and
  Advocate*, 225
Walker, Mr., 112-13, 114, 465
Warren, Ohio, 60, 62, 484
Washing of feet. *See* Dusting of feet
Waterloo, Ontario, Canada, 484
Watertown, New York, 482
Watervliet, Ohio, 484
Watson, Mr., 104, 119, 465
Watterford Lower Village (Lower
  Waterford), Vermont, 485
Watterman, Mr., 122, 466
Weathersfield, Ohio, 484
Webster, Mr., 223, 466
Webster, Vardeman, 223, 466
Welch, John W., and publication of
  McLellin journals, xiii
Wellsville, Ohio, 212, 484
Western Reserve, Ohio, 484
Westfield, New York, 170, 482
Weston, Mr., 218
Weston, William, 466
 subscribes to *Messenger and
  Advocate*, 225
White, James, 117, 120, 414, 466
 baptized, 115
White, Sophia, 414, 466
 baptized, 115
White, William, 30, 41, 466
Whitlock, Harvey, 32, 50, 265, 296-97,
  335, 361, 379, 381, 466

 converts McLellin, 29-30, 79
 encircled with glory of God, 30
 leaves Independence for mission to
  East, 36
 power of testimony of, 30
 preaches, 31
 returns to Independence, 36, 49
 testimony of, of Book of Mormon, 29
Whitmer, David, 32, 50, 80, 165, 207,
  226, 265, 296-97, 312, 314, 324,
  328, 338, 341-45, 352, 354, 366,
  379, 381, 467
 converts McLellin, 29-30, 79
 leaves Independence for mission to
  East, 36
 testimony of, of Book of Mormon, 29,
  49, 264
 travels with McLellin, 33
Whitmer, Jacob, 343
Whitmer, John, 56, 58, 157, 207, 226,
  299, 312, 324, 343, 467
 and background to D&C 45, 239
 McLellin's first encounter with, 45
Whitmer, Peter, Jr., 50
Whitmer, Peter, Sr., 68, 98, 268, 466-67
Whitney, Helen Mar, 232
Whitney, Horace K., 232
Whitney, Newel K., 76, 232, 303, 467
 calls council, 69
Whitney, Orson F., 232
Wickedness, of disciples, 185
Wight, Lyman, 52, 56, 309
Wightman, C., 180, 467
 gives ride to McLellin and Lyman
  Johnson, 181
Wilder, Levi B., 191, 194, 467
Wilhite, Mr., 30, 468
Williams, Frederick G., 50, 68, 76, 155,
  156, 157, 159, 205, 226, 313, 381,
  468
 appointed trustee of Kirtland high
  school, 149
 gives medicine to McLellin, 132
 medical influence of, on McLellin,
  329
 travels with McLellin, 140
Williams, William Wheller, 159
Wills, Thomas, 97, 468

Wilson, Mr., 118, 468
Wilton, Fanny, 468
    baptized and confirmed, 176
Winchester, Benjamin, 336–37, 341–42
Winchester, Indiana, 28, 478
Windham, Ohio, 28, 60, 484
Wissel, Mr., 178, 468
Wolcott, New York, 170, 482
Women, testimonies of, 279
Wood, Mr., 85, 468
Wood, Elder, 188
Wood, Elizabeth, 468
    donation of, to McLellin, 147
Wood, Gideon D., 469
    donation of, to McLellin, 147
Wood, Henry, 207
Wood, Jacob, 207, 468
Wood, Nathan, 30, 469
Woodruff, W. W., 231
Woodruff, Wilford, 287
Word of Wisdom, members' disregard
    of, 183
World, confusion of, 139, 141
Worship
    disagreement about practices of, 392
    modes of, in Mormonism, 279
Wright, Polly, 414, 469
    baptized and confirmed by McLellin,
    193

Y

Young, Brigham, 187, 203, 205, 206,
    276, 316, 346, 350, 381, 469
    absent from conference of Twelve,
    182
    assigned to return to Kirtland, 182
    baptizes, 187
    on Christ in Book of Mormon, 26, 176
    mission of, to Senecas, 179, 276
    preaches, 178
    travels with McLellin, 188–90
Youngstown, Ohio, 60, 484
Youtsey, George, 217, 469

Z

Zabriskie, Lewis, 133, 134, 279–82, 381,
    469
    acknowledges influence of evil
    power, 135

on confusion of world, 136
intends to give up elder's license, 135
interprets tongues, 136, 137
lends McLellin money, 138
preaches, 137
speaks in tongues, 134
travels with McLellin, 139
Zabriskie, Susan, 469
    healed by McLellin, 134
    illness worsened when treated by
        doctor, 134
Zeal
    of brethren, 61
    of elders, 183
Zion, 119, 120, 137, 139, 401, 480. *See
    also* Independence; Jackson
    County; Gathering
    affliction of, 149
    anxiety of members to go to, 216
    committee appointed to purchase
        land in, 176
    common opinions about, 118
    deliverance of, 131, 155, 179, 383
    duty of members to, 144
    early Mormon emphasis on, 271–72
    as gathering for the Saints, 287
    gathering in, 133
    gathering to, in last days, 43, 65
    glories of, 65
    Joseph Smith on, 131
    laws of, 134
    McLellin admonishes people to gather
        to, 39
    McLellin called to bring people to, 46
    McLellin first hears of, 29
    McLellin meets group traveling to, 37
    McLellin not to go to, 46
    members receive recommends to go
        to, 138
    Mr. Scott plans to move to, 116
    people counseled to flee to, 94
    prayers for deliverance of, 149
    prophecies of gathering to, 106, 126–
        27
    redemption of, 154
    as refuge from persecution, 81
    revelations concerning, 48
Zion's Camp, 154, 292, 310–12, 314,
    341, 347, 377